The Institute of British Geographers
Special Publications Series

30 Geography and Empire

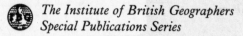 *The Institute of British Geographers*
Special Publications Series

GENERAL EDITORS: Felix Driver and Neil Roberts

In preparation

For a complete list see pp. 403–404

Geography and Empire

Edited by Anne Godlewska and Neil Smith

BLACKWELL
Oxford UK & Cambridge USA

Copyright © The Institute of British Geographers 1994

First published 1994

Blackwell Publishers
108 Cowley Road
Oxford OX4 1JF
UK

238 Main Street
Cambridge, Massachusetts 02142
USA

British Library Cataloguing in Publication Data

A CIP catalogue record for this book is available from the British Library.

Library of Congress Cataloging-in-Publication Data

Geography and empire / edited by Anne Godlewska and Neil Smith.
    p.   cm. – (Special publications series / The Institute of British Geographers: 30)
    Based on papers presented at a conference held at Queen's University, Kingston,
Ont., Apr. 1991.
    Includes bibliographical references and index.
    ISBN 0–631–19384–7 (acid-free). – ISBN 0–631–19385–5 (pbk.: acid-free)
    1. Geography–Philosophy–Congresses.   2. Imperialism–Congresses.
I. Godlewska, Anne. II. Smith, Neil. III. Series: Special
publications series (Institute of British Geographers) : 30.
G70.G443   1994
910'.01–dc20   93–44099
                                                                                          CIP

Typeset in 10½ on 12 pt Plantin
by Apex Products, Singapore
Printed in Great Britain by T. J. Press Ltd. Padstow, Cornwall

This book is printed on acid-free paper

Contents

    Experience
    Harold M. Wesso

17 Post-colonialism, De-colonization, and Geography   333
    Jonathan Crush

    Bibliography of Printed Sources   351
    Index   391

List of Plates

List of Contributors

Horacio Capel is Professor of Human Geography at the University of Barcelona, Spain. He is also the editor of *Geo crítica. Cuadernos críticos de geografía humana*, published since 1976 by the same university. He conducts research into urban geography and the history and theory of the geographical sciences.

Paul Claval (b. 1932) is Professor at the University of Paris-Sorbonne. He is a specialist in the history of geography (*Essai sur l'évolution de la géographie humaine*, 1964; *La géographie humaine et économique contemporaine*, 1984) and in the relations between geography and the other social sciences. He is now working in political and cultural geography.

Lesley B. Cormack, Assistant Professor of History at the University of Alberta, has published several articles on geography at the universities and court of early modern England. She is working on a social and institutional study of geography and the mathematical sciences at Oxford and Cambridge, as well as beginning a project examining patronage of the mathematical sciences at the Stuart courts.

Jonathan Crush is Professor of Geography at Queen's University, Canada. He is author of *The Struggle for Swazi Labour* (McGill-Queens Press, 1987) and *South Africa's Labour Empire* (Westview Press, 1991) and editor of *Liquor and Labour in Southern Africa* (Ohio University Press, 1992).

Lucio Gambi taught political and economic geography in the universities of Messina (1953–1960) and Milan (1960–1975). He is now Professor Emeritus at the University of Bologna. His chief research interests include the history of geography, urban history, agrarian landscape history and regionalism.

Anne Godlewska is a member of the Faculty of Geography at Queen's University, Canada. Her publications include *The Napoleonic Survey of Egypt* and numerous articles both in English and French on the map and the evolution of spatial understanding; the French scientific expeditions to Egypt and Algeria; disciplinarity and geography in France (1790–1830); and ideology as expressed in text, map, and art. She is currently working on a book about pre-1870 developments in social scientific geography in France.

Michael J. Heffernan lectures in geography at Loughborough University in the UK. His research interests focus on the political and cultural geography of European imperialism in the nineteenth and twentieth centuries and on the history of European geographical and environmental thought since the Enlightenment. Recent publications include (with Chris Dixon) *Colonialism and Development in the Contemporary World* (Cassell, London, 1991) and (with Alec Hargreaves) *French and Algerian Identities: A Century of Interaction* (Mellon, New York, 1993).

Andrew Kirby is Associate Dean of Social and Behavioural Sciences at the University of Arizona. He has written or edited over a dozen books, including *Nothing to Fear*, *The Pentagon and the cities*, and *Power/Resistance: Local Politics and the Chaotic State*. His chapter 'The great desert of the American mind: concepts of space and time and their historiographic implications' appeared in *The Estate of Social Knowledge* (Johns Hopkins Press, 1991).

David N. Livingstone is the author of *Nathanial Southgate Shaler and the Culture of American Science* (1987), *Darwin's Forgotten Defenders* (1987), *The Preadamite Theory and the Marriage of Science and Religion* (1992), and most recently *The Geographical Tradition* (1992). He has written many articles on the history of geography and the history of science, and is Reader in the School of Geosciences at Queen's University Belfast.

David T. Murphy is Assistant Professor of History at Anderson University, Anderson, Indiana. Material for his essay was drawn from his dissertation, 'The Heroic Earth: The Flowering of Geopolitical Thought in Weimar Germany, 1924–1933', which was completed in 1992. He has published articles on subjects including geopolitics, the history of geography, and the German Zollverein.

Garth Myers is Visiting Assistant Professor of Geography at Miami University in Oxford, Ohio. He received his PhD in 1993 from UCLA. His main research interests are the politics of urban planning and urban development in East Africa.

Tamar Y. Rothenberg is a doctoral student in geography at Rutgers University in New Jersey. She received her BA from Wesleyan University in Middletown, Connecticut. In addition to pursuing a feminist cultural historical approach to popular geography, she also indulges in contemporary urban geography.

Mechtild Rössler is currently working as an environmental sciences expert in the UNESCO World Heritage Center in Paris. Her main interests are in political geography, history of geography, ecology and feminist geography. She has published 3 books and over 40 articles on these and other subjects. She received her PhD in 1988 from Hamburg University.

Dr Gerhard Sandner is Chair of the Department of Economic Geography at the University of Hamburg, Germany. His areas of expertise include Latin American Studies – particularly Central America and the Caribbean – political geography and history of German geography.

Neil Smith is Professor and Chair of Geography at Rutgers University. He has published widely on urban geography, social theory and the history of geography, and is the author of *Uneven Development: Nature, Capital and the Production of Space*. He is currently working on a book about Isaiah Bowman's role in establishing the geography of the Pax Americana.

Olivier Soubeyran was until 1989 Visiting Professor of Urbanism at the Université de Montréal. He is now Professor of Geography and Planning at the Université de Pau, France. He is also a researcher at the SET. (CNRS). His research and publications are devoted to the history of geography and planning at the turn of the last century.

Keiichi Takeuchi was born in 1932. He studied geography at the University of Tokyo and the University of Milan. Currently Professor of Social Geography at Hitotsubashi University, Tokyo, he specializes in the social and economic geography of Mediterranean countries and in the history of geography. He has published books and papers in his fields of study in Western and Japanese languages with particular emphasis on the Mezzogiorno and the history of modern Japanese geography. Since 1988 he has been President of the Commission on the History of Geographical Thought of the IGU/IUHPS.

Harold M. Wesso is Chair of Geography and Environmental Studies at the University of the Western Cape, Bellville, South Africa.

Acknowledgements

This book is the result of international collaboration. It was born in a discussion between the editors at the 26th Congress of the International Geographical Union (Commission on the History of Geography held in Bundanoon, Australia, in August 1988). A list of potential contributors was drawn up and the editors decided that a small conference would help to integrate different ideas around the theme of 'Geography and Empire.' The conference was held at Queen's University in Kingston, Ontario in April 1991, and was attended by participants from at least ten countries including most of the authors. The essays included in this book, then, are the fruits of individual research, public exchange, and numerous exchanges between the authors and editors.

This work and the conference from which it derived was made possible by the financial support of the following institutions: the Social Sciences and Humanities Research Council of Canada; the National Science Foundation (USA); Queen's University, the Queen's Geography Department, and the Rutgers University Research Council. The editors would also like to thank the Donald Gordon Centre for helping with the conference arrangements; Eric Moore, who was of considerable assistance behind the scenes; the geographers who chaired the sessions in the 1991 conference, Barry Riddell, George Lovell, Peter Goheen, John Holmes, and David Knight; Brian Osborne for leading a field trip to Imperial Canada as manifested in the Kingston countryside; Betty Ann Abbatemarco at Rutgers and Sharon Mohammed at Queen's who provided major technical assistance; Annie Zeidman who assisted with editing; the Blackwell reviewers, and of course John Davey, who patiently cajoled us into getting the project finished as he became more and more convinced of its worth.

Finally, our major debt is to the contributors themselves who have been extremely patient while we manoeuvered through the editing and translation process. Among those presenting work at the conference but not represented here, we would especially like to thank Brian Hudson, Carlene Stephens, Tom Bassett and Julie Tuason.

Introduction:

Critical Histories of Geography

Neil Smith and Anne Godlewska

> It is ... surprising to realize that the history of geography is completely neglected. Geography constitutes the taking of possession of the earth, and the intellectual domination of space. It represents a decisive dimension of human consciousness.
>
> Gusdorf, *De l'Histoire des Sciences à l'Histoire de la Pensée*, 1977

When Joseph Conrad, reflecting on his journey up the Congo River, referred to the late nineteenth-century European colonization of Africa as 'the vilest scramble for loot that ever disfigured the history of human conscience and geographical exploration', the connection between geography and empire was starkly evident, both to him and to his readers. Imperial conquest – whether in ancient Rome, dynastic China, or capitalist Britain – invariably involved the geographical expansion of states into other territories: the extent of their territorial acquisition was a rough and ready measure of their global power. Written at the end of his life, Conrad's 1924 essay on 'Geography and Some Explorers' recognizes the symbiosis of geography and empire by dividing the history of European exploration into three geographical phases. 'Geography Fabulous' was marked by speculative mixes of pre-scientific magic and mythology with graphic and verbal representations of new worlds. The second phase, 'Geography Militant' took over in the eighteenth and nineteenth centuries, leading a more practical exploration and conquest of foreign seas and territories, exotic species and resources. The fruition of this search, Conrad hissed, was 'Geography Triumphant'.[1]

For us today, the connection of geography and empire is less vividly apparent. In the first place, the historicism of western intellectual discourse encourages us to think of empire as an historical more than a geographical question. Surprising as it may seem, otherwise excellent stories of the 'Age of Empire' generally either erase the geography of empire and the role of

[1] Joseph Conrad, 'Geography and Some Explorers', 1926, pp. 1–31.

geographical knowledge in imperial expansion or else treat geographical questions as an inert backdrop to historical events.[2] Not just historians but geographers too are implicated in this invisibility of geography, because although the history of geography clearly reflects the evolution of empire, geographers have done very little to unearth and reconstruct this history. In general, as our quote from Gusdorf at the start of this introduction suggests, geographers have registered a striking indifference to the history of their pursuit. Until very recently, those histories of geography that did exist were largely descriptive, recounting disciplinary events, the careers of the great men of geography, and the origins and evolution of geographical ideas. The history of geography, more often than not, became a story of how specific ideas about space and environment, foreign places and global processes, evolved to their present, superior scientific state. How else can one characterize the majority of geographers' writings on Ptolemy and Mercator, Alexander Humboldt and Halford Mackinder?

In such conservative and defensive histories, geography's umbilical connections with empire are usually treated with a certain ambivalence. The explorations and 'discoveries' of individuals, from Alexander the Great or David Livingstone to Louis Agassiz or William Morris Davis are lauded as heroic disciplinary achievements. Yet the violence and villainy of empire that Conrad recalls and the realities of imperial oppression and exploitation are equally an embarrassment. These political and intellectual tensions spawned idealist histories that isolated individuals and ideas from their social context, and failed to confront the intimate links between geography and empire. Ironically, geographers have abstained from asserting their central historical role in constructing what Mary Louise Pratt refers to as a 'European planetary consciousness'.[3] But empire was nevertheless a quintessentially geographical project.

If the geography of empire was widely disregarded in historical reconstructions of imperialism, so literary critical discourse has dissolved the explicit imperial context of much western literature. 'Nearly everywhere in nineteenth- and early twentieth-century British and French culture we find allusions to the facts of empire ... As a reference, as a point of definition, as an easily assumed place of travel, wealth, and service, the Empire functions for much of the European nineteenth century as a codified, if only marginally visible, presence in fiction, very much like the servants in grand households and in novels, whose work is taken for granted but scarcely ever more than named'.[4] For these and other reasons, therefore, there was a parallel

[2] See for example Eric Hobsbawm, *The Age of Empire*, 1987.

[3] M. L. Pratt, *Imperial Eyes*, 1992. Pratt adopts and adapts from geography the notion of a 'contact zone'. A major exception to this depiction of traditional histories of geography is Clarence Glacken, *Traces on the Rhodian Shore*, 1967, a momentous study of nature and culture in western thought from antiquity to the eighteenth century and a prodigious intellectual history of the idea of nature. See also D. R. Stoddart, *On Geography*, 1986.

[4] Edward Said, *Culture and Imperialism*, 1992, pp. 62–3.

displacement of geography and empire in geographical, historical, and literary discourse throughout much of the twentieth century.

More recently, however, the deficiencies of these various visions of the world have been highlighted. As regards geography, several things have happened over the last two decades to reinvigorate the history of geography and to make it a subject of considerable interest, beyond – as well as within – academic geography. In the first place, the discipline itself has changed dramatically. No discipline ever has a single research agenda, but among the most powerful agendas in human geography today is a sustained commitment to understanding the social construction of geographical space and environment: how do specific societies produce equally specific geographies and, conversely, how do these geographies help to shape social change? But conversely, the traditional historicism of western thought since at least the eighteenth century is now openly challenged – whether in social theory or cultural studies, feminist theory or postmodernism – involving 'a geographical turn' in social theory. A previously missing geographical sensibility is emerging.[5]

The resulting rapprochement of a revivified geography with a spatially informed social discourse, broadly conceived, has focused considerable attention on the history of geography as the intellectual 'site' where many questions of history and politics, space and environment intersect. The two watchwords of these newer histories of geography are 'contextual' and 'critical', and this collection aims to contribute to such a contextual, critical history of geography. Berdoulay suggests that a contextual approach to the history of geography involves consideration of changing systems of thought and social ideologies, historic wrong turnings of geographic investigation, the constitution of the 'geographical community', and the functional importance of specific geographical ideas in specific places in specific times.[6] To this we might also add that a contextual approach to the history of geography is centrally concerned to relate the history of geographical ideas, which is Berdoulay's main interest, to the material geographical changes – practical geographies – that societies both create and experience; European imperialism did indeed create a very different 'context' within which geography developed.

As for *critical* geographies, this follows in many ways from the issue of contextuality. 'Critical geography' in the 1990s means a wide range of social theory that informs the ways in which social relations generate specific geographies. Beginning with Marxist and feminist work in the early 1970s, many geographers have become intensely engaged with the gamut of social theories: poststructuralism and postmodernism, the Frankfurt School and

[5] Edward J. Soja, *Postmodern Geographies*, 1989. In his first two chapters, Soja provides a summary of the mutual interpolation of geography and social theory, although the later argument tempts an indefensible disciplinary exceptionalism; and Derek Gregory, *Geographical Imaginations*, 1994.

[6] Vincent Berdoulay, 'The Contextual Approach', in D. R. Stoddart (ed.) *Geography, Ideology and Social Concern*, 1981, pp. 13–14.

postcolonial theory – together with reformulated Marxisms and feminisms – have all enriched the rediscovery of histories of geography. Even where a suspicion of theory remains, the influence of theory is undeniable.[7]

And yet as events like the 1991 Gulf War remind us, geography has never been simply a contemplative, passive or unengaged study. Contemporary political, military, economic and cultural shifts are expressed in equally shifting geographical landscapes, and this recognition has fuelled the resurgence of interest in geography. The Gulf War, for example, was only possible as a result of the implosion of the Soviet Communist Party in 1989, its control of the state, and the dissolution of the Cold War in favour of an avowedly capitalist new world order. This in turn brought a dramatic political and economic realignment within what used to be called the Third World as well as the (equally euphemistic) 'West'. By the same token, the Gulf War might well be seen as the first full-scale 'GIS war' – a war in which computerized Geographic Information Systems (GIS) technology facilitated the construction, preparation, and deployment of the US 'smart bombs' that devastated Baghdad; base geographic data was supplied by such agencies as the Defense Mapping Agency, the largest employer of geographers in the US; and parallel GIS technologies were employed in the virtually simultaneous representation of the war to the global consumers of CNN. Indeed historically, nothing characterizes geography so tellingly as its close contacts with those either seeking or holding territorial power. Sustained efforts to block the writing of Palestinian geography are another case in point.[8] As Hudson has said of *fin de siècle* geography, 'the study and teaching of the new geography at an advanced level was vigorously promoted at that time largely, if not mainly, to serve the interests of imperialism in its various aspects including territorial acquisition, economic exploitation, militarism and the practice of class and race domination.'[9]

Geography's 'colonial encounter' is only beginning to be re-evaluated critically, but it is already clear that the very formation and institutionalization of the discipline was intricately bound up with imperialism. This said, it should also be kept in mind that geography has always pursued a wide range of intellectual agendas simultaneously and that not all of these can be traced directly to concerns of empire. This perhaps differentiates geography from anthropology, for instance, for which the 'colonial encounter' was even more central to the discipline's self-definition, and remained so – however implicitly – into the 1970s if not to the present. This has lent a certain urgency to the recent critical re-evaluation of anthropology's 'colonial encounter',[10] an urgency already felt for some years in geography.

[7] D. R. Stoddart, *On Geography*; D. N. Livingstone, *The Geographical Tradition*, 1992.

[8] See Ghazi Falah, 'Scholarly Openness', 1991; 'The Israelization of Palestine Human Geography', 1989.

[9] Brian Hudson, 'The New Geography and the New Imperialism', 1977. On geography and war specifically, see D. R. Stoddart, 'Geography and War', 1992.

[10] Talal Asad (ed.), *Anthropology and the Colonial Encounter*, 1973.

Hudson's 1977 *Antipode* article, quoted above, was the first major critical engagement with geography's imperial heritage. Arguing from an extensive survey of original sources, Hudson explored the intricate connections between geography and militarism, pointing especially to the Franco–Prussian War of 1870–1, which stimulated the expansion of geography teaching in German and French universities, and the institutionalization of European national schools of geography. He documented the connection between geographical explorations, the geopolitical self-interest of European states, and the exploitation of both recoverable economic resources and local populations; pointed out the ideological underpinnings and assumptions of the emerging discipline (especially the racist underpinnings of environmental determinism); connected this wider social project to the development of university geography; and revealed the central organizing role of elite geographical societies, especially the Royal Geographical Society.[11]

The investigation of geography and empire announced by Hudson was only taken up seriously at the end of the 1980s as critical and contextual histories of geography began to take off. In the meantime new modes of historical interpretation have developed along with the evolution of social theory over the last two decades. David Livingstone, for example, suggests a more pluralist approach to the history of geography and empire, eschewing any single theoretical inspiration but drawing cautious support from post-modernism. He makes the useful suggestion, too, that we begin to talk about the 'practice of geography', although in his own exposition this seems to imply mainly discursive practice. Similarly, Felix Driver wants to refocus this research away from the multifold connections of empire and capitalism to those of empire and 'modernity' – 'the place that geographical knowledge has had in the construction of modernity'. Indeed the admixture of class, race and gender as constituents in the motives and meanings of empire, rather than traditional nationally based narratives that take such social relations for granted, is very much to the point.[12] Of these, gendered reconstructions of geography and empire are probably least developed, although the recent debate on feminist historiographies of geography may well redress the balance. There can be no doubt that imperial geographies were gendered practices, and much work is needed to reveal the dimensions and extent of

[11] Hudson, 'The New Geography': for an early step in the same direction, see Donald V. McKay, 'Colonialism in the French Geographical Movement', 1943.

[12] Felix Driver, 'Geography's Empire', 1992; David N. Livingstone, *The Geographical Tradition*, 1992. Many of the contributors to this volume have been involved in rethinking geography and empire, and it would be redundant to attempt a full review of their writing here. Rather let us mention some other work that is not directly represented in the present volume: Gerry Kearns, 'Closed Space and Political Practice', 1984; Richard Peet, 'The Social Origins of Environmental Determinism', 1985; Donna Haraway, 'Teddy Bear Patriarchy', 1985; Mark Bassin, 'Imperialism and the Nation State', 1987; Felix Driver, 'Henry Morton Stanley', 1991; C. A. Lutz and J. L. Collins, *Reading National Geographic*, 1993.

this gendering, but it is important that what we already know and are still discovering in terms of race and class constructions of empire is not thereby relegated to the sidelines. How, for example, did white women explorers negotiate their class and race 'privilege' amid the realities of gender-based oppression?[13] How, in short, did race and gender as well as class relations interweave in the construction of empire, albeit in very different ways in different places and times?

The year after Hudson's *Antipode* paper appeared, Edward Said published *Orientalism*, and it is no exaggeration to say that this book established a whole field of literary re-evaluations of empire. Over the next decade and a half, subaltern studies, postcolonial studies, travel writing and what we might call 'exile studies' all emerged as part of a wide reconsideration of empire.[14] This literature is too vast to review here, but two examples will suffice to demonstrate the larger point that there is a broad convergence of interest in 'geography and empire' across a range of literary, cultural and social scientific discourses. Mary Louise Pratt's *Imperial Eyes* uses both European travellers' accounts (women as well as men) and the testimony of colonized peoples to displace the traditional nationalist framework within which so much empire writing is set. 'The systematizing of nature, in the eighteenth and nineteenth centuries', she writes, 'represents not only a European discourse about non-European worlds ... but an urban discourse about non-urban worlds, and a lettered, bourgeois discourse about non-lettered, peasant worlds.' Her reliance on local testimony offers a rich picture of the complexity of social relationships that constitute the experience of empire, and, in particular, reveals how various apparently 'anti-conquest' narratives – Livingstone's anti-slavery campaign for example – represented a coherent strand in imperial conquest.[15]

If Pratt's work gives a visceral feel for the tangible geographies of empire, Said conveys a more abstract geographical sensibility. In *Orientalism*, and especially in his more recent work, geographical difference, conquest, the migration of ideas and peoples, and the rootedness of place all combine to fashion geography as a vital lens on empire. 'None of us', he argues, 'is completely free from the struggle over geography', and he describes his most recent attempt to reveal the connections in *Culture and Imperialism* as 'a kind of geographical inquiry into historical experience'. Said's vivid geographical sensibility emerges most clearly in discussions of imagined political geographies, whether of Camus's Algeria or Conrad's Congo. As he observes, 'most

[13] Mona Domosh poses this question but answers still remain illusive; 'Towards a Feminist Historiography', 1991; David Stoddart, 'Do we Need a Feminist Historiography?', 1991; Mona Domosh, 'Beyond the Frontiers of Geographical Knowledge', 1991.

[14] The literature here is vast and the following are only the merest of introductory references: Edward Said, *Orientalism*, 1978; *Culture and Imperialism*; Salman Rushdie, *Imaginary Homelands*, 1991; Ranajit Guha and Gayatri Chakravorty Spivak (eds), *Selected Subaltern Studies*, 1988; Homi K. Bhabha (ed.), *Nation and Narration*, 1990; Tim Brennan, 'Cosmopolitans and Celebrities', 1990; Timothy Mitchell, *Colonizing Egypt*, 1991.

[15] Pratt, *Imperial Eyes*, 1992, pp. 34–5.

cultural historians, and certainly all literary scholars have failed to remark the *geographical* notation, the theoretical mapping and charting of territory that underlies Western fiction, historical writing, and philosophical discourse of the time.'[16] Yet in the end geography plays an uncomfortable role for Said. The brilliant vista of Said's work is constrained by an ambivalence towards geographies more physical than imagined, a reluctance to transgress the boundaries of discourse and to feel the tangible historical, political and cultural geographies he evokes.[17] Yet precisely this connection of histories *of* geography with historical *geographies* is what needs to be explored.

Whatever the discrepancies in the various geographical, historical, and literary inquiries into geography and empire, the dramatic convergence of interest endures. This collection of essays seeks, quite simply, to push this interest in geography and empire a step further. Intellectually, we adhere to a broad, inclusive definition of empire; 'imperialism' encompasses the gamut of state-centred relations of military, political, economic and cultural domination. Likewise we recognize the historical range of empires, but with one exception, the papers in this collection focus on the last two centuries. There are two reasons for this, one practical, one intellectual. The practical reason is simply that the scale, intensity and range of imperial intrusion into the economies, lives and cultures of conquered peoples is unparalleled in this period. Intellectually, despite earlier forays, the practice of geography really became institutionalized as an academic discipline only since the late eighteenth century, which accordingly produced a particularly intense brew of geographical ideas, practices and institutions. It goes without saying that in earlier times and in different places, the mutual constitution of geography and empire would take very different shapes. Different societies practise different kinds of geography.

The geographical range of the essays is also necessarily limited. This period was, as Mary Louise Pratt suggests, the era in which a 'European planetary consciousness' was established, and geography was a part of this process. It may therefore be true, as Stoddart has suggested, 'that in method and in concept geography as we know it today is overwhelmingly a European discipline',[18] but we should not treat this claim narrowly nor indeed as inevitable. For as Pratt, Said and many others point out, the imposition of a European planetary consciousness was not unopposed, and the result bears all the intellectual scars of the conquest from which it emerged. This of course is the point of 'orientalism'. Inevitably, however, the focus of this work *is* on the engagement of various European empires with non-European peoples and territories. The inclusion of Japan only partly offsets this geographical concentration.

[16] *Culture and Imperialism*, 1992, pp. 7, 58.
[17] For an unrelenting critique of Said, see Aijaz Ahmad, *In Theory*, 1992, ch. 5. See also Neil Smith, 1994 'Geography, Empire and Social Theory'; Felix Driver's cautious questioning of Said in 'Geography's Empire', pp. 30–4.
[18] David Stoddart, 'Geography – a European Science', in *On Geography*, 1986, p. 39.

Equally important is the related question of whose geography is represented and discussed here. These are largely essays about the dominant geographies and geographical practices of European colonizers. This focus is deliberate. With so little exculpation of geography and empire yet accomplished and since we ourselves are representatives of this European-based tradition, it seemed appropriate to begin by developing a critical self-awareness. But we also see this as only a first step toward a fuller portrait of geographical practices in imperial contexts. Opposition to imperial conquest inevitably also embodied geographical practices, what Said refers to as 'rival geographies', that compete in building the imperial terrains of the city and countryside as well as the mind. The final two essays in this collection touch on this question, but it remains to be developed. It is worth stating the obvious, however: namely that the difficulties of reconstructing rival geographical practices, the vast majority of which were never recorded other than in group memory, are extraordinary. Nevertheless, these essays, while covering new ground, also represent a reinterpretation of a disciplinary past that does not shy away from the ambiguity, complicity, cruelty and ugliness of much European geography. We believe that only through a full acknowledgement of the past can we begin to understand the role of geographers in the maintenance of a certain privileged order of things. By this same token, although this collection is largely historical, the earlier mention of geography in the Gulf War should be sufficient to ward off any sense that geography's imperial duplicity was merely a thing of the past. As some of the later essays suggest, we fully intend this historical study to embody and encourage a critical reflection on contemporary geographical practices.

Finally, it should be obvious that we do not imagine that we are offering the whole story of geography and empire in this collection. Indeed we shall have been successful if the reader concludes this volume with the sense that much remains to be done – and if this volume in fact helps to focus that work.

Plate 1 'Billy looks at Boney's carving tool, and opening his eyes with amazement, says to himself, – "O! O! Mr Greedygut! To be sure he is helping himself to a slice where the plums are found to be thickest …".' From Gillray's commentary to his *Caricatures*, London: John Miller and Edinburgh: W. Blackwood, facing page 56. By permission of the Bibliothèque nationale, Paris.

PART I

Establishing Traditions

Introduction

Geography, as earth description and mapping, has been associated, from its earliest archaeologically recorded moments, with territoriality, war and attempts to manipulate and dominate both the natural and human environment. Over the centuries, as the scale of geographic knowledge and control expanded, as the concept of territory grew in sophistication to encompass a more refined array of physical and human resources, and as demands for accuracy, rigour and completeness increased, geography and mapping necessarily became more expensive. Consequently, from early in the history of state formation, geography has been closely controlled by the powerful and particularly by the state. As such, it has been substantially shaped by the attention, support, and demands of governments. The chapters in this section look at two moments in geography's proto-disciplinary phase, prior to the establishment of disciplinary structures designed to shield scholars from the most immediate and blatant interference. In this phase, geographers unselfconsciously and unapologetically served the interests of the state. In periods of extreme state expansion and aggression, such as those associated with European colonial conquest and the Napoleonic wars, geographers, euphemistically proclaiming the 'Era of Exploration' or 'Modernization', became the most vociferous imperialists.

In the first chapter, Lesley Cormack demonstrates the connection between English imperialism and national identity. She traces both to a sixteenth-century drive for a sovereign state distinct from the Holy Roman Empire and to England's role as defender of the Reformation. However, the English national imperialist identity was not born fully formed but was constructed in the writings of both political theorists and geographers. Through the examination of their texts she shows that, whether by conviction or participation in the discourse of patronage, geographers played a key role in the establishment of the mentality of separateness and superiority which lies at the heart of English imperialism. Further, by thus championing the cause of English expansion, geographers gained both status and security for themselves.

Anne Godlewska also links French imperialism to French nationalism, or to the construction of a centralized state fundamentally intolerant of local autonomy both within France and in conquered and colonial territories. She explores the activities of geographers who served in Paris, Italy and Egypt in the revolutionary and Napoleonic periods as military intelligence officers, information brokers, administrators, and straightforward glorifiers of battle, the conquest, French civilization and the French state. These geographers fully embraced the imperialist ideology, believing that they were bringing rational government and commercial prosperity to oppressed and backward peoples. In addition, however, through their attempts to serve the imperialist ambitions of the state, they developed more rigorous mapping techniques and the beginnings of the social scientific inquiry which so characterizes modern human geography.

1

The Fashioning of an Empire: Geography and the State in Elizabethan England

Lesley B. Cormack

INTRODUCTION

In the nineteenth century, the British Empire dominated world affairs. No part of the globe was untouched by British control or exploitation. This empire had not been created from nothing; rather it had been constructed, often explicitly, by politicians and geographers beginning in the sixteenth century. The first step in this process was the creation of an imperial mentality – a sense of independence, separateness, and superiority which would then allow the English to expand outwards. The home country is thus the source of the empire, both ideologically and pragmatically. As we examine imperialism, we often tend to concentrate on colonies and exploitation; important though this is, we must first understand the empire at home before we can grasp its consequences abroad.

The idea of empire, that is, of a state which was self-contained and had the right and ability to govern its own affairs and which attempted to dictate the affairs of client states, had long been in use on the Continent, especially by the Catholic Church and the Holy Roman Empire. Because of England's client relationship with the Church and its subordinate position in relation to other continental powers, this idea was new to sixteenth-century English political theory. Indeed, historians have often traced the origins of the British Empire to the introduction of concepts of empire by political and religious writers in the sixteenth century in defence of the break with Rome and the adoption of a new Protestant religion. This, I would argue, is only half the story. While a definition of England as self-sufficient, able to handle her own political, religious, and social affairs, was fundamental in creating an imperial identity, so too was the depiction of England as a country that had the right and responsibility to govern and control other sections of the globe. While isolationist definitions came from politicians and political theorists, expansionist ones came from geographers. Imperial images of expansion and exploration were used by sixteenth-century geographers to advise, endorse and coerce Tudor sovereigns. This communication between geographers and the court, especially the Elizabethan court, resulted in the parallel development of models of the globe and of the state, and was fundamental to the creation of that consciousness of an outward-looking empire which became so important in the centuries to come.

By examining the geographers' calls to empire, especially as compared to the more inward-looking definitions supplied by politicians, we can begin to understand the relationship between the physical and economic maps which they drew and the image of the English Empire which Elizabeth and her government desired. And to see how the development of an English Empire, expansionist and exploitative, as well as omnicompetent and autonomous, owes its articulation in no small measure to the imperial mentality of Elizabethan geographers.

THIS REALM OF ENGLAND IS AN EMPIRE

During the sixteenth century, England began to develop an identity separate from that of the Continent. In part, this was caused by political and religious controversies that forced England to stand alone. As well, it was a conscious choice by the English to fashion themselves as other than and superior to their continental cousins.[1] One of the ways in which this new-found autonomy was developed and articulated was through the political definitions of England as an empire.

From Henry VII's accession in 1485, English ideas of sovereignty and separateness had been developing. In 1517, when Henry VIII attempted to gain the title of Holy Roman Emperor, Archbishop Cuthbert Tunstall (also a mathematician, interested in the mathematical construction of the globe) advised him:

> Oon of the cheffe points in the Election off th'emperor is that he which shal be electyd must be off Germanie subgiet to [the] Empire; wheras your Grace is not, nor never sithen the Cristen faith the Kings of Englond wer subgiet to th'empire. *But the Crown of Englond is an Empire off hitselff mych bettyr then now the Empire of Rome.*[2]

---

[1] Greenblatt, *Renaissance*, 1980, provides a literary analysis of this growing isolationism. More specifically concerned with geography, see Cormack, 'Good Fences', 1991.

[2] Guy, 'Thomas Cromwell', 1986, p. 177. Emphasis added.

In other words, Tunstall was claiming that England was separate from Germany (and Rome) and sovereign unto itself. This was an important concept, especially in light of the marital problems Henry was soon to face.

From 1525, Henry VIII had wanted to divorce his first wife, Catherine, and marry Anne Boleyn. The Pope refused to grant a divorce (which Catherine did not want) or an annulment. With an intransigent Pope, Clement VII who was, especially after 1527 under the thumb of Catherine's nephew, Emperor Charles V, Henry eventually felt he had no choice but to declare the English Church separate from that of Rome.

Henry was aided in this separation and eventual Reformation by his principal secretary Thomas Cromwell, who in the process of drafting the Act in Restraint of Appeals in 1532 (bill passed, 1533), used the term 'empire' to refer to a national sovereign state:

> Where by divers sundry old authentic histories and chronicles it is manifestly declared and expressed that *this realm of England is an empire*, and so hath been accepted in the world, governed by one supreme head and king having the dignity and royal estate of the imperial crown of the same, unto whom a body politic, compact of all sorts and degrees of people divided in terms and by names of spirituality and temporality, be bounden and owe to bear next to God a natural and humble obedience; he [the king] being also institute and furnished by the goodness and sufferance of Almighty God with plenary, whole and entire power, pre-eminence, authority, prerogative and jurisdiction to render and yield justice and final determination to all manner of folk residants or subjects within this realm, in all causes, matters, debates and contentions happening to occur, insurge or begin within the limits thereof, without restraint or provocation to any foreign princes or potentates of the world.[3]

Cromwell was thus claiming that England was completely autonomous, both in temporal and spiritual matters, with the King at the head and Parliament owing him obedience. Of course, this was political posturing and did not necessarily reflect the actual state of affairs, but it does demonstrate that English governors were already interested by 1532 in establishing the island kingdom as inviolate and omnicompetent in managing its own political and religious policy.

The historiographical debate which has raged since Geoffrey Elton suggested these words of Cromwell's were significant need not concern us here.[4] Such ideas may well have had precedents in earlier Tudor history; recognizing that the historical precedents dredged up by Cromwell and his legal associates

---

[3] Elton, *Tudor Constitution*, 1982, pp. 353–8. Emphasis added.
[4] See Elton, *Tudor Revolution*, 1953; *Tudor Constitution*, 1982; *Reform*, 1977; Guy, 'Thomas Cromwell', 1986, pp. 151–78; Williams and Harriss, 'Revolution', 1963 and 1965; Coleman and Starkey, *Revolution Reassessed*, 1986.

attempted to disguise innovation as tradition, we begin to see how important the English felt it was to develop an image of themselves as self-sufficient and autonomous. In order to separate from Rome and to take their stand as the defenders of continental Protestantism, the English had to convince themselves that this role was theirs by legal and divine right. In part, this imperial definition reflected a growing continental movement, which witnessed the increasing centralization of power by Charles V in Germany and Francis I in France.

England, however, became more successful at imperial posturing than its continental rivals, in spite of a parliamentary system which did not allow the successful growth of absolutism. This was partly due to England's island isolation and to the successful expansion of its empire, beginning with Wales and Ireland, in the latter part of the sixteenth century.[5] But more important for England's imperial success was the portrayal of England as an expansionist empire, an image promoted especially by geographical writers under Elizabeth and later James.

Indeed, the English imperial movement gained a huge impetus with the accession of Elizabeth in 1558. Under Elizabeth, the English Reformation became a reality, causing an irrevocable split between England and Catholic Europe, especially Spain. This isolation forced the English to define themselves as separate from and superior to the Continent, while encouraging them to look to the further reaches of the world for trade, commerce, and conquest. In other words, this was the period during which the English ceased to define their country merely as an empire with the right to self-government, as articulated by the early Tudors, and began to claim their ability to develop an empire of external clients which they could control. And in this transformation geographers were essential.

In the second half of the sixteenth century, an interest in understanding the globe, mathematically and descriptively, was growing both for academics and merchants. The work done by geographers in England helped convince the English of the vast untapped resources contained in the world around them and at the same time encouraged a picture of England itself as sovereign, superior and privileged. Thus geographers built on the work of political theorists, but expanded the concept of English Empire beyond the island shores to make comparisons with other European countries and to point out the potential of non-European countries as sources of materials and colonies.

In order to understand the role of geography in establishing these concepts of empire in sixteenth-century English minds, let us first turn to sixteenth-century geography itself. This was not the closed and structured discipline it was to become in the nineteenth century and must be defined by its practice as much as by its body of theoretical knowledge. This fluidity offers us a

[5] Shakespeare's *Henry V*, first performed *c.*1594, is a telling example of this imperial view. In the play, Henry V's army contains Irish, Scottish and Welsh elements, as well as the English — a truly British army (unlikely to have been the case in the fourteenth century).

wide variety of geographical writing which we can then use to assess the imperial messages encoded. Finally, a closer look at the expansion advice given to Elizabeth, concerning both the discovery of the Northwest Passage and North American planting, reveals the extent to which expansionist, as opposed to the politically isolationist, imperial images had been developed by the turn of the seventeenth century. This process demonstrates the important role played by geography in encouraging the English to consider their country as an empire and the rest of the world as open for conquest and exploitation.

WHAT WAS GEOGRAPHY IN SIXTEENTH-CENTURY ENGLAND?

During the late sixteenth century, the study of geography gained popularity in England.[6] Geography was taught at the universities, geographical works were read by merchants, courtiers, and country gentlemen, as well as investors and explorers, and it was practised by academics, writers, and courtiers, as well as those who ventured forth to see for themselves. In examining the people and ideas involved in the sixteenth-century study of geography, it becomes clear that in the course of this period, it developed into three related branches of mathematical, descriptive, and chorographical geography, each with distinct practitioners and different topics of investigation. Each branch helped develop the ideology of geography and the image of English men and women as unique and separate from other peoples.

Mathematical geography was most closely akin to the modern study of geodesy, that branch of applied mathematics which determines the exact positions of points and the figures and areas of large portions of the earth's surface, the shape and size of the earth, and the variations of terrestrial gravity and magnetism. Cartography, the study of maps and map-making, was related to mathematical geography, although cartography depended far more on guild methods of transfer of knowledge and less on any systematic development of theories or models.[7] Studied by a small group of men who were also interested in other mathematical topics, this was the most rigorously theoretical form of geography.

The second branch, descriptive geography, portrayed the physical and political structures of other lands, usually in an inductive and relatively unsophisticated manner. Because of this relative lack of rigorous analysis, and because its primary goal was utility of knowledge, descriptive geography was the most easily accessible of the three geographical sub-disciplines. It encompassed everything from practical descriptions of European road conditions to outlandish yarns of exotic locales, providing intriguing reading and practical information alike.

[6] For an investigation of the academic discipline of geography, see L. B. Cormack, *Non Sufficit*, 1988.

[7] T. Smith, 'Manuscript', 1978.

The final type of geography, chorography, developed in the course of the late sixteenth century, combining a medieval chronicle tradition with the Italian Renaissance elaboration of local description. Chorography was the most wide-ranging of the geographical sub-disciplines, since it included an interest in genealogy, chronology and antiquities, as well as local history and topography. Chorography thus united an anecdotal interest in local families and wonders with the mathematically arduous task of genealogical and chronological research.[8]

All three sub-disciplines of geography attracted practitioners from within and outside the halls of academe. Most men interested in geography pursued careers which called for a combination of practical and theoretical experience, placing the study of geography within the context of the new scientific methods and ideologies developing in the seventeenth century. As well, many of the men interested in geography pursued active careers which required the support of patrons, either noble or royal.[9] Although a discussion of the patronage of geography is beyond the scope of this chapter, it is clear that much of the imperial rhetoric used by these geographers was designed to impress and flatter patrons. Thus, imperial images, expansionist rather than isolationist, as portrayed by geographers were intimately linked with the political state.

THE MESSAGE OF EMPIRE: RICHARD HAKLUYT

Although all three branches of geography provide instances of patriotic and imperial ideology, it is in descriptive geography that we find the clearest indication of imperial thinking. In order to describe other lands, it was necessary to establish a standard of comparison; the rest of Europe and the Middle East had to be seen as different from (and inferior to) England. Likewise, descriptions of the New World demonstrated the superiority of the Old. The wondrous abilities of past English explorers showed Elizabethans the divinely ordained necessity of English hegemony in the New World and superiority over the Spanish and Portuguese at home and abroad. Thus we see quite a different focus from the political claims to imperial status.

The most significant contribution made by English descriptive geographers to this growing sense of superiority and otherness was in the collection of tales of exploration and adventure. In a genre dominated by such giants as Giovanni Battista Ramusio, Petrus Martyr Anglerius, Acosta, Linschoten, and de Bry,[10] the Englishman Richard Hakluyt takes his place as a significant

[8] See Mendyk, *Speculum*, 1989. See also Levy, 'The Making', 1964.

[9] For a discussion of the system of patronage for science which can be applied to other historical situations, see Biagioli, 'Galileo's system', 1990. For a description of the patronage of geography at one court, see Cormack, 'Twisting', 1991.

[10] Ramusio, *Delle Navigatio*, 1563; Anglerius, *De Orbe*, 1530; Acosta, *De Natura*, 1589; Linschoten, *Itinerario*, 1595–6; de Bry, *America*, 1590–1634; de Bry (son), *India Orientalis*,

and popular contributor to the whole European field of descriptions of voyages and new lands, while providing a particularly English vision.

When Thomas More encountered Raphael Hythlodaeus and questioned him concerning that until then unknown island of Utopia, he fancifully adopted the vocation of Richard Hakluyt. Hakluyt, a Master of Christ Church, Oxford and a diplomat, spy, and churchman, spent his life interviewing mariners, navigators, and travellers and collecting stories of new countries, hair-raising adventures and sea dramas.[11] His great work, *The Principal Voiages and Navigations of the English Nation*, enumerated the voyages and discoveries of Englishmen in the Americas and the East.[12] Hakluyt's collection, seen with Spenser's *Faerie Queene* and Camden's *Britannia* as the cornerstone of both the mature English language and nascent English patriotism, encouraged Britons to view themselves as leaders in the exploration of, and trade with, the wider world. Rather than reading tales of the valour of the Spanish or Dutch, *Principal Navigations* supplied the English with reflections of themselves. Hakluyt used the words of people who had been there, a style of reporting that lent great verisimilitude to his stories and allowed his readers to see the real passion and poetry, as well as hard-nosed business sense, of England's travellers. His book let the English mariner or merchant develop an awareness of his role in the world and encouraged him to risk life and limb for the glory of queen, country, and purse. Thus Hakluyt's book provided an ideological foundation for a descriptive study of the wider world. It combined an energetic and often dramatic literary style, and patriotic and pragmatic pride, with a huge collection of fascinating descriptive and navigational information.

Hakluyt's great work encouraged the English to see themselves as separate from the Continent and the rest of the world in two different ways. First, he stressed the primacy of English exploits and contacts, beginning with Arthur's voyage to Britain, and including the trade of Britons in the Mediterranean 'before the incarnation of Christ', and the 'ancient trade of English marchants to the Canarie Isles, Anno 1526', among others.[13] Second, Hakluyt stressed the dissimilarities between the English and other peoples, by describing the

---

1598–1613. For a discussion of Hakluyt's place in the ranks of these great compilations, see Parks, 'Tudor Travel', 1974.

[11] The authoritative biography of Hakluyt, though now old, continues to be Parks, *Richard Hakluyt*, 1930. For more modern treatments of this important geographer, see Taylor, 'Richard Hakluyt', 1947, and *The Original Writings*, 1935; Lynam, (ed.), *Richard Hakluyt*, 1946; and Quinn, (ed.), *Hakluyt Handbook*, 1974.

[12] Hakluyt, *The Principal Navigations, Voiages and Discoveries of the English Nation*, 1589 was largely concerned with explorations of America. His later work was too much enlarged and revised to be seen as an edition of the first, *The Principal Navigations, Voyages, Traffiques, and Discoveries of the English Nation*, 1598–1600. The 1600 edition dealt with exploration of the whole world.

[13] Hakluyt, *Principal Navigations*, 1598–1600 vol. I, p. 1; vol. II, part I, p. 1; vol. II, part II, p. 3. See also vol. II, part I, p. 96.

latters' strange customs and practices.[14] By stressing odd and foreign attributes, he drew a distinction between 'the other' and the modest English reader. The very essence of Hakluyt's work was imbued with values of the supremacy of England, of Protestantism, and of the power of the Old World over the New. *Principal Navigations* must be seen as an important contribution to a growing awareness of England's imperial greatness – her autonomous sovereignty and ability to export that power for the control of commerce and, potentially, colonies.

The more general and inclusive expression of English hegemony, available in the work of Hakluyt, was consolidated by the work of many other geographers as they described Muscovy, the Middle East and the New World to create an image of England as separate and sovereign.[15] This descriptive geography helped the English to identify themselves as separate from the continental unrest they saw before them and encouraged them to regard the world as an endless source of wondrous tales and new goods, thereby creating a mentality which would condone and encourage the exploitation of foreign peoples and resources. In the short term, this study provided court polish, skill in vernacular languages, economic information, and political comparisons. In the long run, it set in place a mentality of separateness and exploitation that would facilitate the growth of the English Empire.

[14] For example, the Lappians and 'Scrickfinnes' 'are a wilde people who neither know God, nor yet good order ... they are a people of small stature, and are clothed in Deares skinnes, and drinke nothing but water, and eate no bread but flesh all raw.' Hakluyt, *Principal Navigations*, 1598–1600, vol. I, p. 233; or 'The king of Persia (whom here we call the great Sophy) is not there so called, but is called the Shaugh. It were there dangerous to cal him by the name of Sophy, because that Sophy in the Persian tongue, is a begger, & it were as much as to call him, The great begger.' Hakluyt, *Principal Navigations*, vol. I, pp. 397–8.

[15] Accounts of Russian exploits included Horsey, 'Coronation of the Emperor of Russia', 1598–1600; Edward Webbe (servant at Moscow to Anthony Jenkinson), *The rare and most wonderful things*, 1590; and Giles Fletcher, 'Of the Russe Commonwealth', British Library, Lansdowne, MS. 60, London 1591. There is some doubt about this last date. According to Taylor, *Late Tudor and Early Stuart Geography*, 1934, p. 202, it was 'written 1583 and temporarily suppressed' until 1591. According to the *Dictionary of National Biography*, vol. 7, p. 301, the book was 'suppressed and partially printed only in Hakluyt and Purchas'. Both Horsey and Fletcher were reprinted in *Russia at the Close of the Sixteenth Century*, ed. Bond, 1856. Tales concerning the Middle East included those of Sir Anthony Sherley, who travelled to Venice, where he received the title 'Count', proceeded to Persia, and acted as envoy for the Shah to Czar Boris in Russia, to Rudolph II and to Clement VIII. This was reported in several works, including his own *A true report of Sir A. Shierlies*, 1600; his *Relation of his travels into Persia*, 1613; Parry, *A new and large discourse*, 1601; and Cottington, *A true Historical discourse*, 1609. Sandys' travels were recorded in *A relation of a journey*, 1615, while Lithgow's appeared in print in *A most delectable and true discourse*, 1614. Tales of the New World include Brereton, *A briefe and true relation*, 1602; Johnson, *Nova Britannia*, 1609; and Smith, *A description of New England*, 1616; Smith, *A True Relation*, 1608; Symonds, ed., *The proceedings*, 1612; Whitaker, *Good newes from Virginia*, 1613.

THE BREADTH OF IMPERIAL PROJECTS

Perhaps more influential than these general accounts, in terms of governmental policy, were the specific tracts written to Elizabeth to convince her of the possibility and desirability of exploration and colonization. These projects, most of which were not successful, were proposed as part of the patronage connection between geographers and the Queen. In many ways, they constituted a similar kind of advice to that offered by Cuthbert Tunstall earlier in the century. The image of England, however, had changed fundamentally. England was now represented, not as an empire self-sufficient and alone, but as an empire with world hegemonic pretensions. Geographers who desired the financial support of Elizabeth made use of the growing imperial ideology at court (the so-called 'Cult of Elizabeth'[16]), and also actively contributed to its creation. The advice offered to the Queen, both concerning the possibility of discovering a Northwest or Northeast Passage and the desirability of settling North America, was inculcated along with the idea of England as an imperial power. Some explicitly referred to this English right to sovereignty over other parts of the world and the superiority of the English to continental powers, while others contained at least a tacit hegemonic message.

As Richard Willes, a Master of Arts from Oxford and literary executor to Richard Eden, pointed out in 1577, there were four possible paths from Europe to China and the Far East, the source of all wealth and therefore power: one could travel around Africa, as the Portuguese had done; one could travel south-west through the Straits of Magellan, as the Spanish did; ships could sail north-east around Muscovy; or they could sail north-west around the land of America.[17] Since the two southern routes were controlled by Portugal and Spain, only the northern routes remained a possibility for a nation now struggling to assert its imperial independence. Thus many of the geographical proposals that crossed Elizabeth's and her privy councillors' desks suggested the desirability of these north-east or north-west passages.

> Experience proveth, moste gracious Soveraigne, [extolled Anthony Jenkinson in 1565] that Naturally all Princes ar desyrous to Imploye theire study and theire power to advance theire dominions Kingdoms and Terrytories. Wherefore it is not to be marveyled at to see them every daye ready to pruve the same not regardinge any costes perylls or laboures that thereby may chaunce.[18]

[16] Strong, *The Cult of Elizabeth*, 1977.

[17] Willes, 'Certain other reasons, or arguments to prove a passage by the Northwest', 1598–1600. Most of the biographical information for this section comes from the *Dictionary of National Biography* and Taylor, *Tudor Geography*, 1930, *Late Tudor and Early Stuart Geography*, 1934, and *Mathematical Practitioners*, 1954.

[18] Anthony Jenkinson, 'A proposal for a voyage of discovery to Cathay, 1565', British Library Cotton Galba D 9, f. 4a.

Jenkinson, an agent for the Muscovy Company and the first Englishman to set foot in Central Asia, proposed that an English route past Muscovy to Cathay would assure Elizabeth of great wealth and prestige and would confirm the special place which God gave to the English nation. As well, Jenkinson produced as proof of the Northeast Passage the fact that unicorn horns were displayed at the court of Ivan the Terrible. Since everyone knew that unicorns came from China, the horn must have floated to Muscovy, claimed Jenkinson.

Likewise, William Borough, an agent for the Muscovy Company before transferring his services to the Queen in about 1579, and Michael Lok, a governor of the Cathay Company and agent for the Levant Company, proposed Russian routes to China in 1568 and 1575 respectively.[19] Elizabeth's court astrologer and mathematician, John Dee, advised Arthur Pet and Charles Jackman on their 1580 attempt to find such a passage.[20] Borough, after his voyage to Russia, presented Elizabeth with a map of the area in 1578.[21] This interest in the Northeast was in part caused by a desire for the wealth and prestige of eastern trade, as well as the more obvious trade with Muscovy. In fact, Lok suggested that all of the riches of Persia and the Far East could come to the English through Russia.[22] This would allow England to gain a pre-eminent economic position in Europe, surpassing the Italians, Spanish and Portuguese, while trading with a northern empire with which England had much affinity. Thus, claimed these geographers, knowledge of the globe could help England gain economic and political superiority.

Parallel to these north-eastern developments (and continuing long after they had proven futile) were attempts to find the other northern route to Cathay, via the north west. During the 1570s and 80s, several adventurers and geographers proposed paths to the Far East through what is now Canada. Earliest of these was that unfortunate knight, Sir Humphrey Gilbert. Gilbert,

[19] 'Advise of William Borrowe for the discerning of the sea and coast byyonde. Perhaps whether the way be open to Cathayia, or not', *c.*1568. British Library, Lansdowne MS. 10, ff. 132–3b; 'Certayn notes, made by me Michaell Lok, the 8 of May: A° 1575 in London. Touching the Benefit that may growe to England, by the Traffique of English Marchants into Russia; through a firme Amity betwene both the Princes', British Library, Harley MS. 541, ff. 165–73. The document by Borough may have been the first overtures to his moving from the Muscovy Company to the patronage of the monarch.

[20] John Dee, 'Instructions for the two Masters, Charles Jackman and Arthur Pet', MS 1580 cited in Taylor, *Tudor Geography*, 1930, p. 187. Dee is the most famous and least understood of these court geographers. Clulee, *John Dee's Natural Philosophy*, 1988, provides a clear analysis of some of Dee's more difficult work, as well as drawing an interesting picture of Dee's attempts to fit into the early modern patronage network.

[21] Borough, *Plat of Russia*, 1578. 'Given to Queen Elizabeth with an autobiographical address, the latter printed by Hakluyt' in Taylor, *Tudor Geography*, p. 184.

[22] Lok, British Library, Harley MS. 541, ff. 170–3. This advice may represent Lok's feud with the Levant Company, which did not pay him the money he felt he was owed. 'List of debts owed to Michael Lok by the Turkey Co', British Library. Add. MS. 12,504, ff. 293–4.

part of the Sidney circle through his connection with his step-brother Sir Walter Ralegh, was an Oxford-trained mathematical geographer. In 1576, Gilbert wrote *A Discourse for a Discovery for a new Passage to Cataia*, which he directed 'To the Queenes most excellent maj^{ie} our Dread Sovereign Ladie' and in which he mustered the arguments for the existence of a Northwest Passage.[23] Gilbert was convinced of the existence of this passage and petitioned Elizabeth to grant him a monopoly once he found it. Unfortunately, Gilbert did not live to use this monopoly. His ship foundered off the coast of Newfoundland, leading to perhaps the most famous passage from Hakluyt's great work, which demonstrated that even in defeat, English sailors died for the greatness and glory of their kingdom and empire.

Munday the ninth of September, in the afternoone, the Frigat was neere cast away, oppressed by waves, yet at that time recovered: and giving foorth signes of joy, the Generall sitting abaft with a booke in his hand, cried out unto us in the Hind (so oft as we did approach within hearing) We are as neere to heaven by sea as by land ... The same Monday night, about twelve of the clocke, or not long after, the Frigat being ahead of us in the *Golden Hinde*, suddenly her lights were out, whereof as it were in a moment, we lost the sight, and withall our watch cryed, the Generall was cast away, which was too true. For in that moment, the Frigat was devoured and swallowed up of the Sea.[24]

As is well known, many other adventurers tried their hand, and although none found a passage, proposals to the monarch continued largely unabated. For, as Willes had pointed out, if a way could be found into the western sea, who better than the valliant English to make their way there?

The rude Indian Canoa halleth those seas, the Portingals, the Saracenes, and Moores travaile continually up and downe that reach from Japan to China, from China to Malacca, from Malacca to the Moluccaes: and shall an Englishman, better appointed than any of them all (that I say no more of our Navie) feare to saile in that Ocean: What seas at all doe want piracie: What Navigation is there voyde of perill?[25]

With a pause for the Armada engagement, when most people involved with navigation and geography were busy preparing for and harassing Spanish fleets (William Borough, for example, accompanied Drake on the raid of Cadiz and commanded a small vessel at the Armada battle), proposals to search for a Northwest Passage continued well into the seventeenth century. In 1597 William Barlow, an Oxford divine, dedicated a proposal to the Earl

[23] Humphrey Gilbert, 'A Discourse', 1598–1600.
[24] 'The maner how the sayd Admirall was lost', Hakluyt, *Principal Navigations*, 1598–1600, vol. 3, p. 159.
[25] Willes, 'Certain other reasons', 1598–1600, p. 28.

of Essex, and this was followed in the next reign with petitions from mathematician and geographer Thomas Harriot, geographer Edward Wright, mathematician and chronologer Thomas Lydiat, natural philosopher Sir Dudley Digges, and mathematician and Gresham professor Henry Briggs.[26] None of these proposals was brought to fruition, but they clearly fit into the gift-giving system which was so much part of patronage in the early modern period. It was important to these geographers and mathematicians that they be seen by potential patrons to be furthering the cause of English expansion and empire. This was particularly important for Elizabeth during the years of the Anglo–Spanish war (1580–1604) and for Prince Henry in the years before his untimely death in 1612.

Though the search for a Northwest Passage to Cathay proved futile, the land itself was not unappealing and therefore proposals began to reach Elizabeth for the planting of colonies in North America. Probably the most important of these was Richard Hakluyt's *Notes on the Planting of North America* (MS. 1578, printed as *Divers voyages touching the Discoverie of America* 1582, dedicated to Philip Sidney). In this book were the seeds of Hakluyt's later volumes, but his agenda was much more explicitly articulated.

> I Marvaile [began Hakluyt] not a little ... that since the first discoverie of America ... after so great conquests and plantings of the Spaniardes and Portugales there, that wee of Englande could never have the grace to set fast footing in such fertill and temperate places, as are left as yet unpossessed of them.[27]

Just as Anthony Parkhurst did concerning Newfoundland,[28] Hakluyt extolled the benefits, economic, political, and social, which would accrue to England through establishing colonies in North America, including a list of 'Certaine commodities growing in part of America'.[29] Not only would petty criminals be provided with occupation and trade be improved, but America would also provide a safe haven against Spanish incursions, as well as a base from which attacks against the Spanish could be launched. Thus, in one simple proposal, the idea of an overseas colonial empire was born.

Likewise, John Brereton's short tract, *The Discoverie of the North Part of Virginia* (1602), stressed the imperial designs of the growing English mercantile community. Brereton was an Oxford-trained traveller to Virginia

---

[26] e.g. Barlow, *The Navigator's Supply*, 1597, f. b1a; Thomas Lydiat, Oxf. Bodl. MS Bodl. 313 f. 32; Digges, *Of the Circumference of the earth*, 1612; Briggs, 'A Treatise of the NW Passage', 1625. Most of these men were involved with the court of Henry, Prince of Wales. For an analysis of this coterie of geographers at the prince's court, see Cormack, 'Twisting the Lion's Tail', 1991.

[27] Hakluyt, *Divers Voyages*, 1582, f. P1a.

[28] Anthony Parkhurst, 'Report of Newfoundland', 1598–1600. Nothing is known about Parkhurst's life or career.

[29] Hakluyt, *Divers Voyages*, f. R4a.

and dedicated his proposal for a permanent colony there to Sir Walter Ralegh (a man rather out of favour with Elizabeth at the time).[30] Brereton began his proposal with the claim that England already had rights to America:

These lands [of America] were never yet actually possessed by any Christian prince or people, yet often intended to be by the French nation, which long sithence had inhabited there, if domesticall warres had not withheld them: notwithstanding the same are the rightfull inheritance of her Maiestie, being first discovered by our nation in the time of king Henrie the seventh, under the conduct of John Cabot and his sonnes: by which title of first discovery, the kings of Portugall and Spaine doe holde and enjoy their ample and rich kingdomes in their Indies East and West.[31]

He then, as Hakluyt had done, listed the commodities of the New World, the usefulness in supplying English navies for military action, the relative friendliness of the natives, the possibility of a Northwest Passage and the clear superiority of the English in attempting this.

No nation of Christendom is so fit for this action as *England*, by reason of our superfluous people … and of our long domesticall peace.[32]

Brereton was even more convinced than Hakluyt of the superiority of the English and their right to an imperial portion of the New World.

The colonies actually attempted in Virginia, failing under Elizabeth and marginally succeeding under James, became the focus of the last group of proposals directed towards the monarchs by those interested in studying the globe. Thomas Harriot's description of Virginia, seen in his *Brief report of …Virginia* (1588),[33] was 'the first broad assessment of the potential resources of North America as seen by an educated Englishman who had been there'.[34] Harriot was well-connected, as mathematics tutor to Ralegh and later as pensioner to Henry, Earl of Northumberland (the 'Wizard Earl'). Thus, his words carried authority when he described the potential of Virginia as the first outpost of the English Empire. He listed native plants and animals which could be domesticated and minerals which could be mined. His description of the native 'lesser Virginians' was surprisingly sympathetic, acknowledging their superior ability to survive in this locale and their possession of a legitimate culture and religion. He did not wish to convert them but rather

[30] Parker, *Books to Build an Empire*, 1965, p. 169. Ralegh was attempting to win back the Queen's favour in the first years of the century, but ultimately would be thrown back in the tower (and was executed in the next reign for plotting against James).

[31] Brereton *A briefe and true relation*, 1602, p. 15.

[32] Ibid., p. 19.

[33] Harriot, 'A briefe and true report', 1598–1600.

[34] Quinn, 'Thomas Harriot and the New World', ed. Shirley, 1974, p. 45.

to develop a mutually beneficial *modus vivendi*.[35] Harriot compiled the first word list of any North American Indian language,[36] illustrating that inductive spirit never far from the heart of even the most mathematical geographer. He saw Virginia's great potential for English settlement, provided that the natives were treated with respect and that missionary zeal and English greed were kept to a minimum.[37] Thus, Harriot's descriptive geography was less driven by Protestant enthusiasm than by the spark of inductive inquiry, united with enlightened, self-interested patriotism. As well, Harriot's proposal embodies the idiosyncratic, individualistic efforts of English empire-builders, interested in their own prosperity while furthering the Empire of England as a whole.[38]

Literary works were also composed to convince those paying for the enterprise that the settlement of Virginia would be a noble and divinely-ordained enterprise, demonstrating the superiority of England and its right to control the Amerindians.[39] Thus the Virginian settlements were a tangible demonstration of the belief in England's innate superiority and ability to develop a Protestant hegemony in the wider world.

All of these proposals shared a number of characteristics. All were produced by men with some pretensions to court preferment.[40] Several were connected with the spy ring set up by Francis Walsingham and taken over by the Earl of Essex.[41] Although three of the men named were connected

[35] Most of the early encounters with Amerindians by English explorers were relatively non-aggressive. Attitudes towards the natives only began to change as the Europeans had more infrastructures in place and some hope of surviving the winter on their own. Indeed, it would be most informative to trace the deteriorating and increasingly racist attitudes towards Amerindians in the seventeenth century in North America. The Spanish story is quite different. See, for example, Pagden, *The Fall of Natural Man*, 1982.

[36] Shirley, *Thomas Harriot. A Biography*, 1983, p. 133.

[37] The manuscript information concerning this expedition is gathered together in Quinn, *The Roanoke Voyages, 1584–1589*, 1955. Shirley discusses Harriot's desire for non-interference, in *Biography*, pp. 152 ff.

[38] The private and individual nature of England's early Empire may have been the cause of the odd and powerful configuration of the Empire in the centuries to come. One might even call it the 'Invisible Hand' theory of empire-building. The creation of this empire is beyond the scope of this chapter. This observation does suggest, however, an explanatory model for an empire which often seemed to have 'growed like Topsy', causing the English crown some embarrassment, called on as she was to deal with problems not of her own making.

[39] Drayton, *Ode to the Virginia Voyage*, 1606; Crashaw, *A Sermon preached on 21 February 1609/10*, 1610, (which sermon, Strong claims, 'Casts both King and Prince in an imperial messianic role as "new Constantines or Charles the Great"', Strong, *Henry, Prince of Wales*, 1986, p. 62) and Chapman, *The Memorable Maske*, 1613.

[40] For example, William Borough was in the Queen's navy; John Dee was Elizabeth's astrologer and mathematician; Thomas Harriot was mathematics tutor to Ralegh and pensioner for the Earl of Northumberland.

[41] Michael Lok's father had been a spy for Thomas Cromwell in Henry VIII's reign: Richard Willes knew Walsingham; Anthony Jenkinson dedicated his book to Sir Henry

with trading companies (Jenkinson and Borough with the Muscovy Company and Lok with the Levant), the court connections were really the significant ones. Over half had university education and half wrote essentially theoretical treatises. Six could best be described as mathematical geographers with the other four essentially descriptive geographers. What they shared was a need to develop a discourse that would resonate with the desires of the court and government; what they developed was an ideology of overseas imperialism that gained them status and security.

All the proposals themselves contributed to this expansionist ideology of empire. They began by stressing the glory to the English and to Elizabeth that would result from the success of these enterprises, as well as, of course, the numerous financial rewards to be reaped (especially for the proposers, either in terms of patronage or monopolies). All of the proposals demonstrated the economic and military advantage to imperialism and painted a picture of an England that deserved the role of hegemonic exploiter through superiority and native intelligence. Few Elizabethan proposals stressed missionary motivations, something that would change under James and his son Henry. Finally, all of these proposals and reports stressed the innate superiority of the English over both aboriginal peoples and rival European powers. England was subject to no other nation, as Cromwell had said fifty years earlier. But now, added these late Elizabethan geographers, due to the clearly superior ability, knowledge, and virtue of English voyagers, England would be bound to achieve control over both the mathematical and cartographic knowledge of the globe and the peoples and natural resources encountered. The maps were not yet coloured pink, but the idea of imperial control had been developed.

CREATION OF AN IMPERIAL IDEAL

I do not mean to imply that the men here cited actually believed all of the propaganda it was necessary for them to espouse. Just as early articulations of the concept of England as an autonomous empire were more wishful thinking than reality, so too these later claims to the right to expansion and exploitation were overstated. Clearly, much of the rhetoric of superiority and hegemony was part of the discourse of patronage and was considered necessary for an effective proposal. But, as Stephen Greenblatt has shown us (*Renaissance*, 1980), words can help create realities, and if geographers repeated often enough that England was superior, so it would become. Thus the ideal of imperial autonomy and control was first created in principle rather than proven in practice. Those who ventured forth with the witness

---

Sidney (the household Essex grew up in); Sir Humphrey Gilbert, step-brother to Ralegh, was part of the Sidney circle as well; and William Barlow dedicated *The Navigator's Supply* to the Earl of Essex.

of Hakluyt ringing in their ears did so with the ranks of past English achievement standing firmly behind them. Even relative failures – Martin Frobisher's diversion with fool's gold, or Thomas James' inability to find a passage – could be turned to good account and added to the crowds of witnesses who had gone before.

Early modern geography thus helped continue the creation, begun by political theories, of an English awareness, a belief in English isolation, autonomy and omnicompetence. Perhaps more important, it encouraged the English to see the world as theirs by right of conquest. This mentality of exploitation was to have far-reaching effects.

2

Napoleon's Geographers (1797–1815): Imperialists and Soldiers of Modernity

Anne Godlewska*

GEOGRAPHY, THE STATE, MODERNITY, AND IMPERIALISM

There is a close, although complex, association between 'modernity', the rise of the modern bureaucratic state and the development of the discipline of geography. Many of the scholars who use the term 'modernity' associate it with the Enlightenment and its legacy.[1] Although there is considerable disagreement about the implications, consequences and benefits of the Enlightenment and 'the project of modernity', as Habermas describes it, most authors would agree that essential to western 'modernity' is a profound faith in rational thought; a commitment to and belief in universal principles of social organization (encompassing religion, government, and economic organization); an intolerance and suspicion of religious experience and modes of explanation; and a deep conviction that the European traditions of science, technology, art and government are demonstrably superior to all others. Linked to and integral to the development of this mentality was the ascendancy of the centralized, rationalized and controlling state which became radically more centralized, bureaucratized and controlling in France during the late revolutionary and Napoleonic periods.

* The author would like to acknowledge the stimulating input of all of the authors in this collection and of the conference participants. In addition, Brian Ray, John Agnew and Peter Goheen provided constructive and well-timed criticism and suggestions.
[1] Of particular interest on 'modernity' are Harvey, *Condition of Postmodernity*, 1989; Habermas, 'Modernity an Incomplete Project', 1983; and Horkheimer and Adorno, *Dialectic of Enlightenment*, 1972.

Geographers played a significant role in the early aggressive stages of the development of the modern western state, prior to the discipline's institutionalization, or to the entry in large numbers of geographers into universities. Surprisingly, however, as the discipline became entrenched in universities, since approximately the 1870s, geography gradually lost its purchase in the corridors of political, social and economic power. This apparent correspondence between a declining political profile and institutionalization is not entirely fortuitous. Prior to its institutionalization, geography won its right to survive by either demonstrating its social utility (generally through cartography, statistical description, or universal geographies supportive of the ideals of the 'modern' state) or less commonly by suggesting its intellectual value (generally through the activities of individual scholars). This is not to imply a simple equation between institutionalization and political involvement. While a lack of institutional security may encourage efforts at legitimation through conscious demonstration of the discipline's utility, clearly many other factors are also of importance in shaping a discipline's relations with political power. For example, since the Second World War, geography has substantially lost control over the technologies and knowledge most useful in the exercise of modern warfare and governance. In earlier times these were well within the domain of geographers. Similarly, increasing awareness of the importance of the movement of capital, information and goods has led to extremely close ties between government and the discipline of economics in the post-war era.

In this chapter we will explore the role that geographers played in France in the Napoleonic period. This was a time in which geography was not only *not* institutionalized but was, in addition, undergoing something of a crisis of identity and credibility. This crisis revolved around the realization that most mapping problems (the primary preoccupation of geographers since the seventeenth century and which had won a small number of them positions in the Academy of Sciences) were theoretically and practically soluble. This amounted to a demotion of geography, as it was then practised, from a science to a technology. Geographers gradually began to look for a new focus and a new source of legitimation. Through the Napoleonic period, however, geography retained a very strong identification with mapping and associated activities. This period of 'crisis but continuity' for geography coincided with a time of French political aggression so extreme that it demanded on the one hand the elaboration of a particularly virulent imperialist ideology[2] and on

---

[2] Ideology is an extraordinarily elastic term and hence both powerful and provocative. It is used here more broadly than the sense adopted by Adas (borrowing from Skocpol) as 'idea systems deployed as self-conscious political arguments by identifiable political actors'. Adas, *Machines as the Measure of Men*, 1989, p. 9, citing the debate between Sewell, Jr and Skocpol in *The Journal of Modern History*, 1985, 57, 1: 91. In particular, I would add that ideologies are not always coherent, that their expression is often only partial, and that their derivation and implications are frequently not clear to those who share them. The Adas/Skocpol definition does, however, capture the sense that ideologies are composed of

the other the militarization of the entire society. It is argued that this combination of disciplinary predisposition and a larger context dominated by a powerful imperialist ideology, supported by the relatively new mentality of 'modernity', engendered a particularly imperialistic geography.

At the base of the imperialist ideology of the revolutionary and Napoleonic periods was a powerful and – newly fervent[3] – nationalism, a keen belief that the aim of national aggression was civilization and liberation, and a conviction that only scientific rationalism universally applied could lead to peace, order, and good government, both in France and in the realms conquered by France. It is a little unusual to link eighteenth- and nineteenth-century nationalism to imperialism. Nevertheless, it seems clear that French imperialism was an extension overseas of concepts elaborated for the construction and consolidation of a centralized state – particularly when one considers the manner in which a national identity and culture was imposed on the peasantry within France from the sixteenth to the nineteenth centuries. As Robert Muchembled details, the primary aims of this imposition were the creation of a hierarchical and stable social system principally favouring the elite, the expansion of the tax and economic base and, in order to secure these, the eradication of locally-based popular culture.[4] The French nation and the ideology of nationalism were created, then, through the concerted actions of the crown and, into the eighteenth century, the church. Legislation and its enforcement were the principal means by which cultural conformity was achieved. However, science and technology played an increasingly important role in this imposition – particularly space-annihilating science and technology such as cartography (then known as geography), and engineering (e.g. roads, postal systems, etc.). Thus, even before the revolutionary and Napoleonic periods, geography had an important role to play in the annihilation of space and local culture in France and in the shrinking of the many 'pays' of France into a single 'pays' with a universal measurement-based culture.[5]

By the end of the eighteenth century and as a result of the pressures and conflicts surrounding the French Revolution, French nationalism was beginning to assume its most aggressive form, international imperialism. Now the French state turned its attention to the integration of foreign regions into

---

a network of ideas not always easy to identify and that they are associated with relations of power. In addition, following Habermas, I see ideology as a form of 'systematically distorted communication' arising from the contradictions inherent in the society as a whole. For a good discussion of the many meanings of 'ideology' see Eagleton, *Ideology*, 1991.

[3] Beaune describes the ancient roots of French nationalism in *Birth of an Ideology*, 1991, but readily admits that the modern French ideology of nationalism dates from approximately the late eighteenth and early nineteenth centuries, pp. 4–5.

[4] Muchembled, *Popular Culture 1400–1750*, 1985.

[5] For a fascinating discussion of the revolutionary desire to rationalize, 'naturalize' and lend uniformity to time and space through the establishment of a new calendar and metric measures see Sewell, 'Ideologies and Social Revolutions', 1985; for ideas rich in meaning for geographers see also the section in Adas's book *Machines as the Measure of Men* on

its realm. This integration was to be achieved by the introduction of French technology[6] and rational government into the conquered realms and the re-orientation of their economies to serve the interests of France. It was part of the imperialist ideology to argue that technology, economies and even political systems could be radically reformed with no significant disturbance to culture (e.g. religion). Culture, once separated from its material basis, however, was soon seen to be absurd and open to apparently justifiable ridicule and attack.

Geography's predisposition to imperialism was derived from more than its own disciplinary crisis. Also of paramount importance was the often commented upon strength of the historic tie between the discipline and the state.[7] As will be discussed, the long-standing participation of geographers in the design and implementation of the national space- and culture-anni-hilating technologies – both military and civilian – gave them knowledge and skills that were invaluable in foreign conquests. As a group, geographers also played a role which reflected their affiliation and training. Many were middle class and engineers, with a strong sense of the primacy of French scientific culture. Some had recently graduated from the École Polytechnique, the school of higher engineering, established in 1795, through which passed most of France's nineteenth-century scientific elite. Napoleon, a ruler who aggressively sought to shape and direct France's educational and scholarly institutions, shared this image of French science and engineering and clearly expressed his conception of geography's appropriate intellectual and social role. The imperialistic participation of the Napoleonic geographers was above all shaped by the spatial nature of many of the problems engendered by imperial conquest – that is, the ongoing problem of annihilating greater and greater geographic and cultural distances.

THE NEW RELATIONSHIP BETWEEN GEOGRAPHY AND THE STATE

Military Innovation

Apart from the changes internal to the discipline (which I have discussed elsewhere[8]), there were also socio-technological changes which created a

---

'Space, Accuracy and Uniformity,' pp. 259–65. At the time of the Revolution, this process was substantially incomplete. For a discussion of the process in the course of the nineteenth century see Weber's controversial *Peasants into Frenchmen*, 1976 and his critics.

[6] 'Technology' as it is used here refers to an entire method and system of production including the human organization necessary to make it work. This is the usage favoured by Franklin, *Real World of Technology*, 1990.

[7] On this see especially Lacoste, *La géographie*, 1976; and more recently Bergevin, *Déterminisme et géographie*, 1992. Bergevin also comments favourably on Dion's treatment of this theme in classical times in the latter's *Aspects politiques*, 1977.

[8] Godlewska, 'Traditions, Crisis, and New Paradigms', 1989. This question also forms one of the themes of a book I am currently writing on the French discipline of geography in the first half of the nineteenth century.

demand for a geographic research of a slightly different kind. The nature of warfare was changing in the last third of the eighteenth century. The Revolution was the source of a number of important innovations but others were the culmination of technical and theoretical developments in eighteenth-century warfare whose significance only became apparent in the course of the revolutionary and Napoleonic wars. The increasing emphasis placed on the rapid movement of troops in smaller units, such as divisions and brigades, and their reuniting for combat *en masse*, together with the development of lighter and more accurate artillery, gave cartography and road construction a new importance.[9] The rapid movement of smaller units required the careful guidance of troops through rough and irregular terrain. As these new self-sufficient fighting units moved through or near enemy terrain, they could never be sure when they might encounter superior numbers of enemy forces. Thus, their movement had to be informed not merely by a cartographic knowledge of the terrain but by a strategic sense of the implications of terrain features, human landscapes and combinations of both for offensive and defensive operations. This required a knowledge of terrain and society that went well beyond traditional cartography and began to extend into what we would recognize today as social scientific preoccupations.[10]

It is generally agreed that the Revolution gave European warfare a strongly ideological character, although not for the first or the last time. This ideology amounted to a collective illusion closely tied to a new nationalism which argued the coherence and superiority of the French social and political order, French civilization and French science. This social and cultural superiority warranted the domination of neighbouring peoples who, once conquered, would not only no longer pose a threat but would share in the benefits of French rule and French science and technology while expanding the power of France and the depth of French civilization.[11] Thus, in the eighteenth century, war in Europe had been directed by aristocrats who had identified at least as much with each other as they had with their sovereign's state, and had been fought by soldiers whose sentiments were treated as substantially irrelevant.[12] With the Revolution, however, the transborder identification between officers was to break down, to be replaced with a new emphasis on the nation and nationalism.

[9] As is clear in 'Mémoires sur les reconnaissances militaires attribués au général Bourcet', 1875 (first published in 1827, but written and widely circulated before 1780); and Allent, 'Essai sur les reconnaissances militaires,' 1829. See also Quimby, *Napoleonic Warfare*, 1957.

[10] The works which have explored some of these developments in terms of their impact on cartography include Harley, Petchenik and Towner, *Mapping the American Revolutionary War*, 1978 and McNeil, *Pursuit of Power*, 1982. Although, the subject is far from exhausted.

[11] This sense of capturing a historic past and then claiming it for France was very clear in the writings of the scholars involved in the expedition to Egypt 1798–1801.

[12] On this and on the role of population growth and changing social structure in military innovation see McNeil, *Pursuit Of Power*, 1982, especially chapters 5 and 6.

In addition, the attitude to the commitment of the average soldier changed. France's financial difficulties and the government's need to defend the new revolutionary social order required, at least in the early years of the Revolution, reliance on a conscripted army – an army that could only be kept in the field through ideological conviction.[13] It also required the mobilization of the entire society: from the recruitment of scientists, scholars and artists for military expeditions, to the request that every basement owner collect saltpetre for the manufacture of gunpowder, to the Napoleonic militarization of the École Polytechnique, the country's premier scientific educational institution.[14] The ideological tone was further raised when one of France's stated military aims became the export of revolution: a more equitable system of government and a better way of life.[15] The French revolutionary ideology, then, permitted and encouraged direct attack on the social system of the country being invaded – in particular on any aspect at variance with the French economic, governmental or social system. This general atmosphere of social reform, which can also be seen as social intolerance, had, as we will see below, a significant effect on the activities and writings of geographers charged with studying the newly conquered regions.

The combined development of a more highly educated (and, thus, expensive) middle-class officer corps and the ideologization of the army had another effect ultimately of significance to geography. France's inability to pay its soldiers regularly and to keep them in clothing and shoes meant that the army had to live off the countryside it was invading. This led to what Geoffrey Best has described as 'war addiction': an army on foreign soil could be kept functioning by predation of a more or less institutionalized sort. What began as a necessity evolved into a profitable venture.[16] In its least institutionalized form, it amounted to looting – an activity obliquely (and no doubt courageously) condemned by one geographer.[17] Institutionalized predation (which to my knowledge was never condemned by a geographer) entailed the assumption of the previous regime's tax farming system, local conscription (which became essential as the French government encountered increasing resistance to conscription among its own people[18]), and a less pecuniary theft: the plundering of art works and historical monuments[19]. A conquest, then, entailed not only mapping phenomena of strategic importance but mapping

[13] Lynn, *Bayonets of the Republic*, 1984.

[14] See *École polytechnique livre du centenaire*; Fourcy, *Histoire de l'École polytechnique*, 1987, (1828); Hayek, *The Counter Revolution of Science*, 1952.

[15] On the impact of this ideologization of war see von Clausewitz, *On War*, 1984, pp. 592–3.

[16] Best, *War and Society 1770–1870*, 1982, pp. 92–3.

[17] Malte-Brun, 'Aperçu de la monarchie Prussienne', 1808.

[18] Corvisier, *Dictionnaire*, 1988, p. 721.

[19] There is a substantial literature on this peculiarly Napoleonic brand of pillage including Quynn, 'Art confiscations of the Napoleonic Wars', 1945; Boyer, 'Les responsabilités de Napoléon', 1964. On its effects in Italy see Fugier, *Napoléon et l'Italie*, 1947, pp. 39–40.

and commenting on actual and potential wealth. The urgency of this activity and the precise definition of wealth was in the end largely shaped by the economic war waged between France and England and the effects of Britain's blockade and France's continental system.

Political and Social Change

The nature of civil society and particularly the French government's sense both of its ability and its right to control day-to-day and local activities also underwent radical, if gradual, changes in the course of the eighteenth century. These were both directionally similar to, and had as significant an effect on geography, as those taking place in the military realm. Whether examined from the perspective of the historical geography of France, the history of statistics or the history of geography, it is clear that in the course of the eighteenth century, the French government developed Colbert's initial desire to have a general description of the kingdom for the purposes of administration into a commitment to increasingly centralized, regular, consistent and exhaustive statistical and cartographic surveys of the realm. This commitment was not complete by the time of the Revolution and was not realized – in part due to the disruption caused by the Revolution and the Napoleonic wars – until well into the nineteenth century.

One of the characteristics of the state's growing awareness of its realm had also been an evolution in understanding of what constituted national wealth and, thus, what merited the attention of the government. From a primary preoccupation with territory and tax, a more sophisticated appreciation had evolved of the relationship between population and population change; agriculture and agricultural practices; industry; commerce and its structural obstacles; and wages and poverty. The effect of this was a growing belief at all levels of government in the value of statistics including population, industrial, agricultural, commercial and, to a limited extent, social measurements. In the revolutionary and Napoleonic period statistical inquiry became something of a universal preoccupation.[20] Geographers, whether specializing in graphic or textual description, could not fail to be strongly influenced by this general atmosphere and were soon not only convinced of the state's need and fundamental right to collect such statistics but increasingly saw the endeavour as an integral part of their mission.

[20] This was almost certainly in part the result of a number of government circulars in 1799 which tried to mobilize functionaries and a variety of organizations behind this collective effort including, for example, engineers, tax officials, road inspectors, the agricultural societies, and the professors and librarians of the *écoles centrales*. Gille, *Les Sources Statistique de l'histoire de France*, 1980, pp. 119–20. The birth of the *Annales des statistiques* provides a sense of this increasingly general interest.

Direct Pressure from Napoleon

Long-term socio-historical forces were not alone in suggesting to geographers the appropriateness of a close marriage between geography and the modernizing, imperialist state. There was also a more immediate pressure from Napoleon himself. Napoleon's appreciation of maps and cartography is legendary. What is less well known is that he had a clear sense of what descriptive, non-cartographic geography could offer the state and, further, that he expressed those views in writing. It is equally likely that he conveyed this sense verbally to key geographers with whom he came into contact – although this cannot be proven absolutely.

Napoleon had little time for the humanities which he felt had reached their pinnacle in classical times and were therefore unworthy of a place in institutions of higher learning. Anyone with a sound education could acquire all the insight such subjects had to offer by reading the classics themselves. Napoleon reserved his respect for the sciences – in particular mathematics, physics and chemistry. These formed the basis for engineering – perhaps the most useful of sciences. In fact, Napoleon shared the middle-class conviction (which developed and hardened through the nineteenth century) that it was the applied sciences rather than poetry, law or philosophy which were responsible for Europe's global dominance.[21] Geography, a proto applied science, taught in special schools to graduates of the elite science school for engineers, the École Polytechnique, benefitted from this conception of the intellectual hierarchy. Napoleon saw geography (and to a degree history, by virtue of the critical approach necessary to its study) as scientific – or reasonably so. In his view, geography revolved around facts, not interpretations or style. Yet not all the necessary facts had been established and there were points of dispute that could involve scholars in advanced research. In addition, its domain was a changing and expanding one by virtue of exploration, the growth of human understanding, and the constantly changing political and physical nature of the world.[22]

Together with his minister of the interior, Champagny, Napoleon planned the establishment of a school of geography and history within another elite institution, the College de France. His description of this new school makes clear, however, that he was less concerned with making geography part of the College's research and teaching agenda than in reforming the College de France, together with the sciences, including geography and history, into

---

[21] I have not explored the middle-class origins and views of many of the geographers that I have read from this period, but I strongly suspect that most would fit Adas's characterization of them as 'individuals who through hard work had risen above their modest family origins [and who] placed a high premium on improvement...' Adas, *Machines as the Measure of Men*, 1989, p. 184.

[22] The main source for Napoleon's views on descriptive geography is Lefranc, *Histoire du Collège de France*, 1893.

a useful appendage of The Great State. The school of geography was to be a central information bureau which would gather information on different parts of the world, trace and record any changes, make these known, and provide guidance to those who sought more information. The chairs of geography were to be four: maritime, European, extra-European and commercial and statistical geography. This last chair was to be devoted to the study of the source of the power of states, in the cameralist tradition and in keeping with the primary concerns of contemporary statistician–bureaucrats. For reasons that remain unclear, Napoleon's school of geography and history at the College de France was never instituted. As we shall see, however, there was an influential geographer who was to adopt Napoleon's concept of a central geographic information bureau devoted to the gathering and dissemination of new geographic information and to counselling the state on geopolitical and related matters.

It is clear then, that although geographers had long had strong ties to the centralized State in France[23], those ties intensified towards the end of the eighteenth century. This was, in part, a consequence of developments internal to science and to shifts in disciplinary territory. These encouraged geographers to expand their focus from the production of cartography on the one hand and regional description on the other to field- and text-based research into the material basis of the state. This coincided with and was related to changes in the nature of warfare and an evolving sense of the role and capacity of the state to monitor and control ever more local and particular aspects of social, political, and economic life. Geographers' traditional cartographic skills were of importance to these developments as were their newer preoccupations. As a result they became increasingly involved in state activities. This involvement, often in the vanguard, so to speak, of France's conquering forces, brought – and perhaps necessitated – participation in the ideologies fostering state aggrandizement.

THE NATURE OF GEOGRAPHIC PARTICIPATION IN IMPERIALISM

The pre-professional nature of the discipline of geography in this period – a characteristic of most modern disciplines in the early nineteenth century – meant that geographers, or people who called themselves geographers and wrote works of geography, were dispersed in a wide variety of professions. Their principal revenue-generating occupations ranged from military officer, to state

[23] The best examples of this close relationship are Buache and the Cassini dynasty. Buache served as tutor to the three kings of France, Louis XVI, Louis XVIII, Charles X. On this see Drapeyron, *Les deux Buaches*, 1888. See also Gille, *Les Sources Statistique*, 1980, p. 29; and Bourguet, *Déchiffrer la France*, 1988, pp. 23–30. The Cassinis were scientist–bureaucrats who worked with the permission and occasional support of the crown. The closeness of their ties to the dynasty is apparent in the fate of Cassini IV (Jacques-Dominiques) at the time of the Revolution.

administrator, to petty bureaucrat, to journalist, to impoverished or independently wealthy scientist. Their geographic skills were valued in each of these occupations and, whether or not they were in the immediate employ of the state, the state sought to secure the benefit of these skills. Military geographers were used to assess and improve the fit between conquered territory and France. Civilian geographers became involved in information gathering and easing acceptance of the sacrifices necessary for conquest both at home and in the conquered regions. Administrators oversaw the construction and imposition of a physical, economic and political infrastructure which was to link the conquered territories to France indissolubly.

All of the geographers studied in this chapter participated not only in the fact of imperialism but also in the elaboration and implementation of a nationalist imperialist ideology. The geographical engineers believed in their ability to *measure* the value of the peoples and cultures they were invading. This was fundamentally related to a growing western sense that the essence of western superiority lay in the accuracy and measurement of which the non-European cultures appeared incapable.[24] The civilian geographers did not fail to defend French aggression on the grounds that it was bringing peace, security, economic development, good government and finally 'civilization' to peoples unable to bestow these benefits upon themselves. Perhaps most strikingly common among the geographers was a view of local and indigenous culture as inherently less valid than the universal scientific culture of France (and if anyone had cared to mention it, of Britain – but for obvious political reasons no one did care to mention that during much of the revolutionary and Napoleonic periods). Geographers were not incidental participants in imperialism and imperialist ideology. They were central to the continued spatial expansion of France's universal scientific culture.

The most obvious service to the state and to imperialism was that of Napoleon's military geographers, the *ingénieurs-géographes*. These geographers were to be found wherever Napoleon's forces were engaged in combat, sometimes in advance of the army but most often either alongside or behind the army and employed in mapping operations designed to consolidate French control. Already in existence by the end of the seventeenth century as *ingénieurs des camps et armées*, under Napoleon they assumed far greater importance in terms of the sheer volume of their production, the manner in which it was coordinated and organized, and the new social scope of their research which gave them a special sense of participation in their state's imperialism.

It is hard to exaggerate the contribution made by the *ingénieurs-géographes* to the conquest of territories invaded by Napoleon's forces. They mapped rivers, mountains, canals, towns, cities, roads and ways, monuments, and the movement of armies all over Europe from Italy, Piedmont and Savoy to

---

[24] The veritable obsession with measurement among the French geographers in Egypt is discussed but without reference to its relevance to imperialist ideologies in Godlewska, 'Traditions, Crisis, and New Paradigms', 1989.

Elba, Corsica, Bavaria, Austria, Russia, Spain and Egypt. They even carried out mapping missions on special assignments beyond the reach of the army in Persia, Algeria, Santo Domingo, Louisiana, and Greece. They must have produced tens of thousands of maps in the course of Napoleon's reign. A report by Alexandre Berthier, written in October 1802, stated that in the last war alone[25], these geographers had produced 7278 engraved maps, 207 manuscript maps, 51 atlases and 600 descriptive memoirs.[26] For the expedition to Egypt (1798–1801), they sketched hundreds of manuscript maps and ultimately published an atlas of 50 topographic sheets together with innumerable town plans, maps of monuments, a hydrographic map of the country and a map of the ancient geography of Egypt.[27]

Prior to the Revolution the military engineers had had a tenuous administrative status. Fading in and out of existence as they were subsumed into other corps, and then once again given autonomous existence, they and their central office, the Dépôt de la guerre, had little continuous direction. The *ingénieurs-géographes*, who sometimes dwindled to fewer than twelve officers, generated maps upon the command of superior officers, the État Major, and the military engineers, while the Dépôt collected any maps made by these geographers and any other officers and civilians in the context of warfare. However, with the increasing importance accorded cartography and geographic information, the Dépôt became a more aggressive institution. It not only directed the geographers more closely but became something of a military geographic research and dissemination centre. It generated a journal designed to give the geographers a sense of identity, to keep them up to date on the latest technology and techniques, and to involve them in debates about military strategy and history. It fought for the introduction of a school for geographical engineers (the special school of geography mentioned above). Finally, it became the spearhead of an important movement to reform the language of geography in all the cartographic services, civilian and military. By 1802 there were 87 *ingénieurs-géographes* working for the Dépôt.

This stronger direction also contributed to making the geographical engineers into a more powerful instrument of national imperialism and the post-conquest consolidation of French domination. It was through the Dépôt and its many exceptional commanding officers,[28] who were in tune with current intellectual, military and political concerns, that the geographers were taught how to assess the conscription potential of a particular region, how to determine its crop yields, its human, animal, vegetal and mineral resources and the key aspects of its infrastructure, its commerce and its industry. It

[25] Presumably either the war of the Second Coalition or the campaign against Austria.

[26] Berthier, 'Rapport du Ministre de la guerre', 1802, p. 213.

[27] For more on the mapping carried out in Egypt see Godlewska, *The Napoleonic Survey of Egypt*, 1988.

[28] Including Chevalier Pierre-Alexandre-Joseph Allent, 1772–1837; Joseph-Secret Pascal-Vallongue, 1763–1806; Etienne-Nicolas de Calon, 1726–1807; Comte Antoine-Francois Andreossi, 1761–1828: Nicolas-Antoine Sanson, 1756–1840.

taught them how to question the local peasants so as to be sure to obtain undistorted information, how to procure information and cooperation from semi-hostile local administrations, and what aspects of local customs might prove of importance to the governance of these peoples. Under the guidance of the Dépôt, the engineers composed memoirs in which they summarized their observations and reported to the government on the newly conquered territories, and commented on what reforms, political, economic and social, were needed to improve the fit between the conquered region and France. Infusing their research was a developing certainty that the inherent value of a region, terrain or people could be accurately measured through the use of French scientific methods. Some of their observations and analyses were published (although Napoleon blocked the publication of many due to their potential strategic value) and in some cases they helped to form perceptions about the invaded regions and cultures well beyond military circles.

More impressive than the involvement of military geographers in such activities was the participation of their civilian counterparts. One geographer in particular deserves attention, both for his ready support for national imperialism (which was not exceptional), and for the way in which he created, with a less formal structure, the central geographic information bureau that Napoleon so desired. In 1807, in precisely the year that Napoleon was discussing the possibility of founding a school of geography and history at the College de France, Conrad Malte-Brun founded a geographic journal called the *Annales des Voyages*. [29] There is no way of proving that the idea for this journal came from Napoleon. Malte-Brun certainly had contact with Napoleon as the latter had asked him to write a book on Poland to explain the necessity and value of the French conquest. That book, published in 1807, suggests that Malte-Brun was more than prepared to serve and support Napoleon's imperialism. While it constituted an analysis of the political, social and economic slump into which Poland had fallen, his book emphasized the evil wrought by the partitioning powers and the need for a new constitution and a new social structure. It was written to justify the French action and to win the support of patriotic Poles. The Poles, Malte-Brun announced, were a great people, brave, noble, strong, tolerant, but whose country was in a complete shambles. He described how Poland had suffered as a result of the passions that agitated the capitals of Europe, but remarked that fortunately for Poland:

> There is a Great Man who has placed HIMSELF above all of those interests, who no longer has to desire or fear anything, who has identified HIS glory with the happiness of the human species. HE will know from the height from which HE contemplates the centuries and the universe, HE will know how to understand all circumstances, how to judge all interests and how to master passions. In raising HIS fellow monarchs up to HIS height, HE will gather them together around the

[29] Malte-Brun, *Annales des Voyages*, 1807.

altar of peace. HE will certainly combine in his vast plans all that is the greatest with all that is the most stable and the most just.[30]

Here we have evidence of a geographer's full participation in the deification not just of Napoleon the imperialist but indeed of imperialism itself.

That there were commonalities in the way Malte-Brun and Napoleon looked at geography is beyond doubt. Napoleon was interested in the practical assistance that geography could provide for his geopolitical and military musings. Malte-Brun saw the comparison of the strength of states as one of geography's principal concerns.[31] Napoleon respected geography because it dealt with facts and controversies and because new discoveries were a daily occurrence. Malte-Brun devoted his journal to presenting geographic facts and controversies and excluded from it all that was not new.[32] Napoleon expressed the need for a central office where information could be sought when it was needed. Malte-Brun described his journal as a 'dépôt'.[33] Malte-Brun argued that geography and his *Annales* were above particularist interests and that as a science it was above politics and 'embraced no other interests than those of humankind'.[34] Yet he described Napoleon as 'The Protector of the Sciences'.[35] The contemporary perception of the journal appears to have been that it was closely linked to the state – or at least that it had the ear of those working high up in the state. An author who published in the *Annales* declared that he did so in order that his interests might gain 'the protection of the government and all of the signs of its goodwill – to which it has a right by virtue of the usefulness and constancy of its work'.[36]

The *Annales* was not entirely devoted to geopolitics and the glorification of the regime. Malte-Brun published travel descriptions, natural histories, works on physical geography and pieces of pure erudition by recognized specialists. There was, however, a tendency to publish articles that revealed information of value to the state either in terms of the natural resources it described or in terms of geopolitics: certainly this was the case with the many articles (most of which were by Malte-Brun himself) on the Black Sea area, Spain, Austria, Prussia and two Danish Islands in the Baltic Sea.[37] Malte-Brun occasionally played the role of unofficial advisor to the sovereign. He

---

[30] Malte-Brun, *Tableau de la Pologne*, 1807, p. 486.

[31] Malte-Brun, *Précis de géographie universelle*, 1810–1829, 2, p. 601.

[32] Malte-Brun regularly congratulated or castigated authors in the review sections of his journal for the novelty or lack thereof in their research and writing.

[33] Malte-Brun, *Annales des voyages*, 1807, 1: 7.

[34] Ibid., 1807, 1: 14–15.

[35] Malte-Brun, *Tableau de la Pologne*, 1807, p. 1.

[36] Colin, *Extrait des Procès-verbaux de la Société d'émuation de l'Île-de-France*, 1809, p. 378.

[37] Malte-Brun, 'Periple de la Paphlagonie', 1810; '[A review of Lapie's] "Carte reduite de la Mer Mediterranée et de la Mer Noire"', 1810; '[A review of] "Campagnes des armées françaises en Espagne"', 1810; 'Apercu de la monarchie Autricienne', 1810; 'Description de l'île de Bornholm et des islots', 1810.

republished and thus vastly expanded the circulation of a pamphlet on the internal organization of a unified Poland. In so doing he may have been urging Napoleon in the direction of a sovereign unified Poland. [38] He suggested a particular route through the Middle East to attack the British in India. [39] He recommended a work on colonization in the Caribbean to those who claimed that France could not and should not hold colonies. [40] Finally, he devoted a long article to the argument that France should take the island of Taiwan, fortify it and use it as a commercial base to counter the British naval and commercial power in the Far East. [41] Apparently, no thought was given to the rights of the islanders to self-determination:

> What reason could possibly prevent Europeans from establishing themselves on an island that is at once beautiful, fertile and susceptible to all manner of civilization? [42]

He concluded this article with the observation that although he could provide a description of precisely how to undertake this colonization 'that would perhaps entail serving those that we would least want to serve'. (In other words, the English). Presumably, anyone in a position of authority had only to consult Malte-Brun.

In sharp contrast to Volney and the *ideologues* [43], Malte-Brun demonstrated little interest in and even less genuine empathy for non-European cultures. Civilization was a narrow corridor only wide enough to include the states of Europe – and by no means all of them. He published an article which argued that the Chinese civilization was no older and certainly less impressive than that of Europe. [44] He published and mocked an article by an Islamic specialist who was trying to answer the perennial European accusation that Islam is barbaric towards women. [45] Lest we be tempted to see Malte-Brun as a latter-day feminist, it is well to note that elsewhere, he commented 'What principally characterizes the savage state is the enslavement of women, just as at the other end of the chain the too great influence of the fair sex announces the corruption of the civilized state'. [46] During the French invasion

---

[38] Malte-Brun, '[A review of] "Coup d'Oeil sur la statistique de la Pologne" ', 1808.

[39] Malte-Brun, 'Nouvelle description de la Kwarizmie', 1809.

[40] Malte-Brun, 'Sur un voyage inédit fait aux États Unis', 1810.

[41] Malte-Brun, 'Analyse de quelques Mémoires Hollandais', 1810.

[42] Ibid., p. 369.

[43] On these and their relevance to geography see Gaulmier, *L'idéologue Volney 1757–1820*, 1951; Désirat and Hordé, 'Volney', 1984; Godlewska, 'Napoleonic Geography', 1990; E. Kennedy, 'Destutt de Tracy', 1977; and Moravia, 'Philosophie et géographie', 1967; amongst others.

[44] Guigne, 'Réflections sur les observations astronomiques', 1810.

[45] Khan, 'Preuves de la liberté des femmes en Orient', 1809.

[46] Review of *Voyage de découvertes aux Terres Australes*, 1809; Muchembled draws a connection between the concerted attempt to annihilate local culture in France and the

of Spain he commented on the natural savagery of the Spanish, attributed it to the southern sun and noted that the invading Romans had also found the Spaniards barbarous.[47] In general, those resisting French conquest were either deficient in civilization or misguided.

The fundamental lack of empathy for non-European peoples is nowhere more clear than in a description by Malte-Brun and his associate Mentelle of the French conquest of Egypt. Writing about the French invasion of Egypt and the city of Cairo, they reported:

> In the month of messidor, year 7, Cairo gave itself up to the French. The city in no way suffered at the hands of its conqueror and its *monuments, customs, religion* were respected. Its commerce lost nothing and the sciences and arts advanced to increase the happiness of the inhabitants.[48]

Some paragraphs later, however, they quote one of the generals on the expedition describing the 'reforms' that were attempted:

> It was necessary to organize the justice system, to establish municipal authorities, a general police force and an administration entirely devoted to the public good; *to wipe out all political and religious distinctions*, to accustom men of different religions to obey the same laws and to *change the nature of property* ...[49]

There is little doubt that what we have here is a basic incomprehension of the nature of culture, and its diversity. This incomprehension is, however, fundamentally related to the prevailing imperialist ideology and to a self-serving and uneven interpretation of civilization and culture. French civilization, which encompassed language, legislation, art, technology, economy and polity could easily swallow whole the local and indigenous cultures which were understood only as occurrences of monuments, customs and religions.

Chabrol de Volvic is another example of a civilian geographer who served the state. In contrast to Malte-Brun, however, he was directly attached to the state as a paid administrator. Although, to my knowledge, Chabrol never declared himself a geographer, he worked closely with geographers all his life, in Egypt, Italy and Paris, and wrote a number of important geographical statistical studies. Chabrol began his career as a civil engineer but through the good offices of Napoleon rapidly became a senior government administrator. Endowed with a well-developed sense of political balance, he managed

---

suppression of women which is one of a number of possible explanations for the many and apparently unwarranted anti-women outbursts one reads in the European literature of this period. Muchembled, *Popular Culture and Elite Culture*, 1985, pp. 165–70.

[47] Malte-Brun, 'Moeurs et usages', 1810, pp. 278, 316.

[48] Mentelle, and Malte-Brun, *Géographie mathématique*, 1803, pp. 107–8.

[49] Ibid.

to retain his post and even to continue to climb under the Restoration of the monarchy (1815–30). He wrote both as a geographer (often with other geographers[50]) and as a trusted servant of the state.[51]

Until 1812 and his substantial promotion to Prefect of the Department of the Seine, Chabrol's skills were repeatedly called upon to assist in the integration of recently conquered territories into the French realm. In Egypt he was still a young man and one of the many part-scholar, part-engineer, part-military officer types on the expedition. We know that he worked on supplying Alexandria with a permanent source of water; exploring, mapping and commenting on antiquities; and determining the extent of the population, the cultivable land and the number of villages in Egypt as an administrative tool and as the basis for a cadaster to regularize the system of taxation.

The aim of the cadaster was to wrestle control of the taxation system from the Copts so as to cut out the middlemen and render taxation both more efficient and more lucrative for the French rulers of Egypt. The Ottoman-dominated Mameluke system of government, which had been in existence in Egypt since the sixteenth century, had always suffered periods of disruption. As a result, Egypt had developed a Mafia-style system of government which spawned complex relations of protection and fealty (based on an on-going process of negotiation) between different groups: the Fellaheen (the Egyptian peasantry), the settled Arabs, the Bedouin, the Mamelukes, the Pasha and his entourage, the foreign traders, and the Copts. Over the course of the expedition to Egypt, the French moved back and forth between wanting all or some of the middlemen to assist in the government of the country, to wishing to eliminate them altogether. The French conception of the ideal Egyptian society clarified over time but was already evident in the writings of the members of the expedition. Egyptian society would be composed of rulers and producers. There would be a small French elite directing the country, a small governing class composed principally of former Mamelukes, and beneath them peasants, merchants, and industrialists. There was no room for semi-settled Arabs, for Coptic officials and least of all for the Bedouin.

The Muslim system of land ownership of the Iltizam, the Talaq and the Waqf, which was at the heart of relations between the Pasha, the Mameluke, the Sheik and the peasants, was seen as an impediment to the rational development of agriculture and industry for export. Prior to his departure for

[50] He acknowledges the assistance of Jomard for his work in Egypt; the heavy use of the statistics and field work of the military geographers for his work in Italy; and there are suggestions that his publication on the Department of the Seine was as much the work of the famous Baron Von Walkenaer as it was Chabrol's. See Lacroix, 'Walckenaer, Charles Anathase', n.d.

[51] That Chabrol was assigned responsibility for the internment, care, and control of Pope Pius VII from 1809 to 1811 is an indication of Napoleon's trust. Prévost, 'Chabrol', 1936.

France, Napoleon had attempted to institute private property by decree (or the confiscation of all lands not registered as private). [52] The result had been had been a revolt in which, interestingly, the office of the chief geographer–topographer on the expedition was attacked and the geographer himself killed. The cadaster, which became the primary responsibility of the expedition's cartographer–geographers, was an attempt to introduce private property (or the registration of land ownership) slowly, systematically and irremediably. All the essays written by the officials with geographic affiliations, such as Edme François Jomard, General Andréossy, Du Bois Aymé, Lancret, Louis Costaz, and Chabrol de Volvic, on the population, agriculture, industry, commerce, and landownership system of Egypt were directed toward this end. [53]

If Chabrol's role was relatively minor in Egypt, he was to embody the state in the new French Province of Montenotte as Prefect there from 1806 to 1811. Montenotte was a French administrative creation that upset the traditional trade and administrative patterns of Northern Italy. Liguria, formerly under Genoa, and Piedmont formerly under Sardinia were combined to create an extension of France into Northern Italy. Through Montenotte, Chabrol attempted to redirect these two independent economies into a littoral-appennine symbiosis such that the trees and charcoal of the hills could feed the iron, and ceramics industries of the coast with both agricultural and industrial produce being exported (via a heavy tariff) either directly to France by road

[52] There is some scholarly disagreement over the nature of property rights under the Egyptian Islamic system and under the French regime. Al-Rahim considers that the French moved Egypt further toward private land ownership through the confiscation of some Mameluke lands and their redistribution among the peasantry capable of paying the land taxes. Abd Al-Rahim, 'Land tenure in Egypt', 1984. Cuno considers that while Egyptian peasants did not enjoy 'private property' rights prior to the nineteenth century, their usufruct rights were so extensive that they may be considered tantamount to private property rights. He further argues the continuity of development between the traditional Islamic land law of the seventeenth and eighteenth centuries and the developments of the early nineteenth century. Cuno, 'Egypt's wealthy peasantry', 1984. While reviewing many of the same facts, Debs sees the early nineteenth century and the French invasion and subsequent French influence through the rule of Muhammad Ali as a rift with Islamic development and the beginning of a strong 'western' and 'modern' influence. Debs, *The Law of Property in Egypt*, 1963, p. 48.

[53] I would not be comfortable describing all of these individuals as geographers. Chabrol was more inclined to describe himself, and anyone who 'studies the many factors which influence climate ... the action of that climate on animate beings, the new men that he finds himself surrounded by ...", as a philosopher. Chabrol, 'Essai sur les moeurs', 1822, p. 361. For the most part in this period – although this was changing in precisely this generation of geographers – the science of geography was still seen as primarily map focused. This meant that while a man working on the cadaster saw himself as a geographer, an individual writing the articles exploring the aspects of the social, production or administrative structure to be modified by the introduction of the cadaster, might well describe himself as a philosopher – unless he had a tendency to employ a cartographic methodology in his study. See Godlewska, 'Traditions, Crisis, and New Paradigms', 1989.

or to France or elsewhere by sea. Montenotte was to produce and export primary products and to import manufactured goods from France.[54] To that end, Chabrol proposed the construction of a road from Nice to Genoa and a major Mediterranean port and town at Spezzia. The first step, however, in any such reform, as the French government had come to recognize, was the collection of information on the actual or potential wealth of the countryside: its natural resources, population (including calculations concerning the average strength of workers in particular regions and industries), agriculture (olives, silk, fruit trees, grain etc.), industry, and commerce. In what remains a valuable geographical study, Chabrol used the research carried out by the military geographers working in that area together with his own observations to create a remarkably detailed picture of the society and economy of the region.

Chabrol made few grand statements about the benefits of French government in Italy. He was not concerned to stand back and assess the pros and cons of French rule in the region, even at a distance of ten years. Rather, he assumed the whole imposed structure was sound and positive, and a simple matter of good administration. Here, as in Egypt, it was clear that what was needed was 'a benevolent authority'[55] to overcome the difficulties presented by the climate and physical geography of the region and by 'the old customs and above all ... institutions of the country'.[56] Never before had this people had the benefit of an administration that, with firmness, held itself above all local interests ('a multitude of little passions in a constant state of agitation'[57]) and moved the region forward in a single direction. As a result of this, he was convinced that French rule had 'spread ease and comfort among almost all the classes and particularly among the people.'[58]

Just as French geographers shared in Napoleon's military conquest of foreign cultures, in the collection and dissemination of information useful to, or supportive of, that activity, and in the post-conquest activity of fitting the conquered regions into the French economic and administrative structure, so too did they take part in the glorification of imperialism. In a world without television and film, paintings and maps were among the few means by which images of conquest could be brought back from the front. Thus, they were a much more powerful medium of expression than similar works would be today. It was primarily geographers who produced the magnificent landscape paintings and maps which glorified and celebrated both conquest and French rule in Italy. Pietro Giuseppe Baghetti's landscapes were among the most famous in the genre. Baghetti was a rationalist, who believed that with clarity of vision, accurate measurement, and the rational use of conventional and figurative codes, the human and physical landscape could be reproduced to

[54] Chabrol de Volvic, *Statistique*, 1824, 1: p. v.
[55] Ibid., 1: p. i.
[56] Ibid., 1: p. ij.
[57] Ibid., 2: pp. 466–7.
[58] Ibid., 2: p. 275.

express not only its beauty but its utility.[59] As a painter, he exemplified the fundamental faith reigning among the military geographers and the graduates of the École Polytechnique in their ability to understand the world and to shape it according to their ideals. Baghetti's work embodied this faith, celebrating both the daring of troops engaged in mountain battles and the extraordinary beauty of the territory that Napoleon had won for France.[60]

Working alongside Baghetti in Northern Italy was a team of military geographers. This team, and geographers like them elsewhere in the zones of conquest, was assigned the task of producing maps to record battles for the benefit of military history, instruction in strategy, and the glorification of Napoleon. The maps recorded Napoleon's brilliant strategy and the astounding topographical variety and fertility of the region.[61] The time and effort that went into this production, its rigour and, indeed, its striking visual quality speak not only of the geographers' commitment to their profession but of the importance Napoleon accorded the task.[62]

In Egypt, the 22-volume *Description de l'Egypte*, edited and compiled by Edme Jomard (an active geographer and one of the founders of the Paris Geographical Society) with the considerable support of Napoleon and the French government is one of the best possible examples of what Edward Said has called intellectual imperialism.[63] The authors, and French scholars in general, clearly saw themselves as bestowing French civilization on a barbarous modern Egypt and, generously and courageously, by virtue of scientific dominance rescuing, inheriting and continuing the ancient civilizations of Egypt, Greece and Rome.[64] Through the dismantling and removal of some monuments; through the many maps and drawings of monuments which could not be moved; through the studies of the backward state of Egypt's agriculture, industry and commerce; and through countless large-scale topographic maps, the French scholars sought to bring back the evidence which reinforced this conception of the course of human, and specifically, scientific development. This particular myth is still alive and well and lives, in a variety of forms, thinly disguised, in most of the educational institutions of western civilization.

[59] Baghetti, *Analisi della unita d'effetto*, 1827.

[60] For a list (unfortunately not exhaustive) of Baghetti's works, see: Ministère de la guerre, *Liste chronologique des tableaux*, 1901.

[61] These manuscript maps are available at the Service historique de l'armée de terre, Vincennes, under the call numbers L III 433 and L II 758.

[62] The correspondence surrounding the production of these maps and the quality sought by the government is to be found at the Service historique de l'armée de terre, Vincennes MR 1366.

[63] Said, *Orientalism*, 1979.

[64] A good clear example of this is to be found in Jacotin, 'Mémoire', 1822, p. 1, but it echoes through much of the *Description*.

ALSO SOLDIERS OF MODERNITY

From the perspective of the twentieth century, the Napoleonic geographers seem remarkably unconcerned about the disruption they were bringing to the societies they invaded. Yet these were not uneducated and thoughtless men. On the contrary, many had been to the best schools in France, gave every sign of reading widely, were curious about ways of life unlike their own, and thought carefully about the venture they were engaged in.[65] In fairness, however, while their education was technically superb, neither it, nor the regime, taught them the value of critical thought. The time for soul-searching and philosophizing about systems capable of overturning or improving the French social or political order had passed with the Terror. Intellectual individualists, such as Volney, who could think his way through, for example, the prevailing belief in the fixed 'character' of peoples and the European ideology of cultural superiority, were soon to fade altogether from the scene.[66]

Napoleonic geographers were not blind to the brutality and injustice of conquest and colonialism. Nevertheless, at no time did they see themselves as pillagers. They were, both in Italy and in Egypt, soldiers of modernity and civilization. This is nowhere clearer than in the writings of the geographers (and the engineers and administrators who worked alongside them) on the expedition to Egypt. They were missionaries of human progress as well as the high priests of science.

The critical link between imperialism and modernization lay in the argument that what was local or regional or indigenous was demonstrably inferior, and indeed an unacceptable obstacle to the national and supra-national uniformity that was the primary benefit of imperialism. Diversity was associated with degeneracy and uniformity with civilization. It was clear to the expedition scholars that 'civilization' [in the form of uniformity] would 'penetrate into the Middle East':

> Already our expedition in Egypt has familiarized its inhabitants with ways of life other than theirs; it has expanded their ideas, and weakened their prejudices; they have seen the superiority that the practice of our modern arts gives us and they are better disposed to practice these themselves than they were.[67]

[65] My sense of who these engineers were and of what their education and training consisted is derived from the XEM and MR files at the Service historique de l'armée de terre, Vincennes; from Berthaut, *Les ingénieurs géographes 1624–1831*, 1902; from the *Mémoriale du Dépôt de la guerre*, vols 1 and 2, 1829, 1831; entries by Balteau, Barroux, and Prévost *Dictionnaire de biographie française*, 1936; and *Biographie universelle* in *Ancienne et moderne* ...; in addition to a variety of published necrologies.
[66] These views and sensitivities are most clearly expressed in Volney, *Voyage en Syrie et en Égypte*, 1787.
[67] Girard, 'Mémoire sur l'Agriculture', 1809, p. 699.

Similarly, the tax system which the French sought to impose was described as administratively democratic in its uniformity while the Mameluke/Coptic system was seen as tyrannous and, thus, diverse. Variety was the natural outcome of 'an oppressive system' because in such a system 'the diverse landowners, each masters in their own district, are not consulted in order to establish equal taxes and procedures which are uniform in all parts of the state ...'[68] The geographers were convinced that uniformity and civilization could not be successfully imposed in Egypt as long as the European concept of private property met with serious opposition. Freehold tenure was 'the very basis and guarantee of social happiness'.[69]

It is in this light that the virtually unanimous hostility to the Bedouin, and settled and semi-settled Arabs must be seen. In spite of the fact that they were acknowledged to be superior cultivators, when they settled, and extremely successful raisers of horses, camels, and dromedaries, when they remained nomadic, Jomard, for example, argued that the Bedouin and the semi-settled Arabs should be driven from Egypt and that the settled Arabs should be disarmed, dismounted and have their tribal structure destroyed.[70] As Costaz explained,

> The agricultural way of life renders men more sensitive to the concepts of justice, order and property. Those who have embraced it are more easily touched by the action of the law. By contrast, the facility of movement of the pastoral life guarantees the impunity of almost all crimes. That is why that life, which is so precious to poets and so desired by men who have not observed human nature, incites brigandage.[71]

Uniformity was also threatened by the role of middlemen that the Bedouin had long played. In the atmosphere of conflict reigning in the periods of instability under the Mamelukes, they had provided an element of local protection. Further, the French recognized that they were highly successful conquerors and governors in their own right:

> The villages which, in spite of their limited strength, attempt to defend their independence, undergo a sudden Arab invasion. They kill the sheiks and replace them arbitrarily. They destroy the homes of those that they describe as their enemies, steal their land, and conduct themselves so cleverly and skilfully that they end by winning the friendship of the others.[72]

---

[68] Lancret, 'Mémoire sur le système d'imposition', 1809, p. 240. In reality, the French system was no more uniform than previous systems — the ideal was nevertheless uniformity.

[69] Volvic, 'Essai sur les moeurs', 1822, p. 478.

[70] Jomard, 'Mémoire', 1809, pp. 568–9.

[71] Costaz, 'Mémoire', 1809, p. 401.

[72] Jomard, 'Mémoire', 1809, p. 564.

It was noted that because they were also skilled merchants and lived frugally, they consistently drew more money from Egypt than they ever returned.[73] Much was made of the damage done by the Arabs to Egypt's agriculture and industry and their predations on the Fellaheen.[74] Is it possible that the roles of the Bedouin and the French invaders were so similar as to be antithetical? Jomard's assessment of the danger they represented would suggest this:

> The money that the Arabs thus accumulate ... must contribute to establishing their domination in Egypt as much as does the growth of their population and of their cavalry. And is it not evident that that influence must, by the nature of things, continue to grow and one day put Egypt into the hands of the Arabs?[75]

In the final account, according to Jomard, whether the Bedouin, the Copts, and the Mamelukes were to be eliminated or not should depend on their usefulness to France and their cooperation in the 'improvement of the country' or, otherwise put, in the economic and political linking of Egypt to France.[76] Agriculture was to be improved and redirected to production for export and profit. Industries based on primary agricultural production were to be encouraged and mechanized as soon as possible so as to prevent the price rises which would result from excessive dependence on an increasingly well-off labour force. Islam was to be discouraged and laws were to be introduced to protect and encourage agriculturally-based industry and commerce.[77]

CONCLUSION

Geography's close relationship to the state in France is far older than the revolutionary or Napoleonic periods. Nevertheless, it was under Napoleon that changes in the nature of warfare, together with an increasing awareness of the impact of the state on the daily activities of its citizens, began to reveal to a discipline, already in quest of a new role, the potent possibilities of deep involvement in the imperial ventures of the day. Although Napoleon had little interest in social scientific research, and indeed was suspicious of

[73] Ibid., p. 561.
[74] Much of the literature which explores the impact of the French invasion and subsequent French influence on Egyptian land ownership patterns is based on, and is consequently somewhat uncritical of, the research carried out by these French engineers while they were in Egypt. That is, it does not take into account the effect that Western prejudices with regard to Muslim law, religion and society might have had on the analysis.
[75] Jomard, 'Mémoire', 1809, p. 561.
[76] Ibid., pp. 558 and 561.
[77] Girard, 'Mémoire', 1809.

its tendency to criticism, his insistent demands for mapping, his constant need for geographic information, and his general encouragement of utilitarian research further served to stimulate the discipline.

Geographers responded by serving according to their particular skills, training and posts. Military geographers continued to function as cartographers but expanded their operations into social scientific research. Geographers, such as Malte-Brun, with high public visibility became state propagandists and informal state advisors. Administrators with geographic interests and skills became indispensable to the post-conquest social, political and economic integration of the conquered regions into France or into the French system. More than mere supporters of national aggression, these geographers became instruments and advocates of imperialism. In so doing, they saw themselves as both advancing French civilization and heralding and effecting a new and better order.

Since the Napoleonic period western societies have more consistently demonstrated their commitment to modernity than to reflection on its contradictions and cost. As such, the activities of Napoleon's geographers traditionally have been seen and continue to be described as significant contributions to the advancement of science and to the study of European and non-European cultures, both ancient and modern.[78] There is no doubt that the scholars on the expedition to Egypt, with the geographers figuring largely among them, did reveal ancient Egypt to western eyes and indirectly to the modern inhabitants of the country. They also, however, placed Egypt and its people into a context, political, economic, and cultural from which they have never emerged. Certainly, it is clear that the French demonstration of the potential strategic and economic importance of the country had everything to do with its ultimate invasion by the British later in the century. In the course of the nineteenth and twentieth centuries Egypt underwent radical social, political, economic and ecological revolution – by no means all of which could be described as positive.

To Italy, Napoleon's forces, with geographers among them, brought roads, innovations in agriculture, the seeds of unification, stimulation of nascent industries, the fundamental weakening of feudal structures, the destruction and theft of art works, monasteries and convents, and a period of economic dislocation and intense social misery. Geographers as military engineers and disseminators of information, state advice, administration and plaudits played a key role in Napoleonic imperialism. The recognition of their dual contribution on the one hand to the advancement of science and on the other to the advancement of imperial aggression and cultural domination constitutes a recognition of the ideological nature of modernity.

[78] An excellent recent study in this vein is Laurens et al., *L'Expédition d'Égypte, 1798–1801*, 1989.

Plate 2 This caricature by Raffet, is entitled 'Nous civiliserons ces gaillairds-là ...' ('We're going to civilize these strapping fellows.') From Gabriel Esquer, *Iconographie historique de l'Algérie depuis le XVIe siècle jusqu'à 1871*, (Paris: Plon, 1929) plate 138. By permission of the Bibliothèque nationale, Paris.

PART II

Geography's Scramble

Introduction

The nineteenth century was in many ways the century of empire, culminating in a scramble by virtually all European powers to demarcate colonial
territory especially in Africa. Colonialism, a distinct form of imperial expansion, came to represent the global geography of modern capitalism. Across
five continents, European states, private corporations, and individual explorers
sought to identify and to exploit natural resources, precious metals, markets
and local labour power. They imposed political and military control, battled
or bargained with local ruling elites, confronted or diverted local opposition,
implanted foreign cultural practices and participated in the development of
new hybrid cultures in the 'contact zone'. Geographers played many roles in
these pursuits. They were explorers, mappers, and surveyors; scientific cata-
loguers of places and resources; colonial administrators and military advisors;
and they participated in the multifold debates about the advisability and
rationale of imperial expansion, the justifications for conquest, and about
appropriate places to conquer. And geographers' own experiences of empire
helped set agendas for research. Colonial or tropical geography became a
distinct sub-field in many national schools of geography.

Not surprisingly, given the large time period, the many national traditions
and considerable territorial extent comprised by European imperialism, the
particular experiences and styles of empire were diverse. Indeed, much as it
was the century of empire, it was also home to the first decolonizations in
modern history, namely the independence of several Latin American states
from one of the earliest colonial powers, Spain. In chapter 3 in this section,
Horacio Capel explicitly connects Spain's early imperial expansion to an
enlightenment vision, and shows how large-scale mapping and geographic
research projects in Spanish colonies as well as independent states contributed to Spain's spasmodic attempts to hold and unite the remnants of its
empire. But it was the scramble for colonies towards the end of the century,
and the internecine battles between European powers induced in part by
this scramble, that had the most decisive influence on the development of
geography. Throughout Europe, a myriad geographical societies, exploration
societies and other scientific bodies were established in pursuit of different
aspects of empire; and especially following the Franco–Prussian War and

Paris Commune of 1870–1, this institutionalization of geography reached into the academy with existing offerings in geography greatly expanded, chairs and departments founded and journals published. In countries like Germany and Italy, where the nation–state was still forming, the connection of geography and empire with nation building was clear; and as the chapters 4 and 6 by Lucio Gambi and Gerhard Sandner and Mechtild Rössler show, the nineteenth-century colonial movement in these countries survived defeat in World War I and contributed, in the 1930s, to the practical and ideological contours of a new form of imperial claim: fascism. In the more established states such as Britain and France, geographers' imperial zeal was no less nationalistic, but the rhetorical connection to nation-building may have been more muted. In chapter 5, Michael Heffernan shows that several threads of imperial justification – some stronger than others – ran through French society and were expressed in the geographical literature. In France as elsewhere, however, outright anti-imperialism seems to have been missing in the geography of this period, despite the existence of an anti-imperial movement in French civil society. Why, we might ask ourselves, was geography in France and elsewhere apparently so immune from the anti-colonial movement?

3

The Imperial Dream: Geography and the Spanish Empire in the Nineteenth Century

Horacio Capel*

The sudden collapse of the Spanish Empire during the Napoleonic invasion concluded a period in which geography had played an essential part in re-ordering the country's eighteenth-century American possessions. Nevertheless, many territorial projects in the now independent America were a continua-tion of Spanish initiatives begun during the Enlightenment and Spain main-tained its links with the overseas provinces of Cuba, Puerto Rico and the Philippines. In these territories Spain launched new surveys and geographical reconnaissance projects which were to serve as the basis of a new adminis-trative structure. The difficulties at home of imposing the bourgeois regime in nineteenth-century Spain hindered Spanish participation in the race for African dominions. Nevertheless, politicians and intellectuals alike aspired to an African empire. Geography played a crucial role in the elaboration of this dream by stimulating ideological debates and studies focusing on the northern and western parts of the continent.

GEOGRAPHY AND SCIENCE IN THE RE-ORDERING OF SPANISH AMERICA

In the last three decades of the eighteenth century, the administrative, eco-nomic, and social structures of the Spanish Empire in America underwent profound transformation. This change was closely related to the increasingly

* This chapter is based on a larger research project being carried out under the auspices of the Interdepartmental Commission on Science and Technology of the Spanish Ministry of Education and Science (Project PB87–0462–C05–02).

important part played by science and scientists in rationalizing the exploitation of the colonies through a more rigorous appreciation of their resources. Geography was an important facet of the enlightenment programme
of scientific research, producing not only precise cartography but also regional
descriptions, geographical statistics, studies of the natural environment and,
in collaboration with others, analyses of political economy.[1] Scientific expeditions organized by Spain were a factor in both the diffusion of enlightenment ideas and the development of emancipationist ferment.[2]

The process of independence, which began in 1810 during the Napoleonic
invasion of Spain and was concluded twenty years later, interrupted the
programme of reform and led to the fragmentation of joint initiatives with
the different republics. As a result of the tension between centralism and
federalism, a similar fragmentation occurred within the borders of some of
these republics. The old colonial administrative divisions frequently served as
the basis for a new political and administrative organization and were even
maintained at the regional and municipal levels but with essential denomina-
tive changes.[3]

In spite of their separation from Spain, the new states pursued cartographic
and territorial studies in the tradition of the enlightenment programme of
reform and with the participation of former members of the Spanish administration, the Creoles or Spaniards who remained on the American continent
after independence. Some technical bodies were established on the Spanish
model. This was the case with the military engineers who for many years
were entrusted with tasks associated with the territorial organization of the
state – tasks similar to those they carried out under Spanish rule.[4] Particular
scientific projects interrupted by independence were later continued as institutional endeavours whose enlightenment origins can be easily detected: from
coastal cartography which was a continuation of the great surveys of all the
coasts of the empire initiated by the Spanish Navy in 1787, to the maintenance of specific institutions such as the Escuela de Náutica de Cartagena
de Indias. The latter was re-established in 1822 by Rafael Toro, an ex-officer
of the Fidalgo expedition who was born and educated in Spain but who later
served the newly independent Americas.[5]

In general it can be stated that the chorographic, natural, and economic–
statistical approaches developed at the end of the eighteenth century and
the beginning of the nineteenth by the participants of the various botanical
expeditions, by Félix de Azara and other technicians commissioned to establish the boundaries between Brazil and Spanish territory, and by sailors,
officers and naturalists, served as the model throughout the first half of the

[1] Capel, *Geografía y Matemáticas*, 1982; Sellés, Peset, and Lafuente (eds), *Carlos III*, 1988.

[2] Peset, *Ciencia y libertad*, 1989.

[3] Orozco y Berra, *Apuntes para la historia de la Geografía*, 1881; facsimile edition, p. 345.

[4] Capel, Sánchez, and Moncada, *De Palas a Minerva*, 1988.

[5] Lucena, *Ciencia y crisis política*, 1990.

nineteenth century for territorial studies undertaken in the Americas. The chorographic commissions which were established in some countries were a good example of this.[6]

GEOGRAPHY AND THE RECONSTRUCTION OF THE REMAINS OF THE EMPIRE IN AMERICA: CUBA

After the Declaration of Independence by Spanish American provinces, Spain ceased to be an important colonial power and retained only Cuba and Puerto Rico, situated as they were in an economic and geopolitical position of considerable interest. They also retained the Philippines which had had ties with the Americas since the sixteenth century and was now obliged to look for new channels of communication with Spain.

The rapid growth of Cuba's black slave population, the result of continued breaching of anti-slave-trade measures, assured considerable wealth for the owners of sugar plantations. If the maintenance of their ties with the mother country, Spain, had been influenced by fear of a slave revolt, the growth in the number of slaves and freed slaves nevertheless increased the probability of a revolt. By 1841 the total number of black slaves was more than double the figure at the beginning of the century. If this number (436,000 people) is added to the number of freed slaves (152,000), it amounted to 59 per cent of the total population of the island with a volatile age structure dangerous to whites, and large areas in which the black population had a comfortable majority. It was in this context that the introduction of a white labour force and other non-black workers (from Yucatan and China) together with the increasing application of steam technology to sugar machines and the development of new communication systems, such as the railway (1837), became a broadly discussed and applied alternative with resulting economic, social and territorial consequences.

Slavery was corrupting the entire political system. Landowners would not even accept the political equality of free blacks. It was for this reason that special political concessions had been made by Spain to Cuba and other overseas territories since 1837. The nineteenth century was full of debates about the application of successive Spanish constitutions in these territories and, consequently, about assimilation and autonomy, and about the equality or inequality of their inhabitants with Spaniards.

Throughout the nineteenth century, measures to reorganize the administration required the compilation of maps and statistical works, but these were also necessary for defence and for promoting whatever development policies Spain or the island authorities chose to undertake. It was in this context that between 1821 and 1828 work on the *Geographic and Topographic Map of Cuba*

---

[6] On Chile, see Gangas, *La evolución de la geografía chilena*, 1985; and on Colombia see Restrepo, 'La Comisión Corográfica', 1984 and Obregón, 'La sociedad de Naturalistos', 1992.

was carried out by a large group of military engineers and public and naval surveyors under the direction of José Gaspar J. de Valcourt.[7] Their efforts produced a large map of the whole island and several partial maps and plans, as well as statistical data and physical and political reports drawn up by the specially created Sección de Estadística y Topografía. Other hydrographic surveys of the coasts (1830–3) were executed under the direction of the Navy, and led to the publication of a spherical map of the Antilles by the Dirección de Hidrografía – another late fruit of the great enlightenment plan to chart the empire's coasts.

The political reforms undertaken from 1837, which ought to have led to the drafting of special laws, stimulated geographic, statistical and cartographic research. The need to centralize, integrate, and rationalize the various branches of the administration (judicial, military, taxation, etc.) according to the provincial model developed within Spain (drawn up in 1833) led to the creation of the Comisiones de Estadística y División Territorial in the 1840s. This commission was to study the condition of Cuba in a manner similar to the research being carried out in Puerto Rico, and to conduct censuses (1841), compile statistics, compose maps, and draw up territorial divisions. This last objective led, in the 1850s and 1860s, to a wide-ranging debate. There were those who suggested that, with the increase in wealth and population, there should be more administrative units but of smaller size. Others considered that, for reasons of strategy and cost, the number of administrative units should not be increased. There were even those who preferred the retention of the traditional administrative structure rather than of enlightenment-inspired boundaries fixed along natural landmarks or astronomically-established lines. Added to all this, there was the question of how to maintain a strong centralization with regard to Spain and, internally, with regard to the island's government, while allowing for some degree of municipal or provincial autonomy that would not be used to the advantage of the autonomists or, later, the independentists.

The key figures in these debates and in the geographic and cartographic works of the period were the brigadiers Juan Herrera Dávila and Juan Rodríguez de la Torres, directors of the Comisiones de Estadística. There were also surveyors like Mariano Carles and Esteban Pichardo, the author of *Geografía de la Isla de Cuba* (1854), and employees of the Comisiones de Estadística such as Tranquilino S. Nodal and José María de la Torres who wrote a *Diccionario Geográfico Cubano*.

The extensive cartographic production of the nineteenth century in Cuba, and to a lesser extent in Puerto Rico and the Philippines, was for the most part carried out by the military: engineering, artillery, navy and army staff. The work of the military engineers is particularly important. Under the direction of figures like Antonio Ventura Bocarro (from 1819), Anastasio Arango (1835), Mariano Carrillo (1841) and others, these engineers not only took charge of cartography and the elaboration of defence plans but also of civic

[7] Nadal, 'La formación de la Carta Geógrafo-Topográfica de Valcourt', 1989.

and public building projects. These ranged from the projects drawn up at the beginning of the century by Félix and Francisco Lemaur for the Güines and Batabanó canals and the Vejurcal River Reservoir – which could be considered a result of the measures proposed by the Mopox Expedition[8] – to the economic development ventures promoted on the island in the nineteenth century. This cartography, for the most part unpublished, continued the corporate tradition of the eighteenth century into the first few decades of the nineteenth, but it changed with the 1830s and 40s. The military engineers were entrusted by decree with the production of territorial maps at a variety of scales and were also charged with drawing up plans of the principal towns and fortresses and their surrounding areas. It goes without saying that they accomplished their work diligently. Apart from these military engineers, it is worth mentioning the public surveyors and their participation in urban planimetry. Some of these were also master builders: apart from Carles and Pichardo mentioned above, we should note Alejo Helvecio Lanier, Juan O'Conor or Vicente Sebastián Pintado. These and others collaborated on the urban reforms carried out in Havana and other Cuban cities from the time of General Tacón.[9]

Geography, natural science, statistics and political economics often went hand in hand in the intense debates on the reforms to be undertaken in Cuba. These debates were rooted in the enlightenment tradition[10] and such influential works as Alexander von Humboldt's *Essai politique sur l'Île de Cuba* (1826), which would later be reinforced by the impact of positivism. An 'objective' knowledge of reality was the starting point for controlling or transforming it. Numerous publications attacked problems of the Cuban economy: modernization and the sugar farmer's monoculture markets – the source of the island's wealth; free trade; the substitution of slave labour by wage labour; the privileged relationship with Spain; and the appraisal of a colonial pact which was attempting to turn Cuba into a closed market and a supply area for certain products (the 'ultra-marinos'). The works of Ramón de la Sagra[11] or Ramón María de Labra are good examples of an analytical approach to social phenomena which displayed an absolute faith in science, the need for observation, and the utility of statistics.

THE DISTANT COLONIES OF ASIA AND OCEANIA

In the thirty or forty years after the collapse of the Spanish Empire, Spain's main colonial problem was to hold on to and to unite the dispersed remains of empire in America (Cuba and Puerto Rico), Asia and Oceania (the

---

[8] The Mopox expedition had been sent to Cuba in 1796, returning in 1802.

[9] Fraile, 'La necesidad de remodelar un espacio', 1988.

[10] On the development of enlightenment thought in Spain in the second half of the nineteenth century, see Capel, 1982; Sellés, Peset, and Lafuente, 1988.

[11] Fraile, 'Ciencia y utopía', 1989.

Philippines, the Caroline, Mariana and Palaos islands) and Africa (the sovereign outposts in northern Africa and Fernando Po in Equatorial Guinea). The difficult consolidation of its domestic bourgeois order absorbed all of Spain's energies and for some time there was little interest in the far-flung colonies. The initial perception was that these marginal possessions meant little in comparison to what had been lost. Some even advocated the sale or lease to other foreign powers – an idea made more attractive by such offers as the United States made for Cuba in 1845 and those that the English and the Germans made for islands in Asia and Oceania later in the century.

Communication with the Philippines and the small Pacific archipelagos created new problems. These areas, as dependencies of Mexico, had been connected to Spain through the Americas since the sixteenth century. New routes had to be found which would arouse interest in possible ports of call on the African continent. After the opening of the Suez Canal, the Red Sea route became more important and in the 1860s negotiations were begun to obtain ports of call and refuelling stations on the African coast of the Red Sea. Victor Abargués de Sostén's journey to Ethiopia and subsequent lectures at the Sociedad de Geográfica de Madrid in 1883 reaffirmed interest in this route. This was further supported by the *Congreso Español de Geografía Colonial y Mercantil* which insisted that Spain must have trading posts on the Red Sea, 'in order to protect our interests and provide support on the route to the Philippines and the Far East'.

Despite three centuries of Spanish occupation of these islands, the Philippines and its dependent islands (the Caroline, Mariana and Palaos islands) continued to be a distant colony in the nineteenth century, not entirely dominated and little known. Manila and some other cities certainly were well developed urban nuclei with a typically European aura. Outside the cities there was a busy regional hinterland where the presence of European religious orders continued to be important. The development of rural property was minimal, however, and associated with the imposition of state-run reservations for the indigenous population as well as large church properties. The development of commercial agriculture was also minimal, except in the case of tobacco.

From the middle of the century, interest in the Philippine archipelago began to revive and found a new lease on life with the opening of the Suez Canal. The Dirección General de Hidrografía encouraged the charting of the coastline as well as the establishment of new navigational routes. There was also an effort to stimulate commerce and agriculture and exploit the great wealth of the island's timber, traditionally used for ship building. It was in this capacity that a group of mountain or forestry engineers was sent to the islands. Their activities were to have considerable scientific and organizational impact. [12]

The forestry engineers concentrated their research on the flora of the Philippines and on the scope for its exploitation. Within a few years they

[12] Casals, 'Montes e ingenieros en Ultramar', 1989.

had considerably advanced botanical knowledge, announcing 1,804 previously unknown species (from 2,779 known species in 1878 to 4,583 in 1882).[13] They also studied the territory, its natural resources, botanical geography, agricultural development and the native and immigrant populations, producing proposals for economic advancement. S. Vidal, head of the Inspección de Montes de Filipinas and Ramón Jordana, director of the Comisión de la Flora Forestal produced significant examples of this type of work. Vidal's *Memoria sobre el Ramo de Montes en las Islas Filipinas* (1874) looked at social and economic problems and agricultural development while Jordana in *Bosquejo Geográfico e Histórico-Natural del Archipelago Filipino* (1885) produced an excellent natural, geographic, statistical, and ethnographic description of the islands. Jordana lamented the fact that islands were 'less than unknown, at least with regard to scientific knowledge' and that Spain had not followed the example of other colonial powers in entrusting the study of the terrain and its vegetation 'to enlightened and competent officials'.

Similar regrets were expressed at one time or another by members of the Sociedad Geográfica de Madrid from 1876, but especially after 1880. These were related to the awakening of an active Spanish pro-colonial feeling, to which we will turn shortly. In addition to the traditional threat which England posed for the islands, there were also conflicts with Germany over the Mariana and Caroline Islands in this period which nearly resulted in armed confrontation in 1885. Concerned about these threats so close to hand, and stimulated by the geographers, the government decided to reorganize the administration and economy of the colonies. The Sociedad Geográfica de Madrid held many sessions and lectures to debate these problems and to propose concrete reforms, which were published in the pages of its *Boletín*. In one of these, entitled 'Algunas observaciones prácticas sobre colonización', the Marqués de Reinosa, who had considerable experience in the Philippines, proposed an ambitious plan of reform on the premise that 'the increase in the population of old Europe, whose impoverished soils do not produce enough to sustain its inhabitants, naturally leads to people emigrating to young America or even younger Oceania in search of the necessary sustenance which is lacking here'. The Marqués chose this forum because, he said, the Sociedad Geográfica had been a pioneer on the subject of colonization, and had welcomed colonial ideas 'with such enthusiasm and good will that it [had] given all possible support to every colonial project of however small or grand a scale'.[14] The Marqués proposed an ambitious colonization plan for the Philippines, based on the activities of a private company with economic and commercial privileges, as well as the following additional measures:

1 'Take a sufficient number of Chinese to the country to clear the land of trees and then plough it thoroughly, an impossible task for whites where Chinese convicts would be of great assistance;'

[13] Jordana Morera, *Bosquejo Geográfico e Histórico*, 1885, p. 446.
[14] Marqués de Reinosa, 'Algunas observaciones prácticas', 1892, pp. 186–96.

2 'When this job is finished, after a few years of ventilating the land and having grown the odd easy crop merely to prevent forest vegetation taking root again, the fields will then be in a condition for the colonists to go there, bearing in mind that they will always need the help of the Chinese or natives – if there are any – for many jobs. Otherwise many tasks would be impossible for them to perform on their own;'

3 Attention was to be paid to health conditions, for these were a fundamental problem as was the provision of a diet similar to that in Spain 'for in an enervating country in which there is a certain tendency towards anaemia, if the food supply consists mainly of rice, as it does for the Indians, the colonists will soon waste away.'

4 Finally. 'it is known that our colonization of the Philippines is founded on the superiority of the white race over the indigenous race; without this it would be impossible to sustain ourselves and so it is very important to preserve this superiority. All Spaniards occupy superior positions with respect to the Indians. Even the soldiers themselves, who are treated in a different way. White supremacy, without which the archipelago would be lost to us, must be preserved at all costs.'[15]

THE AFRICAN HORIZON AND THE NEW IMPERIALISM

Since the sixteenth century Spain had maintained military outposts in North Africa in an attempt to forestall any Muslim invasions (Ceuta, Melilla and Orán in the eighteenth century). It had also been interested in the north Atlantic coasts for their proximity to the Canary Islands and the consequent access to fishing grounds. On a more limited scale, it had also kept an eye on the coasts of the Gulf of Guinea which it had inherited from the Portuguese and where it had intended to position slave-trading posts. The 1835 Anglo–Hispanic Treaty to control the traffic of black slaves gave a legal pretext for the English to capture and register ships on these equatorial coasts, a practice which allowed them to take effective control of the Atlantic and to drive the Spanish out.

The Spanish–Moroccan War of 1860 represented Spain's first African colonial initiative but had no immediate consequences. The African dream, which can be seen as a late continuation of the medieval Reconquista, inevitably languished with Spain's internal convulsions. These were caused by economic problems and the changes in political regime, from the Monarchy in 1868, to the First Republic in 1873 to the Restoration of 1875. Apart from the cartographic operations connected with the war, prior to 1860 and in the following decade the only more or less sanctioned imperial activities were individual explorations which had missionary or espionage objectives. Among these were the voyage of A. Badía Leblich (known as Ali Bey) and those of Murga, Gatell, Benitez and Lerchundi.

[15] Ibid., pp. 186–96.

From the 1870s a new European imperialism began to unfold, corresponding to a new phase in the development of capitalism. Coinciding with this, in the last three decades of the nineteenth century, and in particular after the Restoration in 1875, there was a renewed interest in colonial matters in Spain. Several different groups readied themselves for the race for Africa and concentrated their attention on three areas of the African continent: tropical Atlantic Africa; the Saharan coasts; and the Maghreb. Exploration, the expansion of geographical knowledge, and the ideological manipulation of spatial concepts each played a fundamental role in these undertakings.

The foundation of the Sociedad Geográfica de Madrid in 1876 had a significant influence on the shape of Spain's new colonial mentality. The Society was founded on the initiative of Francisco de Coello, a military engineer and key figure not only in the development of nineteenth-century Spanish cartography and statistics – along with Carlos Ibañez de Ibero – but also in the organization of the Instituto Geográfico y Estadístico.[16] The objectives listed in the founding charter of the Society, apart from the task of 'promoting the advancement and diffusion of geographical knowledge', included the study of Spanish territory 'and her overseas provinces'. A vague and non-committal supplement declared as another of the Society's aims the study of 'those countries with which Spain already has important connections or where it appears opportune to promote them'. The Society was formed during a change of regime when there was a prevailing feeling of distrust for the country's political forces. Great attention was to be paid to forgotten glories because, as Coello argued in his inaugural speech on 2 February 1876, 'we are fated to live in distressing times in which there is neither the tranquillity nor the resources to dedicate to the search for new glories, and in which we must be content to live only with memories; we can, however, count on the advantage of being able to explore the wealth which our ancestors built up for us in their daring expeditions.'[17]

Before very long, however, colonial interests became better served. In that same year, 1876, the Society participated in the Brussels conference which set up an International Association for the Exploration and Civilization of Central Africa, promoted by King Leopold II. This participation gave them direct knowledge of European plans for the penetration and partition of Africa for apparently 'scientific, charitable, and philanthropic' reasons, and which purported to 'introduce civilization' into the Continent. On the initiative of Coello and shortly after the conference (February, 1877), the Asociación Española para la Exploración del Africa was founded in Madrid at a meeting presided over by King Alfonso XII. A number of members of the Sociedad Geográfica joined the Asociación. By April 1877, the *Boletín* of the Society had already published an article by Coello on

---

[16] Nadal and Urteaga, 'Cartography and State', 1990; Muro, *El pensamiento militar*, 1992.

[17] Muro, *El pensamiento militar*, 1992.

Spain and the exploration of Africa in which he defended the country's future participation in the African market, which was just about to open.

From that moment, against a background of general apathy toward African expansion on the part of leading Spanish groups, interest in colonial matters continued to grow in the Society. E. Hernández-Sandoica has demonstrated the predominance of officials, scientists and members of the 'petite bourgeoisie' in a project which lacked the active support of both industrialists and major traders.[18] The 1880s played a decisive role in this evolution and in the crystallization of a colonial plan for Africa. Encouraged by the activity of Joaquín Costa and other intellectuals, a colonial ideology began to take shape whose aim was the opening of markets for Spanish products and the quest for cheaper and alternative sources of products destined for consumption by the lower classes. At the same time, this ideology promised opportunities for the urban and merchant middle classes. Intellectuals argued that this African enterprise would diminish social conflict and lead to the discovery of places where the 'surplus' Spanish peasant population, noticeably affected by demographic changes and the rigours of the agrarian infrastructure, could be sent. In addition, there were without doubt issues of political prestige and of a more geostrategic nature to which the military members of the Sociedad Geográfica were sensitive.[19] In particular, the Saharan coasts and the intervention in Morocco were seen as essential for the security of the Peninsula and the Canary Islands.

From the beginning of the 1880s, the Sociedad Geográfica de Madrid, while concerned with the diffusion of geographical science, also aimed to persuade public opinion to support geographical exploration and published historical documents to support its territorial claims. Some members, such as C. Fernández Duro and R. Torres Campos, even proposed that the Society abandon its purely speculative projects and dedicate more energy to 'problems of some practical use such as the relations with commercial geography'. The Society declared that it was ready to promote a 'trial commercial venture' which would serve as a model for other initiatives.[20]

In 1883 the Congreso Español de Geografía Colonial y Mercantil, sponsored by the Sociedad Geográfica, gave a public airing to the pro-colonial position in economic, social, and intellectual circles, a position encouraged by those in favour of free trade. Immediately afterwards, in those crucial months which coincided with the Congress of Berlin (1884), a whole series of African and colonial issues were put forward. Geography was an important factor in all of these. In Barcelona, the Sociedad de Geografía Comercial, at the instigation of the merchant seaman José Ricart Giralt, also tried to enhance colonial and commercial geography. It published commercial and production statistics and studied 'the present condition of our colonies, their promotion, and the convenience and practicality of founding new ones and of stimulating

[18] Hernández-Sandoica, *Pensamiento burgués y problemas*, 1982.

[19] Muro, *El pensamiento militar*, 1992.

[20] Duro and Torres Campos, *Boletín de la Sociedad Geográfica*, 1883.

explorers to undertake journeys with the aim of opening up new commercial markets'. In Seville, there was the short-lived Sociedad de Africanistas which brought together traders, military men, and intellectuals. In Madrid the Sociedad Española de Africanistas y Colonistas, of which Francisco de Coello was president and Joaquín Costa 'director of explorations', was founded to encourage private initiatives in African colonization and to compensate for minimal official involvement. This Society was a tireless promoter and sponsor of expeditions to the continent. It was later transformed into the Sociedad Española de Geografía Comercial which produced the *Revista de Geografía Comercial* (1885). As its initiatives flourished, the Sociedad Geográfica de Madrid could focus more directly on the tasks of promoting and disseminating scientific knowledge – geographical, natural, and historical – although it never abandoned, as we shall see, its interests in colonial matters.

AREAS OF INTEREST IN AFRICA

After 1880 and the emergence of a pro-African movement, the colonial urge became very clear. The whole of Europe including Spain was ready to conquer and 'civilize' the continent. In 1882 the secretary of the Sociedad Geográfica de Madrid wrote in the Society's journal:

The storm, which for years has threatened the more or less savage countries of Africa and their inhabitants, has begun to break in 1882. Providence has issued her instructions and the civilized countries dutifully obey, each from its own particular viewpoint, as if they wanted to demonstrate the alliance between free will and divine decree. This continent must be the future and irrevocable source of comfort for the population of Europe. Today the entire world has its gaze fixed on Africa. [21]

Despite the fact, as this same geographer complained, that Spain 'does not like adventures and seems tired of putting her own house in order', Spain joined the race for Africa, concentrating her effort in three particular areas: Morocco, the Saharan coast, and the Gulf of Guinea. Spain, in direct competition with France and indirectly with Great Britain, sought political influence in Morocco and with it strategic security, new markets, and territories where peasants could settle. Ceuta and Melilla, over which Spain had sovereignty, served as excellent bases from which to install an infrastructure for the penetration of the continent.

As the members of the Sociedad Geográfica and the Sociedad de Africanistas y Colonistas saw it, Spain's relations with Morocco were based on the cultural superiority of the Europeans and their civilizing role, which was eventually to include the introduction of Christianity into the area. But

[21] *Boletín de la Sociedad Geográfica*, 1872.

this role also had a commercial component. Competition for African markets was fierce and Spanish products were not competitive, either in price or in quality. Making commercial and political inroads into Morocco would allow Spain to take advantage of its proximity to the country and establish a market for its products. At the same time, agricultural products and live-stock could be imported from Morocco – a possibility which evidently worried Spanish producers. E. Hernández-Sandoica has analysed the proposals of the Madrid geographers and has argued convincingly that there was a link between Spanish colonial plans of the eighties and the free trade ideas espoused by small and medium-sized traders and other groups who wanted to feed the urban population with cheaply-imported grain.

The conquest of Morocco, and northern Africa in general, would allow the establishment of farming colonies around the sovereign bases and this, the geographers argued, would also soothe demographic tensions inside Spain. Interest centred on Algeria, to which large numbers of Spaniards were already emigrating. The debates in the mid-eighties about the fall and the possible partitioning of the Moroccan empire, about French, British, and German pretensions in Morocco, and about the Algerian–Moroccan border, occupied the minds of geographers and the columns of the *Revista de Geografía Comercial*. All these initiatives and arguments were naturally accompanied by geographical works on Morocco and by exploratory expeditions, and a rich, extensive and long-lasting bibliography evolved. [22]

The Sociedad Geográfica de Madrid also played a major role in encouraging the occupation of the Saharan coasts. The north-western African coast had been important to Spain since the sixteenth century because of its rich fishing grounds and its proximity to the Canaries. With the signing of the 1860 treaty which ended the war with Morocco, Spain obtained the concession of Santa Cruz de Mar Pequena, an old factory settlement which had appeared in historical documents but was of uncertain location. At the beginning of the Restoration, news that the British had designs on the Sahara caused the Spanish navy to dispatch the ship *Blasco de Garay*, under the command of Cesáreo Fernandez Duro, a naval captain and an active member of the Society. The aim was to reinforce the Spanish presence, to undertake some cartographic work, and to ascertain the exact location of the old factory settlement. The expedition's findings appeared in the Society's journal in 1878. Shortly thereafter the tribes of the Ifni Delta recognized the old settlement and the sovereignty of Spain, although without the agreement of the Sultan of Morocco.

In 1884, with the awakening of Spanish colonialism and the new encroachments of the British into the Sahara, the Sociedad Geográfica, on the initiative of Francisco de Coello and Joaquín Costa, managed to persuade the government to finance another expedition, led by the sailor Emilio Bonelli. From the Canaries he could ensure the Spanish presence along the Saharan coasts as far as Cape Blanc.

[22] Mensua, *Bibliografía geográfica de Marruecos Español*, 1956.

The creation of the Sociedad Hispano–Africana de Río de Oro, enjoying trading privileges along the Saharan coasts, was criticized in 1885 by the Sociedad Española de Geografía Comercial, which was linked to the Sociedad de Africanistas in Madrid and which, through the columns of the *Revista de Geografía Comercial*, supported direct government involvement and free trade. The members of the Sociedad Geográfica even offered to become directly involved in trade themselves, through the creation of a limited company. Bonelli was appointed government representative in the Sahara that year and his brief was to ensure legal possession. In 1886 the Sociedad de Geográfica Comercial obtained government funds for further expeditions into the Sahara. The first of these was led by an engineer, Captain Julio Cervera, and the naturalist, Francisco Quiroga, who mapped and studied the territory between the 22nd and 24th parallels. But the discovery that natural resources with any commercial potential were scarce, and more importantly, that agricultural development, which would allow people to settle in the area, was impossible, limited Spanish activity in the area following sovereignty. Nevertheless, the regions remained part of Spain until 1975.

South of the Sahara, the Spanish maintained a presence in the Gulf of Guinea on the islands of Fernando Po (Bioko), Annabón, and Corisco which had been ceded by the Portuguese in the eighteenth century and of which Spain had taken effective possession in 1853. There was also limited tribal recognition of Spanish sovereignty on the neighbouring coasts, for example in Biafra in 1843. But after 1835 Spain's commercial presence, as has already been noted, was limited by the actions of the British navy. The islands and territory of the Muni River in the Gulf of Guinea were explored between 1875 and 1877 by the Basque Manuel Iradier, founder of La Exploradora, a 'travelling society' that had been created in 1868 to launch African expeditions. Described as a 'totally charitable, scientific and philanthropic' plan, and designed to amass experience for future companies, it collected the earliest geographical and ethnographic information on the region.

In 1880 France and Germany rushed to establish companies in the Gulf of Guinea and shortly afterwards the Congreso Español de Geografía Colonial y Mercantil, which met in Madrid in 1883, discussed the need to encourage exploration in the area. The geographers' initiatives, although they received little official support, had been essential in stimulating exploration of the Guinea region. Meanwhile between 1884 and 1886, Iradier together with Osorio and Montes de Oca as representatives of the Sociedad de Africanistas, developed further objectives which were much more specific and ambitious. This is how Iradier, himself, described them:

As a result of the meeting I held with the President of the Sociedad [de Africanistas], Don Francisco de Coello, and the Director of Exploration, Don Joaquín Costa, I agreed to lead an expedition to the Gulf of Guinea. The object of the expedition was to acquire for Spain and in the name of the Society those independent territories which the funds given me for the purpose allowed. If possible, I was to establish a research post and commercial station. We felt it wise, therefore, to ask the government to abolish the visiting rights that England had been granted in 1835, and to begin herewith a process in Spain which would inform people of the potential advantages for Spanish commerce in those regions and consequently to suggest to producers that they establish factory settlements without delay in the acquired territories. If resources are not forthcoming from them, the Sociedad de Africanistas should establish and sustain the settlements until commercial trends are properly determined, the occupation of the coasts is consolidated, and Spanish domination in the area is recognized.[23]

The aim of the expedition, as Iradier himself declared, was to ensure 'the foundation of an Hispano–African empire four times as big as Spain' in the region. Secret instructions from the Sociedad de Africanistas recommended caution, for the territory had to be explored under 'the pretext of studying its scientific and commercial aspects and to collect samples of natural history and exportable raw materials'. The results were published by the Sociedad Geográfica de Madrid and the ethnographic collections were given to the Museo Ethnológico Nacional. Meanwhile, exploration and tribal recognition ensured a continued Spanish presence. But later diplomatic conflicts with the Germans, French, and British limited the Spanish colonial initiative. After the agreement with France in 1900, Spain was left with the continental territory of the Muni River which, together with Fernando Po, makes up the modern republic of Equatorial Guinea.

THE EMPIRE AND THE TEACHING OF GEOGRAPHY

Spanish geographers and geographical societies, as we have seen, played a decisive role in fomenting public opinion and in promoting a colonial policy as well as in organizing exploratory expeditions and appropriating territory. But, as in other countries, they went further than this. Through teaching geography and spreading propaganda they contributed to the implantation of colonies in the public imagination.

There were two dimensions to this task: one was the contribution that it made to Spain's knowledge of its colonial and imperial interests and the second was the Spanish influence on the indigenous cultures of the colonized territories. Both sides received the energetic attention of members of the Sociedad Geográfica de Madrid, which for a quarter of a century discussed strategies which might increase the presence of geography in education, both in Spain and in her colonies, and which might improve teaching methods.[24] The secretary of the Sociedad Geográfica de Madrid saw the consequences

---

[23] Iradier, *Africa*, 1887, p. 346.
[24] Capel, et al., *Geografía para todos*, 1985, p. 87ff.

of a weak presence for geography in Spanish education and culture in the following terms:

> The earth, we repeat, will belong to whoever knows it best. It is not possible to use the wealth that a country contains, nor to govern its inhabitants in a manner in keeping with the innate, historical condition of their race, without a profound knowledge of the people and the land. If we lack this knowledge, we will continually face economic and political questions with false or incomplete information, we will commit errors, we will persevere with it, and there will come a time when people will protest, the land will be lost and the various national groups divided. [25]

source —

A basic idea of the empire and the reasons for Spain's colonial weaknesses were transmitted through history and geography textbooks. In history textbooks from the second third of the nineteenth century, after most of the Americas gained their independence, the general tone was one of indignation at losing those nations as a result – according to a text of 1826 – of 'the instigation of ambitious men who have ignited in these countries a fratricidal war and brought upon themselves the horrors of anarchy'. After the middle of the century and the triumph of liberal ideas, a different vision emerges in which the most progressive authors saw the independence process as an inevitable but painful step towards freedom, prosperity, and democracy, or one which at least led Spain to reflect on her responsibilities in these events. [26]

Geography texts used in basic Spanish education (primary and secondary) show a similar but perhaps more rapid development. Since the sixteenth century, descriptions of Spanish America had included a chorographic description of their administrative units. As these units became the foundations of the new independent states the original descriptions were easily adapted to the new situation. It very quickly became apparent that the American nations were 'different members of the same family, with the same interests and conditions', and there was confidence that despite the internal conflicts, the future of these countries would ensure them 'an important place in the history of mankind'. [27] During the nineteenth century, geography texts mentioned the Spanish territories in America, Asia, and Oceania, albeit briefly, in chapters on Spain devoted to the state's administrative system. There was a fuller description in the chapters on the corresponding continents where these territories were described as the 'property of Spain' or 'part of the Spanish Kingdom'. In the case of Cuba, more positive assessments were sometimes made: 'the island enjoys a very modern prosperity and in certain areas the colony displays a greater opulence than the mother country.' [28]

[25] *Boletín de la Sociedad Geográfica*, 1889, p. 17.
[26] Garcia Puchol, 'América en los libros escolares de Historia', 1989, vol. III.
[27] Palacios, *Tratado elemental de Geografía astronómica*, 1850, p. 269.
[28] Avendaño, *Manual completo*, 1844, p. 445.

In the Spanish colonies themselves, geography also played a significant educational role. Geographic education normally took the form of Spanish geography, the geography of the region itself, and general or astronomic geography. Knowledge of the geography and history of the 'mother country' was a logical way of trying to ensure political and cultural unity.[29]

Generally speaking, and as in other countries, geographers were convinced that most people knew little geography and that this had serious cultural and political consequences. In 1897, on the eve of colonial disaster, R. Torres exclaimed in his annual report to the Sociedad Geográfica de Madrid:

> The lack of geographical knowledge of our own country for want of decent teaching, has been seen as one of the reasons for the great disaster of 1870 [in France]. But add to this our ignorance of the colonies – a natural state of affairs given the deplorable state in which the teaching of our science now finds itself, a fact which explains the aimlessness, improvisation and indecision with which we have proceeded in foreign affairs – and our combined ignorance must be seen as one of the reasons for our current misfortunes.[30]

The following year, after the defeat at the hands of the Americans and once the remains of the Spanish American and Spanish Asian Empires had finally melted away, the same geographer complained: 'it was not possible to have colonies without appreciating them, nor could their value be properly appreciated without first knowing them.' He went on to conclude pithily, 'we lost the colonies because we didn't know any geography.'[31] Henceforth, only Africa would be left. In the first third of the nineteenth century, members of the Sociedad Geográfica de Madrid and other Spanish geographers devoted their energies to highlighting the importance of this colonial route and in particular the significance of the occupation of Morocco.

[29] Melcón, 'Geografía en el sistema de instrucción de España', 1989; Capel, Solé, and Urteaga, *El libro de Geografía en España*, 1988.

[30] *Boletín de la Sociedad Geográfica*, 1897, p. 121.

[31] Ibid., 1899, p. 19.

4

Geography and Imperialism in Italy: From the Unity of the Nation to the 'New' Roman Empire

Lucio Gambi

From the awakening of humanism in the middle of the fifteenth century, the whole matter of Italy's physical and national geography has been fraught with interest and difficulty. Over the next two to three centuries, stimulated by the commercial interests of the many and various city states, and by scholars' thirst for knowledge, progress was made in some branches of geography. Such early studies included: (a) chorographic and topographic descriptions heavily laden with the learning of the classical age, determining the difference between modern and classical versions of the earth; (b) the production of maps, at first only of the sea coast, but gradually extended to cover inland areas and eventually the whole of Italy; (c) accounts of journeys by land or by sea to countries either completely 'new', or well-known in ancient times but little in the present.

In the seventeenth century the internal political and economic troubles of the Italian city-states led to a commensurate decline in geography. It revived only in the eighteenth century with the first great wave of interest in natural history, especially in the sciences of geology, hydrology and botany. The geography of the age tackled pragmatic issues such as agricultural land use; the economics of food; and road network design.

In the Napoleonic era interest in such areas of research intensified and became more specialized, as geography retained its statistical and descriptive character. Paralleling the most important years in the process of Italy's unification, from the 1830s to the 1860s, geography focused on those issues that marked the emergence of a modern bourgeoisie: liberalism in agriculture leading to a better use of the land and a more careful choice of crops; the proper drainage of marshlands; the creation of close bonds between industry and agriculture, important given Italy's poverty in natural mineral resources; the increasing numbers and movements of the workforce; the communications network, especially the railways, as a means to improve commerce and link together the previously fragmented parts of the nation; the cities as the focal points of the political and administrative structures of the regions.

In these same years prior to unification, despite the country's long-standing history of division into small and mutually antagonistic states, which meant that such initiatives had little prospect of success, various political and cultural movements sought to rouse a patriotic nationalism in the Italians. One result of such policies was assiduous reference to epochs, individuals, and institutions in Italian history that could be termed 'glories' or 'forerunners' of the modern nation. Prominent among the favourite myths was inevitably that of ancient Rome, the vast empire it had conquered, and the forms of rule over its many colonies; but there were other illustrious ancestors deemed, as the geographer Francesco Costantino Marmocchi wrote in 1840, 'the precious relics of the might of our particular national genius, which it would be a disgrace not to think upon and venerate'.[1]

These heroes included many Italians who, between the thirteenth and sixteenth centuries, were involved both in the commercial development of lands dominated by Genoa and Venice and in the exploration of lands previously unknown to Europeans. The evocation and exaltation of these historical precedents stood at the heart of Italian imperialism, and thereby made it different from that of other European nations. Of dubious historical validity these myths were nevertheless a source of fascination.

Once the unity of the nation, at least in name, had been achieved in the period between 1860 and 1866, with Rome added in 1870, many political initiatives of the new-born state owed their inspiration to these same forerunners and glorious predecessors. This inspiration made itself felt, not so much in the internal politics of Italy, where there was little room for such grandiose language or intentions, but rather in foreign policy *vis-à-vis* Italy's neighbours in the Mediterranean. Especially after 1870, the Italian ruling class felt the need for political dominance and mastery in what it called *mare nostrum* (the Mediterranean), with particular regard to the lands to the south and the east. This same gaze over the Mediterranean passed easily on to the African mainland, where the major European nations, having opened up the continent with commerce and trading expeditions, were now carving it into colonies, often established by force. In 1872 Luigi Campo Fregoso, one of the last members of a great and ancient family of Genoese merchants argued:

it is Italy who, by her history and her very nature, is destined to gather the peoples of the Mediterranean together with those of Europe in her lap; it is she that will give the others life, being and civilization;

[1] Marmocchi, *Raccolta di viaggi*, 1840, vol. 1, p. 13.

if only she learns how to govern herself, she will be the star that will guide them on their way. Egypt, Tunisia, Tripoli, Algeria: all these countries lie at only a little distance from us; they are our natural colonies; they have, in every age of history, been the first places to be occupied by Italian commerce or colonies.[2]

The international ambition of Giuseppe Mazzini, the nationalist leader of the short-lived 1849 Roman republic was even more expansive:

How are we going to open up for Italy the roads leading into Asia, and at the same time fulfil the civilizing mission that history has marked out as ours – this is the question our foreign policy must now deal with...The means are an alliance with the southern-most countries of the Slavs and the Hellenes as far as these last go; a strong Italian presence, systematically increased, in Suez and in Alexandria; and, whenever the opportunity presents itself, the conquest and colonization of Tunisia. The unstoppable movement that summons Europe to the task of civilizing Africa, just as Morocco falls to the Iberian peninsula and Algeria to France, means that Tunis, the key to the central Mediterranean, the physical continuation of Sicily and Sardinia and a mere twenty-five leagues from the former, falls to Italy. Tunis, Tripoli and Cirenaica are a major part ... of that portion of Africa which, up to the Atlas mountains, is really a continuation of Europe. And there on the top of Atlas flew the flag of Rome when after the overthrow of Carthage, the Mediterranean was called 'our sea'. We were the masters, up to the end of the fifth century, of the whole of that area.[3]

THE SOCIETÀ GEOGRAFICA ITALIANA AND COLONIAL POLICY: 1867–1896

An understanding of this background is essential to any study of the 1867 foundation and subsequent history of the Società Geografica Italiana (SGI). The SGI was believed by many important figures in Italian cultural and political life to be the right and proper solution to two major problems in contemporary Italian geography: first, the need to supervise and coordinate research, and second, the need to support studies of the regions of Italy that could eventually be brought together in a complete portrait, still sadly lacking, of the physical and economic character of the peninsula.

But the SGI never became such an organization. In its first thirty years, despite its name, the SGI's members and leadership were only in small part involved in professional geography. In 1870 geographers represented only 11 per cent of members, and only in the early years of the present century

[2] Campo Fregoso, *Del primato italiano*, 1872, p. 169.
[3] Mazzini, 'Politica internazionale', 1871, p. 2; republished in Mazzini, *Opere*, 1939, vol. 2, p. 871.

did it rise as high as 20 per cent. Soon after its foundation the SGI boasted over a thousand members from very diverse professions: politicians, senior diplomats and army officers (these three categories alone accounted for a quarter of the members), doctors, industrialists and businessmen, as well as various scientists. They were men who for intellectual, personal, or professional reasons, showed an interest in the problems of contemporary geography, its information and insights.

The declared purpose of the SGI was the promotion 'of every branch and form of the science of geography'[4], and specifically, albeit with the reservation that it was never to exceed the bounds of pure research, in maritime issues, international commerce and industrial progress and expansion. In the years of Suez Canal construction these last aims were formulated in a context which already anticipated the colonization of the future: insistence on an expansion of the navy, demands for the conquest of new markets, requests for expeditions to explore and map out new territories. Thus the naturalist Giacomo Doria, one of the leading members of the SGI, explained the purpose of the SGI: 'our Society, like its sister organizations abroad, was founded in order to undertake exploration, and therefore to reject the advice of those who urge that, before studying other countries, we should get to know our own.'[5] By statute the Society was obliged to have its seat in the capital city of Italy, and thus in 1871 it moved from Florence, where it had been founded, to Rome. Less than fifteen years after its foundation as an independent body, the SGI had obtained a greater degree of prestige than similar associations established in Milan, Florence or Naples, and it was very closely tied to the Italian government and its policies. The SGI was therefore the scientific body that represented those industrialists and others who, while not always in agreement, advocated and lobbied for the acquisition of colonies.

But an early, hard-fought, internal struggle on colonial policy constrained the Society's participation in foreign exploration prior to 1882. Until then, the few professional geographers who made their voice heard in the SGI were not advocates of colonialism. They argued instead that it was more important to carry out comprehensive studies of Italy itself, and to improve the poor standard of living that still existed in many parts of the country. In their opinion the young state was ill-prepared financially or politically to cope with adventures in other continents. The only activity outside Europe that some of them would contemplate was the acquisition of wider markets for Italian goods which would enhance domestic economic development. To that end, the SGI established a sub-section to deal with commerce and trade, but it was hardly successful and was soon overshadowed by the foundation at Milan in 1879 of a rival and antagonist Società di Esplorazione Commerciale.

The most vociferous if not always rational colonialists in the SGI were the politicians. Among them was one of the most important figures in the

---

[4] *Bollettino della Società Geografica Italiana*, (hereafter *BSGI*) 1868, p. 3.
[5] Doria, *BSGI*, 1896, p. 225.

government of the day, Cesare Correnti, Minister of Education up to 1872. In 1867 he had been one of the founding members of the SGI, and was president of the Society from 1873 to 1879. Before the unification of Italy he had written some useful local geographies, especially on the Po valley; but afterwards, once he had been elected to the Italian Parliament, he was among the most tenacious expansionists. He supported a colonialism that would show just how much, in his own words, 'Columbus was the very incarnation of an Italian idea.'[6] During the years of his presidency, the Society sought to become the national body which with government approval acted as the flagbearer of the colonialist lobby and directed much of the military and commercial penetration into the African interior. In the Society's journal the articles devoted to 'the dark continent' take up well over half the space available, while the pioneering expeditions in Tunisia (1875), Morocco (1876), and into the Scioa in Ethiopia (1876–81), dominated the SGI's meetings. In an 1875 speech to the SGI, Correnti declared that Africa 'is for our Society a kind of vocation'. He maintained that, given the Italian interest in trade and commerce, and as both countries 'look out on to the same waters, and are only a few hours distance apart, it is endowed with irresistible fascination for us Italians ... and it [Africa] is something to which we are unstoppably drawn. It is destined so to be.'[7]

But the results of these first expeditions were at best disappointing. They concerned regions already politically unstable, such as the Maghreb where the French were already competing for domination, or an Ethiopia lacerated by internal strife. Even after the acquisition of Italy's first proper colonies in East Africa, the bay of Assab (Aseb) in Dancala (Dancalica) in 1882, the Sultanate of Massaua (Mesewa) in Eritrea in 1885, and Obbia and Migiurtina in 1890 the results were uninspiring. From the larger SGI expeditions to the horn of Africa – in the Somalian peninsula 1891, the basins of the rivers Scebeli (Shebelle) and Giuba (Juba) 1892–3, and Lake Rudolph and the River Omo 1895–7 – the only useful results were the collection of botanical or zoological specimens, and some pioneering maps of the mountain and river systems. The real objective of these missions was all too obvious. Although they purportedly sought to develop commerce and carry out scientific research, especially in East Africa, and specifically denied any other purpose, they were clearly embroiled in the web of European imperialism that spread through the Continent toward the end of the nineteenth century.

The conflicting interests embodied by the SGI are well demonstrated by the letters written in 1890 between the Marquis Francesco Nobili Vitelleschi and the Prime Minister, Francesco Crispi. The former was president of the Society and a natural conservative, protective of the cultural traditions and the scientific *raison d'être* of the SGI; the latter, from his youth in the heady days of the Risorgimento was a fervent supporter of colonial expansion overseas, which he, as a true Sicilian, also saw as a means to relieve the

[6] Correnti, *BSGI*, 1875, p. 618.
[7] Doria, *BSGI*, pp. 211, 226.

pressures brought by the rapid growth of population in the south of Italy. The ruling body of the SGI applied to Crispi for a three part grant from the government: first, to publish a world atlas, something which Italy as yet lacked; then to do a proper study on the large-scale emigration from the country, which had begun several years previously and was increasingly recognized as a national problem; and, finally, to provide backing for scientific expeditions in Africa. The Prime Minister gave his support only to this last item, or, in his own words 'to any fruitful and patriotic expedition ... so long as it is clear that, as it seems that it will do, the enterprise will have objectives that are not just scientific, but also political, and so long as in its preparation and execution the Society works together with the Foreign Ministry'.[8]

Thus did the SGI become the pioneer, or self-declared pawn in the government's plan for colonial occupation of East Africa. Attitudes within the SGI might well have been lukewarm and undecided in their support for such schemes, and the president might well have declared that the Society wished no part in any 'enterprise in which the interests of the state might give rise to violence',[9] preferring to support expeditions organized by private citizens. Yet, those who travelled to Africa in these years under the auspices of the Society were often soldiers by profession and were sooner or later obliged to be on good terms with the organs of government there. In addition, most government representatives, diplomats and traders in the kingdoms and sultanates around the Nile and along the coast of the Indian Ocean were already members of the Society.

To better understand the direction taken by the SGI, it is important to remember just how few of the members were actually geographers or even persons who dealt with geography in some form. Among officers of the Society up to the turn of the century, the only professional geographer was Giuseppe Dalla Vedova, appointed in 1875 to the Chair of Geography in the University of Rome, and secretary of the SGI. In other words geographers had no real say in the decision-making of the SGI, which from its foundation was dominated by members of parliament, high-ranking diplomatic or military staff, senior civil servants and the like. Geographers and other exponents of the earth sciences become a visible presence in SGI committees only after 1890 when their expertise was recruited for the administration of the newly-acquired colonies of Eritrea (1890) and Somalia (1891–4 with later additions). Their influence was greatly increased following two military setbacks: final defeat at Adua (March 1896) ending the ill-considered conquest of Ethiopia; and the unhappy end in the desert, between Cafa (Caffà) and the Scioa, of the expedition led by the army captain Vittorio Bottego (March 1897). The political objectives of this last venture had been concealed by the public sponsorship of the SGI, so that after the disastrous outcome the latter was compelled to justify its role, and

[8] Quoted in Carazzi, *La Società Geografica Italiana*, 1972, pp. 124–6.
[9] *BSGI*, 1887, p. 428.

found itself unable to avoid the blame directed at it by Parliament and by a good part of the press.

The consequence of these events was the election in 1900 of a geographer of considerable reputation to the SGI presidency, Dalla Vedova. For decades Dalla Vedova had argued in vain that besides research the Society should concentrate primarily on how to teach and interpret geography, leaving other organizations to apply geographical insights to political and commercial prospects. Scholarly rigour prevailed during his six-year presidency as it did in the Società di Studi Geografici of Florence, founded only a few years earlier by Florentines with a colonial background.

OPPOSITION AND REAFFIRMATION, 1890–1918

But this last phase was short-lived. The thirty years following the Conference in Berlin meant increasing rivalry between the various European countries, the birth of strong nationalist feeling, economic competition, rapid population growth, and increasing and more obvious disparities between classes in terms of wealth and prosperity. These changes were felt in the world of scholarship, above all by the younger generation. Among some geographers, there emerged an open opposition to the whole theory and practice of colonialism. Their hostility was either inspired by ideas spread half a century earlier by the democrats of the Risorgimento, or by socialist principles of egalitarianism expounded at the end of the nineteenth century. Several different arguments and attitudes surfaced.

First, in 1891 Arcangelo Ghisleri, creator and founder of a huge number of magazines and reviews (three of them geographical) raised 'a cry of horror, protest and indignation ... against the barbarous manner in which so-called civilized men have destroyed or are in the process of destroying the last remnants of the indigenous civilization and cultures' of Africa[10]. This outburst focused an already angry debate in which Ghisleri had declared:

> a respect for man as an individual, both in private relationships and in those between races, is the principal feature of modern civilization. It is why we believe ourselves to be civilized. In violating this rule – and it is irrelevant whether the destined victims happen to be savages or less civilized than ourselves – while pretending that we are spreading it more widely, we are contradicting a fundamental principle of our whole civilization.[11]

The second attitude is illustrated by the review *La Cultura Geografica*, published by Cesare Battisti and Renato Biasutti, who in 1899 professed themselves 'die-hard anti-Africans. In other words we believe that it should

[10] Ghisleri, 'Le razze inferiori e la civiltà', 1891, p. 7.
[11] Ghisleri, *Le razze umane e il diritto*, 1888; citation from Milan edn, 1972, p. 92.

be left to its own devices, since the only future there for Italy is one of mounting and useless expense...There is nobody who today still believes that it has a viable commercial future; and there are few that argue with conviction that farming colonies can be established there.' [12] When at the beginning of the twentieth century, the question of dominion over the Adriatic and the whole related matter of the Balkans gave rise to strong feelings, the wave of nationalist sentiment, inspired more by nostalgia for long-departed glories than by any real perception of the present, was lucidly combatted in a similar fashion by Carlo Maranelli, a geographer and specialist in the problems of the south of Italy [13].

Such anti-colonial arguments did not find much support among fellow geographers. Up to the outbreak of World War I most geographers (even when ostensibly democratic in their politics) were all too readily caught up in the general fervour of nationalist sentiment. Similar excesses of enthusiasm were widespread in Europe at the time, and the outward symptoms in Italy were little different from those in countries to the north of the Alps. This historically distorted celebration of the nation's former grandeur combined with a modern desire for dominance led to demands for increasing military and economic strength capable of rendering Italy competetive with other nation–states. Yet, at least during the first decade of the century, the most boisterous and aggressive assertions of Italian nationalism came from small groups, mostly among the bourgeoisie, but generally fell on deaf ears. Although the Italian government certainly entertained plans for some form of colonial expansion, it acted with greater circumspection. Up to 1910 more diplomatic and ostensibly peaceful methods were preferred, above all an insidious but gradual economic or cultural dependence. Once Dalla Vedova relinquished the presidency and control had passed back again into the hands of the politicians and the senior military men, the policies of the SGI followed those of the state.

Once again expeditions into Africa were partly financed, but more importantly patronized and directed, by the SGI or by the less scholarly societies with an interest there. These expeditions often rubbed shoulders with rival operations sent by other European countries. They explored either territories adjacent to Italy's existing colonies (in 1902 between the Scioa and Lake Rudolph; in 1904 between the Eritrean plateau and the basin of Dancalia; in 1908 Lake Tana; in 1911 Dancalia); or those areas along the Mediterranean coast where there was already a struggle for dominion among the imperialist powers, especially in Cirenaica (Baqah) in 1901 and Tripolitania (Tarabullus) in 1905. These last two areas were known from explorations in the 1880s by the Società di Esplorazione Commerciale of Milan.

Developments in North Africa, however, marked an important change in the relations between geographers and the authorities. For the first time

---

[12] Battisti and Biasutti, 'Giardini sperimentali nell' Eritrea', 1899, p. 94.
[13] Maranelli, 'Sui rapporti economici', 1907; Maranelli, 'Il problema dell'Adriatico', 1915; Maranelli and Salvemini, *La questione dell'Adriatico*, 1918.

geographers were directly involved in the process of colonization itself. Their scientific prestige was exploited to show that conquest and invasion were not only economically beneficial but also vital to the nation's political and geographical development, and to its increased impact on the international stage. In tones ranging from boundless optimism to cautious prudence, some geographers became public mouthpieces for the government's colonial policies. They orchestrated a whitewash, albeit with less shameless impudence than that of the poets, politicians and other public relations men.

The SGI had close links with the banks that revolved around the Vatican and controlled Italy's commercial dominance in the south-east Mediterranean. In the first decade of the twentieth century, the SGI Bulletin published articles on the economic potential of Tripolitania, the importance of the Lybian coast as the origin of Saharan trade routes, and reaffirmed Italy's right to rule over North Africa since the area was adjacent to Sicily. After the conquest of Libya in 1911, the Society held eight public lectures to illustrate and comment on the new possession. Apart from the obvious military, economic, and physical features, the speakers dwelt on the new civilization that, after centuries of Turkish rule, Italy would introduce there.

During Mussolini's invasion of Ethiopia in 1935, the behaviour of the SGI differed very little. The SGI supported the conquest with the publication of a volume of studies written largely by geographers.[14] If praiseworthy in terms of layout and content, this particular scholarly contribution only too readily countenanced all the horrors of the infamous war that followed the historically indefensible act of colonial annexation. Yet in the years that followed World War I and, above all, once the fanatical nationalism of the Fascists had invaded the echelons of government, even virtues such as technical competence and meticulous scholarship become all too rare. For the many geographers, especially students of political geography, who threw in their lot with the regime, scholarly truth had to take second place to displays of patriotic enthusiasm.

Several years before World War I a number of men in the Partito Nazionalista were already on the governing body of the SGI: the businessman Giuseppe Vigoni who for many years had also been president of the Società di Esplorazione Commerciale at Milan; Giacomo Agnesa who directed the colonial office which in 1911 expanded to become the Ministry for the Colonies; the fiery sea-captain, then businessman, member of parliament and journalist Piero Foscari. One such nationalist, Luigi Federzoni, was Minister for the Colonies when elected president of the SGI in 1923. He was succeeded as president by another Minister for the Colonies, Pietro Lanza di Scalea, while Corrado Zoli, president from 1933 to 1944, was a former colonial governor of Eritrea. Once Fascism took over the state, instead of remaining true to the original ideal of representing the best in Italian geography, the SGI and other geographical organizations increasingly took up the banner of official imperialism.

---

[14] *L'Africa Orientale*, 1935, pp. 408.

Even from such a brief survey it can be seen how and why, in the decades between the two wars, much of Italian geography came to identify itself more and more openly with the ideology, plans and political measures of the ruling imperialist faction. From 1925 all legal opposition to the Fascist regime was abolished.

WORLD WAR I AND AFTER, 1914–1926

The persistence of the Risorgimento in Italian political thinking meant that, even after the horrors of the First World War, there were still those who argued for the inclusion in the Italian state, if necessary by force, of the few remaining areas of Italian language and culture still outside Italy itself. But at the same time a different kind of imperialism began to emerge, a political more than cultural imperialism which sought an expansion of the territory of the nation-state and the seizure for military reasons of the northern mountains surrounding Italy. Some 30,000 Italian place names, generally superfluous and often completely fictitious, were imposed on towns, villages and mountains in areas acquired after the war. These names were the product of committees organized under the auspices of the SGI, most conspicuously in the southern Tyrol and other places incorporated into the kingdom of Italy in September 1919.

This political expansion was already apparent in the seizure of Libyan ports, but now aimed at a wider dominion over much of the Mediterranean, especially in the East along the coasts of Dalmatia, Albania, Greece, Anatolia, and inland along the Danube. Geographers seized the opportunity to compare these ambitions with the glories of ancient Rome. The lack of respect for historical fact and the pulpit-thumping rhetoric are typified in this 1916 passage by Paolo Revelli:

So grandiose are the signs left by Rome and Venice on the eastern seacoast of the Adriatic that anyone who seeks to oppose our claim on these shores will have to try to minimize the significance of those traces, and call them the mere remnants of a state of affairs lost forever in the sweep of time. But Rome and Venice did not just found colonies there to have them swamped in the barbarian flood of the dark ages, then engulfed in the later wave of Turks, and finally to have every last vestige cancelled by the artful greed of the Hapsburgs. They have set their mark, the symbol of their inner selves, on all the peoples along that coast in the lasting influence of their civilization.[15]

The war, and increasingly the peace, gave rise to almost ritual outpourings of the same kind. The distortion of geographical reality and historical fact was occasionally quite cynical:

[15] Revelli, 'Una questione di geografia', 1916, pp. 111–12.

If we hear in these days a great deal about the military importance of
the broken and indented coastline of the eastern shore of the Adriatic
compared with the opposite western shore, devoid of natural ports for
shipping, this interest derives from the finely balanced political situation
of the Adriatic in critical periods of history such as the present. For
this reason it is in the political interest of that nation which occupies
the exposed side of the Adriatic to annex Dalmatia, so as to deprive any
enemy of a perilous natural advantage. [16]

In an ever more explicit enlistment of physical geography:

Dalmatia may well be a physical part of the Balkan peninsula ...
but ... it is an area to itself, whose natural character links it closely to
nearby Italy ... The strip of land that makes up Dalmatia and the steep
mountain range that closes it off are the geological – one could also
say morphological – continuation, without any interruption or other
change, of the mountains at the back of Venice ... Opposite Dalmatia,
along the whole eastern coast of Italy, appear a series of outcrops ...
that can be seen as the remnants of the Dalmatian promontory that
has otherwise sunk into the sea. In these areas, down as far as the tip of
Leuca in Puglia, we find the same kind of landscape, the same geological
features and structures, the same lack of surface water, the same rivers
emerging just before the sea. [17]

By the end of World War I problems of increasingly rapid population
growth and consequent increase in emigration, especially to the New World,
were widely discussed. Since 1890 several proposals had been made to direct
emigrants to Italy's colonies rather than have them lost forever to other
nations. Such emigration represented a vast export trade in men and women
to the growing countries of the New World, and it gave to Italian colonialism
a decidedly lower-class character (one recent commentator talks about 'ragged-
trouser imperialism'). [18] If Italian colonialism was on a smaller scale than
that of northern and central Europe, and was fiercely opposed prior to 1910
by the Nationalists as destructive of cultural values and the dignity of labour,
emigration policies found significant support among Italian geographers; the
Italian geographical associations were represented at the conferences of Italian
emigrants in 1908 and in 1911.

Never at odds with colonization by political conquest, colonization by
transfer of population enhanced later developments. In particular the economic depression of the 1930s and the conquest of Ethiopia in the middle
of the decade gave rise to a wildly optimistic scheme to drain the excess
population of southern Italy into the lands along the Libyan coast and into

[16] Toniolo, 'A proposito di un mio schizzo antropogeografico', 1915, p. 154.
[17] Dainelli, 'La Dalmazia', 1917, pp. 133–40.
[18] Sori, *L'emigrazione italiana dall'unità*, 1979, pp. 152–8.

the Ethiopian highlands. But otherwise, in the period between the two wars most geographers dedicated their energies to, and were often directly involved in, an older and better-tried kind of political imperialism, namely political government of the colonies. Geographers were active at the conferences in Naples (1917) and Rome (1919) on the administration of the colonies, as well as the 1921 Rome conference which discussed the extent and success of Italy's presence in Anatolia and along the eastern Mediterranean coast. In the spring of 1926, consistent with the Fascist harangues delivered in eleven Italian cities to celebrate the anniversary of the foundation of Rome, geographers spoke at a 'colonial day' intended both to stir up the colonial ambitions of the nationalists, and to re-establish in the colonies an Italian dominion, which the conflict in Europe had weakened. These speeches, published in a special issue of the journal of the SGI, held Fascism as the inspiration and doctrine of a state destined to growth, and as the severe protector of weaker peoples unable to govern their own destiny; but they also included some rather obscure allusions to the general instability of the international situation, where, if opportunities were grasped, Italy might expand and even unite its colonial possessions into a single dominion. The following extracts give the flavour of the discussion:

No one can argue that Italy's colonies are comparable to her importance in the world. Everybody therefore accepts that they are inadequate ... Italy therefore feels more strongly than any other nation the anguish that, not within several but rather the next generation, there will not be enough room for her own citizens to live in. The most alarming fact is in fact the rise in population which is more rapid than the country is able to cope with.[19]

There is in fact a huge difference between colonies in Africa and those in America. There the kind-hearted Anglo-Saxons were able to colonize North America by destroying the native Red Indians ... But there the white man can live instead of the native and thus the disappearance of the native does not damage the community as a whole. In Africa things are different. Only certain races, above all the black ones, can live and work there. The destruction of the black peoples therefore means the ruin of the colony because, in those hostile regions the white man cannot take the place of the native ... The right attitude of mind for Africa must therefore be to learn how to live together with the inferior race, but nevertheless to learn how to maintain, unchallenged and unchallengeable, the superiority of the white race.[20]

We must necessarily admit that our colonial problem, even when our older colonies are put to their maximum use, will not be solved ...

[19] Maranelli, 'Il problema coloniale', 1926, pp. 366–9, 372.
[20] Vinassa de Regny, 'Mentalitá e coscienza coloniale', 1926, p. 375.

The full history of a nation and a people covers many centuries, while the political situation of the world sometimes changes more quickly than people think. This nation therefore has to keep itself ready, all the time, so that a change to its advantage occurring in the political and economic situation elsewhere in the world finds us with our colonial plans ready.[21]

It is hardly surprising that geographers were closely caught up in the bloody and ruthless Italian re-conquest of Libya between 1926 and 1931. Whether intended or otherwise, their scientific expeditions served to draw a veil over the atrocities perpetrated by the military occupation, for example the massacres in the winter of 1926–7 at the oasis of Giarabub (Al-Jaghbub), and later between 1930 and 1935 in Fezzan, the oases of Cufra (Al-Kufrah), Tibesti Ghat, and around Mount Tibesti. The SGI directed several expeditions to Libya in this period, and published a good part of the resulting scientific material. It was therefore responsible for disguising the real political objectives of these expeditions, while representing to the public that they were simply surveys of mineral deposits (none of which were in fact discovered in these years).

GEOGRAPHY AND FASCISM: THE 'NEW' ROMAN EMPIRE, 1926–1943

As a doctrine of state, Fascism identifies itself totally with the systematic economic expansion that is the basis of any colonial policy. As a philosophy of the individual it identifies itself with the real and unavoidable model of the colonialist, which during past centuries all the other countries with some sort of imperialist standing in Africa have turned out in their thousands ... It is true that we have had a foot in Africa. But up to now we have never understood what going to and staying in Africa might mean. All this has now been laid down according to precise and properly determined plans, both ethnic and economic. Now we have, for our colonial being, a will and a state doctrine, and we have a philosophy of the individual. This is the strongest foundation Fascism could possibly give to the colonial desire of Italy.[22]

By 1936, when Mussolini officially declared that the Roman empire was born again in Fascist Italy, the SGI was no longer such a prominent apologist for colonial expansion. That function had now passed to new institutions, either generated anew under Fascism or grafted on to existing bodies. Geographers participated in all of these institutions: the Istituto Coloniale (in 1938 re-baptized the Istituto dell'Africa Italiana); the Istituto Agronomico per l'Africa; the ubiquitous and watchful Istituto Nazionale di Cultura

[21] Dainelli, 'Le ragioni del problema coloniale italiano', 1926, pp. 460–2.
[22] Cantalupo, 'Il fascismo e la coscienza coloniale', 1926, pp. 345–6.

Fascista; and above all the new Accademia d'Italia, which, with the collaboration of geographers, established a Centro di Studi per l'Africa Orientale devoted to colonial expeditions.

The dark and troubled years leading up to World War II saw the bond between geography and imperialism at its closest. Geographic scholarship now concentrated on the analysis and exposition of the geopolitical principles underlying imperialism. But there was little or nothing original in these writings, since their theses were largely a reworking or a wholesale borrowing of the best known geopolitics of the previous half century in Northern Europe. Generally intended for use as textbooks in the universities, the first substantial writings in Italian on geopolitics expounded the relationship between population and state, but much space was also given over to economic or demographic increase and the expansion of the territories ruled over by the nation, as well as the related issues of colonization and empire.[23]

The views of imperialism that emerge from these works are divergent. At times they limit themselves to a mere exposition of the economic and demographic pressures; elsewhere they urge the takeover of territories outside the nation's existing frontiers and the need to conquer a position of international strength. Demarchi, for example, contrasts those states that are rich in empire with those that are not:

The sovereignty of a state in some cases is extended to comprehend new territories [involving] a real increase in the territory of the state, which is no longer all of one piece, but is made up of different parts, some far even from the rest...Such complexity of different kinds of sovereignty, exercised at a distance, can only with difficulty be comprehended in the usual definition of a *state*: it is better covered in the concept of an *empire...Every state in a phase of growth tends to build its own empire* so as to provide territory, prime materials, food, and new markets for a population that is not only increasing in size but also developing new forms of economic activity.[24]

This type of imperialism is practised by major powers such as Britain, France, Holland, Portugal, according to Demarchi, and dominated Europe in the first quarter of the century. But there are also countries of similar standing with no empire worth speaking of: 'in Europe, Germany and Italy are the nations that feel most keenly the economic and demographic pressure to expand their influence and territorial possessions beyond the frontiers of the state.' And, with particular reference to Italy, 'a state poor in natural

---

[23] Of course individual approaches differed. There were studies on environmental determinism: Demarchi, *Fondamenti di geografia politica*, 1929; on social and economic dynamics: Roletto, *Lezioni di geografia*, 1933; on the embodiment of such principles in the state: Almagià, *Elementi di geografia*, 1936; or on principles such as biological bond and *spazio vitale* (living space) see Toschi, *Appunti di geografia politica*, 1937.

[24] Demarchi, *Fondamenti di geografia politica*, 1929, pp. 70–4.

resources' (p. 160), this same expansion cannot be met by its existing colonies, in part made up of desert and wilderness. But if these same possessions 'will never, or at least only to a very limited degree, be able to meet our need for prime materials or for land to populate, or to serve even as important markets for the nation's exports' how is the country going to relieve the increasing economic and demographic pressure? Demarchi prefers not to pronounce explicitly on this last question, or its imperialist implications. He will only say that:

the sight of naturally rich areas left to be exploited by peoples who are few in number rouses in other peoples, who find themselves having to live tightly packed together in territories that are less productive or have a large number of people to support, a sense of envy and an awareness of injustice, that can become a source of conflict. [25]

Apart from the strongly-voiced resentment that distinguishes the nationalist outlook, this passage reflects an official position that ostensibly sought to air opinions and promote discussion. Though by definition an imperialist creed, in its early years in power Fascism made much of its supposed interest in innovative forms of colonialism.

The language of Toschi a few years later is very different. Still redolent of the sort of muddled thinking typical of Fascism after the regime had obtained international recognition, it also displays the first signs of a harsher ideology of colonialism, the early traces of racial discrimination, and a eulogy to the ruling power and the force behind it:

Imperialism is the aptitude for expansion particular to those peoples which believe that they are able to carry everywhere a universal concept that will constitute a norm of civilized society. For them it is a mission ... And political geography, a science of facts rather than precepts, must study such empires in the broadest sense...

The concept of empire is here above all geographical. [26] In this respect Toschi invokes the notion of *spazio vitale* (living space) as a central rationale of imperialism:

A certain people happens to be located on a certain part of the world's surface: this is the space in which it lives, its living space ... but this idea is faulty, and extremely so, because of the limitation, or prior assumption, that the proportions of a people are going to remain static. Even in terms of mere numbers, this is an arbitrary and utopian prior assumption. Can the space in which a people of 30 million lives be said to be the living space of the same people when they number 60

[25] Demarchi, *Fondamenti di geografia politica*, 1929, p. 174.
[26] Toschi, *Appunti di geografia politica*, 1937, pp. 20–1.

million?...It is obvious therefore that one is tempted to affirm that the living space of a people is not just *that in which it lives*, but rather *that which it needs in order to live*. And to live means to grow. Therefore the room which is sought is that *which a people needs in order to grow freely according to the rhythm of its own potential for growth*...Wherever one recognizes that there is an unquestionable difference in the level of civilization achieved, or rather an obvious incapacity to bring about, rapidly and efficiently, a modern society, there is no question about the subordination of the living needs of lower peoples to those of higher peoples. In the end the distinction rests on the differences between the races.[27]

Complete with carefully chosen quotations from Mussolini, Toschi's arguments are not exceptional for the time. Similar terminology and ideas can be found in university *dispense* (printed summaries of courses) for geography courses, and in a series of about 15 monographs, published under the auspices of the SGI between 1941 and 1943, illustrating the countries sought by Italian imperialists. All these writings show the extent to which scholarship had allowed itself to become a political tool. They also showed the far-reaching change, as regards geopolitics and international relations, that had occurred in Italian geography under Fascist rule, especially after the latter's alliance with Nazism.

The crescendo of imperial ideology came at the beginning of the Second World War with the journal *Geopolitica*, which drew its inspiration from the German school of political geography and was in some ways an Italian imitation and counterpart of the *Zeitschrift für Geopolitik*. Founded by Giorgio Roletto and Ernesto Massi, with an inaugural message from Karl Haushofer in the first number, *Geopolitica* was published up to the end of 1942 and almost all the best known Italian geographers contributed in some form or other. Editorials and articles alike grovelled for disciplinary approval from the ruling regime. This meant close links with the political and cultural institutions of Fascism which, as the founders of the review hoped, promoted geopolitics as an official doctrine. Quite differently from the catholic taste of the discipline's more traditional journals, *Geopolitica*'s subject matter focused explicitly on the concept of 'living space', interpreted, in the words of the periodical's manifesto, as the 'geographical doctrine of empire'. Its coverage spanned the ancient Roman empire and Fascist ambitions for its renewal, the elaboration of the rules governing international politics, and the laws that direct the growth of cities; it permitted rapid sketches of politics and economies in other countries, and case studies of race and population. But all these themes were handled with the verbosity, harshness and clangour typical of Fascism at its worst.

The first number of *Geopolitica* declares, in appropriately portentous manner, that a distinction must be made between political geography, which 'assesses

[27] Toschi, *Appunti di geografia politica*, pp. 87–9.

the value and relative supremacy of nations on the basis of the peoples living therein, the amount of surface territory, size of population, natural resources and the sorts of production at its disposition', and geopolitics, which 'has far greater scope, and considers spiritual and cultural factors, the desire for power and for empire'.[28] Imperialism is therefore seen no longer as the mere consequence of a national need for territorial and political expansion, nourished by over-production or over-population, but instead as inspired primarily by an intellectual desire. Frequent recourse to the 'genius of Mazzini, interpreter of the will of heaven, [who] achieved the unity of Italy and marked out her future living space', sought to convince the general public of the historical validity of the nationalist claims, while the popularity of the same Mazzini at all levels of Italian society, and his reference to the parallel situation of the oppressed peoples of the Balkan peninsula in relation to the North African coast, were exploited to justify the plans for expansion with which Fascism intended to satisfy its desire for greater space in the Mediterranean.[29] Power must belong to whoever is naturally the strongest; 'the strength, vitality and desire to expand the race that can no longer be held back, all bring Italy back to her dominating role in the Mediterranean. It is not a conquest, but a rightful return'. Here, after all in the Italian peninsula, lives the 'race of Rome, which formerly held dominion over other peoples'.[30]

The cultural and biological supremacy of ancient Rome rationalized the imperialist adventure in Africa, and refracted a contemporary racial hierarchy. According to one geographer the African peoples are biologically unsuited 'not only to absorb a foreign culture of a higher order, but also to keep their own intact. It is therefore unreasonable to argue in favour of the evolutionary improvement of peoples who by invincible forces in their background are destined to decline'. For this reason the Africans 'will never understand what has to be done to exploit properly for the benefit of mankind the immense natural resources that they have within their reach'.[31]

In retrospect, the sort of garbled and shameless deceit which these exponents of *spazio vitale* practised in the Italian universities, with the advent of World War II, is all too evident. As the two founders of *Geopolitica* declared, 'the definition [of geopolitics] and its method were fixed for us by the Duce' in a 'brief, lucid and constructive' meeting in February 1939, where Mussolini 'expounded the principles according to which the review must express as fully as possible the geographical, political and imperial conscience of the Italian people'.[32] Not even the first reverses of the war in East Africa two years later taught the journal to act with more restraint, or to reflect more carefully on events. As late as July 1941 by which time

---

[28] *Geopolitica*, 1939, p. 10.
[29] *Geopolitica*, 1940, pp. 486–90.
[30] *Geopolitica*, 1941, p. 470.
[31] *Geopolitica*, 1939, pp. 337–8.
[32] *Geopolitica*, 1939, p. 75, p. 109.

the East African colonies had been wholly lost, it could still, incredibly, be argued in *Geopolitica* that:

> The work of Italy, once she had conquered her place in the sun, has been to place on the rude, naked and shapeless body of barbarous Ethiopia, the first clothes of civilization. Now British Imperialism, the crushing tyrant of helpless peoples, has revealed her innermost designs and real nature, and is attempting to destroy everything that has been done there in the name of civilization. But the work will begin again soon, after the final victory. [33]

There was no victory of course, only defeat. And in the years immediately after the defeat, despite the occasional intemperate reference to *spazio vitale* in national congresses of geographers and Africanists, colonialism and imperialism virtually disappeared from Italian geography. A defeat is sometimes more useful and more beneficial than a victory, and in this case we can be glad that there was indeed a defeat.

[33] *Geopolitica*, 1941, p. 347.

5

The Science of Empire: The French Geographical Movement and the Forms of French Imperialism, 1870–1920

Michael J. Heffernan*

INTRODUCTION

It has frequently been observed that nineteenth-century European imperialism was sustained and legitimated by European scholarship about the colonial world. The history of disciplines such as anthropology, geology, botany, medicine and philology have all been reconsidered in the light of the imperial assumptions and values which informed their early development during the nineteenth century.[1] A connection has also been drawn between the rapid development of geography as a discipline, particularly after 1870,

* The author would like to thank Felix Driver, the editors of this volume, and the other participants at the Kingston conference for their comments on an earlier draft of this chapter.

[1] See, Arnold, *Imperial Medicine*, 1988; Asad (ed.), *Anthropology*, 1973; Brockway, *Science and Colonial Expansion*, 1979: Cohen, *The French Encounter*, 1980; Leclerc, *Anthropologie et Colonialisme*, 1972: Lorimer, 'Theoretical racism', 1988; MacKenzie (ed.), *Imperialism*, 1990; MacLeod and Lewis (eds), *Disease, Empire, and Medicine*, 1988; Nordman and Raison (eds), *Sciences de l'Homme*, 1980; Pyenson, 'Astronomy and imperialism', 1984, pp. 39–81: Said, *Orientalism*, 1978; Said, 'Orientalism reconsidered', 1985, pp. 1–15; Said, *Representing the Colonized*, 1989, pp. 205–25; Said, *Culture and Imperialism*, 1992; Secord, 'King of Siluria', 1982, pp. 413–42; Stafford, *Scientist of Empire*, 1989; Stocking, *Victorian Anthropology*, 1987, and Vatin (ed.), *Connaissances du Maghreb*, 1984.

and the political and intellectual climate of aggressive imperial expansion which developed within Europe during the later 1800s.[2]

The simultaneous development of geography as a science, and imperialism as an ideology, has led some commentators to claim that the geographers of late nineteenth-century Europe – both the amateur travellers and explorers, and the professional, university-based scholars – were willing and capable agents of European imperialism. They provided, it has been suggested, both the practical knowledge necessary for overseas conquest and colonization through their explorations and overseas travels, and the intellectual justification for European expansion through their geopolitical writings, their informed assessments about the commercial worth of different overseas regions, their social Darwinian theories about the necessity and inevitability of European colonization, and their related ideas about the influence of climate and environment in the formation of different races.[3] Several important works have suggested unambiguously that, for much of the late nineteenth and early twentieth centuries, geography was little more than a form of racial and imperial propaganda.[4] Indeed, for some observers, the overlap between imperialism and geography, particularly when considering the individuals active in each arena, was so great that any attempt to separate them in order to assess the impact of the former on the latter is itself a doomed exercise. From this perspective, European geography was European imperialism, albeit dressed up in a slightly more academic and scholarly guise.

Although there is plenty of irrefutable evidence to support this interpretation, such an assessment tends to gloss over both the complex and contested nature of European imperialism, and the fierce debates and conflicts within the emerging discipline of geography. The purpose of this chapter is to examine in greater detail the connections between French geography and French imperialism in the years between the Franco–Prussian War and World War I. There is, of course, already a substantial body of work on both the rise of a convincing policy of French imperialism during the late nineteenth century[5] and on the rapid development of French geography in these same decades.[6] To some extent, this literature already points to the connections

[2] Hudson, 'The new geography and the new imperialism', 1977; Driver, 'Geography's Empire', 1992, pp. 23–40. See also Livingstone, *The Geographical Tradition* 1992, pp. 216–59 and Stoddart, *On Geography and its History*, 1986.

[3] See, Bassin, 'Imperialism and the nation state', 1987, pp. 473–95; Kearns, 'Closed space and political practice', 1984, pp. 23–34; Naciri, 'La géographie coloniale', 1984, pp. 309–43; and Peet, 'The social origins of environmental determinism', 1985, pp. 309–33.

[4] This is the thesis skillfully developed in MacKenzie, *Propaganda and Empire*, 1984.

[5] See, Betts, *Assimilation and Association*, 1961; Betts, *Tricouleur*, 1978; Bouvier, 'Les traits majeurs', 1974, pp. 99–128; Brunschwig, '*French Colonialism, 1871–1914*', 1966; Comte, *L'Aventure Coloniale de la France*, 1988; Ganiage, *L'Expansion Coloniale*, 1968; Girardet, *L'Idée Coloniale*, 1972; and Marseille, *Empire Colonial*, 1984.

[6] Berdoulay, *La Formation de l'École*, 1981, is an indispensable introduction. See also Berdoulay, *Les Mots et les Lieux*, 1988. Also of relevance are Andrews, 'The Durkheimians

between French geography and French imperialism in this period.[7] However, the relationship between geography and imperialism in France has generally been seen in entirely functional terms, as an inchoate science bolstering an emerging ideology. Yet as both the discipline of geography developed and the ideology of imperialism gained momentum, so the nature of the relationship between the science and the ideology became more complex. I hope to tease out the different aspects of the symbiotic relationship between geography and imperialism beyond those suggested by a broadly contemporaneous chronological development. I seek, in particular, to draw attention to the various forms of French imperialism which developed over this period and to indicate how they influenced, and were themselves influenced by, the debates which took place within French geography.

This problematic raises several questions, chief amongst them being the perennial problem of defining what constituted the discipline of geography in this period. This is, of course, an intractable and effectively unanswerable question as the discipline – if the word 'discipline' can be used in this respect – embraced everything from the 'heroics' of overseas exploration, the technicalities of mapping and cartography, the 'rational', scientific analysis of the human and physical resources of different localities and the almost poetic description of the regions and landscapes of different parts of the world. Any attempt to distil from all this an essential definition of geography is probably, as David Livingstone has recently argued, an impossible and meaningless quest.[8] For Livingstone, the term 'geography' has no universal, fixed transhistorical meaning or essence; rather, the word – and the discipline itself – has always been understood in different ways in different historical and geographical contexts. Indeed, even within a particular historical and geographical context, there has rarely been anything like a consensus on the defining parameters of the subject. However, it is precisely the protean nature of geography – as a term in popular usage and as a discipline within the academy – which makes the study of its history such a fascinating one. According to Livingstone, the history (or as he puts it, the historical geography) of geography must necessarily be a contextual reading of the subject's emergence. Yet this emphatically does not mean interpreting geographical texts and social, economic, cultural or political contexts as causally related – as though they were essentially separate and static factors, the latter

---

and human geography', 1984, pp. 315–26; Andrews, 'The early life of Paul Vidal de la Blache', 1986, pp. 174–82; Andrews, 'Les premiers cours de géographie de Paul Vidal de la Blache', 1986, pp. 341–67; Baker, 'Paul Vidal de la Blache', 1988, pp. 189–201; Berdoulay, 'Vidal–Durkheim debate', 1978, pp. 77–90; Broc, 'L'Établissement de la géographie', 1974, pp. 545–68; Broc, 'La pensée géographique en France au XIXe siècle', 1976, pp. 225–47; Buttimer, *Society and Milieu*, 1971; and Rhein, 'La géographie, discipline scolaire', 1982, pp. 223–51.

[7] Berdoulay, *La Formation de l'École*, 1981, pp. 45–75; MacKay, 'Colonialism and the French', 1943, pp. 214–32; and Murphy, *The Ideology of French*, 1948, esp. pp. 1–40.

[8] See Livingstone, *The Geographical Tradition*, 1992, pp. 1–31.

in some way explaining the former. Rather, it requires a recognition of the reciprocal or dialectical relation between text and context as interwoven forces, each constituting and reconstituting the other. It is also necessary for the historian of science to acknowledge that this interaction between text and context – in this case, between French geography and French imperialism – was also a contested and disputatious process, involving considerable and often vehement debate.

For the purposes of this chapter, therefore, I shall define French geography largely – though not exclusively – as encompassing the activities of the principal French geographical societies during the late nineteenth and early twentieth centuries. The activities and interests of the members of these societies were, of course, extremely wide-ranging and sometimes mutually incompatible. This serves, however, both to demonstrate the variety of rival perspectives within French geography at this time and to indicate the complexity of the interconnections between the French geographical movement and French imperialism. In the next two sections, I shall attempt to describe the principal characteristics of French imperialism and French geography before examining in greater detail, in the following five sections, the nature of the collision between them.

THE NATURE OF FRENCH IMPERIALISM

Our understanding of French imperialism during the late nineteenth and early twentieth centuries has been substantially expanded by the innovative research of C. M. Andrew and A. S. Kanya-Forstner. In a recent article, they argue that although France acquired a huge colonial empire, beginning with the conquest of Algeria in the 1830s and 1840s and ending with the establishment of the French mandates in the Middle East after World War I, for most of this period, French public opinion and the majority of France's political leaders remained unconvinced of the need for overseas colonies. Indeed, many of France's most influential political figures were actively and consistently opposed to imperial expansion.[9]

According to their analysis, this paradox arose from the limitations and instability of French political institutions throughout this period. During the middle decades of the nineteenth century – from Bugeaud's campaigns in North Africa in the 1840s through Faidherbe's conquests in West Africa during the 1850s and 1860s – the drive to expand the French Empire came from within the ranks of the French army operating on the colonial periphery. These military empire-builders ran roughshod over the wishes of Parisian politicians and were effectively beyond the control of their civilian 'masters' in France. Insubordination and the refusal to obey ministerial instructions was raised to an art form in some sections of the colonial army. Imperial objectives and colonial policies were, in this early period, fashioned

[9] Andrew and Kanya-Forstner, 'Centre and periphery', 1988, pp. 9–34.

largely in response to local strategic considerations. In these circumstances, the progressive expansion of France's empire up to 1870 assumed an inexorable dynamic of its own, fuelled partly by military adventurism and partly by the desire amongst senior military figures to protect and enhance their new-found and relatively well-paid positions of power as colonial administrators. As each sector of land was conquered and pacified, so the unconquered and unpacified sectors further afield seemed to threaten the colonial army's control of its existing territorial base. The unimaginative solution to this imagined threat was yet more conquest and military campaigning. Once conquered, territory proved extremely difficult to surrender and even the most resolute anti-imperialist ministers in Paris were often reduced to the status of impotent onlookers. [10]

Andrew and Kanya-Forstner argue that, after 1870, the centre of gravity of the French imperial impulse began to shift from the colonial periphery to the metropolitan core, and from the army to various sections of the middle-class intelligentsia in France. Yet this did not mean that the French political leadership as a whole became more committed to overseas expansion. While the establishment of the Third Republic reintroduced democratic government, the disastrous events of 1870–1 – the defeat of the French army in the Franco–Prussian War, the collapse of Napoleon III's Second Empire, the long siege of Paris, the loss of Alsace-Lorraine to the new German Empire and the bloody interlude of the Commune – disorientated and polarized French political opinion. Governments and ministers came and went with bewildering frequency through the early decades of the Third Republic and, in the interstices, small and well-organized pressure groups like the emerging colonial lobby assumed an influence well beyond the popular support they enjoyed from the public at large. [11]

By the 1880s, a few republican politicians, notably Léon Gambetta and Jules Ferry, had been persuaded of the need to develop and extend France's global imperial presence. With the support of these powerful allies, the colonial lobby developed into a considerable political force. At its head was Eugene Étienne, the charismatic deputy for Oran and a faithful disciple of Gambetta. During the 1890s, an informal alliance established itself around Étienne known as the 'Parti Colonial', comprising around sixty different colonialist societies based in Paris and the provinces, many of which were little more than hearty dining clubs. Some of these societies were organized according to the region into which they advocated greater French colonial expansion, notably the Comité de l'Asie française, the Comité de l'Orient

---

[10] On different episodes in this process in North and West Africa, see Brunschwig, 'French exploration and conquest', 1969, pp. 132–64; Danziger, *Abd-al-Qadir and the Algerians*, 1977; Julien, *Histoire de l'Algérie*, 2nd edn, vol. 1, 1979, pp. 64–163; Kanya-Forstner, *The Conquest of the Western Sudan*, 1969; Porch, *The Conquest of the Sahara*, 1984 and Sullivan, *Thomas-Robert Bugeaud*, 1983.

[11] A most stimulating history of the French Third Republic in English is provided by Elwitt, *The Making of the Third Republic*, 1975 and *The Third Republic*, 1985.

and the Comité du Maroc. Others, like the Comité d'Action Républicaine aux colonies, La France colonisatrice and the 'Société de colonisation française', promoted the need for French overseas colonization and settlement around the world.[12]

Despite its small size – somewhere between 5,000 and 10,000 members – the Parti Colonial played a decisive role in promoting the cause of overseas expansion and in formulating the key components of France's imperial policy. It could rely on committed representatives in the Chamber of Deputies, in the Senate, at the heart of the French civil service and within the expanding universities. From these bases, the colonial lobby could directly influence the decision-making process, in the face of continuing opposition. According to Andrew and Kanya-Forstner, it was largely through the activities of this amorphous pressure group, rather than through the efforts of elected governments, that the second largest European empire of the imperial age was carved out in the name of France.

THE GEOGRAPHICAL MOVEMENT IN LATE NINETEENTH-CENTURY FRANCE

The French geographical movement was intimately involved in the debate about the imperial question. French geographers were certainly in the vanguard of the colonialist lobby and were amongst the more eloquent and sophisticated advocates of empire. However, the initial rapid expansion of geography at all levels in the French educational system after 1870 was not primarily connected to the subject's obvious relevance to French imperial ambitions. Rather, French geography benefited considerably from the widespread desire for domestic educational reform as a means of national rejuvenation in the wake of the Franco–Prussian War. A conviction developed across all shades of political opinion – and education was usually one of the most divisive areas in French political life – that France's defeat in 1870, and all that had flowed from it, had been the result of the country's inadequate educational system, particularly when compared to Germany. German troops had seemed better prepared morally and intellectually, more aware of their environment and more knowledgeable in subjects of relevance to modern warfare. Most alarming for patriotic Frenchmen, the generation of German soldiers that had fought in 1870 seemed more deeply imbued with an inspirational nationalist belief in the justness of their cause. If carefully and judiciously taught, subjects like geography and history were identified as

[12] On Gambetta and Ferry as colonialists, see Ageron, 'Gambetta et la reprise', 1972, pp. 165–204; Ageron, 'Jules Ferry et la colonisation', 1986. On Étienne and the rest of the colonialist movement, see Abrams and Miller, 'Who were the French colonialists?', 1976, pp. 685–725; Andrew and Kanya-Forstner, 'The French Colonial Party', 1971, pp. 9–128; Andrew and Kanya-Forstner, 'The Groupe Colonial in the French Chamber', 1974, pp. 837–66; Andrew, Grupp and Kanya-Forstner, 'Le mouvement colonial français', 1975, pp. 640–73, and Persell, *The French Colonial Lobby*, 1983.

being of central importance to any concerted attempt at national regeneration through education and were tirelessly promoted by French educational reformers, at all levels from the primary schools to the universities.[13]

Institutions like the Société de Géographie de Paris (SGP), still the only geographical society in France in 1870, acquired a new lease of life in these circumstances. The SGP had emerged as an important focus of Parisian intellectual life during the preceding decade, thanks largely to the energetic activities of Charles Maunoir, who had been its secretary since 1864, and to the Marquis de Chasseloup-Laubat – Napoleon III's Minister for the Navy, and the head of the short-lived Colonial Ministry between 1858 and 1860 – who was the Society's president through the late 1860s. Despite the difficulties of the Franco–Prussian War and the siege of Paris, the SGP survived the 1870–1 period with 600 members. In 1873, Vice-Admiral de la Roncière de Nouy succeeded de Chasseloup-Laubat as president on the latter's death and, aided by the indefatigable Maunoir, he set about increasing the size and significance of the SGP. By 1875, its membership had leapt to 1,353. The overwhelming majority of new members were drawn from the ranks of the Parisian liberal professions. Sixteen per cent of members were army or naval officers and a further five per cent came from the world of politics. The SGP could also boast several influential newspaper proprietors and journalists amongst its membership, including Charles Buloz, the directeur of the *Revue des deux mondes*, Robert Gauthiot, the editor of the *Journal des débats* and Guillaume Depping, the editor of the *Journal officiel*.[14]

One can identify two overlapping, but slightly different constituencies within the SGP during the early years of the Third Republic. The first group, dominated by Maunoir, was the driving force behind the announcement, in 1871, that the SGP was substantially to expand its objectives. In particular, it would seek henceforth to promote geography at all levels in the French educational system. This meant providing much firmer and more respectable scientific foundations for geography so that it could stand alongside other emerging disciplines in the natural and social sciences. The climate was right for such an expansion and the teaching of geography increased significantly, firstly in the schools and colleges and, particularly after 1890,

---

[13] The fear of national decline and moral degeneration surfaced in many forms: see Nye, *Crime, Madness and Politics*, 1984 and Pick, *Faces of Degeneration*, 1989, especially pp. 37–106. On the 'redemptive' educational qualities of geography, see Andrews, 'A French view of geography teaching in Britain', 1986, pp. 225–31; Berdoulay, *La Formation de l'École Française*, 1981, pp. 17–43, 109–39 and Broc, 'Histoire de la géographie et nationalisme en France', 1970, pp. 21–6. On Franco–German rivalry in education and science after 1871; Broc, 'La géographie française face à la science allemande', 1977, pp. 71–94 and, more generally, Digeon, *La Crise Allemande de la Pensée Française*, 1959 and Paul, *The Sorcerer's Apprentice*, 1972.

[14] Membership figures and other factual details about the SGP are available in Fierro, *La Société de Géographie*, 1983. See also, Lejeune, 'La Société de Géographie de Paris', 1982, pp. 141–63.

in the universities. In 1870, there was only one official chair of geography in French higher education. Twenty years later, there were still only four chairs of geography but by the turn of the century, a dozen has been established across the university sector, together with around 40 other posts involved in teaching the subject.[15]

Maunoir and his supporters were determined to modernize the discipline intellectually and purge it of its gentlemanly, amateur and eclectic ethos. They were therefore rather suspicious of encouraging close and direct contact between the discipline and the world of politics. The second group within the SGP had no such reservations. For these enthusiasts, geography should be more than an educationally prominent and scientifically respectable discipline; it should also be directly relevant to the commercial and political needs of the nation. It was this group which became increasingly associated with the cause of French imperial expansion. Many of the earliest advocates of French imperialism had joined the SGP under the Second Empire. Jules Duval, for example, one of the most articulate and humane advocates of French colonialism was elected vice-president of the SGP a few months before his accidental death in 1870.[16] Over the next 20 years, many of the leading architects of French imperial policy joined the SGP, so that by 1890 it was firmly established, in the words of Andrew and Kanya-Forstner, as 'the elder statesman of the colonialist movement'.[17] Certainly, their detailed prosopographic survey of the principal personalities in the Parti Colonial lends credence to this view. Of the two hundred names they identify, 54 per cent were members of the SGP and, of the 45 leading colonialist societies in the Parti Colonial, 26 were chaired by SGP members.[18]

However, as this geo-imperialist discourse gathered momentum, so it increased in range and diversity. By the 1880s, the debate within the SGP was no longer concerned with whether France should expand its colonial empire. Rather, discussion concentrated on the more difficult and contentious question of how, and on what basis, this expansion should occur. At the risk of erecting arbitrary categories, I think it is possible to identify five overlapping perspectives on the imperial question within the burgeoning French geographical movement of the late nineteenth century. Although it is often difficult to identify individuals or distinct groups associated with one position as against another, each of these different attitudes influenced the broader debate about imperialism within French intellectual and political life and each contributed to the formulation of France's imperial ambitions between

[15] Berdoulay, 'La Formation de l'École', 1981, pp. 77–108, especially pp. 91–106. On the general expansion of French higher education during the Third Republic, see Clark, *Prophets and Patrons*, 1973 and Weisz, *The Emergence of the Modern Universities*, 1983.

[16] On Duval, see Girardet, *L'Idée Coloniale*, 1972, pp. 43–5 and Vallette, *Socialisme Utopique*, 1976.

[17] Andrew and Kanya-Forstner, *France Overseas*, 1981, p. 102.

[18] Andrew, Grupp and Kanya-Forstner, 'Le mouvement colonial français', 1975, pp. 658–73.

the 1870s and the 1920s. For want of better terms, these five positions can be identified as utopian imperialism, cultural imperialism, economic imperialism, opportunist imperialism and, finally, anti-imperialism.

UTOPIA AND EMPIRE

The first position – that of utopian imperialism – was influential during the 1870s and 1880s, though it became less important thereafter. To an extent, it was a legacy of early nineteenth-century utopian thought though it was also strongly influenced by the values and ethos of the Second Empire. Within the SGP, this position was particularly associated with Jules Duval until his death in 1870; thereafter with Henri Duveyrier and, to a slightly lesser extent, with Ferdinand de Lesseps. [19]

All three of these men had been deeply affected by early nineteenth-century Saint-Simonian thought. Henri Duveyrier, perhaps the leading French Saharan explorer of the late nineteenth century and the president of the SGP during the 1880s, was the son of Charles Duveyrier, one of the leading members of the Saint-Simonian sect in Paris during the 1820s and 1830s. This movement, associated particularly with the École Polytechnique, had developed a radical, crypto-socialist philosophy which had certain features in common with the contemporaneous utopian ideas of Robert Owen, Étienne Cabet and Charles Fourier. [20]

By the early 1830s, the movement included some of the finest young minds in France, many of whom were to achieve fame and fortune under the Second Empire. The leaders, including Prosper Enfantin and Charles Duveyrier, were convinced that industrial technology and communications should be used to overcome the physical barriers separating religious and cultural spheres. This faith in the transformative and beneficial power of technology rested on a firm conviction that the scientifically advanced civilization of Europe was essentially male, while the civilizations of Africa and Asia were fundamentally female. The rationale for this belief was sketched out only in very general terms, but the Saint-Simonians were convinced nevertheless that a fruitful union between these two realms, facilitated by the spread of canals, railways and other means of communications, would generate a new and more vigorous 'hybrid' culture, containing the best qualities from each 'parent' civilization. [21]

[19] On Duveyrier, see Heffernan, 'The limits of utopia', 1989, pp. 342–52. On de Lesseps, see Beatty, *Ferdinand de Lesseps*, 1956, and Bonnet, *Ferdinand de Lesseps*, 1959.

[20] Charlton, *Secular Religions*, 1963; Derré (ed.), *Regards sur le Saint-Simonisme*, 1986; Iggers, *The Cult of Authority*, 1958; Manuel, *The New World of Henri Saint-Simon*, 1963, and Manuel, *The Prophets of Paris*, 1965.

[21] Morsy (ed.), *Les Saint-Simoniens*, 1989. The utopian motive of European imperialism is the theme of Baudet, *Paradise on Earth*, 1965. The theme of sexuality and imperialism is taken up controversially in Hyam, *Empire and Sexuality*, 1990.

The French conquest of Algeria, which began in 1830, was warmly welcomed by the Saint-Simonians as a first step on the path towards this desired union of Europe and Africa. To begin with, however, their attention focused on Egypt. Prosper Enfantin, the self-styled leader of the sect, spent three fruitless years between 1833 and 1836 in and around Cairo trying to persuade anyone who would listen of the need for a canal link between the Red Sea and the Mediterranean. Whilst in Egypt, Enfantin met and greatly impressed Ferdinand de Lesseps, the young French pro-consul in the region. De Lesseps was subsequently to devote most of his considerable entre-preneurial skill to raising sufficient French capital to construct the Suez Canal and was finally to achieve his ambition in 1869. Like Henri Duveyrier, a lifelong friend and confidant, Ferdinand de Lesseps became a prominent member of the SGP and served as its president during the late 1870s. [22]

Duveyrier, de Lesseps and Duval were all committed imperialists, but their brand of imperialism was founded on rather romantic, utopian ideals. From their perspective, French overseas expansion should point the way to a new and more humane imperialism, based on the idea of reciprocal, mutually beneficial commercial and spiritual exchange between the whole of Europe and the entire non-European world.

It is possible to see more than a trace of this utopian imperialism in some of the more misguided and over-ambitious imperial projects which were supported by French geographers and imperialists during the 1870s and 1880s. These included, for example, the attempt to create a huge inland sea deep in the Sahara desert by means of canals which would introduce water from the Mediterranean, [23] and the equally unsuccessful attempt to construct a great Saharan railway linking French colonial possessions in North and West Africa. [24]

Although some sectors of the French military retained a measure of sympathy with Saint-Simonian ideals, the more mystical and utopian brand of imperialist thought was rarely well received by senior colonial army officers, preoccupied as most were with quotidian difficulties of maintaining imperial control. For Duveyrier, however, imperialism based solely on military control was morally and ideologically indefensible and he clashed repeatedly with

---

[22] On the Saint-Simonian involvement in Algeria and in Egypt, see Carré, *Voyageurs et Écrivains*, 1956, vol. 1, pp. 261–77: Émerit, *Les Saint-Simoniens en Algérie*, 1941; Émerit, 'Les explorateurs saint-simoniennes', 1943, pp. 92–116; Émerit, 'Diplomates et explorateurs', 1975, pp. 397–415: Fakkar, *Reflets de la Sociologie Pre-Marxiste*, 1974. On their particular role in the construction of the Suez Canal, see Kinross, *Between Two Seas*, 1968: Marlowe, *The Making of the Suez Canal*, 1964: Taboulet, 'Aux origines du Canal de Suez', 1968, pp. 89–114 and 361–92; Taboulet, 'Le rôle des saint-simoniens', 1971, pp. 1295–1320 and Taboulet, 'Ferdinand de Lesseps et l'Égypte', 1973, pp. 143–71 and 364–407.

[23] Heffernan, 'Bringing the desert to bloom', 1990, pp. 94–114 and Murphy, *The Ideology of French Imperialism*, 1948, pp. 70–5.

[24] Carrière, 'Le Transsaharien', 1988, pp. 23–38; Heffernan, 'The limits of utopia', 1981, pp. 347–8 and Porch, *The Conquest of the Sahara*, 1984, 83–125.

the army and naval officers within both the SGP and the broader colonialist movement. During the controversy surrounding Flatters' expedition to cross the Sahara in early 1881 – the mission was investigating the best route for the proposed trans-Saharan railway and was brutally massacred by the Touareg – Duveyrier was widely criticized in the press for the naively optimistic counsel he had offered the expedition and for his persistent opposition to excessive military involvement in exploration. Depressed by his harsh treatment in the media and by the rise of what he saw as crude and aggressive imperialism, Duveyrier eventually committed suicide in 1892.

NATION, CULTURE AND EMPIRE

Overlapping with this utopian imperialism was a rather less mystical and more nationalistic strand of cultural imperialism which ultimately dominated the colonial discourse in France and became one of the major influences on French geography. Geographers associated with this position saw their educational and imperial roles as inextricably interwoven. While the carefully directed study of France's rich and varied regional geography was to be a central educational component in fostering the spirit of patriotism and devotion to the Republic, the expansion of France overseas was interpreted as crucial to the nation's future survival as a vibrant culture and civilization.

Many of the early prophets of imperial expansion during the Second Empire based their arguments on this cultural rationale. Chief amongst them was Anatole Prévost-Paradol, the author of the 1868 polemic, *La France Nouvelle*.[25] In this book, Prévost-Paradol painted a dark and foreboding portrait of a stagnant and decadent French culture. The cure for this, he insisted, was aggressive colonial expansion, particularly into Africa. 'If our population', he wrote, 'obstinately attached to our native soil, continues to grow so slowly, then we shall inevitably become as Greece is now – an ancient though dead civilization, an historical and cultural artefact'.[26] He pointed, in particular, to France's relatively sluggish population growth as evidence that the nation had become insular, sick and impotent. Reversing what might seem the logical argument – that if there were insufficient people within France, there was little point in encouraging them to colonize the far-flung regions of the globe – Prévost-Paradol insisted that it was only through colonization that cultural and national vigour could return to France.

For Prévost-Paradol, the example of Britain was illuminating. Britain had not become a great imperial power because of its rapid population growth, as was often postulated. Rather, Britain's greater demographic buoyancy – a constant source of embarrassment to virile Frenchmen – was a result of the

---

[25] Prévost-Paradol, *La France Nouvelle*, 1868, reprinted as Prévost-Paradol, *La France Nouvelle et Pages Choisis*, 1981, pp. 155–291. On Prévost-Paradol, see Guiral, *Prévost-Paradol*, 1955.

[26] Prévost-Paradol, *La France Nouvelle*, 1981, p. 286.

psychological and cultural prestige brought by empire. If France could colonize more energetically, it would replicate the success of the British and, by spreading French language, culture and civilization around the world, would challenge the growing cultural hegemony of Britain. This would restore the country's damaged *amour propre* and enable it to incorporate indigenous colonial peoples into a greater France, a France that would one day stretch from Calais to Lake Chad and contain 'one hundred million Frenchmen'.[27]

These ideas, which were echoed by Paul Leroy Beaulieu, Gabriel Charmes, Pierre Raboisson, Paul Gaffarel and other converts close to the geographical movement, were voiced more loudly after 1870.[28] The crisis of 1870–1 seemed to confirm the worst fears about France's declining potential as a great nation. Although attention initially turned to the reconstruction of the country after its defeat, colonial expansion was soon being advocated by many geographers both as a solution to the cultural malaise which seemed to have gripped the nation during the decadent 1860s, and as a means of compensating for the territorial loss suffered by the German annexation of Alsace-Lorraine.

The liberal and largely republican geographical movement within the rapidly expanding universities of the Third Republic was particularly attracted to this strand of imperialist thought. Paul Vidal de la Blache, the doyen of the French school of geography in the last decades of the nineteenth century, interpreted French colonialism in these cultural terms, as did more reactionary and conservative nationalist geographers such as Marcel Dubois, the founding co-editor, with de la Blache, of the *Annales de Géographie* and Professor of Colonial Geography at the Sorbonne from the early 1890s.[29] The career of Pierre Foncin is amongst the most revealing of this brand of French imperialist thought. Foncin was a geography teacher, an educational inspector and a founder member of both the Bordeaux and Lille Geographical Societies.[30] He insisted that, if based primarily on cultural foundations, French

[27] There is a huge literature on French fears of population decline in this period. For different aspects of this anxiety see, for example, and from the English literature alone, McLaren, *Sexuality*, 1983; Nye, *Crime, Madness and Politics*, 1984, esp. pp. 132–70; Nye, 'Honor, impotence, and male sexuality', 1989, pp. 48–71; Offen, 'Depopulation, nationalism, and feminism', 1984, pp. 648–75; Ogden and Huss, 'Demography and pronatalism', 1982, pp. 283–98: Schneider, 'Toward the improvement of the human race', 1982, pp. 268–91; Splenger, *France Faces Depopulation*, 1979. The expression 'one hundred million Frenchmen' became a rallying cry of the pro-colonialist, 'assimilationist' lobby and was in part an attempt to reconcile the idea of overseas colonization with the apparently pressing need to increase the reserves of manpower available to France, particularly in time of war. See Lewis, 'One hundred million Frenchmen', 1961–2, pp. 129–53. On Duval's attempts to reconcile French colonial emigration and the long-term demographic prowess of the nation, see Charbit, *Du Malthusianisme*, 1981, pp. 185–92.

[28] See Murphy, *The Ideology of French Imperialism*, 1948, pp. 103–75 on Leroy-Beaulieu, pp. 176–91 on Charmes, pp. 191–208 on Gaffarel and pp. 208–22 on Raboisson.

[29] On Vidal de la Blache, see the references in note 6. On Dubois, see Broc, 'Nationalisme, colonialisme et géographie', 1978, pp. 326–33.

[30] Foncin is discussed in Bruézière, *L'Alliance Française*, 1983.

imperialism was destined to be more benign and beneficial than other forms of imperialism, notably that developed by the commercially motivated British. Like Louis Blanc, the famous French socialist and historian, Foncin believed that, while 'England has set foot in no country without setting up her counting houses, France has nowhere passed without leaving the perfume of her spirituality'.[31] To foster this 'perfumed spirituality', Foncin co-founded the Alliance Française in 1883 to promote French language and culture around the world. Later, like other leading geographers such as Vidal de la Blache and Lucien Gallois, Foncin became a prominent member of the Fédération Régionaliste Française, a largely ineffective society which was established in 1900 to preserve, celebrate and encourage the regional identities of France in the face of the centralizing and homogenizing cultural influence of Paris. Although this organization embraced a wide range of political perspectives, including old-style anti-republican and anti-Jacobin conservatism, the ideas of Foncin and other republican liberals on the need to conserve the regional diversity within France were linked directly to their ideal of a greater colonial France, in which all the disparate peoples and environments of the French empire could be linked to, and would then enrich and be enriched by, the culture of metropolitan France.[32]

The idea of cultural reciprocity, in which France's civilization would be enhanced by interaction with its overseas colonies while at the same time spreading the immense benefits of France's unique culture and language amongst the people of the colonies, was a central component of the cultural imperialist position and was repeatedly emphasized as the key distinguishing feature in the rhetoric – if not in the reality – of French imperialism. In its avowedly cultural perspective, this second strand of French imperialism clearly overlaps with some aspects of the utopian imperialist project. It departs from the latter, however, in its strongly nationalist line. It was probably this perspective, though, which remained the most influential on French imperial thought into the middle years of this century. Many of the central aspects of French colonial policy after the 1890s – the ideas of *mission civilisatrice*[33] and of assimilation[34] – were couched explicitly in these cultural terms.

[31] Quoted in Andrew and Kanya-Forstner, *France Overseas*, 1981, p. 26.

[32] The role of academic geographers in the conflict between regionalism and centralism under the Third Republic is an intriguing topic. On this, see Berdoulay, *La Formation de l'École*, 1981, pp. 109–39, especially pp. 132–7 and Guiomar, 'Le Tableau de la géographie de la France de Vidal de la Blache', 1986, vol. II, part I, pp. 569–97. Several of the other essays in this huge edited work explore, in different ways, this same theme, especially those by Pomian, vol. II, part I, pp. 367–429: Nordman, vol. II, part I, pp. 529–67; Roncayolo, vol. II, part I, pp. 487–528 and Weber, vol. II, part II, pp. 96–116. See also Flory, *Le Mouvement Régionaliste*, 1966.

[33] The idea of the French imperialism as a *mission civilisatrice* is discussed in Burrows, 'Mission civilisatrice', 1986, pp. 109–35.

[34] On the idea of assimilation, and the subsequent policy of association, see Betts, *Assimilation and Association*, 1961 and Lewis, 'One hundred million Frenchmen', 1961–2. See also, Chipman, *French Power in Africa*, 1989.

Some writers, such as Franz Ansprenger, have suggested that this rather emotive emphasis on culture and language as the basis of French imperialism was partly responsible for the special difficulties which France faced in the process of decolonization. The British Empire, it is claimed, based on commerce and trade and ruled 'indirectly' according to the British model of imperial management, could evolve relatively painlessly into a looser union like the Commonwealth. In France, where the emphasis was on direct rule and on the necessity for cultural assimilation, anti-imperial pressures and the movement towards independence often met with fierce opposition, most disastrously in Indochina and in Algeria. For the supporters of French Algeria, for example, reared on decades of French imperial propaganda about the unity of France and North Africa and the impossibility of the two existing separately from one another, any attempt to establish an independent Algeria was a profound and unimaginable assault on the integrity of French culture and civilization.[35]

TRADE AND EMPIRE

This rhetorical emphasis on the cultural and nationalist objectives of French imperialism is the dominant theme in many of the standard histories of French colonial ideology, notably those by Henri Brunschwig and Raoul Girardet.[36] In the words of Ronald E. Robinson, the historian of British imperialism, Brunschwig's idea of French imperialism rests on the belief that: 'the liberal Anglo-Saxon painted the map red in pursuit of trade and philanthropy, and the nationalistic French painted it blue, not for good economic reasons, but to pump up their prestige as a great nation'.[37] According to this argument, France did not need the markets and raw materials of overseas colonies as Britain did because its economy was less industrialized and it was largely self-sufficient for much of the nineteenth century. Yet France sought colonies nevertheless in order to keep its place amongst the great powers, regardless of the economic costs involved, and was thereby also involved in economic imperialism.

The debate about the economic costs and benefits of empire remains an area of great contention today as it was throughout the late nineteenth century.[38] To some extent, the dispute was not only between those anti-imperialists who insisted that empire would be a net drain on France's economy and those who argued the opposite case, but also between economic

[35] Ansprenger, *The Dissolution of the Colonial Empires*, 1989, especially pp. 208–52.
[36] See Brunschwig, *French Colonialism*, 1966 and Girardet, *L'Idée Coloniale en France*, 1972.
[37] Robinson, Introduction, in Brunschwig, *French Colonialism, 1871–1914*, 1966, p. vii.
[38] On French imperialism and the French economy, see Marseille, *Empire Colonial*, 1984; Andrew and Kanya-Forstner, 'French business', 1976, pp. 981–1000, and more generally, Fieldhouse, *Economics and Empire*, 1973.

imperialists and cultural imperialists. Although there was no hard and fast division here, the economic imperialists sought to demonstrate the commercial advantages of overseas colonies, while many cultural imperialists spent their time celebrating the costs of empire as evidence of France's commitment to the cultural advancement of the colonies.

As William Schneider has recently indicated, this division was evident within French geography and was one of the reasons why the SGP lost its unique position as the flagship of the discipline.[39] The split began in 1873. For some time, a section of committed colonialists within the SGP had been attempting to forge links with the Paris Chambres Syndicales and, towards the end of 1873, a joint Commission de Géographie Commerciale was established with members from both institutions. The objective was to foster economic contact between France and other parts of the world, particularly in the expanding colonial realm.

In the following year, Eugène Azam, a professor of medicine in Bordeaux, and Pierre Foncin applied to the SGP for permission to establish the first provincial geographical society in France under the aegis of the SGP.[40] The impulse for this – notwithstanding Foncin's cultural imperialist tendencies – had come from the local business community. Indeed, the new society proposed to call itself the Société de Géographie Commerciale. Some elements within the SGP were worried about establishing close ties with the grubby world of commerce and, while the SGP vacillated, a group of like-minded local politicians, liberal professionals and businessmen in Lyon established their own geographical society without bothering to contact the SGP. Again, the initiative had come from local commercial agencies, particularly those associated with the silk industry. Inspired by this and impatient with the attitude of the SGP, the geographical enthusiasts in Bordeaux decided in 1874 to proceed without formal recognition from Paris. The following year, local businessmen, academics and liberal professionals in Marseille followed suit and established their own geographical society. As John Laffey has shown, in port towns like Bordeaux, Marseille and Lyon, local business communities had become increasingly aware that, regardless of the overall costs or benefits of empire to France, the local economic advantages which would accrue from increasing imperial trade were likely to be considerable. Local chambers of commerce therefore threw their full weight behind the colonial lobby, a phenomenon which Laffey refers to as 'municipal imperialism'.[41]

The SGP was unable to contain the rising separatist instincts of the commercially-motivated geographers in its own ranks. The Commission de Géographie Commerciale eventually established itself as a separate entity in 1876 called the Société de Géographie Commerciale de Paris. Reflecting its more exclusive concerns with imperial matters, the new society went on to

[39] Schneider, 'Geographical reform', 1990, pp. 90–117.

[40] On Eugène Azam, see Roth, 'Remembering forgetting', 1989, pp. 49–68, especially pp. 61–5.

[41] Laffey, 'Municipal imperialism', 1974, pp. 81–114.

set up colonial and overseas branches in Tunis (1896), Hanoi (1902) and Constantinople (1904). [42]

Although the SGP continued to increase in size, its membership eventually peaked at around 2,500 in 1885 and thereafter declined slightly. [43] Most of the considerable growth in the size of the French geographical movement after the 1870s occurred in the provinces and new geographical societies were established in most of the larger French cities. By 1909, there were 27 independent geographical societies in France and a further four in French Algeria. Following Bordeaux's lead, several of these, particularly those in the larger ports, styled themselves commercial geographical societies, including those at Nantes, Le Havre and St Nazaire. The Marseille society called itself the Société de Géographie et d'Études Coloniales de Marseille. By the turn of the century, the total membership of French geographical societies was 16,508, out of a world total of 47,968. [44]

The spread of geographical societies around France stands in marked contrast to the situation in Britain. In London, the Royal Geographical Society (RGS) – easily the largest geographical society in the world with over 3,500 fellows in 1890 – managed to retain much of its central power within British geography, notwithstanding the establishment in 1884 of both the Royal Scottish Geographical Society and the Manchester Geographical Society, and the subsequent foundation of smaller and relatively short-lived societies in Liverpool, Southampton, Newcastle and Hull. [45] The RGS continued to increase rapidly up to the First World War, when it could boast a fellowship of nearly 5,500.

Thus despite the numerical dominance of French geography compared with other countries, membership was dissipated into a large number of relatively small, provincial societies, and this runs counter to what one might expect in centralized, Paris-dominated France. Yet it reflects a significant division between different sections of the French geographical community over the nature of France's engagement with its colonies. While the imperialists in the SGP tended to speak in terms of France's colonial responsibilities, those in the provincial societies looked unashamedly to the commercial profits from imperial trade. They were more unambiguously supportive of overseas conquest and of geographical research which was obviously geared towards this objective, particularly in areas of special commercial interest to the local

[42] Details on the establishment of the Société de Géographie Commerciale can be found in Archives nationales F[17] 13034.

[43] Fierro, *La Société de Géographie*, 1983, p. 287.

[44] Based on figures in Kollm, 'Geographische Gesellschaften', 1897, 403–13, especially pp. 411–13. Also quoted in Schneider, 'Geographical reform', 1990, p. 91.

[45] The Royal Scottish and Manchester Geographical Societies are discussed in Brown, *The History of the Manchester Geographical*, 1971; Freeman, 'The Manchester Geographical', 1984, pp. 2–19 and Freeman, 'The Manchester and Royal Scottish', 1984, pp. 55–62. The figures on the RGS membership are listed in Fierro, *La Société de Géographie*, 1983, p. 287.

region. A classic illustration is the active promotion by the Société de Géographie de Lyon of French colonial expansion into Tonkin and Indochina in the 1880s in the anticipation that this would open up a new supply of cheap, high-quality silk for the local mills.[46]

THE FIRST WORLD WAR, THE GEOGRAPHERS AND THE CLIMAX OF FRENCH IMPERIALISM

The fourth kind of imperialism within the French geographical movement – opportunist imperialism – was associated specifically with the First World War. Although many of the standard works on European imperialism end in 1914 in the belief that the Great War brought to a close the age of European empire-building, such a view is not entirely justified. Indeed, Lenin's influential views on imperialism, formulated in Zürich as the war reached its most brutal climax in 1916, claimed that the conflict raging around him was directly linked to, and inspired by, the imperial aspirations and ambitions of the great European powers. Although challenged by more recent accounts of European imperialism and by other analyses of the war itself, Lenin's assessment sought to demonstrate that the crisis was 'on both sides an imperialist (i.e. an annexationist, predatory and plunderous) war for the partition of the world and for the distribution and redistribution of colonies, of "spheres of influence", of finance capital.'[47]

By mid-1915, the opposing armies were bogged down in a war of attrition on the Western Front. With the prospect of a swift and dramatic allied victory receding with each week, a few French political leaders began seriously to consider possible terms for future peace accords with Germany and its allies. To an extent, this was prompted by a growing realization that France had no clearly-defined war aims on which to base future negotiations, apart from the simple desire to drive German forces back across the 1914 French boundaries and the generally accepted claim that Alsace-Lorraine should be returned to France as an atonement for German aggression. The desire to formulate a more complete list of intellectually and morally compelling French war aims intensified after the United States began to put pressure on belligerent nations to define their objectives during 1916.[48]

The French government of Aristide Briand, which came to power at the end of October 1915, began to make confidential plans to define French war aims more fully and to prepare the ground for future peace negotiations.

---

[46] Laffey, 'Roots of French imperialism', 1969, pp. 78–92; Laffey, 'The Lyon Chamber', 1975, pp. 325–48 and Laffey, 'Municipal imperialism in decline', 1975, pp. 329–53.

[47] Lenin, *Imperialism*, 1966, p. 12. See also Koch, 'Social Darwinism', 1984, pp. 319–42.

[48] The debate about war aims continues: see, for example, Fischer, *Germany's War*, 1967; Fresh, *British Strategy*, 1986; Koch, 'Social Darwinism', 1984; Nelson, *Land and Power*, 1963; Rothwell, *British War Aims*, 1971; Stevenson, *French War Aims*, 1982 and Stevenson, *The First World War*, 1988, especially pp, 87–138.

The colonial lobby, still a very active force within French politics, was particularly eager to ensure that France's empire should be at the centre of any future peace negotiations. Under pressure from influential colonialist *députés*, particularly the ultra-nationalist Louis Marin, the government agreed to set up a series of expert commissions to consider the issues which were likely to be raised in the peace discussions.[49]

In February 1916, Baron Hulot, the secretary of the SGP, was approached by Marin and asked to establish four commissions. These were to consider, firstly, the future boundary between Germany and France, and in particular, the vexed question of Alsace-Lorraine; secondly, the future political boundaries of Central and Eastern Europe; thirdly, the possibility of French territorial claims in Africa after the war, especially in relation to the German colonies; and, fourthly, the possibility of French territorial claims in Asia and the Middle East, especially in the Ottoman Empire. The working assumption was that, even if the Central Powers did not lose the war outright, they would ultimately be forced to negotiate from a position of relative weakness and that a punitive peace settlement could, and should, be imposed, to the benefit of France and, if possible, the other Allies. It was also generally accepted that Austro–Hungary would have to be divided into a number of smaller states and that the Ottoman Empire in the Middle East would likewise be dismantled.[50]

The SGP was selected to organize and host these confidential commissions in part because it held one of the largest map collections in France and possessed an enormous geographical library in its headquarters on the Boulevard St Germain. However, it is also a measure of the significance of the French geographical movement and the power of the French colonial lobby that these highly significant commissions were entrusted to the geographers within the SGP. Forty-five senior members of the SGP were co-opted onto these commissions, including Hulot (who worked indefatigably on all four), Emmanuel de Martonne (who sat on the European and Asian–Middle Eastern commissions), Emmanuel de Margerie (who contributed to both the non-European commissions and to the work on the future Franco–German border), Lucien Gallois (who worked on the two European commissions), Louis Raveneau (who was active on all four commissions), Augustin Bernard (who

[49] The political background is outlined in detail in Andrew and Kanya-Forstner, 'The French Colonial Party and war aims', 1974, pp. 79–106: Andrew and Kanya-Forstner, 'France and the repartition of Africa', 1977, pp. 475–93; Andrew and Kanya-Forstner, 'France, Africa and the First World War', 1978, pp. 11–23; Andrew and Kanya-Forstner, *France Overseas*, 1981, especially pp. 33–54 and pp. 83–115, and Grupp, 'Le "parti colonial" français', 1974, pp. 377–91. On the remarkable career of Louis Marin, who was to become the dominant personality in the Société de Géographie Commerciale, see Lebovics, *True France*, 1992, pp. 12–50.

[50] The details on these commissions can be found in the archives of the Société de Géographie housed in the Bibliothèque nationale (Hereafter BN-SGP), *Colis* 9, 16 bis, 24, 41 and in the *Fonds Auguste Terrier* in the Bibliothèque de l'Institut de France.

concentrated on the African commission), Franz Schrader (who worked on all except the African commission), together with a number of leading political and military figures.[51] Throughout 1916 and early 1917, as millions were slaughtered at Verdun and on the Somme, these four commissions met regularly to hear evidence from expert witnesses and to debate specific issues. Each commission produced a mass of documentation on every conceivable topic pertaining to their area of investigation and ultimately submitted a series of specific recommendations to the government as the basis of France's future policy.[52]

The two European commissions were eventually disbanded, though several of the leading members continued their efforts to define and justify France's European war aims as members of the so-called Comité d'Études. This committee, also established by the Briand government, was concerned mainly with the geopolitical questions raised by a new European post-war order and with the historical validity of France's territorial claims in Europe. It was therefore less dominated by geographers and was chaired by Ernest Lavisse, the great historian. Its secretary, however, was Paul Vidal de la Blache and, to begin with, its regular meetings were held at the Institut de Géographie at the Sorbonne, though it later moved to the Foreign Ministry at the Quai d'Orsay. Its reports and recommendations, which were of central importance to France's negotiating position at the Paris Peace Conference, were published in two huge volumes after the war.[53]

While the European commissions sought to develop historico-geographical and ethnographical arguments for a new geopolitical order in Europe, the reports of the other two commissions – on Africa, the Middle East and Asia – dealt primarily with contemporary questions of colonial policy. Although their reports were never published, the archives left by the African and Asian commissions make fascinating reading and demonstrate not only the vast erudition of the French geographers involved but also the sheer scale of their imperial ambitions. The objective of these colonial commissions, predicated on the assumption that Germany would lose all its overseas colonies, was to establish a clear set of claims which could form the basis of a negotiating position with other interested colonial powers on the allied

[51] On some of these men, see Dresch, 'Emmanuel de Martonne', 1985, pp. 73–81; Sutton, 'Augustin Bernard', 1979, pp. 19–27 and Broc, 'Franz Schrader', 1977, pp. 97–103. Lists of the membership of each commission are reproduced in Grupp, 'Le "parti colonial" français', 1974, pp. 388–91.

[52] BN-SGP, *Colis* 9.

[53] Comité d'Études, *Travaux du Comité d'Études*, vol. 1: *L'Alsace-Lorraine et la frontière du Nord-Est* and vol. 2: *Questions Européenes*, 1918–19. It is a significant, though little-known, fact that Vidal de la Blache's *La France de l'Est*, 1917, a book frequently interpreted as the crowning achievement of the Vidalian school of regional geography, is based almost entirely on the research carried out by the author while working on this official commission. To an extent, this most famous of geographical texts can be interpreted as a very elegant and subtle form of French propaganda against German claims to this disputed region.

side, particularly Britain, Italy and Belgium. From the tone and content of
these reports, it is clear that the traditional colonial rivalries between France
and the wartime allies were still uppermost in the minds of the French
geographers. The idea that Germany might win the war or at least emerge
from it undefeated – a distinct possibility as late as the spring of 1918 –
was simply not entertained by either of the colonial commissions. Germany
was simply ignored as a future colonial power. The clear objective was
to reach an amicable agreement around the world with the British, while
resisting as forcibly as possible the imperial claims of other powers, particularly Italy. Indeed, the French government was sufficiently alarmed by
the huge territorial claims being articulated in sections of the Italian press
with respect to Africa and the Ottoman Empire, to ask the African commission to reconvene during the summer of 1917 to help formulate a firm
response to Italian ambitions. [54]

The African commission, dominated by Auguste Terrier and Augustin
Bernard, made long and detailed claims for Togo and the Cameroons while
accepting British claims to German possessions in south-east and south-west
Africa, subject to France receiving colonial concessions elsewhere. [55] In the
Middle East, strong arguments were rehearsed for French control of 'la
Syrie intégrale', meaning all of Syria, the Lebanon and much of Palestine.
It should be noted, of course, that this commission was meeting at the
same time as the secret Sykes–Picot negotiations were cynically mapping
out British and French spheres of influence in the Middle East after the
predicted collapse of the Ottoman Empire, in direct contradiction to the
stated British policy of support for Arab independence. [56]

The French government's reliance on the geographers during the Great
War demonstrates the influence of the subject and confirms the pro-colonialist
position of most of the leading practitioners. However, I have dealt with this
episode as a separate form of French imperialism because it is associated
with the particular circumstances that prevailed during the Great War.
Although clearly informed by the earlier debates about the nature and form
of French imperialism, the attempt to expand the French empire by acquiring
German colonies or Ottoman territory as a result of the war was motivated,
at least in part, by the general spirit of revanchism that gripped France
in 1916 and 1917. This persuaded even those who otherwise would have
doubted the long-term benefits of this dramatic extension of the French
empire, that such a policy was necessary in order to weaken Germany and its
allies.

[54] BN-SGP, *Colis* 9.
[55] Ibid.
[56] Ibid. On the Sykes-Picot negotiations and subsequent accords, see Andrew and Kanya-
Forstner, *France Overseas*, 1981, pp. 87–97; Fromkin, *A Peace to end all Peace*, 1989;
Kedourie, *In the Anglo–Arab Labyrinth*, 1976 and Kedourie, *England and the Middle East*,
1978.

AGAINST EMPIRE

The final perspective on imperialism – that of outright anti-imperialism – was, it must be stressed, virtually non-existent in the French geographical movement. There were doubtless a few professional geographers who objected to French imperial expansion, but I have encountered very little sustained and direct anti-imperial argument within the geographical literature.

As I have tried to emphasize, however, anti-imperial sentiments were deeply felt in many other sections of French political and intellectual life and, before the 1890s, hostility or indifference to empire was probably the norm. However, as Charles-Robert Ageron reminds us, opposition to empire in late nineteenth-century France did not come from a consistent political direction.[57] To be sure, once the Left began to recover its momentum after the post-Commune purges, some radical socialists began to challenge the morality of French colonial conquest. Yet in general, socialists in France remained rather ambiguous about the French empire. Indeed, the utopian and cultural arguments in favour of empire discussed earlier still commanded considerable support on the left.[58]

Even the towering presence of Élisée Reclus, a publicly renowned geographer who was forced into exile during the early Third Republic because of his anarchist beliefs and his open support for the Paris Commune, felt unable to challenge wholeheatedly the morality of France's imperial ambitions. Although he wrote with his usual brilliance and fervour against imperialism in general, he deliberately exempted from criticism France's colonial achievements in North Africa.[59] To a large extent, Reclus still believed in the utopian imperialism of his friend and colleague Henri Duveyrier, the man who persuaded the SGP to honour Reclus with its Gold Medal in 1892 but who, having cajoled the great man to come and accept it, did not live to witness the ceremony.

In fact, for much of the 1870s and 1880s, the most consistent and vociferous opponents of French colonialism were economists associated with the conservative Right. From this perspective, the issue was clear. France had too few people and too few resources to sacrifice any in speculative overseas colonization. The real danger to France clearly lay in Europe and, more particularly, in Germany. France should therefore concentrate all its resources

[57] Ageron, *L'Anticolonialisme*, 1973, and Ageron, *France Coloniale*, 1978. See also Brunschwig, 'Vigné d'Octon et l'anticolonialism', 1974, pp. 265–98.
[58] See, alongside references in notes 21 and 22, Émerit, 'L'idée de colonisation', 1967, pp. 103–15. On anti-imperialism and the left in general, see Porter, *Critics of Empire*, 1968 and, for an earlier period, Merle, *L'Anticolonialisme*, 1969.
[59] See the rather odd translation of Giblin, 'Élisée Reclus and colonisation', 1989. On Reclus in general, see Giblin, 'Élisée Reclus', 1979, pp. 125–32; Dunbar, *Élisée Reclus*, 1978; Fleming, *The Anarchist Way*, 1975; Sarrazin, *Élisée Reclus*, 1985 and Stoddart, *On Geography*, 1986, pp. 128–41.

and 'manpower' in France itself rather than squandering these precious gifts overseas. This argument remained a compelling one, at least until the 1890s, and the colonial conquests that took place in the 1880s – the establishment of a French protectorate in Tunisia in 1881 and the expensive colonial wars in Tonkin in the mid-1880s – remained sufficiently controversial to precipitate the fall of the otherwise successful administration of Jules Ferry in 1885.

CONCLUSION

Although most geographers were committed advocates of French imperialism, there was no single and universally accepted version of French imperialism within the geographical community. To be sure, the differences between the various groups of imperialist geographers were sometimes simply a matter of tone and emphasis and all of these groupings could unite on many fundamental issues, as appears to have occurred during the 'national emergency' of World War One.

Although one must guard against the temptation to reify these tendencies into coherent and opposing factions, the distinctions between these different groupings were nevertheless based on firmly held and sometimes mutually exclusive and divisive commitments. To seek out a relationship between geography and imperialism is perhaps therefore a misguided endeavour, for there were, it seems, many complex connections between different imperial-isms and different geographies. Like most ideologies, French imperialism was essentially discursive and rhetorical. All one can discern is a series of over-lapping and sometimes competing imperialisms, each connected to a shifting constituency within the social, political and cultural life of France.

At one level this conclusion, accepting as it does the inherent diversity and incoherence of historical ideologies, re-casts the history of geography in ways which conform to a postmodern re-reading of the history of the human sciences. It challenges head-on the tendency to construct neat and simple equations between text and context, between science and ideology. It rejects the tendency to erect a master-narrative through which ideological and intellectual formations can be seen to have developed in the past in relation to one another, and emphasizes instead the ruptures, fissures and discon-tinuities which punctuate this collision.

This certainly expands our understanding of the complexity of the his-torical relationship between intellectual and ideological formations, but such a deconstructive (even destructive) postmodern reading comes dangerously close to being a celebration of ironic complexity and a rather uninspiring refusal to make moral or political choices about differing values and beliefs in the past (or the present). At its extreme, it seems to deny the very possi-bility of a critical reinterpretation of geography's history. I would insist that, although complex and often contradictory, the various imperial geographies which developed in France during the nineteenth century all carried with

them – in different ways and to varying degrees – an identifiable set of
moral and political values which command critical attention and which
speak directly to our contemporary values. One must accept that, despite the
nuances, French geography in the late nineteenth century was, to a large
extent, a science of empire. Morever, despite its discursive and incoherent
nature, the discourse on imperialism which took place within French geography was sufficiently all-embracing to allow the cause of empire to be
promoted in a variety of different ways, according to circumstance and
locality. Far from weakening the moral and political force of French imperialism, the plurality of different geo-imperialist voices – the polyphony
of the discourse – became itself a source of power.

6

Geography and Empire in Germany, 1871–1945

Gerhard Sandner and Mechtild Rössler

INTRODUCTION

German imperialism was not simply the fruit of the German Reich in 1871.
Its manifold roots lead far back into the nineteenth century, nourished by
a mix of ideologies and experiences, national dreams and social contradictions. Yet the search for empire intensified significantly after 1871. Within
a single lifetime the contentious construction of a national identity underwent
several fundamental phases: from the Bismarck era to aggressive Wilhelmian
politics in 1890; World War I and the consequent loss of colonies; the re-
emergence of imperial dreams during the Weimar Republic; and finally the
aggressive modernism of National Socialism. But change does not preclude
continuity nor the persistence and periodic reappearance of concepts and
ideologies from the past. In this respect, geography provided a continuous
and deep-seated language for German imperialism.

Both the descriptive details and the institutions of geography were appropriated on behalf of German imperialism. In the first place, there was a use
and misuse of geographical facts – of spaces and boundaries, distance and
contiguity – to legitimate aggressive imperial strategies. This chapter will
focus more on the involvement of geography as a discipline. Arguably, the
explosive institutionalization of German geography immediately after the
foundation of the Reich in 1871 has had a lasting effect. The discipline's
intensive search for recognition and legitimacy as a university science in this
period encouraged a conformist political approach that is still evident today.

This paper concentrates on colonialism and the expansion of German
Lebensraum – the concept of a territorial living space beyond the nation's
borders which was to allow the 'natural' expansion of the state. These two
were essentials of imperialist ideology and strategy in the three-quarters of

116   *Gerhard Sandner and Mechtild Rössler*

a century since the foundation of the Reich. Geographers involved themselves in different ways in these two aspects of the German imperial movement, but they shared a general intention to strengthen the new academic institution of geography at universities and in the school system. While the effects of geography on colonial politics and on the political application of the *Lebensraum* strategy were rather limited, geography consolidated itself and underwent considerable expansion at the university level and became increasingly differentiated into specialized sub-disciplines.

THE RISE OF ACADEMIC GEOGRAPHY AND THE GERMAN REICH, 1871–1914

The specific character and the problematic nature of German identity, nationalism and imperialism is rooted in the long-lasting and conflictual endeavour to create a nation state in the centre of Europe. This region has always been characterized by extreme fragmentation, frequent changes in the territorial pattern of sovereignty and power, and by a complex mosaic of peoples and minorities. When in 1871 the German Reich was founded as a unified and centralized state from several existing territorial units, German nationalism intensified with the new combination of territorial claims, deep-seated cultural identity and search for recognition. Several elements of German imperialism can be traced to this specific amalgam, especially the late emergence of colonial ambition, and the persisting and problematic incongruity of national identity being created via the state and cultural identity reaching far beyond.[1]

German geography developed as a university science within this context. In 1871 the only functioning chair of geography was at Göttingen University. By 1885 there were twelve and in 1910 23. This rapid expansion of geography was mandated from above, by state decree which in some cases acted against open resistance from faculties and universities. It was motivated in part by expectations of geography's *Bildungswert* – its potential educational value at school and for the public in general. Geography had played a prominent role in popular science ever since the publicity – by means of family magazines, societies, and lectures for the bourgeois public – given to Alexander von Humboldt's explorations and research. The expansion of geography also reflected the growing importance of the educational system in transmitting political ideologies such as the national ambitions of the German intelligentsia.

The German government's interest in geography was made explicit in an 1875 debate in the Prussian Parliament. According to one delegate, defending

[1] For German imperialist ideologies and politics see Wehler, *Bismarck und der Imperialismus*, 1969; Wehler, *Das deutsche Kaiserreich*, 1977; Smith, *The German Colonial Empire*, 1978. For the specific performance of geography see Schulte-Althoff, *Studien zur politischen*, 1971; and Schultz, *Die deutschsprachige Geographie*, 1980; Bassin, 'Imperialism and the nation state', 1987, pp. 473–95.

government policy: 'Since geography is a very important discipline for general education, particularly for the education of teachers, the government had no hesitation in creating geographical chairs extensively without asking the universities if they were inclined to incorporate a professor of geography'. A school administrator responded that 'geographical education at school is, in most of the secondary schools, nothing but ridiculous, due to the lack of university trained teachers'[2]. The same debate was re-enacted when the Education Ministry demanded the expansion of geography to all German universities in 1883.[3] In the first national meeting of geographers in Berlin in 1881, Alfred Kirchhoff (1838–1907, who held the chair of geography at Halle University, and was one of the most influential geographers of the period) advocated a strengthening of geography at school because of the patriotism, and love of fatherland and *Heimat*, so readily imparted by 'that most German of all sciences'.[4] Friedrich Ratzel (1844–1904, the highly influential geographer, founder of anthropogeography, who held the chairs of geography at Munich and later at Leipzig Universities) for his part introducted his textbook on *Deutschland* with the following: 'First of all, the German should know what he has got in his country. The present intent is based on the conviction that this purpose can only be achieved by showing that *Boden und Volk* [soil and people] belong together. May this book have a stimulating influence on the lessons of *Vaterlandskunde*'.[5] New terms were introduced to describe various aspects of an increasingly nationalist geography: *Vaterländische Erdkunde, völkische Erdkunde, Nationale Erdkunde, Deutsche Kulturgeographie*. At the same time the global perspective was intensified, albeit subordinated to a German purview, leading to such taxonomic extremes as *Deutsche Weltwirtschaftsgeographie* (German global economic geography).[6]

Ratzel's *Politische Geographie* had the same nationalist function. A constant feature of nineteenth-century German political theory was the attempt to understand the state as detached from civil society, an authority above society. Ratzel offered a physical basis for this ideology. His political geography was largely determinist, assumed the state's direct dependence on the 'soil', and employed an organismic perspective which accentuated the dependence of state power on spatial 'size'. Bassin has pointed out the two sides of Ratzel's determinism, the first referring to the post-Darwinian scientific materialism adapted to 'the laws of the territorial growth of states', the second related to the physical space (and not to ethnic or racial affinity) as a basis for national

---

[2] Schultz, *Die deutschsprachige*, 1980, p. 66–7.

[3] The most comprehensive studies on school geography in German imperialism are those from Schulte-Althoff, *Studien zur politischen*, 1971; Schultz, *Die Geographie*, 1989. On institutional development see Engelmann, *Die Hochschulgeographie*, 1983.

[4] Kirchhoff, *Schulgeographie*, 1882, p. 91.

[5] Ratzel, *Deutschland*, 1898, p. v.

[6] Harms, *Vaterländische Erdkunde*, 1897. This book went through 17 editions by 1926 and was dedicated to the 'strengthening of national consciousness'.

unity.[7] Both elements formed the roots of later geopolitical concepts and strategies. Ratzel's originality and influence beyond geography were an exception; the majority of the geographers simply reacted to political discussions of the time.

German colonial ambitions were initially motivated primarily by economic issues such as access to raw material and markets. Until the early 1880s these were still the central arguments for colonial expansion. Bismarck favoured trading colonies rather than mere political possessions, and a system of combined management involving concessions to private enterprise. But in the early 1880s the 'colonial question' erupted in virtual hysteria. In the first place hopes of rapid colonial acquisition after the foundation of the Reich were not realized. Equally important, the intensive social and cultural transformation accompanying the transition from an agrarian to an industrial society expanded German trade and deepened demands for colonial expansion. Further, massive emigration (about 1.5 million from 1871 to 1885) aroused Pan-German feelings and sharp political pressure to secure new settlement areas and stabilize 'Germandom abroad'. Especially in the years leading up to World War I, expectant visions of a colonial future integrated notions of *Lebensraum* and *Weltpolitik*, Pan-Germanism, racism and anti-semitism, and described the establishment of a German Empire including Southern Russia, large areas in Latin America, Africa and South East Asia.[8]

In the 'Scramble for Africa' in the mid 1880s, Germany acquired several African colonies but fundamental controversies persisted over land use, settlement schemes and administration, as well as the effectiveness of German colonial politics *vis-à-vis* Great Britain and France. After Bismarck's dismissal in 1890, the German colonial empire was consolidated around Kaiser Wilhelm's militant and aggressive *Weltpolitik*. After initiating a huge naval construction programme (1898) and the *Flottengesetz* of 1900, the Kaiser instigated a fundamental reform of colonial politics and management designed to meet expanding needs for raw materials and trade. This reform became effective in 1906, just eight years before the outbreak of World War I.

For geography the 'colonial question' opened substantial opportunities. The discipline's traditions and competence in overseas exploration and field research could be combined with its pretention as a universal regional science, to demonstrate its practical relevance for national and patriotic projects. Different geographers responded differently and many of the outstanding geographers of the period became active in newly founded associations and societies. When in 1873 the Deutsche Gesellschaft zur Erforschung Zentralafrikas (the German Society for the Exploration of Central Africa, generally referred to as Deutsche Afrika-Gesellschaft, the German Society for Africa) was founded by Adolf Bastian (1826–1905), the renowned explorer and ethnologist, Ferdinand Freiherr von Richthofen (1833–1905) who specialized

[7] Bassin, 'Imperialism and the nation state', p. 117–18. See also Peet, 'The social origins of environmental determinism', 1985, pp. 309–33.

[8] Sandner, 'The Germania-triumphans-syndrome', 1989, pp. 341–51.

in physical geography and held chairs at Bonn, Leipzig and Berlin Universities, became vice-chairman. The shift during the eighties towards open colonialism and geographers' explicit involvement is especially apparent in the 1882 appeal for a Deutscher Kolonialverein (DKV, the German Colonial Society), signed by geographers Ratzel, Theobald Fischer (1846–1910) who specialized in Africa and held chairs at Kiel and Marburg Universities, Kirchhoff and Georg Gerland (1833–1919) who held the chair at Strasburg University. Fischer was also the co-founder of the radical Alldeutscher Verband (the All-German Association) dedicated to the pursuit of *Lebensraum* in Europe and overseas; Ratzel and other geographers were active members. On the other hand, prominent geographers were entirely missing in liberal anti-colonial organizations like the *Fortschrittspartei* (Progressive Party) which strongly criticized colonial politics.

Variations in the intensity and style of 'imperialist response' by geographers are well illustrated by the three personalities: Ratzel, Fischer and Siegfried Passarge (1866–1957). Ratzel was deeply involved in the colonial question, defending Bismarck's colonial politics from anti-colonial attacks in the decisive period of the mid-1880s.[9] Unlike Fischer and Passarge who carried out colonial explorations and empirical research, Ratzel's support for colonialism derived from his determinist political and human geography and from a fundamental support for imperialism. This general orientation enabled him to deal with colonial issues as just one element among imperialist strategies, as demonstrated by his activities in the newly developing research field of oceanography.

With the transition to a resolute imperialism after Bismarck's ouster, and the Kaiser's formula that 'Germany's future lies on the Sea', there was an immediate response from oceanographic research. This was further fueled by a huge naval construction programme and the *Flottengesetz* of 1900. Ratzel had already edited a two-volume study of oceanography, and responded to the Kaiser's mobilization with a volume on the sea as a source of national greatness.[10] In the same year the Berlin Institut für Meereskunde was founded with von Richthofen as president. Oceanographic research became strongly related to global political strategies and, with it, colonialism.

Theobald Fischer, by contrast, possessed a strong regional orientation.[11] His research focused on the Mediterranean, especially Morocco and the Maghreb. A nationalist favouring rapid transformation of the German Reich to a world power controlling large colonial areas, Fischer was extremely disappointed by German colonial politics in fighting French interests in the first 'Morocco crisis' of 1905. This and the second Morocco crisis in 1911 created

[9] Smith, 'Anthropology and German colonialism', 1987, p. 41. Smith explains that Ratzel was one of the 'most dynamic' figures of a 'newer generation of academics' involved in the whole colonial question. See Ratzel, *Wider die Reichsnörgler*, 1884; See also Bassin, 'Race contra space', 1987, pp. 115–34.

[10] Ratzel, *Das Meer als Quelle*, 1900.

[11] See Engelmann, *Die Hochschulgeographie*, 1983, p. 98.

a diplomatic disaster for Germany, resulting in a nationalist outcry about the incapacity of German politicians, and strong demands that the entente of European powers blocking German expansion be broken up. Based on his regional knowledge, Fischer made concrete proposals for a German foothold in Morocco and for transforming Mogador into a German naval base. In a series of lecture tours, and in journal and newspaper articles, he constantly tried to generate public interest in Morocco, earning himself the nickname of '*Marokko-Fischer*'. When all this propaganda proved ineffective, he transferred his efforts to the Alldeutscher Verband, fighting for the expansion of German *Lebensraum* on a global scale. Simultaneously, however, he used his political activities to expand the tiny geographical department he chaired at Marburg University.

Siegfried Passarge admirably illustrates the convergence of science and politics on the colonial question.[12] His schooldays ended in 1886, the year many Germans hailed the acquisition of colonies in Africa. After finishing his studies in geology, geography and medicine, he was anxious to begin scientific research in order 'to serve the fatherland in the colonies'. His teacher Pechuel-Lösche, introduced him to the private Kamerun-Kommittee and Passarge began a Cameroon expedition straight away. Founded in 1893 in Berlin to 'rescue' the hinterland of Cameroon from French expansion and to expand the German colony, the Kamerun-Kommittee operated by courtesy of a secret agreement with the British Royal Niger Company. Passarge was eventually appointed to the Chair of Geography in the newly founded Hamburger Kolonial-Institut (1908), the only geography department in Germany dedicated exclusively to colonial geography. Eleven years later the colonial institute was transformed into the University of Hamburg.

In his scientific and political work three distinct threads can be distinguished. First, prior to his appointment as chair, he levelled radical criticism at the failure of German colonial politics compared with the success of British colonial companies. Second, his medical knowledge combined with social Darwinism led to a radical racism. He specifically opposed the 'disastrous effects of Christian missionaries' and their 'soft treatment of negroes'. His African experiences were decisive for his later ethnographic writings, his racist and deterministic *Geographische Weltanschauung*, and for his 'law of development of the character of peoples', which after 1918 was transformed into radical anti-semitism. Third, his field observations and empirical research in physical geography, particularly in Southern Africa, combined with the development of his notion of *Landschaftskunde* – an integral, though mostly descriptive and deterministic approach to landscape research, defined the fundamental paradigm of geography. Passarge belonged to that second generation of geographers occupying chairs after 1871, who were trained as geographers and who acted as academics, and his outstanding contributions on geomorphology and *Landschaftskunde* persist today.

[12] Passarge, *Aus achtzig Jahren*, 1951; Sandner, 'The Germania-triumphans-syndrome', 1989.

Ratzel, Fischer and Passarge represented different versions of imperialist and colonialist ideology in geography, and different involvements in colonial politics. In school geography, meanwhile, colonial issues figured in the fight for a greater role for geographical teaching. The 1892 reformed curriculum for secondary schools included colonial themes, but continued demands by geographers for a specific teaching area (*Kolonialkunde*) were not immediately effective. This changed, however, when the *Reichstag* initiated a more coherent and dynamic colonial policy in 1906, reflecting the growing economic importance of the colonies. Colonial education was immediately intensified, combining economic and commercial geography with nationalist colonial policies. Due to a belief in the fundamental necessity of colonial possessions for world powers, colonial studies survived World War I and the loss of all German colonies.

At the beginning of the twentieth century, geography began to fragment into various sub-disciplines. It was less intensely linked to imperialist issues, but the imperialist political context and its influence on geography and its sub-disciplines persisted.

THE LOST EMPIRE: GEOGRAPHY AND NATIONALISM DURING THE
WEIMAR REPUBLIC

The First World War was fought not only in Europe, where it led to the defeat of the Central Powers, but in the German colonies as well. Germans fought in Togo, Samoa and German Southwest Africa, and the war in East Africa continued even after the last gunfire in Europe.[13] The close of war meant the end of the German world empire proclaimed by Wilhelm II in 1896 and the end of this specific form of imperialism. Germany was forced to relinquish all colonies in the Armistice and was excluded from the Treaty of Versailles.

Geographical research and teaching nevertheless remained intricately interconnected with the different forms of imperialism after the war. The *Lebensraum* question re-emerged in a new form after the Treaty of Versailles; geographers' research focused more on the German people and their territory. *Kolonialforschung* (colonial research) was significantly circumscribed, and geographical research was virtually impossible in the former German colonies, now mandated to Britain, France and the USA. The 1931 Geographentag (Conference of German Geographers), for example, deeply regretted the loss of research areas in the tropics and sub-tropics and expressed the need for new German colonies.[14] German researchers were excluded from the exchange of scientific knowledge because Germany was banned from membership in many international scientific organizations.[15]

[13] See Westphal, *Geschichte der deutschen Kolonien*, 1987, p. 304.
[14] Haushofer, *Verhandlungen und wissenschaftliche Abhandlungen*, 1932, p. 31.
[15] Colonial research was discussed at colonial congresses and geographical congresses as

Nevertheless, colonial geography was still taught at schools, some university specialists continued their work, and geographical societies all over Germany popularized the subject during the period from 1919 to 1933. Based on a long tradition of exploration, travel and geographical discoveries, Africa remained the focus of colonial interest and various expeditions were actually organized or joined by German scientists. In addition to tropical Africa, German geographers explored the Arctic and Antarctic and some interior regions of New Guinea and the Amazon. There were also alpine expeditions, like the German–Russian Alai-Pamir Expedition in 1928, the Andean and Cordillera Real Expedition in 1928, and one to Peru in 1932,[16] as well as the German Atlantic Expedition on the research ship Meteor 1925–7. These expeditions fueled the new specialization of the discipline into such fields as geophysics, climatology, hydrology and oceanography. Alfred Wegener, originator of the continental drift theory, made several expeditions to Greenland in this period until his fatal excursion of 1930–2.

As in the pre-war period, motives of disciplinary and national prestige were closely entwined. In a 1930 survey of German science, Albrecht Penck chose not to present specific scientific results nor to rehearse theoretical debates such as that on *Landschafts-* or *Länderkunde*.[17] Instead, summarizing the progress of modern geography, he recounted the aims and activities of German or international expeditions to the Arctic, Antarctic and alpine regions of the world. Such expeditions had wide popular appeal, after all. In addition to producing special measuring instruments for meteorological and geophysical research, and stimulating new theories in highly specialized fields like glaciology, they aimed not only to fill in undiscovered blanks on the map but to claim them in Germany's name. These expeditions in fact constituted a form of 'scientific imperialism' insofar as they sought to occupy the world's last blank spots. Scientific imperialism is partly a symbolic action, but it also had a territorial component, especially in the Arctic and Antarctic. It established real as well as symbolic occupation with national flags, research stations (part of the national territory), and new scientific records (in speed, height, depth etc.) for the state.[18]

Geographers were centrally involved in important pressure groups which lobbied for imperial expansion and which paved the way for National

---

well, but Germany was excluded from the international geographical congresses in 1925 (Cairo), 1928 (Cambridge) and 1931 (Paris). The Cairo Congress especially led to a diplomatic scandal because German geographers were first invited and then excluded after the International Geographical Union (IGU) joined the International Council of Scientific Unions (ICSU) which did not allow German membership. See Rössler, 'La géographie aux congrès internationaux', 1990, p. 188–9.

[16] For a summary of the expeditions see the report made by Troll, 'Die Geographische Wissenschaft in Deutschland', 1947, pp. 3–47.

[17] See Abb (ed.), *Aus fünfzig Jahren Deutscher Wissenschaft*, 1930.

[18] See Katz and Kirby, 'In the nature of things', 1991, pp. 259–71.

Socialism.[19] Erich Obst (1886–1981), a contributor to this Weimar phase of German colonial aspirations, was an important figure in public as well as scientific discourse. He combined *Lebensraum* and *Weltpolitik* visions in an emerging *Geopolitik*.[20] A co-founder of the *Zeitschrift für Geopolitik* in 1924, Obst came to Hamburg after the foundation of the Kolonial-Institut and worked with Passarge for several years, specializing in Africa.[21] He also worked for the Geographische Gesellschaft in Hamburg (the Hamburg Geographical Society), which financed important expeditions to that continent. While he retained an interest in colonial research after 1933, the political situation led him to other questions, especially the *Großraumidee*, the idea of an expanded German Reich in central Europe.

If the period of the Weimar Republic exhibited different forms of a muted imperialism, it nevertheless paved the way for Nazi expansionism after 1933. Radical anti-semitism and racism, as in the geography of Siegfried Passarge, political involvement in the colonial debate, and appeals for *Lebensraum*, kept geographers in the political arena.

'TO NEW FRONTIERS', 1933–1945: THE RE-EMERGENCE OF A GERMAN EMPIRE

With the National Socialist 'takeover' the nature of the colonial question changed: the government of the Third Reich explicitly sought new colonies for Germany as well as the revision of the Versailles Treaty. The question of German colonies was complex. There was no obvious consistency in German foreign policy and Nazi imperialism across this period, but one can distinguish three stages: first, the official 'peace policy' of the first years of the Third Reich until 1935–6; second, preparations for expansionism; and third, the stage of actual expansion with the occupation of the eastern European countries. Different colonial and imperial interest groups and organizations of the Weimar Republic were increasingly shaped to these agendas, in part under the auspices of the newly founded *Reichskolonialbund* (Reich Colonial Union). The dream of a German empire in Africa was increasingly voiced.

If the roots of colonial research and politics were laid down before the turn of the century, and some geographers now continued this work with new energy derived from Nazi support, a younger generation of geographers with a more technocratic approach also developed new concepts of area research and spatial organization that would later be applied in urban, regional and colonial planning.

[19] See Smith, *Ideological Origins*, 1986. See also Heske, 'Der Traum von Afrika', 1987, pp. 205–6.

[20] On the history of the geopolitical discourse during the Weimar Republic see Murphy (Chapter 15 in this volume). For the earlier period: Korinmann, *Continents Perdus*, 1991.

[21] Obst gave seminars on German East-Africa, Cameroon and the history of discovery in Africa. See Passarge, 'Das Geographische Seminar', 1939, p. 27.

The advent of National Socialism boosted geography's importance in the academy and in public discourse, and it led to new subjects of research especially in cultural geography. Or so argued Carl Troll in a 1939 survey of German science.[22] Troll specifically cites research on race, German ethnic studies and environmental issues as being renewed in the late 1930s. The most important fields of inquiry, for Troll, were the German *Lebensraum*, the geography of the 'frontier of Germandom' and the German *Volk* overseas, area research, spatial planning and military geography. He announced a rebirth of German research on Africa and the planned collection of genetic plant material by geographical expeditions to various alpine regions.[23] In this popular survey, he also emphasized the contribution made by the Leipzig Museum für Länderkunde (Museum for Regional Studies), which presented exhibitions on areas like the Saar and the Sudetengau, newly incorporated into the Reich.

In a second essay in the same survey, Erich Obst focused more on colonial geography and argued that the lie of war guilt damaged German colonial geography. He invoked the 'will to fight', and rehearsed colonial geographers' 1926 plea in the *Zeitschrift für Geopolitik*: 'We are asking for our Colonies'. He suggested that 1933 was a real turning point in colonial issues, and that Hitler offered colonial geographers new self-confidence. Many geographers took the opportunity to travel and to do research especially in Africa: Troll (Eritrea, Abyssinia), Obst (German East and Southwest Africa, Natal, Angola, Mozambique), Jäger (Algeria), Kayser (East Africa), Dietzel (Kamerun), Mai (Nigeria), Schultze (East and South Africa), Schmieder and Wilhelmy (Libya). That year, too, a colonial exhibition was included in the Berlin agricultural show visited by Hitler, and colonial organizations met in Frankfurt where General Ritter von Epp was a member of the Nazi party from 1928 and represented the party's colonial branch. He spoke at the same event in 1934 in Kiel and made a strong demand for a new German colonial empire. A year later these organizations met in Freiburg, where von Epp addressed ten thousand people in the central market place. Von Epp was appointed head of the newly formed Reichskolonialbund in May 1936. Thereafter colonial questions were very prominent in the broader Nazi agenda. The need for tropical and colonial space, providing colonial goods, labour and markets were now emphasized in Nazi brochures and the chancellor of Hamburg University asked for new chairs in colonial geography, colonial soil sciences and colonial economic geography.[24]

With the beginning of World War II, the idea of a new colonial empire emerged in a new way. With the quick victory over Poland the first steps

[22] Troll, *Deutsche Wissenschaft*, 1939, pp. 48–50.

[23] Troll himself was involved in several expeditions to Nanga Parbat and the Himalayas. He had close contacts with the *Ahnenerbe* organization of the SS, which was responsible for SS expeditions during the Third Reich.

[24] See Fischer and Sandner, 'Die Geschichte des Geographischen Seminars', 1991, p. 1199.

were made towards an agrarian German empire in Europe. Geographers, who had worked on the 'German East' – the German-speaking territories to the east of the German border – during the twenties and early thirties were suddenly back in vogue. They intensified regional research on the new German territory in the East and in the administrative area of the General-gouvernement which was created in 1939 and covered much of occupied Poland from its headquarters in Krakow. In 1941 it was enlarged to take in areas of Russian Galicia.[25] They worked in regional research units geared to post-war planning, together with historians and sociologists, but were soon reorganized for military purposes. The focus on non-European colonies remained strong however. Where geography was a 'national science', colonial geography was a science for the future, the science of colonial planning.[26]

The first serious steps towards real 'colonial planning' were taken in October 1940 when the Reichsforschungsrat (the Reich Research Council) created a Kolonial Wissenschaftliche Abteilung (the Colonial Scientific Department). Headed by Günther Wolff, it included 27 specialist groups and about 500 scientists, among them several geographers. Because Wolff was also a staff member in the Kolonialpolitisches Amt (the Colonial Policy Office) of the Nazi Party, this department had a very active role:

> The activities of the Colonial Scientific Department were by no means confined to arranging meetings and awarding scholarships. The Department organized scientific research on problems of the projected colonial economy, e.g. the best methods of exploiting the African population, Africa's role as a producer of raw materals and foodstuffs and as a market for capital goods and manufactured goods, as well as medical and technical problems.[27]

At about the same time, the Reichsarbeitsgemeinschaft für Raumforschung (the Reich's Study Group for Area Research) also embarked on a programme of colonial research under the heading, 'Koloniale Raumforschung' ('Colonial Spatial Research'). Several geographers were employed including Erich Obst who became editor of their Africa handbook.[28] In the words of Stoecker, 'the geographers Obst and Dietzel', and 'the geopolitical expert Schmitthenner worked for a Nazi 'new order' in Europe and the planned redistribution of African colonies in favour of Nazi imperialism'.[29] The

[25] See Rössler, *Wissenschaft und Lebensraum*, 1990.
[26] Kraus, *Unsere Kolonien*, 1941, p. 44.
[27] See Stoecker (ed.), *German Imperialism in Africa*, 1986, p. 400.
[28] Obst (ed.), *Afrika*, 1941–3.
[29] Stoecker, *German Imperialism*, 1986, p. 401. Dietzel held the chair for Kolonialgeographie at Leipzig. Schmitthenner also held a chair in geography at Leipzig but was hardly an expert in geopolitics. Stoecker's volume was compiled during a period of research on imperialism in the former GDR, when every statement of the Nazi period received the label 'geopolitical'.

Reich's Study Group for Area Research held successive meetings on colonial policy. Noting at one meeting that 500,000 people had already been sent to Africa by the Fascist regime in Italy, the geographer Schmieder argued that 'Germany should send to German colonies a number of those Germans who already emigrated overseas'. He suggested that 200,000 Germans out of the 1.2 million already in South America might be sent to new German colonies in Africa. Schmitthenner advised that development possibilities in Africa should be analysed in relation to British and Belgian experience in the Congo area.[30] Central Africa should be taken as a basis for colonial research.

A year later in Berlin, 32 geographers, cartographers and administrators attended a session of the Reich's Kommittee für Koloniale Kartographie (the Colonial Cartography Committee). The geographer Behrmann, Professor at Frankfurt University, argued that this committee should direct all colonial sciences, support colonial cartography and set up a central information office. If such coordination did not come to fruition, the files of the meeting reveal the interconnection between several political, colonial and scientific institutions: the Reich's Research Council, the Colonial Political Office of the Nazi Party (led by von Epp) the Reich's Amt für Topographischen Dienst (the Office for Topographical Survey) and other institutions. The Reich Research Council was however commissioned to publish a handbook of African cartography for which Behrmann was responsible, though this was, in fact, never published.

Colonial research peaked in 1942, when the Nazi empire became one of the most rapidly expanded land empires in history.[31] But as the war against the Soviet Union intensified and the German advance was halted, colonial research and planning for a new empire was reduced. Geographers were drafted into various military organizations in defence of the 'German *Lebensraum*'. Some geographical research in tropical regions continued involving the application of new techniques in aerial photography and remote sensing, among other things, but colonial ambition faded with adverse news from the Front.[32]

CONCLUSION

In school and in university, German geography was always a much more practical science than is generally admitted. It was practical not so much in the sense of an applied science or an adjunct to politics, though there were some important contributions in this sense; it was practical in reflecting and adapting to prevalent political and ideological issues and to the state. For the nation as a whole however, the end of World War II meant the end

---

[30] Bundesarchiv Koblenz (BAK), Sektion Forscherarchiv R113/1586–1, *Bericht über die Sondersitzung Kolonialforschung zur Arbeitstagung*, 1940, p. 2.

[31] See Freeman, *Atlas of Nazi Germany*, 1987.

[32] See Troll, 'Die Geographische Wissenschaft', 1974, pp. 3–47.

of imperialistic dreams which had survived World War I and the loss of the colonial empire. It also meant the end of the modernized concepts of Nazi imperialism: '*Lebensraum* in the East' partly and briefly realized with the occupation of Poland and the Soviet Union; and the economic expansion zone in Africa, for which planning ceased in 1943. Geographers were involved in both projects. Their knowledge was appropriated by the institutions and political organizations of the Nazi state in different ways, but geographers also promoted the application and usefulness of their own work.

The rewriting of Nazi-period geography began almost immediately. In 1946, Karl Dietzel prepared a report on German colonial research during World War II.[33] The report was destined for the Field Information Agency (Technical) organization (FIAT) of the Allied Occupation Command in Germany. Apart from physical geography (which he described as 'colonial geoecology'), he studiously emphasized cultural geography – the polarization between Europeans and natives in the colonial context, questions of cultural change, acclimatization, and settlement. Dietzel thereby reduced colonial geography to a supposedly scientific pursuit, largely devoid of the political engagement with Nazi imperialism. This research was easily absorbed as 'geoecology' and the geography of 'underdeveloped countries' after 1945.

[33] Dietzel, 'Kolonialgeographie', 1946, pp. 205–12.

Plate 3 Mrs Shay's method of fording a crocodile-infested stream, 1925, reproduced by kind permission of Felix Shay. © National Geographical Society.

PART III

The Rhetoric of Race and Gender

Introduction

The physical conquest of foreign territories is generally accompanied by a rhetoric of superiority, and European imperialism of the eighteenth to twentieth centuries is no exception. The apologia of empire permeated the range of public discourses – scientific and artistic, literary and economic, popular and political – and helped frame the patterns of response to imperial expansion. As that language of empire lost credibility in the middle decades of the twentieth century, however, the imperial epoch was widely relegated to an embarrassing anomaly in western history. The major discussion of imperialism was carried on by Marxists for whom the connections between global expansion and class domination at home were paramount. If the racial dimensions of empire were widely acknowledged, there was less discussion of the geographical and gender contours of imperial expansion.

As a racial project, European imperialism was permeated by an enlightenment morality that intertwined science, religion and economics. As David Livingstone shows in chapter 7, post-Darwinian British and American geography were part of this wider discourse, and they contributed centrally to the vocabulary connecting climatic environment and social type. Hierarchial social differences were naturalized as the product of climatic and environmental differences; conversely, placing people geographically became a means of typecasting their social and political identities. This collusion of identity and place was worked out not simply in the arcane pages of scientific journals but equally in popular visions of the world such as those presented by the *National Geographic Magazine*. Under the guise of scientific realism, as Tamar Rothenberg argues in chapter 8, the *National Geographic*'s coding of colonial 'others' projected a patronizing racism and sexism that directly reaffirmed the people and places of the colonies as available resources. The inversion of this racism against the 'other' comes of course with xenophobic nationalism, and none was more virulent than the geopolitical nationalism of Nazi Germany. In chapter 9, David Murphy traces the connection between a frustrated German colonialism, following World War I, and the geographically inscribed racism that became official ideology following 1933. If Japanese geopolitics of the same period also combined geography and xenophobia, the situation there was complicated by the clash of imperialisms. A Japanese imperial tradition was confronted in the late nineteenth century by European and American ambitions of empire, and this clash sharpened the racism of Japanese geographical writings. The geographical tradition that emerged by the early decades of the twentieth century expressed, as Keiichi Takeuchi points out in chapter 10, a reluctant hybrid of both imperialisms.

7

Climate's Moral Economy: Science, Race and Place in Post-Darwinian British and American Geography

David N. Livingstone

ON DOING GEOGRAPHY'S HISTORY

What are we speaking of when we refer to 'critical studies in the history of geography'? Are we talking about the history of a body of knowledge, or of a community of people calling themselves geographers, or of institutional arrangements transacted within academia? I do not raise these questions to resurrect that hoary old chestnut, 'What is geography?' That, I think, is actually a misconceived question. But I mention this definitional matter because reflecting on what the label 'geography' actually names, if indeed it names anything at all, takes me to the heart of the argument I want to present in this chapter.

It will be helpful, I think, to start with Wittgenstein's dictum that we shall make more progress in our investigations if we begin by looking at how words are used, rather than working with static definitions. If Wittgenstein's reflections are even in the neighbourhood of a correct analysis then we need to shelve any notions about geography having some timeless 'essence' and proceed by looking at how the word was and is used in different contexts.[1] This is the assumption that I will work with in this chapter, namely, that the label 'geography' has meant different things to different people, at different times, and in different places. Just as it does not make much sense to ask

[1] Saying this, of course, should not be taken to imply any wholesale commitment to Wittgensteinian philosophy.

whether a particular belief is rational independently of certain specific conditions, so, I argue, it does not make much sense to think of the nature of geography as eternally fixed. Clearly what it is to be rational is different for an eleventh-century monk, a fifteenth-century navigator, a seventeenth-century astrologer, and a twentieth-century laboratory scientist. Similarly, what it was to be geography in sixteenth-century England was rather different from its counterpart in, say, Renaissance Italy, Jeffersonian America, enlightenment France, Victorian England, or inter-war Germany. Just as there can only be a situated rationality, so too can there only be a situated geography. The 'nature' of geography is thus always negotiated and the task of geography's historians, at least in part, is to ascertain how and why particular practices and procedures come to be accounted geographically legitimate and hence normative at different moments in time and in different spatial settings.[2] What is required, I submit, is a genuinely historical geography of geography.[3]

Accordingly, my claim is that it is not enough to say that geography was practised in a particular social context; rather social conditions insinuated their way into the very heart of the theorizing. If indeed this is so, then it is not just the scope of disciplinary identity that reflects the crystallization of social forces; the cognitive content of the subject's substantive 'findings' and the methods devised to interrogate the empirical are no less negotiated entities. This suggests that the geographer's traditional craft-skills – such as cartographic competence, regional survey, statistical methods, and so on – turn out to be rhetorical devices of persuasion by which geographers have reinforced the authority of their assertions.[4] Just how and why these particular sets of practices came to be accorded cognitive privilege within the geographical community is certainly a question worthy of consideration.

On this reading, geography is to be thought of as a social practice. In saying this, of course, I do not intend to imply that geographical thought is to be considered a mere epiphenomenon of society. What I do mean is that theory is always located in social and intellectual circumstance. As with my rejection of an 'essential' geography, I should want to speak of situated theory. This will mean, for example, that it would never be wrong to ask of any theory: Why was it put forward? Who benefited from it? Who lost out? Whose interests did it advance or retard? In what kind of cultural and intellectual arena was it conceived and communicated? How adapted was it to its conceptual and social environment? Certainly this is not to imply that these are the only ways in which theory may be cross-examined. But that these are legitimate questions is certainly the case I want to make.

[2] These paragraphs are drawn from my 'In defence of situated messiness', (in press).

[3] A fascinating contribution to what I would call the historical geography of science is available in Shapin and Schaffer, *Leviathan and the air-pump*, 1985. In this work the authors trace the diffusion of Boyle's air-pump, and its associated scientific philosophy, across Europe.

[4] My phrasing here relies on Golinski, 'The theory of practice and the practice of theory', 1990.

In the light of what I have been saying thus far it is clear that the conventional distinction between text and context needs to be transcended. As I see it, text and context are inextricably intertwined in disciplinary history. Thus it is not just that the social context explains the geographical texts, or even contextualizes them. Contextual approaches to intellectual history have frequently been little more than an apologia for a politicized reductionism that accords explanatory privilege – frequently in an unexamined fashion – to the socio-political domain. What we need, I believe, is something far less reductionist and far more symmetrical, a greater sense of how texts and contexts are constituted reciprocally. For defining what constitutes geography's intramural domain – the text – in part determines what composes the extramural space – the context. What too few historians of geography have engaged, I believe, is this very question of just how the reciprocity of text and context is to be understood. And yet it seems to me that it is only as we grasp how they are interwoven that we can begin to understand the history of the geographical tradition. Thus to say that in sixteenth-century England geography was practised in a magical context – astrology, alchemy and all that – is not perhaps the correct way to speak of it; surely it is rather that geography just was part of magical discourse.[5] Here, to separate out geographical 'text' from magical 'context' and to explain one in terms of the other is to put asunder what was originally joined together.

With these observations in mind I want now to turn to the discourse of English-speaking geography in the nineteenth century. If my suspicions are well founded, we will find in the geographical talk of the time, modes of communication that today we might all too comfortably allocate to other conceptual categories – and in particular to the realms of politics and religion.

THE GEOGRAPHICAL CONVERSATION IN THE NINETEENTH CENTURY:
THE 'PURPOSES OF PROVIDENCE' AND THE 'PUBLIC FAITH OF EMPIRES'

There is much to be said for the view that Victorian geography was the science of empire par excellence. For one thing the Royal Geographical Society of London (RGS) was inaugurated in the early 1830s on the explicit grounds that geography's 'advantages are of the first importance to mankind in general, and paramount to the welfare of a maritime nation like Great Britain, with its numerous and extensive foreign possessions'.[6] Moreover, its subsequent history revealed the RGS as more perfectly representing 'British expansionism in all its facets than any other institution in the nation', to use Robert Stafford's words, and as 'an extra-parliamentary venue for debate on empire and peripheral exploitation'.[7] Not surprisingly, by the end of the

[5] I discuss this issue in 'Science, magic and religion', 1988; 'Geography, tradition and the scientific revolution', 1990.
[6] *The Journal of the Royal Geographical Society of London*, 1831, vii.
[7] Stafford, *Scientist of Empire*, 1989, p. 212.

Society's first decade its presiden̄t, W. R. Hamilton, a diplomat and a fellow of the Royal Society, reflected on the scope of geography in militaristic, commercial, and imperialistic terms. Geography, he insisted:

> ... is the mainspring of all the operations of war, and of all the negotiations of a state of peace; and in proportion as any one nation is the foremost to extend her acquaintance with the physical conformation of the earth, and the water which surrounds it, will ever be the opportunities she will possess, and the responsibilities she will incur, for extending her commerce, for enlarging her powers of civilizing the yet benighted portions of the globe, and for bearing her part in forwarding and directing the destinies of mankind.[8]

Geography, apparently, was not merely engaged in discovering the world; it was making it. Nor were such stirring manifestos confined to early nineteenth-century Britain. At the inaugural meeting of the Scottish Geographical Society in December 1884, H. M. Stanley hoped to excite his audience's 'regard for geography by showing ... how it has been and is intimately connected with the growth of the British Empire'.[9] At the other end of the century and on the other side of the Atlantic, Thomas Jefferson's own patriotic enthusiasms – the warp and woof of his *Notes on the State of Virginia* – had surfaced just as dramatically in the Lewis and Clark expedition that he himself orchestrated. Here too, imperial and political interests were never far below the surface. The economic possibilities and geopolitical potential of the West – with all its savour of Manifest Destiny – began to be realized as the rich upper Missouri countryside was opened up to traders and trappers. Besides this, the fact that their enterprise was a government-sponsored one meant that its broad-ranging discoveries were seen as belonging to the people of the new democracy. Thereby geography played its role in the democratization of knowledge in the new republic as a whole clutch of entrepreneurs and naturalists caught the exploring bug.[10]

Geography in both Britain and America, then, was part and parcel of the conversation and conduct of empire. By and large the interlocutors were geographical practitioners, directly engaging in muscular exploration and reporting their adventures to the dining club set at the RGS. Geography's theoreticians, by contrast, were participating in a somewhat different conversation – that of natural theology. In 1929, for instance, H. R. Mill,

---

[8] Hamilton, 'Presidential Address', 1842, pp. lxxxviii–lxxxix. See also the discussion of geography and militarism in Hudson, 'The new geography and the new imperialism', 1977.

[9] Stanley, 'Inaugural address', 1885, p. 6. Stanley's comparable 1884 address to the Manchester Geographical Society is discussed in Osborne, *The Société Zoologique d'Acclimatation*, 1987.

[10] Greene, *American Science in the Age of Jefferson*, 1984; Bedini, *Thomas Jefferson*, 1990; Goetzmann, *New Lands, New Men*, 1986; Van Orman, *The Explorers*, 1984.

reflecting on earlier developments in geography observed that 'Teleology or
the argument from design had become a favourite form of reasoning among
Christian theologians and ... was tacitly accepted or explicitly avowed by almost every writer on the theory of geography.'[11] Mill's judgements certainly
have much to commend them. In the United States, Arnold Guyot's Lowell
Lectures in Boston on 'Comparative Physical Geography' – subsequently
published as *The Earth and Man* – were fashioned on a Ritterian template.
The work, rife with the organic metaphors of idealist natural theology,
was presented as a geographical testimony to the harmonies of nature and
history that everywhere expressed the control of a beneficent providence.[12]
Meanwhile, on the other side of the Atlantic, Mary Somerville was assuring
her readers that the pattern of human centres of civilization, mirroring as
they did the moral configurations of climate, exhibited 'the arrangement
of Divine Wisdom'; that the earthquake and the torrent were 'the august and
terrible ministers of Almighty Power'; and that irresponsible agricultural
methods brought inevitable decline in yield because the 'works of the Creator
are nicely balanced, and man cannot infringe His laws with impunity.'[13]
While the explorers and theoreticians were, by and large, talking different talk, it would be quite mistaken to think that their vocabularies never
overlapped. To the contrary. The British colonial adventure overseas was
periodically cast in the language of providential teleology. Nowhere, perhaps,
is this more clearly displayed than in reflections on Livingstone's missionary–
imperial ventures in Africa. In his prefatory remarks to Livingstone's Cambridge lectures in 1858, for example, Adam Sedgwick, geologist and then
vice-master of Trinity College, Cambridge, expressed his hope that the volume
in hand would advance 'the great and good cause of civilization, brotherly
love and Christian truth – and ... encourage the Missionary of the Gospel
in carrying the message of peace to poor benighted Africa.' Not surprisingly his commentary was replete with references to the workings of divine
providence – a doctrine with religious, imperial and scientific possibilities.
While claiming the approbation of Britian's favourite missionary, Sedgwick
could legitimate Livingstone's evangelism and the nation's imperial exploits,
by affirming that Livingstone 'practically believed that no parts of true
knowledge, whether sacred or profane, can, when rightly used, ever be in
mutual antagonism.'[14]
A range of vocabularies – scientific, imperial, and religious – were woven
into the very fabric of geography in the Victorian period. This is the issue
on which I wish to focus using the conversation about climate as the vehicle
for exploring the ways in which scientific claims were constituted by, and
then made to bear the weight of, moralistic judgments about both people

[11] Mill, 'Geography', 1929, vol. 10, p. 147. See also my discussion of this in 'Natural
theology and Neo-Lamarckism', 1984, and 'Of design and dining clubs', 1991.

[12] Guyot, *The Earth and Man*, 1897, p. 82.

[13] Somerville, *Physical Geography*, 1858, pp. 486, 2, 492.

[14] Monk, *Dr. Livingstone's Cambridge Lectures*, 1858, pp. ii, vi.

and places. Affirming that geographical science is a social practice does not pre-judge the question of how it is so. That geography was the science of empire is one thing; just how it was so is quite another. This is illustrated nicely in Sedgwick's Livingstone Cambridge lectures. The belief, shared by Livingstone and Sedgwick, that Christianity and commerce were the two inseparable 'pioneers of civilization', for example, did not prevent them condemning slavery or quarrying African customs for resources with which to engage in national self-criticism. [15] Reflecting on 'the fantastical decorations of [the African's] outer person', Sedgwick proceeded to observe: 'There is not one among them comparable in absurdity to those monstrous stacks of perfumed and powdered hair that were worn last century by the fairest daughters of England.' Similarly, 'If Africa have its wretched slave gangs; we once had slaves in England, and sent them in gangs to the markets of civilized Europe ... If Africa have its quacks, we too have a plentiful crop from the same vile seed. If we have no rain-doctors ... we have our rain prophets, and our weather-wise impostors in plenty.' [16]

The geographical conversation of the nineteenth century, then, incorporated and integrated the languages and practices of the imperial and the teleological – the 'public faith of empires' and 'the purposes of Providence', to use Roderick Murchison's own words. As regards empire, Murchison gleefully gibed that 'political economists and politicians [might well] now beg for knowledge at the hands of the physical geographer and geologist, and learn from them the secret on which the public faith of empires may depend.' As for Providence, he was certain that resources exploitation in the colonies would further 'the purposes of Providence [by] providing for a great augmenting population, and in converting wild track into flourishing hives of human industry.' [17]

CLIMATE'S MORAL ECONOMY

Geographical discussions of climatic matters throughout the nineteenth, and well into the twentieth century were profoundly implicated in the imperial drama and were frequently cast in the diagnostic language of ethnic judgment. To put it another way, the idioms of political and moralistic evaluation were just part and parcel of the grammar of climatology in the period with which I am concerned. For the sake of convenience I propose tackling the problem on two fronts, although the two themes that I have isolated – anthropo-climatology and white acclimatization – frequently rode in tandem.

[15] Ibid., p. 21.
[16] Ibid., p. xix.
[17] Murchison, 'Address to the Royal Geographical Society', 1844, p. lxix; Ibid., 1853, p. cxxvii. Both extracts are cited in Stafford, *Scientist of Empire*, pp. 38, 39.

Race and Region: Climate and Race Character

The idea that climatic regions on both global and local scales found expression in what might be called an ethnic moral topography snakes its way throughout the corpus of nineteenth- and twentieth-century geographical writings.[18] Geography's mid-nineteenth-century links with anthropology, helped facilitate such conceptual manoeuvres. Numerous members of the Ethnological Society of London, for example, were also fellows of the Royal Geographical Society.[19] So it was not surprising when, on the Tuesday evening of 19 November 1861, John Crawfurd rose to address the Ethnologists, his subject should be 'On the connection between ethnology and physical geography'. His purpose was simple, namely, to catalogue the effects of regional climate on racial constitution. The moralistic complexion of his project is clearly visible: Australia's inauspicious climates had only produced 'the feeblest ... hordes of black, ill-formed, unseemly, naked savages', while in Africa, 'the races of man ... correspond with the disadvantages of its physical geography.'[20] To be sure, it was not clear whether climate had produced such racial degenerates, or whether they had been placed by nature or God in climatically appropriate regimes. No matter. Race and region were, in the eyes of Crawfurd and his colleagues, very tightly, tied together. Thus three months later James Hunt could tell the same audience that in the tropical climates 'there is a low state of morality, and ... the inhabitants of these regions are essentially sensual'; by contrast the 'temperate regions', he insisted, were characterized by 'increased activity of the brain'.[21]

Among the anthropologists one implication of the connection between race and place was the conviction that human origins and, by extension, racial character were polygenic.[22] Thus Josiah Nott, could affirm in 1857 that 'each realm possesses a group of human races, which, though not identical in physical and intellectual characters, are closely allied with one another, and are disconnected from all other races' and that 'the climates of the earth may be divided into PHYSICAL and MEDICAL; and that each species of man, having its own physiological and pathological laws, is peculiarly affected by both climates.'[23] Such affirmation, as we will presently see, bore directly on the whole question of acclimatization.

---

[18] I have discussed this topic more fully in my 'The moral discourse of climate', 1991.

[19] The standard history of anthropology in the period is now Stocking, Jr, *Victorian Anthropology*, 1987.

[20] Crawfurd, 'On the connection between ethnology and physical geography', 1863, pp. 5, 6.

[21] Hunt, 'On ethno-climatology', 1863, p. 53.

[22] See the discussion in Stocking, Jr, 'The persistence of polygenist thought', 1982; Gould, *The Mismeasure of Man*, 1981, pp. 30–72.

[23] Nott, 'Acclimation', 1857, p. 401.

Among geographers the idea that race and region were umbilically connected surfaced both in theodicean and naturalistic depictions of human racial history. The naturalization of geographical vocabulary thus had little effect on the legitimating moves that were afoot. This is nicely brought out when we compare Arnold Guyot's portrait of racial geography with those of the Michigan geologist Alexander Winchell. To Guyot, it was 'the Creator' who had 'placed the cradle of mankind in the midst of the continents of the North ... and not at the centre of the tropical regions, whose balmy, but enervating and treacherous, atmosphere would perhaps have lulled him to sleep, the sleep of death in his very cradle.'[24] For Winchell, it was 'Nature, conscious of their [the blacks'] irremediable estrangement, [that] had contented herself to herd them in regions where they would never mingle in the stir and strife of social and national struggles.'[25] Either way, whether courtesy of Creator or Nature, racial constitution was moored to climatic circumstance.

The construction of a moral–climatic idiom by which racial difference could be portrayed also operated at a much more localized scale. Consider, for instance, the analysis of the Edinburgh geologist, naturalist, and explorer Joseph Thomson who during a short life travelled extensively in East Africa.[26] In 1886, during a period of convalescence between trips, he spoke to the Birmingham meeting of the British Association about his experience in Niger and Central Sudan, an address that appeared later that year in the *Scottish Geographical Magazine*. Here he paused to reflect on the moral-evolutionary impact of climatic conditions:

> It is a fact worthy of our attention that, as the traveller passes up the river [Niger] and finds a continually improving climate ... he co-incidentally observes a higher type of humanity – better-ordered communities, more comfort, with more industry. That these pleasanter conditions are due to the improved environment cannot be doubted. To the student with Darwinian instincts most instructive lessons might be derived from a study of the relations between man and nature in these regions.

Here the 'struggle for existence' had produced a 'higher type of man, both mentally and physically'. Evidently the changing topography of the moral economy could be mapped straight on to climatic regime. To be sure, he felt he must admit that in the upper reaches of the Niger,

> We are still dealing with negroes, but how different are they! Behind us are the unwashed barbarous sans-culottes of the Coast region, with fetishism, cannibalism, and the gin bottle in congenial union; before

[24] Guyot, *The Earth and Man*, 1849; reprinted, 1897, p. 251.
[25] Winchell, *Preadamites*, 1880, pp. 156–7. A general history of the preadamite theory is available in my *The Preadamite Theory*, 1992.
[26] See Thomson, *Dictionary of National Biography*.

us lies a people astir with religious activity and enthusiasm, and wonderfully far advanced in the arts and industries.[27]

The intertwining of specific and sermonic modes of speech are clearly to be heard here. And yet Thomson's fine-tuning of moral climatology on a sub-regional range did not prevent him from issuing moral imperatives on a far grander scale. That same year he also told the readers of the Scottish Geographical Magazine that the 'Negro ... requires to be treated by the State as a child is by the father, only, instead of years, the negro must undergo his moral and mental discipline for two or three generations before he can be trusted to rely upon himself.'[28] Echoes of the recapitulationist strain in biology are clearly audible.

Such moral obligations, of course, were at the same time political mandates too. Judgements about the present moral standing of ethnic groups had direct implications for their future in a new imperialist world economy. Tutelage under 'superior' races or, failing that, sweat equity, represented the policies that James Bryce, Britain's distinguished transatlantic ambassador, advocated at the inaugural meeting of the London Branch of the Scottish Geographical Society in April 1892. Save for the Chinese, Bryce mused:

> none of these tropical peoples ... has a native civilization, or is fitted to play any part in history, either as a conquering or as a thinking force, or in any way, save as producers by physical labour of material wealth. None is likely to develop towards any higher condition than that in which it now stands, save under the tutelage, and by adopting so much as it can of the culture, of the five or six European peoples which have practically appropriated the torrid zone, and are dividing its resources between them. Yet the vast numbers to which, under the conjoint stimuli of science and peace, these inferior black and yellow races may grow, coupled with the capacity some of them evince for assimilating the material side of European civilization, may enable them to play a larger part in the future of the world than they have played in the past.[29]

The idea that climate had stamped its indelible mark on racial constitution, not just physiologically, but psychologically and morally, was a motif that was both deep and lasting in English-speaking geography. Space does not permit a complete chronicle of this strain in the history of geography here, though such a survey would certainly be instructive. Instead I should like to direct you to Austin Miller's standard textbook on climatology, first published in 1931, just to demonstrate something of the idea's intractability. Here I will refer to the fifth, 1947, edition of the work, though other

[27] Thomson, 'Niger and Central Sudan', 1886, pp. 582, 584.
[28] Thomson, 'East Central Africa, and its commercial outlook', 1886, p. 74.
[29] Bryce, 'The migrations of the races', 1892, p. 420.

editions would doubtless merit scrutiny. According to Miller, climate and character were intimately related. 'Psychologically,' he explained, 'each climate tends to have its own mentality, innate in its inhabitants and granted on its immigrants.' And of course there were direct behavioural correlates of climatic governance: 'The enervating monotonous climates of much of the tropical zone, together with the abundant and easily obtained food-supply, produce a lazy and indolent people, indisposed to labour for hire and there-fore in the past subjected to coercion culminating in slavery.'[30] What is remarkable here is the way moralistic terms – enervating, monotonous, lazy, indolent – are still being presented as settled scientific maxims with the result that human mental and moral behaviour is thoroughly naturalized through the deployment of 'climate's moral economy'.[31]

The notion that ethnic constitution was riveted to climatic circumstance, of course, implied that racial character was spatially-referenced and could thus be presented in cartographic form. The whole business of what might be called anthropometric cartography was a project that was taken up with varying degrees of ideological gusto by anthropologists and geographers alike. I have examined aspects of this manoeuvre elsewhere.[32] Suffice at this juncture to observe that the mapping of human trait occurrences could run the gamut from depicting the pattern of blood groups and skin colour to the scurrilous charting, by George Gliddon, of what he called the 'Geographical Distribution of the *simiae* in relation to that of some inferior types of men'. In the latter case Gliddon's cartographic portrait was designed to demonstrate that 'within the black circumvalling line which surrounds the zone occupied by the *simiae*, no "civilization" ... has ever been spontaneously developed since historical times' and that 'the most superior types of Monkeys are found to be indigenous exactly where we encounter races of some of the most inferior types of Men.'[33]

Here, the cartographic enterprise turns out to be a rhetorical device of persuasion to justify the authority of its practitioners' assertions. This can be illustrated further from a brief consideration of Ellsworth Huntington's use of cartographic presentation in his 1924 *The Character of Races*. Other aspects of Huntington's writings will presently attract our attention, but for the moment I propose focusing on the maps he compiled to illustrate his chapter on the 'The Character of Modern Europe'. The details are easily reviewed. Huntington drew up charts of the distribution of genius, of health, of civilization, and so on, and correlated these with a chart of what he termed 'climatic energy'. The conclusion? 'The similarity of the maps of civilization, genius, health, and climatic energy', Huntington remarked, 'is so clear that

[30] Miller, *Climatology*, 1947, (first published 1931), p. 2.

[31] As Wesso's chapter in this volume makes clear, precisely the self-same ideological buttress for imperialism, manifest in the writings of Hutcheon, surfaced in the literature of South African geography.

[32] See Livingstone, 'The moral discourse of climate', 1991.

[33] Gliddon, 'The monogenists and the polygenists', 1857, p. 650.

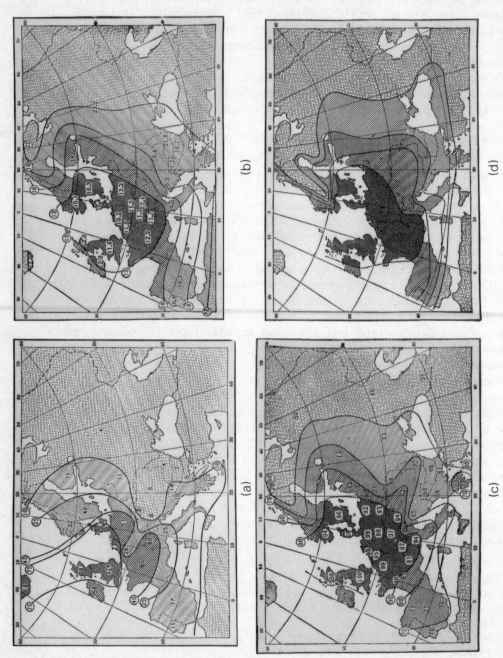

Huntington's charts of the distribution of eminent Europeans per 10,000 of the population in 1800 (a), health (b) and civilization (c) compared with 'climatic energy' (d). From Huntington *The Character of Races*, 1924.

it speaks for itself. In each map there is the same dark area around the North Sea.' How simple. Huntington's claim that 'climate influences health and energy, and these in turn influence civilization' was thus backed up by the traditional craft competence of the geographer – cartography – and the correlations were so plain that the suite of maps – well – just 'spoke for itself'.[34]

Of course the distributional data did not just speak for themselves. Huntington had to extract the information for his map of the distribution of civilization – to isolate just one example – from numerous willing accomplices. Over fifty scholars – geographers, anthropologists, historians and so on – had assisted in the exercise. Huntington, it turns out, had written to the intellectual elite of his day asking them to rank whole countries on a graduated scale of civilization. Some, if J. Russell Smith is representative, relished the task. He apparently had taken 'a half day off to sit in judgment upon the world', and confessed that it gave him 'a sense of a sort of tyrannic despotism to hold a country in his hand'.[35] Many a true word is spoken in jest! James Bryce was also predictably enthusiastic and found Huntington's idea 'ingenious'.[36] But others were not convinced. George Chisholm, for example, admitted to 'a peculiar incapacity for forming judgments about peoples' while A. L. Kroeber had to 'frankly confess that I believe you will obtain misleading results'.[37] W. Z. Ripley wrote to him saying that he did 'not conceive that the method you suggest is possible of scientific results. One must choose between statistics which are definite and mere judgments which are general. To apply the geographic method to a compound of statistics and loose generalization may be productive of grave error.'[38] Even more telling was Franz Boas's eschewal of the cultural imperialism that undergirded Huntington's entire scheme in words that, paradoxically, demonstrate just how dignifying to the human subject a positivist methodology could be:

I feel ... quite unable to comply with your request, for several reasons ... It has been my endeavor, in my anthropological studies, to follow down [sic] the same principles that are laid down for natural sciences;

[34] Huntington, *The Character of Races*, 1924, p. 232.
[35] Letter from J. Russell Smith to Ellsworth Huntington, 3 July 1914, Huntington Papers, box 6, folder 34, Yale University Archives. The previous year Russell had written to Huntington praising his 'chart showing the relation of human output to temperature' as 'real geography'. Letter, J. Russell Smith to Ellsworth Huntington, Huntington Papers, box 31, folder 612, Yale University Archives.
[36] Letter from James Bryce to Ellsworth Huntington, 15 November, 1913, Huntington Papers, box 6, folder 34, Yale University Archives.
[37] Letter from George G. Chisholm to Ellsworth Huntington, 13 November 1913, Huntington Papers, box 6, folder 34, Yale University Archives; letter from A. L. Kroeber to Ellsworth Huntington, 6 December 1913, Huntington Papers, box 6, folder 34, Yale University Archives.
[38] Letter from W. Z. Ripley to Ellsworth Huntington, 3 November 1913, Huntington Papers, box 6, folder 34, Yale University Archives.

and the first condition of progress is therefore to eliminate the element
of subjective value; not that I wish to deny that there are values, but
it seems to me necessary to eliminate the peculiar combination of the
development of cultural forms and the intrusion of the idea of our
estimate of their value, which has nothing to do with these forms. It
seems to my mind that in doing so these obtain subjective values,
which in themselves may be the subject of interesting studies, but
which do not give any answer to the question you are trying to solve.[39]

Huntington's cartographic constructions were therefore just that – constructions, rhetorical devices by which he could legitimate what were even
in his own time profoundly contested judgements about the moral economy
of climate. Their power no doubt derived both from the fact that cartography was an established piece of equipment in geography's repertoire,
and because maps could impose visual clarity on empirical opacity. Precisely
the same moves, I would argue, undergirded the climographs Griffith Taylor
prepared for the purpose of backing up his assertions about 'The control of
settlement by humidity and temperature'.[40] At the centre of his graph of
wet-bulb temperature and humidity was a 'composite white climograph' –
a shaded area – where conditions were 'close to the ideal'. This piece of
graphic rhetoric, of course, pleased Huntington enormously, and he asserted
that 'as representation of the various effects of climate...Taylor's diagrams
are much the best yet available.'[41]
Besides providing cartographic rationale for their anthropo-climatic credo,
both Taylor and Huntington also wanted to situate their theories within the
deep historical framework of Darwinian theory. The role of climate in racial
evolution thus occupied their attentions. In his consideration of 'climatic
cycles and evolution' for the *Geographical Review* in 1919, Taylor repeatedly
made reference to climates as 'strenuous', 'favorable', 'healthful', 'energy-
promoting', and so on, and authenticated the whole undertaking with an
impressive piece of coloured cartographic rhetoric depicting the 'zones of
migration showing the evolution of the races, based mainly on the cephalic
indices of the most primitive tribes in each region'.[42]
Further commentary on such linguistic and cartographic ploys would be
to merely multiply testimonials, however. Instead I want to mention three
metaphors to which Taylor resorted that betray much about the ideological
orientation of moral climatology. First was his use of the recapitulationist

[39] Letter from Franz Boas to Ellsworth Huntington, 5 November 1913, Huntington
Papers, box 6, folder 34, Yale University Archives. It is significant too to note, I think, that
in his review of *The Character of Races* for the *Scottish Geographical Magazine*, Chisholm
observed that Huntington had ignored Boas's celebrated studies on the modification of the
immigrant head form. Chisholm, 'Perplexities of race', 1925, p. 300.

[40] Taylor, 'The control of settlement', 1914.

[41] Huntington, 'Graphic representation of climate', 1917.

[42] Taylor, 'Climatic cycles', 1919, pp. 298, 299, 307.

analogy of racial inferiority and infancy. This application of the youth-maturity-old-age scheme produced such racial stereotypes as the following:

> The childlike behavior of the negro has often been referred to as a primitive characteristic. The white races are versatile, gay, and inventive – all attributes of youth. The yellow races are grave, meditative, and melancholic – which possibly indicates their more mature position in the evolution of races.[43]

Secondly, there was Taylor's bizarre analogy between race migration and class-correlated crowd behaviour at a sporting event.

> First come the lowest classes and pariahs, who wander freely over the ground long before the general public arrives. They have arrived there by the usual roads and tracks but ultimately are found perched in tree tops and in the least attractive positions. Then the proletariat advances along the same road and corridors. They are driven out of the best seats, which are reserved for the last comers.[44]

Some years later, in 1936, he returned to this subject when he produced for *Human Biology* his 'zones and strata theory'. In a nutshell Taylor urged that ever-more-highly evolved stock migrating sequentially outward from a central core provided the key to unlocking race history. Hence his third geological metaphor of zones and strata which depicted racial groups diffusing over earlier cultures and in turn being subsumed under yet later migrant peoples. The implication of this scheme, of course, was that the earliest expansion had not only spread farthest, but had encompassed the least evolved specimens. Assuming the cradle of humankind to have been somewhere in central Asia, Taylor suggested that prior climatic change had ushered out of south central Asia various early forms of primitive hominoid most of whom ended up in Africa. Blacks by this reading were a very ancient type of humanity akin to Neanderthal man.[45] As he put it in 1951: 'My suggestion is that a Neandertaloid type lived in southern Asia and gave rise to the negroes far back in the Pleistocene – perhaps in the Gunz-Mindel interglacial.' This is not, to be sure, polygenism, but it asserts such early racial differentiation that it might as well be. Moreover the moral censure associated with the proposal is evident: 'The writer believes that it is precisely because the negro was thrust into the stagnant environment of the Tropics ... that he preserves so many primitive features.' 'Racial evolution', he concluded, has left the Negro 'far behind'.[46]

---

[43] Ibid., p. 300.

[44] Ibid., pp. 300–1.

[45] Taylor, 'The zones and strata theory', 1936. See also Taylor's 'The evolution and distribution of race', 1921 and his 'Racial migration-zones', 1930.

[46] Taylor, 'Racial Geography', 1957, pp. 455, 454.

Several decades earlier, Huntington had detailed a similar story of the cumulative enregistration of climate on racial constitution. According to him, those migrants who ended up in the tropics where 'evolution ... has stagnated', were psycho-biologically disadvantaged 'because during all the hundreds of thousands of years of man's existence there have been few great changes, few new types of selection whereby mental specialization has been accelerated.' As a result, black Africans 'represent our primitive ancestors'. 'Their characteristics', he went on, 'are those which unspecialized man first showed when he separated from the apes and came down from the trees. It is not to be expected that such people should ever rise very high in the scale of civilization.' The tropical world was thus relegated to the moral margins of history and its people cast out from the mainstream chronicle of evolutionary advance. [47]

The same was true of the American Indians who had come to the New World via the wastes of northern Siberia and across the Bering Strait. Here they had been 'subjected to a repressive evolution', and forever carried with them the stamp of this subversive phase in their evolutionary past. Moreover in the wilds of northern Siberia they had picked up 'arctic hysteria', an affliction to which women were apparently most susceptible:

> The natural selection due to this disease together with the great premium which the Arctic environment places upon passive endurance may have been an important factor in moulding the mental equality of most of the people of America. If we compare the Amerinds with European races, one of the most striking differences is not only a lower degree of originality and initiative, but a certain passivity. The emotional types have been eliminated. [48]

In this extract, we find a particularly clear instance of the discourse I have been tracking in post-Darwinian geography, namely, the deployment of climate's moral economy for the purposes of regionalizing racial character. A closely related issue centred on the question of human migration between different regional climates, and raised the whole matter of human acclimatization.

Mortality and Migration: The Acclimatization Question

With European penetration into the sub-tropical and tropical worlds the whole question of human acclimatization assumed increasing importance towards the end of the nineteenth century. Sir John Kirk, for example, reported to the Sixth International Geographical Congress, which met in

[47] Huntington, 'Environment and racial character', 1924. Reprinted in Count, *This is Race*, 1950, pp. 339–50.
[48] Ibid., p. 350.

London in 1895, that 'Climate is the most important of all considerations in the choice of a home for Europeans in Central Africa'.[49] E. G. Ravenstein concurred, insisting that the 'colonization and climatology of a country were closely connected.'[50] Readers of the *Scottish Geographical Magazine* were kept informed of climatic–colonial matters by reports on the German experience in tropical Africa, the new British colony in South Africa, and reviews of various writers on the subject.[51] As I have argued elsewhere the problem of – and attitudes towards – acclimatization crystallized a host of scientific, institutional, and imperial interests at the time.[52] A whole spate of acclimatization societies emerged during the nineteenth century across Europe and in America to monitor different social, biological, environmental and economic aspects of the question.[53] Considerable debate on the subject already took place in the pre-Darwinian period, particularly in view of Britain's interests in the Indian sub-continent and the death toll exacted from British troops and administrators there; a tropical hygiene industry flourished, manufacturing such items as the cholera belt (a flannel strip worn around the abdomen to counter post-perspiration chills) and the solar topi or pith helmet to protect the head and neck from the tropical sun.[54]

Such imperial interests and accompanying moralistic discourse were constitutive of late nineteenth- and early twentieth-century geographical treatments of acclimatization. My argument is that these issues provided a common framework of exegesis even among those who took up widely differing stances on the matter. That there was a moral economy of climate was a very largely uncontested presupposition among participants in the conversation.

For those who were sceptical about the possibility of white acclimatization to the tropics there was, by the end of the nineteenth century, a substantial body of corroborative medical opinion drawing on supposed evidence of racial degeneration, statistics of infant mortality, cases of hybrid sterility, the injurious physiological effects of heat, and so on. Geographers were certainly aware of this corpus of commentary. Thus E. G. Ravenstein simply took the judgements of the anti-acclimatization partisans as conventional wisdom

---

[49] Kirk, 'The extent to which tropical Africa', 1896.

[50] Ravenstein, Discussion, *Report of the Sixth International Geographical Congress*.

[51] Anon., 'German colonisation in tropical Africa', 1885, p. 263; Anon., 'The new British colony in South Africa', 1885, p. 383; Anon., Review of 'Zur Klimatologie und Hygiene Ostafrikas', by Rohlfs, 1886.

[52] See my 'Human acclimatization', 1987. For a perspective on the treatment of acclimatization outside geography, see the following works: Weiner, 'The roots of "Michurinism"', 1985; Curtin, *Death by Migration*, 1989; Osborne, *The Société Zoologique*, 1987; Crosby, 'Ecological imperialism', 1988.

[53] Sir Christopher Lever is currently preparing a book on this subject.

[54] See Renbourne, 'The history of the flannel binder', 1957 and 'Life and death of the solar topi', 1962.

when he came to draw up his map of 'lands of the globe still available for European settlement'.[55] Demographic decline of the British in India, the Dutch in Java, and the Portuguese in Brazil clinched the argument for him. Moreover when Silva White produced in the same year, 1891, a comparable map of the 'comparative value of African lands' he also built a climatic component into his assessment, for, he declared, it was only in the sub-tropical or temperate zones of Africa that European colonization was possible. White's map, we should note in passing, constituted another case of cartography as imperial rhetoric. After all he himself described it as a graphic illustration of 'the relative value of African lands to any European power' and explicitly declared that 'all humanitarian motives may be set aside as not being pertinent to the present inquiry.'[56]

Medical and demographic concerns were certainly of crucial importance in the geographers' assessments of acclimatization. But as often as not the issue ultimately turned on the question of labour. Was the white race able to labour in the tropics? That was the question. And if not, then what policy should be adopted? Thus Henry O'Neill, British Consul in Mozambique and an RGS gold medallist, told the Edinburgh geographers in 1885 that coastal East Africa just 'will not admit of the labour of the white'. This was an issue of first importance, he considered, and not least because the laws of England no longer tolerated 'coercion or compulsory labour in any shape or degree'.[57] In the same year the Scottish geographers also learned, courtesy of a certain Dr Fisher's work, that tropical Africa's climate was 'decidedly unsuitable for Europeans' and consequently that 'agriculture or other plantation work can only be done by Negroes or other natives.'[58] Eleven years later the London geographers heard the same thing from Graf von Pfeil: 'Manual labour cannot be carried on [in tropical Africa] to any considerable extent by white inhabitants.'[59] And so given this sad state of affairs Sir Harry Johnston acknowledged that the trick was to find out 'how a limited number of Europeans may rule the tropics...how, without unreasonable loss of life, our fellow-countrymen can govern tropical regions'.[60] In 1947 students of climatology were still learning from Austin Miller's textbook that:

India, with its excessive heat and moisture from the tropical monsoon, which is one of the danger-points in the British Empire, because it cannot be settled by Europeans ... must be ruled by a transitory autocracy of British officials whose real home is elsewhere.[61]

[55] Ravenstein, 'Lands of the globe still available', 1891.
[56] White, 'On the comparative value of African lands', 1891, p. 192.
[57] O'Neill, 'East Africa, between the Zambesi and the Rovuma rivers', 1885, p. 348.
[58] Anon., 'German colonisation in tropical Africa', 1885, p. 263.
[59] Von Pfeil, 'On tropical Africa in relation to white races', 1896, p. 542.
[60] Johnston, Discussion, *Report of the Sixth International Geographical Congress*, 1896.
[61] Miller, *Climatology*, 1947, p. 3.

As late as 1951 readers of *Geography in the Twentieth Century* heard from Karl Pelzer that the 'main problem of white settlement in the tropics is that of acclimatization, and closely related to this is the question of whether white settlers are able to perform manual labour in the tropics.'[62]

Among geographers, then, the medical queries about acclimatization were typically translated into imperial imperatives about white labour in the tropics. But what gave particular bite to the anti-acclimatization crusade, I believe, was again the deployment of moralistic talk. The influence of the moral economy of climate was not restricted to its role in the construction of race character; it also acted with relentless efficiency on trans-climatic migrants.

American treatments of the subject in the early decades of the twentieth century will serve to illustrate this claim. Huntington understandably provides our first port of call. Writing in 1914 for the *Journal of Race Development*, he spoke of the tropical inertia that afflicted those who migrated to the tropics. Just what was 'tropical inertia'? It was essentially moral degradation as manifest in a lack of will power, a lack of industry, 'irascible temper', drunkenness and sexual indulgence.[63] Nor was Huntington alone in such judgements, however much subsequent geographers have tried to portray him as marginal and atypical. For one thing Arthur Balfour, Director of the London School of Tropical Medicine from 1923 until 1931, used Huntington's research to support his judgements about degeneration and tropical climate. Besides, a few years earlier Ellen Churchill Semple had warned of the 'derangements in the physiological functions of heart, liver, kidneys and organs of reproduction' because they induced 'intense enervation' in white settlers in the tropics. The consequences were truly far-reaching. 'The conquering white race of the Temperate Zone is to be excluded by adverse climatic conditions from the productive but undeveloped Tropics, unless it consent to hybridization' – presumably a cost too great to bear.[64] And then in the *Geographical Review* for 1926, Glenn Trewartha took it upon himself to bring his colleagues up to date on recent medical work on the acclimatization question.[65] Noting again that the 'European cannot carry on sustained heavy muscular labor in the wet tropics' and that 'the brown man is superior to the white in his economy of sweating', Trewartha went on to speak of the impact of a tropical regime on the nervous system. The terrible nervous exhaustion of the condition known as neurasthenia was certainly a direct effect of climate; but just as significant were the indirect effects. The moral topography of the white tropical experience was summarized thus:

[62] Pelzer, 'Geography and the Tropics', 1951, p. 330.
[63] Huntington, 'The adaptability of the white man', 1914, pp. 199, 211.
[64] Semple, *Influences of Geographic Environment*, 1911, pp. 626–8.
[65] Among the sources he reviewed were Balfour, 'Sojourners', 1923; Balfour, 'Problems of acclimatisation', 1923; Balfour and Henry Scott, *Health Problems of the Empire*, 1924; Eijkman, 'Some questions concerning the influence of tropical climate on man', 1924; Charles, 'Neurasthenia', 1913; Spinden, 'Civilization', 1922–3.

[the] tendency towards excessive use of intoxicating liquor, altered social state, close association with so-called inferior races, with the temptation to sexual indulgence which this situation makes possible, and the difficulty of obtaining a correct and balanced diet make normal healthy living among whites in the tropics a difficult problem.[66]

Similar judgments had been issued a few years earlier on the climate of Liberia when Emory Ross had dilated on the 'nervous strain of the tropics': 'The odors, the mists, the sights, the sounds get on the nerves; the heavy, drooping, silent, impenetrable green forest everywhere shuts one in like a smothering grave; the mind grows sick, and the body follows. For these reasons, largely mental, no one should stay on the West coast longer than eighteen months at a time.' All of these judgements pointed to one inevitable conclusion: 'acclimatization at present is all but impossible.'[67]

The neurasthenia of which these writers spoke, and which supposedly scotched all hopes of acclimatization, however, turns out to have been a rather flexible piece of medical nomenclature. The term had begun life back in the 1870s to describe the condition of nervous exhaustion brought on by modern urbanization and industrialization. Originally identified in this context by George M. Beard, its application to the tropics was largely courtesy of Charles Woodruff author in 1905 of *The Effects of Tropical Light on White Men*.[68] Woodruff had isolated what he termed actinic rays which were supposedly dangerous to fair-skinned Europeans. Exposure to these rays brought such perils as 'tropical inertia', 'tropical amnesia' and the condition that had long been described as 'Burma head' – a rag-bag assortment of ailments subsumed under the label 'tropical neurasthenia'. Soon the term had found its way into the conventional medical lexicon and generated a considerable literature. But it was an exceedingly flexible concept as Dane Kennedy has recently pointed out:

> Studies of the disorder described a bewildering range of symptoms: fatigue, irritation, loss of concentration, loss of memory, hypochondria, loss of appetite, diarrhoea and digestive disorders, insomnia, headaches, depression, palpitations, ulcers, alcoholism, anemia, sexual profligacy, sexual debility, premature and prolonged menstruation, insanity, and

[66] Trewartha, 'Recent thought on the problem', 1926, pp. 473, 472.

[67] Ross, 'The climate of Liberia', 1919, p. 402; Ross of course repeated the now standard axiom that 'in the humid tropics the white man cannot sustain manual labour', p. 400. Much earlier there had been considerable debate about the acclimatization of American ex-slaves and free blacks in Liberia. See Kass, 'Dr. Hodgkin, Dr. Delany, and the "Return to Africa" ', 1983. It was on account of 'the inertia which came over white people living in an isolated community in the tropics' that Swayne recommended the establishment of a hill station in British Honduras to which white settlers could resort. See Swayne, 'British Honduras', 1917, p. 176. See also Osborne, *The Société Zoologique*, 1987.

[68] Woodruff, *The Effects of Tropical Light*, 1905.

suicide. What did this miscellany of afflictions share apart from an intangibility that placed it beyond the grasp of empirical investigation? Tropical neurasthenia, for all its aura of medical certitude, was exceedingly nebulous, a convenient repository for whatever bundle of obscure and often value-laden complaints otherwise eluded classification and explanation. It was precisely this feature of the diagnosis that made it prone to climatic interpretation.[69]

Given these neurasthenic ailments it is hardly surprising that Woodruff would soon produce a text on the *Expansion of Races* (1909) in which standard environmental determinism was integrated with Darwinian vocabulary to produce the paradoxical conclusion that, as Kennedy puts it, 'natural laws drove the white race to control, but prevented them from populating the tropics'.[70]

These discussions of acclimatization by geographers reveal just how integral moral evaluations of the tropical world were. Indeed it became commonplace to actually build a moralistic component into the very definition of acclimatization, that is, to insist that successful acclimatization had to incorporate the maintenance of assumed white moral excellence. Robert DeCourcy Ward, for example, himself a leading light in the Boston Immigration Restriction League around the turn of the century, and a distinguished climatologist at Harvard, believed that acclimatization 'in the full sense of having white men and women living for successive generations in the tropics, and reproducing their kind without physical, mental, and moral degeneration – i.e., colonization in the true sense – is impossible'.[71]

None of this should be taken to imply, of course, that the pro-acclimatization position found no representation within the geographical literature. In 1898 a certain Luigi Westenra Sambon, a medical practitioner from Rome who was to become a lecturer in the London School of Tropical Medicine and an advocate of the germ theory, addressed the RGS on the subject and repeated the arguments he had advanced the previous year in the *British Medical Journal*.[72] One by one Sambon picked up the superstitions about the tropics that had dominated scientific discussion about acclimatization for too

[69] Kennedy, 'The Perils of the Midday Sun', 1990, p. 123.

[70] Ibid., p. 124. Kennedy also has a valuable discussion of Dr Aldo Castellani's discussion of neurasthenia in his *Climate and Acclimatization*, 1931.

[71] Ward, 'Can the white race become acclimatized in the tropics'? 1931, p. 157. The previous year Ward had resorted to the new science of genetics to oppose the immigration of certain racial groups and to argue that no process of Americanization could make certain races 'true to the American type'. Ward, 'Fallacies of the melting pot idea', 1930, p. 231. That the question of climate's influence on human culture was never far from his mind is evident from his discussion of Köppen's climatic classification scheme in which he included some reflections on Köppen's comments on climate and civilization. Ward, 'A new classification of climates', 1919.

[72] Sambon, 'Remarks on the possibility', 1897.

long, and relegated them to the slag heap of scientific folly. He exposed many
of the problems in comparing the death rate in England with mortality in
India, not the least of which was the fact that such general comparisons
ignored the sub-regional geography of demographic statistics. And on the
labour question he did not mince his words: 'The truth about the labour
problem is that white men will not work; they go with a fixed resolve to
gain wealth by coloured labour, which only too often is another word for
slave-labour.'[73] Needless to say his viewpoint did not go down well. Harry
Johnston, in a characteristically anecdotal mode, reminisced on his experience
of the atrophy of Britons born and brought up in India; J. A. Baines spoke
about the degeneracy of white children in the tropics; and Robert Felkin
found Sambon's arguments about rapid acclimatization frankly dangerous.[74]
For all that, J. W. Gregory could, a quarter of a century later, report that
Sambon's remarkable paper had been endorsed by Sir Patrick Manson and
was 'supported by the general trend of medical opinion during the past
seventeen years'. Earlier prejudice about tropical climates, he announced,
was without foundation.[75]

And yet, even among pro-acclimatizationists, climate's moral economy could
still surface. Gregory's own 1924 paper certainly did not refrain from racial
stereotyping: the 'affectionate, emotional Negro, the docile, diligent Asiatic,
and the inventive, enterprising European' all made their appearance. Clearly
there was still, to Gregory, a regional geography of ethnic character. Besides,
there were immediate racial policies to be derived from such geographical
realities. 'Close association' of the races was no success because inter-marriage
and inferior offspring were the inevitable outcome; co-residence had been no
more successful; only separate existence remained as practical politics.[76]

Consider too in this regard the judgements of Robert Felkin, the Edinburgh expert on tropical diseases who lectured on 'climatology and the
diseases of the tropics' at Minto House School of Medicine and regularly
authored articles on his African travel experiences for the *Scottish Geographical Magazine*.[77] Felkin was a fellow of both the RSGS and RGS and
clearly saw it as duty to keep the geographers informed about the medical

[73] Sambon, 'Acclimatization of Europeans', 1898, p. 594. Sambon, however, was later
to find Woodruff's theory about actinic rays convincing and actually produced a fabric
supposedly impervious to them. See Sambon, 'Tropical Clothing', 1907. This is discussed
in Kennedy, 'Perils of the Midday Sun', 1990, pp. 122–3.

[74] Discussion remarks, *Geographical Journal*, 1898.

[75] Gregory, 'Inter-racial problems', 1924, p. 270.

[76] Ibid., p. 281. The combination of views that Gregory held – that acclimatization
and white labour in the tropics were certainly possible, and that races must develop in an
apartheid fashion – meant that he was enthusiastic about the future possibilities that
Australia held for white Europeans.

[77] Felkin's course was reported in the Geographical Notes section of the *Scottish
Geographical Magazine*, 1886, p. 124. He was the author of 'The Egyptian Sudan', 1885;
'Uganda', 1886; and *On the Geographical Distribution*, 1889.

aspects of acclimatization. His own position, spelled out at the British Association, represented a half-hearted endorsement of acclimatization. What it amounted to was that acclimatization was just about possible over several generations, but that for the meantime European colonization needed to be restricted to upland areas. Indeed he made proposals for a whole scheme of rapid transportation from the unhealthy coastal zone to temporary inland receiving stations enabling emigrants to escape the pernicious effects of the coast within a single day of arriving in Africa. Indeed he observed that tropical uplands were better even for indigenous peoples than the swampy coastal belt. The inhabitants of coastal Bengal he thus stigmatized as 'timid, servile, and superstitious', while those living on the higher table land of Mysore were 'brave and courteous'.[78]

Finally, those who urged the possibility of acclimatization frequently presented their advice on how to survive in the tropics in the moralistic language of prudence, abstemiousness, circumspection, and hygienic discipline. Here again was a moral economy of climate – not in this case that climate conditioned standards of behaviour, but rather required them. The sermonic tincture of much of this 'travel advice' literature would certainly merit closer inspection. All I have space to say here is that earlier medical works on how to survive conditions in tropical India included prophylactic advice on exercise, bathing, alcohol consumption and the conduct of the 'passions'.[79] As H. M. Stanley concluded, speaking of a different continent and to a different generation, and approvingly referring to this earlier medical literature:

> with good food, with work to amuse or interest the mind, with due means to check the influences resulting from such a total change in life as the tropic climate demands, and with proper moral conduct, I maintain ... the European [will be able] to thrive in a hot climate as well as in any climate under the sun.[80]

CONCLUSION

The burden of what I have been trying to argue in the preceding pages can be reduced to two fundamental issues. The first concerns the project of doing this history of geography. If my suspicions are well founded, then it is impossible to extract the substance or essence of geography from the

[78] Felkin, 'Tropical highlands', 1892, p. 162. Felkin had also announced his findings in 'Can Europeans become acclimatised?', 1886, and 'On acclimatisation', 1891. These articles were the written version of presentations he had made to the British Association for the Advancement of Science.

[79] Johnson, *The Influence of Tropical Climates*, 1821; Martin, *The Influence of Tropical Climates*, 1856.

[80] Stanley, *The Congo and the Founding of the Free State*, 1885, vol. 2, p. 294.

broader social, religious and ideological networks in which it was transacted. The very stuff of geography, its language, its methods, its theories, and its practices were constituted in the midst of the messy contingencies of history. Imperialism no more provides the context for geography, than geography provides the context for imperialism. It is, rather, a question of reciprocal constitution.

Secondly, moral climatology was clearly able to set crucial boundaries between civilization and barbarism, between the white and black races, and of course between virtue and vice. By deploying the legitimating discourse of scientific climatology it located the imperial drama within what Kennedy describes as 'a world unalterably bound by the imperatives of race, evolution, and climate'.[81] As I see it this whole project of rooting human values, potential, morals, and worth in regional climatic circumstance, or insisting that the exigencies of climate contained compelling behavioural norms that would be transgressed at one's peril – the naturalization of human values as Bob Young refers to it – is a deeply scientistic move in which the 'non-reversible flow of diagnostic knowledge' is dramatically revealed.[82] The discourse of climate's moral economy thus flourished because it facilitated the elaboration of a moral topography that was crucial to the project of the racial ideologue,[83] and because it employed scientific language to diagnose and treat the sicknesses of a colonial regime.

[81] Kennedy, 'The Perils', 1990, p. 137.
[82] Bann, *The Inventions of History*, 1990, p. 16.
[83] The implications of the racist debate for moral philosophy are the subject of an arresting paragraph in Taylor, *Sources of the Self*, 1989, p. 8.

8

Voyeurs of Imperialism:
The National Geographic Magazine before World War II

Tamar Y. Rothenberg

National Geographics always gave us the giggles. We would look through the magazines in the school library, and stamped across the breasts was 'Property of P. S. 156, Queens – Joseph Baron, Principal'. The principal was sort of balding and serious-looking, and the idea of him going through all the magazines so he could stamp the breasts as his was hysterical. The idea, of course, was to cover up their nakedness, but we thought he was stamping them his property.

Judy Mann Rothenberg[1]

My own favorite, for what it's worth, was a photograph of an exceptionally nubile, perhaps Nubian, young woman who was identified as a Sudanese slave girl, 'the property of an Arab merchant in Mocha', that appeared with a splendid article, 'Pearl Fishing in the Red Sea', in 1937. I looked her up in a dusty bound volume of Geographics not long ago. She was still there, head erect, hands on hips, shoulders thrown back in proud servility, the stuff of multidimensional sexual fantasy beside whom the girls in *Playboy* are poor plastic things indeed.

Tom Buckley[2]

The National Geographic Magazine holds an almost mythic place in American society. With its easy readability, pretty pictures, high educational purpose and aura of unquestioned respectability, *National Geographic* has been welcomed into homes, schools and libraries for decades. Approximately 50 million people

[1] The author's mother, November 1989.
[2] Buckley, 'With the National Geographic', 1970, p. 19.

read each monthly issue.[3] As Howard Abramson, author of the first critical book on the National Geographic Society, puts it, 'it is always perceived as a nice homespun organization that publishes that distinctive yellow-bordered magazine that adorns doctors' offices everywhere and features those trademark harmless photographs of all those memorable brown breasts.'[4]

That they are memorable indicates both their erotic value and fetishized objectification; it is not the women who stand out, only their breasts. The idea that the photographs are 'harmless', however, removes any possible taint of pornography; it reinforces the message that these pictures are not crude and tasteless, but naive and natural.[5]

Much of the magazine's reputation entails just that seemingly odd juxtaposition of stodgy respectablity and half-naked women. Before *Playboy* appeared in the 1950s offering over-the-counter boobs, *National Geographic* served as the accessible and acceptable format for breast ogling. Humorous jabs at the magazine suggest that for some, it served as 'the equivalent of an anthology of breasts'.[6] When *National Geographic* published its first photos of women 'in their native dress' at the turn of the century, American women were still wearing full length, long sleeved, and often high-necked dresses. Gilbert H. Grosvenor, editor of the magazine from 1899 to 1954, refrained from drinking and smoking, and kept the magazine's advertisements similarly in line. 'So unquestioningly genteel was the magazine, and so patently pure its anthropological interest, that even at a time when nice people called a leg a limb it never occurred to anyone to accuse Grosvenor of impropriety.'[7]

National Geographic shared with its audience – whom Grosvenor depicted as 'the lonely forest ranger, the clerk at his desk, the plumber, the teacher, the eight-year-old boy or the octegenarian – a range of conventions.[8] Specifically important to *National Geographic* was its status as a scientific society and the belief in science as an objective quest for pure information about the world. Other conventions took the form of shared, familiar narratives

---

[3] Abramson, *National Geographic*, 1987, p. 5.

[4] Ibid., pp. 4–5. A second book, published after this chapter was written, presents a critical analysis of the content of the magazine from 1950 to the present with particular emphasis on the photographs: Lutz and Collins, *Reading National Geographic*, 1993.

[5] The distinction between erotica and pornography is by no means clear. Kappeler, *The Pornography of Representation*, 1986, p. 1, calls it 'notorious that there exists no clear-cut definition of pornography; instead, different discussions identify different characteristic elements as their basis for a discussion of the phenomenon.' Burt, *Erotic Art*, 1989, p. 32, comments that 'virtually every entry' in his bibliography has its own definition of erotica, including the differentiation from pornography.

[6] Alloula, *The Colonial Harem*, 1986, p. 105. While Alloula is refering to the colonial Algerian postcards in his book, the phrase seems applicable to *National Geographic*. The magazine acknowledged its reputation in its anniversary issue: Blount, Jr, 'Spoofing the Geographic', 1988, pp. 352–7.

[7] Buckley, 'With the National Geographic', 1970, p. 19.

[8] Quoted in Pauly, 'The world and all that is in it', 1979, p. 530.

such as the heroic epic of the explorer or the American myth of manifest destiny.

Racism must also be seen as a convention. It was race that distinguished the women who could be photographed topless from those who could not. Brown women were women; that was why they had breasts and that is why the pictures have been fetishized as they have.[9] But they were a different kind of woman. The articulation of gender differentiated by 'race' or class status has a long tradition in western thought. Elizabeth Spelman finds precedents in Plato and Aristotle, noting that Aristotle pointedly distinguished women from slaves, even though many of the slaves were female; gender identity came from the combination of sexual identity and 'race' identity. For Aristotle, 'there were at least two different genders females could become, depending on whether their function was to be a "woman" or to be a "slave" ... a difference in "race identity" has to mean also a difference in gender identity.'[10] As the *Geographic* itself might have said, there were distinctive 'types' of women, women who were so different from the American woman – meaning white, preferably Protestant, and at least middle-class – that they could comfortably be placed in another, inferior, category. The contrast between the restrained, civilized American woman and the uninhibited, uncivilized woman who bared her breasts 'without the slightest suspicion in her manner of any impropriety',[11] made revealing pictures of these 'other' women easier for the *Geographic* and its audience to justify.

Racism fits another narrative convention of which *National Geographic* has been a major conduit in the twentieth century – what Tiffany and Adams call the 'romance of the wild woman'.[12] This mythic story centres on the equation of primordial nature with wild woman, creating and sustaining analogies between the temptations of unknown, unexplored land and unknown, unexplored woman. Nature and woman, both constructed by men as the 'other', elicit a desire laden with the urge for conquest and possession.[13] In this male tale, mysterious females and remote lands are alluring and sexual, offering men riches and pleasures but also unpredictable dangers. Men who are brave, strong and smart enough to tame and control them can remove much of the threat and extract much of their seductive wealth. Race is a critical element of this story.[14] The 'romance of the wild woman' makes non-European women from unknown territory emblematic of the mystery and

[9] The study of the fetishization of women's breasts/bodies/body parts is itself a massive project that will not even be attempted here.

[10] Spelman, *Inessential Woman*, 1988, pp. 168–9.

[11] Bailey, 'A new Peruvian route', 1906, pp. 445–6.

[12] Tiffany and Adams, *The Wild Women*, 1985.

[13] See also Kolodny, *The Lay of the Land*, 1975; Merchant, *The Death of Nature*, 1980. Halpin, 'Scientific objectivity', 1989, pp. 285–94, and Stepan, 'Race and gender', 1986, pp. 261–77, emphasize race as well as gender and nature in formulations of the 'other'.

[14] On representations of race and sexuality, see for example Gilman, 'Black bodies, white bodies', 1985, pp. 204–42; De Groot, ' "Sex" and "race" ', 1989.

potential riches of remote lands. The reader's eyes perceive a young African woman, clothed in little more than beads, smiling at the camera; the mind interperets: Africa.[15] *National Geographic* bought the romance of the wild woman wholesale and sold it at a hefty profit to millions of Americans.

The cornerstone of *National Geographic*'s appeal has been its photography. Like *National Geographic*, photography itself brought together art and science in a package designed for the education and entertainment of a particular audience. Photography – or to be more fair and accurate, photographers – continued many of the conventions of representation already established in western visual art.[16]

Americans were already familiar with the well-formed body as art object. The one place in American culture where nudity was acceptable was in the art museum. The nude, as opposed to the naked, says art historian Kenneth Clark, is a classical (Greek) art form that embodies the search for the ideal. Not only do we have a 'distinctive desire ... to perfect', according to Clark, but human nature ordains 'the desire to grasp and be united with another human body'.[17] Consequently, 'no nude, however abstract, should fail to arouse in the spectator some vestige of erotic feeling ... and if it does not do so, it is bad art and false morals.'[18] One of the threads tying together the great artists of the female nude is 'the belief that the female body was the token of a harmonious natural order'.[19] It is but a small step from the graceful nudes of Renoir – one of Clark's great artists – to the graceful, posed, demi-nudes of Sarawak. Clark's 'classic' of classical art reiterates long-held views likely shared by *National Geographic* photographers, editors and readers alike. Properly executed, such photographs emulate Clark's 'good art', striving to gather together qualities of eros, beauty and 'type', and fostering (a bit of) desire through one-way visual connections. And if 'classical art' considers a European female body symbolic of harmonious nature, how much more may African, Asian or Amazonian female bodies be deemed 'closer to nature' by virtue of their embodied cultures or dark skin tone. Brown people of every hue in *National Geographic* were described as 'bronze', a material often used for statues. A full-page photo of an Eskimo woman in one issue is 'A Study in Bronze'. Forty-six pages later is another full-page

---

[15] For more on feminine icons and allegories, especially woman as a national symbol, see Ryan, *Women in Public*, 1990; Schiebinger, 'Feminine icons', 1988, pp. 661–91; Warner, *Monuments and Maidens*, 1985.

[16] For example, see Cagan, *Photography's contribution to the 'Western' vision of the colonized 'other'*, 1990; Graham-Brown, *Images of Women*, 1988.

[17] Clark, *The Nude*, 1956, pp. 33, 29.

[18] Ibid., p. 29. There is a great deal of feminist, psychoanalytic, literary and postmodern analysis regarding the spectator, the look, and the imaged object, the general gist being that images of women are made by (heterosexual) men for (heterosexual) men. See for example, Kaplan, 'Is the gaze male?', 1983, pp. 309–27. Kappeler, *The Pornography of Representation*, 1986, presents a materialist analysis of this construction of representation.

[19] Clark, *The Nude*, 1956, p. 232.

portait photo, labeled 'Bronze Beauty – Trinidad'.[20] The brief captions make a point of emphasizing skin colour.

The reference to classical art forms in ethnographic photography is even more striking in a browser's comparison of a photograph of 'An [almost naked] Australian Aboriginal with sea hawk's eggs' with a photograph of an ancient Greek statue. After seeing so many ideal male physiques either completely nude from the back or with loincloths from the front, it is a bit startling to see, on another page, a photograph of a well-built male with full frontal nudity – a statue of Eros by Praxiteles. This image emphasizes the fact that the handsome young Australian in the photo looks like a statue himself, centred in the photo, standing on a 'pedestal' of rock, silhouetted against the sky and holding the eggs in his hands.[21]

Many of the photographs in the first few decades of the magazine owe a great debt to the European orientalists of the nineteenth century; the overt eroticization of women of non-European cultures and ethnicities was as effective in twentieth-century imperialist America as in nineteenth-century imperialist France and Britain.[22] John Berger has suggested that photography took up the oil painting's tradition of visual representation, a way of seeing intrinsically linked to the development of capitalism and the desire for tangible things that money could buy.[23] Or as Alan Sekula puts it,

> Photography is haunted by two chattering ghosts: that of bourgeois science and that of bourgeois art: The first goes on about the truth of

[20] *National Geographic Magazine*, 1907, pp. 464, 490.

[21] Adams, 'Australia's wild wonderland', *National Geographic Magazine*, 1924, p. 339; the statue of Eros is in *National Geographic Magazine*, 1937, p. 351. Another good example is a full-page photo in an article by Grosvenor on 'The Hawaiian Islands', 1924, p. 159. The scenic picture, which focuses on the nearly-nude, muscular man posing in the centre, is captioned 'A Hawaiian Landscape. In the Hawaiian Islands to-day only fishermen when in action wear this abbreviated costume.' (A dated photo becomes a good excuse for showing some skin in an 'artistic' format.)

[22] See De Groot, ' "Sex" and "race" ', 1989; Graham-Brown, *Images of Women*, 1988.

[23] Berger, *Ways of Seeing*, 1972. The tradition, using the ability of oil paint to show detail and texture, focused largely on depictions of wealthy men and the things they owned; fine clothes, luscious food, elegant homes, *objets d'art*, livestock, family members – especially wives and daughters. '[P]ainting itself had to be able to demonstrate the desirability of what money could buy. And the visual desirability of what can be bought lies in its tangibility, in how it will reward the touch, the hand, of the owner' (p. 90). Berger's analysis features paintings explicitly related to European exploration and colonialism, including one by De Witte in which a kneeling African slave holds up an oil painting – of a castle above a West African slave trading centre – to his European master (p. 95). Berger also discusses how oil paintings tended to depict women, allegorical/religious figures in particular (he focuses on Mary Magdelene), as 'takeable and desirable' (p. 92). Kappeler, whose analysis is informed by Berger's work, picks up on his ideas of representation to construct her understanding of the 'pornography of representation'; 'the behaviour comes first, the desire to represent it after' (Kappeler, *The Pornography of Representation*, p. 61–2).

appearances, about the world reduced to a positive ensemble of facts, to a constellation of knowable and possessable *objects*. The second spectre has the historical mission of apologizing for and redeeming the atrocities committed by the subservient – and more than spectral – hand of science.[24]

Photography gave visual representation a distinctive realism that paintings could not produce, using the camera as technological and scientifically 'neutral' mediator between photographer and subject.[25] 'The camera cannot be deceived ... [therefore, it has] enormous scientific value', explained wildlife photographer Martin Johnson in 1923.[26]

The half-naked women of *National Geographic* most likely did walk around without covering their breasts; the realism of photography and the scientific mission of *National Geographic* caused few to doubt that the pictures were anything but honest and educational. *National Geographic*, however, has specialised in selective truths, including omitting mention of black Americans in extensive articles on US states and regions, ignoring the various ill-effects of Fascism in Germany and Italy in the 1930s, and doctoring photographs.[27]

The *National Geographic Magazine* of the late twentieth century is more attentive than its Victorian-mannered predecessor to world problems ranging from pollution and pesticides to apartheid, urban poverty and nationalist separatist movements, a shift that caused controversy around 1977.[28] It still features articles on the barely-clad peoples of the world, although the authors of such stories tend to be anthropologists rather than tourists or white administrators; naked white Europeans can also be seen – from the back – enjoying a nudist beach.[29] Even today *National Geographic* retains its early reputation for 'all those memorable brown breasts' although nakedness is somewhat more accessible today, even in a relatively puritanical America. To understand how 'those trademark ... photographs' became 'trademarks' requires us to focus on *National Geographic Magazine* before World War II.

[24] Sekula, 'Traffic in photographs', 1984, p. 78; quoted in Graham-Brown, *Images of Women*, p. 1.

[25] Cagan, *Photography's contribution*, 1990.

[26] Haraway, *Primate Visions*, 1989, p. 44.

[27] Cagan, *Photography's contribution*, 1990; Haraway, *Primate Visions*, 1989; Abramson, *National Geographic*, 1987; Buckley, 'With the National Geographic', 1970. The history of American media is rife with the presentation of selected and retouched facts, but *National Geographic*'s purported scientific mission to show 'the world and all that is in it' makes its obvious omissions all the more flagrant.

[28] Bryan, *The National Geographic Society*, 1987, pp. 381–99.

[29] Photograph by Curry for Danforth, 'Yugoslavia', *National Geographic Magazine*, 1990, p. 113.

IMPERIALIST MUSEUM OF NATURAL HISTORY

In what some might call a fortunate accident of fate, or others attribute to the standard structure of the ruling class, Gilbert H. Grosvenor was second cousin to William H. Taft, US President and Chief Justice. In 1905, Taft, then Secretary of War, informed his cousin of the impending release of the first 'Census Report of the Philippines', to be filled with photos. 'If Grosvenor would inform Society members [subscribers] of this interesting publication,' Taft told the young editor, 'the National Geographic Society could help both the government and the people of the Philippines.'[30] Taft wanted to trumpet the economic charms of the newly acquired territory and to lure American business with all its trappings to the Philippines. Although Grosvenor was more excited by the treasure of over a hundred ready-to-print photographs, he was as patriotically imperialist as could be expected from a man of his class. When the magazine published the photographs, the accompanying text evaluated and generally lauded the country's natural resources, a common approach in *National Geographic* at the time.[31]

Natural resources here included the native human population. By the nineteenth century, western science and culture conceptualized nature as set apart from the humans perceiving it.[32] Nature was equated with wilderness, by definition uncontrolled by 'man', and like every other wild thing it had the potential to be tamed. Those people who lived in the wild had not tamed nature but were part of it. It remained for white people to tame nature – and the people living within it as well.

Isolated for the purpose of study, elements of nature were classified and arranged to fit within the appropriate taxonomic hierarchy. Like a museum of natural history with exhibition rooms dedicated to educationally enshrined minerals, stuffed animals and grass-skirted mannikins, *National Geographic* merged enthnology with zoology and botany. All natural elements of note were to be explored, studied and preserved for posterity – at least in print or photographs. All ethnic peoples were defined by 'type': a Hungarian type, a Negrito type, a Zulu type. On one page the reader would find a photo of a 'Typical Eskimo Dog', on the following page a 'Typical Face of Eskimo Woman'.[33]

---

[30] Bryan, *The National Geographic Society*, 1987, p. 94.

[31] Grosvenor, 'A revelation of the Filipinos', *National Geographic Magazine*, 1905, pp. 139–92.

[32] See for example Smith, *Uneven Development*, 1991, especially chapters 1 and 2; Frykman and Löfgren, *Culture Builders*, 1987, especially chapter 2.

[33] Atkins, 'Arctic expeditions commanded by Americans', *National Geographic Magazine*, 1907, pp. 462, 464. Ethnographic taxonomy was a mainstay of late nineteenth-century scientific and pseudo-scientific thought. Photography, the scientific method of representation, was put to use in anthropometric 'mug shots' by physical anthropologists as well as by travel writers. Americans, particularly white American women, were also subjected to

Natives could be portrayed as one might a strain of plant or species of bird. Reporting on his travels through central Africa, E. Torday noted:

> In the north, the women are not very good-looking, but farther to the south, where the males approximate a feminine type, there are real beauties among the softer sex. As the traveler goes eastward he observes that the features of the natives become more refined. In some types very few of the characteristics usually attributed to negroes are found. The black color, so common on the west coast, is replaced by a soft chocolate-brown, which in certain individuals merges into dark yellow ... All blacks are born traders, but the female of the species is more clever than the male. [34]

Objectification of native peoples was easy if they were considered a part of nature, and they were. 'The Shillook, tall, lithe, and usually wearing only a string of beads, frequently not even that, is a true child of nature', wrote Herbert L. Bridgman in 'The new British Empire of the Sudan'. 'With head plastered with red mud and body with wood ashes, he toys with his murderous spear, surveying the newcomer, one is inclined to treat him with every outward appearance of respect.' [35]

Civilized people wore layers of clothing and lived and worked in structures more than one story off the ground; they created layers of distance between themselves and nature. Natives of tropical lands – referred to as 'wild', 'savage', and 'children of nature' far more frequently than the well-bundled natives of colder regions – walked around '*au natural*', or nearly so. Their humble abodes were generally one-room huts made from a combination of reeds, leaves or twigs, and mud. While they were sheltered, they were 'in' nature, as might a bee or beaver be. They hunted and gathered their food. They had no knowledge of 'civilization', or mechanized weapons; their spears could kill, but they were toys compared with the guns of white men.

'As wild as the world's wildest', reads the caption of a photo showing two completely naked men, backs to the camera, talking to each other on a western boat deck. The sub-caption continues: 'These inhabitants on a small island on the north-east coast of Western Australia live entirely in the open, build no huts, and when first approached by white men dashed into the scrub, later appearing armed with spears.' [36] One story speaks of the Buduma, who 'live in villages of carelessly constructed reed huts and have little culture

---

typing. Representation of 'types' reflected the quest for the 'ideal' long expressed by Euro–American artists. See Gould, *The Mismeasure of Man*, 1981; Graham-Brown, *Images of Women*, 1988, pp. 48–54; Banta, *Imaging American Women*, 1987.

[34] Torday, 'Curious and characteristic customs', *National Geographic Magazine*, 1919, pp. 345, 347, 362.

[35] Bridgman, 'The new British Empire of the Sudan', ibid., 1906, p. 255.

[36] Adams, 'Australia's wild wonderland', ibid., 1924, p. 354.

worth mentioning'.[37] The caption of a photo of 'Fijians doing a club dance' goes on to say that 'these most cruel and barbarous of the South Pacific islanders show a human love for song, dance, and storytelling.'[38]

In the numerous lands where the US or western European countries had vested economic interests, articles catalogued the region's resources, from climate and port locations to the average number of dates produced by a single tree. The inhabitants, as much a part of nature as a tree and just as cataloguable, were evaluated in terms of their capacity for labour. A 1910 article on 'Guatemala, the country of the future' featured a picturesque, unposed photo of women in a village square carrying large vessels on their heads. Beneath the caption – 'Indian women of Cantel coming from the fountain' – lurks the sub-caption: 'These women make excellent workers in the cotton factory.'[39]

In 1908 the magazine published a report by Beatrice Grimshaw, 'an enterprising young English woman who recently passed several years in Fiji and the New Hebrides in search of good opportunities for investment'.[40] She finds the land quite fertile for vanilla beans, maize, coffee, millet and copra, but the natives bad labour prospects for the present. The New Hebridean:

> is supposed to be, and is, treacherous, murderous, and vindictive. He is to the full as sensual and indolent as the Eastern Islander and lacks almost every virtue possessed by the latter. He is almost inconceivably clumsy and stupid in a house or on a plantation; almost devoid of gratitude, almost bare of natural affection, ready to avenge the smallest slight by a bloody murder, but too cowardly to meet an enemy face to face.[41]

Miss Grimshaw has high hopes for the future, however. She continues:

> Like the Fijians, who were at one time the fiercest and most brutal cannibals of the Pacific, and who are now a peaceful and respecting nation, worthy of the crown who owns them, the Tannese will in all probability 'train on' into a really fine race, as soon as they can be restrained from continuously murdering each other on the slightest provocation and induced to clean their houses and themselves and live decently and quietly.[42]

---

[37] Wilson, 'Three-wheeling through Africa', ibid., 1934, p. 73.
[38] Hildebrand, 'The geography of games', ibid., 1919, p. 97.
[39] Tisdel, 'Guatemala, the country of the future', ibid., 1910, p. 616.
[40] Grimshaw, 'In the savage South Seas', ibid., 1908, p. 1.
[41] Ibid., p. 14
[42] Ibid., p. 18

National Geographic openly admired the efforts and effects of colonialism. Under white domination everything was under control; nature was tamed, and resources, including native labour, were being mined with great efficiency in comparison with the prior lack of productiveness. The entire February 1925 issue was devoted to Felix and Porter Shay's journey across Africa. In central Africa they found that

> [t]his soil was black and rich and the natives lived easily. No one yet has devised a plan for making the native Africans work. They seem to wish for nothing that is not free and under their hands. They wear practically no clothing, live in grass and mud huts, and find amusement in having children, hunting, fishing, frolicking, singing, dancing, and decorating their bodies ... Meanwhile, the land and civilization languish. [43]

It was the white man's burden to teach the ignorant, childlike natives how to live and labour productively. While curious about the traditional ways of the native peoples, numerous authors extolled the virtues of 'civilization'. Reporting on Sumatra five years after the Shays' adventure was published, W. Robert Moore noted:

> Today, thanks to the efforts of the Dutch government and the missionaries, the trip to Toba Lake and its surrounding territory can be made in perfect safety. In the last 50 years the Bataks have undergone a great change. They are no longer hostile to the white man and have long since ceased the practice of the ceremonial eating (a fine distinction between cannibalism) of their elderly relatives and their enemies.

They are now a peaceful agricultural and pastoral people. [44] The French were complimented on their resorts and gardens in French Indochina, the Italians were admired for their cafes, railroads, and 'excellent highways' in Italian Libya. In British-ruled Sudan, 'further evidence of modern improvements is given by the policeman who, laying vigorously about himself with a whip, charges a crowd of a hundred ragged and dirty urchins crowding around the English ladies and blocking the way so that progress is almost impossible.' [45]

[43] Shay, 'Cairo to Cape Town, overland', *National Geographic Magazine*, 1925, pp. 141–2.

[44] Moore, 'Among the hill tribes of Sumatra', ibid., 1930, p. 207.

[45] Moore, 'Along the old Mandarin Road', 1931, p. 175; Adams, 'Cirenaica', 1930, pp. 689–726; Bridgman, 'The new British Empire', 1906, p. 252.

CHILDREN OF NATURE

Romanticization and exploration of native populations went hand in hand. Like nature itself, indigenous people were threatening until controlled. Firmly under control, the natives became quaint, anachronisms in their own time and place. Noting the colonizers' shift from gun to camera, Susan Sontag observes: 'When we are afraid, we shoot. But when we are nostalgic, we take pictures.'[46]

> The people inhabiting the settlements around Victoria Nyanza will be probably for a year or so still a source of amusement to the excursionists whom the Uganda railway will bring from the east coast of Africa to the Victoria Nyanza; for they will see before them coal-black, handsomely formed negroes and negresses without a shred of clothing, though with many ornaments in the way of hippopotamus teeth, bead necklaces, earrings, and leglets of brass. They are very picturesque as they strut about the streets in their innocent nudity decked with barbaric ornaments.[47]

The romantics of the nineteenth century, reacting to industrialization, deified nature. Nature was pure, unspoiled, the Garden of Eden. If economic development and colonization corrupted the purity of nature, it likewise corrupted the nature-people who lived within it. They in turn had to be romanticized:

> Their ideas in regard to propriety were satisfied by a loin-cloth, and several young women of modest mein and rather dignified presence stood and attempted to talk with us dressed in this fashion ... The Garden of Eden still lingers here. These Amazonian Eves have evidently never heard of The Fall.[48]

Of all the peoples deemed romantic by the *Geographic*, none were more so than the poor doomed Marquesan islanders of the South Pacific:

> Lacking the ambitions and desires which constitute such a large part of the mental make-up of civilised man, and free from any commercial or competitive strife, they simply failed to develop many unpleasant traits common to civilisation, and remained to a great degree good-natured, impulsive children in their temper and conduct.[49]

---

[46] Sontag, *On Photography*, 1977, quoted in Haraway, *Primate Visions*, 1989, p. 42.
[47] Johnston, 'Where Roosevelt Will Hunt', *National Geographic Magazine*, 1909, p. 233.
[48] Bailey, 'A new Peruvian route', ibid., 1906, pp. 445–6.
[49] Church, 'A vanishing people of the South Seas', ibid., 1919, p. 296.

But as the *National Geographic* records, the Marquesans were all but wiped out by colonization. One article relates how the happy natives were stricken by European diseases and their social innocence corrupted, while co-mingling between the whites and the natives irreversibly diluted the purity of the Marquesan race. Their story illustrated 'the danger of destroying the primitive customs and harmless occupations of pagan races simply because the white man knows that he can employ his own time better'. [50]

The October 1919 issue features a full-page photo portrait of a topless young woman sitting demurely against a blurred background. She holds a bouquet of flowers in her hand and a long necklace of shells is carefully draped over her breasts. The photograph is reminiscent of turn-of-the-century 'studio fantasies' of partially unclothed women. [51] In this case, the caption explains: 'A daughter of a dying race – Beautiful, luxuriant hair, fine eyes, perfect teeth, a slender, graceful form, a skin of velvet texture and unblemished figure – these are the attributes of the few Marquesannes who survive as worthy representatives of a people seared by the sins of the white man.' [52] Virtually in paradise, according to John W. Church, the life of a Marquesan girl was nigh perfect:

> I doubt seriously if a more carefree or contented maiden ever existed. Her domestic duties were light and agreeable. ... The making of tappa cloth was her only tedious occupation, and, as the girls gathered in groups and discussed matters of interest to the feminine mind while they worked, I doubt if it proved to be more onerous than the modern sewing circle. [53]

The Marquesanne's male counterpart, meanwhile, was 'a magnificent savage'. [54]

Innocence and purity were not the only attitudes encouraging whites to treat people of colour as children. Conquered native peoples also lacked authority, requiring the paternalistic guidance of their white caretakers. Accordingly, white colonizers were invariably pictured with native servants, treated as children, even pets: 'Migli was a companionable, good-natured little fellow, with velvety brown skin, a laughing face, and boyish figure – a constant stimulus to the good spirits of the party,' wrote Harrison W. Smith in 1919. [55]

The straightforward Shays appear to have enjoyed their relationship with the natives:

[50] Smith, 'Sarawak', ibid., 1919, p. 147.

[51] Graham-Brown, *Images of Women*, 1988, pp. 40–1.

[52] Church, 'A vanishing people of the South Seas', *National Geographic Magazine*, 1919, p. 276.

[53] Ibid., p. 289.

[54] Ibid., p. 285.

[55] Smith, 'Sarawak', *National Geographic Magazine*, 1919, p. 143.

We surely learned to like these black boys. To be afraid of them seemed absurd. We spoke to them and ordered them about as if they were seven-year-olds. They reacted dutifully to that treatment. They required a minimum of blame and a maximum of direction and instruction. Like all the savages whom we had met in Africa, these boys had no manual dexterity. They made a sorry job of trying to put up camp beds, chairs, and a camp table. They had to be instructed every time. Yet they all were eager to help fumble. There was no order or system to their minds.[56]

The Shays also recommend 'to travelers in Africa that they do not include black women on their safaris. They are the cause of much trouble and annoyance.' They get tired, they get sick and whine and 'los[e] [their] social instinct'.[57] From today's perspective, the Shays' irritated description of the women's behaviour hints intriguingly at specifically gendered and deliberate ways of dealing with uncustomary labour demands.

'THAT OLD-TIME NEGRO DEFERENCE': RACISM

Imperialism would never have worked without racism. Whether crudely exploitative, gently paternalistic or just plain nasty, racism provided the base logic for whites controlling the brown and black people of the world. In a rather simplistic equation, imperialism was racism plus capitalism. *National Geographic* condoned the former, despite occasional articles deploring prejudice, and actively advocated the latter.

Travellers, white and at least middle-class, brought their American-bred racism with them wherever they went. 'We discovered that the American Negro's love for watermelon is a hereditary influence', wrote Felix Shay. 'All these black people were excessively fond of melons. To the Sudanese they were food, drink, and refreshment, all combined.'[58] Or here in 1910 is Edgar Allen Forbes on 'the only American colony in the world':

I shall not soon forget a feeble, grey-haired negro who hobbled up the steps and held out a hand that trembled with excitement. 'I seed you on the porch', he said, apologetically, with that old-time negro deference, 'an' I knowed you wuz sum o'mine, an' I'm some o'yourn.' And I should like to remark right here that the negroes of Liberia are as polite and respectful to the white man as they are in Kentucky.[59]

[56] Shay, 'Cairo to Cape Town, overland', 1925, p. 215.
[57] Ibid., p. 227.
[58] Ibid., p. 137.
[59] Forbes, 'Notes on the only American colony in the world', *National Geographic Magazine*, 1919, p. 723.

Black Americans rarely appeared in the *Geographic*'s pages, omitted entirely, for example, from a 1949 regional survey of 'Dixie industry'. Two photos of blacks did appear in a 1960s paen to 'North Carolina – Dixie dynamo'. Even as the civil rights movement stirred the South, one photo showed a uniformed black maid handing a flower to a white woman in long white dress and white gloves. The other photo showed a ragged tobacco farmer. [60]

An earlier survey of the American Virgin Islands by DuBose Heyward (who wrote *Porgy and Bess*) and Daisy Reck was accompanied by a photo of well-dressed black children singing and banging on tambourines; it is captioned 'They all got rhythm – In the W.P.A. nursery school at Charlotte Amalie little natives sing and play in a percussion band.' Beyond the implication of a race-based propensity for 'rhythm', the assumption that black residents are 'native' while whites are settlers indulges a racist stereotype as much as it denies the history of settlement. [61]

Articles repeated racist hierarchies of racial types:

> The cross of the East Indians in the New World is the enforced association with the Africans. These 'lords of all creation' look with contempt upon the orientals. 'He only a coolie man!' says the lazy, ignorant negro, disgust written on every line of his face. The brown man – this descendent of an old and proud race, who regards the negro as little more than a savage – does not retaliate, but goes steadfastly on with his work. [62]

The Japanese and Chinese, as white-honoured civilizations, generally fared better than other foreign peoples in *National Geographic* coverage – as long as they were not in the USA. Japan gained points because it was becoming an imperialist power itself. A 1910 article went so far as to comdemn 'race prejudice in the Far East', railing against 'European snobs in Asia' who shut the host peoples (of the equivalent class) out of their private clubs. [63]

'THE DAYAK GIRL AND THE AMERICAN BELLE'

American women in the pages of the *Geographic* generally represented an ideal of white gentility, projected by the upper- and upper-middle-class WASP men who ran and wrote for the magazine. Indeed it is in the depiction of women that the articulation of race and class is most evident. Karl

---

[60] Buckley, 'With the National Geographic', 1970, p. 16.

[61] Heyward and Peck, 'The American Virgins', *National Geographic Magazine*, 1940, p. 307.

[62] Adams, 'The East Indians in the New World', ibid., 1907, p. 491.

[63] Stone, 'Race prejudice in the Far East', ibid., 1910, p. 977.

Krederick Geiser relates a 1908 conversation with a Black Forest peasant woman who tried to help him with his bags. He refused her assistance, explaining that in America, women don't carry suitcases, let alone men's suitcases. The poor peasant shed a tear, the author tells us, when she thought of what a paradise America must be.[64] Of course, had this German woman emigrated, she would likely have become a factory labourer, one of the many varieties of American working women who must have slipped Geiser's mind when he was thinking of what American women do and do not do.[65]

When American women of the *National Geographic* variety travelled abroad to exotic places, they expected at least the same deferential and preferential treatment bestowed on white men. On treks through Africa, they too were invariably carried in some sort of litter by native 'boys'. Mrs Shay was no exception. To cross a stream, she takes to the shoulders of a young African man, and the caption accompanying the photograph reads: 'Mrs. Shay's method of fording a crocodile-infested stream'.[66]

Sensitive to the debate over women's suffrage in the USA in the first decades of the twentieth century, *National Geographic* explored women's rights and lives in Turkey, Persia, Finland, Bulgaria and later Japan in stories authored by women.[67] *National Geographic*'s American women emerge as refractions of women in other lands insofar as foreign women's lifestyles were often explicitly compared with those of American women. Intended to cast light on the lives of foreign women, such analogies also illuminate central assumptions about American women. In addition to highlighting differences between US and foreign women, the magazine also presented apparent universals of gender. Photographed together, 'the Dayak girl and the American belle are equally anxious to look their best when posing for the photographer.'[68] Elsewhere, topless women walking with baskets on their heads are 'off on a shopping expedition in the Congo'. The sub-caption elaborates: 'Marketing is one of the duties of the women in Central Africa; it is also one of her great pleasures. Thus it appears that the joys of bargain hunting are not the exclusive prerogative of western civilization's womankind.'[69] In Western Africa, another writer is taken by the similarities between a 'comely young native woman, naked to the waist', and the sort of

[64] Geiser, 'Peasant life in the Black Forest', ibid., 1908, p. 646.

[65] Cf. Sojourner Truth's famous retort: 'That man over there says women need to be helped into carriages, and lifted over ditches, and to have the best place everywhere. Nobody ever helps me into carriages, or over mud-puddles, or gives me any best place! And ain't I a woman?', 'Ain't I a woman?', 1976, p. 235.

[66] Shay, 'Cairo to Cape Town, overland', *National Geographic Magazine*, 1925, p. 195.

[67] Patrick, 'The emancipation of Mohammedan women', ibid., 1909, pp. 42–66; Korff, 'Where women vote', ibid., 1910, pp. 487–93; Sykes, 'A talk about Persia and its women', ibid., 1910, pp. 847–66; Nourse, 'Women's work in Japan', ibid., 1938, pp. 99–132.

[68] Smith, 'Sarawak', ibid., 1919, p. 117.

[69] Torday, 'Curious and characteristic customs', ibid., 1919, p. 362.

woman he would meet back home. The wife of his host's employee, this African woman 'greeted me in excellent French with as much social ease and grace as would have been shown by a socially experienced young matron in a suburb of an American city.'[70] In general, the discovery of salubrious values and attributes among the women of the world mirrors the virtue and fortitude of American womanhood.

THE EROTIC ELEMENT: 'THE SAVAGE INSIDE EACH OF US'

The 'traditional American woman', the civilized woman, modest and proper, was the queen of control. She could control her temper, the family's morality, and her own sexuality.[71] In fact, the white 'native-born' American woman controlled her sexuality so well that eugenicists worried that the races who supposedly had no civilized control over their sexuality – Southern Europeans, blacks, Jews, the poor – would overrun the country with their progeny.[72]

Presented as part of nature or at least closer to nature, the brown peoples of the world were expected to express more fully their animal instincts. In the USA this logic was played out in various myths of black sexuality. Black men were supposed to have greater sexual potency than white men, and black women were supposed to be more eager to have sex than white women.[73] In one sense, many *National Geographic* articles downplayed the image of the highly-sexed native. Almost every story expressing unease about scanty apparel found ways to suggest that nudity did not necessarily imply more overt sexuality. In this way the portrayal of nakedness could be justified as 'harmless', while the same articles could commend the 'perfectly developed brown bodies' or 'beautiful rippling muscles' of colonized subjects. Whatever the putative intent of editors and authors, *National Geographic* readers would find it difficult to escape their own cultural concepts of nudity and its connection to sexuality.

Simultaneously blatant and surreptitious, the expression of sexuality in *National Geographic* suffuses even the text of Felix Shay's description of a ceremonial dance in Nimule, central Africa. Following a dance by 'black bucks', and in Shay's own words:

[70] Atkins, 'French West Africa in wartime', ibid., 1942, p. 385.

[71] A fiery temper was the one big flaw, the bane of existence, of all the best gutsy heroines between the Civil War and World War I – Jo March and Anne of Green Gables, for instance. Their maturity and ladyhood were contingent on their mastery of their temper.

[72] Alexander Graham Bell who was president of the National Geographic Society from 1898–1903 and Gilbert H. Grosvenor's father-in-law, was a eugenicist who authored articles on eugenics in *National Geographic*.

[73] See Wallace, *Black Macho*, 1979; Davis, *Women, Race and Class*, 1981.

Now we were to see something! Women had joined the dancers. All were innocent of apparel except for the usual little fringe. They gyrated in front of the men – extraordinary dancers, their glossy bodies performing contortions that would start a vice crusade in any civilized city; yet in this atmosphere, among these savages, it seemed all right, proper, and respectable ... One woman in particular made her body gyrate and squirm, vibrate and quiver, until one felt impelled to break his neighbor's hat and let the nebular hypothesis prove itself. We wondered whether the 'savage' inside each of us is really dead.[74]

The overt eroticism of Shay's experience clearly made him uncomfortable as he struggled to keep his own sexuality under control. Although he was accompanied by his wife, the social mores of his own 'civilized' world threatened to burst his internalized nature, to explode into the nature in which he now found himself.

James Wilson, one of two young American men who in the early 1930s crossed Africa by motorcycle, was less inhibited:

We stopped to watch three well-muscled young wenches rhythmically battering away at a gigantic wooden mortar of clay with mighty six-foot pestles. Their sturdy shoulderblades rippled pliantly beneath black satin skin, and they smiled coyly and displayed their clean, white teeth when we told them in sign language what good figures they had.[75]

An accompanying photo captures a young woman from her breasts to the top of her head. She is smiling and very blurred faces in the background appear to be laughing. The caption reads: 'Health and erect carriage mark the Hausa girl – She walks gracefully and unconcernedly with loads on her head that would tax a man's strength.' One wonders in retrospect whether the caption refers to a man's physical strength or moral strength, and whether it is something other than the woman's carriage that is erect.

In fact, this photograph was taken neither by the author nor his companion, but was selected by editors from *National Geographic*'s extensive photo collection. Nor was this an isolated case; printing photos of bare-breasted women that had nothing to do with the article they illustrated was part of a larger policy acknowledged by the *Geographic*.[76] In a 1907 article on Liberia, three photographs by a certain David Hume, unconnected to the article, depict women naked to the waist in the country's interior.[77] Even after traditional topless costumes were no longer common, the *Geographic*

---

[74] Shay, 'Cairo to Cape Town, overland', *National Geographic Magazine*, 1925, p. 162.

[75] Wilson, 'Three-wheeling through Africa', ibid., 1934, p. 40.

[76] 'Photographs often appeared in the middle of articles that bore no relation to them whatever', cf., McCarry, 'Three men who made the magazine', ibid., 1988, p. 297.

[77] Johnston and Lyon, 'The Black Republic, Liberia', ibid., 1907, pp. 336, 340.

reached back for historical photos of topless women. Gilbert Grosvenor illustrated his own description of Hawaii's 'volcanic and floral wonderland' with such obsolete illustrations, including one of a Hawaiian woman with only a grass skirt and a ukelele.[78]

Grosvenor was a shrewd businessman. According to all accounts, the mail he received regarding depictions of nudity in *National Geographic* was almost always positive. A 1943 *New Yorker* profile proclaimed that:

> to judge from their letters, *Geographic* readers look with favor upon Grosvenor's policy of running a good many pictures of lightly-clad young people, generally of the colored races in far-off lands. Grosvenor knows that the *Geographic* is read by a great many ladies, so, in addition to pictures of girls, he makes a point of running occasional photographs, or paintings, of handsome young men, some of whom, being natives of tropical regions, are dressed in next to nothing. 'One of the Chief's hobbies in the magazines is to see that both sexes are well represented on looks', a Grosvenor associate said.[79]

National Geographic took its readers to exotic places and showed them the 'other' – the wild antithesis to 'civilization'. Printing pictures of bare-breasted native women was acceptable because they were a breed apart from American women. Breasts were fit to be educationally ogled as long as they were a discernable shade of brown. 'On one occasion, a frolicking Polynesian girl appeared suspiciously fair-skinned', reported Tom Buckley in a later retrospective. 'The problem was taken care of in the *Geographic*'s laboratories. "We darkened her down", said Melville M. Payne, the president of the society, "to make her look more native – more valid, you might say"'.[80] Natives are brown, imperialists white; dark-skinned bosoms are quite all right.

[78] Grosvenor, 'The Hawaiian Islands', ibid., 1924, p. 125. See also footnote 21.
[79] Hellman, 'Geography Unshackled III', 1943, p. 29.
[80] Buckley, 'With the National Geographic', 1970, p. 19.

9

Space, Race and Geopolitical Necessity: Geopolitical Rhetoric in German Colonial Revanchism, 1919–1933

David T. Murphy

One of the striking aspects of German colonial propaganda during the Weimar era is the dramatic incongruence between the actual significance of the empire for German society, which was very small, and the huge amount of words, paper and ink, and energy expended on its recovery after the Versailles peace settlement. In the four decades or less in which they were ruled by Germany, the colonies never played more than a marginal role in German economic and social life. German emigration to the colonies in Africa and the South Pacific, for example, was not significant. The most populous German colony, Southwest Africa, had fewer than 15,000 German residents in 1914. The independent countries of North and South America were always much more popular among German emigrants than were Germany's own colonies. Nor were the colonies of much importance economically, save of course to those small elites whose livelihoods derived directly from them. They furnished small quantities of raw materials and, 'tropical products', but not at advantageous prices, nor did they provide significant markets for German exports.[1] Only the German base at Tsing-Tao gave access to a potentially promising export market, but the fabled 'China Market' remained for Germany, as for most of the other western powers at the time, no more than a fable.

[1] For statistics on population, see Duems et al., (eds), *Das Buch der deutschen Kolonien*, 1937, p. i; on trade and population see Petzina, et al., *Sozialgeschichtliches Arbeitsbuch*, 1978, pp. 24–7.

Perceptions, nevertheless, can be as important historically as realities. This seems to be particularly true where relations between states are involved. The objective benefit derived from influence in or possession of a particular area is, for the course of national politics, often less relevant than its perceived value. Since it is clear that many Germans of the Weimar era viewed the colonial empire as vitally important to the German nation, the significant issue therefore becomes the source of this perception.[2] The historian Thomas Childers, writing in a different context, has called for a thoughtful reconsideration of political language to expand our historical sense of the Weimar era.[3]

This chapter examines the language of Weimar era arguments for a German overseas colonial empire, and argues that a part of their political success was due to the gradual absorption into colonial rhetoric of geopolitically-influenced theories linking *Raum*, or space, *Lebensraum* or living space, and the survival of the German 'race'. This represented a significant departure in German colonial revanchism from early legalistic and economic claims to the colonies. Colonial agitation of the period certainly showed a good deal of continuity with colonialist propaganda of the Wilhelmine era, but it differed in important ways as well, particularly in its increased reliance on demographic and racial arguments. From a critical examination of pro-colonialist arguments by some colonialist geopoliticians and by colonialist organizations, it will be seen that geopoliticians and colonialists increasingly exploited concepts of *Raum*, *Lebensraum* and racial survival to convince Germans of the need for a revival of their erstwhile colonial empire. The rhetoric of *Raum*, especially, forged a conceptual link between colonialists and geopoliticians; and an emphasis on race, cultural superiority based in technological achievement, and ethno-biological paranoia merged to form a shared language of geopolitics and colonialism.

It was once commonly argued that Weimar geopoliticians were, in general, opposed to a renewal of German overseas colonialism. Both Lothar Gruchmann and Klaus Hildebrand, for example, advanced this view in important studies of German imperialism published in the 1960s.[4] Even then, however, some historians dissented from this judgement, which was founded on an overly-homogenized view of the geopolitical movement and

---

[2] The widespread significance of the empire is suggested in the National Assembly's protest vote on 1 March 1919 against the confiscation of the colonies. In a rare example of Weimar political unity, the vote was 414–7, and included the support of many members of the leftist Independent Social Democratic Party (USPD). See Grunder, *Geschichte der Deutschen Kolonien*, 1985, p. 217. Grunder also points out that the popularity of colonial literature peaked in the 1920s and 1930s, rather than in the era when the Germans were in actual possession of colonies.

[3] Childers, 'The Social Language of Politics', 1990, p. 358.

[4] Gruchmann, *Nationalsozialistische Grossraumordnung*, 1962, pp. 20–1; Hildebrand, *Vom Reich zum Weltreich*, 1969, p. 375.

an identification of 'geopolitics' with the views of Karl Haushofer.[5] None familiar with the recent historiography of the topic, particularly with the work of Klaus Kost, would now make such an argument.[6] What has become clear in recent years is the heterogeneity of views concealed beneath the rubric of geopolitics.

The concept of geopolitics' was introduced in 1899 by the Swedish political scientist and journalist Rudolf Kjellén as part of a supposedly empirical system for understanding the state, but it remained largely the property of a circle of specialists until after 1918.[7] Germany's defeat in the First World War stimulated a popular explosion of geopolitical thought. The *Zeitschrift für Geopolitik* was founded in 1924, courses on geopolitics began to appear in German universities, geopolitical articles were featured in major geographical and political journals, geopolitical ideas and terms were applied in German history and geography texts, geopoliticians were even featured in regular radio broadcasts.[8] Although Haushofer, as the guiding spirit behind the *Zeitschrift für Geopolitik*, was and remains the best-known of geopoliticians, it became popular with a wide circle of writers, some geographers and some not. They interpreted geopolitics broadly as the science of the state as an organism in *Raum*, or space, whose social, political, cultural and economic developments were linked to and dependent upon its geography.[9]

---

[5] A different view was expressed in Gerstenberger, *Der Revolutionäre Konservatismus*, 1969, p. 27.

[6] See the extensive discussion of geopolitical colonialist ideas in Kost, *Die Einflüsse der Geopolitik*, 1988, pp. 193–233.

[7] Kjellén in *Ymer*, 1899, vol. 9, p. 283. For a good example of its use in his writings for a German audience prior to the end of the First World War, see Kjellén, *Der Staat als Lebensform*, 1917, pp. 46–93. The explosion of its popularity after the war was noted in many places, for instance by Maull, Professor of Geography at Frankfurt and a co-founder of the *Zeitschrift für Geopolitik*, who wrote in 1929: 'There probably has never been a time, probably not even in the second era of great discoveries, in which geographic thought has encountered so much interest among those standing outside the science of geography as this momentary period, determined by the high market value of geopolitics'. See Maull, 'Review of R. Hennig's *Geopolitik*', 1929, p. 61.

[8] As an editorialist for the *Frankfurter Zeitung* wrote in 1926: 'The press can note with satisfaction the gratifying degree to which an understanding of political geography has developed in the German people in recent years. The geopolitical view of political problems prevails more and more; the word "geopolitics" appears to have become a basic requirement of the modern editorialist.' *Frankfurter Zeitung*, 4 February 1926. Among others, Haushofer lectured monthly on Bayerischer Rundfunk between 1924 and 1931, when the broadcasts were cancelled briefly. See Jacobsen, *Haushofer, Leben und Werk*, 1979, vol. 1, p. 183; vol. 2, p. 121.

[9] Many definitions were offered for geopolitics. Kjellén wrote 'Geopolitics is the teaching of the state as a geographic organism or a manifestation in space: Therefore, the state as land, territory, district or, most pronouncedly, as an empire.' See Kjellén, *Der Staat*, 1917, p. 46. Hennig defined it simply as 'The science of the state as a life form'; Hennig, *Geopolitik*, 1928, p. 1. Haushofer defined it as 'the science of the political life form in its

The conceptual lowest common denominator here, a geopolitical baseline applicable across disciplines, was geodeterminism, sometimes nuanced and sophisticated, often crude.

This broad theoretical framework afforded room for a variety of opinions, and despite the disagreement of Haushofer, many geopoliticians were impassioned advocates of the re-acquisition of colonies.[10] They came from various backgrounds. Erich Obst, a geographer whose academic career in Germany spanned 45 years and two world wars, and who from 1921 occupied the first Chair in Geography at the Technical University of Hannover, was a prominent colonial propagandist during the Weimar era. From his position as chair of the Geographical Institute at Hannover and a long-time editor of the *Zeitschrift für Geopolitik*, Obst was in a position to popularize his colonialist views. Richard Hennig, a professor at the University of Düsseldorf, and member of the German National People's Party and the right-wing Stahlhelm, the war veterans' organization, also wrote of the geopolitical need for renewed German colonialism. Another prominent geopolitical agitator on behalf of colonialism, Arthur Dix, was not a geographer at all, but a journalist educated before the war in economics and *Staatswissenschaft*, the forerunner of political science. A self-described 'geographic autodidact', Dix had an extensive pre-war background in journalism and was already publishing widely in geographical journals.[11] After the war, he would take a leading role in exploiting geopolitical concepts to demand the return of the colonies. Other geographers, among them Josef März, Franz Thorbecke and Karl Sapper, also advanced geopolitical justifications for renewed colonialism.

Raum and *Lebensraum* were crucial to the geopolitical view of state development and state relations. The centrality of the concept of *Raum* to geopolitical thought can hardly be overstated. Translated into English simply as 'space' or 'area' the word is deflated, losing the variety of meanings and thick layers of nearly mystical connotations with which it resonated for German geopoliticians. *Raum* combined topography, climate, arability, maritime access and other elements with a given people, or *Volk*, to create a mystical unity from which was derived the state. As Otto Maull saw it, *Raum* itself was thereby elevated from the position of a simple geographical

---

natural *Lebensraum*, which seeks to understand it in its earth-dependence (*Erdgebundenheit*) and its conditioning by historical factors', Haushofer et al. (eds.), *Bausteine zur Geopolitik*, 1928, p. 59; Kost has argued that a lack of conceptual clarity is one of the defining characteristics of geopolitics: Kost, *Die Einflüsse*, 1988, p. 110.

[10] Haushofer was more interested in the 'German East', or central Europe, than in Africa, and felt that Germany ought not to raise the colonial issue until in a position to enforce its demands. See his contribution to the special issue 'Should Germany Pursue Colonial Politics? A Poll', 1927, pp. 638–9. His view is reiterated at length in the letter 'Haushofer to N. N.' 10 September 1927, in Jacobsen, *Karl Haushofer*, vol. 2, p. 82.

[11] Dix, *Politische Geographie*, 2nd edn, 1923, p. 111. See also Dix, 'Geographische Abrundungstendenzen', 1911. For a characteristic example of his pre-war colonial writing, see Dix, *Deutscher Imperialismus*, 1914.

setting to the status of a fully-fledged actor, endowed with progenitive powers. 'The state in its total spatial structure and in its manifold incarnations must be the object of geographical research', he wrote, 'not only as an organism *in* space, but in a much deeper sense as a spatial-organism (*Raumorganismus*) grown out of space'.[12]

Not only could space thus call forth the state, which was seen as having a life history analogous to that of a biological organism, but it also played a decisive role in shaping the *Volk* who developed within it. Wilhelm Volz, a geographer who combined volkish and geopolitical ideas during the Weimar period (and who had been Rector of the University of Berlin for a year during the war) argued that 'every space has its people, and history teaches emphatically that the space is a co-determinant of history where spaces and peoples pressure one another...The people make the space their own, but the space also creates its people'.[13] Such geographic determinism, couched in terms of *Raum* and applied to peoples and states, was typical of geopolitics in the period. Some geopoliticians even went so far as to define *Geopolitik* as '*Raumpolitik*',[14] while critics warned of the new mysticism of *Raum*. As the conservative German journalist Paul Fechter wrote in 1929, '*Raum* has become current to a heightened degree in the last few years ... One begins to sense that it is more than the divinely ordained residing place of our small life, that in the one word "*Raum*" a sum of the most wonderful things and concepts has been summarized'.[15]

The most important variant of *Raum* for geopolitical theories was *Lebensraum*. This term was coined two years before the word 'geopolitics', in 1897, by Friedrich Ratzel, who came to geography after a formal education in zoology, and who was later eulogized by Maull as the father of geopolitics.[16] While to Ratzel the term simply denoted the space necessary for a state to enjoy security in its independence, and had connotations pertaining more to the German role in central Europe than to an overseas empire, *Lebensraum* acquired a broader and conceptually less clear meaning for geopoliticians in the wake of German defeat in 1918. In the hands of more radical theorists, *Lebensraum* came to acquire overtones of space sufficient for

[12] Maull, *Politische Geographie*, 1925, p. vi; emphasis in the original. For a perceptive analysis of new views of the meaning of space which emerged in the years before World War One, and of the ways space came to be considered not a mere void but a 'positive constitutive factor' in politics and culture, see Kern, *The Culture of Time and Space*, 1983, pp. 152–9.

[13] Volz, 'Lebensraum und Lebensrecht', 1925, p. 174.

[14] Kohl, *Ursprung und Wandlung*, 1932, p. 7. Kohl insisted that Germany would of necessity expand again, despite the peace settlement, since central Europe formed the natural *Raum* of the Germans and '*Raum* is stronger than human caprice', p. 565.

[15] Fechter, 'Der amerikanische Raum', 1929, p. 47.

[16] Ratzel, 'Über den Lebensraum', 1897, pp. 363–7. He developed the term in 'Der Lebensraum, eine biogeographische Studie', 1901; Maull, 'Friedrich Ratzel zum Gedächtnis', 1928, p. 617.

an autarchic existence for the German state of central Europe, and it came to symbolize the necessity of settlement areas, particularly in eastern Europe but also for overseas colonies.[17] In keeping with the organic and often crudely Darwinist view of the state which they promoted, geopoliticians viewed the struggle for more *Lebensraum* as an eternal and inherent part of the state system.[18]

The Weimar geopolitical colonialists were able to depict overseas colonies as a necessary adjunct to, and extension of, the German *Lebensraum*. Before the war *Lebensraum* was associated primarily with 'easterners', while *Weltpolitik* was the rallying cry of overseas colonialists. After the war, some geopoliticians attempted to synthesize these two approaches. In 1926, for example, the *Zeitschrift für Geopolitik* published a special issue devoted to the colonial question, in which Obst wrote the keynote article under the title 'We Demand Our Colonies Back!' While many of the articles stressed traditional *Weltpolitik* arguments depicting colonies as an economic and security necessity, Obst added a comparatively new spatial twist. Today, he wrote, 'we lack the land to be able to settle the uprooted part of the ethnic community in German lands', and he concluded that the lack of settlement colonies forced thousands of Germans into emigration each year. Germany's exclusion from potential 'settlement colonies' likewise constituted a threat to European peace by keeping population density within Germany at dangerously high levels, so that 'in consequence of its gigantic population pressure [Germany is] naturally the source of an inundation of foreign ethnic soil'.[19] In the same issue, Hans Meyer applied the term '*Grösserdeutschland* of the future' to the colonial empire, invoking a term normally associated in the German context with expansion on the continent rather than overseas.[20] Other writers, conceding that German colonies in East Africa and the South Seas could not support many white settlers, focused on German Southwest Africa as *Siedlungsraum*, or settlement space for the German 'race' constricted in central Europe. Leo Waibel, for example, used this argument and contended further that the presence of German settlers in the *Südwest* had rendered it a part of German ethnic soil, pointing out that the colony had only 275,000 native inhabitants in any case (compared to perhaps 15,000 German settlers), and that these natives were unfortunately of 'low quality'.[21]

[17] See Smith, *Ideological Origins*, 1986, pp. 83–93.

[18] Maull, *Politische Geographie*, 1925, pp. 87–8; Hennig, *Geopolitik*, 1928, p. 98. The World War was, as early as 1919, being analysed by German geographers as a manifestation of the inter-state struggle for *Raum*. See Wegener, *Die geographischen Ursachen*, 1920, pp. 20–7.

[19] Obst, 'Wir fordern unsere Kolonien zurück!', 1926, p. 155. This article was reprinted under the title 'Warum brauchen wir Kolonien?', or 'Why Do We Need Colonies?' in the company magazine of the Continental Caoutchouc- und Gutta-Percha-Compagnie of Hannover, pp. 3–6.

[20] Meyer, 'Geopolitische Betrachtungen', 1926, p. 174.

[21] Waibel, 'Südwestafrika', 1926, pp. 187, 191.

Waibel, a member of the conservative German National People's Party and a respected geographer who taught at Kiel and Bonn, used here a standard geopolitical tactic for claiming overseas colonies for the German *Lebensraum*. Emphasizing race, he argued that the presence of ethnic German settlers made the colony a part of the German *Volksboden*, or ethnic soil. Others invoked updated versions of the 'white-man's-burden' argument, common to all the western imperialist countries, arguing that it was Germany's moral duty to 'take up the burden' of governing and improving the supposedly benighted natives of the colonies. Still others argued that the survival of the German race depended upon the acquisition of more space.

Although geodeterminism of this sort occasionally collided with racial theories during the Nazi period, they generally co-existed harmoniously in the works of many Weimar geopoliticians, especially those with a colonialist agenda.[22] Popular throughout this period was the cry of *Volk ohne Raum!*, or people without space, the title of Hans Grimm's enormously popular novel of German colonists in Southwest Africa. Published in 1926 and selling hundreds of thousands of copies, the book's title became a motto for both geopoliticans and colonialists. In the same vein, Hans Simmer writes:

All nations which possess a will to live wish or strive for spatial expansion. The will to live alone often categorically demands an enlargement of the *Lebensraum*. This occurs if a) the *Lebensraum* is constricted by covetous enemies, so that the necessities of life of the conquered people are curtailed (Germany, Hungary, Bulgaria); or b) the growing, steadily increasing population needs elbow room, because the *Lebensraum* is too small. Here it is above all the colonies which should take up the excess population, whose run-off into foreign lands is thereby hindered or at least ameliorated, and so that the immigrants remain protected within their own nationality and domestic economy ... We Germans are today especially the *Volk ohne Raum*, and we must sooner or later procure the lacking *Raum*, if we do not wish to perish. No people of the world has therefore a morally founded claim to more

---

[22] On the clash of racial and geodeterminist theories see the persuasive argument by Bassin, 'Race contra space', 1987, pp. 115–34. While this may be correct for the Nazi period, however, Bassin's focus on the scientific materialist and determinist roots of German geopolitics overlooks the roots of geopolitics in nineteenth-century romantic conceptions of geography. In this sense, geopolitics shared important non-rationalist elements with the racial ideology of the Nazis, which developed out of the so-called 'volkish' movement. These roots of geopolitics in romantic thought were clearly recognized by geopoliticians and critics of geopolitics in the Weimar period. As de Battaglia wrote in 1932, 'In all areas we observe today, together with the advance of undisguised materialism, the triumphant rise of a new romanticism, mysticism, of an irrational world sensibility ... in history, in political theory, in regional geography and in the youngest of these disciplines, which has splintered something off from each of these just named, in geopolitics.' Battaglia, 'Geopolitik', 1932, p. 24. A similar modern view is found in Faber, 'Zur Vorgeschichte der Geopolitik', 1982, pp. 389–406.

Raum like that of the Germans. For our people and our economy an expansion of *Lebensraum* must remain the most important goal. Our very destiny is dependent upon maintaining the will to a greater *Lebensraum*, which may be won by economic penetration, or by revision of the borders and return to the colonies.[23]

Franz Thorbecke, a Cologne geographer who advocated German re-colonization of Africa introduced the 1931 resolution which put the German Geographic Congress officially on record as supporting the return of the colonies.[24] He later demonstrated a disregard for geographical precision unusual in a geographer, claiming that 'the African expanses of *Raum ohne Volk* stand in immediate juxtaposition to the German *Volk ohne Raum* in over-populated Europe: Africa lies before the gates of Europe and has for Europe the same significance which it had earlier during the *Imperium Romanum* and again acquired in the Age of Discoveries: it was and is colonial land'.[25]

However, a serious weakness in the colonial demands associated with *Volk ohne Raum* rhetoric appeared in the 1920s as the German birth rate declined sharply and population expansion was expected to cease.[26] It is revealing for geopolitics, and for the colonialist movement, that this did not lead to a reconsideration of the presumed need for expanded *Lebensraum*. On the contrary, geopoliticians and colonialists who even took cognizance of birth rate declines either argued that Germany was still, for the time being, over-populated, or else inverted the *Lebensraum* arguments, suggesting that the declining birth rate was itself symptomatic of the lack of space and thereby proof of the need for more. Arthur Dix, for example, foresaw a 'twilight of the Germans':

Viewed from the densely populated industrial centres and the great cities, we are *Volk ohne Raum*. We have at the same time, with the unfavourable contemporary development of agriculture, *Raum ohne Volk*. We must fill up our unpopulated *Raum*, and must provide more *Raum* for the landless people.[27]

[23] Simmer, *Grundzüge der Geopolitik*, 1928, pp. 83–4.
[24] See the account of the meeting in Langhans, 'Die 24', 1931, pp. 195–9. A complete account of all the sessions is in Behrmann (ed.), *Verhandlungen des Deutschen Geographentages*, 1932, p. 24; The resolution was co-sponsored by Schmitthenner of Leipzig and Troll of Berlin.
[25] Thorbecke, 'Warum Kolonien?', 1934, Beilage.
[26] See Knodel, *The Decline of Fertility*, 1974. The main geopolitical analyst of the birth rate decline in these years was Burgdörfer, director of the Reich Statistical Office. He argued for lands in the East to offset the problem, and for colonies as a counter-measure to declining fertility. See Burgdörfer, *Volk ohne Jugend*, 1932, pp. 423–4; on Burgdörfer see Murphy, *The Heroic Earth*, ch. 2 (forthcoming).
[27] Dix, *Weltkrise und Kolonialpolitik*, 1932, pp. 25, 28.

Dix concluded that in addition to re-colonizing the German lands in eastern Europe, Germans needed space in Africa. This represented a clear evolution in his argument. Since before the war he had used over-population as an apology for German colonization, and had for a period after the war concluded reluctantly that the colonial era was ended.[28] By the late 1920s, however, he had resumed a passionate colonial advocacy, and could argue that whether Germany was over-populated or heading toward under-population, both facts constituted elements of a sound geopolitical argument for the return of the colonies. Dix favored a vague European condominium over Africa rather than a simple return to the African status quo.[29]

Traditional colonialist claims founded on the supposed superiority of European culture were also updated by the geopoliticans who emphasized technological achievement. Technology served a two-fold purpose in the geopolitical colonialist rhetoric of the era, both as proof of the continued superiority of the white nations and as a catalyst for a new global age from which Germany could not afford to be excluded. Weimar Germany indulged an enthusiasm for new technologies such as zeppelins, airplanes, and wireless telegraphy that altered the geography of global power.[30] 'In the age of air travel not a speck of the earth's face can remain hidden', wrote Dix, adding that 'geopolitics is the product and the requirement of a new age.'[31] A particularly striking and sinister example of this geopolitical exaltation of technology was published in the *Zeitschrift für Geopolitik* under the laconic title 'Capital, Technology and Geopolitics'. Max Krahmann rhapsodized on the future use of machines:

> Technology wants to master nature. Technology is a continuation of nature in the spiritual sphere, to which nature adapts itself. Technology is new creation or continuation of creation by man, by the *ingenium*, by the engineer. Technology is embodied capital, is tool, machine,

[28] For his pre-war use of the population theme and birth rate decline, see Dix, *Deutscher Imperialismus*, 1914, pp. 90–4. For his early Weimar disillusion with the era of colonization, see Dix, *Politische Geographie*, 1923, p. 560.

[29] Dix, 'Wirtschaftsstruktur und Geopolitik', 1927, Zentrales Staatsarchiv Potsdam: Nachlass Dix; 90 Di 2; 63, 1, pp. 240–49.

[30] Pommrich, 'Geopolitische Ziele in der Luftpolitik', 1927, pp. 558–9, who laments that 'the loss of the German colonies has had a catastrophic impact on aviation.' Likewise, even Haushofer likened the loss of colonies in the Pacific with the loss of radio and air bases: Haushofer, *Geopolitik des Pazifischen Ozeans*, 1924, pp. 39, 216. On the obsession with technological progress and the heroism of science, see Gay, *Weimar Culture*, 1970, pp. 30–1; Kuhn, 'Das geistige Gesicht', 1980, pp. 216–18.

[31] Dix, *Geopolitik, Lehrkurse*, no. 16, undated, probably 1927, pp. 4, 17. Dix also used the term 'the global village' ('Das Dörfchen Erde') in an essay in 1927 to describe the changes which radio, telegraph, telephone, cinema and changes in travel technology were creating. See Nachlass Dix, 'Wirtschaftsstruktur', 1927, Zentrales Staatsarchiv Potsdam: p. 242.

explosive, system, disciplined army, warship, press, routine, in short, a means of power, new against old, human-power against nature-power, dominance over the earth, and therefore – a powerful geopolitical factor... Politics ... is decisively determined by the earth-space of a state with its natural resources, its flora and its climate. Politics is the power-deployment of stored capital of any type in the form of technology against resistant nature, including more natural, capital-deficient humanity without technology – for example, in the form of the ships of Columbus against America, or present-day machine guns against the rebellious Incas in Bolivia or future aeroplanes over South America, all working to fulfil the vision of the 'engineer' Columbus.[32]

That this geopolitical rhetoric of race and space, as well as culture and technology, penetrated the colonialist movement proper is clear from a variety of sources. Weimar political life witnessed a proliferation of organizations dedicated to propagandizing the colonial cause. Some of these groups, such as the Deutsche Kolonialgesellschaft (German Colonial Society), (DKG), dated back to the 1880s, but newer ones also emerged, often with overlapping membership: the Deutscher Kolonialkriegerbund (German Colonial Serviceman's League), the Bund für koloniale Erneuerung (League for Colonial Renewal), the Koloniale Frauenhilfe (Colonial Womens' Aid), the Bund deutscher Kolonialpfadfinder (League of German Colonial Scouts) and a bewildering array of others had different emphases but were all devoted to the preservation of the German colonial grievance. Usually small, these groups nevertheless disposed of a good deal of money and used it to fund a variety of newspapers, journals, popular magazines, and yearly colonialist congresses, and to foment support for the demands of the Interfraktionelle Koloniale Vereinigung (Interfactional Colonial Coalition) in the Reichstag.[33] Many of the leading colonialists had personal connections with geopoliticians, and groups such as the Colonial Economic Committee brought together geographers and colonialists of all political stripes, from writers and businessmen to socialists and right-wing members of the German National People's Party.[34] Geopolitical colonialist arguments appeared regularly in

[32] Krahmann, 'Kapital, Technik und Geopolitik', 1927, p. 859.

[33] A complete overview of the various organizations allied under the umbrella of the Koloniale Reichsarbeitsgemeinschaft (KORAG) can be found in 'Übersicht über die kolonialen Organisationen, 11.1.1930', (Zentrales Staatsarchiv Potsdam: DKG, 61 Ko 1; 1108, B1. 55–9). See also Hildebrand, *Vom Reich*, 1969, pp. 57–63, Grunder, *Geschichte*, 1985, pp. 219–21 and Schmokel, *Dream of Empire*, 1964, pp. 1–2. These colonial enthusiasts were predominantly male, and members of the former colonial bureaucracy, academia or the military, but included a sprinkling of exporters, importers, planters, etc. Hildebrand, pp. 102–3.

[34] The governing board of the committee, was an extremely mixed bag, including Dix, the geopolitical demographic expert on the birth rate decline, Burgdörfer, the writer Grimm, the DNVP deputy Laverrenz, the socialist Cohen-Reuss, the geographer Rohrbach, representatives of exporting industries and many others. See the list of members in *Verhandlungen des Vorstandes des Kolonial-Wirtschaftlichen Komitees*, 1932, pp. 1–3.

such colonialist organs as the Koloniale Rundschau and the Übersee- und Kolonial-Zeitung.

The appearance of pro-colonial arguments based on the need for space and the maintenance of the German population, next to more traditional economic and cultural arguments, was part of an articulate and deliberate shift in the official colonial propaganda programme. The yearly congresses of the Koloniale Reichsarbeitsgemeinschaft (Reich Colonial Task Force, or KORAG) were the high point of the German colonialist year, and at the 1925 meeting in Munich – a glittering social event attended by Crown Prince Ruprecht – they agreed upon so-called 'Guidelines for Colonial Propaganda', whose primary emphasis was still the legal claim to the old colonies. 'The colonial movement of our day', the guidelines declared, 'is founded on two facts: one, on the illegal seizure of our colonies, carried out under violation of the Wilsonian promise, and which is to be justified by the lie of our inability and unworthiness to colonize. After that, on the political, economic and cultural grounds of irrefutable necessity'.[35] Under the influence of Erich Duems, however, who became general secretary of the KORAG in 1928, a new 'General German Colonial Programme' was approved in which pragmatic claims to the colonies founded on economic, cultural, and demographic necessity were accorded an equal status with formal legalistic claims. This allowed greater tactical flexibility in popular propagandizing, according to the programme, which expressly demanded overseas colonies suitable for white settlement which would be able to provide agricultural land for Germany's excess population. 'The timely procurement of our own large settlement areas in the still free earth-spaces (*Erdräumen*) is a duty of national self-preservation', according to the 1928 guidelines.[36]

Strengthened in 1930 by the DKG with an emphasis on the need for raw materials and settlement space, this pragmatic approach was not entirely new.[37] The issue of economic necessity had been an integral part of the colonial revanchist movement from the beginning, and the rhetoric of space, at times geopolitical in tone, had also been present. Under Heinrich Schnee, however, who had been the last governor of German East Africa, a German People's Party deputy in the Reichstag, and leader of the DKG after 1930, geopolitics assumed greater prominence. Schnee was a popular writer (his book *The Colonial Guilt-Lie* sold over 150,000 copies) with close connections with many political activist groups and a wide circle of geopoliticians whose

[35] 'Richtlinien für koloniale Propaganda'. Bundesarchiv Koblenz (hereafter BAK), R 43 1; Reichskanzlei, Kolonien; 625, frame 178; See the account of the congress in 'Große Koloniale Kundgebung', 11 June 1925, p. 4.

[36] See the reprint of the programme for the Cologne Congress in Koloniale Reichsarbeitsgemeinschaft, *Wesen und Ziele*, 1928, pp. 13–18. This and other evidence renders questionable Schmokel's assertion that the colonialists did not take seriously the acquisition of overseas settlement space. See Schmokel, *Dream of Empire*, 1964, p. 49.

[37] 'Richtlinien für die Behandlung der deutschen Kolonialfrage, 1930', ZSTA Potsdam: DKG, 61 Ko 1; 553, BI, pp. 51–3.

thinking clearly influenced his own.[38] He too stressed the influence of *Raum* on declining birth rates:

> In general it must be said that the population–political situation of Germany is unfavourable, and is being exacerbated by a series of special tendencies ... We must keep in mind that the diminution of *Lebensraum* has brought with it intensified antagonisms ... Germany requires a large, self-renewing population, precisely because of its position, or it will not be able to avoid inundation by foreign elements ... It must be recognized that a contradiction exists between the national necessity to keep the population growing and young and the actual economic and political situation, which compels a slowing of population growth ... The most important task falls to foreign policy, which must try to effect an expansion of subsistence areas. Toward this end it must strive, for example, for the re-acquisition of the colonies ...[39]

For the next several years, until the fall of the Weimar Republic, strains of both population arguments appeared regularly in colonial propaganda. While several authors, such as Dix, embodied an uneasy reconciliation of both arguments, others clearly took sides. In the case of Friedrich Ebeling, the need for *Raum* was connected to a eugenic argument and to the fear of working-class revolution:

> The quality of the young generation has decreased, and will according to the laws of racial hygiene further deteriorate. It is statistically proven that it is not the families with high-quality racial properties but on the contrary, in the best case, the average, and usually the inferior classes who compose the main contingent of the births ... This hard destiny befalls a people which will be yet more densely populated, since the prediction that the *Volk ohne Raum* will, due to sinking birth rates, devolve into a *Raum ohne Volk*, does not yet apply ... it gives rise

---

[38] See, for example, the correspondence with Grimm over colonial affairs in Geheimes Staatst Archiv (hereafter GStA): NL Schnee; Ha 1, Rep. 92, 38/114: Grimm to Schnee, 1931 and 38/115, Schnee to Grimm (copy), 1931; 57/4, Obst to Schnee, 1924 and 57/5, Obst to Schnee, 1928; 40/16, Hennig to Schnee, 1934 and 40/17 Schnee to Hennig (copy), 1934. See as well Schnee's speech delivered to the Interparliamentary Conference of October, 1925, in New York City, which emphasized space for population surplus and economic necessity, in NL Schnee; 24/40. As president of the Arbeitsausschuss Deutscher Verbände (ADV) from 1924, Schnee also had links to around 2,000 German organizations ranging from the German Civic Congress (Deutscher Stadtetag) to the volkish Deutscher Schutzbund. See Heinemann, *Die verdrängte Niederlage*, 1983, pp. 120–54 for a treatment of the ADV and Schnee's role therein.

[39] Saenger, *Das Bevölkerungsproblem*, in BAK: NL Külz; BI, pp. 17–18. During the war, Hoetzsch had also warned of the threat of 'inundation' of the Germans, although he was arguing on behalf of eastern rather than colonial expansion; Burleigh, *Germany Turns Eastwards*, 1988, p. 20.

to thoughts that the overburdened future generations, packed like sardines, will themselves conquer with the sword the *Raum* they require.[40]

Other colonialists too saw colonial settlement as a form of eugenic therapy for the German ethnic body. While some argued that settlement overseas would reduce class antagonisms in Germany and stabilize their own class positions by diverting the excess of the labouring classes to new lands, the geopolitical colonialists were more likely to emphasize the benefits colonialism would confer on the German race by strengthening the racial stock.[41] Relying heavily on geopolitical terms and concepts cited from the works of Ratzel and Haushofer, Julius Lips argued that colonial politics and the acquisition of new space would play a vital role in shaping, as he put it, the relation of ethnicity to state life. His advocacy of the term '*Ethnopolitik*', and his belief that German colonial policy would necessarily become more ethnopolitical, is a measure of the colonialist debt to geopolitical thought, since the term received one of its first extended treatments in German by Kjellén.[42] 'That portion of anthropology which transcends the purely methodological formulation of the cultural disciplines, which does not content itself with the mere cultural–historical working out of historically determinable cultural processes, I call ethnopolitics', Lips wrote, describing it also as 'dynamic anthropology' (just as some geopoliticians called their field 'dynamic political geography').[43]

Lips's definition of 'ethnopolitics' closely paralleled the contemporary discussion of 'biopolitics'. Louis von Kohl, for example, envisaged biopolitics as concerning the 'interaction of *Volk* and *Raum*', and investigating 'the development of a *Volkskörper* [ethnic body] and its *Lebensraum* over time'.[44] The pursuit of sound 'ethnopolitical' or 'biopolitical' policy would also have important ramifications for the position of women in German society, of course, and while the impact of ethnopolitics on the significance of gender went largely unexplored by the geopoliticians, it was later the object of considerable attention from the Nazi administrators who succeeded Weimar's bureaucrats.[45]

[40] Ebeling, 'Schafft Raum zur Überwindung', 1930, pp. 407–8. Zimmermann has pointed out that the colonialists also viewed colonies as an antidote to the social dislocation they claimed arose from overcrowding. See Zimmermann, 'Kampf um den Lebensraum', 1976, p. 166. Around the turn of the century, Rhodes made a similar observation following a trip to London's East End, a connection picked up explicitly by Lenin. See Lenin, *Imperialism, the Highest Stage of Capitalism*, 1975, pp. 93–4.

[41] For a discussion of the role of class relations and class struggle in fostering enthusiasm for German colonial renewal, see Rüger, 'Der Kolonialrevisionismus', 1977, pp. 248–53.

[42] Kjellén, *Der Staat*, 1917, pp. 43ff.

[43] Lips, 'Ethnopolitik und Kolonialpolitik', 1932, pp. 532, 538. See the treatment and criticism of the concept of geopolitics as 'dynamic political geography' in Hettner, 'Methodische Zeit-und Streitfragen', 1929, pp. 332–6.

[44] Kohl, 'Biopolitik und Geopolitik', 1933, p. 308.

[45] For an analysis of the links between concepts of 'biopolitics' and the significance of gender in the Nazi era, see Koonz, *Mothers in the Fatherland*, 1987, pp. 3–17 and for

Attempts to reconcile the contradictions between the overcrowding and under-population arguments foreshadowed a parallel reconciliation in imperialist ideology during the Nazi era. At that time, the conflict between the supporters of *Ostpolitik*, who favoured expansion in eastern Europe, and the advocates of *Kolonialpolitik* would be resolved by arguing that the two forms of expansion were complementary rather than mutually exclusive, a resolution suggested in the Nazi-era slogan of '*Kolonialpolitik und Ostpolitik*'.[46] This view characterized the colonial empire as an adjunct to the eastern expansionism embodied in the radical agrararian '*Blut und Boden*' ideology of Walther Darré.

In conclusion, the relationship between geopolitics, the colonialist movement and colonial agitation generally should be placed in historical perspective. The support which the colonial agitators managed to foment for the re-acquisition of colonies was often purely *pro forma*. As a part of general German agitation for revision of the harsher aspects of the Versailles peace settlement, it was a convenient tool to drum up a little foreign sympathy and some resentment among Germans. The German woman or man in the street did not think too much about the colonies, however, a fact frequently lamented by the colonialists but one hardly surprising in light of the intensity of economic, social and political turbulence during the Republic's short life.[47] This did not mean, however, that if asked, the average German woman or man would have opposed a renewed colonial empire for Germany. On the contrary, a good case can be made that colonialist sentiment resonated, as one of its supporters hoped it would in 1920, as the 'common property of the broadest classes of the people'.[48] The ideal of a renewed colonial empire, for example, clearly retained a powerful fascination throughout the era for a considerable contingent of academics, government officials, journalists and politicians. All the political parties to the right of the Social Democrats felt that a formal commitment to the re-acquisition of the colonies was in their electoral interest. Many deputies of the Reichstag were committed to German colonial activism, and the subject came up for frequent debate. The pressure exerted by the colonial movement also had a demonstrable influence on the conduct of German diplomacy by Stresemann and the other foreign ministers of the Republic – usually a deleterious one in that it further

---

the links between these ideas and Nazi racism see Bock, 'Racism and Sexism in Nazi Germany', 1984, pp. 271–85.

[46] Schmokel, *Dream of Empire*, 1964, pp. 50–1. See also Sandner and Rössler, chapter 6 in this volume.

[47] 'The negligible popularity of colonial thought is in itself a surprising fact. One would have supposed that a people like the German, which disposes of too little space, would have seized the possibility of winning great new spaces with passion and resolution...' Duems and von Stuemer (eds), *Fünfzig Jahre deutsche Kolonialgesellschaft*, 1932, p. 99.

[48] Solf, *Afrika für Europa*, 1920, p. 5.

constricted their already limited freedom to manoeuvre.[49] Finally, most of the colonialists welcomed the Nazi regime when it took power in 1933, and it is probably true that the colonialist obsession with a genuine but not very important colonial grievance contributed to popular receptivity when the colonial grievance was exploited by the National Socialists in similar language.

As this chapter has tried to show, the rhetoric and concerns of a vague geodeterminist view of culture, states and politics, linked to the colonialism of some geographers and geopoliticians, created a rhetoric of space, race and living space that was easily exploited to buttress the illusion that Germany's crisis could be solved in the colonies.

[49] See Schmokel, *Dream of Empire*, 1964, pp. 76ff; Rüger, 'Der Kolonialrevisionismus', 1977, pp. 243–72.

10

The Japanese Imperial Tradition, Western Imperialism and Modern Japanese Geography

Keiichi Takeuchi

THE BIRTH OF MODERN GEOGRAPHY AND NATIONALISM

Geography and empire have two distinct facets in Japan. On the one hand there was the economic and cultural imperialism of the 'West' which affected indigenous Japanese geography. On the other, there was Japanese imperialist expansion on the Asian mainland and the Pacific islands. Both influenced the practice of geography.

Today, the Japanese word for 'geography' – *chiri* – is a term comprised of the combination of two Chinese ideograms, pronounced *di* and *li*, respectively. The term appears for the first time in an ancient Chinese book, the *Yijing* (also *I Ching* or 'Book of Changes'), dating back to the second century BC, and means the description of, and the logic governing the earth. It was only at the beginning of the nineteenth century, however, that Japanese scholars of western culture (*yogaku-sha*) started to use the word *chiri* as a translation of the western word 'geography'. At this time, then, a rupture developed between the indigenous tradition of geographical thought and practice, which since the ancient period had embraced both the knowledge of various places and the consciousness of spatial differentiation, and geography as a socially recognized branch of knowledge, an institutionalized academic discipline imported from the West. From the nineteenth century, specialists in geography were trained according to western culture but not in the traditional and indigenous intellectual disciplines involving regional description or the human–environmental relationship.[1]

[1] Takeuchi, 'Some remarks on the history of regional description', 1980.

In 1853, Commodore Perry, commanding an American fleet, arrived in Japan and asked for the opening up of the ports. As is well known, a so-called 'isolationist policy' had been in force until that time. In fact, it would be more accurate to call the policy one of shogunate monopolization of commercial and cultural exchanges with foreign countries. In the face of the threat posed by Perry's 'black ships' (*kurofune*), the political and economic leaders of the shogunate government began to discuss ways of negotiating with the Americans: should they comply with the request to open up the ports or reject it and continue to maintain the policy of isolation? These discussions can be regarded as the first instance of geopolitical deliberation in modern Japan, in the sense that the Japanese intelligentsia discussed appropriate foreign policies in the light of the geographical situation.

Adhering to an isolationist policy and opening the country to commercial and cultural intercourse with foreign countries were apparently opposite policies, each with their supporters. The common concern of all, however, was to maintain national independence in the face of western colonialism, that is, to avoid the Chinese 'folly' of the Opium Wars. This concern lasted, at least in the consciousness of the Meiji intelligentsia, throughout the 1860s and 70s.

The first modern geography textbooks were largely interpretations of western works. But while the sources behind world geographies were undeniably western, their style was derived from indigenous works. In 1872, the newly-established centralized Meiji government introduced compulsory education, with geography as one of the most important subjects in the school curriculum. The first geography textbooks were written in the traditional style of a tourist guide. For example, Yukichi Fukuzawa's *Sekai Kunizukushi* (World Geography),[2] first published in 1869 and used widely during the early years of compulsory education, was written in a five–seven–five syllable verse style, which made it easy to read aloud and easy to memorize. In this book, Fukuzawa claimed that Europe was actually the centre of the world, and continued:

Their industries are successful and their trade prosperous; their armies are strong and well-armed. They enjoy a peace of which they are proud. If we seek the source of all this prosperity, we find that it is the blossom on the branches of a tree, whose trunk is learning. Never envy the flowers which blossom on branches without a solid trunk. Devotion to learning may look like a diversion, but it is the only way to arrive at progress. Let us take this path so that we might see the western flower in our country.[3]

This description, in a primary school textbook, is a clear expression of the views of the Meiji occidentalists, who advocated studying western culture in order to uncover the foundations of western prosperity. Thus in the early

[2] Fukuzawa, *Sekai Kunizukushi*, 1869; see also Takeuchi, 'The origins of human geography in Japan', 1974; Takeuchi, 'How Japan learned about the outside world', 1987.
[3] Fukuzawa, *Sekai Kunizukushi*, 1869, vol. 2, p. 617.

Meiji period, geography was utilized exclusively by occidentalists to advocate western ways of life and thought. A certain number of traditionalists or shintoist fundamentalists opposed the early Meiji occidentalists, but as the former could not support their advocacy with either geography, or cosmology, their influence was minor.

While Japanese geography emerged as a compulsory school subject in the 1870s, it coincided with the rise of European academic geography. There is no doubt that authors of school textbooks in both Europe and Japan sought to indoctrinate. Japanese authors did this by flavouring conventional western school textbooks with an original combination of occidentalist ideology and nationalist sentiment. Nevertheless, the development of Japanese school geography in the 1870s had no relationship to the emergence of 'academic' or 'scientific' geography in the Western world in the 1870s. [4]

Another distinctive feature of the early Meiji geography textbooks was a strong faith in the possibility of economic development through, not surprisingly, sustained economic expansion. Backwardness was never ascribed to physical factors such as climate: the fatalism implied by a physical explanation of backwardness was incompatible with the dominant ideology of modernization imposed from above. Rather, backwardness in traditional Japan was attributed to the laziness of the people, misgovernment and so on. China, for instance, had been defeated in the Opium Wars and had become a semi-colonial country because it had been subjected to despotism and its people were apathetic. By contrast, the United States, thanks to its democratic system and the industriousness of its people, had become comparable to Great Britain in industry and to France in culture. In the school textbooks of the 1870s, geography and nationalism were strongly interwoven and the impact of the threat of western imperialism was very much in evidence.

Along with the wide diffusion of geography in school curricula by the late 1880s, a certain number of publications appeared which systematically introduced and applied the methodology of 'modern' western geography. Readers of these publications were generally intellectuals, but it was the geography teachers who made extensive use of them. In contrast with authors of the early Meiji period (1868 to 1880s), who were usually self-made scholars dependent on standard and sub-standard textbooks from the West, the authors of these new publications had generally received their higher education in Japan and had carried out further systematic studies in geography. Moreover, they applied geographical methods pertaining to human–environment paradigms which, while available in indigenous Japanese geographical thought, were more often imported independently from nineteenth-century western sources. They developed and shaped these imported methods to fit the geographical realities of Japan. Although these new geographical works exercised considerable influence, their authors were not yet academic geographers in the strict sense of the term; prior to 1895 there were no courses in geography at the post-secondary level.

[4] Isida, *Nihon ni okeru kindai chirigaku*, 1984, chapter 5.

These late nineteenth-century authors, who included Kanzo Uchimura, Inazo Nitobe and Shigetaka Shiga, adopted distinct ideological stances, but certain common features recur in their works. Known in Japan as an assiduous advocate of Protestantism, Uchimura wrote *Chirigaku-ko* (Considerations on Geography)[5] in 1894, after studying for three years in the United States where he came under the strong influence of Arnold Guyot. Nitobe was an agronomist who encouraged studies in human geography and folklore. Shiga was mainly engaged as a journalist but lectured in geography at Tokyo Technical College (Tokyo Senmongakkō, now Waseda University) and published books on the subject.[6] All three share a disciplinary base either of agronomy or earth sciences, which they studied at the Sapporo College of Agronomy founded in Hokkaido, in 1876. All were strongly influenced by William Smith Clark (1826–86), President of the Massachusetts Agronomical College, who had been invited to teach and serve as Vice-Principal at the Sapporo College of Agronomy. Their interpretations of the human–environment relationship were practical rather than metaphysical and their approach may have been shaped by the political context. In this period Japan had begun to exercise economic and political influence on the Asian continent and, with its victories in the Sino–Japanese War (1894–5) and the Russo–Japanese War (1904–5), it had taken its place among the world's political and military powers.

Japanese authors of geographical books of this period were unquestionably internationally-minded and opposed to overt and chauvinistic imperialism. They were, however, nationalist in their own way, in that they hoped that Japan could occupy an appropriate global position and act so as to deserve respect and confidence. Always of paramount concern to them was the 'Japanese nation'. Shiga, for instance, wrote in 1889:

It is vital for all Japanese to cultivate knowledge of geography. If each one of the 47 million people of this country is familiar with the world situation and has a proper understanding of the advantages and disadvantages of the foreign powers in all matters including trade and armaments – that is, if every one of the 47 million becomes something of a geographer and something of a diplomat, no confusion would occur no matter what emergency might happen.[7]

Shiga like Uchimura discussed the advantages and disadvantages of Japan's island status, and the relationship between the geographical conditions of an island and human activity. They pointed out the easy maritime access to

---

[5] The work is generally known under the title of the second edition, 1895; *Chijin-ron*.

[6] On Shiga, the most reliable bio-bibliographical studies are: Minamoto, 'Shiga Shigetaka', 1984, and Nicola-O et al., *Shigetaka Shiga*, 1992; I have discussed Shiga in the following two papers: Takeuchi, 'Paysage, language et nationalisme au Japon du Meiji', 1989; and Takeuchi, 'Nationalism and geography in modern Japan', 1988.

[7] Shigetaka Shiga, *Chirigaku*, 1908 in *Collected Works*, vol. 4, p. 237.

the United States, the Pacific islands and Southeast Asia. While for the
Japanese military, at least up to the 1920s, the paramount concern had always
been Asia, geographical authors emphasized the desirability of a friendly
relationship with the United States and the expansion of Japanese influence
in the Pacific. These three graduates of the Sapporo College of Agronomy
all declared support for the Sino–Japanese War believing, simply, that the
increased influence of China on the Korean Peninsula would threaten Japan.
Confronted with the Russo–Japanese War, their attitudes diverged: while Shiga
belonged to the hawks and went to the Front as a news reporter, Uchimura
openly protested against the war. Nitobe was more equivocal: as professor
at the Imperial University of Kyoto, he was not in a position to express
overt anti-government opinions. To judge from his writings on colonial policy
and pacifism, however, he was fully aware that Japan's was an ugly role; a
puppet of the British Empire in the worldwide struggle amongst imperialist
powers. His attitude was shared by a small number of internationally-minded
Japanese intellectuals.

After World War I, Shiga became increasingly pessimistic about Japan's
future in the face of the strengthening of Japanese military aggression and
territorial expansion, a growing anti-Japanese sentiment typified by immigration quotas in the United States together with the racial discrimination
which he himself experienced in South Africa. Nitobe worked for six years
(1920–6) in Geneva as Deputy Secretary-General of the League of Nations,
but his work grew more difficult as Japan began to impose her imperialist-
chauvinist policies in the international as well as the domestic sphere. In
Japan the intellectual stance of the Meiji nationalists, who were simultaneously cosmopolitan and internationalist, became increasingly isolated.

The establishment of chairs of geography at higher normal schools took
place at the end of the 1890s, and the chairs of geography at imperial
universities were created in 1907 (Kyoto) and 1911 (Tokyo). The new generation of academic geographers completely ignored the earlier Meiji authors,
who had contributed a great deal to the diffusion and popularization of the
knowledge of *chiri*. The establishment of academic geography in the true
sense coincided with the arrival of imperialist Japan on the international
scene. In order to secure and extend the number of outlets for its industrial
products, Japan adopted expansionist policies which resulted in military
conflicts in Asia, and diplomatic difficulties with the western powers. Institutionally, the emergence of imperialist Japan and the appearance of academic
geography in Japan were closely related, both marking the arrival of Japan as
a modern state. Along with history, ethics and Japanese (language), geography
was considered one of the most important means of awakening students to a
recognition of national identity. Government control over national education
was constantly being tightened; in 1886, a government approval system was
applied to all primary and secondary school textbooks, and from 1903 (until
1947) all primary school textbooks were uniformly edited by the Ministry of
Education which also supervised teacher training. Nevertheless, there was
a perennial shortage of qualified geography teachers for secondary schools.

Consequently a teaching licence examination for non-graduates was instituted, with newly-established academic geographers playing an important role on the examining committee.

Apart from this institutional link, academic geographers made some indirect contributions to the Japanese empire. First, although trained in the disciplines of geology or history, most of this generation of academic geographers were active members of the Geographical Society of Tokyo (founded in 1879) and specialists in natural history. Moreover, as politicians and military men, they were often social celebrities in much the same way as geographical society members were in western countries. The Geographical Society of Tokyo, in line with the interests of the government and the Japanese military, organized lectures and published numerous papers on various places on the Asian mainland. After 1910 it dispatched scientific expeditions, mostly geological surveys, overseas.[8] Takuji Ogawa, first head of the Department of Geography, Imperial University of Kyoto and editor-in-chief of its journal, who had conducted a geological survey in China in 1903, was promotor of these projects.

The second indirect contribution to the Japanese empire was a result of the fact that the majority of graduates in geography before World War II went on to become teachers in secondary schools and institutions of higher education. Some taught at the Military or Naval Academy, or other military establishments. Most of those who engaged in work for the military were assigned to the Geographical Survey Section of General Headquarters. A small number of geographers worked in other sections of the army and navy. The Japanese armed forces were comparatively independent of ministerial control, and the geographers working for them as skilled specialists in turn retained considerable independence. By the 1930s, an increasing number of young geographers began finding jobs in the colonial administration in Formosa, Korea, and Northeast China (Manchuria).

Another indirect contribution to Japanese imperialism came about as a result of the post-World War I peace settlements. During World War I, Japan captured Chintao and the German islands in the Pacific with comparative ease and gained huge economic profits by penetrating Asian markets while European countries were preoccupied with war. At the Paris Peace Conference, Japan's sole concern was the re-confirmation of the concessions made in Shantung and the mandate for the former German islands north of the equator that had been promised to Japan by Britain, France, and Italy in secret agreements made in 1917.

Unlike geographers of the United States, France, and Britain, the three major protagonists at the Paris Conference, Japanese geographers played a marginal role and in general were less well prepared. Had they, as Asian geographers, dispassionately assessed the situation, they would have found

---

[8] Isida suggests there was a relationship between these expeditions and government policies towards China, noting the scientific achievements of the geological survey. Isida, *Nihon ni okeru kindai chirigaku*, 1984, p. 261.

themselves compelled to denounce the victors in the war, including Japan, for their failure to apply the principles of self-determination to the Asian nations concerned. Such a denunciation would have provoked a frontal clash with Japanese government authorities, since Japan herself was violating Chinese and Korean rights of self-determination. But no Japanese geographer had the courage to protest and, as in many other countries, Japanese academic geographers remained attentive to the state's agenda. One might condemn those Japanese geographers who, for one reason or other, opted to maintain the status quo. At the same time, a number of tough-minded economists and political scientists did offer a biting criticism of the establishment. They were subjected to suppression in all its forms, losing their jobs, suffering imprisonment, and in the worst cases, perishing in prison. Only two academic geographers were arrested and detained in custody for several days: Keishi Ohara,[9] for his involvement in Marxian studies, and Hiroshi Sato for the introduction to Japan of the geographical materialism of K. Wittfogel.[10] Other geographical writers were religious dissenters. The Christian Kanzo Uchimura, who was professor at the First Higher School (the present Faculty of Arts, University of Tokyo), refused to recognize any living being as superior to God. This was at a time when the emperor of Japan was considered a god by his subjects. Japanese subjects were required to bow during the reading of imperial rescripts. On one occasion Uchimura refused to bow during a reading by the director of the school of the Imperial Rescript on Education. For this he was forced to resign his professorship. The Buddhist Tsunesaburo Makiguchi experienced more drastic repression. He was a self-educated teacher of geography and author of three important geographical works, *Jinsei chirigaku* (Geography of Human Life) written in 1903, *Kyōju no tōgōchūshin toshite no kyodoka kenkyū* (Study of the Homeland as the Centre of Integrated Teaching), 1912, and *Chiri kyōju no hōhō to naiyō no kenkyū* (Study on the Method and the Contents of Geographical Education), 1916. In 1930, he founded the Sōka Kyōiku Gakkai, literally the Association for Creative Education. This was the origin of the present Sōkagakkai, a militant Buddhist sect which today has considerable social and political influence in Japan. For his activities as a militant Buddhist, he was subjected to severe suppression. In fact he died in 1944 under the totalitarian militarist regime inspired by nationalist Shintoism.[11]

---

[9] Ohara was the author of *Shakaichirigaku no kisomondai*, 1936, p. 359. I have discussed Ohara in further detail in Takeuchi, 'Geopolitics and geography in Japan', 1980.

[10] Sato, *Keizaichirigaku soron*, 1933, pp. 70–83.

[11] I have discussed Makiguchi in further detail in Takeuchi, 'Strategies of Heterodox Researchers', 1984–5.

JAPANESE IMPERIALISM AND THE GEOPOLITICAL MOVEMENT[12]

Kjellén's *Geopolitik* was introduced to Japan comparatively early in 1925 when the *Journal of International Law and Diplomacy* reviewed *Staten som Lifsform*, published in Stockholm in 1916. By that time, the geopolitical movement in Germany was already underway. Mitsuo Fujisawa, reviewing the book, knew nothing of the German movement and made a positive appraisal of this geopolitics as a Swedish product: 'It takes into consideration the reality of international politics rather than conventional political doctrines'. In fact, in view of the changed nature of international relations in the imperialist era in the early twentieth century, this is an extremely accurate appraisal of the character of Kjellén's geopolitics.

Some newly-emerging Japanese academic geographers, especially graduates of the Imperial University of Tokyo, such as Nobuyuki Iimoto and Hikoichiro Sasaki, began to demonstrate an interest in geopolitics at almost the same time.[13] In the latter half of the 1920s they reviewed a number of works published by German geopoliticians, but they generally regarded geopolitics as a branch of political science rather than as geography, and opposed those Germans who considered geopolitics either a development of political geography or a new kind of geography. Geographers such as Nobuyuki Iimoto, Gorō Ishibashi and Takuji Ogawa considered that geopolitics lacked a precisely defined object of study. However, Iimoto also recognized the utility of geopolitical studies for policy-making.[14]

After the Japanese invasion of Northeast China (Manchuria) in 1932 which marked the beginning of what was to be, for Japan, a 15-year war, international opinion severely criticized Japanese expansionist policies. This resulted in Japan's withdrawal in 1933 from the League of Nations. The invasion of Manchuria both advanced the profit-making schemes of industrial leaders and was designed to divert popular attention from internal economic and social difficulties. The Manchurian invasion involved such enormous Japanese and Chinese losses, that Japanese leaders found themselves forced to justify themselves before both international and domestic opinion. Seeking a convincing pretext for the military and political manoeuvres in Manchuria, they found geopolitical arguments attractive. These defined East Asia as some kind of 'sphere of influence' or *Lebensraum*. So it was that by the end of the 1930s, geopolitics (*chiseigaku*) came to be hailed in the journalistic world as an 'up-to-date' science.

[12] This section is a revised and abbreviated version of Takeuchi, 'Geopolitics and geography in Japan', 1980.
[13] Iimoto, 'Jinshutōsō no jijitsu', 1925; Sasaki, 'Geoporichiku to ekonomikku jeogurafi', 1927.
[14] Iimoto, 'Iwayuru chiseigaku no gainen', 1928, pp. 76–9; Ishibashi, 'Seijichirigaku to chiseigaku', 1927; Ogawa, Jinmonchirigaku no ikka to toshite no seijichirigaku', 1933.

Japanese geopolitics was not, however, a homogenous movement. It was composed of various cultural and social subgroups due largely to the vagueness of geopolitics as a doctrine. Nevertheless, it is possible to group Japanese geopoliticians into the following three schools according to their research and praxis: the Kyoto school, which was oriented towards indigenous Japanese geopolitics; academicians who were strongly influenced by German geopolitics; and finally, the academicians, politicians, and military men who founded the Japanese Society for Geopolitics.

The Kyoto School

The first school, developed by geographers at the Imperial University of Kyoto, concentrated on the search for a geopolitics appropriate to the Japanese empire. From the time of its establishment in 1907, the Department of Geography of the Imperial University of Kyoto had leaned towards studies in historical and settlement geography and had developed an interest in human and social geography. This was in contrast to the Department of Geography of the Imperial University of Tokyo which emphasized physical geography and the direct importation of western geographic ideas. The Kyoto school's position is summarized by Saneshige Komaki, Head of Department, in his Manifesto of Japanese Geopolitics:

> Now it is true that our national policies find one of their bases in geography. This necessitates a new Japanese geopolitics which must develop upon the basis of a geographical study of Japan and must constitute the basis of Japanese policies enhanced by the Japanese spiritual tradition. [15]

Komaki's manifesto is pervaded by a belief in the ultimate decline of western civilization and a reaction to evolutionism in western culture. In the intellectual history of contemporary Japan after 1853 there are repeated recurrences of traditionalism in reaction to Western civilization's manifestation of supremacy through political and military predominance and cultural Eurocentrism. The early Meiji period (mid to late 1880s), witnessed just such a reaction against occidentalization. Again, in the 1920s and 30s, in a Japan beleaguered by economic difficulties, social unrest, and international political isolation, occidentalization aroused something verging on a fundamentalist movement in both intellectual circles and the popular consciousness. This constituted the social background to the rise of the Kyoto school of geopolitics.

Kyoto school geopolitics under the leadership of Komaki had three aspects. First, it involved pinpointing the geopolitical tradition in Japanese culture

[15] Komaki, *Nihon chiseigaku sengen*, 1940, p. 5.

especially in the Togukawa period (1600–1867). This was found in the writings of Shoin Yoshida[16] and others of the Togukawa period who confronted the increasing menace of the Western powers and monetary economics.[17] Second, the Kyoto geopolitics exalted a peculiarly Japanese spiritual tradition, tennoism. According to tennoist ideology, Japan was unique and its geopolitics were equally unique. For Komaki:

> In this way Japanese geopolitics is different from the many world geopolitical currents imitating German geopolitics, from the colonialist in the British style and also from the old-fashioned type of Chinese geopolitics; it is a distinctively Japanese type which has existed since the beginnings of the imperial family and will develop in line with the prosperity of the imperial family as a truly creative science of Japan.[18]

At first glance, these writings seem merely illogical and fanatic, but careful examination shows the leaders of the Kyoto school, such as Komaki and Nobuo Muroga, to be very well read in German geopolitics. One of their claimed distinctions from German geopolitics was their rejection of environmental determinism.[19]

The third aspect of the Kyoto school's geopolitics was its attempt to clarify the history of the western imperialist invasion in East Asia. Contributing to the development of regional studies in Kyoto, this work largely consisted of bibliographical surveys, without reinforcement by field work, in the 'Greater East Asia Co-prosperity Sphere'. The work undertaken had no direct connection with political or administrative authorities in the region and remained restricted to the moral and intellectual sphere. The remarks made by these geographers on the economic problems caused for Japan by the dominance of the western powers in East Asia and on racial discrimination against Japanese, (especially that displayed by Nazi Germany) had a considerable effect on the Japanese public. At the same time, these authors sensed that the mere exposure and condemnation of western imperialism was not enough to legitimize similar imperialist policies implemented elsewhere by Japan. As an alternative ideology, they had to construct 'Asianism', the idea of a communalistic unity binding Asian people together. This was an extension of the idea of the communal state centred on the tenno family applied to the 'Asian community' as a whole. To exalt this communalism, they mobilized an indigenous ideology which underlined familial and pseudo-familial ties as the basis of social organization. This was ideology derived from feudal Japan which the Kyoto geopoliticians applied to the vagaries of competition

[16] Yoshida (1830–59) was the ideological percursor of the Meiji Restoration.

[17] A typical example of the plentiful quotations from Togukawa thinkers is: Muroga, 'Daitōa chiseigaku shinron', 1943.

[18] Komaki, 'Nihon chiseigaku no shūchō', 1940, pp. 3–6.

[19] Muroga was fully conscious that geopolitics inherited Ratzel's romantic view of the world rather than his environmentalism. See, Muroga, 'Chirigaku no dōkō', 1942.

among nation-states in the twentieth century. In a certain sense, therefore, this constituted a revival of traditional indigenous ideology; but it was not simply a reaction to modernity as the old ideology was thoroughly adapted to support national policies at the height of the imperialist era.[20]

The German Influence

The second group of Japanese geopoliticians comprised those who introduced and were influenced by German geopolitics. From an international point of view they argued that Germany was in a position fundamentally similar to that of Japan, and so German geopolitical theories, especially that of *Lebensraum*, were valid for Japan. They also sought to apply the concept of spatial planning, *Raumordnung*, to Japan itself and especially to the Japanese colonies of Manchuria, Korea, and Formosa. Starting in 1939, numerous translations and interpretations of German geopolitics were published. Haushofer's special interest in East Asia stimulated the adoption of German geopolitics in Japan.[21] These geographers and political scientists saw the consistent development of Kjellén's state-as-an-organism theory in German geopolitics and adopted it as the most appropriate for explaining the political reality of the imperialist era. In one sense, they followed the Meiji (1868) intellectual tradition which gave priority to an uncritical study of western science. The organic concept of the state involved a biological analogy, and the spatial organization of the state was interpreted as a mechanistic interaction of various socio-economic forces.

For those Japanese geographers inspired by German geopolitics it was not necessary to integrate a traditional universalist Japanese ideology into geopolitical analysis, nor was it necessary to exalt, in order to legitimize, national policies. Thus, the economic geographer Joji Ezawa defined the geopolitical movement as based on 'the romantic thought that overcomes a debatable universalism' and he stressed 'the necessity of understanding the concept of economic space which differs from physical space'.[22] For Ezawa, geopolitics

[20] In his study on Japanese geopolitics as an aspect of the intellectual history of Japan in the 1930s, Hatano clearly pointed out the logical connection between this ideological emphasis on indigenousness and advocacy of Asian 'chauvinism'. See Hatano, 'Toa shinchitsujo to chiseigaku', 1980.

[21] Thanks to his experience in Japan as military attaché, Haushofer was able to write six books on Japan alone between 1913 and 1938. Between 1939 and 1943 two Japanese versions of *Bausteine zur Geopolitik*, 1928 in co-authorship with E. Obst, H. Lautensach and O. Maull were published in addition to three Japanese versions of *Geopolitik des pazifischen Ozeans*, 1925. Also, Haushofer's, *Weltmeer und Weltmacht*, 1937 and *Geopolitische Grundlage*, 1939 were translated in 1943 and 1940, respectively. Abdel-Malek has noted that the geographical position of Japan is highly conducive to the flourishing of geopolitics. See Abdel-Malek, 'Geopolitics and national movements', 1977.

[22] Ezawa, 'Keizaichirigaku ni okeru kūkan-gainen', 1939.

provided the theoretical analysis behind *Lebensraum* and *Raumordnung*; it was a practical science devoted to mechanistic and geometric spatial analyses. Ezawa was critical of the contention, associated with Haushofer, that geopolitics was an 'artistic handicraft' rather than a science.[23] It would seem that the identification of geopolitics with the study of spatial logic ought to have been more acceptable to academics than the transcendent approach of the Kyoto school. In the field of geography, however, those who advocated geopolitics as spatial analysis and spatial praxis constituted a minority. One reason for this was, perhaps, that deductive spatial analysis was not familiar to geographers of that time. In addition, in the Japanese academy under a totalitarian regime, most university geographers avoided involvement with social and political issues. Consequently, many academic geographers never developed a critical approach to either the geopolitics of the Kyoto school or German-type geopolitics. Those academic geographers who advocated the geopolitics of the German school tended to be outside the inner circle of academics – professors at small or private universities, or journalists. Furthermore, they were fundamentally Eurocentric, and were incapable of taking a critial stand against colonialism or against Japanese racial discrimination and militarism directed at other Asian peoples. They were, indeed, indifferent to these problems and were unconcerned with the dubious applicability of Western analyses to their own non-western field. They failed to demonstrate the relevance of their theories to the realities of East Asia.

The Japanese Society for Geopolitics

The third branch of Japanese geopolitics was represented by academics including geographers, journalists, military persons and politicians who comprised the founding members of the Japanese Society for Geopolitics established in November 1941. Coming immediately prior to the outbreak of the Pacific War, the founding of the society marked the culmination of nationalist sentiment. It also reflected the increasing necessity for the mobilization of scientists to implement national policies. The society's charter declared that: 'The purpose of this society consists of the study of geopolitics, geopolitical surveys of the terrestrial and marine spaces of Japan and her *Lebensraum*, and in contributing to the national policy to construct and defend a highly-developed state'. Almost all the scholars who had advocated a German-type geopolitics joined this society together with other geographers who had heretofore shown reluctance to embrace geopolitics. The latter included university geographers who had criticized the lack of coherence of geopolitics, or who had questioned its scientific nature.[24] The fact that no

---

[23] Haushofer, *Geopolitik des pazifischen Ozeans*, 1938, p. 13; Ezawa, *Chiseigaku gairon*, 1943, pp. 140–1.

[24] Iimoto, who became the secretary-general of the society, never agreed that geopolitics could constitute a coherent science. See, Iimoto, 'Iwayuru chiseigaku no gainen', 1928.

geopoliticians of the Kyoto school attempted to join this society tells us more about its orientation. Its main activities included the publication of a journal aimed at popularizing geographical knowledge of Asia and the Pacific areas (strategically important in the context of the Pacific War), and the various doctrines of German geopolitics, as well as promoting geographical surveys of the newly-occupied areas of Southeast Asia. Unsurprisingly, given the composition of its membership, the society never expressed a unified view of the nature of geopolitics. All arguments concerning spatial aspects of Pacific War strategies and administrative measures of that period were bundled together under the term 'geopolitics'. Before the establishment of this society, Ezawa and some other geopoliticians had clearly refuted geographical determinism as an explanation of spatial organization, but in the society's journal *Chiseigaku*, geographical determinism was freely applied to descriptions of occupied areas and in the interpretation of military strategies.

The Japanese Society for Geopolitics promoted, but did not directly finance, numerous surveys of colonial lands and newly-occupied territories. In fact, many leading social scientists of post-war Japan had their first field experiences in surveys in China and Southeast Asia under the aegis of the society. In some cases these involved collaboration with other institutions and companies, such as the Southern Manchuria Railway. That no consistent methodology or ideology governed the society's surveys demonstrates its heterogeneous composition. On the one hand, studies were conducted in the name of economic efficiency and large-scale regional planning in the East Asian autarkic sphere.[25] On the other hand, there was a certain ruralist orientation, a sort of physiocracy fighting 'the battle against urbanism in modern capitalist civilization'.[26] The geopoliticians' arguments exerted some influence on the bureaucrats and administrative bodies responsible for wartime policies.

Critiques of German geopolitics were published in the 1930s which, as already suggested, did not receive wide support among academic geographers and political scientists. Some researchers pointed out, at times implicitly, the connection between geopolitics and totalitarianism, and the threat that this represented to academic freedom.[27] Others condemned it for its colonialist

---

Also in 1939, Sato, who wrote numerous papers for the the society's journal, severely criticized the arbitrariness of geopolitical reasoning and the unsystematic nature of geopolitics. See, Sato, *Seijichirigaku gairon*, 1939, pp. 324–8. Watanabe, who joined the society as Professor of Geography at the Military Academy, always maintained his critical stand against geopolitical arguments which seemed to him 'intuitive rather than analytical'. See Watanabe, 'Chiseigaku no naiyō ni tsuite', 1942, p. 269.

[25] Ezawa, *Chiseigaku kenkyū*, 1942, pp. 277–83.

[26] Iwata, *Chiseigaku*, 1942, p. 123. Ezawa also expressed his anti-urbanist views in his *Kokudo-keikaku no kisoriron*, 1942, p. 25. In his case, he discussed, on a purely theoretical basis, the economic loss brought about by urban and industrial over-concentration.

[27] See for instance, Watsuji, *Fudo, ningengakuteki kōsatsu*, 1935, pp. 238–9. This was originally published in *Shisō* in 1934.

character. In 1933, for instance, Masakane Kawanishi, citing Karl Wittfogel, dismissed 'an explanation neglecting the intermediate mechanism of the connection between existing natural conditions and political patterns' and characterized geopolitics as 'the theory heralding a fascist-type dictatorship based on the utilitarian and invasionist ambitions of an imperialist power of the Caucasian race'. [28] Geopolitics here was somewhat narrowly understood as German geopolitics; nobody took much notice of the practice of political geography outside Germany. Important as it was, liberalist antipathy towards geopolitics had its shortcomings. Despite their insistence on political neutrality and ideological pluralism in scientific matters, these critics failed to grasp that such neutrality was impossible in the Japanese academy of the time. Moreover, the condemnation of geopolitics on the basis of its connection with western colonialism contained a dangerous weakness in that it harboured an Asian racism or ethnocentrism. This academic racism was echoed in the strong prejudice and discrimination inflicted by the Japanese people at large against other Asian peoples. Nevertheless, given the totalitarian nature of the Japanese government, under which freedom of speech was drastically curtailed, it is worth documenting opposition to geopolitics alongside the record of Japanese geopoliticians.

Among the very small number of Japanese geographers who strongly opposed geopolitics was Keishi Ohara:

The fundamental method of a geopolitical approach still continues to be one involving an explanation of the nature of the state and the process of its political development, not in terms of the development of social productive forces or other socio-economic factors such as the pursuit of profit or of capitalist economies, but directly and one-sidedly through natural conditions. This masks the socio-economic factors existing behind the activities of the state and justifies the claims and the acts of exploitation on the part of the state in regard to existing natural conditions ... Geopolitics and present-day political geography are thus based on an organic view of the state and on the geographical materialism of past times. Only the social and economic situations of present-day Germany have restored these conventional theories ... Political geography expressed in present-day Germany is an ideological reflection of the recovery of German capitalism and its nationalistic development, and serves as a scientific instrument for its development. [29]

Ohara was purged from a teaching post in higher education in 1937 for, among other things, publishing the book from which this quotation was taken. Thereafter, criticism of geopolitics became more and more difficult with increasing restrictions on the freedom of speech imposed under censorship.

[28] Wittfogel, *Geopolitik, geographischen Materiarismus und Marxismus*, 1929; Kawanishi, 'Fassho-chirigaku, geoporichiku hihan', 1933.

[29] Ohara, *Shakaichirigaku no kisomondai*, 1936, pp. 311–14.

With Akira Watanabe and Koji Iizuka, criticism was veiled, couched in slavish terms which seemingly catered to the political dicta of the times. Thus according to Watanabe in 1942: 'when the territory is one which does not affect the interests of their country, it is treated analytically as it would be by political geographers', [but] 'when territory pertinent to the interests of the country is involved, there is no scientific analysis, but only interpretations based on a naive determinism'.[30] In this way, Watanabe implied that, on the theoretical level, geopolitics had contributed nothing whatsoever to political geography. Iizuka was more prudent. In a series of papers published in 1942 and 1943, he analysed the German geopolitical literature of the 1920s, and with reference to Demangeon,[31] came to the conclusion that, as far as geography was concerned, geopolitics was nothing new.[32]

Since the end of World War II, very few studies of geopolitics have been carried out in Japan. Most criticism of geopolitics has attacked its support of the militarist, ultra-nationalist regime, rather than its scientific claims. The principal advocates of the Kyoto school of geopolitics and the social scientists who played important roles in the Japanese Society for Geopolitics resigned their offices immediately after the war, or were purged from public posts at the order of the Allied Forces. This situation prevailed until the end of the occupation in 1952.[33] This created the impression in the intellectual world that geopolitics was dead. The purge was naturally an administrative measure, influenced by the social and political circumstances in universities and academic circles, and did not involve a scientific evaluation of geopolitics. Investigation of university professors was entrusted to the faculty and the criteria of judgement differed. At colleges (including the teacher training colleges) and among the teachers of preparatory courses for the university, investigations and decisions were made directly by the Allied authorities. They attached importance not to geopolitical theories

[30] Watanabe, 'Chiseigaku no naiyō ni tsuite', 1942, p. 269.

[31] Demangeon, 'Géographie politique', 1932.

[32] Iizuka, 'Geoporitiku no kihonteki seikaku', in *Keizai Ronsō*, vol. 12, 1942, pp. 816–44; vol. 13, 1943, pp. 288–314, 486–96; I discussed Iizuka in Takeuchi, 'Two outsiders', 1984.

[33] For those who were purged, life up to 1952 was very hard. Komaki ran a secondhand bookshop in Kyoto, and many others practised farming in their native villages. After 1952, with an increase in the number of posts in higher education resulting from the post-war reform in the educational system, most of them obtained posts in national or private universities. Among the active members of the Kyoto school, Komaki obtained a post at the National University of Shiga and was president of the University for several years; Muroga became professor at Tokai University and Yonekura became professor at Hiroshima University. In Tokyo, Ezawa obtained a professorship at Senshu University and played an important role in the development of regional science in Japan. He was also president of the Japanese Association of Economic Geographers. He retained his approach: the mechanistic treatment of the spatial system.

per se but to the social influence wielded by the person in question. [34] As for primary and secondary schools, the situation differed greatly in different prefectures. Where the local government tended to ingratiate itself with the Allied authorities, many teachers were purged simply because they had been officers of the Japanese army or navy. The scientific examination of geopolitics was also hindered for many years because a large number of persons involved in geopolitical affairs were still alive and exercised a certain influence in academic circles. No critical or summary appraisal of Japanese geopolitics, along the lines of those made in Germany by Troll, has ever been carried out in Japan.

Ohara's comprehensive 1936 critique of geopolitics was republished after the war. Thorough in its treatment of the social and ideological basis of German geopolitics, it came too early to discuss the development of geopolitics in Japan. Iizuka's critique, in a revised edition of his papers written during the war, has come to be considered the definitive frame of reference as regards criticism of Japanese geopolitics. These papers confront the theoretical and social bases of geopolitics, i.e., the state-as-organism theory, and the marginal place of geopolitics *vis-à-vis* the academy.

Later theoretical criticism of Japanese geopolitics has never surpassed Ohara's and Iizuka's writings. Japanese geographers thoroughly criticized the environmental determinist aspects of geopolitics, though they sometimes seemed to rely on its 'possibilism' which seemed to preclude the establishment of causal explanations. Preoccupied with criticizing environmentalism, Japanese geographers did not properly explain the connections between geographical conditions and social circumstances. Thus, because the conditioning of social life by environmental influences and geographical position was apparent even to the naive perceptions of the common people, the criticism voiced by Japanese geographers failed to gain the wide support of either popular opinion or intellectual thinkers. Furthermore, they never succeeded in challenging the communalistic claims of the modern state in general and the Japanese nation-state in particular. Even after the collapse of Japanese geopolitics with the defeat of Japan in World War II, the ideological justification of the violence of state power remained, and still remains,

[34] In 1986 Masai and I conducted interviews with 20 senior Japanese geographers, 16 of which were published. See, Takeuchi and Masai (eds), *Chirigaku wo manabu*, 1986; Iimoto (1895–1989) who had been secretary-general of the Japanese Society for Geopolitics, spoke eloquently on how he was able to escape the purges of the occupation authorities. We also recorded a dialogue with Komaki (1898–1991), but only on the condition that the interviewers would not refer to 'geopolitical affairs'. At the Tokyo Commercial University (the present Hitotsubashi University), Ezawa, who had been professor on the preparatory course, was purged after submitting to the direct examination of the Allied authorities. At the same time, many faculty professors of economics and political science, who had actively collaborated with the military administration and the military intelligence services in Southeast Asia, escaped from the purge because the faculty refused to recognize that they had been 'responsible for war crimes'.

unchallenged, and all sorts of ethnic claims, albeit in changing guises, continue to be made. In other words, the ideology of the pseudo-consanguinity of the Japanese Empire was easy to criticize, but ethnicity was, and is, a product of the contemporary world, which the critics of Japanese geopolitics have never adequately been able to handle.

For historians of geography, both the social practices of professional geographers and the contributions to geographical theory by practitioners who were not formally trained in the discipline are very important. From this perspective, it is clear that the criticism of Japanese geopolitics has not acknowledged the social relevance – both of a pernicious or beneficent nature – of geographical studies. It has not acknowledged that a critique based merely on an 'ivory tower' viewpoint, which legitimizes only the avoidance of a commitment to real politics, encourages continued confusion. Those academic geographers who have criticized Japanese geopolitics have never considered it necessary to develop a counter-geopolitics or an alternative geopolitics. All the critiques have so far failed to point out what prompted researchers and practitioners of geography to support an imperialistic geopolitics. They have failed to point out, too, that this geopolitics encouraged a blindness to the social contradictions in Japan itself, and to Japan's attitude towards other Asian peoples.

GEOGRAPHY AND EMPIRE AFTER WORLD WAR II

In the history of modern Japan, 1945 was a turning point, as was 1868, the date of the Meiji Restoration. As a result of political, economic and administrative reforms carried out at the instigation of the occupying Allied forces, the Emperor was deprived of political power, remaining only nominally and symbolically head of state. The Imperial Army and Navy were dissolved and in the new constitution of 1946 Japan renounced military force as a means of settling international disputes. The *Zaibatsu*, or financial combines, which had supported Japanese imperialism were also dissolved and the peasants of rural Japan, which had once been an important source of the Japanese soldiers notorious for wartime cruelty, became owner-cultivators following the land reforms.

But the administrative reform most important for geographical studies after the Second World War was that which involved the education system. In 1949 former higher educational institutions such as upper secondary schools, professional colleges, and the former national and private universities were all reorganized into a new system of more than 200 universities on the American model. Many departments of geography were established in these universities; even those universities without departments of geography had at least one chair of geography in the liberal arts. This resulted in a great increase in the number of professional geographers in universities and also in the number of geographical societies and publications.

Institutionally, therefore, Japanese geography is firmly entrenched. This does not mean however, that geography is highly influential in applied fields or that there are many geographers engaged in jobs outside research and education. The strength of geography in academia derives mainly from its importance in the school curriculum and less from the activities of geographers in applied fields. In post-war Japan, now deprived of the military forces and the centralized, totalitarian political power of old, the possible contributions of geographers to the 'empire' underwent a total change.

After World War II, with the new concept of public intervention in the market economy, many economists became actively involved in economic, as well as town and regional planning. The remarkably rapid growth of the national economy after World War II and the changing industrial structure were necessarily accompanied by the reorganization of the spatial structure of the Japanese economy and the emergence of new problems such as environmental pollution and increased regional disparity. In comparison with specialists in economics and civil engineering, few geographers have been actively involved in government policy-making as administrative officers or members of consulting bodies. Moreover, in the private sector, only a small number of specialists in economic geography have been concerned with locational problems. These economic geographers have certainly contributed to putting new industrial sites at the disposal of private firms, first on a domestic scale and later, after the mid 1960s, on a world-wide scale. An increasing number of geographers are also now interested in social issues. They have analysed government locational policies and the spatial behaviour of private firms but, at best, they have voiced mild criticism without proposing counter-policies. Regarding environmental problems, which became very serious as a consequence of the rapid industrial development from the mid-1950s up to the oil crisis in 1973, specialized techniques and knowledge not possessed by geographers became necessary. Among geographers who, since the introduction of modern geography in this country, had consistently purported to be specialists in environmental studies with their 'man–environment' paradigm, only a few were actively engaged in grappling with environmental questions of increasing social relevance.

Many Asian peoples still feel the menace of Japan as a military power. However, Japanese public opinion is strongly against the bestowal of offensive power on the 'self-defence' forces. In addition, the members of the 'self-defence' forces themselves are reluctant to engage in military operations outside Japan, even under the designation of Peace Keeping Operations (PKO). There is little possibility that Japan will revert to a military power. In this sense, the Allied demilitarization of Imperial Japan was successful, to the disappointment of certain Japanese right-wing leaders. As a by-product, the demilitarization came to constitute an important factor in the economic prosperity of post-war Japan. Entrusting military matters to the United States according to the terms of the Security Treaty, Japan has concentrated on economic growth in both domestic and global markets. As a paradoxical consequence, one of the biggest debtor countries, the United States, is today obliged to answer for the defence of one of the world's biggest creditor countries. Now with the end of the Cold War, the situation is changing. For the time being, however, while the Japanese military empire may not exist, there is nevertheless, a Japanese economic empire whose geopolitical impact is far from negligible.

In comparison with pre-war times, Japanese field researchers, including geographers, engage in a good deal of foreign field research. These are generally funded by grants from government and public or private foundations. These tend to be given for studies undertaken in areas and countries with a close economic relationship to Japan, that is Asian and Pacific countries and the United States. In 1962, the Institute for Developing Economy was established as an extra-departmental organization of the Ministry of International Trade and Industry (MITI). The staff of this Institute, including several geographers, has played a leading role in social and economic research involving developing countries. These studies are not directly connected with Japanese economic expansion nor do they directly support the country's economic imperialism, it is necessary to recognize that regional studies by Japanese geographers in foreign countries have been biased by the latter's economic relationships with Japan. Most of the geographers concerned are, however, relunctant to admit this fact. Furthermore, many new and relevant geographical issues of international scope are now emerging. For instance, an increasing number of foreign workers are making their way into Japan; some 4 million have already arrived, in addition to the descendants of the Chinese and the Koreans brought to Japan by force during the Japanese colonial administration. There is also growing concern among Asian peoples over the ecological destruction resulting from the Japanese economic 'invasion', such as the exhaustion of tropical forest resources and the environmental pollution caused by Japanese-built factories. No Japanese geographer has yet seen fit seriously to take up these significant geographical issues.

We can conclude, therefore, that since World War II, the attitude of Japanese geographers with regard to the 'empire' has remained a passive one, much as in pre-war days. It is for this reason that it is so necessary to examine the involvement of geographers in the contemporary Japanese empire. Why have modern Japanese geographers failed to step out of their ivory towers and, in a spirit of self-criticism, place their discipline in a wider context?

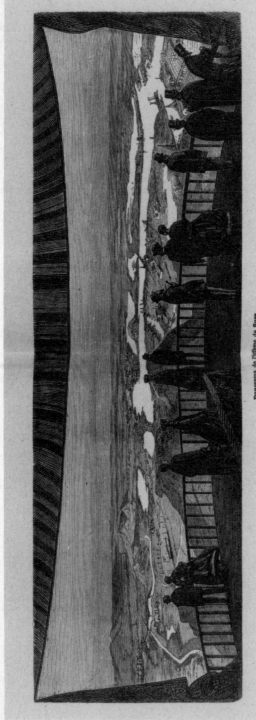

Panorama de l'Isthme de Suez

Plate 4 Europeans at the Paris *Exposition Universelle*, 1867, viewing a panorama of the construction of the Suez Canal, the global planning project of the nineteenth century which perhaps best reflected Europe's imperial aspirations and technical pride. From *Grand Album de l'Exposition Universelle*, (Paris, 1867), p. 60. By permission of the Bibliothèque Nationale, Paris.

PART IV

Planning and Reflecting

Introduction

Micro-scale planning and social and economic restructuring were an important part of late nineteenth-century imperialism and led to a radical alteration of space and place in the colonial world. Indeed, the European hegemonic approach to colonial space extended well beyond the physical manipulation of space, to the manipulation of the human use of space, and, indeed, to the manipulation of mind. But the application of a European planning mentality to the colonial world not only restructured colonial territory but served to change the geographic discipline by providing geographers with a new set of problems and by altering the internal politics of the discipline.

In the diverse chapters in this section each author explores some of the consequences of the new focus on micro-scale planning and restructuring. Beginning from Gramsci's concept of 'hegemony', Garth Myers draws on the work of two African historians on colonial Cairo and Mombasa to examine British attempts to restructure the town of Zanzibar. This restructuring was shaped by a desire to reorient the economy of the region to fit Zanzibar's evolving geopolitical role in the British Empire. It entailed the functional redesign of the port, roads, and sewage system, the 'beautification' of the city to enhance its appeal to European tourists, and the reform of the educational system with a view to staffing these various endeavours. There is little doubt that these 'reforms' reached into and transformed the lives and thoughts of the dwellers of Zanzibar. Olivier Soubeyran looks at a disciplinary power struggle toward the end of the nineteenth century between Vidalian regional geography and Dubois's colonial geography. The struggle centred on the concept of colonial geography and the extent to which it would be a planning discipline which sought to analyse and transform colonial space through social and political institutions. Similarly, but at a slightly later period, Paul Claval looks at a rationalist critique of imperialism produced by the French geographer Albert Demangeon in the context of the British Empire. Demangeon, in Claval's view was not only making a political statement but was advocating an altogether new type of colonial geography. One which was neither historical reconstruction nor transplanted regional geography but which explored the complexities, dynamics and spatial patterns arising from the interaction of peoples with radically different material, economic and social cultures. The colonial realm, then, and the possibilities it offered for social and economic transformation, changed colonial geography in both senses of the term.

11

From 'Stinkibar' to 'The Island Metropolis': The Geography of British Hegemony in Zanzibar

Garth Myers*

> The stench [of the town]...is quite horrible. At night it is so gross or crass, one might cut out a slice and manure a garden with it: it might be called 'Stinkibar' rather than Zanzibar
>
> David Livingstone in 1869

> It is a town of rich merchants and busy streets; of thronged market places and clustered mansions. Over all there is the din of barter, of shouts from the harbour; the glamour of the sun, the magic of the sea, and the rich savour of Eastern spice. This is Zanzibar ... the island metropolis of Eastern Africa
>
> F. B. Pearce in 1920[1]

Pearce's representation of Zanzibar in 1920 as a glamorous metropolis instead of a compost heap marked a reawakening in the geographical literature about the city made infamous by Livingstone and his peers a half century or so before. The outpouring of geographical scholarship which followed Pearce's book into print was quite distinct from the writings of Livingstone,

The author would like to acknowledge some of the many people who helped in thinking through different elements of this chapter. Neil Smith, Anne Godlewska, Terence Young, Steve Herbert, Ed Soja, Gerry Hale, Ned Alpers, Judith Carney, Abdul Sheriff, Tom Spear, Issa Shivji and Michael Curry have given invaluable advice, though they bear no responsibility for the final product's faults or shortcomings.

[1] Both quotations can be found in Pearce, *Zanzibar: The Island Metropolis of Eastern Africa*, 1920, p. 199.

Burton or Speke, and not just in terms of the character of its imagery. First, the chief authors of this new geography were administrators of, or paid consultants to, the British Protectorate of Zanzibar. Second, the works of these new geographers were unambiguously geared toward the direct application of geographical knowledge to the local articulation of colonial power.[2]

This chapter analyses four geographical texts from the 1920s and 1930s in an effort to place them in the context of the full expression of British colonial power in Zanzibar. Each of the four works – G. M. Stockley's geological survey, H. V. Lanchester's town plan, L. F. Hollingsworth's Zanzibar geography textbook, and G. H. Shelswell-White's tourist guide – was linked to the administration's attempts to deal with a period of economic crisis in the Protectorate.[3] The British were also in the process of solidifying their rule in Zanzibar in the aftermath of the First World War, and much of this literature – especially Lanchester's town plan – furthered the process. Yet taken as a whole, there is something more in their works than the obvious objectives of the colonial administration for economic gain and political rule. I contend that in these colonial geographies we can see the elements, both physical and social-psychological, which constituted the geography of an attempted British hegemony in Zanzibar.

I use the word hegemony here, following Gwyn Williams's interpretation of Gramsci, to refer to 'an order in which a certain way of life and thought is dominant, in which a concept of reality is diffused throughout society in all its institutional and private manifestations'.[4] According to Gramsci, 'the normal exercise of hegemony in a particular regime is characterized by a combination of consensus and force', both dominative power and consensual persuasion.[5] The construction and maintenance of hegemony depends on the largely ideological work of an intellectual vanguard, who translate the ideas of a ruling elite to the ruled, thus becoming the 'creators of consciousness' for the social formation.[6]

[2] Burton, *Zanzibar: City, Island and Coast*, 1872, and Speke, *Journal of the Discovery of the Source of the Nile*, 1863, are especially representative of the earlier geographies. Although the geographical knowledge gathered by Burton, Speke and Livingstone certainly served the interests of the British Empire, the applications were not always direct, and Britain was as yet not an official colonial power in East Africa. Some of the nineteenth-century European adventurers, most pointedly Burton, in fact had very ambiguous feelings about British colonialism.
[3] Stockley, *Report on the Geology of the Zanzibar Protectorate*, 1928; Lanchester, *Zanzibar: a Study in Tropical Town Planning*, 1923; Hollingsworth and Seif, *Jiografia ya Unguja na Pemba*, 1932; and Trade and Tourist Traffic Bureau, *A Guide to Zanzibar*, 1932. The original guide was compiled by Shelswell-White; it was reprinted in 1949, 1952 and 1962.
[4] Williams, 'The Concept of "egemonia"', 1960, p. 587.
[5] The quotation is actually an interpretation of a passage from Gramsci's, *Selections from the Prison Notebooks*, 1971. See Bates, 'Gramsci and the Theory of Hegemony', 1975, p. 363.
[6] See Femia, 'Hegemony and Consciousness', 1975, pp. 29–48, for a discussion of notions of consciousness and the role of intellectuals developed by Gramsci in the *Selections*, 1971.

A number of geographers have begun to suggest, though usually implicitly, that hegemonic power within a particular social formation is very much a matter of geography. Some, like Denis Cosgrove, have analysed the ways in which cultural power is expressed and maintained in the 'landscape' of European cities and the English countryside.[7] Others, such as Mark Billinge or Charles Withers, have dealt with transformations in cultural dominance among broad 'historical blocs' in Britain.[8] For colonial Zanzibar I take these suggestions of what might be called a Gramscian geography with caution, recognizing that there are aspects of the adoption of a Gramscian analysis that are more complex than this short chapter can suggest.[9] However, colonial Zanzibar represents an opportunity to take a step further the idea that hegemony has a certain geography. I am arguing here that the colonial authorities attempted to assert themselves in Zanzibar not only through particular constructions or reconstructions of physical space but by more subtle means as well: by efforts to shape the prevailing spatial consciousness of the city's residents – their 'idea' of urban space – as well as the representations of urban space in the European and American tourist market.[10] The intellectuals at the core of my study were the agents of these attempts.

HEGEMONY, INTELLECTUALS AND GEOGRAPHY

The Gramscian idea of 'hegemony' characterizes the ways in which power is exercised in society short of violent repression. It is often seen as a

[7] Cosgrove's ideas have evolved in many published pieces on these themes, but the most pertinent works to my study, because they are works in which he is bringing a Gramscian–Williamsian framework to bear on 'landscape', are: Cosgrove, *Social Formation*, 1985, and 'Geography is Everywhere', 1989, pp. 118–35.

[8] See Billinge, 'Hegemony, Class and Power', 1984, pp. 28–67; and Withers, *Gaelic Scotland*, 1988. The concept of 'historical bloc', which is Gramsci's way out of the sometimes confining box of structuralist conceptions of classes, has been expanded upon in Williams, *Problems in Materialism*, 1980.

[9] As Crush suggests in this volume, Gramscian analysis has been applied to African contexts only in limited cases, and even in these situations there are problems with the Europeanness of the framework and with the question of *post-facto* voices for the 'subaltern' (see Spivak, 'Can the Subaltern Speak?', 1988). Nevertheless, I am arguing that Gramscian hegemony theory may be especially appropriate to understanding the nature of dominance and of the dominant cultural and political forces in African settings (see also Lears, 'The Concept of Cultural Hegemony', 1985, pp. 567–93).

[10] Western has written an intriguing pair of articles in which he develops ideas and concepts that seem to bear the influence of Gramscian thinking and to bring a certain consciousness of geography to that manner of thinking: Western, 'Autonomous and Directed Cultural Change', 1984, pp. 205–36; and 'Social Engineering', 1984, pp. 113–40. His idea of 'the power of definition', which is quite suggestive of hegemony theory, has been used by other authors in the analysis of colonial planning, especially by Anderson, 'The Idea of Chinatown', 1987, pp. 580–98.

complement to Marxist political economy, though Raymond Williams has argued that its understanding of the 'forms of domination and subordination more closely approximate normal processes.'[11] Hegemony involves 'a complex interlocking of political, social and cultural forces' that are 'active in the imposition of values designed to confirm the legitimacy of a dominant group.'[12] Political actors and administrators as well as artists or educators are essential to the projection and communication of hegemony because they articulate and disseminate the dominant group's values.[13] As Cosgrove has written, the hegemony of a ruling group's ideas is:

> sustained and reproduced ... by [its] ability to project and communicate by whatever media are available and across all other social levels and divisions, an image of the world consonant with [its] own experience, and to have that image accepted as a true reflection of everyone's reality.[14]

If hegemony were simply a matter of projection and communication, it would not have been nor would it continue to be struggled for so violently in the colonial and post-colonial capitalist world. Hegemony, as Jackson Lears reminds us, means nothing as an analytical tool unless consent is 'paired with the notion of domination'.[15] Force and consent intertwine in the efforts of a dominant bloc to sustain its dominance. Consent is not at all universal: in Gramscian thought, there are always alternative and oppositional forces which resist the hegemonic bloc. Geographers influenced by Gramscian thinking have begun to tackle this complexity. They have shown that dominant groups are complex and fragmented, and that there is an equally complex panorama of non-hegemonic groups.[16] This type of approach would be useful for understanding the complex alliances the colonizers tried to forge with elite elements of Zanzibari society and for addressing the nature

---

[11] Williams, *Marxism and Literature*, 1977, p. 110.

[12] The first quotation comes from Williams, *Marxism and Literature*, 1977, p. 108; the second comes from Billinge, 'Hegemony, Class and Power', 1984, p. 32.

[13] Both Gramsci, *Selections*, 1971, and Williams stress the significance of a broadly-defined set of 'intellectuals' for social consciousness. They include within this group 'ecclesiasts' as well as academics, politicians and artists.

[14] Cosgrove, 'Geography is Everywhere', 1989, p. 128. This ability to project and communicate hegemony is, to Cosgrove, the very 'definition' of ideology.

[15] Lears, 'The concept of cultural hegemony', 1985, p. 592.

[16] Cosgrove, 'Geography is Everywhere', 1989 for example, has provided a model for a Gramscian geography that would explore the meanings imparted to landscapes by dominant, alternative, oppositional or excluded cultural forces. Billinge, 'Hegemony, Class and Power', 1984 identifies a bourgeois counter-hegemony resisting the alliance of aristocracy, nobility and gentry in 1780, and a working-class counter-hegemony in 1850 opposing landed interests, industrial capital and the urban gentry in England. Both are sensitive to the processual and contested character of hegemony, as a whole, and the fragmented nature of the dominant bloc within it.

of opposition, and I readily admit that my concentration here on British intellectuals is a substantial simplification of the 'dominant bloc'. This chapter is only a sketch of what would of necessity be a larger, more complex model, one that would need to bring out the voices of Zanzibaris – those who acquiesced as well as those who resisted.

As Billinge is quick to admit, his work on hegemony is a study of 'period far more than of place'.[17] In other words, like many geographers working with Gramscian ideas about power, he does not attempt an exploration of things that might be 'geographical' about hegemony. Cosgrove's emphasis on landscape brings us much closer to geography, but it may be easier to use the literature of the 'colonial city', which has emerged largely outside of geography, as a starting point for my analysis of colonial Zanzibar.[18] For example, African historians like Fred Cooper and Timothy Mitchell have focused on the colonial city in an intriguingly spatial way.[19] In Cooper's Mombasa, the colonial state attempted to define 'who could be where', and to redefine space within the city, arguing that the kind of working class it sought to create could not be housed any old way, but that neighbourhoods and housing types had to be shaped by state authority.[20] The physical construction of space in the colonial city was central to the maintenance of control. From the design of 'residence housing' for dock workers and 'village layouts' for migrants in early years to the creation of zoning controls and high density estates at the end of the colonial era, town planning, housing, health and 'development' schemes in Mombasa more generally 'served to emphasize ... domination'.[21]

Although at one point Cooper says that 'the mask of city planning and urban architecture' was important to colonial authority as a 'symbol of hegemony', he does not fully explore the importance of symbolism for the transformation of social consciousness about space. Cooper argues that the quest of Mombasa's colonial officials 'for a more "modern" society demanded

[17] Billinge, 'Hegemony, Class, and Power', 1984, p. 30.

[18] See King, *Colonial Urban Development*, 1976; and Ross and Telkamp (eds), *Colonial Cities*, 1985, for samples of this literature. Zein, *The Sacred Meadows*, 1974, takes something that might be called a 'Cosgrovian' approach in analysing the symbolic–spatial structure of Lamu, Kenya, but the complexities and shortcomings of Zein's work only serve to reinforce my feeling that a short, exploratory essay such as this one could only begin to do justice to the intricacies of symbolism in Swahili urban society.

[19] Cooper's earlier work was concerned with agricultural labour history on the East African coast (Cooper, *Plantation Slavery*, 1977; and *From Slaves to Squatters*, 1980). Even there he displayed a keen appreciation for the spatial dimensions of colonialism, but it is his more recent work that is my main concern ('Urban Space, Industrial Time', 1983; and Cooper, *On the African Waterfront*, 1987). Mitchell uses a Foucauldian framework in colonial Egypt (Mitchell, *Colonizing Egypt*, 1988), but as Cocks (*The Oppositional Imagination*, 1989) has shown, Foucault and Gramsci were never far apart in their understandings of the workings of power in society.

[20] Cooper, *On the African Waterfront*, 1987, p. 176.

[21] Cooper, 'Urban Space, Industrial Time', 1983, p. 20.

planning and regulation of urban neighborhoods', but he deals sparingly with the instruments or pathways for transforming Mombasa residents' conception of 'modernity' into spatial terms; the 'hegemony' he seems to have in mind thus appears to be much closer to dominative force than to consensual persuasion.[22]

Similarly, Mitchell's work on Cairo presents a colonial city 'enframed', where 'the apparent neutrality of space, as the dimension of order, is an effect of building and distributing according to the strict distinction between container and contained...producing and codifying a visible hierarchy.'[23] Colonial town planning made the apparent divisions of space in Cairo 'absolute' in the interests of separating the 'containers' ('well-to-do, rich and foreign') from the 'contained' ('ordinary peasants').[24] Yet the 'enframing' or containerizing of Cairo that Mitchell describes is also an intellectual process taking place in the consciousness of at least some Egyptians as well as Europeans. On the one hand, 'colonial power required the country to become readable, like a book', because this is how it 'was able at the most local level to reproduce theatres of its order and truth'. Hence there were broad plans to reorganize cities, villages, schools and houses to meet European criteria. On the other hand, colonialism created 'the appearance of a structure, a framework that seemed to exist apart from, and prior to, the particular individuals or actions it enframed'.[25] Consequently, it was in fact elite Egyptian modernists who were at the forefront of a movement to reorganize social consciousness on matters as diverse as health, the status of women, street life and the nature of 'order' in the city. There was an enframing of Cairo going on in the minds of Egypt's educated male elite – a certain way in which other Egyptians were now supposed to think of the city, of urban order, of the internal structure of a house, and so forth.

It is this transformation of the manner of thinking about space on a number of fronts which seems to me to be suggestive of a geographical element within the Gramscian idea of hegemony. Colonial authorities desired the construction of a particular built environment conducive to political or economic domination; yet they also seem to have worked towards a containerizing of social consciousness about space. If a certain spatial order conducive to the colonialists' interests were to be perceived by elite Kenyans, Egyptians or Zanzibaris as a 'common sense' order of things, to which in 'normal times' workers and peasants would give their consent, then we can say that the hegemonic bloc had achieved a measure of success in containing the latent forces of resistance.[26] Cooper tells us that British spatial policies

---

[22] Cooper, *On the African Waterfront*, 1987, p. 185.

[23] Mitchell, *Colonizing Egypt*, 1988, p. 44.

[24] Ibid., p. 45. Specific housing and zoning codes were enacted and enforced according to this differential scale.

[25] Ibid., pp. 33, 171, 14.

[26] The best discussions that I have found of the Gramscian concepts of 'common sense' and 'normal times' in relation to hegemony are in: Williams, *Marxism and Literature*,

in Mombasa backfired in the eruption of worker militancy in the port city during the 1940s. From Mitchell, we get more of a sense of the colonial 'success' in enframing Cairo, perhaps because the process was so reliant on the 'self-help' movement among Egyptian intellectuals.[27] In Zanzibar during the 1920s and 1930s, the tall task of 'enframing' or containerizing in both physical and psycho-social terms was left to a handful of British officials and consultants with, it seems, little assistance from indigenous intellectuals. Hence the picture which emerges of the attempted hegemony seems much closer to Cooper's Mombasa than to Mitchell's Cairo.

THE VIEW FROM THE TOWER: BRITISH ZANZIBAR, 1923–1932

Some time in 1929, the British administrator R. H. Crofton left his office in the protectorate's headquarters, the Beit el Ajab (House of Wonders), and climbed up the building's tall tower. He wrote down what he saw. His account gives us a marvellous view of how the British saw themselves and their Zanzibar in the inter-war years:

> When the climber reaches the summit of the tower a grand panorama of sea and land bursts upon his gaze; the long line of coast stretching to the North; westward, the faint outline of the Continent – so eagerly scanned by the explorers; close in, the series of islands marking the line of the reef as far as the lighthouse on Chumbe. In the stream rides at anchor the Bombay mail maintaining the long connection with Hindostan ... In the immediate foreground, the flagstaff, from which floats, as it did a century ago at Mtoni, the 'blood red flag of the Sultan' ... At the back, the courtyard of the seminary where Mrs. Johnson is fashioning the daughters of the land that they may become the 'polished corners of the temple'. Farther north, the little peninsula of the new port, with the cranes on the wharf suggestive of giant giraffes looking askance at the sheds behind, which yield them so little sustenance these days...In the channel, the cable store ship that always seems to be coming but never arrives – symbolical of these days of depression ... Eastward stretches the city with its close-packed houses and labyrinthine ways up to the edge of the green field ... and northward

---

1977; Femia, 'Hegemony and consciousness', 1975; and Cocks, *The Oppositional Imagination*, 1989. An important analysis of Gramscian conceptions of resistance applied to East Africa is Feierman, *Peasant Intellectuals*, 1990.

[27] Cooper, *On the African Waterfront*, 1987; see also Janmohammed, 'African laborers in Mombasa', 1975, pp. 154–76; Clayton, *The 1948 Zanzibar General Strike*, 1976, gives a detailed account of the similar uprising in Zanzibar. There are fascinating connections yet to be explored between this 'self-help' in Egypt and the 'Harambee' movement which has been so instrumental to the success of the post-colonial Kenyan regime in cementing its legitimacy in rural areas.

a sea of brown huts spreading out into the distance. The eye roving south again catches the Union Jack flying over the Residency, the dome of the Court, the dome of the Museum, the red-tiled roofs of schools, and over all the sun reigns in splendour.[28]

When Crofton climbed the tower to give us this view, the British protectorate of Zanzibar was scarcely 30 years old, but the Colonial Office was worried. To begin with, there was a depression running around the empire, and this place, Burton's 'filthy labyrinth', was not paying its way.[29] The clove industry was suffering and, in the Zanzibar of the 1920s, this was the only industry from which the administration or its allies extracted any revenues.[30] The protectorate's alliance with the island's Arab aristocracy was on shaky ground, with this 'planter class' deep in debt to Indian merchants.[31] The strategic significance of the port was apparently waning with the rising importance of Kenya and Tanganyika. Alternative revenue sources were needed, and a renegotiation of the colonial relationship with the island was of the utmost importance; this is where our British intellectuals came in.

The first order of business was economic. In the preface to Officer Stockley's geological survey we are told the main reason behind his visit to the island: 'was an enquiry into the nature of a gold occurrence, with a view to determining its economic possibilities.' Assessing the marketability of gum copal supplies and ilmenite sand deposits as well as the potential agricultural productivity of island soils were stated as secondary goals.[32] Lanchester, who had already served as a town planning consultant to other strategic cities in the empire, had as his main task the redesign of the port and the roads connecting it to the suburban clove plantations, with an eye

[28] Crofton, *Zanzibar Affairs*, 1953, pp. 110–11. Crofton is one of a host of British colonial officials who to wrote fairly drab memoirs of their Zanzibar services, lending credence to Anthony Clayton's characterization of British agents in Zanzibar as, at the very least, 'unimaginative' (Clayton, *The Zanzibar Revolution*, 1981, p. 5).

[29] Burton, *Zanzibar: City, Island and Coast*, 1872; see also Rice, *Captain Sir Richard Francis Burton*, 1990, p. 362. In spite of the romantic vision of some primeval Africa with which Burton is commonly associated, his lively account of Zanzibar is of a city that is anything but lovely or romantic.

[30] The clove industry is the pivot around which the political economy of Zanzibar has revolved since the middle of the nineteenth century. Cooper, *From Slaves to Squatters*, 1980, gives a slice of this story, as do the doctoral dissertations of El Sheikh, *State, Cloves and Planters*, 1986 and Welliver, *The Clove Factor*, 1990. The broad picture of the economic cornerstone of colonial Zanzibar emerges more fully in Sheriff, *Slaves. Spices and Ivory*, 1987.

[31] Besides the three authors also cited in note 30 above, Bennett, *A History of the Arab State of Zanzibar*, 1978 also analyses these tenuous relationships, albeit with something of an 'Arabist' approach that El Sheikh and others reject rather forcefully.

[32] Stockley, *Report on the Geology*, 1928, p. 4. Stockley was on loan to the Zanzibar administration from the Uganda Protectorate.

towards improving the efficiency of the protectorate's methods of wealth extraction.[33] Cruise ships began unloading tourists in Zanzibar in earnest in the 1920s, and Shelswell-White, with the newly-formed Trade and Tourist Traffic Bureau, aimed to sell the city to these tourists as an adventurous, mysterious and exotic vacation. With the diversification of the economy (and the British protectorate's role in it), the educational system for Zanzibaris also needed to be revised to train a diverse labour force. Hence in the 1920s, four special educational tracks beyond primary school were established, corresponding to the four employment-generating sectors of the economy: agricultural, clerical, industrial and teaching. Hollingsworth came to Zanzibar to start the Teacher Training School.[34]

These economic concerns were intertwined with political and strategic objectives. The development of a fuller understanding of the hydrology of the island was a major goal of the Stockley survey, because by 'the end of 1920 the Zanzibar government became concerned for ... the water supply of the capital', and 'the future of Zanzibar as a watering station for ships appeared to be in some measure of jeopardy.'[35] Maintaining that 'long connection with Hindostan' that Crofton described depended on watering British ships in Zanzibar. Lanchester tells us that the port had 'the best water between Alexandria and the Cape', but his own goals were more terrestrial: 'to enhance the efficiency and amenity of Zanzibar as a civic organism'. His notions of efficiency were employed in the distribution of police lines and the design of police stations as well as in a reorganization of social and economic activities that made markets, shops, houses and neighbourhoods more amenable to police surveillance.[36] Shelswell-White went to great lengths, in his map and in his description of the town, to highlight the manifestations of British power and to assure visitors of the safety and security inherent in Zanzibar's connection to the empire. In pointing out the wireless office, for example, the guide tells us that, because it connects South Africa with Aden, 'the Station is the most important on the coast'.[37] Hollingsworth similarly reminds his students of the role of the British resident: 'He is the representative of the Queen, and from the top of his residence flies the British flag, which is called the Union Jack.'[38]

[33] Lanchester, *Zanzibar: a Study*, 1923, p. 41.

[34] See Crofton, *Zanzibar Affairs*, 1953, for the details of Hollingsworth's work in education in Zanzibar. While he dabbled in geography, Hollingsworth considered himself an historian. For examples of his works, based on his experiences as head of the Teacher Training School and later as head of the Secondary School, see Hollingsworth, *Zanzibar Under the Foreign Office*, 1953 – this is a reworking of his doctoral dissertation; and Hollingsworth, *A Short History of the East Coast of Africa*, 1965 (1929).

[35] Stockley, *Report on the Geology*, 1928, p. 4.

[36] Lanchester, *Zanzibar: a Study*, 1923, p. 10.

[37] Trade and Tourist Traffic Bureau, *A Guide to Zanzibar*, 1949 (1932), p. 16.

[38] Hollingsworth and Seif, *Jiografia ya Unguja*, 1932, p. 41; my translation from the Kiswahili: 'Yeye ndiye wakili wa mfalme wa Kiingereza na juu ya nyumba yake hutundikwa bendera ya Kiingereza inayoitwa "Union Jack".'

In Shelswell-White, Lanchester, and Hollingsworth, an apparently conscious effort was made to affect the way that people in Zanzibar were to think of the urban structure of 'the island metropolis'. With Shelswell-White's guide, of course, this effort was directed toward tourist readers. The guide was part of the process of producing and maintaining a representation of the city as an exotic, yet thoroughly pacific place. This geographical representation in the 1920s and 1930s was markedly different from the writings of the nineteenth-century explorers; if Burton, Speke, or Livingstone would ever have agreed on anything about the geography of East Africa, it might have been about the character of the 'wretched', 'ruinous', 'lurid' city of 'Stinkibar':

> a closely packed, reeking, suffocation of dirt-caked stone and coral-lime houses, divided into a crossword puzzle of dark, fetid alleys whose open drains, abundant night soil and busy vermin helped erase any image of oriental glamour.[39]

This is hardly the timeless tropical paradise that was conjured up by the Tourist Bureau in 1932.[40] Although many years of story-telling probably had transformed the popular Euro-American image, the western idea of the city, at least to some degree, moved from 'a reeking mass of abomination' in

---

[39] From Christie, *Cholera Epidemics*, 1869; the quotation appears in UN Center for Human Settlements, *The Stone Town of Zanzibar*, 1983, p. 1/4. See also Hollingsworth, *Zanzibar Under the Foreign Office*, 1953, p. 192; Pearce, *Zanzibar: The Island Metropolis*, 1920, pp. 196–9; Burton, *Zanzibar: City, Island and Coast*, 1872; and Headley, *The Achievements of Stanley*, 1878, which is a popularized version of the diaries of Stanley and Livingstone, among others. See also: Menon, *Zanzibar in the Nineteenth Century*, 1978. Both Menon and the UN study give summaries of the explorers' writings on the city.

[40] The timeless, romantic Zanzibar lives on in the travel writings of today. Diamondstein, *New York Times*, 30 April 1989, writes of Zanzibar's 'exotic medley'; Rule, *New York Times*, 22 April 1987, portrays Zanzibar as an 'easygoing Isle' where people are 'more than laid back'; *Time* magazine 18 September 1989, in addition to a misinformed, patronizing swipe at the current regime as 'a tiny citadel of Marxist doctrine and xenophobia', writes of the 'fabled Isle of Cloves'; the *Wall Street Journal* 18 June 1990, makes fun of the current state of affairs in Zanzibari development with reference to the period of myth-making to which Shelswell-White belonged, by saying, 'there is no road to Zanzibar'; but the prize for exotic othering and vacuousness goes to *Business Traveller*, March 1986: 'For over a century and without really trying, the name of Zanzibar has evoked the kind of romance that national tourism organizations across the globe would pay dearly to link with their own products. Like a battered oil lamp, when rubbed by the mind's eye, it seems to conjure up the smells and sensations of both the sultry South and the East. Though few Europeans have been there, Zanzibar is the grandfather, the ancestor of a dynasty of beach resorts and the place that launched a thousand look-alikes.' For examples of the story-telling of an earlier time, see Headley, *The Achievements of Stanley*, 1878; and Stigand, *The Land of the Zinj*, 1913.

the 1860s to a mysterious 'isle of cloves' by the 1930s through the work
of colonial agents like Shelswell-White.[41]

New, polished, romantic images emerged in the guidebook. Shelswell-
White's Zanzibar was an exotic place to visit and be adventuresome:

> If the visitor should cross the Creek he steps into a different world or
> to be more precise, into a different town. Between the waterfront and
> the Creek is the Stone Town' of two-, three- and four-storeyed houses.
> Beyond the Creek lies Ngambo (sic) – the 'Other Side' – a thousand
> acres of light sandy soil, alternating between occasional narrow open
> spaces and hectic crowded quarters of African houses. You need a
> compass and a clear head to penetrate it, for the huts straggle around,
> conforming to no coherent scheme, a confusing maze of endless twisting
> alleyways.[42]

This type of representation of the urban structure of the Other Side was
essential to the development of the tourist industry, upon which the economic future of Zanzibar was said to depend, because it made the tourist
comfortable with the spatial form of the city. Shelswell-White's Ng'ambo
might be a 'confusing maze,' but not a 'filthy labyrinth': if you have a
compass (and a clear head), make an 'incursion'.[43]

Lanchester was also communicating with a European audience, the British
administrators of the island. His work seems to have had representational
dimensions beyond simply promoting tourism. The 'othering' of Zanzibar's
African population in his plan created a framework for superiority and
inferiority in political–cultural terms which could justify not just colonial
rule but the replacement of chattel slavery with corvée labour and wage
labour by the British:

> Physically the Zanzibar Swahilis are well fitted for rough manual labour,
> and are freely employed in loading and unloading ships, and in the
> transport of heavy goods. They work better in unison, and when extreme
> bodily exertion is required, than at less violent and isolated labour.
> Normally they are not energetic, and do not care as a rule to apply
> themselves indefinitely to one task.[44]

Lanchester and the professional town planning mechanisms and apparatuses
established in his wake also communicated a particular vision of urban space
to the Zanzibari audience. Nowhere is this more clear than in what were

[41] Pearce, *Zanzibar*, 1920, pp. 196–9.
[42] Trade Bureau, *A Guide*, 1949, p. 25.
[43] Ibid., p. 42.
[44] Lanchester, *Zanzibar*, 1923, p. 15. One cannot help but note how this description
of African labourers compares with those of African–Americans by slaveholders in the
American South (see Genovese, *Roll, Jordan, Roll*, 1974, pp. 7–24, for example).

seen all over the empire to be the intimately intertwined spheres of housing and health. [45]

The urban form of neighbourhoods associated with various groups in Zanzibar society were seen by Lanchester as organic embodiments of a hygiene problem. Indians had 'overflowed into all the bazaars running eastward', while 'the real Swahili quarter' had 'irregularly scattered huts ... packed along irregular and narrow lanes'. This irregularity, overcrowding and overflow in urban form was attributed to the 'ingrained habits' of poor hygiene among the non-white races. Although 'in the matter of house accommodation the Swahili show[ed] his superiority over his pagan cousins the negro', the Swahili had 'bad housing', and it was badly arranged. And bad housing bred bad health. [46]

Lanchester's extensive proposals on housing, a number of which were not fully enacted, revolved around four themes: 1) institutionalizing and increasing the spatial extent of segregation of Europeans from 'natives' in the interests of health; 2) establishing stricter building codes to regulate, in particular, the sanitation systems of Ng'ambo; 3) using the frequent fires in Ng'ambo as 'opportunities for remodelling the arrangement of huts' until a more comprehensive planned community could be organized; and 4) importantly, educating the public to 'a fuller appreciation of the possibilities of life resulting from better business organization, improved housing and general facilities'. [47]

Until the appointment of a town planning officer in the 1950s, much of Lanchester's programme of change was enacted through the health department. Health officers often went further than Lanchester in decrying the city's conditions in epidemiological metaphors: 'The town as a whole is a parasitic growth on the island', wrote one officer in 1935. [48] The 'disarranged maze of huts' in Ng'ambo were seen to provide 'more acceptable material for the operations' of the Department, mainly because of the physical ease with which neighbourhoods could be uprooted. Two model villages were laid out in the 1930s with streets that followed a modified grid pattern, with well-aligned houses and a local police station. Although the villages conformed to the garden suburbs of Lanchester's imagination, the Health Department found that 'few people could be persuaded to live there', largely on account of the alien nature of housing and neighbourhood design. [49]

The government devised several strategies for persuading Zanzibaris to adopt British ideas about housing types and neighbourhood form. First, an

[45] Frenkel and Western, 'Pretext or prophylaxis?' 1988, pp. 211–28; Swanson, 'The sanitation syndrome', 1977, pp. 387–410; and Sundiata, 'Twentieth century reflections on death in Zanzibar', 1987, pp. 45–60.

[46] Lanchester, *Zanzibar*, 1923, pp. 13, 54, 70. For a comparison with colonial planning in mainland Tanzania, see Alexander, 'European planning ideology in Tanzania', 1983, pp. 17–36.

[47] Lanchester, *Zanzibar*, 1923, pp. 58, 77.

[48] Zanzibar Protectorate, *Annual Medical and Sanitary Report*, 1935, p. 41.

[49] Zanzibar Protectorate, *Annual Medical and Sanitary Report*, 1937, p. 30.

exhibition was organized – one of five permanent exhibitions – at the Zanzibar Museum (open to and popular with the public at the time) which focused on the interconnections between urban form and public health. Second, a civic centre was constructed in the heart of Ng'ambo, where films and lectures were given on matters of housing and health. The 1936 lecture series was aimed at 'contrasting satisfactory and unsatisfactory forms of native premises' but included informal talks on diet, disease avoidance, maternity and child welfare. This approach was taken because the department believed that 'it is rather by personal talk, personal example ... that education of the African has to proceed.'[50]

Perhaps more than on external images or even physical constructions, hegemony depended upon the construction of a geography of the mind among Zanzibaris, but this meant doing something more than the occasional lecture on health or housing. 'Because the spontaneous consent on which hegemony depends must be gotten from the mind and the heart', Gramsci wrote, 'every relationship of hegemony is necessarily an educational relationship.'[51]

When the government elementary and primary school was finally built and operational in 1925, its curriculum consisted of the following courses: reading, writing, arithmetic, geography and hygiene for the first three years; and these same classes, with the addition of history and drawing for the next four years. Advanced geography, commercial geography or agricultural geography were required courses of the different special tracks. Why was geography so important to the education of Zanzibaris in the protectorate, and what was the geography that was being taught? Geography loomed so large in the curriculum because it was a big part of all British schooling; but geography, more than any subject, put the different elements of Zanzibari society in their place. Geography textbooks informed them of the overwhelming might of the empire, its splendorous gifts to their city and their inferior role in its affairs. Geography was central to a curriculum which, as one of its most ardent internal critics put it, was 'fitted only to produce clerks, typists and printers ... mere automatons who will ever be a dependent class'.[52]

Hollingsworth and Seif's geography textbook for the Zanzibar Teacher Training School shows us much of what was geographical in the British quest for a hegemonic educational relationship. Entitled *A Geography of Zanzibar and Pemba*, the text was introduced by Hollingsworth:

[50] Zanzibar Protectorate, *Annual Medical*, 1935, p. 49 and 1937. The civic centre buildings were actually constructed in the early 1940s as part of the Holmwood Estates housing project. Holmwood, with its curved street designs and neighbourhood unit theme, amounted to a transferral of new concepts in British town planning theory to Zanzibar, (Great Britain, Colonial Office Annual Report on Zanzibar, 1949; and Alexander, 'European Planning Ideology in Tanzania', 1983).

[51] Cocks, *The Oppositional Imagination*, 1989, p. 42.

[52] Jivanjee, an Indian Zanzibari and the lone non-white or non-Omani member of the curriculum committee at the time. Africans had no representative on the committee until the final decade of the colonial era. See Crofton, *Zanzibar Affairs*, 1953, p. 42.

I have put this little book together in order to assist all teachers in Unguja [the Kiswahili name for Zanzibar island] and Pemba in teaching the geography of these islands. In teaching my own students at the Teacher Training School, I am continually astonished to see that they don't know very much about their own islands. I hope that this book will help all those who want to know more about these islands.[53]

Hollingsworth tells his students how water is piped into their city thanks to British ingenuity; he explains the type of work Zanzibaris of different races do, and where they do it. The reader/student is reminded constantly of British power in the islands. Eight of the book's 48 pages describe the workings of British government in Zanzibar, while only one discusses the island's cultures.[54] The difference between the Pemba coastline and that of Unguja (Pemba has a jagged edge on its west coast) is described through a reminder of the past: 'British warships cruised these islands to capture slaving ships. Slavers would flee into Pemba's creeks when they saw the warships chasing them, while hiding their slaves below decks.'[55]

CONCLUSION

In 1930 British colonial administrators in East Africa established the Inter-Regional Swahili Committee to promote the development of officially approved literature in Kiswahili, for dissemination on Zanzibar and the coast. Its first act was the translation of western children's books 'to teach about geography'.[56] The first novel ever written by a Kiswahili speaker (a non-Zanzibari), published by the committee in 1934, dealt favourably with British colonialism and Christianity as agents of liberation. The Zanzibari literary scholar Maulid Mohammed Omar has reflected on the assumptions implicit in British education policy: it was as if the British expected that 'the African

---

[53] Hollingsworth and Seif, *Jiografia ya Unguja*, 1932, p. 2. My translation of: 'Nimetunga kitabu hiki kidogo ili niwasaidie walimu wote wa Unguja na Pemba kufundisha habari za jiografia za visiwa hivi. Mara kwa mara ninaposomesha wanafunzi wangu wa Skuli ya Walimu hustaajabu sana kuona kuwa hawajui mambo mengi ya visiwa vyao wenyewe. Natumaini kwamba kitabu hiki kitawafaa watu wote wanaotaka kujua zaidi habari za visiwa hivi.'

[54] Even then, the discussion of culture is demographic and classificatory. See Hollingsworth and Seif, *Jiografia ya Unguja*, 1932, p. 38.

[55] Ibid., p. 4. My translation of: 'Manuwari za Kiingereza zilivinjari karibu na visiwa hivi ili kuyateka madau yenye watumwa. Watu waliochukua watumwa katika madau walikimbilia ndani ya hori walipoona manuwari inawafukuza wakajificha wakateremsha watumwa wao.' Sheriff, *Slaves, Spices and Ivory*, 1987, demonstrates how British writers wildly exaggerated the significance of the export of slaves from the Zanzibari empire, for ideological reasons.

[56] Omar, 'Historia ya Hadithi (Riwaya) na Maendeleo Yake', 1981, p. 58. My translation of: '... hadithi za kitoto zinazofunza jiografia'.

had gone from one form of oppression [slavery] to another [colonialism] without the conscious understanding that inside [the head] there was still an internal acceptance of being ruled.'[57]

This represented one means by which the 'consent of the led' was to be built; it was to be constructed on 'an internal acceptance of being ruled' that was to be as geographical or spatial in form as it was historical or temporal. Lanchester, Shelswell-White and Hollingsworth were the articulators of the geographical dimension of this effort to effect consent. But their images and ideas never fully took root among more than a thin stratum of Zanzibari society. An oppositional identity emerged among both Swahili and mainland Africans, especially after the Second World War which, in spite of the best efforts of traditional British divide and rule, brought these groups closer together.[58] British rule failed in Zanzibar, of course, for a variety of reasons, but[59] I would only suggest that one part of the failure of British rule might be found in the dearth of active participation in what Mitchell called the 'enframing' of the colonial city by a broader element of Zanzibari society.

It is delightfully symbolic that the *Geography of Zanzibar and Pemba* was written in English by a British scholar and translated into Kiswahili for Zanzibari readers by an Omani-Zanzibari. But Ahmed Seif's help in translating for Hollingsworth is not part of a large intellectual literature by Zanzibaris supportive of colonial aims. Although there was a touch of Islamic modernism linked to westernization at the surface of the society, the prevailing intellectual climate – beyond the Sultan's retinue – would appear to have been one of seething resistance.[60] Riots and civil disturbances occurred regularly throughout the colonial period and with increasing frequency after 1945. By then it was evident as one British administrator wrote, that the British had been 'found out'.[61] As in Mombasa, a wave of strikes and work slowdowns swept Zanzibar in 1948 as never before, opening the path

[57] Omar, 'Historia ya Hadithi', 1981, p. 8. My translation of: '... Mwafrika alitoka katika unyonge mmoja na akaingia unyonge wa pili bila ya kujifahamu kuwa yumo mlemle, ndani ya kucha za kutawaliwa.'

[58] This tumultuous 'coming together' was not without serious splits, many of which remain in Zanzibari life today. See Lofchie, *Zanzibar*, 1965; Saissy, 'The Role of the Ethnic Factor', paper presented to Department of Development Studies, Uppsala University, August 1979.

[59] Ayany, *A History of Zanzibar*, 1970; Mrina and Mattoke, *Mapambano ya Ukombozi Zanzibar*, 1980.

[60] For a discussion of Islamic modernism in coastal East Africa during this period, see Pouwels, 'Sheikh Al-Amin bin Al-Mazrui', 1981, pp. 329–45. The literature on Swahili and coastal East African Muslim resistance to colonialism is only really beginning, in contrast to the volumes which have been written on other coastal resistance movements. But see Bierstecker, *Post-War Swahili Poetry*, 1990; Salim, 'Early Arab–Swahili political protest', 1974, pp. 71–84; Durrani, 'Kiswahili resistance publishing at the Kenya coast', 1988, pp. 26–34; and Strobel, 'From Lelemama to lobbying', 1976, pp. 207–35.

[61] Clayton, *The 1948 Zanzibar General Strike*, 1976, p. 1.

to outright revolution 16 years later. The British intellectuals, too, were, in effect, found out: they were not a vanguard here. The more Arab-oriented intellectuals of Zanzibar itself were tuned to the pan-Arabism of Nassir; the more African-oriented, to Marxism.

The nature of hegemony is such that, if the dominant bloc is successful, the social order as well as the geographical order appears as common sense to the ordinary majority of people. The Zanzibari masses never really adjusted to the social and spatial reality impressed on them during the British colonial period, however fragmented or ill-defined Zanzibari resistance was until the revolution.

The construction of a particular physical order was important to the economic and strategic goals of the British in Zanzibar. It was also an imaginative order. 'We would not have had empire itself', Said has written, 'without important philosophical and imaginative processes at work in the production ... of space.'[62] This 'geographical disposition' in Said's words, carries us beyond dealing simply with issues of the political economy of planning in the colonial city, to the 'imaginative processes' involved in communicating the geography of hegemony.

[62] Said, 'Representing the colonized', 1989, p. 217.

12

Playing with Mirrors: The British Empire According to Albert Demangeon

Paul Claval

BRITISH COLONIAL EXPANSION AS A PARADIGM FOR FRENCH IMPERIALISM

Throughout the nineteenth century, French colonial development was closely linked to British patterns of expansion. Memory of the centuries of rivalry over North America and India was still alive. After the American Revolution and the Declaration of Independence, which deprived Britain of the most promising part of its first empire, the Treaty of Paris of 1763 had appeared less disastrous. The development of British rule in India in the last decades of the eighteenth century was however, strikingly rapid and profitable and in the same period British territorial expansion continued at an alarming rate (from the point of view of the French) in both Canada and Australia. By the end of the revolutionary and Napoleonic wars France had lost all of its former colonial possessions with the exception of French Guyana, Martinique, Guadeloupe, Saint-Pierre and Miquelon, Saint-Louis and Gorée, Réunion and five ports of trade in India: Yanaon, Mahé, Pondichéry, Karikal and Chandernagor. Although the list seems long, the French Empire in this period consisted of nothing more than scattered islands and ports of trade with no navy to defend or supply them.

The British situation was different. Britain began the century with significant colonial possessions. Colonial expansion was certainly slower in the first half of the nineteenth century than in previous periods but it did not stagnate. The Napoleonic wars allowed Britain to annex some of the former French Lesser Antilles, French Mauritius, the Dutch Cape Colony and Dutch

Ceylon. In addition, Raffles' initiative in Malaysia was paving the way for further expansion in Southeast Asia.[1]

The British never forgot the lesson taught them by the American War of Independence: that expansion in temperate areas open to British settlement would ultimately result in a demand for self-government. This must have acted as a damper on expansion into temperate regions. Australia, however, was a special case in many regards. It was a penal colony and there, settlement was very closely controlled. In addition it was too remote and seemed to offer little in the way of profit through production and export or indeed through consumption of British produce. This changed with the development of the wool trade, but the wool runs employed so few people that free settlement in Australia remained unimportant until the 1830s.

The British navy retained an interest in the possible acquisition of maritime strongholds or key strategic points, but other impulses were needed to foster annexation for colonization. Humanitarian and Christian movements were influential in the development of a new interest in overseas expansion during the early decades of the nineteenth century. The slave trade was banned in 1807 and slavery itself was abolished in the British colonies in 1833. Both enlightenment ideals and a new form of Christian conscience played a significant role in this evolution. Ironically, the enforcement of the ban on slave trading and slavery opened up new opportunities for expansion on the west and east coasts of Africa. The London Missionary Society turned the Protestant world, for the first time, towards a policy of proselytism directed at non-Christian societies. Wakefield's initiatives were, however, also motivated by the desire to offer new ground for the expansion of Christian societies.[2] The creation of Christchurch in New Zealand was supported by the Church of England. Similarly, the Scottish Presbyterians supported the creation of Dunedin. Britain's demographic expansion and Industrial Revolution created a substantial demand for produce and raw materials but were also used as the rationale for seeking new migratory outlets.

By 1850 it was clear that Britain's colonial empire was significantly enhancing its global power and, hence, also its status in Europe. In the European context, the mid-nineteenth century was a period of economic growth. For a number of countries, and particularly for France, while British industry was seen as superior, continental competition and even dominance seemed entirely possible. The perception was altogether different in the context of overseas expansion. French intellectuals pointed to the increasing imbalance in global geopolitical power and especially to the growing number of English-speaking regions and countries. The co-existence of American

---

[1] Raffles, Secretary of the East India Company, decided to maintain the presence of the Company in Malacca (1811) and bought Singapore (1819).

[2] Wakefield founded the South Australia Association (1834) and the New Zealand Association (1840) to settle these colonies. The whole scheme relied on the selling of land at a relatively high price to wealthy people in order to finance the passage of poorer people to Australia.

territorial expansion, demographic dynamism and a democratic system drew
the particular attention of French liberals, among them the influential essayist,
Alexis de Tocqueville.[3] French liberals began to support colonial expansion
as the only means by which to restore France to her former position of
power on the world scene. For these thinkers the British colonial tradition
served as a model. This is not to say that French imperialism was built on
the same principles as the British Empire, but that it evolved with an acute
consciousness of the British model.

France's lack of demographic dynamism was widely perceived as the
reason that she had been pre-empted in all of the world's temperate regions.
For French nationalists such as Rameau de Saint-Père, only Canada (through
the rapidly expanding French speaking population) and Algeria offered real
possibilities for significant demographic and territorial expansion.[4] A more
optimistic conclusion resulted, however, from an examination of the tropical
and sub-tropical world where 'exploitation' colonies might be developed. In
the mid-nineteenth century many regions had still escaped European domination. Vigorous expansion was therefore possible and, indeed, took place from
the time of the Third Empire but especially in the 1880s and the 1890s
when Tunisia, Madagascar, Indochina, and large tracts of central and western
Africa were incorporated into the French colonial Empire.

THE ROLE OF THE BRITISH EMPIRE IN FRENCH COLONIAL STUDIES

Britain's nineteenth-century colonial movement was supported by many of its
intellectuals, but many of these were more interested in Britain's missionary
responsibilities than in economic expansion. The Royal Geographical Society
was created in this context.[5] In addition, in a country where the colonial
tradition had evolved continuously since the sixteenth century, independent
scholarly studies of the nature of empire, its economics and its problems,
were superfluous. Public services with a strong commitment to territorial
expansion and exploitation had developed over the centuries. Scholarly studies
seemed unnecessary since efficient administrative structures and a rich lore
based on experience already existed. As a result, the extant British literature
of this period devoted to the colonial theme is surprisingly poor. It was
only in the last decade of the nineteenth century when the pre-eminence
of Britain in the economic field began to be jeopardized by the acute competition of younger industrial nations such as Germany, the United States
or Japan, that published reflections on the nature of the empire began to

[3] Tocqueville, *La démocratie en Amérique*, 1935–40; Claval, 'André Siegfried', 1989,
pp. 121–35.

[4] A complete discussion of de Saint-Père's influence is provided in Morrissoneau, *De la
terre promise*, 1978, p. 151–61.

[5] On the origins of the Royal Geographical Society and the protestant missionary movement see Freeman, 'The Royal Geographical Society', 1980, pp. 1–99.

appear. This new interest, however, was more concerned with the reorganization of the empire as an economic unity – with the erection of some
form of tariff to protect it against 'unfair' competition – than with its
territorial organization.

In the 1870s colonial expansion became a popular preoccupation everywhere in Europe. However, countries like Germany, Italy, Belgium and even,
to some extent, France lacked colonial traditions. In France, the navy had
inherited some principles from the *ancien régime*, including the use of river
systems for the exploration and organization of colonial space at a minimal
cost. But this in no way broached the difficult themes, concerns, and issues
surrounding the opening of newly-conquered territories to trade and modernization. The experience gained in Algeria was of limited value given the
very particular nature of Islamic societies – and everyone was aware of the
haphazard nature of the Algerian conquest, in spite of its vigorous theoriza-
tion by Alexis de Tocqueville[6] and of the support that it received later from
liberal intellectuals, like Elisée Reclus, for instance.

The European colonial societies were founded in order to provide new
colonial offices, armies and navies with sound colonial doctrines, in addition
to offering businessmen information on natural resources, the quality of the
local labour force, and the existing basic equipment in remote countries.[7]
The first task was to collect information from the travellers, traders and
officers who were exploring the hinterland of the new colonies. These colonial
societies thus attempted to develop a new type of applied geography. The
applied geographers who carried out this work (in France applied geographers
were merchants, officers, or university teachers like Marcel Dubois) were
not particularly attracted by the new preoccupations of academic geography
in France and Germany. 'Man'/milieu relationships were not an object for
intellectual speculation but lay at the heart of very concrete and limiting
health problems. Colonial geographers were concerned to assess the medical
conditions reigning in distant tropical countries. What areas were to be
avoided? Which were the more dangerous contagious diseases? And what was
the risk of epidemics? They were eager to report on mineral resources, on
farming possibilities, and to advise on the best locations for port facilities.
They advocated the building of railways. There was little of a comparable
nature in the British literature of this period. The closest analogy was to be
found in the official publications of the Colonial Office, the Indian Civil
Service and the different British colonies: their directories, gazetteers, reports
to their local parliaments, or the results of their censuses.

---

[6] Tocqueville, *De la colonie en Algérie*, 1988. The book is a compilation of three studies
initially published in 1837, 1841 and 1847.

[7] Good discussions of the nature of these societies and the research they carried out
are to be found in Carazzi, *La Società Geografica Italiana*, 1972 and Kemény, *La Società
d'Esplorazione*, 1973. These societies were seldom directly commissioned by the colonial
offices to prepare specific studies. They volunteered information but were mainly committed
to lobbying.

The tensions between mainstream academic geography and colonial geography are well documented in France in the conflict which soon developed between the two founders of the *Annales de géographie*, Marcel Dubois and Vidal de la Blache.[8] Dubois was the first professor at the Sorbonne to teach colonial geography. As a result of his influence, a sizeable proportion of the new review was, at least in its early years, devoted to colonial expansion. There were travel reports but also assessments of the development potential of particular cities, harbours or regions.

Dubois and geographers like him, however, did not develop a new and original approach to cope with the problems of colonial expansion.[9] Some used mainstream Vidalian geography to uncover colonial realities but it was some time before these attempts produced significant results. It was only during the 1920s that regional description and *genre de vie* analysis began to be used in overseas contexts: Robequain's doctoral dissertation on Than-Hoa province in Vietnam[10], and Emile-Félix Gautier's views on the relations between farmers and nomads in the Maghreb[11] were the first attempts to explore traditional forms of territorial organization in colonized countries through fieldwork, interviews, and the precise description of farming techniques. By the mid-1930s with the publication of Pierre Gourou's doctoral dissertation on *Les paysans du delta tonkinois*[12], the French school of tropical geography had developed its basic approach. This included an emphasis on farming, an awareness of the differences between material and social techniques, the study of the geographical consequences of these, and the use of density maps as the basis for all comparisons. Albert Demangeon was the first and the only French geographer to present an academic vision of colonial problems. Hence the significance of his book.

Dubois was right to seek altogether new geographical approaches appropriate to colonial contexts. The methods of tropical geography could help explain the traditional spatial organization of a country through the description of its different ways of life and the analysis of their complementarity (as there were always some products which did not grow in local environments, people had to rely on exchange with communities exploiting different ecological niches: hence the development of solidarities, first economic and then often social and political), but they were unable to provide recipes for development and for an efficient and harmless integration of the tiny cells of the traditional native societies into a modern open economy.

Economists, such as Paul Leroy-Beaulieu, were developing more interesting tools. Leroy-Beaulieu's book, *De la colonisation chez les peuples modernes* was

[8] Soubeyran, *Les dix premières années*. Typescript.
[9] Their colonial geography amounted to a collection of data and analyses considered useful for colonial expansion. It was in that sense that it foreshadowed the applied geography of the 1950s and 60s.
[10] Robequain, *Le Than-Hoa*, 1929.
[11] Gautier, *Les siècles obscurs du Maghreb*, 1927.
[12] Gourou, *Les paysans du delta tonkinois*, 1936.

principally based on a thorough analysis of the British experience.[13] He was the first to compare 'settlement' colonies (mostly in temperate regions open to European settlement) with the 'exploitation' colonies of the tropics.[14] In the latter, the European population was necessarily small. Its role was to control the country, to import Indian or Chinese labour where the native population was too scarce or refused to work for money, and to develop a trade in staples or in mineral ores. From the contrast between these he deduced different types of policies. The devolution of many of the metropolis's powers would be normal in 'settlement' colonies, but impossible in 'exploitation' colonies because with white settlers a small minority, a democratic regime would eliminate those metropolitan functions.

French colonial geographers adopted this classification. It provided them with some insights into the economic aspects of colonization and explained the difference between direct rule (the system prevalent within the French Empire, at least during the first decades of colonial expansion) and indirect rule (the normal British approach within 'exploitation' colonies, which was increasingly emulated by French colonial specialists). This new orientation was to some extent prepared by the work of Marshall Louis Lyautey, who was almost singlehandedly responsible for the conquest and organization of the Morocco protectorate, and who had also concluded that the survival of the colonies, and the colonized, depended on maintaining a strong identity for native institutions. It is clear that Lyautey's attitude towards Moroccan society was in part rooted in the discovery of the advantages of indirect rule, in particular, its relative non-interference in time-honoured local cultures.[15]

During the 1890s the interest in the new English-speaking countries grew conspicuously. It was a period in which the sons of many businessmen and politicians were sent on a new type of Grand Tour through Britain, Canada, the United States, South Africa, India, Australia and possibly New Zealand. Pierre Leroy-Beaulieu, the son of Paul Leroy-Beaulieu, André Siegfried and others visited these countries during the last years of the nineteenth century.

[13] Leroy-Beaulieu, *De la colonisation*, 1902.

[14] Since in the French Empire, 'settlement' colonies have significant native populations, they were also, in a way, 'exploitation' colonies. But in the publications of colonial geographers, as in the newspapers of the time, 'exploitation' colonies were understood to offer types of food or raw materials that could not be procured in western Europe. For this reason, the use of the term was restricted to tropical environments. Exploitation, then, is here used to refer to the use of resources and not to the treatment of the peoples. This is in conformity with the meaning assigned to the terms 'exploitation' and 'settlement' colony in France between the 1890s and the 1940s.

[15] Early in his career Lyautey secured his public reputation through his book *Le rôle social de l'officier* (1891) in which he developed an original conception of society and of the responsibility of the elites and which had a strong influence on social relations in French industry and on urban and regional planning in France. In Morocco he promoted a strong segregation between native society and the French settlers in order to avoid the collapse of local institutions which he had observed in Algeria and considered to have been disastrous for both the colonized people and the colonizers.

Pierre Leroy-Beaulieu published interesting accounts of *Les nouvelles sociétés anglo-saxonnes* and *Les États-Unis d'aujourd'hui.*[16] Siegfried wrote a doctoral thesis on *La démocratie en Nouvelle Zélande* (note the influence of de Tocqueville on the title) and soon became the premier French specialist on all English speaking countries.[17] Both were fascinated by the fantastic economic and social laboratory that these new countries represented. Leroy-Beaulieu focused on economic achievements, but also examined the condition of the labour markets, investment policies and the search for efficiency. Siegfried was more attentive to political conditions. Both were interested in the influence of democratic and – for Australia and New Zealand, socialist – ideals in these countries.

DEMANGEON AND THE BRITISH EMPIRE

Such was the general context in which Albert Demangeon prepared his book *L'Empire britannique.*[18] Demangeon had come to intellectual maturity in the atmosphere of the 1890s during which France borrowed its scientific paradigms and some of its management methods from Germany but turned to the English-speaking world for economic and political models. Born in northern France, Demangeon's doctoral dissertation had analysed the spatial organization of a region which was but a part of a larger whole: north-western Europe, centred on the Channel and the North Sea. It was there that the main economic achievements of industrial and commercial modernization occurred.[19] As a result, Demangeon always maintained an interest in Belgium, the Netherlands and the British Isles, and Vidal de la Blache requested that he prepare the volumes on these countries for Vidal's new *Géographie universelle.*[20] Demangeon spent several years before and after World War I visiting Britain, conducting research in British archives, and analysing the basis of British success.

Before the turn of the century, there was already evidence of economic decline in Britain. Vidal de la Blache was conscious of it in the 1880s and André Siegfried made it the focus of his study of the British Isles.[21] Britain remained, however, the major world power in spite of the growth of American influence. Indeed, it was thanks to the empire and not to the United States that the country managed to survive the war. Certainly, Demangeon could not ignore the Empire when dealing with British realities. This was why he

[16] Leroy-Beaulieu, *Les nouvelles sociétés*, 1901, and *Les États-Unis*, 1904.

[17] Siegfried, *La démocratie en Nouvelle-Zélande*, 1904.

[18] Demangeon, *L'Empire britannique*, 1925.

[19] Demangeon, *La plaine picarde*, 1905.

[20] Demangeon, *Les Îles britanniques*, 1927 and Demangeon, *Belgique Pays-Bas, Luxembourg*, 1927.

[21] Vidal de la Blache, *Autour de la France*, 1889; Siegfried, *L'Angleterre aujourd'hui*, 1924.

agreed to cover the subject for Armand Colin, the principal publisher of geographic titles which, in that period, was launching a new series of short treatises for students and the educated public.

Demangeon was a Vidalian geographer. His doctoral thesis was considered the best example of the new regional approach (thanks to its balanced treatment of the 'man'/milieu relationship and analysis of the genesis of both small *pays* and larger regions), which he also successfully mobilized in his books on Belgium, Luxembourg, the Netherlands and the British Isles. But he was also more conscious than most of his colleagues of the significance of nations, hence the long, dense chapters devoted to the heritage decisive in the building of national identities and states, and the thorough description of national economies and their international links. On the strength of his doctoral dissertation, the regional descriptions in his books on Benelux and Britain, and his strong interest in settlement patterns, Demangeon is generally presented as the most faithful of Vidal's disciples. But for Demangeon, as for Vidal, geographers were not limited to the study of regions; the regional scale was but one of the scales that geographers must explore.

There was unfortunately no body of methods and concepts for analysing multi-national entities. There was no guide and no model. Political science was still very crude and its issues were raised and examined in essays rather than in erudite publications. There was a tradition of colonial geography, but its theoretical content was poor. Demangeon was well aware of this fact and preferred to imagine new approaches rather than to rely on weak ones. Hence the significance of *L'Empire britannique*. The book was a testimony to the sustained French interest in the British Isles, its history, political institutions, economic experience and its overseas expansion. It used the evidence provided by French authors like André Siegfried, Paul and Pierre Leroy-Beaulieu, Victor Bérard (whose *L'Angleterre et l'Impérialisme* was very influential) and by an extensive English literature.[22] Its originality, however, was that it offered a new perspective on colonization and sought to pave the way for a new model of colonial geography. It was, in fact, the first attempt to conceptualize the ways in which western societies managed to control distant countries, develop their economies and dominate their native populations.

DEMANGEON'S APPROACH TO COLONIAL GEOGRAPHY

Demangeon clearly understood colonial geography as 'an independent discipline'.

> Its purpose is not to tell the story of the conquest. That is the task of history. Nor is it to describe the countries involved. That is the

---

[22] Bérard, *L'Angleterre et l'Impérialisme*, 1901.

function of regional geography. It is essentially to study the contact between two types of people who are to be associated in a colony: an advanced one, well provided with capital and material equipment and searching for new riches, spatially mobile, open to the notion of enterprise, adventure, the unknown, and the exotic; the other, closed in on itself, faithful to old ways of life, with limited horizons, badly equipped with weapons and tools. Research consists of explaining how the colonizing people acted in order to exploit this domain, to create wealth, to dominate and use the natives, and how the colonized country, according to its natural setting and the state of civilization of its inhabitants, reacted to the breath of the new spirit.[23]

It is difficult today to appreciate the novelty of such a programme. For the majority of its practitioners, geography was a natural science which dealt with places, landscapes, and territories and which focused on the 'man'/milieu relationship. Demangeon conceived of colonial geography as a social science: its main emphasis was on the relations between two peoples, on their techniques of spatial organization, and on the way in which they interacted. His very careful statements about the nature and finality of geography are strikingly unusual in the context of the late 1900s. His was truly a new conception of geography. He described its programme in the following terms: 'Within the broad context of human geography, the aim is to show how, on a stage at the same time very peculiar and very diverse, a group of men managed to mobilize their faculties of invention, adaptation, acclimatization and propagation.'[24] *L'Empire britannique* relied mainly on the analysis of a culture: the evolutionary stages of one of its original aspects, how it managed to develop special skills regarding spatial organization and control, and the spatial achievements that it allowed for. What approach was appropriate to such an inquiry? The first step was to present the genesis of the empire. The second was to analyse the tools developed by the process of British colonization and the resulting nature of British civilization overseas. The third was to examine the current problems of the British Empire in the early 1920s. We shall look at each of these in turn.

Demangeon did not undertake a detailed history of the British Empire – that was clearly history's task. The purpose of the first part of his book was to stress the pre-conditions of colonial development, the conditions necessary to the birth of a 'colonial spirit'. He traced back its successive expressions: the motivations behind the first plantations, the search for Northeast and Northwest passages to the Indies and the growth of 'exploitation' and 'settlement' colonies.

Demangeon had been a student at the École Normale Supérieure at the same time as Lucien Febvre, and he had maintained close links with Febvre, as their co-authored work on the Rhine problems attests. His appeal to the

[23] Demangeon, *L'Empire britannique*, 1925, pp. v–vi.
[24] Ibid., p. vi.

notion of a colonial spirit is fascinating since it suggests that Demangeon was as convinced of the significance of 'mentalities' as the founder of the 'Annales School'.[25] The explanation of geographical facts had to rely on the exploration of psychologies, but the focus was not on individuals. It was the collective dimension which was of interest. Demangeon's resort to psychology is often missed since he is widely remembered as the author of a devastating review of Georges Hardy's *Géographie psychologique*.[26]

Following this discussion of the colonial spirit, Demangeon focused the rest of the first part of *L'Empire britannique* on the main structures of the empire. Following Paul Leroy-Beaulieu, he underscored the contrast between 'settlement' colonies and 'exploitation' colonies. The development of each had been characterized by some prominent facts: the high level of British emigration for the former, the role of business communities, as exemplified by the chartered companies, for the latter. The result was a giant conglomerate of scattered possessions. It was through the domination of the seas, through chains of strongholds built on small islands, promontories or capes, and through the use of the most sophisticated communication technologies of the time that unity was achieved and maintained. Demangeon placed great emphasis on communication: 'from relay to relay, from base to base, there is a nearly continuous thread which conducts British ships all over the world through British territory. Straights, inlets, isthmuses, islands, promontories are organized for imperial circulation.'[27] And further, 'The telegraphic cables suppress geographic isolation: all the main pieces are linked together through submarine lines.'[28] He also paid attention to organizations, enterprises, associations and public bureaucracies: 'Many associations, by recruiting their members from all over the empire, contribute to maintaining the cohesion of the whole', and he went on to list these associations.[29] Unfortunately, his

[25] Ibid., pp. 3–18.

[26] Hardy, *Géographie psychologique*, 1939. Reviewed by Demangeon in *Annales de géographie*, 1940, pp. 134–7. Many people consider that Demangeon was eager to restrict geographical inquiries to material facts. His criticism was not, however, targeted at the role of psychic factors in geography, *per se*, but at the poor quality of Hardy's treatment of these factors (Jean Gottmann, personal conversation with the author). Hardy, was unable to address collective attitudes and relied on a naive view of mental factors in social life. In addition, Demangeon had already developed a distinct dislike for Hardy on the basis of the latter's inadequate textbook on colonial geography: *Géographie et colonisation*, 1933.

[27] Demangeon, *L'Empire britannique*, 1925, p. 84.

[28] Ibid., p. 85.

[29] He considered the associations worthy of mention to be the Universities' Office of the British Empire (formed 1912), the Imperial Office of Entomology (formed 1901), the Imperial Office of Mycology (formed 1918), the British Medical Association, the Society of Comparative Legislation, and the British Association for the Advancement of Science ... In the field of economics the Federation of British Industries, the British Empire Producers' Organization, the Empire Resources Development Committee, the Worker's Educational Association and many others are also significant. Demangeon, *L'Empire britannique*, 1925, p. 153.

analysis of the Colonial Office and of the administrative systems of the different colonies and dominions remained sketchy.

The second part of *L'Empire britannique* is certainly the most original. It is a fascinating analysis of what Pierre Gourou later called social techniques, or the systems of social relations and their spatial correlates.[30] Demangeon's analysis was limited by the absence in this period of a pertinent sociological approach. Max Weber's ideas concerning bureaucracies were not known outside Germany and his approach did not, in any case, emphasize their spatial dimensions. French and English sociology had nothing to offer. As a result, Demangeon's analysis remained impressionistic. The first chapter was devoted to the tools of British colonization. It explored the effort involved in constructing from scratch the basic transport infrastructure, together with the introduction and improvement of irrigation which opened impressively large areas to cultivation, particularly in tropical regions where commercial crops such as cotton were profitable. British colonization was also a capitalist venture, with heavy investments coming from Britain, and this explained the rapid development of new crops, and mining activities, the rapid provisioning of basic equipment, and the early appearance of universities and research centres. During the nineteenth century, British colonization relied heavily and from the start on scientific research.

The second chapter was more classical. It described the main types of British colonization both in tropical and temperate areas. The variety was great, from ports of trade such as Aden, Singapore, and Hong Kong to huge pre-developed countries such as India. India was the laboratory where indirect rule was first experimented with, hence its influence on the practices developed elsewhere. British policy was always to create the conditions for an open economy. Within temperate colonies, the native populations were generally quickly disposed of since in most regions they had been few in number and lacked the solid hold on the land of sedentary peoples. The key to the economic development of these regions was the creation of farms, he argued. Demangeon provided a clear picture of the land survey and land property systems, of the bureaucracies which managed them, and of the resulting evolution of democracies based on commercial farmers.

After deciphering the social basis of the British colonial enterprise, Demangeon moved back to questions concerning culture, attitudes, and particularly to the concept of *genre de vie* as appplied to modern urbanized and industrialized society. He described material life, food, clothing, housing as well as the role of sports in British society. His discussion of the main aspects of social life, the role of the English language, and the significance of religion completed the picture: a society cannot be operated only through social organizations. It is made of classes and of interest groups. Hence the significance of political systems, especially the original forms of self-

---

[30] For a systematic presentation of the concept of social techniques see Gourou, *Pour une géographie humaine*, 1973, p. 17–24. It is worth noting, however, that the concept was present prior to Gourou's work on it.

government which were developed very early in the life of British settlement colonies.

In this portion of the book Demangeon did not regard the British Empire as a global economic and political system but focused on how it functioned locally and on how the local cells were integrated into a coherent organization. He saw it as an organization made up of partially autonomous units.

DEMANGEON AND THE FUTURE OF THE BRITISH EMPIRE: AN ASSESSMENT

The third portion of Demangeon's book was devoted to 'imperial problems'. It was the most political section of his book. Its aim was to explain the present organization of the British Empire, the principles according to which it operated, and the probable shape of its evolution. Demangeon was writing at a time in which there was passionate debate about the unity of the empire not only in Britain but in the dominions and in many colonies. The problem had many facets. The operation of such a huge conglomerate on a centralized basis was impossible and did not conform to the traditions of the British people. The American War of Independence reinforced these attitudes. But decentralization, Demangeon pointed out, carries its own dangers, in particular the strengthening of local egotisms and the disappearance of a sense of a common interest worthy of support and defence.

Demangeon saw that there were many common interests within the empire. They were most evident in the field of security: during the First World War, the defence of Britain had not been possible without the help of the whole empire. In that war, the British Isles had been the most vulnerable part of the empire, but in other circumstances, he suggested, the brunt of the danger might be born elsewhere. Australia, New Zealand or South Africa could not rely on near allies and consequently turned to Britain for defence. The situation was different for Canada because the interests of Britain and the United States generally converged.

The common economic interests were obvious: all the components of the empire had open economies which needed foreign outlets. Temperate dominions had to sell their wheat, wool, meat and butter. Tropical colonies were producing sugar, tea, coffee, rubber or cotton. The largest market for all these products was Britain. Demangeon noticed that local colonially-based industrialists suffered from the crushing competition of British industrial goods but considered that the exporters of raw staple products were so strongly tied to their British customers that the British point of view generally prevailed. Tariffs were not high enough to prohibit the importation of a wide range of British domestic and commercial products – the situation was different for other commodities.

With time, the conflict between industrial interests in Britain and in the colonies became more manifest. Demangeon considered that the security provided by Britain would be less effective with the growth of new powers such as Japan. From the end of the nineteenth century it was evident that Britain could not both defend itself against a strong European country and provide security for the most remote parts of the empire. This realization was, on the British side, the principal motivating factor behind the establishment of the dominions. Instead of small colonies completely dependent on Britain, dominions would have responsibility for their own armies and navies which, while they were integrated into an imperial defence system, were also able to cope with regional problems on their own. The various independence movements also evidently played a major role.

Demangeon was aware of both the economic and military implications of these imperial controversies. He reviewed the possibilities of a more thorough economic union and concluded that there would be a natural evolution toward a reinforcement of the local commitments of the dominions. Nationalism would come to the fore. Regional imperialisms would develop – as was already evident in Australia and South Africa.

But the imperial system was not solely composed of white Protestant colonies of predominantly British stock. Demangeon devoted a long chapter to India which was central to the empire due to the sheer size of its population, its strategic importance, and the strength of its nationalist movements.[31] In Demangeon's view, the foreseeable future held the possibility of either 'complete independence or supervised autonomy'. Would the sub-continent constitute one country or several? Demangeon did not broach the question, despite the fact that rivalry between Moslems and Hindus was already acute in many parts of the country. His conclusion was, however, incisive: 'in India a slow process is at work which is creating a national solidarity in the face of European domination. It would be dangerous to ignore the fact that the very principle of this movement threatens the future of the British regime. From the political point of view, the running of the country will pass from the hands of Englishmen to those of Indians. From an economic point of view, when conducting their own businesses, Indians will work for the sake of their own country and not for the benefit of Great Britain.'[32]

Demangeon thought that similar evolutions could be predicted for other tropical colonies in Burma, Ceylon, West Africa, South Africa and Egypt. He was particularly conscious of the growing solidarities between Moslem peoples. 'After long years of impotence and discouragement, an Islamic renaissance of sorts is occurring. It is reclaiming its powers of propaganda, faith in its future, influence over its believers, and consciousness of its universality.'[33] And with considerable insight he predicted that 'The religious dimension is in this sense opening a way to the political dimension: the defence of the faith combines with the defence of freedom: Islam will again tend to become a political power.'[34] Overall, it appeared to Demangeon 'that

[31] Demangeon, *L'Empire britannique*, 1925, p. 224–50.
[32] Ibid., p. 250.
[33] Ibid., p. 260.
[34] Ibid., p. 261.

British prestige is weakening in the Orient where it is confronting national movements supported by religious faith which are preparing the Moslem people for a regime of political liberty.'[35]

Demangeon traced the British Empire's golden years to the First World War. 'Never had the British Empire appeared more united and more coherent than during the Great War when, as colonies gave their men and their money, one got the impression they were defending their threatened homeland.'[36] If internal tensions and conflicts were diminished with the advent of war, Demangeon knew that unanimity is always a provisional state and that divisive forces are the more permanent ones. Writing of India, he commented,

> Just like the dominions, India lives in accordance with its own life, which is not always congruent with imperial life. But the two types of colonies utterly differ. Conscious of their rights, the dominions never refused to recognize their duties: the community of memories and of civilization which attach them to the home country is a factor of union ... Conscious also of its rights, India does not have the same reasons for recognizing its duties. It shares nothing with Englishmen beyond remembrance of a two-century-long domination. In its religions, its races, its customs, its ways of life, it is different from Europe. It is a member of the empire but its adherence to the union relies on force not on free association. If India becomes a force in its own right, what will the nature of its relations with the empire be?[37]

As a theoretician of empire, Demangeon displayed great lucidity concerning the evolution and the fate of specific colonies. He was a liberal. His studies pointed to the trends in the evolution of the bonds which held the empire together. Bold conclusions emerged. Colonial empires were ephemeral constructs partly because it was difficult to manage dispersed territories in a world where competition was becoming tougher, and also because the principles of western democracy were destroying the bases of colonial domination. The only real question was how long the process of disintegration would last and what policies would prolong the process and hence soften its impact for both sides.

CONCLUSION

L'Empire britannique was in many respects an exceptional book. It was ahead of its time in terms of the conception of human geography which lay at its foundation, its explanation of the principles and nature of British

[35] Ibid., p. 262.
[36] Ibid., p. 263.
[37] Ibid., p. 225.

colonial policies and their territorial expression through an exploration of attitudes and institutions, and its critical analysis of both the present and the future of colonial empires.

It was certainly this last dimension which had the greatest impact when the book was first published. Demangeon's conclusions were welcomed by superficial readers as they stressed Britain's coming difficulties and satisfied the jealousy of many of the French concerning the British Empire: isn't it pleasant to discover that one's more successful cousin is finally experiencing difficulties and that his future is apparently not as bright as his past? But for the majority of its readers, the book carried a different message. Demangeon was analysing the largest empire ever built at a time when its power was apparently overwhelming. Yet he clearly perceived its contradictions and weaknesses. They were not rooted in poor political choices or in the poor management of the system. On the contrary, Demangeon stressed the wisdom of Britain's leaders who were ever adapting institutions to the changing nature of relations and power. The fragility stemmed from the very nature of modern European societies and the nature of their expansion. As a result, the threat to the British Empire was a threat to any European empire.

A study of the French Empire would not have succeeded as impressively in undermining the beliefs of the imperialists as did Demangeon's book on the British Empire. The French empire was younger, still expanding in the 1920s (e.g. Morocco) and was mainly composed of 'exploitation' colonies. There was, however, no reason for its evolution to differ from that of the British Empire. North Africa, which was then the only French 'settlement' colony, was facing a growing Arab nationalism. French settlers became more willing to accept a centralized political system, but the French position was not safe as it could be jeopardized at any time by the settlers' quest for autonomy and by Moslem nationalist movements. French geographers, including Elisée Reclus who was happy to have one of his daughters settle in the Dahra region of Algeria, had generally supported colonial expansion. Demangeon was the first to present the modern European empires in an evolutionary perspective and to stress their vulnerability. For him, the time for colonialism was already past.

The originality of the conception of human geography to be found in the book was less clear at the time. Epistemological problems were not central either to students or the informed public. The majority of contemporary geographers were satisfied with the principles provided in newly published books by Vidal de la Blache and Lucien Febvre.[38] They scarcely noticed the shift from a natural science to a social science perspective. In fact, many of the best geographers of the period were undergoing a similar evolution, among them Denis and Emile-Félix Gautier.[39] French geography was entering a phase of schizophrenia which lasted three or four decades.

[38] Vidal de la Blache, *Principes de la géographie humaine*, 1922, and Febvre, *La terre et l'évolution humaine*, 1922.

[39] Denis, *La République Argentine*, 1920 and Gautier, *Les siècles obscurs du Maghreb*, 1927.

Today the book is interesting for its analysis of a culture, its social techniques, and the ways in which these were used for organizing territory. The originality of Demangeon's approach to these is clear but also unsatisfactory. It is at once impressionistic and reveals no attempt at generalization. Demangeon was certainly hampered by the lack of systematic studies of social relations and by his ignorance of Max Weber's most recent work on bureaucracies. There may, however, be a deeper reason for his imperfect exploitation of genuinely original insights. Demangeon believed in a structural–functional approach. His previous works focused, for example, on the minor regional divisions in Picardy and on their permanency, or on the functional organization of farm settlements. He refused to restrict his study to the landscape and its conspicuous features, viewing these as often irrelevant to significant geographic realities. In his presentation of the British Empire, the emphasis was again on global entities, attitudes and cultures.

Demangeon's work was not fundamentally analytical. He was working at a time when Durkheim was writing of the *fait social global*, and given his own parallel interest in *faits géographiques globaux* (global geographic phenomena), it is not surprising that he did not attempt to systematize his inquiries into mentalities and social organization. These were merely seen as details in a larger pattern – or 'typology' (to use the terminology employed by French geographers of the period). Certainly, the emphasis on global approaches must have deterred Demangeon and some of his colleagues from systematically pursuing the fields that they had discovered.

The relationship between geography and colonial expansion could and did take various forms: First, geography could present and support justifications for expansionism; second, geography could provide soldiers, settlers, and merchants with useful information on the look of the land, on its resources, on its climate, on the best way to open an area to trade, and on how to protect it from the ambitions of other imperialist powers; third, geography could study the way in which colonization transformed territorial and social structures and created new types of spatial organization. This third form is the truly scientific contribution. Demangeon was among the first geographers to explore this avenue and in so doing he mobilized efficient conceptual tools. In many respects, his work was completely new. But it reflected the changing forces which western societies were experiencing after the First World War.

13

Imperialism and Colonialism versus Disciplinarity in French Geography

Olivier Soubeyran*

INTRODUCTION

The relationship between geography and empire is not a new area of inquiry in the history of French geographic thought. In a sense, no issue in the history of the sciences is ever definitively resolved. Recently, however, new analytical perspectives have reopened and rejuvenated this theme. A new realization that the relationship between geography and empire was at the very heart of the constitution of French geography as a 'university discipline' gives a whole new impetus to its exploration. Thus, it is appropriate to begin by making clear how this theme is both new and relevant to modern French geography.

Without caricaturing too much the received history of the discipline, until very recently, the conception of how French geography became a university discipline was limited and simplistic. Everything traditionally revolved around the turn of the last century and the founding father of the French school of geography, Paul Vidal de la Blache (1845–1918).[1] Our discipline began its scientific life with Vidal and the history of the institutionalization of geography starts with the formation of his school. Dominant in the universities into the 1960s, Vidal, in geography focused on the national scene.

Vidal's radical break with the past was easily identifiable with three key developments: the creation of the *Annales de géographie* (1891) founded by

---

* Translated by Lorin Card and Anne Godlewska
[1] Among the members of the French school of geography were Gallois (1857–1941), Demangeon (1872–1940) and De Martone (1873–1955).

a master 'already in full possession of his doctrine', according to Gallois; the imposition of the regional method, of which Vidal was to give a marvellous example in his 'Tableau Géographique de la France' (1903); and the appearance of the first dissertations on regional geography directed by Vidal, most notably A. Demangeon's *La plaine picarde* (1905). It was therefore assumed that an evolution in geographic thought separated pre-Vidal (that is to say, 'pre-scientific') and post-Vidal (or 'scientific') thought. Further, according to this view, it was in the pre-Vidal era that all the geography associated with the colonial movement was concentrated. In this historical reconstruction, colonial geography was initially amalgamated with the history of geographic exploration, and then confused with the history of the building of the colonial empire which, after 1870, really took off. Colonial geography, then, was seen as culminating in nothing more than the simple production of practical facts, and was consequently deemed incapable of the disinterested stature which was considered the *sine qua non* of a 'science'.

Seen in that light, there was strictly no common measure between the substance and scientific weight of the Vidalian message on the one hand, and the mediocrity of the practical geography associated with the French colonial empire on the other. From this perspective, then, the relationship between geography and empire was not only not at the heart of the institutionalization of the discipline, but entirely 'irrelevant' to it; its historical role was quickly resolved, so to speak, in the passage from pre-scientific to scientific geography.

This implicit model of French geographic thought, this manner of separating the essential from the residual in the analysis of the establishment of French geography as a discipline, is currently under revision. The aim is not primarily to challenge the mistaken identification of the institutionalization of French geography with the formation of the French school of geography. We have nevertheless distanced ourselves from the Vidalian school[2] and, as a consequence, we can more clearly see that that implicit model was the property of the victors, and in the long run this model too would have to be 'localized', or in turn considered an aspect of the history of geographic thought. A few of the model's assumptions are already under particular scrutiny. In addition, and more directly related to the question of the relationship between geography and empire, an important cultural phenomenon has been taking place in France: there has been a relative loss of guilt with respect to our colonial past. Suddenly the intellectual projects and practices accompanying the colonies are no longer *a priori* suspect and unworthy of scientific interest.[3] Further, the inferiority of geographic thought associated with the colonial movement is not all that obvious. If colonial geography is no longer discredited *a priori* by Vidalian geography, then the

[2] This distancing is different from the frontal attacks inflicted on the Vidalian school beginning in the 1970s by both Marxist and quantitative geographers.

[3] The current move toward ethnographic studies in geography, particularly through the impetus given it by Claval, forms a part, I believe, of that rehabilitation.

passage from colonial geography to Vidalian geography is recovered as a real problem worthy of our attention. Thus re-contextualized, the relationship between geography and empire expressed in terms of a scientific conception of the field of colonial geography becomes an important element in the establishment of geography 'as a discipline'.

This means that we can no longer ignore Marcel Dubois's colonial geography. In fact, we must now explore how and why his colonial geography did not or could not become institutionalized. Why, in the very heart of the French school of geography, was Dubois unable or unwilling to 'discipline' (as he so aptly put it) his project, and to establish his colonial geography as the paradigm for modern geography?

On the other side we must also explore how geography as a university discipline modified the treatment of colonial space and how geography's constitution as a university discipline modified the relations between geography and empire. In order to do this, we should first undertake a review of the relationship between the discipline of geography and the colonial movement in France during the last quarter of the nineteenth century. Finally, despite the general recognition of the 'colonial rootedness' of our geographic tradition and the importance of the historical relationship between geography and empire in that tradition, remarkably few of the major monographs devoted to the birth of French human geography choose to remember this. Why? And is this amnesia particular to our discipline?

THE GEOGRAPHIC SOCIETIES: AN OPEN CONSPIRACY

On one level, the close ties that link geography and the colonial movement and their centrality in the French school of geography are well known, as demonstrated by Vincent Berdoulay.[4] The degree of the collusion is clear from the role and history of the geographic societies (of which the oldest and most prestigious was the Société de Géographie de Paris, created in 1821). The very growth of the societies through the nineteenth century is an indication of the rising importance of colonialism and the colonial movement. Berdoulay demonstrates that the geographic societies were implicated in and concerned to promote the colonial movement. Indeed, it is clear from their stated aims that they constituted significant pressure groups in favour

---

[4] The recognition is, however, only as recent as Berdoulay's *La formation de l'école française*, published in 1981. Today it is a key text, but at its publication it did not receive wide acclaim. Similarly, in the chapter devoted to the institutionalization of the discipline in the most recent account of the last two centuries of French geography (Pinchmel et al., *Deux siècles*, 1984), there is no mention of works related to colonial space or even colonial geography. In keeping with this, no texts written by M. Dubois are listed. To crown it all, the amnesia with respect to Dubois extends to the substitution of Lucien Gallois as the co-founder of the *Annales de géographie*. The significance of this apparent oversight will become clear in the course of this chapter.

of colonization. Due to their confusion of social and scientific roles – a confusion all the more significant thanks to the possible utility of geography to military and commercial interests – their role as propagandists is inseparable from their representation of geography.[5] But why did the number of these societies increase exponentially between 1872 and the 1890's? In order to answer that question we must briefly review the national context and the entirely new position held by geography during that time.

THE NATIONAL CONTEXT AND THE GEOGRAPHERS' ROLE

The French defeat in the Franco–Prussian War of 1870–1 provoked popular, political and academic soul searching. Geography found itself at the heart of a number of discussions on the causes of France's defeat and the conditions under which the country could avoid any similar future humiliation. There was a recognition of the danger to France of German superiority in geography. It was widely said that it was 'the German school teacher who won the war'. The French generals themselves had not known 'whether the Rhine ran from south to north or from north to south'.[6] In 1872 Levasseur commented: 'Indifference to geographic studies can be counted among the causes of our disasters.' Vidal, in the obituary of his friend and colleague Pierre Foncin, described the general mood: 'One of the concerns of public opinion, in the aftermath of 1870, had been to restore the teaching of geography, which had fallen to a very low level, to the position it deserved in our schools: we had experienced a feeling of inferiority which was harmful to the interests of our homeland ...' It was necessary 'to raise our heads and vigorously undertake the long-term project of rebuilding the greatness of our homeland, and of restoring its courage and pride'.[7] The Vidalian school therefore developed a scientific approach to the personality of French territory.

Aware of the disastrous consequences of the absence of a geographic culture, the government planned a series of official measures – we are

[5] 'Apart from the work of the scientists who established doctrines, we must note the work of the learned societies and even of the economic interest groups who, through participation in propaganda activities, prepared the way for reform and who often guided reform with a sure sense of national interest: I designate as such our geographic societies, our chambers of commerce and our maritime and colonial propaganda groups. It would be unfair not to bring to light the important role played by the military geographers in our home army, our colonial armies and in our navy who, isolated and grouped in bodies such as "the geographic service of the army" or of the "colonies", and the "navy map depot", have eminently contributed to our progress.' Dubois, 'Géographie et géographes', 1914, p. 853.

[6] In *La république française*, 27 November 1871 cited in Ozouf, 'Le tour de France', 1986, p. 318.

[7] Vidal de la Blache: 'Nécrologie de Pierre Foncin,' 1917, pp. 67–8.

familiar with the role played by Levasseur in the rebuilding of the secondary-level geography programmes. However, 'explaining the worth of their home-land to the French youth', as Foncin put it, was not incompatible with the desire to engage in colonial expansion. On the contrary, Foncin, a fervent supporter of the colonial movement, founder of the Alliance Française and co-founder of the geographic societies of Bordeaux and Lille, contributed to the inaugural *Annales de géographie* in 1891 with a burning article on 'France beyond her borders' ('La France extérieure').

In fact, love of country mixed with a spirit of revenge had produced a strong nationalist upsurge, which became more and more closely associated with the colonial movement. Berdoulay captured the genesis and logic of that association:

Following the humiliation of 1871, several patriots reconsidered the possibility of restoring the prestige and power of France through its colonies. They tried to demonstrate that there was no contradiction between the desire for revenge and the sending of expeditions overseas, and even that the success of the expeditions would create the possibility of a future revision of the humiliating treaty of Frankfurt. That opinion, which was initially shared by only a minority, became more and more widely accepted by government and then by the public.[8]

A close relationship between the colonial movement and the nationalist upsurge allowed France to compensate for the amputation of Alsace-Lorraine from 'internal' France through the conquest of a larger 'external France'. And it is quite evident that the increase in the role and number of geographic societies is directly related to the size of the French colonial conquests following the defeats of 1870–1.[9]

The personnel heading the geographical societies and responsible for their periodicals also reflect the interweaving of geography and the colonial move-ment. At the head of the Société de Géographie de Paris we find leading figures associated with diplomatic circles, the navy, and the colonial adminis-tration. Thus, Chasseloup de Loubat who was Minister of the Navy from 1859 to 1867, and therefore also in charge of colonial affairs, was also the president of the Society.[10] Major political figures such as Prince Bonaparte and Baron Hulot were responsible for the publication of the Society's journal at different times. These same men were also among the founders of the

[8] Berdoulay, *La formation de l'école*, 1981, p. 97.

[9] According to Berdoulay's calculations in *La formation*, 1981, the establishment of the protectorates of Tunisia (1881) and Morocco (1912), the conquests of Madagascar (1895) and Chad (1900), the Berlin Conference (1884–5), the Franco–English accords (1890), and the Tonkin wars (1883–5) increased the French colonial empire between 1871 and 1914 from 5 to 54 million inhabitants!

[10] The post of Under-Secretary of State to the colonies was only created in 1881. It became a Ministry in 1894.

Comité de l'Asie française. The well-known geographers of the era, Dubois, Levasseur, and the Reclus brothers were also supporters of the colonial movement. As for Vidal, his support of the colonial movement is clear from his involvement in the Comité d'Action Française – the body responsible for the revision of the Franco–English accord of August 1890. As we will see, reaction to that agreement was to colour the inaugural issue of the *Annales*.

Berdoulay notes that between 1893 and 1903 (a crucial period in the history of the *Annales* and which witnessed the emergence of the Vidalian school), the Union coloniale française organized more than 400 conferences which were regularly held at the Geographic Society. Dubois, who obtained the Chair of Colonial Geography at the Sorbonne in 1893, and Vidal frequently figured among the lecturers. If the *Bulletins* of the geographic societies, particularly the Paris society, provide a good picture of the scientific/colonial engagement, the role of propagandist played by the geographic societies was also evident in the granting of funds, medals and awards to the expeditions judged the most important.

Apart from the *Bulletin de la Société de Géographie de Paris*, which constituted the key scientific journal of the period, a large number of other periodicals published towards the end of the century were mere instruments of colonial propaganda. An exception to the rule, the *Revue de géographie*, born of the impetus given it by Ludovic Drapeyron in 1877, had intellectual ambitions both in terms of the advancement of knowledge and the reform of teaching. The journal's attraction to the colonial theme was nevertheless strong: in less than four years, it had published 30 or more articles on North Africa alone. And, as Berdoulay has pointed out, the *Revue* considered itself, in part, responsible for the French occupation of Tunis in 1889. Finally, as in the case of the *Bulletin de la Société de Géographie de Paris*, some of the members of the central administrative committee of the *Revue de géographie* were key leaders in the colonial movement (for example, Félix Faure, head of the Parti Colonial).

SCIENTIFIC CULTURE AND THE COLONIAL MOVEMENT

Traditionally, the exploration movement, which grew significantly during the last quarter of the nineteenth century, has been treated as externally controlled and directed essentially by military and commercial interests. But this is far too naive a view.[11] It is a mistake to separate the process of

[11] It is important to understand that the geographers who sought to carry out scientific studies throughout the colonial movement never hid the collusion between commercial, military and scientific interests. Dubois, in the inaugural issue of the *Annales de géographie* stressed external conditions in the development of geographic knowledge. His long article 'L'Océanie' was based on that idea. The naive view of explorations carried out uniquely in the name of a noble and disinterested science was later championed by those who

exploration from the scientific culture which imbued it with meaning and which, in turn, the exploration movement helped to shape. In that respect, the articles by Schirmer on the evolution of knowledge of Africa between 1880 and 1890 are of particular interest.[12] Schirmer argued that, given the immensity of the land to be explored and the extremely limited means available, the real scientific challenge did not lie in the systematic filling in of 'blank spaces' but in the construction of scientific problems. The resolution of those problems was necessary to eliminate all but the good hypotheses which would combine to form a true picture of the orographic and hydrographic systems and the relations between them. The development of this paradigm depended on individual observations and on observations gleaned along particular lines of march, from which plausible hypotheses about extensive regions could be constructed. The nineteenth-century commitment to exploration can also be seen as closely related to experimental science in so far as the hypotheses were ultimately provable, and in so far as the choice of what to explore was guided by scientific 'logic'. Exploration conducted in that spirit allowed the speedy elimination of the greatest number of competing hypotheses. Thus, even if exploration was shaped by commercial and military interests, it was no less part of a dynamic engagement between hypothesis and discovery.

Africa not only played the role of experimental field station for the development of a planning approach, but also served to test geographic models and ideas conceived in France. Thus, we should not be surprised to find an immense imaginary mountain range (the 'Kong' mountains) on a map of the Sudan. These mountains were analogous to imaginary mountain ranges depicted on maps of France. Both were born of the same predictive cartographic theory, developed by Philippe Buache, which argued that the orography of a country could be surmised from the location of river basins. These fictitious ranges must not be regarded as ludicrous errors but as plausible inferences, supported by theoretical models and based on point observations. Although the colonial movement relied on a process of domination, it nevertheless permitted the fashioning of a geographical culture that went beyond mere empiricism and explored problems, enigmas, theories, hypotheses and discoveries. Certainly, it is interesting to note that what attracted Vidal de la Blache in the explorations he recorded during the first few years of the publication of the *Annales de géographie*, was not the movement from one scientific victory to another but the role of discovery in the creation of uncertainty, and the contesting of established theories. This contrasts sharply with the strict positivism of Gallois who, as will be discussed below, was to lead the 'Bataille des Annales' against colonial geography.

---

fought against colonial geography, among them, L. Gallois. Gallois's contributions to the *Annales* (for example, those concerning North and South America) are quite revealing in that regard.

[12] Schirmer, 'La géographie de l'Afrique,' 1891; 1892.

The collusion between geography and the colonial movement also found expression in the planning approach which evolved and accompanied the alteration, exploitation, and management of the colonies. Many of the papers in the *Bulletin de la Société de Géographie* dealt with the technical and social feasibility of large management projects. Among the technical conditions studied were topography, the location of resources, the development of relay points and linkage routes, the possibility of changing traditional routes, the drain of wealth, the conditions under which cultures could be implanted and could be expected to adapt, anticipation of possible climate change, and adapted transfers of technology. The social conditions discussed included the identification of hostile and friendly ethnic groups, the use of inter-ethnic conflicts, the capacity of the European labour force living in poverty to work in the colonies, and the examination of the economic, environmental, and social impacts of major development projects.

The formation of this social and physical planning approach was only possible in an intellectual context in which the relations between human beings and the environment were not already pre-determined. It was important to be able to describe the countryside not just in terms of what it was but in terms of what it might be and, further, how that condition might be arrived at.

This planning approach also presupposed a conception of space and people, both the colonized and the colonizer, as subject to change; space and people represented potential and opportunity rather than simply unavoidable constraint. Colonization, through its ability to stimulate and direct change in the material environment could advance the well-being of the colonies. There was a belief in social reform as an emancipatory force, and space was to play an active role in this liberation. 'Saint-Simonism' has often been described as the philosophical basis of this reformist attitude to colonialism and the writings and activities of M. Chevalier, P. Enfantin, C. Duveyrier, and F. Delesseps attest to this connection. But it has been less often noted that, especially after 1870–1, this vision of the related potential of humanity and the environment were tightly bound to the neo-Lamarckian conceptions of the time. Experimental transformism was more instrumental in the development of a planning approach within the colonial enterprise, than ever was social Darwinism or environmentalism. [13] Darwinism of course encountered a well-known resistance in France precisely due to the prevalence of neo-Lamarckian theories among French naturalists and biologists, [14] and there

[13] To our knowledge, the only writer who has looked at the neo-Lamarkian influence in colonial thought is Rabinow in his innovative *French Modern*, 1989, especially chapter 5. On the influence of a number of neo-Lamarckian naturalists and biologists on the writings contained in the *Annales* and in particular on Vidal's epistemology see: Olivier Soubeyran, 'Dubois, Gallois, Vidal', 1992 and Berdoulay and Soubeyran, 'Lamarck, Darwin, Vidal', 1991.

[14] Conry, *L'introduction du darwinisme*, 1974 and Roger, 'Les néo-Lamarckiens français', 1979.

were almost no Darwinian references in the *Bulletin de la Société de Géographie de Paris*. The colonial movement concentrated instead on classical themes such as migration, examining different aspects of the problem in detail: under what conditions would emigration, the mixture of populations, the transformation of the races, environmental adaptation hygiene and cultural and linguistic change take place? These were irreducible to either environmentalism or the Darwinian themes of the survival of the fittest, vital competition, etc. [15]

THE BATTLE FOR THE *ANNALES* (1891–1894): AN ANALYTIC PERSPECTIVE

University geography became truly institutionalized at the very end of the nineteenth century. Between 1890 and 1900 the number of chairs of geography quadrupled. This period also marked the emergence of the nascent paradigm of the French school of geography.

The simultaneous evolution of a school of thought and institutionalization of a discipline requires careful attention. The social, political, and academic dimensions of this phenomena are equally valid subjects of analysis. But we can just as legitimately adopt an alternative perspective. It is reasonable to suppose that, in the transformation of a school of thought into a discipline, concurrent paradigms can generate the dynamic of a discourse which in turn leads to the development of a certain 'depth' of thought. This transformation is never totally erratic and arbitrary.

Where can we examine these competing paradigms, the intersection of their discourses and the strategies they employed to convince and to guarantee their superiority? The *Annales de géographie* represents a collection of heretofore unrealized wealth in this respect. Founded in October of 1891, the *Annales* was both the medium through which propaganda was spread and a key instrument in the consolidation of the French school of geography. But contrary to what we may think (and this is where the wealth of the source has been untapped), the *Annales* during the first few years of its existence does not provide a seamless affirmation of its founder's thought. It is, rather the scene of a polemic from which Vidal de la Blache is almost totally absent. The journal hosted a battle between two competing currents of thought. One focused on colonial geography, but it was the other, centred on France, that affirmed itself as the paradigm of the French school of geography. It was therefore within the circle of Vidalians that the fight for paradigmatic dominance took place. The *Annales*, then, was not only the scene but the object of battle since the occupation of the *Annales* was essential to victory. That is why the *Annales* constitutes such an excellent corpus for analysis.

[15] Related material can also be found in the report 'Histoire de l'émigration européenne', by A. de Quatrefages de Breau, 1863, a naturalist, anthropologist, 'transformist-fixist', and once president of the Société de Géographie de Paris, in which he discusses the works of the no less illustrious J. Duval.

THE 'MOMENTUM' OF THE REORIENTATION OF GEOGRAPHY AND SCHIRMER'S ABORTED ATTEMPT

The close relationships between geography and empire, on which critical studies of the history of thought justifiably insist today, together with the emphasis placed on the importance of the geographic societies and their influence on the movement of geography into the universities, suggest that it was inevitable that colonial geography would find its place in the battle for the *Annales*. After all, both Vidal and Dubois were the co-founders of the journal and strong supporters of the colonial movement. The inaugural issue, which set out the particular aims of the journal, included Foncin's 'La France extérieure'. It was a furiously propagandist article in support of the colonial movement, as were Schirmer's long articles on Africa and, in particular, his article on the Sudan in which, in a very polemic tone, Schirmer denounced the Franco–English Accord of August 1890 and French government irresponsibility.[16] Thus, the colonial movement, and its need for defence set the tone for the first issue of the *Annales*.

Yet by the end of the nineteenth century several dimensions of the link between geography and empire seemed to be running out of steam. As Berdoulay has pointed out, by the 1890s the number of geographic societies was stabilizing. This corresponded to a period during which, although colonial conquest continued apace, colonialism itself was no longer an issue. By then, it had found unquestioning acceptance in government circles and in public opinion. Thus it seems possible that, from then on, the geographic societies, whose very existence and nature was closely tied to their role as propagandists, lost some of their social utility and even their reason for existence. This diminution of mission also corresponded to a self-questioning on the part of scientific geographers involved in the colonial movement: Many, following Schirmer's example in France (among them Supan, director of the famous *Pétermann Mittheilungen*), expressed the view in the *Annales* that the time of great discoveries, and great scientific enigmas, and, consequently, of a certain geographic culture, was coming to an end. To what goal should geography now be redirected? The question was all the more delicate as there was general awareness among these scientists of the profound implications of national imperialist competition during the last quarter of the nineteenth century. And although Schirmer argued that it is 'under the spur of competition among the European nations that the most systematic progress has been made with respect to geographic knowledge', he analysed the essential question well: how can colonial geography, which is more and more pre-occupied with practical and utilitarian goals, nevertheless produce a body of knowledge which does not have a particular orientation? Or to quote Schirmer's 'question': 'if their motives are not based on a love for pure science, how can they eventually serve it [science]?'

---

[16] Schirmer, 'La France et les voies', 1891.

The question of disciplinary autonomy was thus posed. What was the future for modern geography? That is what the *Annales* addressed in its inaugural issue. It is clear that Schirmer, as a disciple of Dubois, was a supporter of colonial geography. But his response to the question of autonomy (as he formulated the question) could not serve his own aims.

In the very formulation of the question of disciplinary autonomy, Schirmer implied that the answer must lie in an objective and non-normative vision of geographic knowledge concerning the colonies. He sought this objectivity in a reorientation of geographical knowledge. It was his view that although colonial geography clearly served the national interest, it nevertheless remained in and of itself neutral by virtue of the fact that it was part of the most systematic, fine-grained and exhaustive territorial survey. So far as the map agreed with the terrain, he implied, geographic knowledge was neutral and objective. By thus restricting geography to pure description, Schirmer placed it beyond the criticism of those who had judged it too practical and utilitarian. But Schirmer's gain in neutrality was made at the cost of a three-fold risk.

On one hand, Schirmer was returning to the old, outmoded aim of a scientific geography for which 'the final expression of the total geographic knowledge of a region lies in its topographical map'.[17] This places full trust in what was a stillborn conception of geography. On the other hand in reducing geography to a descriptive knowledge of space, Schirmer was casting aside the fundamental question of the organization of space, and the explanatory power of geographic factors in the organization of space. But this was to be expected; in his 'La France et les voies de pénétration au Soudan',[18] he argued that geographic factors carried very little weight in the explanation of the organization of colonial geographic space. In his view, insight into these phenomena would be the fruit of political explanations. The risk, then, was the development of a geography which while independent could not, as a discipline, be self-sufficient.

Finally, Schirmer's strategic choice of neutral and independent geographic knowledge of colonial space led him to tie the relevance of colonial geography to the geography which was evolving in Europe and France. In fact, Schirmer noted that the great transformation in geographic knowledge associated with colonial space (the end of the great discoveries and the redirection of geographic knowledge), had already taken place in Europe and in particular in France. No differentiation was made between colonial geography and the geography that was proposed and practised in and on France itself. The only distinction was a delay. But de-emphasising the specificity of colonial space entailed a risk. Did this not open colonial geography to those who were appropriating France as their main territorial domain – to those who had a competing view of geography?

[17] V. A. Malte-Brun, 'Aperçu de l'état', 1875, p. 561.
[18] Schirmer, 'La France et les voies', 1891.

Schirmer's position was, then, very fragile and understandably it soon vanished from the *Annales*. But Schirmer was only the second knife in the battle of the *Annales*. The true founder of colonial geography was Schirmer's teacher, Marcel Dubois. It was he who took up arms against the competing vision of a domestic geography.

COLONIAL GEOGRAPHY VERSUS REGIONAL GEOGRAPHY: DUBOIS'S CONCEPTION OF COLONIAL GEOGRAPHY

It was not Dubois's intention, as he clearly stated in the first lesson of his course on colonial geography, to produce a geography of the colonies.[19] In that respect, he distanced himself radically from the perspective defended by Schirmer. In fact, he rejected a purely descriptive conception of geography on both theoretical and rhetorical grounds. In his view, geography should take part in the decisions leading to the organization of colonial space. He opted for a discipline of action, 'an applied science' whose aim was the generation of knowledge necessary to establish 'the laws of a truly rational colonization'.[20] In contrast to Schirmer, Dubois did intend to integrate the question of the organization of space into geography. But as he was aware of the 'extreme mobility of political and social personnel'[21] and the weak effect of geographic conditions on the organization of space, a purely geographic explanation of the criteria of location was far from sufficient.

In any case, the applied science of colonial geography cannot be reduced to a purely utilitarian, practicable and practical activity, as its detractors claimed. It was, in fact, the very opposite. The meaning and depth of Dubois's colonial geography is only clear within the context of the development of a territorial planning and management approach. This approach can be seen as anticipating possibilism – a possibilism (if the term is not too anachronistic) which explored the conditions under which planned utopias could be realized. Colonial geography, then, was to be a science of localization. This also meant, however, that it could participate in both large-scale spatial projects for the colonies as well as local plans of lesser scope. Under what conditions could the grafting of a colonial spatial plan on to an existing spatial sub-stratum succeed? Colonial geography's practitioners hoped to provide a partial answer to that question. What interested Dubois was not a geography focused on the influence of the environment, but a geography which examined the possible use by humankind of all the natural resources. It is in this sense that Dubois's comment that the best naturalist would be the best colonist must be understood.

Dubois's commitment to territorial transformation and reform acquires particular interest when we look at other dimensions which he considered

[19] Dubois, 'Leçon d'ouverture', 1894.
[20] Ibid., p. 125.
[21] Dubois, 'Géographie et géographes', 1914, p. 859.

fundamental to colonial geography. He argued that not only did physical factors play an important role in the organization of space (and after the fact, in its explanation) but so too did the world economy, and the extreme fragility of territorial fixity and mobility. For Dubois, these were irreducible constraints critical to any understanding of modern geography.

With regard to making colonial geography a science of the location of human activities, Dubois was a relativist; for him the determinants of the location of human activities could not be reduced to a (more or less nuanced) physical geography. His *Annales* contributions on coastal and hydrographic resources suggest that physical conditions *per se* could have no influence on the evolution of societies. Rather it was the physical world which was dependent on the civilization which invested it with meaning. Physical geography did not stand above history and the development of peoples. Of interest here was not the relatively banal idea that more advanced civilizations were more liberated from local conditions, but the richer political and scientific relativism according to which 'the values of geographic features change throughout the course of history. The very privileges which nature bestowed on certain countries might change into serious disadvantages.' Suddenly, if we accept Dubois's perspective, there are no longer any 'fixed physical causes'[22] which could explain the superiority of a particular nation and concommitantly there is nothing guaranteeing the immutability of the truth of any particular geographic discourse. Therefore a science of geography based on physical invariants committed not only a scientific error but also a political error. This political error would allow France, for example, to harbour illusions about 'its eternal superiority'. This would lead to a peculiar irony whereby an extraordinarily extreme expression of 'European chauvinism' (to use Reclus's words) would actually work against the homeland. 'And if in order to be a geographer' as Dubois pointed out 'we have to declare that Europe owes much to the beautiful articulations of its coastline, then we would be saying that the commercial and military greatness of the German, Russian, French and Austrian–Hungarian navies lies in the fjords of Norway and the gulfs of Greece. In this way, instead of trying to explain a part of our past, we would appear to be guaranteeing the most distant future. That is pushing love for Europe a little too far.'[23]

Interesting as his relativism may be, the argument that 'truth itself evolves' did not make it any easier for Dubois to demonstrate that his conception of geography could be a science in the classic sense of the term. There was another difficulty, however revolving around Dubois's vision of a 'world economy'. According to Perret, 'Marcel Dubois claims that a geography which is in conformity with the new truth must expose the phenomenon of economical circulation which links the smallest towns to the resources of the universe.' We must begin with (and not ignore) the fact that:

[22] Dubois, 'Géographie et géographes', 1914, p. 848.
[23] Dubois, 'Le rôle des articulations', 1892, p. 141.

even a rural French family, apparently confined to its hamlet, lights its home with oil from Borneo, dresses with cotton from Virginia, works with a plow built at Pittsburgh and fertilizes its field with nitrates from Chile and phosphates from Gafsa [Tunisia]. This is why the explanation for the British Empire is not to be found in England, but in India where jute is harvested for Dundee, in Australia which sends its wool to Bradford, in Manitoba which exports its wheat and in Southern Africa which delivers its nuggets. The time is past in which each of us can live independently of the other.[24]

Was this early analysis of global economic integration capable of quickly and efficiently nourishing a new conception of scientific geography? In less than the time that Dubois needed to pursue his risky gamble, the competing alternative solution had already been boldly proposed. Let us, then, examine the conception put forward by Lucien Gallois, which was to become that of the Vidalian school.

LUCIEN GALLOIS'S CONCEPTION OF REGIONAL GEOGRAPHY

A complete break with previous approaches appears in the second (January 1892) issue of the *Annales de géographie* which opened with by Gallois's 'La Dombes'.[25] This article reflected an altogether different conception of geography than that described in the inaugural issue of the journal. To begin with, the focus was entirely on the territory of France, and there was no longer any hint of a commitment to planning. Gallois presented the reader with a necessary and flawless approach to the description of the plateau of Dombes: 'there is no surer method than following the history of its geological formation into the past.' The geology determines the relief and the nature of the soil which in turn, through the agricultural economy, determine the criteria of the location of human activities (way of life, distributions, groupings, etc.). The only confusion in this flawless unfolding was history, which 'has often separated what nature had united'. There was no methodological dilemma: all that was required was the observation of the countryside, because one can 'read in the soil, the reasons and the laws of population'. The focus here is exclusively on what is and what was. Descriptions were no longer 'potential' as for Dubois, but confined to 'reality'. Nevertheless, Gallois's dogmatism had the enormous advantage of finality and of giving the discipline autonomy by internalizing the criteria of location. And besides, what could be more neutral, more constant and more non-human than geological factors? As for patriotism, there too his approach was different. Gallois did not produce any fiery speeches on the intimate relationship between his

[24] Perret, 'Un grand géographe', 1916.
[25] 'La Dombes' is a plateau region in south-eastern France near Lyon. Gallois, 'La Dombes', 1892.

conception of geography and patriotism. Instead, he discussed the 'rational divisions' of France, emphasizing the harmony and the new-found balance between the earth and 'man'. His articles often ended with a poetic evocation of ten or so lines in which he shared his 'love for his country'.

TWO INCOMMENSURABLE CONCEPTIONS AND THEIR SUPPORT

We now understand the radical difference between the Gallois and Dubois conceptions of geography. But how was it possible to evict Dubois's conception given that, on the one hand, there was no independent paradigm from which to judge their performance rationally (the point of the battle was precisely to institute one) and that, on the other Gallois's and Dubois's conceptions were not always sufficiently distinct to allow empirical evidence to adjudicate between them.

The classical view, which holds that one scientific approach is eliminated in favour of another cannot, by definition, apply here since a dominant paradigm was absent. In fact, this caricature corresponds to the official history of the victors. Yet, if we accept that the eviction of Dubois's conception was not entirely arbitrary, what, then, are the criteria according to which the choice was arrived at?

Part of the response lies in the ability of each conception to satisfy what we might call the dictates of disciplinarity, or their capacity to demonstrate their autonomy and 'disciplinary exclusivity'. At that time, there was more concern that a science be an 'independent and self-sufficient science'.[26] That is, a science capable of claiming convincingly that it had integrated into itself the factors which could explain the phenomena under observation and which were the subject of elucidation. There is no doubt that for any disciplinary conception to undergo institutionalization it must be able to make such a claim. Colonial geography seems to have performed less well in this respect than Gallois's project.

In a bitter text, written late in his life, Marcel Dubois bemoaned his 'excommunication' from the Vidalian school and the disciplinary pragmatism that caused it. Although he refrained from criticizing Vidal de la Blache himself, Dubois made it clear that he considered regional geography an aberration: 'as if all the characteristics of human civilization observed in a region would find their natural explanation there'.[27] He concluded that Vidal's message had been twisted by the race for disciplinary autonomy, and that this had prevented a true discussion between the two conceptions. Dubois resented 'those impatient disciples who demanded autonomy for the geographic sciences, who believed that they were ensuring it by melting it in with geology, who exaggerated the "regional method" founded on that alleged identity, and in short, who placed geography in peril: those mistakes must not be attributed,

---

[26] Dubois, 'Géographie et géographes', 1914, p. 848.
[27] Ibid., p. 856.

I repeat aloud, to the originators of the reform.'[28] He did not blame the 'masters' who 'by their work, and in good faith, believed that they were building by virtue of that single process[29] an original, independent and self-sufficient geography'.[30] But he also reminds us that it is much more difficult to 'discipline' a geography which does not evade the reality of movement and mobility, and which admits that 'provinces [are] temporary combinations of facts which are both historical and physical ... rather we must recognize, as Jean Bruhnes's example shows, that regional descriptions can be the crowning and not the commencement of geographic research.'[31]

In Gallois's conception, natural regions were precisely both the crown and commencement of geographic research. Contrary to the evolutionary approach from which Dubois drew his inspiration, Gallois conceived of 'humanity as contained within bounds which are always identical, and this has been called the regional method'. In summary, even if Dubois regarded these regional geographers as 'old-fashioned doctrinarians', he recognized that 'the disciplinary framing of geographic studies within natural regions'[32] had great powers of seduction. The source of that power is clear if we apply to geography what Durkheim said concerning the rules of the sociological method: 'what should explain a social fact? Another social fact'. Self-validation in geography was encouraged by the placement of physical geography at the uncontested core of explanation. Recognizing the strategic powers of the regional method, Dubois wrote:

I admire, without sharing, the feeling of security among some fellow geographers who declare our science to have arrived at its 'definitive constitution', and our method to have been strictly set in matters of teaching. For more than thirty years, I have approached that dogmatic illusion several times to study it curiously, and the more I meditate on the nature of the science which bears the rather vague name of 'geography', the more I hesitate to dogmatize with such confidence.[33]

In one conception of the discipline, Dubois saw an ability to build dogma, a sense of security and confidence, a sense of the definitive constitution of geography. In the other he saw an open mind, and awareness of the illusion of dogma, a lack of assurance and only a very vague sense of the

[28] Ibid., p. 838.
[29] At issue here is the 'remedy of the regional method', p. 854. That is to say, 'the geography which places at the base of every geographic study a preliminary, regional division, most often determined by the nature of the soil and the relief of the land', Ibid., p. 851.
[30] Ibid., p. 855.
[31] Quoted in Perret, 'Marcel Dubois, un grand géographe', 1916, p. 495.
[32] Dubois, 'Géographie et géographes', 1914, p. 856.
[33] Ibid., p. 852.

nature of geography. Colonial geography's difficulty in effecting disciplinary autonomy was related to a more global system of thought.

FROM DISCIPLINARY AUTONOMY TO A SYSTEM OF THOUGHT

We have thus analysed how two incommensurable scientific conceptions can be compared even as a discipline is in the process of formation. However, it would be wrong to suppose that the dynamics of the *Annales* discourse, and the nature of the dialogue between the two protagonists and their associated contributors, necessarily corresponded to an explicit agenda determined by the constraints of institutionalization. The field in which the seduction took place was of course more diffuse than that. In addition, in the various contributions by Gallois and by Dubois, seduction was not separated and distinct from the presentation of the scientific project. The seduction lay in the statement of the scientific aims and the arguments adduced in support. It is precisely in that zone of the ambivalence of scientific claims and promise that the seduction operates.

Both of these systems of thought were composed of four mutually reinforcing poles: the conceptions; how space is conceptualized; the epistemology; and the rhetoric. The systems of thought set up by Gallois and Dubois are incommensurable, and create contrasting images: Dubois's system suggested insecurity, risk, and an opening up, whereas calm, security and order were suggested by Gallois's system.

It is noteworthy that all of Dubois's contributions explicitly addressed issues of method; he destabilized his readers, calling into question their way of seeing and analysing, and challenging their 'European chauvinism'. Gallois, by contrast, never asked methodological questions. 'He proves movement by walking.' His method was implicit and he proceeded as if the question of methodology were unproblematic, as if all that was necessary was a linear account of the formation of a region.[34]

Dubois's articles provided a relativistic view of past and present conceptual systems in the evolution of geographic knowledge. He insisted on the dialectic between hypothesis and discovery as a way of studying the progress of geographic knowledge. In this vein, he showed how the theory of the 'role of the articulations', could have been true in the past but false today. He also explained how a theory which is true today can become false in the future. Why was geographic truth changing? Because it was always supported by conditions of validation which are of a socio-technical order and which are therefore human and evolutionary. Those conditions defined the nature and importance of geographic factors of a physical type, and of a non-physical type.

Where but in Gallois's contributions could security and stability be found? His geological bias and his physical determinism guaranteed the constancy

---

[34] See, for example, Gallois, 'La Dombes', 1892.

and the 'endo-causality' of geographic explanation. Gallois presented us with a de-humanized nature which directs social customs and in which history and politics are considered de-naturalizing. Gallois countered Dubois's relativity of conceptual systems with a conception of the progress of knowledge based on an evolutionary expunction of error in order to finish today at true, intangible knowledge. Hypotheses existed for Gallois but were always associated with error or with the polluting of the observation of facts. They represented the 'interference' that had to be eliminated at all costs from our process of acquiring knowledge. As soon as it was realized that a given fact was constructed, and thus human, it lost its intangibility, became once again tainted, theoretical, and was to be disposed of. [35]

By contrast, Dubois' colonial geography was premised on the external legitimacy of the political and social system, and he was obliged to justify this external legitimization within the discipline. He proposed geographic science as a 'creative boiling over', which was hardly reassuring for the reader.

FROM COLONIAL GEOGRAPHY TO TROPICAL GEOGRAPHY

The Battle of the *Annales* ended with a definitive victory for Gallois. From the inaugural issue of 1891 to Dubois's doctoral article (1894) on colonial geography, there were eight contributions by Gallois compared to ten by Dubois. But from 1895 to 1905, when the first regional theses under the direction of Vidal began to appear, there were more than 21 contributions by Gallois and none by Dubois. It was in 1895 that Dubois gave up the co-direction of the *Annales* to be replaced by Lucien Gallois.

Thus, from 1895 the change in the orientation of the journal is striking. Colonial territory is still dealt with but in the spirit of Gallois's geography. The focus is on the regional geography of the colonies, or on the influence of the environment on individuals. It is 'a geography which thinks that one can read in the soil the reasons for or the laws governing settlement', a geography which restricts itself to the regional method, 'to the alleged natural regions, which it considers so many pigeon holes in which humanity is embedded'. In this vein, as early as 1897, Emanuel De Martonne produced two articles on the life of peoples on the Upper Nile [36] in which he sought to explain their way of life from the physical geography of the region. The study is, therefore, steeped in physical determinism and naturalism, and invokes Darwinism.

There was also another equally important reversal. Written from within the evolutionist ideology, the geography of the colonies viewed the races to

[35] This difference in point of view is particularly clear in the way in which Dubois and Gallois review works having to do with exploration. See for example: Dubois, 'Le continent Austral', 1894 and Gallois, 'Dr. E. T. Hamy', 1897.

[36] De Martonne, 'La vie des peuples', 1896 and 1897.

be found in tropical regions as close to the 'zero degree' of civilization and thus subject to the influences of external circumstances 'in which man is little tolerated by the nature surrounding him'.[37] Here the weight of local conditions was clearly observable. But what a reversal, for from then on it was in the colonial realm, ironically, that Vidalian geography established and legitimated its paradigm of the relations between 'man' and environment.[38] If establishing a conception as truly paradigmatic means, among other things, imposing it beyond its own chosen domain then Gallois's victory is no longer merely total, it is arrogant. Dubois's colonial geography was not able to form itself into a discipline, and from 1895 it was replaced by tropical geography, which was increasingly formed in the Vidalian mould of 'pure and simple geography'.

CONCLUSION

As Berdoulay has shown, the relationships between geography and the colonial movement represent a dimension of analysis impossible to ignore for those interested in the formation of geography. And as this chapter attests, colonial geography played a role in the emergence of the paradigm of the French school of geography. So why have the few French books which deal with the birth of French geography simply forgotten the colonial connection?

There are several ways to answer this question. First, until Paul Claval's landmark work on the evolution of human geography,[39] critical reflection on the history of our discipline was of little interest to the reigning Vidalian School. Official history (which sets up as sacred the scientific prejudices of the founders of a discipline) was all that was required in a geography mistrustful of theoretical and critical reflection and confident in its methodology and tradition. It was as if Lucien Febvre's *La terre et l'évolution humaine* had established and justified once and for all the foundations and the durability of that school. In Febvre's work, Dubois and colonial geography

[37] Vidal de la Blache, 'La géographie humaine', 1903, p. 223.

[38] It is revealing that in the first lesson of his geography course at the Sorbonne (Vidal de la Blache, 'Leçon de l'ouverture', 1899), Vidal illustrated the meaning and the legitimacy of the geographic vision through examples drawn from the colonial realm (in which he noted the supreme influence of the conditions of the environment on people). This was a course, we learn in the last few lines of his article, on the geography of France. As a result of his argumentative strategy, Vidal later allowed himself to say: 'although it is correct to recognize that in superior societies it does not act in the same degree ... it would nevertheless not be very scientific to abstract from that observation'. Vidal de la Blache, 'La géographie humaine', 1903, p. 236. This was a brilliant strategy of immunization as here Vidal succeeded in painting as non-scientific those who used perceived differences in the degree of nature's influence to create a hierarchy of societies.

[39] Claval, *Essai*, 1964.

were completely forgotten (while Gallois is quoted in abundance). But that 'amnesia' was not an error. Indeed, in the context of the task Febvre's set himself, it was even plausible. Febvre was more interested in the definition, scope, and novelty of the Vidalian message (it was he who first identified the concept of 'possibilism' in Vidal's thought) than in the establishment of that school. Moreover, *La terre* is a pragmatic and polemic work written by Febvre the historian.[40] Its aim was to destabilize 'traditional history' via Vidal. In that sense, there was no need to make reference to the colonial context.

More than 40 years passed before Paul Claval relaunched the history of geographic thought in France. But there was, even in Claval's *Essai sur l'évolution de la géographie humaine* a colonial amnesia. Nevertheless, although the colonial context was not discussed, Dubois was present, but as an historical rather than a colonial geographer. It was in Claval's essay, too, that the theme of 'normative geography', focused on action and planning, was first recognized. For Claval, however, Patrick Geddes was the great precursor. Again, this was not an 'error'. Claval may have introduced radical new ideas, but he too was in part heir to Vidal's possibilism via Febvre. In the rest of the work, Claval argued that the Vidalian geographers of the 1960s were further removed from the thought of Vidal than they were themselves aware.[41] Here again, the history of the collusion between geography and the colonial movement was substantially irrelevant to the argument.[42]

In 1969, a few years before his death, Meynier published *Histoire de la pensée géographique en France*. This work too suffered from almost complete colonial amnesia. It was not until the early 1980s and the publication of Vincent Berdoulay's book,[43] that the colonial context began to be a focus of research and analysis as one of the contextual dimensions essential to the formation of the Vidalian school.

Critical to an understanding of the developments of the last several decades is a sense of the 'the spirit of the times' of the 1960s in France. It was a period of de-colonization characterized by intense feelings of guilt. This was not a time in which geographers would have willingly chosen to find the discipline's roots in a 'history of dirty deeds'. Certainly, the spells of colonial amnesia were not exclusive to geography. Research into the foundations of planning and urban planning has remained strangely silent

---

[40] Febvre, *La terre*, 1922.

[41] That implicitly critical comment concerning what became of Vidalian geography did not escape A. Meynier's attention. In his book review for the *Annales*, he made it clear that he had not much appreciated Claval's swipe at the sacrosanct regional monograph.

[42] However, in 1972, in his excellent article on 'La naissance de la géographie humaine', Claval distanced himself from the Febvre group. By bringing in the notions of 'épistèmé' (Foucault) and paradigm (Kuhn), Claval restored imperialism and nationalism as structuring dimensions in the birth of human geography. He did not, however, discuss the relationship between imperialism and nationalism.

[43] Berdoulay, *La formation de l'École française*, 1981.

concerning the colonial experience. It is only very recently that its importance has finally been recognized. The same phenomenon has also occurred in sociology where, for example, the Le Playsian School has only recently begun to emerge from historical oblivion. Finally, there are the recent contributions of Brochier and Levan-Lemesle on the development of economics into a discipline in France.[44] These still include no mention of the colonial political economy and totally ignore the relationship of the early discipline of economics to the colonial movement. Perhaps it is time to focus our attention more critically and completely on the colonial sciences, those blind spots of modernity.

[44] Brochier, 'Fondements idéologiques', 1988; Lemesle, 'De l'économie politique', 1986; see also Bencheikh, 'Sciences coloniales, sciences du développement', 1991.

WE DO BUSINESS IN ONLY ONE PLACE.

With major offices in North America, Europe, Australia and Asia, we provide clients with opportunities everywhere in the world. So whether you want to raise capital, merge, acquire or divest, either domestically or internationally, keep one thought in mind.

At Salomon Brothers our willingness to go to the ends of the earth for our clients isn't simply a figure of speech.

Salomon Brothers

Plate 5 'We do business in only one place.'
Advertisement by kind permission of Salomon Brothers Inc., New York.

PART V

Post-Colonial Geographies

Introduction

The de-colonization of previously European colonies in Africa, Asia and the Caribbean began in earnest following World War II, but it would be a mistake to conclude that this de-colonization marked the end of empire. It did effectively signal an end to colonialism as a specific form of empire, but imperial interest and global reach continue to the present. In particular, the United States sought to dissolve the European empires as a means of opening up the so-called Third World to US trade and political sway. The Pax Americana that succeeded European colonialism was organized around economic control through the market rather than direct political management of colonized territories, and as Neil Smith points out in chapter 14, US geographers were centrally involved in bringing about this new American world, and with it a new, geographically displaced form of empire. The USA had been involved in various territorial frays, from the seizure of California and Arizona from Mexico in 1846 to the incursions against Cuba, the Philippines and Haiti in 1898, and more recent gunboat diplomacy in Latin America, but the fruition of the American empire after 1945 represented a very different experience. As Andrew Kirby shows in chapter 15, the geographical practices demanded by the war were responsible for the emergence of a completely new species of 'scientific' professional that remains highly influential in US geography and directly tied to local and global projects of the US state.

But the American empire was also short-lived. Fundamentally challenged by revolts in Vietnam, Iran, Nicaragua and elsewhere, and by economic challenges from Japan and Germany, the political power of the US empire was clearly in recession by the mid-1970s and was not reinstated by the desiccation of official communism in 1989. De-colonization remains an on-going struggle in many places but nowhere more so than in South Africa where opposition to apartheid has simultaneously involved opposition to US multinational capital. Official South African geography – Anglo and Afrikaner – has been a product of colonialism, and as Harold Wesso argues in chapter 16, this led to a colonization of geographical thought. Intertwined with the struggle to free South Africa from global capital and the direct power of a minority white ruling class, therefore, is a struggle to de-colonize geography.

In chapter 17, Jonathan Crush discusses some of the contemporary efforts to de-colonize South African geography, and highlights the crucial political dilemmas of this process.

The connections between geography and empire are very different today than they were a hundred years ago. Not only has the nature of empire changed, but so too has the tangible political geography around which geographic research is organized. Specifically, the national schools of geography that dominated the imperial geographies of a century ago are much weaker and more porous. The global fluidity of multinational capital and the multinationalization of US cultures are mirrored by a global interchange of intellectual ideas. Further, while much contemporary geographical research remains tied to the agendas of state and capital, there is today a much larger and more influential critical tradition in the discipline than at any past time. A central goal of these critical geographies is precisely to disconnect geographical practice from the imperial project.

14

Shaking Loose the Colonies: Isaiah Bowman and the 'De-colonization' of the British Empire

Neil Smith

On the eve of World War II, more than 60 per cent of foreign direct investment from the developed capitalist world was targeted at the developing world. It was a matter of faith, therefore, in the circles of American economic and political power, that US global ambition was bound up with the fate of the 'Third World'. Equally a matter of faith for many was the assumption that the coming US empire would be as tied to territorial control as had been its European predecessors. And yet, even towards the end of 1944, as the war itself continued, President Roosevelt either denied or dodged the question of territorial settlements following the war.

Such territorial discussions were of course very actively afoot, and had been since before the first shells were fired between the Allies and the Axis powers. Within the US State Department and in the British and Soviet Foreign Offices, there was eager anticipation and planning for the post-war map of the world. The disposition of Germany was only the most immediate task; it represented a reconciliation with the old world, a settling of historical accounts, that would clear the historical agenda for establishing the geography of a new world. More so than in the past, the geography of this new world would be negotiated on the basis of economic considerations, as the United States struggled to establish a vital global reach for the post-war American economy. This new economic geography was of course established via intense political struggles that pitted the American ruling class's global ambitions against a gamut of opponents: the ruling classes of the declining European Allies, the expansionism of Soviet state capitalism, and insurgent working-class and populist movements from Greece to Indochina. And of course there was a global political structure, to be centred in the United Nations, that would negotiate conflicts in the post-war world. If these arrangements for a new world order – first time around – emerged from diverse locations, ideas and struggles, the central inspiration came from Washington DC between the State Department and the White House.

The term 'Pax Americana' was coined by General George Strong in a 1942 meeting of the security sub-committee of the wartime State Department. A year earlier, Henry Luce, publisher of *Time* magazine had referred to the impending 'American Century'. 'Tyrannies may require a large amount of living space', Luce concluded dryly. 'But Freedom requires and will require far greater living space than Tyranny.' Isaiah Bowman, President of Johns Hopkins University, by now a public figure, and the best known US geographer, anticipated these visions with an even more vivid depiction of the post-war American world. In an early 1940 meeting of the Council on Foreign Relations' territorial committee, as the German military seemed to close in on Britain, the anglophile Bowman railed at Hitler's geopolitical quest for *Lebensraum*. '*Lebensraum* for all is the answer to *Lebensraum* for one', he retorted; 'it is an economic question.' In more vividly geographical terms than Strong and Luce, Bowman envisaged the global economic arrangements that would make the Pax Americana a reality. Edward Stettinius, Bowman's friend and colleague, and later Secretary of State, translated this vision of a global economic *Lebensraum* into the requisite bureaucratic nuts and bolts: [1]

> The question of greatest importance before us at this time is one which has been under discussion with the British and Canadian Officials regarding the negotiation of an International Commercial Policy Convention which all the countries of the world would be invited to join. Such a convention would deal with the difficulties created in the inter-war period as the result of Nationalistic Governmental action. The convention would deal with all important aspects of trade relations such as the reduction of tariffs, the abolition of preferences (those between the British Empire countries, for example), the abolition of quantitative restrictions, the prohibition of export subsidies, and the principles to govern relations between state-trade and free-enterprise countries.

[1] Stettinius to Pratt, 10 March 1944 (Johns Hopkins University, Special Collections, Bowman Collection [hereafter JHU] 2.4, Pratt); Minutes T–A1, 16 February 1940, Council on Foreign Relations [CFR]. Minutes S–3 security sub-committee, advisory committee on post-war Policy, 6 May 1942, National Archives [hereafter NA] NA.NF 76 (Bowman was on the security sub-committee but not at the meeting where 'Pax Americana' was coined). As regards the destroyers and bases, in 1940 the US exchanged 50 destroyers for 8 bases in the British West Indies, Bermuda and Newfoundland; Luce, 'The American Century', 1941, p. 64.

Shaking loose the colonies was a central requirement in this new global economic geography. Nowhere was the clash of post-war visions between the Allies more sharply defined than in the question of so-called 'dependent territories'. It was widely and quickly realized with the onset of war that, apart from the sovereign and independent states of what we would now think of as the developed world, including China and the British dominions, there would be a veritable mess of territories dotted around the post-war globe whose legal, political and economic status would be uncertain.

The fate of the dependent states was an issue that went to the heart of the Allies' competing political aspirations for the post-war world. In the words of William Roger Louis, an historian of de-colonization, 'the future of the colonies was a touchstone of the post-war world'.[2] Despite internal differences and periodic shifts in perspective, it is possible briefly to summarize the positions of the major players. The United States, undoubtedly the most vocal and persistent of the major powers, argued for some means of trusteeship and international accountability for the dependent states, with a view to eventual independence. Britain fought this, vigorously preferring instead a system whereby individual major powers assumed exclusive responsibility for specific dependent territories – a solution that would clearly permit the retention, unmolested, of the British Empire. The Soviet Union, by contrast, stood consistently for immediate independence and self-determination.

The ruling American vision of a new global order was the product of an intense colloid of seemingly selfless altruism and extreme self-interest. Roosevelt and his top state department people shared an antagonism to what they saw as the moral injustice of European imperialism and saw themselves as the champions of the rights of subjected peoples. The prevailing perspective involved a commitment to moral reform in the colonies, to the rightful progress of the 'native peoples', and to the application of the paternalistic as much as the materialistic threads of the Monroe Doctrine. Equally prevalent, and sometimes expressed with unabashed honesty, was the economic rationale for opening up the colonies. 'As I see it', wrote Under-Secretary of State Stettinius to his close friend John Lee Pratt, previously vice-chairman of General Motors and a trustee of Johns Hopkins University, 'the United States will need the greatest international trade our country has ever had following the war. The State Department must be prepared to establish by international agreements and otherwise conditions under which private industry can develop it.'[3] Equally there was a strategic vision concerning the necessity of American military bases around the globe both to protect global economic interests but also to restrain resurgent belligerence from Japan and Germany, and later the USSR.

Isaiah Bowman shared this global vision of American interests and he shared responsibility for implementing it. Shortly after the outbreak of war

[2] Louis, *Imperialism at Bay*, 1987, p. 27.
[3] Stettinius to Pratt, 10 March 1944, JHU, 2.4, Pratt.

in Europe he undertook to warn Henry Wallace, then Secretary of Agriculture, of 'the possibility of an invasion of the South American trade area by foreign powers after the war'. Wallace had helped Bowman to launch the Science Advisory Board seven years earlier and Bowman thought he would try him again with a suggestion that the US get 'on the job now' of cultivating expanded South American trade. The idea of a European trade invasion 'is no longer a scarehead theory', Bowman continued. 'It would be almost as disastrous to have a complete trade invasion as to have armed invasion. An impoverished Europe will fight desperately for trade outlets, undercutting us in price, in organization, and in desperate energy. Partial relief from this situation might be obtained by encouraging the rapid development of industry in Latin America.' Or as Norman Davis, Bowman's colleague at the Council on Foreign Relations and on the State Department advisory committee, put it 'the British Empire as it existed in the past will never reappear and ... the United States may have to take its place.'

Elsewhere Bowman espouses the ambiguous intertwining of economic and geopolitical self-interest with global altruism:

> At home in our own Western Hemisphere we have an opportunity at hand. That opportunity spells out the words Latin America ... It is ... to help in the slow process of industrialization of Latin America, to diversify its production, to enlarge the area of its interest, to raise the standard of living through education and public health measures and thus eventually create a wider and more diversified, in short, a richer trade area that will mean enlarged trade for us. This is a gain all around, not a gain at the expense of somebody else. [4]

The enduring exploitation and political oppression of the peasant and working classes, Bowman comes to recognise by the late 1920s and early 1930s, was now rendered unimportant. The larger purpose of post-war US interests in the end far outweighed questions of the morality of domestic arrangements in the American backyard.

On the question of dependent territories, then, there was not merely a clash of national policies and strategies on a specific issue but a fundamental opposition of world views and ultimately a confrontation between different historical eras and projects of global hegemony. The discord was not confined to the global scale. Typically in the Roosevelt administration, there was general agreement on broad principles but implementing the vision, often eloquently espoused by the President himself, and translating from general Wilsonian sympathies to specific post-war realities, was often arduous. Between the economic and the moral motivations, between the military and

---

[4] Untitled speech, undated but 1940, Robert Bowman collection [henceforth RGB, and subsequently integrated into the Bowman collection at Johns Hopkins]; Minutes S–3 security sub-committee, advisory committee on post-war Policy, 6 May 1942, NA.NF 76; Bowman to Hull, 15 April 1943, JHU RG; Bowman to Wallace, 27 March 1940, RGB.

the political imperatives, between the vision and the application, lay a considerable gulf mined with many explosive political questions. 'From the first to the last', according to one historian, Bowman 'figured prominently' in these events and in the effort to open up the dependent territories to American commerce. British Foreign Office ministers even assumed that on the American side, Bowman was for a time 'the key-man on this particular question'.[5]

FROM TERRITORY AND RESOURCES TO TRUSTEESHIP

At their first stormy summit on the ocean off Quebec, Churchill and Roosevelt released a pronouncement of general principles concerning the post-war world. The first such principle of their Atlantic Charter declared that 'their countries seek no aggrandizement, territorial or other', as a result of the war. They affirmed the 'right of all peoples to choose the form of government under which they will live' and expressed their 'wish to see sovereign rights and self-government restored to those who have been forcibly deprived of them'. It quickly became evident that these fine sounding phrases meant very different things to Roosevelt and Churchill and indeed to the various government departments on both sides of the Atlantic. Roosevelt was already thinking over the possibility of employing plebiscites, much as had been done in 1919 in contested territories, but quickly began to conceive of a more direct role for the major powers. Dependent territories – the 'minor children among the peoples of the world' – perhaps ought to be placed for the sake of their own advancement under the 'trusteeship' of the 'adult nations' who could lead them 'back into a spirit of good conduct'.[6] Along with the Atlantic Charter, this nascent conception of Roosevelt's 'four policemen' and the notion of trusteeship provided the backdrop for state department deliberations on dependent territories.

The earliest state department deliberations on dependent territories were initiated by Bowman in the territorial committee (a sub-committee of the overall advisory committee) on 11 April 1942, and they set the pattern for ensuing policy discussions. Bowman offered a succinct summary of what would become post-war modernization theory with its central thesis of uni-linear development. The 'first consideration', he insisted, was 'that colonies are backward and we must do something about them.' Further, we should assume 'that they are "coming up to something such as we are". These assumptions lead to the conclusion that ... the people of backward areas are going to arrive at some stage of development to the limit of their competence.' But contrary to all published accounts, he warned, the victorious

[5] Richard Law to Oliver Stanley, 11 April 1944, quoted in Louis, *Imperialism at Bay*, 1978, pp. 329, 55.

[6] Sherwood, *Roosevelt and Hopkins*, 1948, p. 572; Russell, *A History of the United Nations Charter*, 1958, pp. 42–3.

powers would not have a *tabula rasa* on which to 'create ideal systems'. Whatever our brave words, 'we cannot expect that the whole world will lie prostrate before us.' Colonial rule will in the beginning be a 'makeshift affair', he suggested, and will be military in nature; trade will be re-initiated under controlled conditions. Despite these realities, a 'broad declaration' of colonial policy was necessary now, one that would embody 'the hope of colonial peoples' for more just treatment and better living standards. But care was necessary even at the start. 'The charge of hypocrisy will be made and will not be forgotten if we do not put the reality of control in the first instance beside the dream and beside the hope of a brighter future.' Pushing further the search for balance, Bowman emphasized that substituting self-reliance for 'acute dependency' would be a 'reciprocal process' between the adult nations and the 'minor children'.

It was simply 'unrealistic to suppose that Great Britain will willingly hand over its colonies to an international authority', Bowman continued. But above all, he emphasized American security. 'The first objective will be security and this will require the holding of strategic points and areas' by the USA. He repeated this point towards the end, with more than a hint of self-serving apology:

> It is no service to dependent areas to let our desire to improve their condition override our desire to keep the world from falling into its present danger again. It is hypocritical to pretend that we are going to make everything safe and easy for dependent peoples at our own expense and risk. Small peoples are onlookers in a world struggle like that of the present ... Their place in the world will be secondary ...

Two essential considerations, Bowman concluded, were the resources, aptitudes and possibilities of a people and a place, and their wider economic role in the world: 'what international economic agreements can be made that will advance world trade' so as to have the dependent countries 'produce wanted products instead of an excess of some products and a deficiency [*sic*] of others'.[7]

This initial survey of the problem of dependent areas is remarkable not so much for any specific details or proposals, more for the tenor and extent of its vista. Bowman's tone of gradual but committed change, the interplay of economic, political and military interests, the supposed mutual self-interest of the dependent peoples and the large powers – these themes survived the bureaucratic process that would follow and were eventually reflected in the wording of the UN articles on trusteeship three years later. They did indeed represent a residue of Wilsonian idealism, but an idealism increasingly enlivened by much more pragmatic American interests in the post-war world. They were not Bowman's alone of course; in initiating the discussion

---

[7] Bowman, 'Dependent Areas' memo, 10 April 1942, JHU 2.1 Dependent Areas; minutes T–5, 11 April 1942, State Department RG 59, Notter file, box 42.

in such a manner he merely synthesized in his own way ideas already afloat if not quite publicly discussed. More than original thought or new ideas, it was Bowman's dexterity at general synthesis that was valued in the State Department and the White House.

The State Department territorial committee gave more systematic attention to specific dependent territories beginning in August, focusing on Indochina, the Near East and Africa. Most significant in these discussions, as indeed in Bowman's opening statement, may have been the issues that were downplayed rather than those that were decisively treated. Specifically, the State Department by 1942 gave only diluted attention to the previously central question of resources and minerals. A vital evolution was taking place, one that expressed the historical distinctness of the emerging American Empire. Resources remained an important issue, but there was never an energetic translation of committee discussions on this topic into policy after 1942. A mineral committee had a brief but undistinguished existence as part of the post-war planning bureaucracy and a petroleum division was established within the Office of Economic Affairs in 1944. If resources remained a clear concern, they had lost some of their centrality in broader foreign policy questions.[8]

The council members drawn into the State Department in 1940 had a clear sense that their work would be more focused than that of the Inquiry in 1918; they were explicitly not, in Bowman's words, attempting 'to blueprint an ideal territorial settlement'. Nevertheless they began, perhaps inevitably, with a traditional expectation that questions of territory, boundaries and resources would define the basis of peace. By 1942, however, with the closer integration of the work into the State Department, the priorities had changed. The factual data on specific territories were of distinctly secondary concern; ad hoc geographical settlements were disavowed in favour of an integrated global policy that could bridge the gap between broad principles and local situations; and the guiding philosophy was less one of achieving or maintaining access to specific resources, important as that was, than one of opening up the dependent territories *en masse* for global economic intercourse. Thus in the territorial committee that Bowman headed, there was indeed discussion of tin and rubber in relation to Indochina and the Dutch East Indies, an assessment of the importance of Near East oil resources in the post-war economy and so forth. But the dominant assumption was no longer that these resources would be controlled by individual colonial powers; the assumption rather was that the resources and indeed the entire economies of the dependent nations were to be opened up to capital investment. In the words of the Atlantic Charter, all nations should have 'access, on equal terms, to the trade and to the raw materials of the world which are needed for their economic prosperity'. For many in Washington, and certainly for FDR, this meant nothing short of dismantling

[8] Read to Bowman, 10 July 1942 JHU 2.3 Minerals; Leith, *Minerals in the Peace Settlement*, February 1940.

the entire system of European colonialism. Under-Secretary Welles went further, announcing in his Memorial Day address of 1942 that 'the age of imperialism is dead'.[9]

Bowman looked forward enthusiastically to the fruition of an American globalism he had long advocated, but not without nostalgia and reservations.

The overall work of the advisory committee, then, aimed at devising an administrative mechanism by which the dependent territories might be governed as part of a new structure of relationships between nations. Between August and November 1942 there ensued intensive discussion devoted to exploring suitable international forms of administration and, as with the German question, it was the political sub-committee that took over the initiative from the territorial committee. The political committee adopted an inductive rather than deductive approach, focusing first on specific territories and seeking to generalize only later. With the territorial committee concurrently examining the dependent territories, Bowman indefatigably repeated to the political committee the enormous disparities between different peoples and places. He repeated earlier sentiments that Angola might offer the most suitable destination for large numbers of European refugees; the diversity of peoples in Burma evoked his pessimism as regards any unified settlement; and he sided with Sumner Welles, advocating an end to the Southwest Africa mandate and the donation of that territory to South Africa. With others on the committee, Bowman highlighted the difficulty of applying a single set of international trusteeship principles to such a diverse range of territories, peoples and conditions, and at the second meeting, on 15 August, suggested an alternative course. Citing the example of the Monroe Doctrine and American stewardship of the western hemisphere under the good neighbour policy, Bowman argued that the diversity of people and places as well as the geographically diverse interests of the major powers could be accommodated through a system of 'regional associations'.

This was the course the committee in fact took. It sought to restrict the number of territories taken under direct international administration in favour of representative regional trusteeship bodies comprising the major powers with significant interests in a given area. Thus the committee advocated a regional federation for Southeast Asia and the South Pacific which would be administered by the Soviet Union, China, Australia, New Zealand and the USA. In sub-Saharan Africa the situation was more complex, and the committee finally approved a two pronged solution, taking some territories under direct international control and allotting the remainder (except Southwest Africa) to a regional body that would obviously include Britain. Northern Africa was considered in the discussions of the Middle East, in which the committee moved much more gingerly. Not only were French and British claims paramount in this region, but the various nations of the region were far more advanced the committee felt, and trusteeship might not be

[9] CFR, 'Progress Report, W and PS', 3 July 1940, RGB; Welles is quoted in Louis, *Imperialism at Bay*, 1978, pp. 154–5.

the appropriate answer. In any case, the fate of Palestine lay at the centre of post-war plans for the region and would require much more detailed consideration. [10]

US security interests were also uppermost in the minds of many committee members, and it was here that potential contradictions in the US position became evident. If trusteeship, international or regional in scale, were to be the solution, and if that trusteeship were to be joint rather than exclusive, what did this mean for the Monroe Doctrine? More specifically, territories of the Caribbean such as Puerto Rico and the Virgin Islands were now held exclusively by the USA, as were the Philippines. And what of Hawaii, Alaska, or the Pacific mandates now under Japanese control, but which the USA increasingly saw as vital to its western security belt? How could the USA justify holding these territories exclusively for so-called security purposes while preaching at the same time the moral imperative of the 'end of imperialism'? In Bowman, the contradiction found its most extreme form. An ardent moralist about the rights of native peoples, he was a stony pragmatist with an intensely geographical vision of American security, and for him the defence of America had virtually no geographical limits. Not only was he concerned about the Caribbean and the Pacific; his concern stretched to the British dominions of Canada and Australia which he saw as grossly underpopulated and appallingly vulnerable to attack. Canada was especially crucial being contiguous to the USA. 'We cannot allow Canada to be taken', he warned the political committee. 'The pressure of the yellow race upon these two great blocks of territory is as much a part of our problem as that of the British Empire.'

By the middle of November, there remained many unresolved problems but the committee had come to an agreement on a core perspective regarding trusteeship. With alterations, they accepted a document on 'international trusteeship' that had emerged from the recently created sub-committee on international organization (on which Bowman also sat). This document was envisaged as the basis for the trusteeship articles in the United Nations organization that was being forged. They had attempted, in Bowman's words, to find a 'mid course ... between pure idealism and [the] pre-war scheme of national responsibility for dependent peoples'. The mandate system following the Great War had been very weak since 'rights and properties were intermingled' to the clear benefit of the European powers; the mandate system left the dominant power in the hands of the 'so-called foreign exploiter'. A system of regional and international administration would solve this problem and encourage the timely self-development of dependent territories, free from domination. Eventual independence was the goal of the trusteeship system.

Yet in Bowman's vision at least, there were shades of a Tocquevillian paradox. All of the high-sounding morality concerning independence and

[10] Minutes, P–22, 15 August 1942, NA.NF 55. For a useful summary of the early discussions see Louis, *Imperialism at Bay*, 1978, pp. 159–74.

trusteeship and the earnest desire to unyolk the 'natives' from European imperialism was not matched by a concern for equality. Quite the contrary; according to Bowman, trusteeship was to become a new means of racism and paternalism rather than equality: 'our symbols and words and idealism [are] not understood by tens of millions that we rule. They think on a low level of comfort, food and work. Government as we know it is not within their range. The concepts and traditions that steady us are unknown to them.' Bowman questioned the 'equality of treatment of peoples that are not equal', arguing that 'tribal organization is a primitive form of society ... Primitive men are children and maintain a rigidity of thought about things that is extraordinary.' With this forthright confusion of ontogeny and phylogeny, Bowman departed significantly from his original Wilsonianism. Undeveloped as it was, the latter's view was that the equality of treatment of peoples was a moral imperative, irrespective of differences and inequalities in terms of material wealth, technology or even level of development. Yet for Bowman, precisely such differences had become the ample rationale for encouraging unequal treatment under the trusteeship proposals.[11]

DEFINING TRUSTEESHIP

'The great enigma in the international political world at the present time', Bowman announced to the political committee in the spring of 1943, is 'the United States'. We can be 'more sure of the course of Great Britain and Russia than ... of our own course. If we remain an enigma it would be disastrous to our international relationship and position in the post-war world.'[12] Bowman's rare moment of national self-evaluation came as the State Department began to sense its own power in the post-war settlement. Yet this only sharpened the concern inside the department regarding concrete solutions. The political committee had not crystallized its own course beyond core generalities, and in any case there was no guarantee that a coherent foreign policy emerging from the political committee and the secretary would be followed or even taken seriously by the President.

From the start of the war, Roosevelt had taken an even dimmer view of European colonialism than his state department advisors. To Soviet Foreign Secretary Molotov he confided 'that there were all over the world, many islands and colonial possessions which ought, for our own safety, to be taken away from the weak nations'. To Queen Wilhelmina of the Netherlands he chided: 'Don't be too sure you will get the Dutch East Indies back unless you do something more for the natives.' And about Indochina he declared that the French had no automatic right after the war simply to walk back

[11] Minutes, P-33, 14 November p. 2; P-37, 12 December 1942, NA.NF 55; Bowman, memo, 2 October 1942, JHU 2.1 Davis.
[12] Bowman, memo, 23-4 April 1943, JHU 2.3 PC; Minutes, P-36, 5 December 1942, p. 7.

in. About the fate of the British Empire, however, FDR was more circum-spect, at least in the beginning. He conceded that along with the Dutch they had been more attentive colonizers, and of course they had borne the brunt of the war until 1942, but this did not prevent him from confronting an angry Churchill head-on at their first meeting in Quebec on the colonial question; indeed it was on this question that Roosevelt and Churchill clashed most seriously throughout the war. Later, after a brief stop-over in Gambia en route to the Teheran conference, FDR's attitude toward the British Empire hardened appreciably. Nothing short of universal trusteeship for all dependent territories became his aim. To administer these territories around the world he wanted China, Britain, the USSR and the USA to be the 'four policemen' of the globe, and he allowed Molotov to inform Stalin that this was his 'final and considered judgement'.

Clearly the State Department intended no such extreme stripping away of the colonies as Roosevelt seemed to have in mind, and Bowman in particular came to feel a real frustration at what he saw as the President's impractical stubbornness concerning dependent territories. He could accept and even endorse Sumner Welles's sentiment that 'the age of imperialism is dead', but he argued that the USA ought to tread very carefully indeed in the dissolution of European power. We criticize Britain, he pointed out, but we ourselves 'have no substitute'. To withdraw from the colonies is certainly not enough since Germany would simply move in, and yet the notion of the 'four policemen' smacks too much of a new imperialism. 'Power there must be to hold the balance', he intoned, 'to support the decisions of a court of justice, to give continuity to a policy of world improvement.'[13] At the end of 1942 Bowman himself was not yet sure what this balanced power politics would look like, but by the time the political committee took up the colonial question again in earnest, in April 1943, his ideas had progressed and crystallized considerably.

When the political committee resumed its consideration of trusteeship, Hull and Welles both attended the Saturday morning meetings. At the first meeting there was little apparent progress as committee members batted back and forwards their different views and perspectives on the best resolution for Ethiopia and Korea. This round of discussions was for the purpose of making more concrete and specific the broad agreement on core principles reached five months earlier, and at the next meeting, on 10 April, the com-mittee rose to the challenge in their exploration of the temporal and geo-graphical limits of trusteeship. The Under-Secretary ruled out the possibility that the western hemisphere would be covered by such agreements, thereby exempting a number of American possessions, from the Caribbean to the Pacific and Alaska, from international interference. There was surprisingly

[13] Bowman, memo 23 February 1943, JHU 2.3 FDR; Sherwood, *Roosevelt and Hopkins*, 1948, p. 572; Louis, *Imperialism at Bay*, 1978, pp. 121, 279; Divine, *Second Chance*, 1971, p. 61. For the Roosevelt-Churchill correspondence see Kimball, *Churchill and Roosevelt*, 1984.

little discussion at such a blunt and potentially controversial exercise of power on the American behalf. Instead there quickly followed an almost surreal discussion on the timing of independence under trusteeship. Congressman Eaton of New Jersey asked how long independence would take, and it was Welles again who supplied the answers, suggesting that in the Congo it would be more than a hundred years before the populace was fit to govern itself while 'in the case of Portuguese Timor it would certainly take a thousand years'. What a 'wonderful' vision, was the sarcastic reply of the congressman whom Welles now sought to mollify by eschewing further foggy generalities. Of course, he admitted, 'everything' in the trusteeship proposal 'is designed to promote world security. The project is motivated not by altruism or idealism but solely by considerations of security.'

In the same meeting Bowman told the committee that there could be 'no doubt that Britain will not relinquish control over its empire at the end of the war'. In fact, Bowman 'had little desire to force Britain to do so'. He then made a crucial distinction that guided the discussion of the next few sessions. Arguing against the all-inclusive coverage of the draft document on trusteeship, Bowman made a fundamental separation between what he called the 'detached territories' – the existing mandate territories together with the Italian colonies – and the colonies of the other European powers.[14] In so doing, Bowman must have known that he was making a basic distinction where Roosevelt sought to establish a general principle. Leo Pasvolsky, a top departmental advisor, had recently overseen the issuance of a 'Declaration of National Independence' which attempted to subsume the distinction within a general policy for the so-called backward countries, but Bowman was eager that this internal distinction between the detached and Ally-controlled territories remain paramount.

Secretary of State Cordell Hull had clearly taken notice. Quite by chance, when Bowman returned to the State Department the next Wednesday he encountered Hull in the elevator. Hull insisted that Bowman come into his office and tell him anything 'that may be on your mind'. Bowman told the secretary that he earnestly hoped the political committee would begin where it left off last Saturday and keep mandated territories and re-conquered territories to the front and not get into the field of colonies and protectorates. In a remarkable retreat from his own erstwhile moral idealism, Bowman then confided to Hull his misgivings about Roosevelt's approach:

> The colonies of other nations are none of our business. If we try to tell Churchill or Wilhelmina how to rule their subjects ethically they and their peoples will be incensed. It is just none of our business. We can't rule in their stead & we can not buy up the world ... The Pres. has gone as far as anyone can or should go in setting up very general moral statements but from now on we must channel, define, interpret & see what is practicable.

[14] Minutes, P–51, 10 April 1943, p. 19.

According to Bowman's account, 'Hull agreed heartily' and in turn the wiley ex-Senator confided his own problems with FDR:

> these brilliant fellows like the Pres. & Sumner (Welles) are always going off on a tangent because they get out ahead of the facts & make speeches and give out interviews that confuse instead of clarify public opinion and congressional debate. I mean no disrespect to the Pres. but I have a devil of a time holding him to a practical political course. He has an idea & in a flash he makes a statement that takes me months to clear up with these congressmen ...

Hull further informed Bowman of his intention to take a more active part in the political committee meetings. He and Bowman agreed that the recent meetings with the President by the informal agenda group (formed by Hull at the beginning of January 1943 to act as a steering committee for post-war planning) had not been a success.[15]

Hull too wanted to separate the colonies of Allied powers from the question of mandates and acquired territories, and so, on the Friday of that week, he invited Bowman to lead the trusteeship discussion the next day with a statement on mandated and re-conquered territories. Bowman took the opportunity to begin with a familiar appeal about ideals and practicality, but in the course of painting an expansive vision, he also went further than at any previous time in disavowing the kind of idealistic proclamations he himself had held so dear. In his preparatory notes he wrote:

> the trouble would begin when we tried to reconcile the practical details of life in mandated and reconquered territories with the Sermon on the Mount. There was a great gulf between the two things. The American people will feel betrayed the instant that one of the Freedoms or one of the conditions of the Atlantic Charter seems to the people to be violated by a concrete settlement. The practical details of oil and other resources and of government of tribal groups put the white man into a condition of superiority and power. The fuzzy-wuzzies of the world do not understand Jeffersonian democracy and are not accustomed to authority, nor to the Australian ballot system. How to bridge the gap between the broad declarations of policy of the United Nations and practical details of rule in a thousand places throughout the world, constitutes the gravest political problem ahead of the American people.

Bowman now believed the moral generalizations of the Atlantic Charter to have been a mistake since it hampered the committee in its search for specific solutions; it narrowed considerably their field of operation. The Atlantic Charter said that territorial changes should be in accord with 'the freely expressed wishes of the people concerned', but there was no such free

[15] Bowman, untitled memo, 14 April 1943, JHU 2.3 PC.

expression under tribal organization, he argued. How then should the Nauru territory be handled? A tiny Pacific island straddling the Equator to the west of the international date line, this mandate had a population of 3,000, but it mined an annual yield of 1,265,000 tons of phosphates that were exported largely to New Zealand. 'The phosphate is of no use to the natives. Whose land is it? What could the natives do with royalties on that amount of phosphate?' Bowman asked. He cautioned that the committee ought to be very careful about using words such as 'imperialism' and 'exploitation'. 'What is exploitation on Naura Island?' he asked. Is it sufficient to 'leave people in their old ways of life' after extracting the resources or 'is it necessary to do more and attempt to modernize people?'

He added as a second example the 90,000 'lousy Arabs' who lived on the Bahrein Islands, and who exported several million gallons of oil per year. In their treatment of such peoples, he argued, the USA might even 'take a leaf from the Soviet book', referring to their principle of cultural autonomy as applied to the Yakuts and other tribes. What Bowman conveniently omitted, of course was that the Yakuts possessed no oil or phosphates and that the Soviet policy was based on cultural as much as economic considerations, whereas Bowman's primary interest clearly lay in access to oil and phosphates. 'We had no right', he concluded, 'to assume that people everywhere around the world wanted to be like ourselves ... We ought to preserve native customs, for the binding cement of native society lies in such customs and institutions ... rather than in the tin-can borrowings and the acquisitions of the white man's outlook.' In the heat of his own rhetoric Bowman went beyond his prepared statement in the actual meeting. The Yakuts, he enthused, represent a celebrated example of an undervalued freedom, the 'freedom to be left alone'. He concluded that 'improvement of the status of such peoples must be at their own expense and not at ours. The United States is not going to revise the living standards and raise the status of all the fuzzy-wuzzies in the world at *its* own expense.'[16]

It is difficult in retrospect not to see here an extraordinary international advocacy of benign neglect. The 'natives' are to be protected from the adulterations of white civilization and graciously allowed to retain their precious customs and their poverty so long as the white nations can have their phosphates. But even in its own time Bowman's abstentionist paternalism, not to mention his multifarious racism, must have given cause for concern among some of the more liberal members of the committee such as Welles or even Hull who, unlike Bowman, advocated international aid to trustee territories. Certainly by this stage he was the most extreme member of the committee in this respect; even Stanley Hornbeck, who admitted in an earlier meeting that 'there are some things to be said in favour of imperialism', now volunteered that it was surely the obligation of the exploiting nations, after the drying up of phosphate resources, to ensure that

[16] Minutes, P–52 17 April 1943, NA.NF 55; Bowman, '–P1–', memo, 17 April 1943, JHU 2.3 PC; minutes, P–21 8 August 1942, p. 11.

the lot of the Nauru people 'was not worse than at the beginning'. Hamilton Fish Armstrong agreed, detecting a retreat from moral commitment on the colonies. But it was Congressman Eaton who worried most bluntly in response to Bowman that the USA may 'merely be substituting a benevolent dictatorship for a selfish dictatorship' and there could never be a guarantee that benevolence would not turn to greed. In the future, he predicted, 'it will be necessary to meet the charge that the trusteeship plan is merely a disguised form of imperialism.' The gravity of his concern was diffused by a series of tense jokes.

In the end, Bowman seems to have swayed the debate. According to one historian he 'crystallized the ideas of important figures not intimately concerned with trusteeship but occupying important policy-making positions', among them Adolf Berle and Leo Pasvolsky. Even Hull went along, drawing out the primary political point in Bowman's presentation: 'How backward must the people be to be excluded from the discussion of their own rights; and how advanced must they be to become participants on some declared level.' [17]

Although Welles harboured reservations about which he could do little given Hull's more active participation, the State Department was reconciled by the spring of 1943 to Bowman's proposal that post-war trusteeship be restricted to the 'detached territories'. Not so the President whose discussions with the British Foreign Minister, Anthony Eden, in Washington that same spring revealed to the British just how indignant the American leader was over colonialism. It is not clear how much thought went into FDR's proposal, but in discussion with Eden, the President revealed a blueprint for the Pacific. The Japanese islands together with Korea and Indochina would pass into international trusteeship while the remaining islands would retain their national (largely British or French) sovereignty but would be covered by a common economic policy akin to that for the Caribbean. Two French mandates, the French Marquesas and Tuamotu Islands, were to be internationalized as necessary stepping stones for civil and military air travel between the Americas and Australasia, a matter of key importance to the geographically minded Roosevelt. In Africa, he suggested that the USA take responsibility for Dakar, for security reasons, while the UK take Bizerte (Tunisia). The British Empire *per se* was not discussed in the same terms but, to Eden, FDR's direction was clear. The President did propose that the British relinquish Hong Kong to the Chinese as a gesture of 'good will', but Eden 'dryly remarked that he had not heard the President suggest any similar gestures'. Eden did consult with Hull, who gave him a second copy of the all-inclusive state department draft on trusteeship, a document which emphasized heavily, if generally, eventual independence and self-government for all dependent peoples.

[17] Minutes, P–52 17 April 1943, NA.NF 55; Bowman, '–P1–', memo 17 April 1943, JHU 2.3 PC; Louis, *Imperialism at Bay*, 1978, p. 241.

Eden recognized the difference between Roosevelt's hard line and Hull's more flexible vision of the post-war dependent territories and thought a meeting of the minds would eventually be possible, but like other British officials in the Colonial and Foreign Offices, he was highly suspicious of territorial avarice by the USA. Although the State Department was moving away from its earlier unilateral approach to dependent territories, its language of independence was to the British outrageous. The Colonial and Foreign Offices saw themselves as protecting British interests from the raw ambition of a youthful and still stretching American Empire, and they persistently treated the moral pretensions of the State Department and the White House as precisely that – pretensions, designed to cover an aggressive policy of global expansionism. The state department draft, from this perspective, was nothing less than an assault on the British Empire.

When he attempted to discuss the colonial issue with Eden at the Quebec conference and at Moscow, Hull was 'strongly rebuffed', and so at the foreign secretaries conference in October he gave Molotov a copy of the trusteeship draft. The British were angry. In the first place they began to sense that on the question of dependent territories at least, the USA and USSR were close to ganging up against the British Empire. Second, the British had arrived for the Cairo Conference at the end of November with a full compliment of officials including the Foreign Secretary and the Permanent Under-Secretary, Sir Alexander Cadogan; by contrast Roosevelt brought not one official from the State Department. Whether by design or oversight is not clear, but as a result, when the Cairo Declaration was released on 1 December 1943, it was as much news to Hull and his team as to the American people. Publicly Roosevelt and Churchill agreed on several non-controversial territorial dispositions. Together with Chiang Kai-sheck, they declared that Japan would be stripped of its mandates at the end of the war, China would regain Manchuria, Formosa (now Taiwan), and the Pescadores, and Korea would 'in due course' be made 'free and independent'. During the conference Roosevelt took it upon himself to offer Indochina to Chiang Kai-sheck, who declined, and so the three leaders decided that it should pass from the French to international trusteeship.[18] Privately, however, despite the Cairo declaration, the beginning of 1944 saw the British and the USA further apart than ever on trusteeship and dependent territories.

SHARPENING THE VISION

Bowman's involvement in the fate of dependent territories would seem to have climaxed in the spring of 1944 with his trip to London with Under-Secretary Stettinius. It was a compact team that Stettinius took to London

[18] Sherwood, *Roosevelt and Hopkins*, 1948, pp. 713, 719; Louis, *Imperialism at Bay*, 1978, pp. 227–8, 354; The wording of the Cairo Declaration can he found in: *Official Documents issued during the Two World Wars*, April 1944.

in March 1944. Apart from Bowman and Pratt, the latter to focus on Anglo–American economic problems, the mission included Wallace Murray of the state department's Near East office, and H. Freeman Mathews of the department's European Office. After Stettinius, Bowman's were the broadest responsibilities. He was to consult on the whole gamut of questions involved in setting up an international organization, including the question of trusteeship.

The delegation for the London mission met in the White House with Roosevelt on St Patrick's Day 1944. This was a crucial meeting. It reveals most clearly not only the breadth of Bowman's brief in the upcoming mission but also his growing disagreement with Roosevelt on the colonial question. More important, as the White House and State Department together began to feel the extent of post-war American power, the geographical vista of the impending Pax Americana was articulated explicitly and with unusual succinctness.

When they entered the oval office, the delegation found the President dressed for the day in a green tweed suit, green striped tie and green and white carnation, and this occasioned a few minutes of St Patrick's Day jocularity. When the serious discussion began, FDR revealed his concern that this mission would elicit from congressmen, senators and the public charges of 'secret diplomacy'. 'They will say that all is underhanded and illegal and even unconstitutional', the President said, 'but we always have to put up with that'. Stettinius emphasized the informal and exploratory nature of the discussions and received the President's permission to talk about any subject that arose. In addition, if the exiled Greeks and Poles in London sought a meeting with the American mission there was no harm in this. Stettinius noted that Bowman in particular 'had an almost limitless sphere of topics which he might discuss', and when Bowman took the cue to ask for instructions concerning trusteeship and dependent territories, FDR renewed his tirade against European colonialism.

Eager for an expansive mandate in the coming discussions with the British, Bowman pressed Roosevelt whether they should bring up the whole colonial issue. Roosevelt admitted he had not got far with the British on the disposition of their colonies, and then turned his ire on the French. They 'had made a complete mess of colonial administration. The people there were worse off than they were 100 years ago. The white man's rule was nothing to be proud of.' It had become clear at the Teheran conference, FDR stressed, that the Russians, Americans and Chinese all wanted French Indochina to become independent, whereas Churchill had objected, presumably with a self-interested eye toward protecting French prerogatives among erstwhile possessions. FDR responded gruffly that it did no good for Churchill to object since the vote would be three to one against him. From the Teheran discussion, FDR shifted to the west coast of Africa where, he said, 'the British and the French have taken $10 worth of goods out for every $1 that they have put in.' He encouraged Bowman to press the colonial question persistently but cautioned that there would be no need to raise the question of colonial sovereignty as it pertained to the Allied powers. Full internationalization of all colonies would not be necessary, he now thought in a substantial retreat from his earlier position; 'ultimate sovereignty' might still lie with the present owners so long as some form of international inspection commission were established. The best control over colonial powers was to 'tell the world' about their administration.

Roosevelt was also concerned about American security. After the destroyers-for-bases deal with the British earlier in the war, the Americans quickly constructed a handful of bases dotted round the Caribbean, touching off British fears that FDR wanted to appropriate the islands outright. Roosevelt replied that he did not 'want to buy a headache' and that before 1929, the British West Indies had cost the British Treasury $20 million annually. Next the President addressed the necessity of bases in West Africa and New Caledonia. Bowman flinched. 'He talked about this and Indo-China and the bases of France and West Africa as if we had them for disposal!'[19]

When he emerged from the St Patrick's Day meeting, Bowman had the mandate he wanted. He could explore virtually any topic he wanted with the British and on the question of dependent territories, he was to take the lead. He was to attempt to draw out the British on this whole issue and, if they tried to push him aside, he was to push back relentlessly. But he also felt a growing disquiet at Roosevelt's view of colonialism. In particular, he rejected the claim that the Europeans had extracted ten times the value of their input to the colonies. Although he raised no objection in the meeting, he believed that with this statement, 'the President fundamentally misunderstands trade'. While the Europeans may indeed have taken too much out and left the local population with insufficient, the absence of trade and production would have meant that 'the native himself would live on a lower scale. The question is not that of disproportion between what is taken out and what is left, but what the balance sheet shows of advantage on the two sides.'

Bowman's resort to the classical economic theory of comparative advantage and his selective amnesia about the realities of colonial exploitation, concerning which he himself had earlier been quite eloquent, is an unusually transparent apology for the British Empire – and even more so for the emerging American Empire rooted more directly in economic intercourse. Thus it was not that Bowman resisted the American assumption of global power while Roosevelt embraced it. Rather Bowman felt it could (indeed should) be accomplished without dissolving the British Empire, while FDR could not tolerate the continuance of British preference. Bowman's sentiments toward Britain and its empire would be telling in the London deliberations,

---

[19] 'Call Made on the President by Secretary Hull, Under-Secretary Stettinius and the Members of the London Mission, Messrs. Bowman, Murray, Matthews, Pratt, Lynch and Hector, March 17, 1944,' JHU 2.3, FDR; 'Report of a conversation with the President,' March 17, 1944, JHU 2.3, FDR; IB, untitled memo, February 10 1944, JHU, Miscellaneous Notes.

for although he had the mandate he wanted, he was less inclined than ever to exercise it at the expense of the British.

Where FDR and Bowman agreed completely was in their vision of the constitutive geography of the Pax Americana. The American Empire would not be organized in the obsolete European fashion as an aggrandizement of 'possessions'. In this, the Americans can fairly be assumed to have been the more honest signatories of the Atlantic Charter, if hardly for altruistic reasons. By the Teheran conference FDR made explicit his historic break with the fading old-world colonialism, leaving implicit the geographical contours of the new American Empire. On the question of Indochina, Stalin and FDR were committed to de-colonization, but they also tried to feel out with Chiang Kai-sheck his post-war aspirations in the region. When Chiang declined any interest or involvement, Churchill scoffed that no one turns down territory. FDR instantly took him to task. The British made their empire by successive acquisitions, he said, and 'you have 400 years of acquisitive blood in your veins', he told the Prime Minister. 'A new period has opened in the world's history. You have to adjust yourself to it.' The British would take land anywhere, Roosevelt continued, 'even if it were only a rock and a sand bar.'[20]

Whatever the liberal morality of FDR's stance against taking over from Europe as imperial overlord, it was equally a pragmatic calculation. In this interchange between Roosevelt and Churchill we see in the sharpest terms the American vision whereby post-war global power is finally disconnected from the assumption of political and military occupation of geographical territory. In day-to-day operation, the Pax Americana was to be an economic before a political or military empire – Bowman's 'economic *Lebensraum* for all'. It was imperialism without colonies, economic exploitation – systematically disproportionate advantage on one side, to use Roosevelt's liberal conception – without direct political responsibility. This certainly was not to preclude multifarious political intervention, as widespread governmental discussions about American security made clear, both at the time and subsequently. Nor, as Indochina would discover, was full scale military invasion ruled out in defence of American control of erstwhile European colonies. Rather, the political and military determination of the geography of the Pax Americana was a back-up of its direct economic determination in the world market.

BOWMAN GOES TO LONDON

Bowman left Baltimore for New York on 28 March 1944 and spent the evening at the University Club reading Churchill's *Marlborough*. When he boarded the new liner, *Queen Elizabeth*, on 30 March, he was joined by other

[20] 'Call Made...' JHU 2.3, FDR.

members of the Stettinius mission and by 13,000 troops bound for Glasgow on their way to the European theatre. The mission members were flown from Prestwick Airport to London on 7 April and checked in at Claridges. From the American side, there were two objectives to the mission. First, its members were to explore the British government's views on a whole front of issues from Germany's surrender terms to post-war international organ- ization; second, they were to push their own (i.e. the American) interpre- tation of desirable solutions. Both sides were feeling each other out at a level high enough to be substantive and to escape bureaucratic routine, but without the constraint of official diplomatic obligation.

On the colonial question, a continuum of issues set the agenda: sover- eignty, self-government, independence, and international administration. The most thorough overhaul of international relations would come from a re- version of sovereignty to the colonial territories themselves, and this was clearly FDR's preference. Short of this, various means for self-government and independence might be arranged that still left ultimate sovereignty in European hands. The mildest alternative envisaged the establishment of international condominia, regional or global in scope, that would be re- sponsible for administering the dependent territories. While retaining a desire for limited self-government and independence, it was to this weakest alter- native that Bowman had gravitated. To the British, even this represented an unconscionable threat to the empire.

The British were ready for Dr Isaiah, as they called him. After several preparatory meetings, his first major appointment was on 11 April with Richard Law, Minister of State at the Foreign Office. On the question of colonies, the British were defensive. They felt that Roosevelt preferred to establish common ground with the Russians before broaching the question with Churchill, and so Law felt that Bowman's inclusion on the mission represented both an opportunity and also a sign that the widening differences between the USA and the UK on the colonial question might be narrowed. With his colleagues in the Colonial and Foreign Offices, Law also speculated on the more pragmatic reasons for Bowman's trip. There was an election to be faced in November of that year and FDR would want to distance himself from any accusations of imperial ambition; and yet the Americans surely wanted control of the Japanese mandated islands in the Pacific for strategic reasons, Law surmised. In any case, as we have seen, he told his colleagues, Bowman seems to be the key-man on this particular question.'[21]

The following day, Bowman met with the American ambassador to Britain, John Winant, and his advisor, E. F. Penrose, who briefed Bowman on British post-war planning proposals. Impressed with Penrose, he imme- diately earmarked him as a possibility for the Hopkins geography programme. Next came discussions with Sirs George Gater and Alexander Cadogan,

[21] IB 'Diary', 28 March 1944, JHU 2.4; IB memo, 11 April 1944; for the British side of negotiations with the Stettinius mission I rely on Louis, *Imperialism at Bay*, 1978, pp. 326–36.

Permanent Under-Secretaries at the Colonial and Foreign Offices respectively. These gentlemen he pressed to agree on the concept of regular colonial reports by the metropolitan power, submitted to a central supervisory body, but without success. On 15 April the mission went to Chequers where they were received by Churchill.

Although the discussions were, by arrangement, non-binding and open ended, Bowman and Churchill never did get around to talking about bananas. In addition to the colonial question, Bowman was to survey the Prime Minister's attitude on arrangements for an over-arching world organization, and it was on this topic that he initiated conversation with a reluctant Churchill. Having been forewarned both by Ambassador Winant and by the Foreign Office about Churchill's violent reaction to any perceived threat to British sovereignty over the Empire, Bowman 'introduced the subject tentatively and mildly'. The American position, of course, was to combine the issues of colonialism and world organization, hoping that some or all of the administration of dependent territories could be prized loose from hitherto imperial European states and vested in a centralized international organization. Churchill predictably demurred. He refused to discuss the question of 'self-government for peoples who are without history or traditions ... We propose to continue to deal with colonial peoples from the standpoint of their interest and world requirements.' In the case of French colonies in the Pacific he conceded the American right to demand military bases so long as the conquered lands (Indochina, New Caledonia, Marquesas Islands) were restored as French possessions. But when he turned to the question of British possessions, Bowman recalled, he grew more strident:

> He straightened up, stuck his chest and belly out and with a wide forward sweep of both hands he retracted them as if embracing every square mile of the British Empire and drew them there toward his belly and pressed them there, saying, '*Now*, our *own* territory, our possessions overseas – *that* is quite a different matter! We will not give up one acre of ground; we haven't the least intention of breaking up the Empire or of letting it fall into ruin.

Churchill became specific regarding his favorite hobby-horse, India, which, he insisted, would be 'defenseless, disunited, and in a state of chaos if Great Britain withdrew. We have a responsibility there and mean to stand by it.' Certainly, something would have to be done to improve the situation there, he conceded, but by no means would he even contemplate relinquishing government to the 'ignorant folk':

> The Indian is a small fellow. They are less well equipped for self-government than the Chinese. They marry young, they are immature mentally, they breed far in excess of reason seeming to think that to stretch their limbs out in the sun and let the light of Heaven shine on them is the chief aim of existence. How can you expect government from such people.

'I would rather have one hundred squadrons of airplanes', Churchill blustered, 'than all India.'[22]

Bowman records of the discussion with Churchill that '[w]e got on well when we talked about colonies.' Clearly impressed by the PM's resolve, Bowman found him 'restrained, though emphatic', at times impatient. If the Prime Minister's mix of paternalism and self-interest and his naked expression of 'the white man's burden' failed especially to trouble Bowman, this may well have been because Bowman himself had voiced a similar vision in earlier state department deliberations. Bowman clearly disagreed with Churchill on India although he chose not to press the claim for self-government or the need to open India up to international trade. Nor did he push for an extension of the mandate system as an option for the dependent territories. Bowman himself had doubts about such an arrangement, and he knew that the British rejected it as both too threatening for their sovereignty over the Empire and as, in any case, a clear failure. Churchill allowed that the USA would take the leading role in the post-war world, but he was reluctant to include among the 'Great Powers' the Chinese, as FDR had of course done with his notion of the 'Four Policemen'. The Chinese he disparaged as 'the pigtails', an epithet that Bowman found sufficiently distasteful to record with pointed tension. Having presumably heard rumours about Churchill's drinking habits, the puritanical Bowman also took it upon himself to provide faithful witness (in his memo of the occasion) to the number of brandies and glasses of wine the Prime Minister consumed during their extended afternoon session.

The meetings with Churchill left a strong impression on Bowman, but he walked a very narrow path. He had neither the political inclination, nor perhaps the heart, and certainly not the authority – although Stettinius would report that Bowman 'met [Churchill] on his own ground of interest' – directly to challenge Churchill for the Empire. In any case, a more intense and meaningful negotiation took place with colonial and foreign office leaders. In the initial meeting with Law, Bowman had confirmed that he wanted to explore the possibility of common ground on a policy for dependent territories, and even gave Law to believe that high sounding moral proclamations, for which the Americans seemed to have such a proclivity, might be left aside in a more serious discussion of the issues. The British sensed well the tension between the President and his State Department, and so Law used Bowman's overture to encourage a reluctant Colonial Secretary, Colonel Oliver Stanley, to talk directly with Bowman. The British minister with direct responsibility for colonial administration, Stanley had once been characterized by Under-Secretary Welles as the 'most narrow, bigoted, reactionary Tory' that he had ever met in his official career.[23]

[22] 'Report by Bowman on Chequers Conversation', April 15, 1944; 'Colonial Policy', undated, JHU 2.4; Campbell and Herring, *The Diaries of Edward R. Stettinius. Jr., 1943–1946*, 1975, p. 52.
[23] Report by Bowman. Wells quoted in Dallek, *Franklin D. Roosevelt*, 1979, p. 429.

When they met on 18 April, the Colonial Secretary's reaction was distinctly frosty. Perhaps anticipating Stanley's hard line, Bowman chose not to begin by repeating his earlier overture, but resorted instead to those general moral principles about which he himself had such misgivings. He particularly emphasized the depth of feeling as regards the fate of the colonies among liberal and church elements of the American electorate. Stanley bristled. He complained that the State Department had not responded to British comments on the American Declaration on National Independence, simply handing them a second copy of the document, and that this had 'been like a dash of cold water' on earlier British enthusiasm. He dug his heels in against further broad generalities, noted that the British position should be quite clear, and then reiterated it: 'Our main plank is a *regional council and no supervision*' by any 'outside authority'. This insistence on a regional rather than global organization was clearly designed to protect British prerogatives and minimize American encroachment.

Mixing projection with genuine insight, the British Colonial Secretary later scoffed that Bowman's position was 'wrapped up in a rather diaphanous cover of the usual idealism', beneath which he sought to rationalize the post-war retention by the USA of Japanese mandates in the Pacific. 'Dr Bowman, who shifts his ground continually, is not easy to pin down', he added.

In this first crucial meeting, Bowman seems to have given too much away and yet not enough. To have made his stand on moral proclamation while having tempted the British with his flexibility on the colonial question, resulted in a hardening of stances just at the time when a reconciliation might have been possible. On the one side FDR had, as Bowman knew from the St Patrick's Day meeting, retreated from the demand that the dependent territories be fully internationalized, settling instead for regional organization and an international inspection commission. Stanley too had retreated perceptibly from the position that the British colonies were impregnable; he now agreed to loosely organized regional associations, and even to an international body as long as its purpose was restricted to passive documentation rather than active supervision – the collecting of paper rather than direct administration. [24]

Bowman was disappointed and frustrated. Among the arguments marshalled to deflect his 'diaphanous idealism', Stanley urged that different colonial possessions had very different circumstances and problems, and therefore required divergent approaches. In addition there were cross-cutting economic versus strategic considerations that varied by country and region. So what use would be a general proclamation? While clearly designed to fragment the colonial question and thereby protect British interests as a whole, this argument must have struck a very responsive chord in Bowman who himself had applied it to Roosevelt's moralism on colonial exploitation. But

[24] IB memo, 'Colonial Problems', 18 April 1944, JHU, 2.4, Colonial Policy, and Louis, *Imperialism at Bay*, 1978, pp. 330–2.

instead of coming together, the British and American positions hardened. In part this was due to Bowman's miscalculation about how to approach Stanley. But at the same time, neither he nor any of his colleagues had seen the British reply to the Declaration on National Independence, since the US Ambassador had never sent it on to Washington. Bowman therefore found himself arguing from a position of strategic weakness and, moreover, against a position with which he largely sympathized.

If there were differences and even confusion between the White House and the State Department, the British too did not operate as a single unit. In particular, while the Colonial Office took a very hard line on the fate of the empire, the Foreign Office, with a much wider purview, could treat colonies as one among a number of important issues. So it was to Sir Alexander Cadogan, Permanent Under-Secretary at the Foreign Office, and to two other foreign office strategists, that Bowman 'poured out his woes about the interview with Stanley'. So ardent was his lament that he conveyed to his British confessors the quite erroneous impression that FDR had put considerable pressure on him to achieve an agreement on colonial policy.[25] Rather it was Bowman himself who wanted to bring home a compromise in which the British at least agreed to submit annual reports to an international colonial bureau. Whether for reasons of politics or pity is not clear, but Cadogan agreed that the Foreign Office should intercede, and so it was arranged that, with Cadogan present this time, Bowman would have another shot with the Colonial Secretary.

When he met with Stanley and a largely silent Cadogan on 24 April for lunch at the Dorchester Hotel, Bowman immediately perceived a very different atmosphere. In a much more convivial meeting, he and Stanley began surveying the issue one colony after another, discussing specific needs and problems. Bowman was more adroit this time. He used the case of Tanganyika, the British East African colony confiscated from Germany in 1919, to try and impress on Stanley that a strictly national policy toward the colonies was unrealistic. His main purpose, he related afterward to Ambassador Winant, was to show that a colonial policy and international agreement already essentially existed:

> The Caribbean Commission was one example. The pre-war Tea Restriction scheme or Tea Marketing Board was another. The restriction of tea in Tanganyika was a restriction upon the standard of living since tea was the principle export. Assuming international control of excess products of commercial agriculture in the tropics, all colonial powers would have to confer on quotas as well as prices. In this way also there would be international collaboration on colonial policies because economic decision affected social welfare, island by island, and colony by colony, the world round.

---

[25] Louis, op. cit., p. 332.

In the stronger language he reserved for a post-lunch memo to himself, he declared that the 'British Government could not keep Tanganyika out of world discussion and call it an interest reserved for the British Government's consideration alone.'[26]

Stanley began to consider the specific regional councils that might be set up. Southeast Asia and the Japanese mandated islands were not particularly controversial, and he was prepared to envisage a third regional council for East Africa. For West Africa, this would not be a desirable solution, he argued, or at least if one were established it ought not to include the USA which, he explained, was quite unpopular in that part of the world. Stanley then returned to the British need to maintain 'authority in the rule of British possessions scattered over the world'. But the cost of raising the standard of living of the colonial peoples must be borne by the local people themselves, he insisted. 'The Metropole will keep order, it will secure the means of justice, it will increase production, it will provide technical assistance, it will teach native peoples to improve their sanitation and health. It cannot give native peoples a blank check.'

Stanley could hardly have known how closely he again mirrored Bowman's own sentiments, expressed in the Saturday morning state department meetings. Bowman now avoided any reference to global ideals, self-government or national independence, and agreed wholeheartedly with the assumptions of power politics Stanley conveyed, while angling his response in favour of American interests. He concurred on the unqualified priority and 'necessity for maintaining order as the first function of government', of world organization and colonial administration, and was even more blunt about the economic rationale underlying the 'white man's burden':

What we were all required to do as a result of the war ... was to look at dependent peoples quite closely to see that they who were at our mercy were not neglected in the general settlement to follow the war. The development of our resources by our superior machinery of development, our capital and our technical personnel was a primary obligation. When the rewards of enterprise were distributed, we should see that dependent peoples were left with a sufficient share to get along.

If Bowman was successful in using the case of Tanganyikan tea to stress the internationalization of colonial policy, and in wedging American ambitions into a global power politics, this did not lead to any major shift in the momentum of the negotiations. It was Stanley who took the initiative to

[26] IB memo, 'Colonial Policy' 24 April 1944, JHU, 2.4, Colonial Policy; IB to Winant, 28 April 1944, JHU 2.4, Colonial Policy. In the letter to Winant, Bowman floats the rather self-serving explanation that it was his (Bowman's) intervention with Churchill that accounted for Stanley's changed attitude, when of course Bowman had seen Churchill three days before the first unhappy interview with Stanley. Cadogan, according to Louis, was the intermediary (Louis, op. cit., p. 332).

summarize the results of the conversations. First, Bowman had succeeded in having any statement on colonial policy linked to the emerging world organization, but only at the expense of disavowing any effort at an independent colonial declaration by Britain and the USA. Second, while Stanley agreed in principle to regional commissions and even entered a more specific discussion about which these might be, he forced the stipulation that they would not be executive in character but simply receive, publish and collect annual reports 'available for inspection'. [27]

Bowman left the Dorchester Hotel a much happier man. To Ambassador Winant he expressed 'the hope that a new start could be made on the discussion of colonial policy'. It was an optimism provoked by the congeniality of the lunchtime discussion, however, as much as its substance, but it sustained Bowman and other members of the mission for several weeks. He had negotiated common ground if not a complete agreement with the notoriously protective Colonial Secretary. Stanley also relished the outcome. He was sufficiently confident of his position that towards the end of their lunch, he asked Bowman a favour. Once Cadogan had left, Stanley asked if Bowman might bring to Cordell Hull's attention the predicament of Barbados. A British colony dependent mostly on agricultural production, Barbados was experiencing large-scale unemployment and Stanley fretted that as a result there may be considerable disturbances: 'violence will ensue'. Could the United States absorb as many as 30,000 Barbadan labourers to work in the American economy? Whether this was an innocent request or not is unclear. But such a blunt request that the US economy support British colonial policy – the very bone of contention in their negotiations – might also be seen as a deftly brazen reassertion of Britain's political upper hand in colonial affairs. Whatever the case, Bowman took the request at face value, duly reported it in his memo of the meeting, and assented to deliver it to Hull. [28]

On his return to Washington, Bowman was reaffirmed in his optimism and in his belief that significant progress had been achieved. He was enthusiastically congratulated by Secretary Hull, who was apparently impressed by a renewed British openness on the colonial question, and he re-entered the Department shrouded in the warm glow of success. 'We found ourselves much closer in our thinking at the end of our several talks than we could have hoped', Bowman exuded in his draft report to the Secretary of State. But the approbation did not come without qualification. A Churchill speech during May included a short paragraph on post-war arrangements that betrayed a closer knowledge of American thinking than Hull and Roosevelt would have liked. 'The question was raised whether some of the members of the mission had "talked too much".' Stettinius defended the mission on the grounds that on innumerable occasions, they were embarrassed by British references to State Department documents that the mission members

[27] Louis, op. cit.
[28] Louis, op. cit., p. 333; and 'Colonial Policy' 24 April 1944.

had never even seen, and that if anything, they talked too little. But this rain on Bowman's parade was enough to draw out his annoyance at both FDR and Hull whose disorganization, he felt, followed from their personal and political rivalry over their respective places in history. An efficient foreign policy was jeopardized in the process.

In retrospect, of course, the mission made much less progress than Bowman wanted to believe. As William Louis argues in his exhaustive archival reconstruction of World War II British–American negotiations over the colonies, Stanley 'had conceded virtually nothing' that had not already been agreed on. Bowman, by contrast, had drawn back from some of the major American positions: a bipartisan declaration on colonial policy, eventual self-government, and the effective internationalization of European posses-sions. Along the continuum from sovereignty to international administration, Bowman had been able to secure only the most watery acknowledgement of the weakest option. Far from managing to 'draw out British officials with respect to colonial policy after the war', as FDR had requested, it was they who drew out Bowman. It was not so much a compromise that was achieved; rather Bowman conceded much of the British position – much with which he already agreed but FDR and the State Department did not.

Subsequent to an official response, Bowman had agreed to enter his agree-ments with Stanley into 'the stream of discussion' in the State Department, and predictably perhaps, he found this a frustrating experience. On the colonial question, the Department was in a state of transition. On the one hand, as discussions necessarily moved toward specific solutions, FDR took less of a lead, leaving the State Department with primary responsibility. On the other hand, the informal political agenda group that led this discussion had not yet reconciled itself on the question of general principles and pro-clamations versus specific solutions. Bowman gave extended reports on his deliberations, but found his state department colleagues more politely indif-ferent than ever to his essentially pro-British pragmatism. 'Forget the general principles', he responded, and 'pass on to what you can do about them.' Returning to a familiar theme, but generalizing this time in terms of national traits, he declared that the problem with Americans is that we talk '*words* instead of figuring out how to deal with *things*'. Our approach has been akin to devising 'the Ten Commandments to fit all dependent areas', he warned, and proceeded to support as merely realistic the Colonial Office's demand that British sovereignty be retained in the colonies. '[E]verything we produced on colonial subjects sounded like the Sermon on the Mount', Bowman concluded, 'and everything we said was "just as good as Jesus". Our papers were always awfully good but awfully unrealistic.'[29]

Bowman failed to convince his colleagues of the propriety of an avowedly pragmatic approach, and in May and June of 1944 the discussion in the sub-committee on international organization turned again to questions of a

[29] 'Colonial Policy', Draft Report to the Secretary of State, n.d., JHU 2.4; untitled memo June 12, 1944.

general colonial declaration and the definition of sovereignty in the dependent territories. The State Department eventually agreed that there ought to be collective sovereignty over dependent territories, shared by the United Nations as a whole. On self-government and independence, Bowman was eager to abandon both concepts, but he comprised a minority of one. He managed only to dilute the moral generality of the eventual list of proposals. Bowman 'held the extreme position on this point.'[30] Little vestige of his habitual 'diaphanous idealism' survived the London mission, at least on the colonial question.

Under other circumstances, Bowman's access to the British might have had more deleterious results. But with the State Department undergoing a further internal upheaval and with FDR following a resolutely independent foreign policy in any case, there is little evidence that Bowman's mission substantially altered the course of post-war colonial planning. There seems to be no record of a response by FDR, or indeed by Hull (beyond the obligatory politenesses), to Bowman's colonial section of the mission's report to the Secretary. The main significance of his mission, Louis concludes, may well have been that it lulled the Colonial and Foreign Offices into 'a momentary sense of false security'. Whatever the preparatory agreements about the informality of the mission, the British continually treated Bowman as an emissary of the President, and must have been heartily disappointed when FDR and indeed the State Department did not dramatically alter course as a result of the London talks. If Bowman can be credited with one thing, his agreements with Stanley on regional councils probably ensured that henceforth, the colonial question was folded under the larger question of an international organization (eventually to become the United Nations). This transition was already underway, especially in the State Department, and the British followed when Churchill's opposition softened. Two weeks after the mission's return, the State Department learned that Churchill had significantly altered his position on world organization. Hitherto a staunch believer in the priority of a fragmented regional structure, the Prime Minister now seemed to concede the necessity of building a world organization first. This did at least seem to represent a little movement on the British side and Bowman was quick to claim credit: the mission 'permitted me to disclose our positions all along the line', whereupon 'the Foreign Office and Eden took heart and were able to oppose the PM', Bowman surmised. 'This *alone* is worth the trip to London.'[31]

CONCLUSION

In 1919 the colonies were a footnote to the Paris Peace Conference. There was no over-riding question of what to do with the 'dependent' territories.

[30] Minutes I.O. (International Organization Subcommittee) 52, May 10 1944; I.O. Minutes 54, May 12 1944, NA.NF Box 142; and Louis, op. cit., pp. 351–65.
[31] Bucknell to Secretary and Under-Secretary of State, Secret Telegram, 18 May 1944; IB accompanying memo, June 13, 1944; JHU 2.4; and Louis, op. cit., p. 334.

Self-determination was certainly discussed, but even Woodrow Wilson, in his Fourteen Points, confined himself to the insistence that competing colonial claims between European colonizers be arbitrated fairly and with an equal view to the welfare of the colonized. It was a very different global vision that confiscated the colonies from one set of European powers only to mandate them to another. Bowman's experience of the peace conference and of the inter-war period taught him, that in and of themselves, neither boundary changes nor territorial switches prevented wars or guaranteed international stability. This negative lesson about the geographical conceits of the old world were foundational in his vision of the new world. If Bowman balked now in 1944 at expropriating British colonies for American trade, this was in no way because he remained wedded to an obsolete geography of empire. Rather, he felt much more strongly than Roosevelt that whatever their colonial transgressions, the British were forever allies and would be a necessary part of the post-war Pax Americana. Who would substitute for them in the 'Third World', as it was about to be dubbed, if the British were dispossessed of their imperial responsibilities? How would American economic interests be protected in such a vacuum?

In FDR, who refused to involve himself in specific colonial solutions, preferring instead to let his State Department explore the possibilities, a more ardent anti-colonialism was retained. 'The widely accepted orthodoxy is that in foreign policy he flew by the seat of his pants and dealt with problems as they came up', according to Warren Kimball who has chronicled FDR's at times tense correspondence with Churchill. 'He saw nothing wrong with great power "leadership", but he was staunchly opposed to formal colonialism, even though he avoided always making an issue of it.' He was 'absolutely consistent in his belief that colonialism was the major post-war problem.' If on the colonial question, FDR espoused an extrapolated Wilsonian idealism, his St Patrick's Day lecture to the Stettinius mission and his concession on regional organization show that any idealism was also tempered by a keen sense of American interests. Indeed Louis argues that 'Roosevelt had a shrewd sense' of what might be politically possible, 'and he refused to pursue an issue that would interfere with wartime cooperation. He aimed at stabilizing, not undermining the colonial world... The demand for timetables [for independence] was a distinctly American contribution to the process of de-colonization.'

Yet as we have seen, the President remained committed to de-colonization and, despite his own patrician anglophilia, retained a particular animosity for the British, less because of the style of their colonial administration and more because of the tenacity with which they intended to defend colonial preference against American expansion. Even as the American forces prepared to fight in Europe, Roosevelt had complained that '[W]e will have more trouble with Great Britain after the war than we are having with Germany now.'[32]

---

[32] Kimball, *Churchill and Roosevelt*, 1984; Louis, *Imperialism at Bay*, 1978, p. 9; Dallek, *Franklin D. Roosevelt*, 1979, p. 429.

Bowman's was a rather different vision. He certainly worried that a re-constructed Germany might succeed a dispossessed Britain in the dependent territories, but his larger geopolitical concern lay further to the east. By 1944 Bowman's antipathy for the Soviet Union stretched well beyond the boundaries of Europe and the question of a German settlement. Though not always openly, he was increasingly alarmed at the effect of 'Soviet propaganda in trusteed areas'. Given 'the immense advantage of Soviet techniques among dependent peoples', he reasoned, the 'field would thus be wide open for Soviet agents – to indoctrinate, to unify, to lead. Thus one after the other the trusteed areas would or might go communist.'

Within the State Department, by 1942, could be found 'the grand design of the United States in the post-war era of de-colonization.'[33] If by 1944 Bowman had moved to the extreme conservative wing of the State Department team this by no means rendered him irrelevant in shaking loose the colonies. He may have travelled farthest from the 'diaphanous idealism' of the Wilsonian heritage, but it was a progressive and internationalist conservatism. Bowman's *'Lebensraum* for all' may have omitted many of the moral trappings but it was recognizably connected to Wilson's project of a global Monroe Doctrine. In Bowman's eyes, it was of course to be an *American* *'Lebensraum* for all', not just in economic but in military terms. What was good for America was automatically good for the security and stability of the world. What has been said of Roosevelt, then, applies equally to Bowman: he 'believed his own rhetoric and saw no contradiction between American security and the world's security.'[34] Where the two men differed was not in the goal but in the means for achieving this American *Lebensraum* for all. In the end, of course, the American *Lebensraum* was only partially implemented. Germany was only partly dismantled and was certainly reconstructed as a bulwark against the Soviet Union. The United Nations rarely fulfilled its state department ambition as an arm of US foreign policy (prior at least to the Gulf War of 1991), stymied by an excess of democracy at the hands of numerous Third World nations and, perhaps surprisingly, the Soviet Union. And yet the colonies *were* shaken loose from their European empires. The irony here is that this quintessentially geographical gambit for global economic power succeeded precisely at the time when global power was to be expressed in the most aspatial terms. Not until the end of the 1980s would the geographical construction of a now declining American empire again become such a prominent political concern.

[33] IB memo, 'Trusteeship', 12 December 1946, JHU 2.4, Trusteeship; and Louis, op. cit., p. 179.
[34] Louis, op. cit., p. 354.

15

What Did You Do in the War, Daddy?

Andrew Kirby*

A real science is able to accept even the shameful, dirty stories of its beginning.

Foucault[1]

La géographie, ça sert, d'abord, à faire la guerre.

Lacoste[2]

PREAMBLE: WAR AS AN INDEPENDENT VARIABLE

In this chapter, I want to explore a simple premise, which involves the salience of war in our thinking. We are used to seeing war as a manifestation of conflict between nation states, war as an expression of geopolitics, and even war as a determinant of urban form. But in each of such cases, war is invoked as an independent variable – a means of accounting for some process or pattern.[3] This seems strange to me, because we would rarely, if

* This chapter has gone through a number of convulsions, and has been improved immeasurably by the comments of those who have been kind enough to read the various versions. The author would, therefore, like to thank the editors for their patience, and John Agnew, Peter Gould and Sallie Marston for their commentary. In addition, he thanks Barry Katz at Stanford and Bradley Smith at Cabrillo College for allowing him to interrogate them, and Barry Katz for sharing his finds in the National Archives. The usual disclaimers apply.

[1] Foucault, 'The minimalist self', 1988, pp. 1–16, especially p. 15.

[2] Lacoste, La Géographie, ça sert, d'abord, à faire la guerre, 1976.

[3] For examples from the geographical literature, see O'Loughlin and van der Wusten, 'Geography, war and peace', 1986, pp. 484–510; O'Tuathail, 'The language and nature of the new geopolitics', 1986, pp. 73–86.

ever, invoke peace in the same way. We would be hard pressed to find reference to a frontier as 'the result of peace', or a nation state as 'ravaged by peace' – even though a little thought could produce examples of both.[4]

In short, peace is seen as shorthand for a complex set of relations, whereas war is a thing in and of itself; moreover, peace is normal, whereas war is an aberration that interrupts and punctuates the normalcy. In consequence, war is dismissed as being of minor importance in shaping either the state or society. Taking the example of the First World War, Giddens notes that:

> It still tends to be assumed by sociological authors analysing social development in the current century that if it had any lasting influence on social organization, the First World War merely accelerated trends that were bound to emerge in the long run in any case. But this view is not at all plausible and could scarcely be countenanced at all if it were not for the powerful grip that endogenous and evolutionary conceptions of change have had in the social sciences.[5]

The reasons for this grip are not, in my view, hard to find. Anglo social science has been cocooned by nearly 50 years of peace, punctuated only infrequently and partially by territorial struggles in distant places such as Korea, Aden, Algeria, Vietnam, Nicaragua and Kuwait. In reality, of course, there is perpetual warfare around the globe, but these wars appear as the struggles of others, even when fought on our behalf and probably with our tax dollars.[6]

This problem is a much deeper one however, and can be traced back to the foundations of modernist science. Michael Mann, for example, states bluntly that 'from the Enlightenment to Durkheim, most major sociologists omitted war from their central problematic'.[7] He continues:

> This was not neglect, it was quite deliberate. They believed the future society would be pacific and transnational. Industrial, or capitalist, or 'modern' society would be unlike the preceding feudal, or theocratic, or militant societies. Power could now operate pacifically, without physical force ... [and] would also operate transnationally ... social classes would also become transnational. Whether classes were defined

[4] For instance, closer economic integration is producing very clear changes in the social and political landscape in the MexAmerican borderlands: see ch. 7 in Kirby, *Power/resistance*, 1993. For discussions of the economic changes in localities that have resulted from reductions in the US defence budget, see ch. 1 in Kirby (ed.), *The Pentagon and the Cities*, 1992.

[5] Giddens, *The Nation State and Violence*, 1985, p. 234.

[6] Watts makes mention of the 'brutal Gulf War, fought with smart bombs against a raggedy-arsed nineteenth-century Iraqi army in the name of a new world order'; 'Mapping meaning, denoting difference, imagining identity', 1991, pp. 7–16, especially p. 7.

[7] Mann, 'War and social theory', 1988, pp. 146–65, especially p. 147.

according to property, the market, or occupation, they could be found interchangeably at both the global level and the level of the individual nation state. These notions dominate the theories of Smith, St-Simon, Comte, Spencer, Marx and Durkheim – our liberal and Marxian founding fathers.[8]

In their studies of state building, both Mann and Tilly have shown convincingly that external affairs – frequently manifested as war making – have been a crucial and constant preoccupation of rulers, and their bureaucratic successors.[9] This historical insight is a vital antidote to the usual functionalist taxonomies of state actions, and it is one that we can apply with equal value to the present. What I want to emphasize in this chapter is the simple proposition that war is everywhere, at all times. Since 1945, there have been hundreds of wars – manifested as *coups d'etat*, civil wars, invasions – scattered throughout the world. To use the terminology of world systems theorists, a majority of these have taken place within nations on the periphery. Many of them have, in their various ways and at varied times, involved representatives from a number of the core nations, interceding in civil struggles. As such, these conflicts are little different from the incursions and invasions that marked the last period of extensive colonialism throughout the nineteenth century.

The connection between war making and state making has become so intermingled that it is hard to separate the two. On a global scale, consider that approximately 40 per cent of the world's population lives in states controlled by military forces. Even in liberal democracies, the growth of the state apparatus has been very closely connected to the expansion of the military–industrial complex. It is little more than a century ago that government efforts to create a standing army in the USA were turned back; since 1945, in contrast, American forces have been stationed across the globe.[10] Throughout the 1970s and 80s, spending on military hardware and personnel expanded steadily, driving nations to the brink of bankruptcy – or in the case of the Soviet Union, perhaps beyond.

Taken together, these and other factors have hidden the positioning of war within our everyday lives. We no longer notice the military planes flying over our heads or the nuclear warships in our ports. Adolescent males no longer have white feathers thrust into their hands if they fail to enlist – we now send our poor, lured into standing armies by promises of a college education. Yet as some feminists have argued, there is a short thread connecting militarism in our communities and violence in the home.[11] In addition, many of the most prosperous local economies in the United States

---

[8] Mann, *War and Social Theory*, 1988, p. 147.

[9] Tilly, *States, Coercion and Capital*, 1990.

[10] Skowronek, *Building A New American State*, 1982.

[11] Enloe, 'Feminists thinking about war', 1987, pp. 526–47; and *Bananas, Beaches and Bases*, 1989.

depend upon the annual injection of billions of dollars of Department of Defense contracts, a fiscal dependency that can generate a militaristic culture within the locality. [12] Furthermore, the educational system in the USA is to some extent tied into the science and engineering needs of our armed forces: universities receive extensive research funds from the Department of Defense and the Office of Naval Research, and a majority of our engineering graduates go into the military–industrial complex in one capacity or another. [13]

These are not the only links between the university and militarism. Here I want to retrieve war as an encompassing influence upon academic geography and show that there exists great continuity between Victorian preoccupations and current concerns. [14] While many of the chapters in this volume have shown convincingly how geography – as academic work – was embedded in that orgy of exploration and colonialism, this tale runs more slowly after World War I, which in many ways brought the era of European imperial hegemony to an end. As our attention has shifted from geographers to geography, from travel to the travails of departments and disciplines, so the concern for war has also slipped from sight. This has occurred because war has become a commonplace, in every sense of the word. For instance, as Meyrowitz has noted, struggles in specific places have been replaced by wars represented as gestalt images via television – with the result that one conflict blurs into another. [15] Although individual geographers may not be involved directly in the usurpation of territory and the like, they still operate within a discipline that has close instrumental links to the state apparatus. The examples I use below emphasize in part the two world wars, but that is hardly the end of the story. The relation between the military state and contemporary geography is also of great interest.

WAR AND ACADEMIC GEOGRAPHY IN THE UNITED STATES

The usual accounts of the discipline tell us that geographers, like other mortals, have done war service – they have given their expertise to their

[12] See Parker and Feagin, 'Military spending in free enterprise cities', 1992.

[13] The connections between what Melman calls the permanent war economy and the development of production relations are discussed by Giddens, *The Nation State and Violence*, 1985; Dumas, *The Overburdened Economy*, 1986; Melman, 'Economic consequences of the arms race', 1988, pp. 55–9.

[14] A recent discussion of the historical record, in particular the impact of the disastrous Boer War upon academic geography in Britain, is given by Stoddart, 'Geography and war', 1992, pp. 87–99.

[15] Meyrowitz, *No Sense of Place*, 1985. Similarly, fact and fiction have commingled as moviemaking capabilities have been perfected; whereas John Wayne was frequently shown amidst actual newsreels of the Pacific war, Coppolla was able to recreate his own Vietnam in the Philippines for *Apocalypse Now*, thus inadvertently reinforcing the jingoistic conceit of the interchangeability of one South East Asian country with another.

country and then returned to their civilian activities. Such accounts, in keeping with the argument already developed, treat war as a punctuation. But the two world wars during this century had profound long-term impacts upon academic geography. As Owen Lattimore observed in the 1950s, the opportunity to work within government proved to be seductive and ultimately 'corrupting': the ability to use classified information, the receipt of research funds, and the chance to influence decision-making processes have all contrived, he argued, to channel the long-term goals of the academic community.[16]

This corruption, in Lattimore's terms, gains its greatest momentum during the second global conflict, but begins in the very earliest years of the institutionalization of the disciplines, in the decade preceding the First World War. In 1912, there were only 76 members of the Association of American Geographers (AAG); nevertheless, 51 of them were involved in some way in the First World War. Several worked in the Shipping Board and others in the War Trade Board.[17] Individuals undertook a variety of war-related tasks, but the most influential involved political geography – several academics, for instance, moved into the 'Inquiry', a large operation run by the American Geographical Society (AGS) and overseen by the State Department, which was responsible for laying the groundwork for US participation in the peace discussions in Paris. Isaiah Bowman acted as executive officer and geographer of the unit, and attended the Versailles talks. He was accompanied by Mark Jefferson, and Lawrence Martin also attended on behalf of G-2 military intelligence.[18]

Geographers had little interest in strategy and warfare in 1914, but by the close of the conflict approximately half the output of the *Annals* was linked to the war.[19] Interest in warfare expired very rapidly after the Armistice but geographers had nevertheless been changed by their roles in organizations like the State Department, the Shipping Board and the War Trade Board, beyond traditional service in the Geological Survey or the Weather Bureau. Wallace Atwood wrote in 1919 about this new instrumental emphasis that grabbed the discipline:

> The war has emphasized the need of more trained geographers in America ... We are entering a period of maritime expansion. More men will be needed to go as representatives of great commercial houses in different parts of the world. Our Diplomatic Service will undoubtedly be increased. Those who attempt to represent us abroad should know

[16] Lattimore, *Studies in Frontier History*, 1959, especially p. 22.

[17] James and Martin, *The Association of American Geographers*, 1978, especially p. 172.

[18] A number of other participants in the activities of 'Inquiry' are listed in Anon., 'War services of members in the Association of American Geographers', 1919, pp. 53–70. See also Gelfand, *The Inquiry*, 1963.

[19] A comparison with journals such as the *American Journal of Sociology* and the *American Political Science Review* indicates a much lower level of interest in the war.

the geography of the country ... we must know better the peoples of the world, and to accomplish this we must know better the geography of the world.[20]

Atwood's prophecy of the links between 'geography and informal empire' was reprised by Whittlesey two decades later on the advent of World War II:

The war ... awakened wide interest in the nature of places where fighting occurred, it brought to public attention the importance of earth resources in the economic life of nations, and in directing national policy, and many geographers had been given stimulating opportunities to view their subject afresh in the practical atmosphere of wartime jobs. The new orientation brought human geography to the side of physical geography which had dominated the field before 1914. Except for the knotty problems presented by social geography, the American student as a result learned to view the earth in all the complexity of its natural and cultural features ... whether they are considered as a platform for peace or a springboard for war.[21]

In short, the Great War, as it was ambivalently christened, was not a brief diversion for academic geography – it was a catalyst. We should not underestimate, for example, the shift of emphasis noted by Whittlesey, from physical to human geography. In a relatively brief period of time, geography's physiographic roots were eclipsed by economic and political analysis which had greater practical applications within government and commerce.

Geographers played various roles within the bureaucratic machines of war, and the intellectual impact of the war workers within the discipline was a lasting one. Consequently, when global conflict re-emerged in the thirties, there already existed a framework of geographers with experience within the state apparatus: 'when Europe burst into war again in 1939, American geographers were ready to speak and move promptly and to the point.'[22]

GEOGRAPHERS IN THE SECOND WORLD WAR: THE OSS

World War I began as a struggle between monarchs and emperors, fought with volunteer armies. By the close, warfare had become complex and industrialized, and Europe itself had a very different political map. Giddens argues convincingly that the changes wrought during four years of war had profound social impacts, and he links the prosecution of war with the escalated power of the state apparatus and the regulation of industrialized economies. Science and technology became central to developments taking

[20] Attwood, 'The call for geographers', 1919, pp. 36–43.
[21] Whittlesey, 'War peace and geography', 1941, pp. 77–82, especially p. 79.
[22] Ibid.

place in industry, urban planning and the home, and the importance of intervention and control increased rather than diminished in importance in the years after the war; as the economic situation worsened and turned into depression, so governments increased their efforts to generate planned, interventionist solutions to social and economic problems. [23]

In consequence, the numbers of universities and, of course, of academics in the US expanded throughout this period. Thus when peace ended in the USA in 1941, there was a large reservoir of faculty and graduate students who were able to move directly into war work. Six hundred and seventy geographers were involved in some way in the wide range of permanent agencies (interior, state, war), the armed services, and temporary agencies. This latter collection was the largest, and the 129 geographers working within the Office of Strategic Services (OSS) was the single biggest group of inductees. [24]

The OSS was one of the most prestigious places for war service open to an academic without experience in the reserves. In its first incarnation, it was created in 1941 by Presidential confidante 'Wild Bill' Donovan as an intelligence organization. Originally begun with just two dozen recruits, the OSS had nearly 2000 staff within the year and became a major player within the already crowded intelligence bureaucracy in Washington. The latter boasted over 9000 personnel by the end of 1945. [25] OSS staff created many of the blueprints for post-war US economic and military hegemony; work done during the 1941–5 period looked explicitly to a new world order. The Research and Analysis Branch (R and A) was especially prominent in the OSS. The R and A presents an effective example of the ways in which significant numbers of academics transformed themselves into workers within the state apparatus, and became closely involved in the most far-reaching aspects of war making. In doing so, they also presided over the emergence of essentially new conceptions of academic labour. [26] It was in the R and A, for instance, that priority was given to economic analysts, whose insights were given a stature that had not been seen before. The rapid rise of economics as a discipline within the USA is due in part to its prominence in the war effort.

Wild Bill Donovan's mandate was to develop an organization that could coordinate the various intelligence activities undertaken on behalf of different US agencies. His goal was to create a unit that could comprehend the new world war emerging in Europe and later in the Pacific; a total war, enmeshed with regional economic conditions and bolstered by complex propaganda and ideology. Intelligence data – the raw – were suddenly less important than interpretation and prediction – the cooked:

[23] Giddens, *Nation State and Violence*, 1985, ch. 9.

[24] Wright, *Employment of Geographers in the War Effort*, report to the Joint AAG-AGS Committee, unpublished manuscript, 1947.

[25] Of this total, R and A represented about 10 per cent of the personnel.

[26] See, for example, Soellner, 'From political dissent', 1990, pp. 225–43.

In modern war, the traditional distinctions between political, economic and military data have become blurred. Enemy armament production or military transportation are not things apart but are aspects of the total economic picture, which in turn reflects manpower problems, administrative machinery and the general state of morale.[27]

Donovan's 'total picture' could not be addressed by the narrow, scholarly insights valued in many parts of the academy at that time. As Katz observes, 'the received division of intellectual labor which compartmentalized and departmentalized the world into reified academic categories had to be repudiated in favor of a collaborative and interdisciplinary practice.'[28] The scale and ferocity of the war necessitated a new research style, although the varied accounts of the R and A branch all indicate the problems that faced the first recruits; Smith notes that 'the use of a team approach, in which groups of researchers worked on a single project, was ... virtually unknown among historians and geographers at the time'.[29]

This was much more than an issue of styles and personalities – it was a matter of fostering methodologies that were consistent with the needs of a state fighting for its life. Historical and geographic description, undertaken on a case-by-case basis, was almost irrelevant in the new era of total war. It was overshadowed by the approach adopted by varied researchers in sociology, government and economics, who often worked together to generate reports on political–economic developments. They self-consciously employed a 'valueless' approach, now more commonly labelled 'positivist'.[30] Here, in the crucible of the wartime state, we see significant foundations of a 'social science', dedicated to the explanation and prediction of aggregate human behaviour.

I do not want to give the impression that those with a regional interest were simply displaced by the nascent 'social scientists'; nor were these the only two identifiable groups of researchers. Within the R and A, there was also a third cluster, whose members embodied complex assumptions and generated controversial conclusions. These were refugees, displaced academics on whom the war had already had an explicit impact. Most had fled from Germany and achieved distinction as representatives of the Frankfurt School, as it became known. Throughout the war, they found themselves in conflict with both the old-style regionalists and the social science positivists.[31] While Marcuse, Neumann and Kirchheimer (to name the most visible) ultimately had only a limited impact on policy generation, their bearing on methodological development and intellectual history remains unequivocal.

[27] Donovan, *Functions of the OSS*, 1949, vol. 2, p. 343; quoted in Soellner, 'From political dissent', 1990.
[28] Katz, *Foreign Intelligence*, 1989, p. 16.
[29] Smith, *Shadow Warriors*, 1983, p. 363.
[30] See Katz, op. cit.
[31] See Soellner, op. cit., p. 229.

They represented an alien tradition – literally – that owed everything to German intellectual thought steeped in materialism and dialecticism, a tradition that was still virtually unexplored within the American academy. [32] They brought to the analysis of Germany and fascism a sophisticated reading of the enemy, expressed most emphatically in Neumann's *Behemoth*. [33] The group ultimately contributed to a restatement of the classic problems of intellectual history that stimulated a generation of thinkers after 1945. Most important of these was Carl Schorske, whose long service in R and A provided the bases for his profound, and critical, studies of modernity and rationality. [34]

The Frankfurt group, already used to a style of collaborative work, was better placed than some American counterparts to contribute to the war against fascism; even in August of 1945, Marcuse was complaining to a colleague, 'may we reiterate our humble request that instead of indulging in personal interviews of isolated personalities that you concentrate your effort on such reports covering one decisive larger area integrating political and economic developments?' [35] Clearly, old habits of piecemeal research persisted throughout the war. However, Marcuse and the others faced their biggest battles with those in the social science camp. The latter struggled to craft 'objective' and value-free methods, and frequently saw the work of 'the aliens' as highly subjective. This interpretation was to be expected, as the latter were dealing with very large, socially-constructed concepts – the nature of the state, relations between fascism and civil society, the place of rationality within politics and the nature of justice. Such work was mistrusted by analysts more comfortable with armaments production and bombing statistics, establishing an interpretive tension that has been accelerating since this period. At its base is the conflict between the social scientists' claims to explanation and prediction on the one hand, and more complex hermeneutic efforts at understanding on the other. Since 1945 and the emergence of the era of total war, the pragmatism of explanation has consistently gained ground at the expense of the process of understanding, often dismissed on the grounds of its soft (i.e. non-numeric) and interpretive (read 'subjective') methodologies. As Katz observes,

> The dream of a pure and presuppositionless logic, abandoned already
> in the thirties by Husserl and on whose ruins the major positions

[32] But see Mills's, 1942 review of Neumann's, *Behemoth*, pp. 432–6. It is another testament to the impact of war – albeit an ironic one – that the materialists of the Frankfurt School were employed in the United States.

[33] Neumann, *Behemoth*, 1942.

[34] An estimated seven historians who worked in R and A went on to be Presidents of the American Historical Association. At least three geographers – Hartshorne, James and Ackerman – were similarly elected by the AAG.

[35] Marcuse, memo to Lt.-Col. Hughes, quoted in Katz, *Herbert Marcuse and the Art of Liberation*, 1982, p. 118.

of postwar philosophy would rise, endured some of its most rigorous reality-testing in the wartime Office of Strategic Services.[36]

THE PROJECTS COMMITTEE

These intellectual questions were fought out in practice within the bureaucracy of the Research and Analysis branch. A projects committee was formed in 1942, a pivotal group of gatekeepers whose job was to police the work undertaken within the R and A, and in particular to screen its products. For much of the war, this was chaired by Richard Hartshorne, described by one historian as a 'hard headed geographer'.[37] Hartshorne clearly took his position seriously, and his memos were famous for their astringent calls for 'objective' and 'scientific' writing: his 'directives to his academic colleagues, models of what has been called "the rhetoric of anti-rhetoric", managed to be simultaneously pointed and blunt'.[38]

Hartshorne was responsible for the close scrutiny of R and A documents. As Katz notes, 'the projects committee fought a rear-guard battle to enforce in practice the objectivist standard of political reporting called for by the positivist theory to which the directorate of the Branch subscribed.'[39] Although this was to be a war fought via 'thoroughly objective and neutral research', neutrality did not spill over into the determination of policy options: and it was here that methodological conflicts revealed themselves.[40] One notable clash occurred towards the end of the European war, with the production of a report on the putative role of the SPD (Sozialistische Partei Deutschlands), which 'pitted Marcuse, Schorske and Sherman Kent against Richard Hartshorne and the projects committee'.[41] The 'aliens', notably Neumann, were keen to generate some measure of German regeneration, which was to involve the dismantling of the Nazi system and its replacement with civilian government – preferably, they argued, under the auspices of the SPD. These proposals generated a heated response from the projects committee.[42] Their document, written by Hartshorne, begins:

[36] Katz, *Foreign Intelligence*, 1989, p. 20.

[37] Katz, 1989, op. cit. p. 16. Hartshorne was a political geographer, who had published in the *American Political Science Review* and had co-authored a work on German geopolitics in 1942: 'Recent developments in political geography', 1935, pp. 785–804, 943–66, and Whittlesey, Hartshorne and Colby, *German Strategy of World Conquest*, 1942.

[38] LaCapra, quoted in Katz, *Foreign Intelligence*, 1989, p. 16.

[39] Ibid., p. 20.

[40] Schlesinger, cited in Smith, *Shadow Warriors*, 1983, p. 362.

[41] Smith, *Shadow Warriors*, 1983, p. 364.

[42] Untitled and undated memorandum from the Projects Committee Correspondence file, RG 226, entry 37, box 5. This brief document is uncredited but has all the marks of Hartshorne's other documents on this theme of objectivity: for example, his 'Draft of proposed guide to preparation of political reports', generated in May, 1944 (RG226, entry 37, box 5).

The problem of objectivity in R and A reporting presents a new aspect in the treatment of post-war Germany, and a peculiarly difficult one, requiring some basic analysis of the whole process of scientific thought in the social field.

The second paragraph continues:

In all problems concerning man, scientific studies involve certain assumptions – commonly not expressed – that are not scientific in character, but rather are, fundamentally, moral or social principles.

Hartshorne continues that there exist certain assumptions which insinuate themselves throughout scientific discourse, such as the value of human life. 'Normally', he says, 'this lack of absolute objectivity creates no difficulties because of universal agreement on the subjective elements.' Problems arise 'the moment that writers and readers are not in agreement'.

This is the current situation with regard to our reports on the treat-ment of Germany. Unconsciously, we write of Germany as we would of any other nation of the world's brotherhood. If certain things are done to Germany, there will be a 'serious lack of calorie intake'; a 'grave deficiency in heating coal', or the economy will be 'unsound'. In a dozen other ways far less easily spotted, we are writing on the assumption that it is best that a people be well-fed, well-housed, efficient and prosperous. These assumptions are not permissible.

The document concludes with an appeal for objectivity at any price:

We could solve this problem if our writing were made completely free of subjective assumptions and absolutely objective in tone ... We must directly state that we are not concerned with the fact that millions of Germans may not get enough of the right food to be healthy, but are only concerned with what those millions may do in whatever efforts they may make to get more.

Hartshorne reveals in the starkest possible terms his commitment to 'scientific thought'. Yet his document ends on a very different note; the 'presuppositionless logic' is abrubtly replaced by a series of rhetorical questions:

If our calculations showed that Germany in post-war years will have no more food per capita than Poland had before the war ... what of it? Why should Germany have more than Poland had? Who got us into this mess anyway?

THE IMPACT OF THE WAR ON THE DISCIPLINE OF GEOGRAPHY

Work in government agencies such as the R and A was not a diversion for those involved: it helped define their subsequent intellectual positions. Just as the First World War had accelerated the eclipse of physical geography at the expense of political and economic study, so the Second World War prompted the demise of regional study and the methodological assumptions on which it was based. In summarizing the role that geographers had played during the conflict, Ackerman (also an OSS alumnus) wrote that 'there may be a lesson on professional training to be derived from our wartime experience.' He concluded:

> As far as research is concerned, our success in meeting [wartime] demands can be measured in terms of two criteria: the extent to which we were able to provide properly trained personnel and the usefulness of the body of facts accumulated by our previous basic research. Our score was not high in either.[43]

The thrust of Ackerman's criticism was directed against regional geography, which had spawned what he identified as technicians lacking insight and originality. In preceding years, non-regional study had been marginalized: 'many systematic studies of the past twenty-five years were undertaken by investigators who were more or less amateurs in the subject'.[44] For the future, he argued, the discipline should turn away from regionalism and work collaboratively on systematic tropes – as had been emphasized within the OSS. Regionalists would be excluded from such interactions, as their skills were insular ones: 'since two geographers with similar regional specialties theoretically have the same background and competence, presumably there is little to be gained by their working together.'[45] With Ackerman we see a strong echo of the collective wartime experience: geographers now had an objective criterion against which to measure their progress – namely their stature within government – and they could use this to generate a blueprint for the discipline. The message was clear: dump regionalism, move to systematic study, and get in step with the other disciplines.

The strength of this feeling can be demonstrated by a specific example, which again invokes the career of Richard Hartshorne. He is not as well remembered as Herbert Marcuse, for instance, but a case could be made that his impact within the R and A branch of the OSS was a good deal greater. On the projects committee, he played a significant part in determining what policy documents were circulated within Washington, including what would

---

[43] Ackerman, 'Geographic training, wartime research and immediate professional objectives', 1945, pp. 121–43; especially pp. 122, 127.

[44] Ibid., p. 124.

[45] Ibid., p. 137.

be seen by the President.[46] It was Hartshorne and his colleagues on the Committee who limited the members of the Frankfurt School to a subsidiary role, restricting them to the task of providing information which was ultimately crafted into more 'rigorous' reports by their American colleagues.

Hartshorne had entered the OSS as a rising star within geography as a result of the publication of his 1939 paper, *The Nature of Geography*. The immediate object of intense scrutiny, and an influential methodological statement in subsequent decades, *The Nature of Geography* still attracts attention including a golden jubilee retrospective.[47] It is now widely held that for the cohort of geographers that filled the burgeoning academic departments after 1945, Hartshorne's work was an already outmoded statement of exceptionalist principles, derived from Kant; Schaefer's 1953 critique of *The Nature of Geography* crystallized this opposition and issued a call for the reconstitution of geography as a nomothetic, spatial science.[48] In light of Hartshorne's OSS activities, however, this interpretation is wide of the mark. Hartshorne was clearly committed to a version of positivism, albeit developed via normative and internalist insights derived within geography itself rather than via philosophy.[49] His stance in the OSS was quite explicitly perceived as representative of objective science, and this explains his antipathy to the work of the Frankfurt personnel much more readily than would any vestiges of exceptionalism on his part. Although the divide between Hartshorne and Schaefer (and their proponents) within geography is widely accepted as a contest between an obsolete exceptionalism and emerging nomothetic research, it also concerned the *objects* of geographical research as well as the *methods*. Here too the war influenced intellectual activity: the global struggle served to downplay the importance of places and peoples, who were swept back and forth with little regard to their individuality. They were replaced in importance by broad ideologies and processes, not least of which was the imperative of post-war economic reconstruction.

Far from detracting from his academic career, Hartshorne's war work cemented his reputation within the profession. He was one of the most senior of the large cohort of geographers in Washington who became very influential in the discipline. For example, the war period saw the emergence of a new geographical organization – The American Society for Professional

---

[46] Anyone interested in taxonomy *à la* Foucault (see, for instance, his preface to the *Order of Things*), should note the structural charts of R and A branch organization (reproduced in Katz, *Foreign Intelligence*, 1989, pp. 242–3). *All* documents had to pass through the hands of the projects committee before they could receive any official designation and be routed to the President or other war departments.

[47] Entrikin and Brunn, (eds) *Reflections on Richard Hartshorne's 'The Nature of Geography'*, 1989.

[48] Schaefer, 'Exceptionalism in geography', 1953, pp. 226–49. See also Morrill, 'Recollections of the "Quantitative Revolution's" early years', 1984, pp. 57–72.

[49] Lukermann describes this as a 'liberal positivist' position: Lukermann, in Entrikin and Brunn, (eds) *Reflections*, pp. 53–68.

Geographers (ASPG) – and its creation neatly captures the distinctions drawn by Ackerman. The ASPG represented an explicit challenge to the Association of American Geographers (AAG), a tiny, elite club of elected members constituting one of the smallest academic professional bodies in the country.[50] AAG membership was supposed to reflect status within the profession and a commensurate publication record. Only this elite had the right to publish in the *Annals*, and the notion of 'right' can be taken literally; refereeing of papers was purely advisory and non-binding.[51] The large, professional cohort in wartime Washington was, for the most part, working in high status positions and using professional skills, but was still unable to interact via the AAG. In consequence, members of this group created the American Society for Geographical Research in 1943, and this in turn became the ASPG. By 1948, there were over 1000 members, who were represented by a complex system of regional officers and a new journal with a significant name, *The Professional Geographer*. The success of the new organization was total; although the AAG had the mandarins, many of those no longer operated within the organization.[52] In confirmation of this unequal contest between tradition and modernity, the ASPG effectively received the surrender of the AAG in 1948, as the latter was folded into the ASPG organization. It is quite indicative that the first president of the new organization – which maintained the name, but little else of the AAG – was Richard Hartshorne. Although he had in no way encouraged the formation of the ASPG, his employment in Washington, coupled with his recent academic eminence, allowed him to straddle the old and the new ages.[53] He was the new Everyman, forged in war.

CONTEMPORARY GEOGRAPHY AND WARFARE

The two global conflicts of the twentieth century shaped American geography in distinct ways, and provided a legacy of objective and instrumental research. To bring this story up to the present would involve a lengthy essay dealing with numerous complex questions.[54] The most central of these is

[50] James and Martin, *The Association of American Geographers*, 1978, p. 98. The AAG had only 167 members in 1941.

[51] There seems something Kafkaesque about a professional association that required publication as a mark of eligibility but restricted the right to publish to those already elected.

[52] The disciplinary history by James and Martin reports somewhat acidly that by this period, neither Barrows, Bowman nor Sauer had attended an AAG meeting in over a decade, op. cit., p. 107.

[53] In fact, Hartshorne had been the object of much criticism as a symbol of the self-perpetuation of the AAG; correspondence of the period shows that both James and Hartshorne were seen as active in the defence of the elite membership model.

[54] The official history of the AAG is of little assistance in this, although it manages to find almost one page to discuss the development of military geography classes for the

the way in which war has been transformed into both a commonplace and a direct reality for most people, while in the USA war has receded to a distance. As its visibility diminished, so have our abilities to grasp the realities of war. Within the discipline this fed the demise of political geography after 1945. Although the bi-polar world order possessed obvious geopolitical structures, there existed a massive silence on this within geography.[55] A number of factors contributed to this, including the close and very public links between *Geopolitik* and the doctrines of National Socialism, that appeared to diminish the ability of geographers to continue to develop geopolitical thinking in other contexts (although, paradoxically, the equally public links between central place theory and the Nazi's forced resettlement of the Ukraine seemed to have had little academic impact).[56]

More important has been the repositioning of the concept of strategy within the discourse of foreign policy. From George Kennan's blueprints of containment onwards, the image of the bi-polar world has been central to American policy, and spatial concepts such as domino theory have been embedded within this image. Crucially, however, analyses of foreign policy have been developed within the field of international relations rather than geography, and it is political scientists such as Kissinger and Kirkpatrick who have played central roles in policy formulation. The appropriation of this role by international relations experts represents a division of academic labour between political science and geography. Political geographers of the stature of Bowman, or even Hartshorne, no longer exist and are no longer represented within government.[57] Instead, their more traditional skills as cartographers for the state have been re-emphasized, albeit in dramatically different ways. The process of surveillance has been passed over to orbiting satellites, so that the panopticon is now truly global in extent. The processing of spatial imagery has become a crucial element in warfare, and the United States Department of Defense has invested heavily in this technology. For instance, the Defense Mapping Agency (DMA) has spent in excess of $2.6 billion since 1982 on a 'Data Integration/Segment' programme. This has involved the creation of an automated system that coordinates the needs of the armed forces in terms of maps and charts, and over 7000 people are employed in this project alone.[58] The DMA recruits actively within 200 US universities, and is a significant employer of students with automated cartography, remote sensing and Geographic Information Systems training.

General Staff school at Leavenworth and political geography for the Air Force ROTC, James and Martin, op. cit., p. 137.

[55] This is well discussed by Dalby, *Creating the Second Cold War*, 1990.

[56] Kristof, 'The origins and evolution of geopolitics', 1960, pp. 15–51.

[57] My exclusion of Demko, formerly of the State Department, is deliberate: his comments on geopolitics can be read in 'Geography beyond the ivory tower', 1988, pp. 575–9.

[58] Correspondence, Defense Mapping Agency, 30 October, 1990.

It is hardly coincidental that these are the largest specialty groups within the Association of American Geographers. [59]

CONCLUSION

I began this chapter with a quotation from Yves Lacoste, which asserts that geography serves to wage war. Peter Gould is correct to respond that 'to label geography a discipline whose major purpose is to wage war is, to my mind, quite absurd.'[60] At the very least, there has long been a tradition of humanist and pacifist work within the discipline, and a strong wing of critical analysis, within which this volume can be placed. What I have aimed to do here is to emphasize the impact that war has had upon American geography, and the ways in which armed conflicts have provided the settings within which specific kinds of intellectual development have taken place. In particular, I want to rescue the links between geography and the expansion of the territorial state – while these have been closely examined with respect to the Victorian era, little has been said about the contemporary discipline and its instrumental links. As I have shown here, these connections are strong, for as Gould reminds us, 'geography (using the word rather broadly), must enter into military strategy – it always has, and presumably always will.'[61] Let us hope that we need never again invert this statement, in order to echo the assertions of an earlier era, when it was proclaimed that 'war has been one of the greatest geographers.'[62]

[59] The four largest specialty groups within the AAG in 1992 were: GIS–962 members; urban–759; cartography–673; and remote sensing–489. It may not be surprising that there has only been one effort within the AAG to investigate links between geographical science and government intelligence agencies 'for clarification of the legitimate and illegitimate roles which may occur in such associations'. It was overturned by popular vote of the membership: James and Martin, op. cit., p. 162.

[60] Gould, *The Geographer at Work*, 1985, especially p. 166.

[61] Ibid., pp. 161–2.

[62] Goldie, 'Geographical ideals', 1907, pp. 1–14; cited and quoted in Stoddart, 'Geography and war', especially p. 88.

16

The Colonization of Geographic Thought: The South African Experience

Harold M. Wesso

The existence of geography in South Africa, both as a school subject and as a university discipline, is fundamentally linked to the contribution it could make to schooling during the period of British colonial rule. In South Africa, education has developed in a unique manner because of particular political–economic developments and can, therefore, not be divorced from a broader understanding of the history of the South African state. Two distinct periods through which the state has developed can be identified: a period of colonialism (1652–1910) and a post-Union (1910–) period. The period of colonialism can again be divided into two phases: the Dutch occupation of the Cape (1652–1806) and the period of British control (1806–1910). Likewise, the post-Union state has evolved through several phases: the period until 1948, when the National Party came to power and the apartheid state was established and the current transitional phase in which apartheid is being dismantled. Much of what we regard as our educational system today is derived from the way the country was colonized and from the social pressures initiated by colonization.

Education during the colonial period was, initially, characterized by the central place of moral–religious principles in Dutch/Boer education, and later, the anglicization of education under British rule. Of particular importance during the latter period, was the inculcation of empire sentiments. Empire education was seen to be important for two reasons: 1) to bolster Britain's world position by reinforcing the unity of the empire; and 2) to inculcate in young people, especially the Afrikaner, an acceptance of their political position under British rule.

In the aftermath of the Anglo–Boer War (1899–1902) the British authorities realized that people could not be ruled by political force alone, but that the control of ideas played an equally important role. It was also necessary to colonize the minds of people, and the best way the ideology of empire could be promoted, was to harness the educational system. Geography, as a school subject, was seen to be an important medium through which imperial ideology could be inculcated in the minds of young people, and it was, therefore, moulded to serve the needs of the colonial rulers. This emphasized the socially produced nature of geographical knowledge. Geography was made, not only in a physical and spatial sense, but it was also made in the mind.

Very little research has been done on the history of geography in South Africa. Especially in the present context of de-colonization, it is necessary also to de-colonize our minds, and this begins with an understanding of how current thinking came to be. We cannot effect a process of change without first knowing how changes came about in the past. This chapter is mainly concerned with the institutionalization of geography in South Africa and in particular the process by which ideas, geographical ideas or ideas about geography, were imposed on people in order to justify imperialism. Firstly, the chapter endeavours to show how, with the intensification of British imperialist influence during the nineteenth century, geography was seen to be an important instrument in establishing British hegemonic control. Secondly, it is suggested that the changing educational environment in South Africa during the early years of this century, prompted by socio-economic and political transformation, provided the basis for continuous British influence in geographical discourse and that this led to the introduction of the 'new' geography and, eventually, the establishment of geography as an academic discipline. Thirdly, it is argued that the study of geography has always been a white man's domain, and that it conveniently served to teach blacks their place in society. In the light of the growing debate regarding the de-colonization of education and scientific discourse in South Africa, this chapter will also, in conclusion, briefly reflect on the de-colonization of geography.

EMPIRE EDUCATION AND THE ROLE OF GEOGRAPHY AS A SCHOOL SUBJECT

Geography was granted official status in the curriculum for the elementary classes when the Cape Education Department was established in 1839.[1] The inclusion of geography in the curriculum was regarded as important, not only in view of the contribution it could make to a more 'liberal education' in South Africa, but also because it was seen to be relevant as

---

[1] The Cape Education Department was established with the white colonists in mind. Black education was left to various missionary societies.

far as the inculcation of empire sentiments in young people was concerned. The geography which was taught was largely physical. The only human geography was topographical, and factual in content.

However, during the mid-nineteenth century, geography was not highly regarded as a secondary school subject in the schools of the Cape Colony.[2] Secondary geography did not exist although geography of secondary standard was offered by the Board of Public Examiners in Literature and Science (previously the Cape Public Service Board) in 1858. It was an optional subject for the Public Service Certificate and after 1863 was included for the Third Class Certificate in Literature and Science. The certificate was designed to correspond to the matriculation examination of London University. In 1873 the examining powers of the Board were transferred to the newly-constituted University of the Cape of Good Hope, which was modelled on the University of London, and geography was gradually phased out as a subject for the University examinations. From 1901 geography was no longer prescribed for the secondary examinations of the university and was, accordingly, relegated to a position of utter neglect in the secondary sphere of Cape education.[3]

Comparable information on the teaching of geography in the other territories (Natal, The Orange Free State, and Transvaal) is not readily available. It could, however, be argued that the nature and content of the geography which was taught in the Cape Colony was merely duplicated in these territories.[4] Of particular importance is the more explicit emphasis that was placed on empire geography[5] in Natal since 1877, and in the Orange Free State and the Zuid Afrikaanse Republiek, since the end of the Anglo–Boer War. The teaching of empire geography should not be seen in isolation. It was part of the overall strategy of the colonial authority to anglicize society and to portray South Africa as part of the British Empire. Its role in frontier expansion, to conquer and civilize the wilderness, was also clearly realized. In 1887, *The Educational Times*,[6] expressed its astonishment at the vanishing of geography from university programmes, realizing the contribution it could make to exploration in Africa.

Despite the peripheral status of geography, i.e., as a subject for elementary school only, the educational authorities remained convinced of the value of geographical education. During the Edwardian period, more than previously, imperial sentiment in Britain and abroad was systematically promoted and mobilized.[7] At the forefront of the 'imperial studies movement'

---

[2] Levy, *Geography Teaching in South African Schools for Whites, c.1800–1980*, 1984.

[3] Knox, *The Historical Development of Geography*, 1958.

[4] Levy, *Geography Teaching*, 1984.

[5] 'Empire geography' consisted of lessons and geographical descriptions of Britain, as a colonial power, and its overseas possessions. The geography of the empire was taught mainly to promote the unity of the empire.

[6] Anon., 'Editorial', 1887, p. 56.

[7] Greenlee, *Education and Imperial Unity*, 1987.

were three London-based imperial societies: the League of the Empire, the
Victoria League, and the Royal Colonial Institute. Both the League of the
Empire and the Victoria League were very active in South Africa, where
the subsequent re-establishment of geography teaching occurred within the
context of the development of the discipline in Europe. There the study and
the teaching of geography was, according to Hudson,[8] vigorously promoted
during the latter part of the nineteenth century, largely to serve the interests
of imperialism in its various aspects including territorial acquisitions, economic exploitation, militarism and the practice of class and race domination.
In the colonies, however, education in general and geographical education
in particular had to respond to imperialism in a very specific way. The
context for geography's contribution to 'empire education' was clearly outlined by Lt.-Colonel H. Elsdale of Natal, in 1895. While complimenting
the London School Board on its efforts in promoting empire education, he
suggested, that all colonies should follow this example and so

> ... widen the horizon of their children, and train them adequately
> for their future duties ... Thus, while England is careful to train her
> children to a better knowledge of each distant colony and its needs,
> the colonies should apply themselves to learn more of the position and
> requirements of England, and of the great question [of federation, see
> below] which must largely determine her future, and vitally affect the
> fortunes of all her colonies in the coming century.[9]

Elsdale proposed a rough curriculum which included the following main
themes:

A – The position of the South African Colonies under Responsible
      Government
   – The more general position and interests of the Cape Colony and Natal
   – The British power elsewhere in Africa

B – The position of England in relation to free trade
   – The grave responsibilities of England
   – The past position of England at the centre of gravity
   – The position of England in relation to the war between Japan and
      China

C – The present position of the continent of Europe
   – The position of various countries in Western Europe
   – The position of the United States

D – The great question of the federation of the Empire.

[8] Hudson, 'The new geography and the new imperialism', 1977.
[9] Elsdale, 'Higher Education', 1895, p. 236.

According to Elsdale, addressing such issues was of vital importance to the future of the British Empire, and could powerfully influence the future of the whole human race. The subjects Elsdale regarded as most suitable for the purpose were geography and history. Regarding the role of geography, he noted:

> Much can be done by an intelligent teaching of geography. For it will be noted that a great deal of the ground above is covered by, and comes properly within the province of an enlightened geography lesson. Thereby the dry bones of geography will be clothed with a much more attractive skin, and the geography lesson will become far more interesting to the boys, and will be much better assimilated and remembered. [10]

Similar sentiments were also expressed in the annual report of the Council of the Royal Colonial Institute in 1898, namely, that,

> ... they were deeply impressed with the fact that it is incumbent on the greatest and most successful colonising nation of the world to impart to the rising generation a full and accurate knowledge of geography, more especially as regards the British possessions. [11]

The Royal Colonial Institute was never directly involved in promoting the teaching of geography in South Africa. However, it was very supportive of the geography department at the University of Oxford and in particular the establishment of The Geographical Association, and its official organ, *The Geographical Teacher*, both of which were influential in South Africa. [12] During the early twentieth century, *The Geographical Teacher* became the sole medium on which the Cape Education Department based its conception of geography. Many articles in this journal were, for example, reprinted in local journals such as *The Education Gazette* (published by the government's Department of Education) and *The Educational News* (the official organ of the South African Teachers Association). Teachers were also regularly urged to subscribe to *The Geographical Teacher*, and the Cape Education Department was even prepared to subsidize subscription fees.

After the Anglo–Boer War, the inculcation in school children of a single-minded loyalty to British rule, emerged as a very high educational priority. The promotion of this was seen as the first object of all education, especially in the new territories. It was regarded as the duty of the state to devote its attention first and foremost to fashioning a loyal and contented population. According to two historians, the purpose of early twentieth-century education

---

[10] Ibid., p. 238.
[11] Andrews, 'Geography and empire education', 1900, p. 103.
[12] Ibid.

was '... to win over the young generation of Dutch Afrikaners to English ways of thought and speech, [and to get them to understand] the greatness of the English Imperial Idea'.[13] The Anglo–Boer War could have played a major role in the establishment of patriotic societies such as the League of the Empire (1901), as the moral credibility of the imperial idea was clearly at stake. Britain had suffered heavy continental criticism, argues Greenlee, 'because this was a war waged not against Zulus or Afghans, who could, it was held, be expected to profit by the imposition of white rule, but against the European inhabitants of two small nation states.'[14]

Geography responded positively to the idea of empire education, and many lessons on the British Empire were included in the school geography syllabuses. A full year was set aside for the geography of the empire in the pupil-teachers' course, and textbooks for use in schools were regularly suggested in *The Education Gazette* and in *The Educational News*. Some of the more popular books included:

The Royal Wall Atlas for South African schools (the Atlas for Stage VII, dealt with the British Empire)
For junior classes: Parkin's Round the Empire
For senior classes: Nelson's Royal Osborne Geography Reader (book VI).

According to an article in *De Unie* (1906) children were taught, from a very early age, that everything painted red on the world map belonged to the British Empire, and that all other areas were treated as if they were unknown and occupied by savages.[15]

While positive attitudes regarding the empire had to be inculcated, there was a parallel need to justify the Anglo–Boer War. Information provided in textbooks, for example Gill's 'Students' Geography', was generally used to create positive images of the English, while the Afrikaners were portrayed as inhuman. The English were presented as the freers of slaves, while the Afrikaners indulged in the killing of blacks. The annexation of the Boer Republics was, therefore, justified, because the Boers were killing blacks, and the war was a necessary punishment for disobedient subjects.[16]

The importance of geography, as far as empire education is concerned, is also reflected in the introduction of the Duke and Duchess Prize for geography which was instituted following the visit of King George V. Money for an endowment fund was made available after the visit for the purchase of school prizes in the Cape Town area. The prizes commemorated the royal visit, and were given for proficiency in an examination on the 'geography of the empire'. These prizes were later combined with the Victoria League prizes for history and geography.

[13] Behr and MacMillan, *The History of Education*, 1966, p. 165.
[14] Greenlee, *Education and Imperial Unity*, 1987, p. 10.
[15] Anon., 'Vakman', 1906, p. 21.
[16] Anon., 'Zo Leren onze Jongelieden Aardrijkskunde', 1908, pp. 385–6.

A major role of geography was, therefore, to foster among the public, particularly the Afrikaners, an acceptance of their status as part of the British Empire. The representation of British interests as universal, constituted a significant component of geographical education. At this very early stage in its development in South Africa, geography, through this assumption of universality, abstracted itself from society. It thereby failed to account for the social relations within the broader society, and by doing so contributed to obscuring current systems of dominations. Marx's theorem that '... the ideas of the ruling class are in every epoch the ruling ideas',[17] is very appropriate in this regard. A concern with sectional interests, introduced into geography a clear ideological component which was enhanced by the distortion of communication. 'Facts' were presented to suit the interests of the English.

Although the Boers protested vehemently against the anglicization of society in general, and the way geography was taught, school geography remained committed to the British ideology of empire, well into the second decade. A major portion of the first syllabus for the matriculation certificate, drafted in 1913, consisted of the geography of the British Empire. In the meantime, however, other needs had also developed within the broader society and these demanded a philosophical and methodological reorientation of geography.

THE CHANGING ROLE OF GEOGRAPHY: INTRODUCTION OF THE 'NEW' GEOGRAPHY

By the turn of the century, various other demands came to be placed on the educational system. It was increasingly realized that in order to facilitate industrial and commercial development in a very competitive world, the development of science would be of paramount importance. This clearly echoed a more general concern with efficiency in British society at the time. Those who were concerned with linking education and imperial unity, according to Greenlee,[18] also took a keen interest in the promotion of scientific education for the sake of efficiency. The two priorities, imperial unity and efficiency were therefore not seen as mutually exclusive, but as two sides of the same coin.

The quest for science education placed a heavy responsibility on the shoulders of those who advocated the necessity of geography in the school curriculum. What follows is a brief outline of the process by which 'modern and scientific' geography was introduced to serve the 'other' needs of colonial society.

The introduction of modern, scientific geography in South Africa dates back to the early years of this century, deeply rooted in the British tradition

---

[17] Marx and Engels, *The German Ideology*, 1970, p. 64.
[18] Greenlee, *Educational and Imperial Unity*, 1987, p. xiv.

of that time. The need for scientific and modern geography, culminated in the publication, in *The Education Gazette*,[19] of the 'syllabus of instruction in geography' produced under the auspices of the Royal Geographical Society in Britain. The Department of Education regarded it as such an important document, that the permission of the Royal Geographical Society was asked to reprint the syllabuses for both the elementary and the higher examinations. The 'man–environment relationship' was presented as fundamental to an understanding of the nature and scope of geography, and this undoubtedly set the scene for the future development of geography in South Africa.

The teaching of geography was further nourished by the establishment of a geographical society in 1905. In September of that year Dr A. J. Herbertson, then Reader in Geography at the University of Oxford, visited the country as the Honorary Secretary of the British Geographical Association. Dr Herbertson addressed a specially convened meeting with the purpose of discussing the advisability of starting a branch of the Association in South Africa.[20] The Geographical Association sought to unite teachers in different parts of the empire in a common effort to further the principles of geographical education, and after the address a resolution was carried that a branch of the association be formed. The establishment of the South African branch of the Geographical Association was welcomed by the Department of Education, but it was short-lived. It ceased to exist in 1907 and its membership transferred to the parent association, furthering direct British influence in the development of geography in South Africa.

Nevertheless, in retrospect, it is evident that Herbertson's visit to South Africa and the establishment of the South African branch of the Geographical Association provided the necessary impetus for the development of geography on modern and scientific lines. This was reflected in the contents of various articles and documents published in *The Education Gazette*. In 1906, for example, *The Education Gazette*, carried an extensive commentary on a British document concerning 'suggestions for teaching geography'.[21] *The Education Gazette* (and by implication the Department of Education) was highly impressed by the document which, it felt, was '... inspired by broad views of the great educational value of the subject even in the elementary school course'.[22] The 'suggestions' reflected the 'new' geography debate in Britain. The following definition of geography was highlighted in the above mentioned commentary:

Geography is concerned with the earth's surface, the condition of its various parts, their relations to one another, and the influence of those conditions and relations on plant life, on animal life and specially on human life.[23]

[19] Anon., 'Syllabus for instruction in geography', 1901.
[20] Anon., 'A geography association for South Africa', 1905.
[21] Anon., 'Suggestions for teachers', 1906, pp. 622–3.
[22] Ibid., p. 622.
[23] Ibid., p. 622.

The British document also provided the Education Department with the ideal opportunity of relating geography to the changing educational environment in South Africa. It was gradually realized that the teaching of science subjects in South Africa should occupy a more prominent place in the school curriculum, and the opportunity was grasped to show how geography could contribute to the mental and intellectual development of the child. The 'suggestions' were employed to give support and authority to some of the principles laid down for the teaching of geography in South Africa. The 'new' geography had, therefore, finally arrived in South Africa towards the end of the first decade of this century.

The idea of a 'new' geography was later taken up by *The Educational News*, which was clearly most impressed by the latest developments in the discipline:

> A great deal of attention is now-a-days being directed to the teaching of geography. The old days of cram are rapidly passing away, and thanks largely to the geographical and similar associations, people are recognising that geography, scientifically taught, can be made an excellent mental training.[24]

To underline this 'modern spirit' in geography, *The Educational News* published in full the new syllabus in Geography for the Elementary School Teachers' Certificate (for 1909) of the Education Department in England. The syllabus included elements of mathematical and astronomical geography, physical geography (climate and geomorphology) and natural regions. Much attention was also given to the geography of the British Isles, Europe and the British colonies.

The first concrete step to implement the new ideas and concepts in geography, came about with the establishment of a committee by the South African Teachers Association in 1910. They were charged to develop a scheme for the 'revision of the syllabus in geography'.[25] The committee's conception of geography was distinctly determinist. As a basis for their own work they adopted, verbatim, the definition of geography in the British 'suggestions for teaching geography', reported in *The Education Gazette* in 1906. The scheme was eventually adopted by the Cape Division of the Teachers' Association, but not throughout the country. The Education Department felt that it would have created chaos since the teachers were not adequately trained to teach the 'new' geography. Instead, it was decided to introduce the 'new' geography on the level of the third year senior pupil-teachers' course.

---

[24] Anon., 'Editorial', 1908.
[25] Anon., 'Suggestions for the teaching of geography', 1910, pp. 47–50.

ENVIRONMENTAL DETERMINISM: A CONCEPTUAL FRAMEWORK FOR
GEOGRAPHY AS AN ACADEMIC DISCIPLINE

Since the Herbertson visit, and the establishment of the South African
branch of the Geographical Association, various geography enthusiasts took
it on their shoulders to promote and facilitate the academic debate regarding
geography in South Africa. With the necessary support from the Education
Department, these enthusiasts became the main advocates for academic geography in the pre-academic phase. The first academic contribution to the
debate came from James Flowers.[26] In a paper delivered at a meeting of
the South African Association for the Advancement of Science, Flowers
addressed the question of 'geography as a factor in higher education', focusing broadly on the nature of the discipline. His main objective was to
stimulate an interest in geography's claims for inclusion in the curricula of
the colleges and the University of the Cape of Good Hope. As a working
hypothesis, he suggested that 'geography is the science which details the
earth's dictation to life'. Flowers quoted freely from the work of prominent
British geographers such as Herbertson, Mill and Sir Clement R. Markham.
The work of writers such as these was also used to generate the necessary
support for the introduction of geography in higher education.

Towards the middle of the first decade of the twentieth century, the
teaching of geography was becoming more and more the work of specialists.
This served as additional motivation for the geography enthusiasts, like
A. Ritter, J. Jamieson, and J. Hutcheon, to pressure the university authorities
to introduce geography as an academic discipline.

Geographical research was never a priority. The discipline was rather
promoted in terms of its status overseas and the contribution it could make
to general education within South Africa. However it was gradually realized
that, in order to make a 'scientific' impact, geographical research and not
simply teaching would have to be put on the agenda. In his address in 1915
to the South African Association for the Advancement of Science, Hutcheon
divulged details of 'several men' who had already formed themselves into
the nucleus of a Geographical Society, with their main aim to consider the
preparation of South African geographical monographs.[27]

Hutcheon himself became increasingly involved in developing ideas for
the study of local geography, and was particularly interested in aspects of
climatic control:

The true sphere of the geographer is the study of man's relation
to his environment, both 'passively' and 'actively', and of all the
geographic controls which constitute that environment, e.g. position,

---

[26] Flowers, 'Geography as a factor in higher education', 1905–6, pp. 213–14.
[27] Hutcheon, 'Geography', 1915.

elevation, area, distance from the sea, rivers, configuration, surface-imposition and climate, the last is the most important.[28]

The importance of climatic control was also emphasized in his paper to the South African Association for the Advancement of Science: 'Of all the external modifying forces which influence mankind, there is little doubt but that climate is, in the main, responsible for the different stages of his physical, mental and moral development.'[29] The focus on climate is significant given its larger role in contemporary environmental determinist ideology which legitimated supposed European superiority in the struggle for survival:

... it was a widely-held view that the character and achievements of the peoples of the world were largely determined by physical or 'geographical' factors, especially climate. The supposed superiority of the European and their descendants in suitable environments overseas had been determined by Nature which had also condemned less fortunate peoples to inferior status. The white man, therefore, saw himself as the natural inheritor of the world's wealth and master of its peoples.[30]

Environmental or geographic determinism was, therefore, a significant ideological buttress for imperialism and racism,[31] and it found fertile breeding ground in South Africa after the establishment of Union in 1910, particularly in view of the concerted effort by the government to eradicate the British–Afrikaner divide in the South African society, and to replace it with a white–black divide. It is perhaps not too far fetched to argue that it was the environmentalist paradigm which rescued geography from its peripheral position within the South African educational system, and which gave it some respectability among academics. Until this time the university authorities and many school principals and teachers could not be convinced that geography was essentially scientific in nature. Many teachers of other subjects also felt threatened by the inclusion of geography in an already overcrowded curriculum. The 'new' geography, and environmental determinism in particular, provided the necessary scientific basis for geography and it was therefore more readily recognized as a science to be institutionalized within the South African context. But the new orientation paved the way for geography's incorporation as an institutionalized discipline in 1916 at The University of the Cape of Good Hope and as a subject for the Matriculation Certificate in 1918. The syllabuses for both the BA Pass Examination and the Matriculation Certificate were clearly in the mould of the environmental determinist philosophy:

[28] Hutcheon, 'Some aspects of climatic control', 1915, p. 74.
[29] Hutcheon, 'Geography', 1915, p. 328.
[30] Hudson, 'The new geography and the new imperialism', 1977, p. 17.
[31] See also, Peet, 'The social origins of environmental determinism', 1985.

FIRST SYLLABUS FOR THE BA PASS EXAMINATION OF THE UNIVERSITY OF THE CAPE OF GOOD HOPE (1916)

First Paper
   Astronomic basis of geography
   Meteorology
   Climatology
   Physiography

Second Paper
   Biogeography
   Anthropogeography and Ethnology
   Social and economic conditions and their dependence upon the physiographic environment
   Political and commercial geography of a selected area
   History of geographical discovery in outline

Practical Examination

SYLLABUS IN GEOGRAPHY FOR MATRICULATION EXAMINATION (1918)

THEORY

A 1 The earth as a part of the solar system
   2 Distribution of land and water
   3 Climatology. General knowledge of the distribution of vegetable and animal life: natural regions
   4 The races of mankind and their chief characteristics; distribution of population; human activities and their relation to geographical environment. Commercial products and the conditions affecting their production and distribution

   (Candidates will be expected to make a practical study of their own districts in relation to the various points dealt with above)

B 1 A general knowledge of the geography of the various continents
   2 The geography of Africa south of the Zambezi in detail

PRACTICAL

The principles on which these syllabuses were based provided the context for geography courses in South Africa (except, to a certain extent, the geography courses at the University of Cape Town) until the late 1960s. Environmental determinism could conveniently explain the dynamics of a racist society. White supremacy, and economic exploitation of blacks in particular, could be justified. This, initially, also served British imperialist needs inside South Africa. The institutionalization of geography as an academic discipline in South Africa should, therefore, be seen as a result of a process in which the needs of society, on the one hand, and the international developments in the nature and scope of the discipline, on the other hand, played an important role. The syllabuses established at South African universities were largely a duplication of what was offered at British schools and universities. The British influence was further entrenched by the fact that many of the academics who were responsible for the teaching of the discipline during the early years, were either British in origin or received part of their geographical education at British universities.

While Afrikaners largely rejected 'empire education' in the British mould, they could identify with environmental determinist geography. The Hebertsonian concept of 'natural regions', for example, became the hallmark of Afrikaner geography in the early decades of the twentieth century.[32] It was, however, not until the late thirties that a specifically Afrikanerized geography emerged. In July 1939, at a congress for Christelik–Nasionale Onderwys (CNO – or Christian National Education), organized by the Federation of Afrikaans Cultural Organizations (a Broederbond[33] offshoot), strategies were discussed to counteract the Hertzog government's plans for dual-medium education. These plans were seen as a renewed attempt to Anglicize Afrikaner children. The congress set up an Institute (ICNO) to investigate issues concerning Afrikaner education. In 1948 the ICNO issued a report in which geography featured very prominently. Fundamental to the report was the recognition of Christian–Nationalist principles in education, i.e., that nationalism ought to be rooted in Christianity, and that a love for one's own language, history and culture should be instilled in the Afrikaner. Concerning the content of education, the report urged that there should be no anti-Christian or non-Christian or anti-Nationalist or non-Nationalist propaganda.

Geography turned out to be one of four core subjects identified by the ICNO. The other three were religious teaching, the mother-tongue, and history. Concerning the content of geography the report stated:

---

[32] Nel, *Die Natuurstreke van die Wêreld*, n.d.

[33] The Broederbond (Association of Brothers) was established in 1918. It was a secret society which has gradually come to assume a dominant position in the affairs of the Afrikaner. Its general mode of operation has been to coordinate activities among Afrikaners and to ensure that members were placed in key positions which can then be utilized for the advancement of the Afrikaner.

Every nation is rooted in a country (Landsbodem) allotted to it by God. Geography should aim at giving the pupil a thorough knowledge of his own country and the natural objects pertaining to it, in such a way that he will love his own country, also when compared and contrasted with others, and be ready to defend it, preserve it from poverty, and improve it for posterity.[34]

The above pertained to white education only, and was meant to include English speakers as well as Afrikaners. As far as blacks were concerned, education was to be based on trusteeship, non-equality, and segregation; its aim was to inculcate the white man's view of life, especially that of the Boer nation, conceived as the senior trustee. An assumption implicit in the ICNO report was that the worldview of the Broederbond was to be imposed on the rest of the population. Although spokespersons for the newly elected nationalist government tried after 1948 to distance themselves from the report, Bunting argues that the government itself proceeded with the implementation of the CNO programme almost to the letter.

GEOGRAPHY AND BLACK EDUCATION

Whilst the Afrikaners were seriously engaged in the de-colonization of education, and with it geography, *vis-à-vis* British control after 1948, they were at the same time ready to impose an extraordinary re-colonization of black South Africa and the black mind. The development of apartheid brought not only a new system of social controls along race lines and new social fissures, but also a new brand of racial ideology. This involved a re-colonization of the mind, asymmetrically organized between blacks and whites. Education was restructured and if environmental determinism remained central to geography, the stage was nevertheless set for a reoriented 'apartheid geography'.

The Government Memorandum on Education of 1839 stipulated a system of public instruction with the white colonists in mind. Elementary education for those who were not white was left to the various missionary societies. At most of the mission stations pupils were taught, apart from religious instruction, basic skills and a little handiwork. No set courses of instruction were followed, though there are indications that some form of geography was taught. When the nationalist government took control of black education, the contents of subjects, like geography were simply based on the syllabuses that were in use in white schools.

With the passing of the Extension of University Education Act in 1959, for the first time provision was made for non-white universities. Except

[34] Quoted in Bunting, *The Rise of the South African Reich*, 1986, p. 246.

for the University of Fort Hare, all black universities,[35] which were established during the 1960s, originated as constituent colleges of the University of South Africa, all of which had Broederbond principals. Most of the lecturers appointed to the departments of geography at the black university colleges were graduates from the University of Stellenbosch or one of the other Afrikaner universities, and most had close links with the Afrikaner establishment.[36] The result was that black students were confronted with a geography with strong ideological and environmental determinist undertones. They had to learn about and repeat their inferiority in relation to whites. This kind of education was perpetuated when they graduated as teachers and they had to teach from textbooks written by white South Africans. In this way geography contributed to the colonization of the black mind.

THE DE-COLONIZATION OF GEOGRAPHY

Much could be said and needs to be said about apartheid geography, but it is a large topic on which research is only beginning to be done. This work has been stimulated with the dismantling of formal apartheid, and comes as part of a larger agenda for the de-colonization of geography. This chapter concludes with a consideration of the current work in this area.

The late nineteenth- and early twentieth-century Eurocentric notion of geography is still deeply entrenched in the minds of many South African teachers and academics alike. The legacy of that period remains in terms of philosophy, ethnocentrism, racism, and support for state activities expressed in geographical education. But apartheid is crumbling at the edges, and this has provoked a consideration of the de-colonization of the geographic mind.

In the late 1960s and early 70s the overt environmental determinist focus of university geography syllabuses was largely replaced by a conception of geography as a spatial science, inspired by developments within the discipline, especially in the United States of America. Geography as a spatial science was in various ways supportive of a utilitarian geography that still buttressed a society built on inequalities of race, class and gender. It was largely a dehumanized and depoliticized geography – to such an extent that it tended to become irrelevant as an academic and political endeavour in which the oppressed of South Africa could engage. Various attempts have been made to address the consequent sterility of recent geographic discourse in South Africa. In 1982, McCarthy[37] invited geographers to engage in

---

[35] During the 1960s several universities were established to cater to the needs of the various non-white ethnic groups: four universities for African students, one for Indians, and one for so-called 'coloureds'.

[36] Blacks had no part in either the institutionalization of geography or the establishment of the discipline at South African universities.

[37] McCarthy, 'Radical geography, mainstream geography and southern Africa', 1982.

critical (Marxist) debate. There was no substantial response. Others ventured to initiate relevant research projects, mostly informed by liberal perspectives regarding the socio-economic and political reality of the South African situation.[38]

Recently, some geographers have specifically considered the de-colonization of geography, but mainly in terms of a 'relevant' research agenda.[39] Others have tried to focus on the extent to which the 'masses', the 'people', or the 'oppressed' could contribute to a decolonized geographic discourse, or how they could be empowered to produce their own geographies.[40] Nothing substantial has crystallized as yet.

The colonization process has been varied and very complex and the de-colonization process will have to be equally rich. The oppressed in South Africa were never permitted a concerted geographic voice. They were colonized into the belief that geography mattered not to them, that geography was made by whites, for whites. Any contribution to the de-colonization of education, and scientific discourse, generally, will have to be tied to a consideration of the contribution we could make to critical thinking and empowerment. Two aspects seem to be of fundamental importance: 1) geography will have to be Africanized, and 2) the current conception of geographical space will have to be reconsidered. Since an exhaustive discussion of this topic is beyond the scope of this chapter, only a brief review of the issue is given.

For imperialism, white domination and capitalist exploitation to flourish, the colonized, the dominated, and the exploited had to be alienated from their indigenous culture and their past. The educational system was the most appropriate means to establish cultural and political hegemony, and geography had a crucial role to play in this regard. While South African society is currently in a process of radical transformation, geography will have to be radically transformed as well. Euro-American theoretical constructs will have to be carefully scrutinized and critically evaluated. The influences of western society, imperialism and racism have been so entrenched in the South African lifestyle that most of the valuable aspects of African culture and experience have been undermined. The South Africa geographical environment (both human and physical), and geographical space and spatial phenomena in particular, are generally interpreted in terms of the legacy of imperialism and apartheid.[41] Such interpretations are also rooted in theories and philosophies developed in western, developed countries.

The de-colonization of geography in South Africa involves a deliberate effort to Africanize the discipline and to empower people geographically.

[38] For a review of literature see: Rogerson and Parnell, 'Fostered by the laager', 1989.

[39] For example: Crush, Reitsma and Rogerson, 'Decolonising the human geography of Southern Africa', 1982, pp. 197–8; Wellings, 'Geography and development studies in Southern Africa', 1986.

[40] Crush, 'Towards a people's historical geography for South Africa', 1986; Wesso, *People's education*, 1989; Wesso, *The colonisation of geography in South Africa*, 1991.

[41] Magi, *Geography in Society*, 1991.

This should form part of the great challenge to transform the established academic culture in order to meet the demands of a changing political and social environment and to reflect the changing power structure in society. The process of transformation within the South African context is denoted by the concept 'Africanization'. As far as geography is concerned, the institutional structures as well as the practice of geography are completely dominated and controlled by whites. The concept of 'Africanization' recognises the imperative of transforming, not only the institutional structures of the discipline of geography in South Africa, but also the nature and scope of the discipline so as to more accurately reflect the racial composition of the population. It is, however, not only about changing the racial composition of institutional structures, but also the curriculum and the whole way in which learning and teaching is organized. Geography and geographies have been socially produced to serve the needs of empire, capital and apartheid. People will have to empower themselves geographically and develop the conceptual tools in order to produce their own geographies. If the restructuring of apartheid space, for example, is regarded as important in a 'new' South Africa, the conceptualization of space needs to be seriously considered within the African context. Geographical space, like geographical knowledge, is socially produced, and is a direct result of material production. It is, however, more than this: the production of space 'also implies the production of the meaning, concepts and the consciousness of space which are inseparably linked to its physical production'. [42] Africanization, therefore, also means the geographical empowerment of the oppressed and disadvantaged in South Africa. People need to understand and realize their capacity to produce their own geographies. In this way a genuinely people's geography can be produced.

To conclude: it is suggested that an understanding of the history of geography in South Africa cannot be divorced from an understanding of the dynamics of the society in which it functions. The Anglicization, the Afrikanerization and the Americanization of geography, resulted in the total neglect of African needs and African culture. Any move to de-colonize geography in South Africa should involve the Africanization of the discipline and the geographical empowerment of the people. Precisely what this might mean and how it might be accomplished is a question of geographical practice as much as theory.

[42] Neil Smith, *Uneven Development*, 1984, p. 77.

17

Post-colonialism, De-colonization, and Geography

Jonathan Crush

> The project of decolonization involves ... a constant vigilance and a consistent transgression of the norms that facilitate, and control, the production of knowledge
> Robert Young, *White Mythologies*, 1990

INTRODUCTION

In his recent study of the 'white mythologies' of Anglo-Saxon scholarship, Robert Young argues that colonial discourse analysis is not a specialized activity reserved for minorities or for historians of imperialism and colonialism.[1] Rather, it constitutes a fundamental point of departure for questioning the categories and assumptions of western thought. The possibility of producing a truly de-colonized, post-colonial knowledge is currently a subject of considerable debate within disciplines such as anthropology,[2] literary criticism,[3] and development studies.[4] Young's own lineage of post-colonial

---

[1] Young, *White Mythologies*, 1990, p. 11.

[2] Clifford and Marcus (eds), *Writing Culture*, 1986; Marcus and Fischer (eds), *Anthropology as Cultural Critique*, 1986; Clifford, *The Predicament of Culture*, 1988; and Rosaldo, *Culture and Truth*, 1989.

[3] Barker et al. (eds), *The Politics of Theory*, 1983; Barker et al. (eds), *Europe and Its Others*, 1985; Miller, *Blank Darkness*, 1985; Ashcroft, Griffiths and Tiffin, *The Empire Writes Back*, 1989; and Eagleton, Jameson and Said, *Nationalism, Colonialism and Literature*, 1990.

[4] Norwine and Gonzales (eds), *The Third World*, 1988; Mathur, 'The current impasse in development thinking', 1989, pp. 463–80; Trainer, 'Reconstructing radical development theory', 1989, pp. 481–516; Rajan, 'The discourse of exploitation', 1990, pp. 29–52; and Marglin, *Dominating Knowledge*, 1990.

scholarship begins with Fanon, and includes more recent writers such as Said, Bhabha and Spivak.[5] Other influential post-colonial thinkers include C. L. R. James, Amilcar Cabral, Amin, Mudimbe, Ngugi wa Thiong'o and Coetzee.[6] In the work of these scholars can be detected the first halting steps towards the deconstruction and de-colonization of the western intellectual tradition.

Much of the effort in this field has concentrated, to date, on tracing the relations between imperialism and the construction of knowledge in the western metropoles. As Young argues, this has not simply been a matter of setting up a critique of colonialism in opposition to metropolitan culture but rather of demonstrating the extent to which they are deeply implicated with each other. One of the aims of this collection is presumably to demonstrate the truth of this statement *vis-à-vis* geography. But the task is essentially unfinished if we do not also ask the question: what would a de-colonized, de-whitened, post-colonial geography actually look like?

Western geography has not, as yet, seriously engaged with the arguments of post-colonial scholars. The very idea that the discipline as a whole needs de-colonizing is likely to be treated with scepticism if not derision in mainstream circles. In South Africa, by contrast, this challenge has been taken extremely seriously since the early 1980s though not, it must be said, in conscious articulation with the literature on post-colonialism. Faced with the painful irrelevance of their own discipline, geographers actually living a process of political de-colonization and rapid social transformation have found the task of intellectual de-colonization to be particularly urgent and necessary. Over the last decade, geographers (like scholars in other disciplines) have struggled to define, and practise, an alternative post-colonial, post-apartheid geography.

POST-COLONIALISM

The growing literature on post-colonialism defies easy summary. It is possible, however, to pick out several strands which are of relevance to the present discussion. The first, and most obvious of these, is the deep suspicion of what is generally known as 'totalizing discourse' – the grand projects and truth claims of enlightenment thinking. The distrust applies equally to the theoretical systems of knowledge of the Right and the Left.

[5] Fanon, *The Wretched of the Earth*, 1967; Fanon, *Black Skin, White Masks*, 1986; Said, *Orientalism*, 1978; Said, *The World, the Text and the Critic*, 1983; Bhabha, 'Difference, discrimination, and the discourse of colonialism', 1983; Bhabha, 'Of mimicry and man', 1984, pp. 125–33; Bhabha, 'Articulating the archaic', 1990, pp. 203–18; Spivak, *In Other Worlds*, 1987; and *The Post-Colonial Critic*, 1990.

[6] James, *Beyond a boundary*, 1983; Cabral, *Return to the Source*, 1973; Amin, *Eurocentrism*, 1988; Thiong'o, *Decolonising the Mind*, 1986; Coetzee, *White Writing*, 1988; and Mudimbe, *Invention of Africa*, 1988.

Writing, for example, of left-leaning global systems of analysis – such as world-systems theory, theories of unequal exchange, and dependency theory – Edward Said recently argued that they 'depend on a homogenizing and incorporating world historical scheme that assimilated non-synchronous developments, histories, cultures, and peoples to it'.[7] The same point was made some years ago by Jacques Depelchin when he argued that the African past was being rewritten by underdevelopment theorists as the story of Europe 'the exploiter' as opposed to Europe 'the developer'. The subject of African history, concluded Depelchin, was still Europe.[8]

One route out of such meta- or, more accurately, master-narratives consists, in Robert Young's words, of 'a relentless anatomization of the collusive forms of European knowledge'.[9] The difficulties inherent in this task are clearly illustrated in Edward Said's influential text *Orientalism*.[10] Said's study of the representation of the East in the West, for all its strengths, refuses to suggest what alternatives there might be to the discourse of orientalism. As a result, argue his critics, Said is unable to break out of the totalizing discourse of which he is such a trenchant critic.[11] Clearly, it is a great deal easier to view the process of de-colonization purely as the subversion of all western forms of representation, than it is to suggest what a de-colonized knowledge might actually look like.

One possible resolution – and a second strand of post-colonial scholarship – is suggested in the work of the subaltern studies group in India.[12] These scholars have argued that the project of de-colonization involves, as a starting point, the recovery of the lost historical voices of the marginalized, the oppressed and the dominated.[13] By giving a voice to the silenced, the scholar participates in the process of de-colonization by subverting and contesting elite and ruling class versions of the past. bell hooks warns, however, that the claim to write counter-histories of the marginalized and the dispossessed is often a rhetorical one. In her view, subalterns often become 'an absent presence without a voice'.[14] Spivak goes one step further to question the possibility of the subaltern ever speaking within the textual

---

[7] Said, cited in Young, *White Mythologies*, 1990, p. 10.

[8] See Crush and Rogerson, 'New wave African historiography', 1983, pp. 203–31.

[9] Young, *White Mythologies*, 1990, p. 9; see also, During, 'Postmodernism or post-colonialism today', 1987, pp. 32–47.

[10] Said, *Orientalism*, 1978.

[11] See for example, Mani and Frankenburg, 'The challenge of orientalism', 1985, pp. 174–92; Parry, 'Problems in current theories of colonial discourse, 1987, pp. 27–58; Young, *White Mythologies*, 1990, pp. 119–40 and Clifford, *The Predicament of Culture*, 1988. For a rejoinder to his critics see Said, 'Orientalism reconsidered', 1985.

[12] See Sen, 'Subaltern studies', 1987; O'Hanlon, 'Recovering the subject', 1988; Prakash, 'Writing post-orientalist histories of the Third World', 1990, pp. 383–408; Prakash, *Bonded Histories*, 1990, and the six vols of Guha and Spivak (eds), *Subaltern Studies*, 1988.

[13] Prakash, 'Postcolonial criticism and Indian historiography', 1992.

[14] hooks, *Yearning: Race, Gender*, 1990, p. 126.

conventions and modes of representation which characterize contemporary academic texts.[15]

In Spivak's view, Said's *Orientalism* is a study not of marginality, nor even marginalization, but the imperial construction of an object for investigation and control.[16] Colonial discourse analysis – taking its cue from Said – has similarly tended to focus on the construction of western knowledges about 'the other'.[17] But there is an implicit assumption that this academic enterprise provides space in which 'the marginal can speak and be spoken, even spoken for'.[18] Spivak quite sensibly warns of the delusion that a post-colonial history merely involves making subalterns the subject of their own history. Rather, to the extent that she (and others) fix marginality in western scholarship as an 'object' of investigation, they reconstruct it as another object for control – hence the danger of what she calls a 'new orientalism'. In these circumstances, great vigilance is required to avoid the dramatization of victimage and the assertion of a spurious identity with the victim.[19]

How, then, can the subaltern speak if the very act of inscription by the 'saviours of marginality' robs them of their voice? This question is at the heart of the crisis of representation which has plagued ethnographic field-work over the last decade.[20] In part the difficulties arise from the deep complicity of anthropology as a discipline with the formal structures of European empire and the 'uses' to which anthropological knowledges were put.[21] In part they come from a thoroughly post-modern suspicion of the referential value of language.[22] But fundamentally, the crisis arises from what we might call the discomforts of distance – the cultural, racial, class, and spatial barriers between the high ground of western academe and the back-streets of the third world.

What relevance does this have for the discipline of geography? Adapting some of the protocols of post-colonial scholarship, the aims of a post-colonial geography might be defined as: the unveiling of geographical complicity in colonial dominion over space; the character of geographical representation in colonial discourse; the de-linking of local geographical enterprise from

[15] Spivak, 'Can the Subaltern Speak?', 1988.

[16] Spivak, 'Poststructuralism', 1990, pp. 221–2.

[17] Miller, *Blank Darkness*, 1985; Mudimbe, *Invention of Africa*, 1988.

[18] Spivak, 'Poststructuralism', 1990, p. 221; Pratt, 'Conventions of representation', 1988; Chisman, 'The imperial unconscious?'; and Trotter, 'Colonial subjects', 1990.

[19] Spivak, 'Poststructuralism', 1990, p. 228.

[20] Clifford and Marcus (eds), *Writing Culture*, 1986; Kapferer, 'The anthropologist as hero', 1988, p. 8; and Polier and Roseberry, 'Tristes tropes', 1989.

[21] Asad (ed.), *Anthropology and the Colonial Encounter*, 1973; Said, 'Representing the colonized', 1989, p. 15; Comaroff, *Of Revelation and Revolution*, 1991, p. xiii.

[22] Sangren, 'Rhetoric and the authority of enthnography', 1988; Spencer, 'Anthropology as a kind of writing', 1989; Fabian, 'Presence and representation', 1990; Birth, 'Reading and the righting of writing ethnographies', 1990; and Atkinson, *The Ethnographic Imagination*, 1990.

metropolitan theory and its totalizing systems of representation; and the recovery of those hidden spaces occupied, and invested with their own meaning, by the colonial underclasses. The next section of the chapter attempts to ground these placeless prescriptions in the local context of South African geography.

THE COMPLICITY OF GEOGRAPHY

Edward Said has suggested that if there is anything that radically distinguishes the imagination of anti-imperialism 'it is the primacy of the geographical'.[23] This is because imperialism itself was an act of geographical violence through which space was explored, reconstructed, re-named and controlled.[24] The nineteenth- and twentieth-century history of Southern Africa is, at one level, an exemplary tale of the geography of territorial violence – of conquest, partition, segregation, enforced controls on mobility, and the extension of colonial dominion over space.[25] As a number of scholars have also begun to demonstrate, at the heart of colonial discourse in the region lies a set of fundamentally geographical representations of space, place and landscape.[26]

Colonial landscapes were never the unequivocal expression of imperial dispossession and domination, however, and could reflect in important ways the resistance and struggles of the dispossessed.[27] In early colonial Swaziland, for example, the British 'protectors' grabbed over two-thirds of the land area for white settlers. Swazi who refused to work for wages on the new white farms were forcibly resettled in scattered reserves demarcated by a colonial officer, George Grey. Grey's thoroughness and skills as an applied geographer garnered him much praise from colonial officials including a local District Commissioner, A. G. Marwick. Not surprisingly, the Swazi saw his activities rather differently: they were 'being killed', 'living in darkness', 'being pushed into the mud' and 'being stripped naked'. Grey's cartographical skills extended to plotting the homesteads of all Swazi royals and chiefs on rudimentary base maps, and drawing the reserves around these locations.

[23] Eagleton et al., *Nationalism, Colonialism and Literature*, 1990, p. 77.

[24] See Carter, *The Road to Botany Bay*, 1987; Carter and Malouf, 'Spatial History', 1989; and Carter, 'Plotting', 1990; Mitchell, *Colonising Egypt*, 1988.

[25] See Marks, 'Southern and Central Africa, 1886–1910', 1985.

[26] The representation of geography and landscape in colonial discourse is not pursued any further in this particular piece, but see Pratt, 'Scratches on the face of the country', 1986; Dubow, 'Race, civilization and culture', 1987, pp. 71–94; Packard, 'The "healthy reserve" and the "dressed native"' 1989; Ferguson, 'Mobile workers', 1990; Hofmeyr, 'Turning region into narrative', 1990; Ashforth, *The Politics of Official Discourse*, 1990; Brooks, *Playing the Game*, 1990, pp. 1–78; and Comaroff, *Revelation and Revolution*, 1991, pp. 86–125.

[27] Crush, 'Beyond the frontier', 1992.

His rationale, and that of his paymasters, was that by appeasing the local ruling class the likelihood of a mass revolt would be considerably reduced. And so it proved.[28] Grey's partition – and the two very different landscapes that resulted – was not, in other words, constructed on a pre-colonial countryside devoid of peoples and lines of power. The subsequent imprint of the imperial imagination on the landscape of the country's white farms was continuously compromised and subverted by the struggles of black tenants, sharecroppers and wage workers.[29]

George Grey left Swaziland in 1909; Marwick remained and became convinced of the iniquity of the policies he had earlier endorsed. His skills were bent to the Swazi cause and he became a fervent advocate of Swazi land rights. South African geographers have traditionally been drawn to serve the geographical enterprise represented by Grey rather than Marwick. As Rogerson and Beavon suggested some years ago, and Harold Wesso has recently begun to demonstrate, there is a largely untold tale of the deep complicity of academic geography with the colonial project of race and class domination in South Africa.[30] As segregation hardened into apartheid after 1948, geography scarcely missed a beat. Geographical skills were bent to the service of the new state and to the entrenchment of race in space. These were the geographers who saw themselves, in Hattingh's revealing phrase, as 'those who make things happen'.[31] There were a few dissenting liberal voices in the 1950s and 1960s, but most seemed content to avoid 'controversial topics' and many had left South Africa for other academic pastures by the 1970s.[32] Those who remained became immersed in an unreconstructed and utterly tendentious spatial science imported directly from the hearth of geography's quantitative 'revolution' in North America and Britain.

South African geography has traditionally exhibited what Chris Rogerson calls a 'cultural cringe complex'; a thoroughly colonial sense that imported theories and methodologies are inherently and necessarily superior.[33] This geography has always sought to define itself by, and seek validation from, the metropole. This suggests that certain questions need to be asked about the usefulness of imported conceptual schemas for understanding local realities and providing guides to post-colonial scholarship and practice. Does the decolonization of the discipline require a rupture with the knowledge industry

[28] The full story is told in Crush, *The Struggle for Swazi Labour, 1890–1920*, 1987, pp. 131–66.

[29] Ibid., pp. 167–88.

[30] Beavon and Rogerson, 'Trekking on', 1981; Wesso, ch. 16 in this collection. See also Rogerson and Browett, 'Social geography under apartheid', 1986; Rogerson and Parnell, 'Fostered by the laager', 1989.

[31] Hattingh, 'Geographers and the political system', 1988.

[32] The role of liberalism in South African geography has yet to be explored. On the liberal impact in other disciplines see Saunders, *The Making of the South African Past*, 1988, pp. 165–91; and Smith, *The Changing Past*, 1988, pp. 155–228.

[33] Rogerson, 'Censorship and apartheid geography', 1985.

of the western heartlands of geographical enterprise, or is there room for a productive, post-colonial interface? A narrative account of the struggle to de-colonize South African geography in the 1980s may suggest some answers.[34]

DE-COLONIZING A DISCIPLINE

The original impetus for the de-colonization of South African geography did not, in my view, originally come from within, though it may be seen, in part, as a response to the perceived need for a new geography more attuned to internal social and political developments. In the 1970s and 1980s, a number of South African-trained geographers moved overseas for further study, mostly to North America. There they were exposed both to the neo-Marxian critique of orthodox development theory and to its geographical variants within radical geography.[35] They also began to engage with a series of seminal Marxist reinterpretations of the South African political economy which began to appear in Britain in the early 1970s.[36]

In the late 1970s many of these scholars began to return to academic posts in South Africa. Simultaneously, and of considerable importance to subsequent developments in geography, a number of South African historians and sociologists were returning to South Africa from graduate work in Britain bringing with them two distinct, and sometimes conflicting, brands of British historiographical influence – the social history of Thompson and the structural Marxism of Althusser.[37]

By the early 1980s, South African social science (in the English-speaking universities at least) was increasingly dominated by a radical scholarship forged in the crucible of British and North American university radicalism.[38] Like radical South African scholars in the 1940s and 1950s, the new generation attempted to put their skills, and theories, at the disposal of trade unions and progressive community organizations (inside the country) and exiled political organizations such as the ANC (outside it).[39]

[34] This narrative could, of course, be constructed in other ways. My stress on the North American connection is, for example, absent in the more personalized narrative of Rogerson and Beavon, 'Towards a geography of the common people in South Africa', 1988, pp. 83–99. Similarly, scholars at other institutions would probably take exception to my characterization of the centrality of Wits and Durban.

[35] Crush, 'Discourse of progressive human geography', 1991.

[36] Ibid.

[37] See Bozzoli and Delius, 'Radical history and South African Society', 1990; Mabin, 'At the cutting edge', 1986.

[38] Murray, 'The triumph of Marxist approaches in South African social and labour history', 1988.

[39] See Lewis, 'Intellectuals, the working class', 1989; Maree, 'Harnessing intellectuals', 1989; and Bozzoli, 'Intellectuals, audiences and histories', 1990.

Through their own research, teaching and off-campus political activity the returning geographers also began to refashion the terrain of South African geographical discourse.[40] Initially, the new South African geography exhibited the heavy influence of its North American roots. David Lincoln's seminal article on ideology and South African geography was heavily indebted to Frankian underdevelopment theory.[41] Rogerson's work on industrial and regional development was recast in terms of world-systems theory and the internal colonialism thesis.[42] Jeff McCarthy (with Dan Smit) began to rewrite the geography of the South African city in the vocabulary of structural Marxism.[43] Others experimented with versions of modes of production theory (such as Wolpe's cheap labour thesis), Amin's unequal exchange model and the settler-colonialism thesis.[44] Beavon and Rogerson predicted in 1981 that the 'new school' of Marxian geography would experience a 'lift-off' in the 1980s.[45]

But there were growing signs of unease. Radical geographers, like the spatial scientists before them, relied heavily on imported theoretical goods. Empirical work consisted, in the main, of 'applying' imported (radical) theory to the South African situation. McCarthy, for example, in an essay on the relevance of North American radical geography for South Africa wondered whether geographers should indeed be following 'some externally defined politico-intellectual agenda illustrated with local example'.[46] In 1982, McCarthy and Wellings went a step further to argue that the role of the radical academic lay as much off-campus as on it. They called, in a much cited statement, for a geography which was as much *for* as *of* the working class.[47] There were also programmatic calls for the 'de-colonization' of the discipline, critiques of the Eurocentrism and androcentrism of neo-Marxian theory, calls for the reorientation of the discipline away from 'first world' to 'third world' theory, and demands for the development of a 'people's geography'.[48]

[40] The research agenda of many leading liberal geographers also appears to have been increasingly radicalized around this time by internal political developments (and the impact of the returnees).

[41] Lincoln, 'Ideology and South African development geography', 1979.

[42] Rogerson and Osborne, 'Conceptualizing the frontier settlement process', 1978; Rogerson, 'Industrialization in the shadows of apartheid', 1981; and Rogerson, 'Internal colonialism', 1980.

[43] McCarthy, 'The political economy of urban land use', 1983; and McCarthy and Smit, *South African City*, 1984.

[44] Wellings and Sutcliffe, 'Developing the informal sector', 1984; and Crush, 'Capitalist homoficence', 1986.

[45] Beavon and Rogerson, 'Trekking on', 1981.

[46] McCarthy, 'Radical geography, mainstream geography and southern Africa', 1982.

[47] Wellings and McCarthy, 'Whither Southern African human geography', 1983; see also Wellings, 'Geography and development studies in Southern Africa', 1986.

[48] Crush, Reitsma and Rogerson, 'Decolonising the human geography of Southern Africa', 1982, p. 73; Crush and Rogerson, 'New wave African historiography', 1983; Friedman

Out of these deliberations and debates emerged two quite distinct geographies. The first – at the University of the Witwatersrand – came heavily under the influence of social history. Attention turned to the mapping of the 'hidden spaces' (hidden to academics) of the apartheid city and to reconstructing the historical geography of the 'common people'.[49] Like the social historians, this geography quickly abandoned the terrain of Marxian high theory, took a strong empirical turn, began to rely heavily on archival and oral research methodologies, and adopted narrative forms of explanation.[50]

The second group – at the University of Natal and latterly Durban-Westville – offered important contrasts. Like scholars in adjacent disciplines, they quickly shed the straitjacket of Marxian structuralism but continued to 'import' new theoretical schemas for local use.[51] Their research focused almost exclusively on present-day concerns and conveyed a strong sense of their own political involvement.[52] Indeed, most of them were drawn into local political struggles in Natal during the 1980s.[53]

By mid-decade, then, radical South African geography had loosened its ties with its North American parent and had begun to assume a rather different trajectory, more attuned to local circumstances and political struggles. Some South African geographers continued to monitor overseas intellectual

and Wilkes, 'Androcentric knowledge and geography', 1986; Crush, 'Towards a people's historical geography', 1986; and more recently, Wesso, *People's education*, 1989. Many of these tendencies and debates are reflected in a recent book of essays which appeared too late for systematic incorporation into this chapter; see Rogerson and McCarthy (eds), *Geography in a Changing South Africa*, 1992, especially essays by Dhiru Soni, Jennifer Robinson, Jeffrey McCarthy, Susan Parnell and Harold Wesso.

[49] For a sample of this literature see the special issues of the following journals: *Journal of Historical Geography*, 1986, 12: 1; *Geojournal*, 1986, 12: 2 and 1990, 22: 3; and *Urban Geography*, 1989, p. 9. A full bibliographic listing is contained in Rogerson and Parnell, 'Fostered by the laager', 1989, pp. 20–6; and Crush, 'Beyond the frontier', 1992.

[50] On the new social history see Crush and Rogerson, 'New wave African historiography', 1983; Marks, 'The historiography of South Africa', 1986; Bradford, 'Highways, byways and cul-de-sacs', 1990; Lewis, 'South African labor history', 1990; and Bozzoli and Delius, 'Radical history and South African society', 1990, pp. 27–35.

[51] The contrast may be a little too starkly drawn in reality. Most of the Wits group also pursued contemporary research agendas. On the other hand, Durban geographers have contributed important work in historical geography.

[52] See McCarthy and Swilling, 'South Africa's emerging politics', 1985; Wellings and Sutcliffe, 'Worker militancy in South Africa', 1985; Sutcliffe, 'The crisis in South Africa', 1986; McCarthy, 'Contours of capital's negotiating agenda', 1986; McCarthy and Wellings, 'The regional restructuring of politics', 1989; Reintges, 'Urban movements in South African black townships', 1990; and Smith, *Apartheid City and Beyond*, 1991.

[53] Sutcliffe and Wellings, 'The widening rift', 1986, 3 : 51–82.

currents and interpret their significance for South Africa.[54] In the main, however, the trends, fashions and 'revolutions' of Euro-America had less and less influence on a geography shedding its 'cultural cringe complex', no longer looking to the metropoles for 'validation' and seeking to make a contribution to the political struggle against apartheid.[55] Euro-American geography, in turn, cast off its offspring, paying less and less attention to the innovative work being done in South Africa. Symptomatic of this de-linking, perhaps, was the special issue of *Antipode* on Southern Africa published in North America in 1983, which did not carry a single contribution from a South African geographer, rehearsed a set of concerns more American than South African, and had precious little impact within South Africa itself.[56]

When South African scholars speak of the need to 'de-colonize' their discipline, they usually mean one of two things. First, the term articulates a process of de-linking from a 'mindless metropolitan slavishness'.[57] South Africa, they argue, should cease to be a 'sink for Euro-American thinking' but should develop its own indigenous and eclectic synthesis.[58] Second, intellectual de-colonization means the shattering of boundaries between campus and community. Spurious objectivity is eschewed and a committed, radical scholarship is proposed which empowers the margins and provides the ideological and pragmatic tools to contest ruling-class domination.[59] There are clear echoes here of the arguments of post-colonial scholarship, outlined earlier. In the following section of the chapter, I therefore want to suggest that 'metropolitan slavishness' aside, there are some important parallels to be drawn between the latest metropolitan 'fashion' – placeless post-colonialism – and the specific practices of South African geography.

[54] McCarthy, 'Research on neighbourhood activism', 1981; Pirie, 'Political philosophy and political geography', 1984; Scott, 'Time, structuration', 1986; and Reintges, 'Philosophy and methodology in geography', 1989.

[55] Rogerson and Parnell, 'Fostered by the laager', 1989.

[56] Personal communication, Chris Rogerson, October 1990; see O'Keefe, 'South Africa in the global division of labor', 1983, p. 15. The beginnings of a new rapprochement may be signalled by the more recent special issue of *Antipode* with contributions by South African and North American scholars: Pickles and Weiner (eds), *Rural and Regional Restructuring in South Africa*, 1991.

[57] Bozzoli and Delius, 'Radical history and South African society', 1990, p. 42.

[58] Crush, Reitsma and Rogerson, 'Decolonizing the human geography of Southern Africa', 1982.

[59] Wellings and McCarthy, 'Whither Southern African human geography?', 1983; Wellings, 'Geography and development studies in southern Africa', 1986; and Rogerson, 'A new South Africa – a new South African Geography?', 1990.

POST-COLONIALISM AND DE-COLONIZATION

The first parallel invokes the post-colonial rejection of totalization and the master-discourses of Right and Left. Traces of this principle can be detected in the South African view of de-colonization as de-linking. Within geography, de-linking (always partial and incomplete) initially involved a repudiation of the models and analytical methods of positivism which had dominated the discipline locally for much of the 1960s and early 1970s. More particularly, it demanded the subversion of neo-classical and liberal analyses of the causes of poverty, inequality, and racial domination in South African society – narratives of the diffusion of modernization, dual economies, backward peasants, progressive white farmers, irrational frontier mentalities, colour-blind capitalists, and a benevolent state.

These narratives were supplanted by counter-narratives drawn from progressive third world thinkers – such as Rodney, Amin, Fanon, Laclau, and the *dependistas* – and radical critics within the metropole – such as Frank, Rey, Mellaisoux, Wallerstein, Arrighi, and (within geography) Slater, Santos and Harvey. South Africa's past and present began to be rewritten as the story of world-economies, of the development of underdevelopment, of articulating modes of production, of internal colonies, of fractions of capital and hegemonic blocs, of states that accumulated and legitimated. The question of who told the 'better' stories is largely irrelevant. What post-colonial scholarship objected to on principle, South African geographers came slowly to realize in practice – the Eurocentrism and androcentrism of both discourses, the evacuation of human agency in the face of intangible but immutable structures, the silencing of subjectivity, and the stunning irrelevance of both to the everyday struggles of the dominated and the dispossessed.[60]

While the Durban group of South African geographers sought to disaggregate and refashion the totalizing discourses of the radical Left, the Wits group increasingly rejected them altogether. Under the strong influence of the social historians, South African historical geography embarked upon a descent into particularity.[61] The persistent focus on the local case study, on the documentation of yet another facet of hidden urban space, meant that each 'case' seemed too unique, and certainly too complex, to permit generalization or the construction of concepts of broader applicability – activities not inherently inimical either to the project of de-colonization or the spirit of post-colonialism.[62]

---

[60] Crush and Rogerson, 'New wave African historiography', 1983.

[61] Crush, 'Beyond the frontier', 1992.

[62] Only the liberal historical geographer, Christopher, has to date developed a comparative research agenda which attempts to situate South Africa's supposed peculiarities within a broader imperial context; see Christopher, *Colonial Africa*, 1984; and *The British Empire at Its Zenith*, 1988.

Central to the arguments of certain branches of post-colonial scholarship is what Spivak calls the 'the saviours of marginality' syndrome.[63] This is the presumption that the textual restoration of marginality (the writing by academics for academics about the struggles of subalterns) turns the authors into subalterns themselves. It is possible that subaltern history (or historical geography) may operate within a discipline as a form of insurgency against conventional forms but that neither makes or allows the self-proclamation of subalternity by the academic. It is surely no coincidence that much of the rhetoric of post-colonialism is impenetrable and obtuse, and is exercised within the sanitized corridors of western universities. The intention may well be, in Robert Young's words, to 'cunningly subvert any comparable impulse towards [colonial] mastery' in the post-colonial text.[64] In practice, the 'pathetic assertion' of a spurious identity and the dramatization of victimage is a constant danger.[65]

This is clearly a temptation from which South African geography has not been immune. During the 1980s, it became increasingly common for geographers to claim for their work an identity with social groups outside the university. In some cases the claim lent authority to the arguments of empirical text, as subsequent 'confessionals' made clear.[66] Thus, for example, John Western suggests that the success of his book *Outcast Cape Town* is directly proportional to his ability to give a voice to those who 'have rarely had the opportunity to speak of *their* contending city'.[67] Similarly, Chris Rogerson and Keith Beavon rest their credibility on a textual relationship with a particular social group (the 'common people').[68] Their research, they claim, is part of an 'insurrection, if not a revolution' which is reshaping South African human geography. This rhetorical device positions them in the vanguard of an in-house revolution, which is producing a 'dewhitened, de-colonized, and critical human geography'. The revolution is itself legitimated by virtue of its connections to social groups outside the discipline.[69]

Geographers divide at this point. Rogerson and Beavon admit that 'we accept the criticism of our detractors that in Nero-like fashion we may be "fiddling" while Soweto and other Black South African townships continue to burn.'[70] They suggest that the imperative in South Africa is to end black suffering, rather than simply to document it and suggest that if progress in human geography is to be gauged solely by its contribution to the overthrow of the white minority regime 'then we have singularly failed'.

[63] Spivak, 'Poststructuralism', 1990, p. 226.
[64] Young, *White Mythologies*, 1990, p. 158.
[65] Spivak, 'Poststructuralism', 1990, p. 228.
[66] Crush, 'The discourse of progressive human geography', 1991, pp. 401–5.
[67] Western, 'Places, authorship, authority', 1986, pp. 23–38.
[68] Rogerson and Beavon, 'Towards a geography of the common people', 1988.
[69] Ibid.
[70] Ibid., p. 96.

The argument of their 'detractors' (primarily the Durban group) is disarmingly simple. Geographers should be researching and writing, they claim, *for* rather than *about*.[71] The consumers vary – 'the working class', 'the common people', 'popular forces'. The obvious corollary of this argument is that research agendas should be defined by and with the people. The practical problems and difficulties of this demand have been debated at length elsewhere.[72] My concern here is not with this question, important as it is, but rather how marginality is actually constructed within academic texts as a form of authority.

In her recent study of the changing discourse of popular culture in Britain, Morag Shiach argues that the rhetorical power of the concept of 'the people' far outstrips its descriptive specificity.[73] There is little attempt to analyse who exactly is being talked about as 'the people'. The same tendency can be seen in geographical writing in South Africa. The imagined community of 'the common people', about and for whom geographers write, has powerful resonances – but it is largely unexamined. In contrast, geographers in the Durban group devoted a great deal of effort to textual identification with other equally powerful (though largely unproblematized) textual constructs, such as 'the working class'.

In the introduction to the 1986 issue on South Africa of the *Journal of Historical Geography*, I suggested that the collection might help contest the 'deliberate and dangerous mystifications of a powerful racist ideology'.[74] On reflection, it is hard to see how texts produced for an overseas, specialized, academic readership can do anything of the sort. However, the legitimacy of the claim rested on a textual association with a social history movement which *is* actively seeking to disseminate the results of academic research and popularize an alternative subaltern view of the South African past.[75]

The attempts of South African social historians in the 1980s to 'popularize' academic research have had a number of underlying motivations: to provide trade unions and community organizations with accessible historical narratives of, for example, their own past struggles; to 'empower' the dispossessed by returning to them historical traditions either lost or distorted and silenced by racist ideology; and to transfer research experience and skills to allow people to 'write their own history'.[76] The success of these efforts is currently a point of reflection and debate. But what is striking is how infrequently

[71] Wellings and McCarthy, 'Whither Southern African human geography?', 1983.

[72] Callinicos, 'Intellectuals, popular history and worker education', 1989, p. 11; and Bozzoli, 'Intellectuals, audiences and histories', 1990.

[73] Shiach, *Discourse on Popular Culture*, 1989; see also Bourdieu, *The Uses of the 'People'*, 1990, pp. 150–5.

[74] Crush, 'Towards a people's historical geography', 1986, p. 2.

[75] Callinicos, 'The "People's Past" ', 1987, pp. 44–64; Witz, 'History of the people', 1989; and Callinicos, 'Popular history', 1990.

[76] Bozzoli and Delius, 'Radical history and South African society', p. 41; and Witz, 'The write your own history project', 1990.

the work of historical geographers is invoked in these discussions.[77] The sense of belonging to a corporate enterprise which both contests the state and empowers the people may help geographers feel more comfortable with their role in apartheid society, but no one has yet demonstrated how historical geography *per se* can be popularized and why it might be empowering. This, I think, was the root of the Durban group's unease with the Wits group, and their demand that geographers become politically active, rather than assume activism by association.

In a recent critical review of popular history in South Africa, Belinda Bozzoli makes several telling observations on local academic experience in this area.[78] She points out that in the South Africa of the 1980s, popular culture tended to engender and sustain ideologies of a nationalist, populist, 'motherist' or racially-defined character, which the post-colonial activist might find troublesome. Schemas and narratives of class action, experience and consciousness can have little resonance in these circumstances: that 'a culturally vacant, economistic Marxism is unappealing ... in the face of a culturally, experientially, and historically rich nationalism is not surprising'.[79] What happens to Marxism, Bozzoli asks, when it engages with populist nationalism? The question might as easily be put about geography in a post-apartheid South Africa which is already positioning itself, in certain quarters, as an aid to governments-in-waiting. The centre may change its hue, but the margins will remain. The real challenge of post-colonialism, as Ngugi wa Thiong'o repeatedly stresses is where the new margins are drawn after political de-colonization is complete and 'freedom' is attained.[80]

Spivak, in her reading of the *Subaltern Studies* group, has argued that in post-colonial writing the subaltern is provided no space in which to speak: 'everyone speaks for her, so that she is rewritten continuously as the object of patriarchy or of imperialism.'[81] Spivak's preferred solution is to reorient post-colonial scholarship away from the 'impossible' task of retrieving subaltern consciousness and will towards 'the location and reinscription of subject-positions which are instrumental in forms of control and insurgency'.[82] The corollary of this position, suggests Young, is an important disaggregation of 'the subaltern' which draws attention to the way in which 'the factors of class and, particularly, gender, create a heterogeneous field that problematizes the general notion of an undifferentiated colonial subject or subaltern – as indeed of a monolithic colonizing power'.[83] It seems highly unlikely that the *Subaltern Studies* group would accept Young's characterization of their project. But how relevant is it to South Africa?

[77] Crush, 'Beyond the frontier', 1992, p. 11.
[78] Bozzoli, 'Intellectuals, audiences and histories', 1990, pp. 239–40.
[79] Ibid., p. 260.
[80] Thiong'o, *Decolonising the Mind*, 1986.
[81] Young, *White Mythologies*, 1990, p. 164.
[82] Ibid., p. 160.
[83] Ibid., p. 161.

Through detailed local-level reconstructions of communities and individual life histories, the South African popular history movement has long demonstrated the ambiguities of colonial domination and the differentiated colonial subject.[84] Historical geographers have added spatial nuance to these representations. Indeed, it could be argued that it was engagement with the living subject, rather than rummaging through the archival traces of the dead, that persuaded historians and geographers to face the forces of culture and consciousness. The subalterns, through the power of oral reminiscence, forced 'a culturally sensitive understanding of class, compelling [scholars] to relate issues of class formation to those of ethnicity, community, gender, youth, and the family'.[85]

Any number of examples might be marshalled in support of this position. Let me mention just one – a social historian whose work shows remarkable sensitivity to 'geographical' issues of ecology and spatiality. William Beinart's influential early narratives of rural transformation in Pondoland stretched but did not break the conceptual categories of class.[86] In 1987, however, he published the life story of a former migrant worker (M) based on extensive interviews with the man in 1982.[87] Beinart's own historical narrative regularly breaks for M:

If a Pondo goes to the Zulu side, the Zulus do not know him and they start abusing him and saying all sorts of things. They hit him and when he comes back to the Pondos then the Pondos start arming ... That is what usually sparked faction fights.

A Shangaan boss boy suggested love to me. Well, I said, 'I think you have made a mistake.' He insisted, he wanted to force me. And then we fought there right on top of the shaft. His friends came to help him and I was driven down.

Why (do) the *indlavini* hate the *amanene*? The *amanene* come from more or less the same Christian families. But they differ in this way. They are not a group. And they believe in fighting with a knife. They believe in stabbing. They believe in bribing parents of the girls ... Since I was a Pondo, I didn't have much trouble. I was regarded just as an African who had come to visit friends. Of course I did not dress

[84] See, for example, the following collections of essays: Marks and Atmore (eds), *Economy and Society*, 1980; Marks and Rathbone (eds), *Industrialization and Social Change*, 1982; Onselen, *Studies in the Social and Economic History of the Witwatersrand*, 1982; Bozzoli (ed.), *Town and Countryside*, 1983; Marks and Trapido (eds), *The Politics of Race, Class and Nationalism*, 1987; Bozzoli (ed.), *Class, Community and Conflict*, 1987; Bonner et al. (eds), *Holding their Ground*, 1989; Walker (ed.), *Women and Gender in Southern Africa to 1945*, 1990; and vols 1 to 6 of the *Southern African Studies Series*.

[85] la Hausse, 'Oral history and South African historians', 1990.

[86] Beinart, *The Political Economy of Pondoland*, 1983.

[87] Beinart, 'Worker consciousness', 1987, p. 307.

like an urban African. I tried to dress like the Pondos: just an ordinary jacket, khaki shirt, khaki trousers with patches.[88]

The experiences of M, 'who prefers to remain anonymous for the present', are used by Beinart to further his own developing critique – begun in earlier work – of unlinear narratives of black proletarianization. More important, M forced Beinart to recognize that 'forms of consciousness, whether national, racial, ethnic or worker are not necessarily exclusive; they are neither self-evident and self-explanatory, nor mere epiphenomena of class categories, to be "read off" from simply abstracted means of production.'[89] Beinart concludes, in a revealing passage:

> M's experiences give some hint as to how difficult it is to pin socio-
> logical categories on to the nature of consciousness or to grasp the
> totality of consciousness, individual or class, at any particular moment.
> Clearly, the responses of a group or class are framed by its position
> in the political economy of the society as a whole. But in the rapidly
> changing world of South Africa's industrial revolution, where people
> could find themselves peasants, workers, lumpenproletarians and petty
> entrepreneurs in close succession, and not necessarily in that order,
> any analysis of the development of political ideas must be able to cater
> for the variety of the conditions of oppression.[90]

Beinart's language would presumably mean little to M, who by this stage has little control over the way he is to be represented in the academic text. But there is a broader issue here. Does the sporadic insertion of the words of the subaltern allow him to speak or is his voice subordinated to the reconstructed narrative – and historiographical concerns – of the narrator; to the 'framing' comforts of the meta-narratives of 'the totality of consciousness', 'the political economy of the society as a whole', and 'South Africa's industrial revolution'?

Both Beinart and la Hausse seem to suggest, contrary to Spivak and Young, that complexity in the conditions of oppression and response does not preclude comprehension of the consciousness of the oppressed. Thus, they see no intrinsic incompatibility between the recovery of subjectivity and the description of subject-positions. The subaltern may speak: it is 'the rich potential of oral histories which recovered the subjective popular experiences of social change wrought within living memory'.[91] Certainly, there has been a growing concern in South African social history and (more recently) historical geography with black culture and consciousness, and the subjective

---

[88] Ibid., pp. 293–301.
[89] Ibid., p. 307.
[90] Ibid.
[91] la Hausse, 'Oral history', 1990, p. 348.

experience of domination and resistance. Here lies the force of Spivak's critique. For la Hausse, and other commentators on oral methodologies, the idea of recovering and representing 'subjective popular experience' – of allowing the subaltern to speak – is unproblematized.[92]

Geographers too are largely silent. The Durban group, for example, used social science questionnaire techniques to solicit and represent the 'opinions' of the oppressed on a range of contemporary political issues. In a fierce critique of other social scientists they also show how the oppressed can be induced, through crafty design and language manipulation, to hold the opinions which, according to the preconceptions of the researcher, they ought to hold. Their solution lies in 'proper', 'objective', 'unbiased' survey procedures.[93] The question of who speaks in their own, quite opposite, survey results is unposed. The Wits group, for all their claims as the chroniclers of marginality, have displayed a refreshing uncertainty about their ability to communicate with, much less provide a space for the voices of 'the common people'.[94]

ENDWORD

In this chapter, I sought to bring two distinct and distanced intellectual projects together in the same space. This seems to me to be a potentially valid exercise not least because both claim discursive authority through reference to the same defining metaphors – de-colonization and marginality. More than that, however, it is apparent that the various discourses of marginality – as practiced in widely scattered locales in all three worlds – could all gain from dialogue. I have tried to suggest areas where fruitful points of contact might be made, at least insofar as geographers are concerned.

One of the more powerful geographical legacies of the imperial experience were the linkages which bound distinct parcels of colonial territory to particular metropolitan powers. Through the spatial demarcation of boundaries the colonial powers also severed pre-colonial links between peoples and places. In the post-colonial period these patterns persist and might be contested – in the intellectual sphere as well as the political and economic – through creative lateral linkage.

My point, then, is not to promote 'post-colonialism' as another metropolitan fashion to fuel the 'cultural cringe complex' of South African geography. Nor is it to suggest that Euro-American geography ought to appropriate South African geography since it addresses critical silences within

[92] For further discussion, see Miles and Crush, 'Personal narratives as interactive texts', forthcoming.

[93] Sutcliffe and Wellings, 'Disinvestment and black workers' attitudes', 1985; 'Black worker "attitudes" and disinvestment', 1985; and 'Attitudes and living conditions in Inanda', 1986.

[94] Rogerson and Beavon, 'Towards a geography of the common people', 1988.

metropolitan geographical discourse. Rather it is to argue for a constructive lateral dialogue within post-colonial scholarship and fuel instead the
transgression of 'the norms of [western] knowledge production'. Only then
can the legacies of empire in geography be superseded.

Bibliography of Printed Sources

Abb, G. (ed.) 1930: *Aus fünfzig Jahren Deutscher Wissenschaft. Die Entwicklung ihrer Fachgebiete in Einzeldarstellungen*. Berlin: W. de Gruyter and Co.

Abd Al-Rahim, A. 1984: 'Land Tenure in Egypt and its Social Effects on Egyptian Society: 1798–1813'. In Tarif Khalidi (ed.), *Land Tenure and Social Transformation in the Middle East*, Beirut: American University of Beirut, 237–48.

Abdel-Malek, A. 1977: 'Geopolitics and national movements: an essay on the dialectics of imperialism'. *Antipode*, vol. 9 no. 1, 28–36.

Abrams, L. and Miller, D. J. 1976: 'Who were the French colonialists? A reassessment of the Parti Colonial, 1890–1914'. *The Historical Journal*, 19: 685–725.

Abramson, Howard S. 1987: *National Geographic: Behind America's Lens on the World*. New York: Crown Publishers.

Ackerman, E. 1945: 'Geographic training, wartime research and immediate professional objectives'. *Annals of the Association of American Geographers*, 35, 4: 121–43.

Acosta, Joseph de, S. J. 1589: *De natura novi orbis, libri duo, et de promulgatione evangelii, apud barbaros … sive de procuranda Indorum salute libri sex*. Salamantica.

Actas 1884: *Actas del congeso español de geografía colonial y mercantil celebrado en Madrid los días 4 al 14 de noviembre de 1883*. Madrid: Fortnet, 2 vols.

Adams, Harriet C. 1907: 'The East Indians in the New World'. *National Geographic Magazine*, 18, 7: 485–91.

Adams, Harriet C. 1930: 'Cirenaica, eastern wing of Italian Libia'. *National Geographic Magazine*, 57, 6: 689–726.

Adams, Harriet C. 1933: 'River-encircled Paraguay'. *National Geographic Magazine*, 63, 4: 385–416.

Adams, M. P. Greenwood 1924: 'Australia's wild wonderland'. *National Geographic Magazine*, 45, 3: 329–56.

Adas, Michael 1989: *Machines as the Measure of Men. Science, Technology and Ideologies of Western Dominance*. Ithaca and London: Cornell University Press.

Ageron, C.-R. 1972: 'Gambetta et la reprise de l'expansion coloniale'. *Revue française d'histoire d'outre-mer*, 59, 215: 165–204.

Ageron, C.-R. 1973: *L'Anticolonialisme en France de 1871 à 1914*. Paris: Presses universitaires de France.

Ageron, C.-R. 1978: *France coloniale ou Parti Colonial?* Paris: Presses universitaires de France.

Ageron, C.-R. 1986: 'Jules Ferry et la colonisation'. In François Furet (ed.) *Jules Ferry: Fondateur de la République*, Paris: Presses universitaires de France, 191–206.

Ahmad, A. 1992: *In Theory*. London: Verso.

Alexander, L. 1983: 'European planning ideology in Tanzania'. *Habitat*, International, vol. 7, no. 1/2: 17–36.

Allent, Chevalier 1829: 'Essai sur les reconnaissances militaires'. In *Mémoriale du Dépôt de la guerre*, Imprimé par ordre du Ministre 1802–3 (reprinted Paris: CH. Picquet) 1: 387–522.

Alloula, Malek 1986: *The Colonial Harem*. Minneapolis: University of Minnesota Press.

Almagià, Roberto 1936: *Elementi di geografia politica ed economica*. Milan: Giuffré.

Amin, S. 1988: *Eurocentrism*. New York: Monthly Review Press.

Anderson, K. 1987: 'The idea of Chinatown: the power of place and institutional practice in the making of a racial category'. *Annals of the Association of American Geographers*, 77, 4: 580–98.

Andrew, C. M. and Kanya-Forstner, A. S. 1971: 'The French "Colonial Party": its composition, aims and influence, 1885–1914'. *The Historical Journal*, 14: 9–128.

Andrew, C. M. and Kanya-Forstner, A. S. 1974: 'The French Colonial Party and French colonial war aims, 1914–1918'. *The Historical Journal*, 17: 79–106.

Andrew, C. M. and Kanya-Forstner, A. S. 1974: 'The Groupe Colonial in the French Chamber of Deputies, 1892–1932'. *The Historical Journal*, 17: 837–66.

Andrew, C. M. and Kanya-Forstner, A. S. 1976: 'French business and the French colonialists'. *The Historical Journal*, 19: 981–1000.

Andrew, C. M. and Kanya-Forstner, A. S. 1977: 'France and the Repartition of Africa'. *Dalhousie Review*, 57: 475–93.

Andrew, C. M. and Kanya-Forstner, A. S. 1978: 'France, Africa and the First World War'. *Journal of African History*, 19: 11–23.

Andrew, C. M. and Kanya-Forstner, A. S. 1981: *France Overseas: the Great War and the climax of French imperial expansion*. London: Thames and Hudson.

Andrew, C. M. and Kanya-Forstner, A. S. 1988: 'Centre and periphery in the making of the second French empire, 1815–1930'. *Journal of Imperial and Commonwealth History*, 16: 9–34.

Andrew, C. M., Grupp, P. and Kanya-Forstner, A. S. 1975: 'Le mouvement colonial français et ses principales personnalités (1890–1914)'. *Revue française d'histoire d'outre-Mer*, 62: 640–73.

Andrews, H. F. 1984: 'The Durkheimians and human geography: some contextual problems in the sociology of knowledge'. *Transactions, Institute of British Geographers*, n.s. 9: 315–26.

Andrews, H. F. 1986: 'A French view of geography teaching in Britain in 1871'. *Geographical Journal*, 152: 225–31.

Andrews, H. F. 1986: 'Les premiers cours de géographie de Paul Vidal de la Blache'. *Annales de géographie*, 95, 529: 341–67.

Andrews, H. F. 1986: 'The early life of Paul Vidal de la Blache and the makings of modern geography'. *Transactions, Institute of British Geographers*, n.s. 11: 174–82.

Andrews, M. 1900: 'Geography and empire education'. *Journal of the Royal Colonial Institute*, 11: 103.

Anglerius, Petrus Martyr 1530: *De Orbe Novo Decades*. 8 Decades. Compluti. London: British Library.

Annales de géographie: Bulletin de la Société de Géographie. 1891: Paris: A. Colin. [inaugural issue]

Anon., 1885: 'German colonisation in tropical Africa'. *Scottish Geographical Magazine*, 1: 263.

Anon., 1885: 'The new British colony in South Africa'. *Scottish Geographical Magazine*, 1: 383.

Anon., 1886: Review of 'Zur Klimatologie und Hygiene Ostafrikas', by Gerhard Rohlfs, *Scottish Geographical Magazine*, 2: 637.

Anon., 1887: 'Editorial'. *The Educational Times*, 2: 56.

Anon., 1889: 'Obituary of Edward Anthony'. *Wilson's Photographic Magazine*, 26.

Anon., 1895: *Germania triumphans! Rückblick auf die weltgeschichtlichen Ereignisse der Jahre 1900–1911 von einem Größtdeutschen*. Berlin: A. W. Hayn's Erben.

Anon., 1901: 'Syllabus for instruction in geography'. *The Education Gazette*, 1: 2, 3.

Anon., 1905: 'A geography association for South Africa'. *The Education Gazette*, 3, 1: 167.

Anon., 1906: 'Suggestions for teachers'. *The Education Gazette*, 5, 27: 622–3.

Anon., 1906: 'Vakman'. *De Unie*, 21.

Anon., 1908: 'Editorial'. *The Educational News*, 8, 9: 20.

Anon., 1908: 'Zo Leren onze Jongelieden Aardrijkskunde en Geschiedenis'. *De Unie*, 3, 385–6.

Anon., 1910: 'Suggestions for the teaching of geography'. *The Educational News*, April, 47–50.

Anon., 1919: 'War services of members in the Association of American Geographers'. *Annals of the Association of American Geographers*, 8: 53–70.

Anon., 1932: *Verhandlungen des Voxstandes des Kolonial-Wirtschaftlichen Komitees*, 1.

Anon., 1944: 'History repeats for Dr. Bowman'. *Omaha Evening World Herald*, 19 March.

Anon., 1989: 'Editorial statement'. *National Geographic Magazine*, 9, 6: frontispiece.

Anon., 1989: *National Geographic Index, 1888–1988*. Washington, DC: National Geographic Society.

Ansprenger, F. 1989: *The Dissolution of the Colonial Empires*. London: Routledge.

Aquarone, Alberto 1977: 'Politica estera ed organizzazione del consenso nell'età giolittiana: il congresso di Asmara e la fondazione dell'Istituto coloniale italiano'. *Storia contemporanea*, 70–119, 291–333, 549–70.

Arnold, D. 1988: *Imperial Medicine and Indigenous Societies*. Manchester: Manchester University Press.

Artz, Frederick B. 1966: *The Development of Technical Education in France 1500–1850*. Cambridge, Mass. and London: MIT Press.

Asad, T. (ed.) 1973: *Anthropology and the Colonial Encounter*. London: Ithaca Press.

Ashcroft, B., Griffiths, G., and Tiffin, H. 1989: *The Empire Writes Back: Theory and Practice in Post-Colonial Literatures*. London: Routledge.

Ashforth, A. 1990: *The Politics of Official Discourse in Twentieth Century South Africa*. Oxford: Clarendon Press.

Atkins, Paul M. 1907: 'Arctic expeditions commanded by Americans'. *National Geographic Magazine*, 18, 7: 458–68.

Atkins, Paul M. 1942: 'French West Africa in wartime'. *National Geographic Magazine*, 81, 3: 371–408.

Atkinson, P. 1990: *The Ethnographic Imagination: Textual Constructions of Reality*. London: Routledge.

Attwood, W. A. 1919: 'The call for geographers'. *Geographical Review*, 36–43.

Austen, R. 1987: *African Economic History*. London: J. Currey.

Avendaño, Joaquín 1844: *Manual completo de instrucción primaria elemental y superior, para uso de los aspirantes a maestros*. Madrid: Imprenta de Hidalgo y J. González y Cia, 3 vols.

Ayany, S. 1970: *A History of Zanzibar*. Nairobi: East African Literature Bureau.

Baghetti, Pietro Giuseppe 1827: *Analisi della unità d'effetto nella pittura e della imitazione nelle belle arti*. Turin.

Bailey, Solon I. 1906: 'A new Peruvian route to the plain of the Amazon'. *National Geographic Magazine*, 17, 8: 432–48.

Baker, S. J. K. 1988: 'Paul Vidal de la Blache, 1845–1917'. In T. W. Freeman (ed.), *Geographers: biobibliographical studies*, 12: 189–201.

Balfour, Andrew 1923: 'Problems of acclimatisation'. *The Lancet*, 205: 84–7, 243–7.

Balfour, Andrew 1923: 'Sojourners in the tropics'. *The Lancet*, 204: 1329–44.

Balfour, Andrew and Scott, Henry Harold 1924: *Health problems of the empire: past, present and future*. London: Collins.

Bann, Stephen 1990: *The inventions of history. Essays on the representation of the past*. Manchester: Manchester University Press.

Banta, Martha 1987: *Imaging American Women: Idea and Ideals in Cultural History*. New York: Columbia University Press.

Barker, F. et al. (eds) 1983: *The Politics of Theory*. Colchester: University of Essex.

Barker, F. et al. (eds) 1985: *Europe and Its Others*. Colchester: University of Essex.

Barlow, William 1597: *The Navigator's Supply*. London.

Barth, Heinrich 1859: *Travels and Discoveries in North and Central Africa*. New York: Harper and Brothers.

Bassett, Thomas J. and Porter, Philip W. 1991: 'From the best authorities: the Mountains of Kong in the cartography of West Africa'. *Journal of African History*, 32, 3: 367–413.

Bassin, Mark 1987: 'Imperialism and the nation state in Friedrich Ratzel's political geography'. *Progress in Human Geography*, 11: 473–95.

Bassin, Mark 1987: 'Race contra space: The conflict between German Geopolitik and National Socialism'. *Political Geography Quarterly*, 6: 115–34.

Bates, T. 1975: 'Gramsci and the theory of hegemony'. *Journal of the History of Ideas*, 36, 3: 351–66.

Battaglia, Otto Forst de 1932: 'Geopolitik'. *Europäische Gespräche*, 10: 24–38.

Battisti, Cesare and Biasutti, Renato 1899: 'Giardini sperimentali nell' Eritrea'. *La Cultura Geografica*, 94–6.

Baudet, H. 1965: *Paradise on Earth: Some Thoughts on European Images of Non-European Man*. New Haven: Yale University Press.

Beatty, C. 1956: *Ferdinand de Lesseps: A Biographical Study*. London: Eyre and Spottiswoode.

Beaune, Colette 1991: *The Birth of an Ideology. Myths and Symbols of Nation in Late-Medieval France*. Berkeley, Los Angeles, Oxford: University of California Press.

Beavon, K. and Rogerson, C. 1981: 'Trekking on: recent trends in the human geography of Southern Africa'. *Progress in Human Geography*, 5: 159–89.

Bedini, Silvio A. 1990: *Thomas Jefferson. Statesman of Science*. New York: MacMillan.

Behr, J. and MacMillan, M. 1966: *The History of Education in South Africa*. Cape Town: Nasionale Pers.

Behramann, W. (ed.) 1932: *Verhandlungen des Deutschen Geographentages: 24 Deutsches Geographentag zu Danzig, 26–9 Mai, 1931*. Breslau: F. Hirt Verlag.

Beinart, W. 1983: *The Political Economy of Pondoland*. Cambridge: Cambridge University Press.

Beinart, W. 1987: 'Worker consciousness, ethnic particularism and nationalism: the experience of a South African migrant'. In S. Marks and S. Trapido (eds), *The Politics of Race, Class and Nationalism in Twentieth Century South Africa*, London: Longman.

Bencheikh, Ahmed 1991: 'Sciences coloniales, sciences du développement'. Mimeographed paper, University of Montreal, spring 1991.

Bennett, James and Brown, Olivia 1982: *The Complete Surveyor*. Cambridge, England: Whipple Museum of the History of Science.

Bennett, N. 1978: *A History of the Arab State of Zanzibar*. London: Methuen.

Bérard, Victor 1901: *L'Angleterre et l'Impérialisme*. Paris: Armand Colin.

Berdoulay, Vincent 1978: 'The Vidal-Durkheim debate'. In D. Ley and M. Samuels (eds), *Humanistic Geography: prospects and problems*, Chicago: Maaroufa Press, 77–90.

Berdoulay, Vincent 1981: 'The Contextual Approach'. In D. Stoddart (ed.), *Geography, Ideology and Social Concern*, Oxford: Basil Blackwell.

Berdoulay, Vincent 1981: *La formation de l'École française de Géographie*. Paris: Bibliothèque Nationale (CTHS).

Berdoulay, Vincent 1988: *Les Mots et les Lieux: la dynamique du discours géographique*. Paris: Éditions du Centre Nationale de Recherche Scientifique.

Berdoulay, Vincent and Soubeyran, Olivier 1991: 'Lamarck, Darwin, Vidal: aux fondements naturalistes de la géographie humaine'. *Annales de géographie*, 561–2: 617–34.

Berger, John 1972: *Ways of Seeing*. London: British Broadcasting Corporation and Penguin Books.

Bergevin, Jean 1992: *Déterminisme et géographie: Hérodote, Strabon, Albert le Grand et Sebastien Münster*. Sainte-Foy: Les Presses de l'Université Laval.

Bernal, Martin 1987: *Black Athena. The Afroasiatic Roots of Classical Civilization*. London: Free Association Books. vol. 1.

Berthaut, Colonel H. 1902: *Les Ingénieurs géographes militaires 1624–1831*. Paris: Imprimerie du service géographique.

Berthier, Alexandre 1802: 'Rapport du Ministre de la guerre au Consuls de la République sur les travaux du Dépôt général de la guerre pendant le cours de l'an X (1802), 14 vendemaire an xi'. In *Mémoriale du Dépôt de la guerre*, vol. 1. Paris: Ministère de la Guerre.

Best, Geoffrey 1982: *War and Society in Revolutionary Europe 1770–1870*. New York: St Martin's Press.

Betts, R. F. 1961: *Assimilation and Association in French Colonial Theory 1890–1914*. New York: Columbia University Press.

Betts, R. F. 1978: *Tricouleur: the French Empire Overseas*. London: Gordon and Cremonsi.

Bhabha, H. K. 1983: 'Difference, discrimination, and the discourse of colonialism'. In F. Barker (ed.), *The Politics of Theory*, Colchester: University of Essex.

Bhabha, H. K. 1984: 'Of mimicry and man: the ambivalence of colonial discourse'. *October*, 28: 125–33.

Bhabha, H. K. 1990: 'Articulating the archaic: notes on colonial nonsense'. In P. Collier and H. Geyer-Ryan (eds), *Literary Theory Today*, Ithaca: Cornell University Press, 203–18.

Bhabha, H. K. 1990: *Nation and Narration*. London: Routledge.

Biagioli, Mario 1990: 'Galileo's system of patronage'. *History of Science*, 28: 1–62.

Bierstecker, A. 1990: 'Post-war Swahili poetry and the construction of a Swahili identity'. Paper presented to the Annual Meeting of the African Studies Association, Baltimore, November 1.

Billinge, M. 1984: 'Hegemony, Class, and Power in late Georgian and early Victorian England: towards a Cultural Geography'. In Baker and Gregory (eds), *Explorations in Cultural Geography*, Cambridge: Cambridge University Press, 28–67.

Billinge, M., Gregory, D., and Martin, R. (eds) 1984: *Recollections of a Revolution*. London: Macmillan.

Birth, K. 1990: 'Reading and the righting of writing ethnographies'. *American Ethnologist*, 17: 549–57.

Blount, Roy Jr 1988: 'Spoofing the Geographic'. *National Geographic Magazine*, 174, 3: 352–7.

Bock, Gisela 1984: 'Racism and Sexism in Nazi Germany: Motherhood, Compulsory Sterilization and the State'. In Renate Bridenthal, et al. (eds), *When Biology Became Destiny: Women in Weimar and Nazi Germany*, New York: Monthly Review Press, 271–96.

Böhmer, Rudolf 1929: 'Kolonialpolitik oder Proletarisierung'. *Deutsche Rundschau*, 55: 65–8.

Boletín de la Sociedad Geográfica Nacional. Madrid 1876 – founded 1876 – title changed 1901 to *Real Sociedad Geográphica* – title changed 1931 to *Sociedad Geográfica Nacional*.

Bollettino della Società Geografica Italiana. 1868: Roma: Reale Società geographica Italiana.

Bond, Edward A. (ed.) 1856: *Russia at the Close of the Sixteenth Century*. London: Hakluyt Society.

Bonelli, E. 1885: 'Nuevos territorios españoles de la costa del Sahara'. *Boletin de la Socidad Geografica de Madrid*, 18, 5: 333–54.

Bonner, P. et al. (eds) 1989: *Holding their Ground: Class, Locality and Culture in 19th and 20th Century South Africa*. Johannesburg: Ravan Press.

Bonnet, G.-E. 1959: *Ferdinand de Lesseps*. Paris: Plon.

Borough, William 1578: *Plat of the Coasts and Inward Parts of Russia*. London, in Taylor, *Tudor Geography*.

Bourçet, Général 1875: 'Mémoires sur les reconnaissances militaires attribués au général Bourcet'. In *Journal de la Librairie militaire*, Paris: Librairie militaire, 1–2 années 1875–6.

Bourdieu, P. 1990: *The Uses of the 'People'. In Other Words: Essays Towards a Reflexive Sociology*. Stanford: Stanford University Press.

Bourguet, Marie-Noël 1988: *Déchiffrer la France. La Statistique départementale á l'époque napoléonienne*. Paris: Éditions des archives contemporaines.

Bouvier, J. 1974: 'Les traits majeurs de l'impérialisme français avant 1914'. *Le Mouvement social*, 86: 99–128.

Boyer, Ferdinand 1964: 'Les responsabilités de Napoléon dans le transfert à Paris des oeuvres d'art de l'étranger'. *Revue d'histoire moderne et contemporaine*, 11: 241–62.

Bozzoli, B. (ed.) 1983: *Town and Countryside in the Transvaal: Capitalist Penetration and Popular Response*. Johannesburg: Ravan Press.

Bozzoli, B. (ed.) 1987: *Class, Community and Conflict: South African Perspectives*. Johannesburg: Ravan Press.

Bozzoli, B. 1990: 'Intellectuals, audiences and histories: South African experiences, 1978–1988'. *Radical History Review*, 46/7: 237–63.

Bozzoli, B. and Delius, P. 1990: 'Radical history and South African society'. *Radical History Review*, 46/7: 13–46.

Bradford, H. 1990: 'Highways, byways and culs-de-sac: the transition to agrarian capitalism in revisionist South African historiography'. *Radical History Review*, 46/7: 59–88.

Brennan, Tim 1990: 'Cosmopolitans and Celebrities'. *Race and Class*, 31: 1–20.

Brereton, John 1602: *A briefe and true relation of the Discoveries of the North Part of Virginia ... made this present year 1602*. With annexed: *A treatise containing inducements for planting*, by Edward Hayes. London.

Bridgman, Herbert L. 1906: 'The new British Empire of the Sudan'. *National Geographic Magazine*, 17, 5: 241–67.

Briggs, Henry 1625: 'A Treatise of the NW Passage to the South Sea, to the Continent of Virginia and by Fretum Hudson'. In Samuel Purchas, *Purchas his Pilgrimes*. London. Part II, 848–54.

Broc, Numa 1970: 'Histoire de la géographie et nationalisme en France sous la IIIe République (1871–1914)'. *L'Information historique*, 32: 21–6.

Broc, Numa 1974: 'L'Établissement de la géographie en France: diffusion, institutions, projets (1870–1890)'. *Annales de géographie*, 83, 459: 545–68.

Broc, Numa 1974: *La Géographie des philosophes. Géographes et voyageurs français au XVIIIe siècle*. Paris: Éditions Ophyrys.

Broc, Numa 1976: 'La pensée géographique en France au XIXe siècle: continuité ou rupture?' *Revue Géographique des Pyrénées et du Sud-Ouest*, 47: 225–47.

Broc, Numa 1977: 'Franz Schrader, 1844–1924'. In T. W. Freeman, M. Aughton, and P. Pinchemel (eds), *Geographers: biobibliographical studies*, 1: 97–103.

Broc, Numa 1977: 'La géographie française face à la science allemande (1870–1914)'. *Annales de géographie*, 86, 473: 71–94.

Broc, Numa 1978: 'Nationalisme, colonialisme et géographie: Marcel Dubois (1856–1916)'. *Annales de géographie*, 87, 481: 326–33.

Brochier 1988: 'Fondements idéologiques et visée scientifique en Economique', *Economies et sociétés*, 10: 169–88.

Brockway, L. H. 1979: *Science and Colonial Expansion: the role of the British botanic gardens*. London and New York: Academic Press.

Brooks, S. 1990: *Playing the Game: The Struggle for Wildlife Protection in Zululand, 1910–1930*. MA Thesis, Department of Geography, Queen's University, Kingston, Canada.

Brown, T. N. L. 1971: *The History of the Manchester Geographical Society, 1884–1950*. Manchester: Manchester University Press.

Bruézière, M. 1983: *L'Alliance française: histoire d'une institution*. Paris: Hachette.

Brunschwig, H. 1966: *French Colonialism, 1871–1914: Myths and Realities*. London: Pall Mall Press.

Brunschwig, H. 1969: 'French Exploration and Conquest in Tropical Africa from 1865–1898'. In L. Gann and P. Guignan (eds), *Colonialism in Africa, 1860–1960: the history and politics of colonialism, 1870–1914*, Cambridge: Cambridge University Press, 1: 132–64.

Brunschwig, H. 1974: 'Vigné d'Octon et l'anticolonialisme sous la Troisième Republique'. *Cahiers d'études africaines*, 14: 265–98.

Bryan, C. D. B. 1987: *The National Geographic Society: 100 Years of Adventure and Discovery*. New York: Harry N. Abrams.

Bryce, James. 1892: 'The migrations of the races of men considered historically'. *Scottish Geographical Magazine*, 8: 401–25.

Buckley, Tom 1970: 'With the National Geographic on its endless, cloudless voyage'. *New York Times Magazine*, September 6, 10–23.

Bunting, B. 1986: *The Rise of the South African Reich*. London: International Defence and Aid Fund for South Africa.

Burgdörfer, Friedrich 1932: *Volk ohne Jugend, Geburtenschwund und Überalterung des deutschen Volkskörpers*. Grunewald, Berlin: Vowinckel.

Burleigh, Michael 1988: *Germany Turns Eastwards: A Study of Ostforschung in the Third Reich*. Cambridge: Cambridge University Press.

Burrows, M. 1986: 'Mission civilisatrice: French cultural policy in the Middle East, 1860–1914'. *The Historical Journal*, 29: 109–35.

Burt, Eugene C. 1989: *Erotic Art: An Annotated Bibliography with Essays*. Boston: G. K. Hall and Co.

Burton, R. 1872: *Zanzibar: City, Island and Coast*. London: Tinsley Brothers.

Buttimer, A. 1971: *Society and Milieu in the French Geographic Tradition*. Washington DC: American Philosophical Society.

Cabral, A. 1973: *Return to the Source*. New York: Monthly Review Press.

Cagan, Steve 1990: *Photography's contribution to the 'Western' vision of the colonized 'other'*. Paper presented at the Center for Historical Analysis, Rutgers University, 10 April.

Caldo, Constantino 1982: *Il territorio come dominio: la geografia italiana durante il fascismo*. Naples: Loffredo.

Callinicos, L. 1987: 'The "People's Past": Towards Transforming the Present'. In B. Bozzoli (ed.), *Class, Community and Conflict*, Johannesburg: Ravan Press.

Callinicos, L. 1989: 'Intellectuals, popular history and worker education'. *Perspectives in Education*, 11.

Callinicos, L. 1990: 'Popular history in the eighties'. *Radical History Review*, 46/7: 285–97.

Campbell, Thomas M. and Herring, George C. 1975: *The Diaries of Edward R. Stettinius, Jr., 1943–1946*. New York: New Viewpoints.

Campo Fregoso, Luigi 1872: *Del primato italiano sul Mediterraneo*. Torino: Loescher.

Candeloro, Giorgio 1970–82: *Storia dell'Italia moderna*. Milan: Feltrinelli, vols. 6, 1871–96 (1970); 7, 1896–1914 (1974); 8, 1914–22 (1978); 9, 1922–39 (1982).

Cantalupo, Roberto 1926: 'Il fascismo e la coscienza coloniale'. *Bollettino della Società Geografica Italiana*, 337–52.

Capel, Horacio 1982: *Geografía y Matemáticas en la España del siglo XVIII*. Barcelona: Oikos-Tau.

Capel, Horacio et al. 1985: *Geografía para todos. La Geografía en la enseñanza española durante la segunda mitad del siglo XIX*. Barcelona: Los Libros de la Frontera.

Capel, Horacio, Sánchez, J. E., and Moncada, O. 1988: *De Palas a Minerva. La formación científica y la estructura institucional de los ingenieros militares en el siglo XVIII*. Barcelona: Serbal.

Capel, Horacio, Solé, J., and Urteaga, L. 1988: *El libro de Geografía en España (1800–1939)*. Barcelona: Ediciones de la Universidad de Barcelona.

Caraci, Ilaria 1982: *La geografia italiana tra '800 e '900*. Genoa: Istituto di Scienze Geografiche dell'Università.

Carazzi, Maria 1972: *La Società Geografica Italiana e l'esplorazione coloniale in Africa (1867–1900)*. Florence: La Nuova Italia Editrice.

Carré, J.-M. 1956: *Voyageurs et écrivains français en Égypte*. Cairo: Imprimerie de l'Institut Français d'Archéologie Orientale.

Carrière, B. 1988: 'Le Transsaharien: histoire et géographie d'une entreprise inachevée'. *Acta Géographica*, 74: 23–38.

Carter, P. 1987: *The Road to Botany Bay: An Essay in Spatial History*. London: Faber and Faber.

Carter, P. 1990: 'Plotting: Australia's explorer narratives as "spatial history"'. *Yale Journal of Criticism*, 3: 91–107.

Carter, P. and Malouf, D. 1989: 'Spatial History'. *Textual Practice*, 3: 173–83.

Casals, Vicente 1989: 'Montes e ingenieros en Ultramar. Las ideas sobre la protección del bosque en Cuba y Filipinas durante el siglo XIX'. In J. L. Peset, 357–88.

Casals, Vicente 1991: 'Del cultivo de los árboles a las leyes de la espesura'. In M. Lucena (ed.), *El bosque ilustrado. Estudios sobre la política forestral española en America, 1750–1810*, Madrid: Instituto de Ingeniería de España, 63–89.

Castellani, Aldo 1931: *Climate and Acclimatization*. London: J. Bale, Sons and Danielsson.

Chabrol de Volvic, 1822: 'Essai sur les moeurs des habitans modernes de l'Égypte'. *Description de l'Égypte*, État moderne. Paris: Imprimerie royale, 2, 2: 361–526.

Chabrol de Volvic, 1824: *Statistique des provinces de Savone, d'Oneille, d'Acqui et de partie de la province de Mondovi formant l'ancien département de Montenotte*. Paris: Jules Didot aîné.

Chapman, George 1613: *The Memorable Maske ... of the Inns of Court*. London.

Charbit, Y. 1981: *Du malthusianisme au populationisme: les économistes français et la population, 1840–1970*. Paris: Presses universitaires de France, 185–92.

Charles, Havelock 1913: 'Neurasthenia and its bearing on the decay of northern peoples in India'. *Transactions of the Society of Tropical Medicine and Hygiene*, 7: 2–31.

Charlton, D. G. 1963: *Secular Religions in France, 1815–1870*. Oxford: Oxford University Press.

Childers, Thomas 1990: 'The social language of politics in Germany: the sociology of political discourse in the Weimar Republic'. *American Historical Review*, 95: 331–58.

Chipman, J. 1989: *French Power in Africa*. Oxford: Basil Blackwell.

Chisholm, George G. 1925: 'Perplexities of race: a review'. *Scottish Geographical Magazine*, 41:

Chisman, L. 1990: 'The imperial unconscious? Representations of colonial discourse'. *Critical Quarterly*, 32: 38–58.

Christie, J. 1869: *Cholera Epidemics in Eastern Africa*. London: MacMillan.

Christopher, A. J. 1984: *Colonial Africa*. London: Croom Helm.

Christopher, A. J. 1988: *The British Empire at its Zenith*. London: Croom Helm.

Church, John W. 1919: 'A vanishing people of the South Seas – the tragic fate of the Marquesan cannibals, noted for their warlike courage and physical beauty'. *National Geographic Magazine*, 36, 4: 275–306.

Clark, Kenneth 1956: *The Nude: A Study in Ideal Form*. New York: Doubleday, Garden City.

Clark, T. N. 1973: *Prophets and Patrons: the French University and the emergence of the social sciences*. Cambridge, Mass: Harvard University Press.

Clausewitz, Carl von 1984: *On War*, edited and translated by Michael Howard and Peter Paret. Princeton: Princeton University Press.

Claval, Paul 1964: *Essai sur l'évolution de géographie humaine*. Paris: Les Belles Lettres (2nd edn, 1969).

Claval, Paul 1972: 'La naissance de la géographie humaine'. In *La pensée géographique contemporaine (Mélanges offerts à A. Meynier)*, Sainte Brieuc: Presses universitaires de Bretagne: 355–76.

Claval, Paul 1989: 'André Siegfried et les démocraties anglo-saxonnes'. *Études normandes*, 2: 121–35.

Claval, Paul and Nardy, P. 1968: *Pour la Cinquanténaire de la mort de Paul Vidal de la Blache*. Paris: Les Belles Lettres.

Clayton, A. 1976: *The 1948 Zanzibar General Strike*. Uppsala: Scandinavian Institute of African Studies, Report 32.

Clayton, A. 1981: *The Zanzibar Revolution and its Aftermath*. London: Archon.

Clifford, J. 1988: *The Predicament of Culture*. Cambridge: Cambridge University Press.

Clifford, J. and Marcus, G. (eds) 1986: *Writing Culture: The Poetics and Politics of Ethnography*. Berkeley: University of California Press.

Clulee, Nicholas 1988: *John Dee's Natural Philosphy. Between Science and Religion*. London: Routledge.

Cocks, J. 1989: *The Oppositional Imagination*. London: Routledge.

Coetzee, J. M. 1988: *White Writing: On the Culture of Letters in South Africa*. New Haven: Yale University Press.

Cohen, W. B. 1980: *The French Encounter with Africans: White Responses to Blacks, 1530–1980*. Cincinnati: Indiana University Press.

Coleman, C. and Starkey, D. 1986: *Revolution Reassessed: Revisions in the History of Tudor Government and Administration*. Oxford University Press.

Colin, Epidariste 1809: *Extrait des Procès-verbaux de la Société d'émuation de l'Île-de-France*, vol. 9, no. 27: 378–89.

Comaroff, J. and J. 1991: *Of Revelation and Revolution*. Chicago: University of Chicago Press.

Comité d'Études 1918–19: *Travaux du Comité d'Études*, vol. 1: *L'Alsace-Lorraine et la frontière du Nord-Est* and vol. 2: *Questions Européenes*. Paris.

Comte, G. 1988: *L'Aventure coloniale de la France*. Paris: Editions Denöel.

Conrad, Joseph 1926: 'Geography and Some Explorers'. In *Last Essays*, London: Dent, 1–31.

Conrad, Joseph 1988: *Heart of Darkness*. New York: W. W. Norton and Company. (First published 1902.)

Conry, Y. 1974: *L'introduction du darwinisme en France en XIXème siècle*. Paris: J. Vrin.

Cooper, F. 1977: *Plantation Slavery on the East Coast of Africa*. New Haven: Yale University Press.

Cooper, F. 1980: *From Slaves to Squatters: Plantation Labor and Agriculture in Zanzibar and Coastal Kenya, 1890–1925*. New Haven: Yale University Press.

Cooper, F. 1983: 'Urban Space, Industrial Time and Wage Labor in Africa'. In Cooper (ed.), *Struggle for the City*, Beverly Hills: Sage, 7–50.

Cooper, F. 1987: *On the African Waterfront: Urban Disorder and the Transformation of Work in Colonial Mombasa*. New Haven: Yale University Press.

Cormack, Lesley B. 1988: *Non Sufficit Orbem: Geography as an Interactive Science at Oxford and Cambridge, 1580–1620*. Toronto, PhD Thesis.

Cormack, Lesley B. 1991: 'Good fences make good neighbors: geography as self-definition in early modern England'. *Isis*, 82: 639–61.

Cormack, Lesley B. 1991: 'Twisting the lion's tail: theory and practice in the court of Henry, Prince of Wales'. In Bruce T. Moran (ed.), *Courts, Academies and Societies in Early Modern Europe*, London: Boydell and Brewer, 67–84.

Correnti, Cesare 1875: 'Relazione al XII congresso degli Scienziati Italiani'. *Bollettino della Societá Geografica Italiana*, 603–18.

Corvisier, André 1988: *Dictionnaire d'art et d'histoire militaires*. Paris: Presses universitaires de France.

Cosgrove, D. 1985: *Social Formation and Symbolic Landscape*. Totowa, New Jersey: Barnes and Noble.

Cosgrove, D. 1989: 'Geography is Everywhere: Culture and Symbolism in Human Landscapes'. In Gregory and Walford (eds), *Horizons in Human Geography*, London: Macmillan, 118–35.

Costaz, Louis 1809: 'Mémoire sur la Nubie et les Barabras'. *Description de l'Egypte*, État moderne. Paris: Imprimerie impériale, 1: 399–408.

Cottington, Robert 1609: *A true Historicall discourse of Muley Hamets rising and the three kingdoms of Morocco, Fes and Sus ... the adventures of Sir Anthony Sherley, and divers other English Gentlemen ...* London.

Count, Earl W. (ed.) 1950: *This is race. An anthology selected from the international literature on the races of man*. New York: Schuman.

Crashaw, William 1610: *A Sermon preached on 21 February 1609/10 before the ... Lord*

Delawarre, Lord Governour and Captaine Generall of Virginea. London: [William Hall] for William Welby.

Crawfurd, John 1863: 'On the connection between ethnology and physical geography'. *Transactions of the Ethnological Society of London.* n.s., 2: 4–23.

Crofton, R. 1953: *Zanzibar Affairs, 1914–1933.* London: Francis Edwards.

Crosby, Alfred W. 1988: 'Ecological imperialism: The overseas migration of Western Europeans as a biological phenomenon'. In Donald Worster (ed.), *The Ends of the Earth. Perspectives on Modern Environmental History,* Cambridge: Cambridge University Press, 103–17.

Crush, J. 1986: 'Capitalist homoficence, the frontier and uneven development in Southern Africa'. *Geojournal,* 12: 129–36.

Crush, J. 1986: 'Towards a people's historical geography for South Africa'. *Journal of Historical Geography,* 12, 2–3.

Crush, J. 1987: *The Struggle for Swazi Labour, 1890–1920.* Montreal and Kingston: McGill-Queen's Press.

Crush, J. 1991: 'The discourse of progressive human geography'. *Progress in Human Geography,* 15: 395–414.

Crush, J. 1992: 'Beyond the Frontier: The New South African Historical Geography'. In C. Rogerson and J. McCarthy (eds), *Geography in a Changing South Africa,* Cape Town: Oxford University Press, 10–37.

Crush, J. and Rogerson, C. 1983: 'New wave African historiography and African historical geography'. *Progress in Human Geography,* 7: 203–31.

Crush, J., Reitsma, H., and Rogerson, C. 1982: 'Decolonising the human geography of Southern Africa'. *Tijdschrift voor Economische en Sociale Geografie,* 73, 197–8.

Cuno, Kenneth M. 1984: 'Egypt's Wealthy Peasantry, 1740–1820: A Study of the Region of al-Mansura'. In Tarif Khalidi (ed.), *Land Tenure and Social Transformation in the Middle East,* Beirut: American University of Beirut, 303–32.

Curtin, Philip D. 1964: *The Image of Africa; British Ideas and Action, 1780–1850.* Madison: University of Wisconsin Press.

Curtin, Philip D. 1989: *Death by Migration: Europe's Encounter with the Tropical World in the Nineteenth Century.* Cambridge: Cambridge University Press.

Dainelli, Giotto 1917: 'La Dalmazia'. *Pagine geografiche della nostra guerra,* Rome: Società Geografica Italiana, 123–45.

Dainelli, Giotto 1926: 'Le ragioni del problema coloniale italiano'. *Bollettino della Società Geografica Italiana,* 447–65.

Dainville, François de 1964: 'Enseignement des "géographes" et des géomètres'. In René Taton, *Enseignement et diffusion des sciences en France au XVIIIe siècle,* Hermann, 481–91.

Dalby, S. 1990: *Creating the Second Cold War.* London: Pinter.

Dalla Vedova, Giuseppe 1904: *La Società Geografica Italiana e l'opera sua nel secolo XIX.* Rome: Società Geografica Italiana.

Dallek, Robert 1979: *Franklin D. Roosevelt and American Foreign Policy, 1932–1945.* New York: Oxford University Press.

Danforth, Kenneth C. 1990: 'Yugoslavia: A house much divided'. *National Geographic Magazine,* 178, 2: 92–123.

Danise, Sandra and Palombino, Rita 1979: 'Il terreno delle colonie'. *L'inchiesta sul terreno in geografia.* Torino: Giappichelli, 193–201.

Danziger, R. 1977: *Abd-al-Qadir and the Algerians: resistance to the French and internal consolidation.* New York: Holmes and Meier.

Davis, Angela Y. 1981: *Women, Race and Class.* New York: Vintage.

de Bry, Johann Theodore (son) 1598–1613: *India Orientalis,* partes 1–10. Frankfurt.

de Bry, Theodore 1590–1634: *America,* partes 1–13. Frankfurt.

De Groot, Joanna 1989: ' "Sex" and "Race": The Construction of Language and Image in the Nineteenth Century'. In Susan Mendus and Jane Randall (eds), *Sexuality and Subordination,* London: Routledge, 89–128.

De Jonge, Alex 1969: *The Weimar Chronicle: Prelude to Hitler*. New York: Meridian.

De Saissy, E. 1979: *The role of the ethnic factor in the politics of pre-revolutionary Zanzibar*. Paper presented to the Department of Development Studies, Uppsala University, Sweden, August 31.

Debs, Richard Abraham 1963: *The Law of Property in Egypt: Islamic Law and Civil Code*. PhD thesis, Princeton University.

Degli Esposti, Anna C. 1987: *La Società Geografica Italiana attraverso il suo Bollettino: 1916–1943*. Bologna: University of Bologna (typed thesis).

Del Boca, Angelo 1976–84: *Gli italiani in Africa orientale*, 4 vols. Bari: Laterza.

Del Boca, Angelo 1986–8: *Gli italiani in Libia*, 2 vols. Bari: Laterza.

Demangeon, Albert 1923: *L'Empire britannique. Étude de géographie coloniale*. Paris: Armand Colin (2nd edn 1925).

Demangeon, Albert 1905: *La plaine picarde*. Paris: Armand Colin.

Demangeon, Albert 1927: *Belgique, Pays-Bas, Luxembourg*. Paris: Armand Colin.

Demangeon, Albert 1927: *Les Îles Britanniques*. Paris: Armand Colin.

Demangeon, Albert 1932: 'Géographie politique'. *Annales de géographie*. 41: 22–31.

De Martonne, E. 1896: 'La vie des peuples du Haut-Nil, I'. *Annales de géographie*, 24: 506–21.

De Martonne, E. 1897: 'La vie des peuples du Haut-Nil, II'. *Annales de géographie*, 25: 61–70.

Demarchi, Luigi 1929: *Fondamenti di geografia politica*. Padova: Cedam.

Demko, G. 1988: 'Geography beyond the ivory tower'. *Annals of the Association of American Geographers*, 78: 575–9.

Denis, Pierre 1920: *La République Argentine*. Paris: Armand Colin.

Derre, J.-R. (ed.) 1986: *Regards sur le Saint-Simonisme et les Saint-Simoniens*. Lyon: Presses Universitaires de Lyon.

Désirat, Claude and Hordé, Tristan 1984: 'Volney, l'étude des langues dans l'observation de l'homme'. In Rupp-Eisenreich, Britta, *Histoires de l'anthropologie: XVI-XIX siècles*, Paris: Klincksieck, (Colloque: 'La pratique de l'anthropologie aujourd'hui', 19–21 Novembre 1981, Sèvres), 133–41.

Dietzel, Karl Heinz 1946: 'Kolonialgeographie'. In Hermann von Wissmann (ed.), *Geographie. Naturforschung und Medizin in Deutschland 1939–1946. Für Deutschland bestimmte Ausgabe der FIAT*, 1 Wiesbaden: Dieterichs'sche Verlagsbuchhandlung, vol. 44, part 1: 205–12.

Dietzel, Karl Heinz, Schmieder, O., Schmitthenner, H. (eds) 1941: *Lebensraumfragen europäischer Völker*. vol. 1 Europa, vol. 2 Europas Koloniale Ergänzungsräume. Leipzig: Quelle und Meyer.

Digeon, C. 1959: *La Crise allemande de la pensée française (1870–1914)*. Paris: Presses universitaires de France.

Digges, Sir Dudley 1612: *Of the Circumference of the earth: or, a treatise of the northeast passage*. London.

Dion, Roger 1977: *Aspects politiques de la géographie antique*. Paris: Les Belles Lettres.

Divine, Robert, A. 1971: *Second Chance*. New York: Antheum.

Dix, Arthur 1911: 'Geographische Abrundungstendenzen in der Weltpolitik'. *Geographische Zeitschrift*, 17: 1–18.

Dix, Arthur 1914: *Deutscher Imperialismus*, 2nd edn. Leipzig: B. G. Teubner.

Dix, Arthur 1923: *Politische Geographie. Weltpolitisches Handbuch*, 2nd edn. Munich and Berlin: R. Oldenbourg.

Dix, Arthur 1927: 'Wirtschaftsstruktur und Geopolitik'. *Volkswirtschaftliche Blätter. Mitteilungen aus dem Reichsverband der Deutschen Volkswirte*, 26: 465–72.

Dix, Arthur 1927: *Geopolitik, Lehrkurse über die geographischen Grundlagen der Weltpolitik und Weltwirtschaft*, (Füssen a. Lech, undated, probably 1927) Athenaeum.

Dix, Arthur 1929: 'Weltgeschichte – Kolonialgeschichte'. *Übersee-und Koloniale Zeitung*, 41: 213–14.

Dix, Arthur 1932: *Weltkrise und Kolonialpolitik. Die Zukunft zweier Erdteile*. Berlin: Paul Neff.

Domosh, M. 1991: 'Towards a feminist historiography of geography'. *Transactions of the Institute of British Geographers*, 16: 95–104.

Domosh, M. 1991: 'Beyond the frontiers of geographical knowledge'. *Transactions of the Institute of British Geographers*, 16: 488–90.

Donovan, W. 1949: *Functions of the OSS*. OSS – War Report, Washington DC., 2 vols.

Doria, Giacomo 1896: 'Notiziario' *Bollettino della Società Geografica Italiana*.

Drapeyron, Ludovic 1888: *Les deux Buaches et l'éducation géographique de trois rois de France, Louis XVI, Louis XVIII, Charles X* ... Paris: Institut Géographique de Paris.

Drayton, Michael 1606: *Ode to the Virginia Voyage. (Poems Lyrical and Pastoral)*. London.

Dresch, J. 1985: 'Emmanuel de Martonne, 1873–1955'. In T. W. Freeman (ed.), *Geographers: biobibliographical studies*, 12: 73–81.

Driver, F. 1991: 'Henry Morton Stanley and his critics: geography, exploration and empire'. *Past and Present*, 133: 134–66.

Driver, F. 1992: 'Geography's empire: histories of geographical knowledge'. *Environment and Planning D: Society and Space*, 10: 23–40.

Dubois, Marcel 1892: 'Le rôle des articulations littorales'. *Annales de géographie*, 2: 131–42.

Dubois, Marcel 1894: 'Leçon d'ouverture du cours de géographie coloniale'. *Annales de géographie*, 10: 121–37.

Dubois, Marcel 1894: 'Le continent Austral'. *Les annales de géographie* 11: 386–87.

Dubois, Marcel 1914: 'Géographie et géographes, à propos d'une thèse'. *Le correspondant*, 86, 255: 833–63.

Dubow, S. 1987: 'Race, Civilization and Culture: The Elaboration of Segregationist Discourse in the Inter-War Years'. In S. Marks and S. Trapido (eds), *The Politics of Race, Class and Nationalism in Twentieth Century South Africa*, London: Longman.

Duems, Erich and von Stuemer, Willibald (eds) 1932: *Fünfzig Jahre Deutsche Kolonialgesellschaft 1882–1932*. Berlin: Deutsche Kolonialgesellschaft.

Duems, Erich et al. (eds) 1937: *Das Buch der deutschen Kolonien*. Leipzig. W. Goldmann.

Dumas, L. 1986: *The Overburdened Economy: Uncovering the Causes of Chronic Unemployment, Inflation and National Decline*. Berkeley: University of California Press.

Dunbar, Gary S. 1978: *Élisée Reclus 1830–1905: Historian of Nature*. Hamden, Connecticut: Archon Books.

During, S. 1987: 'Postmodernism or post-colonialism today'. *Textual Practice*, 1: 32–47.

Durrani, S. 1989: 'Kiswahili resistance publishing at the Kenya coast'. *Ufahamu*, 16, 3: 26–34.

Duveyrier, H. 1890: 'Rapport sur le concours au prix annuel fait à la Société de Géographie'. *Bulletin de la Société de Géographie*, 11: 147–51.

Eagleton, T., Jameson F., and Said, E. 1990: *Nationalism, Colonialism and Literature*. Minneapolis: University of Minnesota Press.

Eagleton, Terry 1991: *Ideology: An Introduction*. London, New York: Verso.

Ebeling, Friedrich 1930: 'Schafft Raum zur Überwindung einer schweren Zukunft'. *Übersee-und Koloniale Zeitung*, 42: 406–8.

École normale n.d. : *Séances des écoles normales. Débats* and *séances des écoles normales recueillies par des sténographes et revues par les professeurs*, vol. 1–4. Paris: L. Reynier, (*c.*1802).

École polytechnique, livre du centenaire, 1794–1894, 3 vols, Paris: Gauthier-Villars, 1894.

Eijkman, C. 1924: 'Some questions concerning the influence of tropical climate on man'. *The Lancet*, 206: 887–93.

Eksteins, Modris 1989: *Rites of Spring: The Great War and the Birth of the Modern Age*. Boston: Lester and Orpen Dennys.

El Sheikh, M. 1986: *State, Cloves and Planters: A Reappraisal of British Colonialism in Zanzibar, 1890–1934*. PhD Dissertation, University of California, Los Angeles.

Elsdale, H. 1985: 'Higher Education: Its Present Deficiencies and Future Improvement'. *The Educational News*, March, 236.

Elton, Geoffrey R. 1953: *The Tudor Revolution in Government: Administrative Changes in the Reign of Henry VIII*. Cambridge University Press.

Elton, Geoffrey R. 1955: *England under the Tudors*. London: Methuen.

Elton, Geoffrey R. 1977: *Reform and Reformation – England 1509–1558*. Cambridge, Mass.: Harvard University Press.

Elton, Geoffrey R. 1982: *The Tudor Constitution*. Cambridge University Press.

Elwitt, S. J. 1975: *The Making of the Third Republic: class and politics in France, 1868–1884*. Baton Rouge: Louisiana State University Press.

Elwitt, S. J. 1985: *The Third Republic: Bourgeois Reform in France 1880–1914*. Baton Rouge: Louisiana State University Press.

Émerit, M. 1941: *Les Saint-Simoniens en Algérie*. Paris: Éditions de l'Empire.

Émerit, M. 1943: 'Les explorateurs saint-simoniens en Afrique orientale et sur les routes des Indes'. *Revue Africaine*, 87: 92–116.

Émerit, M. 1967: 'L'idée de colonisation dans les socialismes françaises'. *L'Age Nouveau*, 24: 103–15.

Émerit, M. 1975: 'Diplomates et explorateurs saint-simoniens'. *Revue d'Histoire Moderne et Contemporaine*, 22: 397–415.

Engelmann, Gerhard 1983: *Die Hochschulgeographie in Preussen 1810–1914*. Wiesbaden: Franz Steiner.

Enloe, Cynthia 1987: 'Feminists thinking about war, militarism and peace'. In B. B. Hess and M. M. Ferree (eds), *Analyzing Gender*. Newbury Park, CA: Sage, 526–47.

Enloe, Cynthia 1989: *Bananas, Beaches and Bases: Making Feminist Sense of International Politics*. London: Pandora.

Entrikin, N. and Brunn, S. D. (eds) 1989: *Reflections on Richard Hartshorne's 'The Nature of Geography'*. Occasional Publication of the Association of American Geographers, Washington DC.

Eyries, Jean Baptiste Benoit 1854–65: 'Mentelle, Francois-Simon'. *Biographie universelle ancienne et moderne*. Michaud 27: 661–3.

Ezawa, Joji 1939: 'Keizaichirigaku ni okeru kūkan-gainen' [The spatial concept in economic geography]. *Hitotsubashi Ronso*, 3: 211–19.

Ezawa, Joji 1942: *Chiseigaku kenkyu* [Studies on Geopolitics]. Tokyo: Nihon-Hyōnom-sha.

Ezawa, Joji 1942: *Kokudo-keikaku no kisoriron* [Basic Theories of Territorial Development]. Toyko: Sogen-sha.

Ezawa, Joji 1943: *Chiseigaku gairon* [Outline of Geopolitics]. Tokyo: Nihon-Hyōron-sha.

Faber, Karl-George 1982: 'Zur Vorgeschichte der Geopolitik: Staat, Nation und Lebensraum im Denken deutscher Geographen vor 1914'. In Heinz Dollinger and Horst Grunder (eds), *Weltpolitik, Europagedanke, Regionalismus: Festschrift für Heinz Gollwitzer*. Münster: Aschendorff, 389–406.

Fabian, J. 1990: 'Presence and representation: the other and anthropological writing'. *Critical Inquiry*, 16: 753–72.

Fakkar, R. 1974: *Reflets de la sociologie pre-marxiste dans le monde arabe: idées progressistes et pratique industrielle des saint-simoniens en Algérie et en Égypte au XIXe. siècle*. Paris: Geuthner.

Falah, G. 1989: 'The Israelization of Palestine human geography,' *Progress in Human Geography*, 13: 535–50.

Falah, G. 1991: 'Scholarly openness and the role of Israeli geographers,' *Journal of Geography and Higher Education*, 15: 81–5.

Falcucci, Clement 1939: *L'Humanisme dans l'Enseignement secondaire en France au XIXe siècle*. Toulouse: Edouard Privat.

Fanon, F. 1967: *The Wretched of the Earth*. Harmondsworth: Penguin.

Fanon, F. 1986: *Black Skin, White Masks*. London: Pluto Press.

Farah, Nuruddin 1986: *Maps*. New York: Pantheon Books.

Febvre, Lucien 1922: *La terre et l'évolution humaine*. Paris: La Renaissance du Livre.

Fechter, Paul 1929: 'Der amerikanische Raum'. *Deutsche Rundschau*, 55: 47–59.

Fehn, Richard 1930: 'Raumnot – Kolonien'. *Bayerische Industrie. Organ des Bayerische Industriellen-Verbandes E.V.*, 14: 14–15.

Feierman, S. 1990: *Peasant Intellectuals*. Madison: University of Wisconsin Press.

Felkin, Robert W. 1885: 'The Egyptian Sudan'. *Scottish Geographical Magazine*, 1: 221–38.

Felkin, Robert W. 1886: 'Can Europeans become acclimatized in tropical Africa'? *Scottish Geographical Magazine*, 2: 647–57.

Felkin, Robert W. 1886: 'Uganda'. *Scottish Geographical Magazine*, 2: 208–26.

Felkin, Robert W. 1898: Discussion remarks for Sambon's 'Acclimatization of Europeans'. *Geographical Journal*, 12: 602–5.

Felkin, Robert W. 1889: *On the Geographical Distribution of Some Tropical Diseases, and their Relation to Physical Phenomena*. Edinburgh and London: Y. T. Pentland.

Felkin, Robert W. 1891: 'On acclimatisation'. *Scottish Geographical Magazine*, 7: 647–56.

Felkin, Robert W. 1892: 'Tropical highlands: their suitability for European settlement'. *Transactions of the Seventh International Congress on Hygiene and Demography*, 10: 155–64.

Femia, J. 1975: 'Hegemony and consciousness in the thought of Antonio Gramsci'. *Political Studies*, 23, 1: 29–48.

Ferguson, J. 1990: 'Mobile workers, modernist narratives: a critique of the historiography of transition on the Zambian Copperbelt'. *Journal of Southern African Studies*, 16: 385–412.

Ferrari, Mario Enrico 1985: 'La rivista "Geopolitica" (1939–1942): una dottrina geografica per il fascismo e l'impero'. *Miscellanea di storia delle esplorazioni*, 10: 209–93.

Fieldhouse, D. K. 1973: *Economics and Empire, 1830–1914*. London: Routledge and Kegan Paul.

Fierro, A. 1983: *La Société de Géographie de Paris (1826–1946)*. Geneva/Paris: Librairie Droz/Librairie H. Campion.

Fischer, F. 1967: *Germany's War Aims in the First World War*. London: Chatto and Windus.

Fischer, Holger and Gerhard Sandner 1991: 'Die Geschichte des Geographischen Seminars der Hamburger Universität im Dritten Reich'. In Eckart Krause, Ludwig Huber and Holger Fischer (eds) *Hochschulalltag im 'Dritten Reich'. Die Hamburger Universität 1933–1945*, Berlin, Hamburg: Dietrich Reimer Verlag, 1197–222.

Fleming, M. 1975: *The Anarchist Way to Socialism: Élisée Reclus and Nineteenth-Century European Anarchism*. London: Croom Helm.

Flory, T. 1966: *Le mouvement régionaliste français: sources et développement*. Paris: Presses universitaires de France.

Flowers, J. 1905–6: 'Geography as a factor in higher education'. *The South African Journal of Science*, 213–14.

Foncin, Pierre. 'La France extérieure', *Annales de géographie*, 1, 1891, 1–9.

Forbes, Edgar Allen 1919: 'Notes on the only American colony in the world'. *National Geographic Magazine*, 21, 9: 719–29.

Foucault, Michel 1980: *Power/Knowledge: Selected Interviews and Other Writings*, (ed.) C. Gordon, New York: Pantheon Books.

Foucault, Michel 1988: 'The minimalist self'. In L. D. Kritzman (ed.), *Politics, Philosophy, Culture*, New York: Routledge, 1–16.

Fourcy, A. 1987: *Histoire de l'École polytechnique*. Paris: Eugène Bellin.

Fraile, Pedro 1988: 'La necesidad de remodelar un espacio: La Habana del general Tacón'. *Estudios de Historia Social*, 44–7: 577–94.

Fraile, Pedro 1989: 'Ciencia y utopía: Ramón de la Sagra y la isla de Cuba'. In J. L. Peset, *Ciencia, vida y espacio en Iberoamérica*, 3: 209–39.

Franklin, Ursula 1990: *Real World of Technology*. CBC Massey Lecture Series (1989). Toronto: Susan Sutton.

Freeman, M. 1987: *Atlas of Nazi Germany*. Oxford: Blackwell.

Freeman, T. W. 1980: 'The Royal Geographical Society and the Development of Geography'. In E. H. Brown (ed.), *Geography: Yesterday and Tomorrow*. Oxford: Oxford University Press.

Freeman, T. W. 1984: 'The Manchester and Royal Scottish Geographical Societies'. *Geographical Journal*, 150: 55–62.

Freeman, T. W. 1984: 'The Manchester Geographical Society, 1884–1984'. *The Manchester Geographer*, 5: 2–19.

Frenkel, S. and Western, J. 1988: 'Pretext or prophylaxis? racial segregation and malarial mosquitos in a British Tropical Colony: Sierra Leone'. *Annals of the Association of American Geographers*, 78, 2: 211–28.

Fresh, D. 1986: *British Strategy and War Aims, 1914–16*. London: Allen and Unwin.

Friedman, M. and Wilkes, A. 1986: 'Androcentric knowledge and geography – examined'. *South African Geographical Journal*, 65: 89–94.

Frisio, M. 1985: 'L'Europa balcano-danubiana nelle riviste geografiche italiane'. In E. Di Nolfo, R. Rainero, and B. Vigezzi (eds), *L'Italia e la politica di potenza in Europa (1938–1940)*. Milan: Marzorati, 227–39.

Fromkin, D. 1989: *A Peace to end all Peace: The Fall of the Ottoman Empire and the Creation of the Middle East*. New York: St Martin's Press.

Frykman, Jonas and Löfgren, Orvar 1987: *Culture Builders: A Historical Anthropology of Middle-Class Life*. New Jersey: Rutgers University Press, New Brunswick.

Fugier, André 1947: *Napoléon et l'Italie*. Paris: J.-B. Janin.

Fukuzawa, Y. 1869: 'Sekai Kunizukushi [World geography]'. In *Fukuzawa Yukichi Zenshu* [Collected Works of Yukichi Fukuzawa], vol. 2, 1959, Tokyo: Iwanami Shoten, 591–668.

Gallois, Lucien. 1892: 'La Dombes'. *Annales de géographie*, 2: 121–31.

Gallois, Lucien. 1897: 'Dr. E. T. Hamy, études historiques et géographiques'. *Les annales de géographie*, 26: 181–3.

Gangas, Mónica 1985: *La evolución de la geografía chilena*. PhD Thesis, Department of Geography, University of Barcelona, 4 vols.

Ganiage, J. 1968: *L'Expansion coloniale de la France sous la Troisième République 1871–1914*. Paris: Payot.

Gannett, Henry 1904: 'The Philippine Weather Service'. *National Geographic Magazine*, 15, 2: 77–8.

Garcia Puchol, J. 1989: 'América en los libros escolares de Historia del siglo XIX'. In J. L. Peset (ed.), *Ciencia, vida y espacio en Iberoamérica*, vol. 3, 241–56.

Gaulmier, Jean 1951: *L'ideologue Volney 1757–1820. Contribution à l'histoire de l'orientalisme en France*. Beirut.

Gautier, Emile-Félix 1927: *Les siècles obscurs du Maghreb*. Paris: Payot.

Gay, Peter 1970: *Weimar Culture: The Outsider as Insider*, 2nd edn. New York: Harper and Row.

Geiser, Karl Krederick 1908: 'Peasant life in the Black Forest'. *National Geographic Magazine*, 19, 9: 635–49.

Gelfand, Lawrence Emerson 1963: *The Inquiry*. New Haven: Yale University Press.

Genovese, E. 1974: *Roll, Jordan, Roll: The World the Slaves Made*. New York: Vintage Books.

Gerstenberger, Heide 1969: *Der Revolutionäre Konservatismus. Ein Beitrag zur Analyse des Liberalismus*. Berlin: Dunker and Humbolt.

Ghisleri, Arcangelo 1888: *Le razze umane e il diritto nella questione coloniale*. Savona: Miralta (new edn 1972, Milan: Marzorati).

Ghisleri, Arcangelo 1891: 'Le razze inferiori e la civiltà'. *Critica Sociale*, 1: 7.

Giblin, B. 1979: 'Elisée Reclus, 1830–1905'. In T. W. Freeman (ed.), *Geographers: biobibliographical studies*, 3: 125–32.

Giblin, B. 1989: 'Elisée Reclus and colonisation'. In P. Girot and E. Kofman (eds), *International Geopolitical Analysis: a selection from Herodote*. London: Croom Helm.

Giddens, A. 1985: *The Nation State and Violence*. Cambridge: Polity Press.

Gilbert, Humphrey 1598–1600: 'A Discourse for a Discovery for a new Passage to Cataia'. In Richard Hakluyt, *Principal Navigations, Voyages, Traffiques, and Discoveries of the English Nation*. 3 vols. London, vol. 3, 11–29.

Gille, Bertrand 1964 (1980): *Les Sources Statistique de l'histoire de France. Des enquêtes du XVIIe siècle à 1870*. Genève: Librairie Droz.

Gilman, Sander L. 1985: 'Black bodies, white bodies: toward an iconography of female sexuality in late nineteenth century art, medicine, and literature'. *Critical Inquiry*, 12: 204–42.

Girard, M. P. S. 1809: 'Mémoire sur l'agriculture, l'industrie et le commerce de l'Égypte'. *Description de l'Égypte*, État moderne. Paris: Imprimerie impériale, 2, 1: 491–714.

Girardet, R. 1972: *L'Idée coloniale en France de 1871 à 1962*. Paris: La Table Ronde.

Glacken, C. 1967: *Traces on the Rhodian Shore*. Berkeley: University of California Press.

Gliddon, George R. 1857. 'The monogenists and the polygenists: being an exposition of the doctrines of schools professing to sustain dogmatically the unity or the diversity of human races; with an inquiry into the antiquity of mankind upon earth, viewed chronologically, historically, and palaeontologically'. In J. C. Nott and George R. Gliddon, *Indigenous races of the earth; or, new chapters of ethnological inquiry*, Philadelphia: J. B. Lippincott, 402–602.

Godlewska, Anne 1988: *The Napoleonic Survey of Egypt. A Masterpiece of Cartographic Compilation and Early Nineteenth-Century Fieldwork. Cartographica Monograph*, vol. 25: nos 1 and 2, Spring and Summer 1988, Monograph 38–9.

Godlewska, Anne 1989: 'Traditions, crisis, and new paradigms in the rise of the modern French discipline of geography 1760–1850'. *Annals of the Association of American Geographers*, 79, 2: 192–213.

Godlewska, Anne 1990: 'Napoleonic Geography and Geography under Napoleon'. *Nineteenth Consortium on Revolutionary Europe*. Athens, Georgia: University of Georgia, Department of History, vol. 1, 281–302.

Goetzmann, William H. 1959: *Army Exploration in the American West, 1803–1863*. New Haven: Yale University Press.

Goetzmann, William H. 1986: *New Lands, New Men. America and the Second Great Age of Discovery*. New York: Viking.

Goldie, G. T. 1907: 'Geographical ideals'. *Geographical Journal*, 29, 1–14.

Golinski, Jan 1990: 'The theory of practice and the practice of theory: sociological approaches in the history of science'. *Isis*, 81: 492–505.

Gould P. R. 1985: *The Geographer at Work*. London: Routledge and Kegan Paul.

Gould, Stephen Jay 1981: *The Mismeasure of Man*. New York: Norton.

Gourou, Pierre 1936: *Les paysans du delta tonkinois. Étude de géographie humaine*. Paris: Éditions d'Art et d'Histoire.

Gourou, Pierre 1973: *Pour une géographie humaine*. Paris: Flammarion.

Graham-Brown, Sarah 1988: *Images of Women: The Portrayal of Women in Photography of the Middle East 1860–1950*. New York: Columbia University Press.

Gramsci, Antonio 1971: *Selections from the Prison Notebooks*. Q. Hoare and H. Smith (eds). New York: International Publishers.

Grazioli, Regina 1972: *Storia della Società di Studi Geografici e della sua Rivista dal 1893 ad oggi*. Milan: State University of Milan (typed thesis).

Great Britain. 1950: *Colonial Office Annual Report on Zanzibar, 1949*. Zanzibar: Government Printers.

Greenblatt, Stephen 1980: *Renaissance Self-Fashioning: From More to Shakespeare*. Chicago: University of Chicago Press.

Greene, John C. 1984: *American science in the Age of Jefferson*. Ames: Iowa State University.

Greenlee, J. G. 1987: *Education and Imperial Unity*. New York: Garland Publishing, Inc.

Gregory, D. 1994: *Geographical Imaginations*. Oxford: Basil Blackwell.

Gregory, J. W. 1924: 'Inter-racial problems and white colonisation in the tropics'. *Scottish Geographical Magazine*, 40: 257–82.

Grimshaw, Beatrice 1908: 'In the savage South Seas'. *National Geographic Magazine*, 19, 1: 1–19.

Grosvenor, Gilbert H. 1905: 'A revelation of the Filipinos'. *National Geographic Magazine*, 16, 4: 139–92.

Grosvenor, Gilbert H. 1924: 'The Hawaiian Islands – America's strongest outpost of defense – the volcanic and floral wonderland of the world'. *National Geographic Magazine*, 45, 2: 115–238.

Gruchmann, Lothar 1962: *Nationalsozialistische Grossraumordnung. Die Konstruktion einer 'deutschen Monroe-Doktrin'*. Stuttgart: Deutsche-Verlags Anstalt.

Grunder, Horst 1985: *Geschichte der Deutschen Kolonien*. Paderborn: Schöningh.

Grupp, P. 1974: 'Le "Parti Colonial" français pendant la première guerre mondiale: deux tentatives de programme commun'. *Cahiers d'Études Africaines*, 14: 377–91.

Guaiti, Giorgio 1974: *Una rivista di geografi fascisti: Geopolitica (1939–1942)*. Milan: State University of Milan (thesis).

Guha, R. and Spivak, G. C. (eds) 1988: *Selected Subaltern Studies*. New York: Oxford University Press.

Guigne, de (fils) 1810: 'Réflections sur les anciennes observations astronomiques des chinois, et sur l'état de leur empire dans les temps les plus reculés'. *Annales des voyages*, 8: 145–189.

Guiomar, J.-Y. 1986: 'Le Tableau de la géographie de la France de Vidal de la Blache'. In P. Nora (ed.), *Les Lieux de memoire: La Nation*, 2, 1: 569–97. Paris: Gallimard.

Guiral, P. 1955: *Prévost-Paradol: pensée et action d'un libéral sous le Second Empire*. Paris: Presses universitaires de France.

Gusdorf, Georges 1977: *De l'Histoire des Sciences à l'Histoire de la Pensée*. Paris: Payot.

Guy, John 1986: 'Thomas Cromwell and the Intellectual Origins of the Henrician Revolutions'. *Reassessing the Henrician Age, Humanism, Politics and Reform 1500–1550*. Oxford: Blackwell.

Guyot, Arnold Henry 1849: *The Earth and Man: Lectures on Comparative Physical Geography in its Relation to the History of Mankind*. New York (reprinted 1897).

Habermas, J. 1983: 'Modernity an Incomplete Project'. In *The Anti-Aesthetic: Essays on Postmodern Culture*, Port Townsend, Wash.: Bay Press, 3–15.

Hahn, Roger 1971: *Anatomy of a Scientific Institution, The Paris Academy of sciences, 1666–1803*. Berkeley: University of California Press.

Hakluyt, Richard 1582: *Divers Voyages Touching the Discoverie of America*. London.

Hakluyt, Richard 1589: *The Principal Navigations, Voiages and Discoveries of the English Nation*. London.

Hakluyt, Richard 1598–1600: *The Principal Navigations, Voyages, Traffiques, and Discoveries of the English Nation*. 3 vols. London.

Halpin, Zuleyma Tang 1989: 'Scientific objectivity and the concept of the "other"'. *Women's Studies International Forum*, 12, 3: 285–94.

Hamilton, William R. 1842: 'Presidential Address'. *Journal of the Royal Geographical Society*, vol. 12: lxxxviii-lxxxix.

Haraway, Donna. 1985: 'Teddy bear patriarchy: taxidermy in the Garden of Eden, New York City, 1908–1936'. *Social Text*, 11: 20–64.

Haraway, Donna 1989: *Primate Visions: Gender, Race and Nature in the World of Modern Science*. New York: Routledge.

Hardy, Georges 1933: *Géographie et colonisation*. Paris: Librairie Gallimard.

Hardy, Georges 1939: *Géographie psychologique*. Paris: Gallimard.

Harley, J. B. 1987: 'The Map and the Development of the History of Cartography'. In *The History of Cartography*, vol. 1, *Cartography in Prehistoric, Ancient, and Medieval Europe and the Mediterranean*, J. B. Harley and D. Woodward (eds.) Chicago: University of Chicago Press, 1–42.

Harley, J. B. and Woodward, D. (eds) 1987: *The History of Cartography*, vol. 1, *Cartography in Prehistoric, Ancient, and Medieval Europe and the Mediterranean*. Chicago: University of Chicago Press.

Harley, J. B., Petchenik, B. B. and Towner, L. W. 1978: *Mapping the American Revolutionary War*. Chicago and London: University of Chicago Press.

Harms, H. 1897: *Vaterländische Erdkunde*. Leipzig: List and Bressendorf.

Harriot, Thomas 1598–1600: 'A briefe and true report of the new found land of Virginia', with preface by Ralph Lane, and map 'Americae Pars, nunc Virginia dicta: autore

J. White'. In Richard Hakluyt, *Principal Navigations, Voyages, Traffiques, and Discoveries of the English Nation*. 3 vols. London, vol. 3: 266–80.

Hartshorne, R. 1935: 'Recent developments in political geography'. *American Political Science Review*, 29: 785–804, 943–66.

Harvey, David 1989: *The Condition of Postmodernity: An Enquiry into the Origins of Cultural Change*. Oxford England, Cambridge Mass.: Blackwell.

Hatano, Sumio 1980: 'Tōa shinchitsujo to chiseigaku' [Geopolitics and the new order of East Asia]. In Miura, Kimitada (ed.), *Nihon no 1930nendai* [The 1930s in Japan], Tokyo: Saikokusha, 13–47.

Hattingh, P. 1988: 'Geographers and the political system or "there are those who make things happen"'. *South African Geographical Journal*, 70: 3–19.

Haushofer, Albrecht (ed.) 1932: *Verhandlungen und wissenschaftliche Abhandlungen des 24. Deutschen Geographentages zu Danzig 16. bis 28. Mai 1931*, Breslau: Ferd. Hirt.

Haushofer, Karl 1924: *Geopolitik des Pazifischen Ozeans. Studien über die Wechselbeziehungen zwischen Geographie und Geschichte*, Berlin: Kurt Vowinckel Verlag (2nd edn 1927, 3rd edn 1938).

Haushofer, Karl 1927: 'Soll Deutschland Kolonialpolitik treiben? *Europäische Gespräche*, 5: 638–9.

Haushofer, Karl 1928: 'Politische Erdkunde und Geopolitik'. In K. Haushofer et al. (eds): *Bausteine zur Geopolitik*, Berlin: Kurt Vowinckel Verlag, 49–80.

Haushofer, Karl 1936: 'Geopolitische Grundlagen'. In H. H. Lammers and H. Pfundtner (eds), *Grundlagen, Aufbau und Wirtshaftsordnung des NS-Staates*, 1: 14, Berlin: Industrieverlag Spaeth and Linde.

Haushofer, Karl 1937: *Weltmeere und Weltmächte*, Berlin: Verlag Zeitgeschichte.

Hayek, F. 1952: *The Counter Revolution of Science: Studies on the Abuse of Reason*. Glencoe, Ill.: The Free Press.

Headley, J. 1878: *The Achievements of Stanley and Other African Explorers*. Philadelphia: Hubbard.

Heffernan, M. J. 1989: 'The limits of utopia: Henri Duveyrier and the exploration of the Sahara in the nineteenth century'. *Geographical Journal*, 155: 342–52.

Heffernan, M. J. 1990: 'Bringing the desert to bloom: French ambitions in the Sahara desert during the late nineteenth century – the strange case of "la mer intérieure"'. In D. E. Cosgrove and G. E. Petts (eds), *Water, Engineering and Landscape: water control and landscape formation in the modern period*, London: Belhaven Press, 94–114.

Heinemann, Ulrich 1983: *Die verdrängte Niederlage, Politische Öffentlichkeit und Kriegsschuldfrage in der Weimarer Republik*. Göttingen: Vandenhoeck and Ruprecht.

Hellman, Geoffrey T. 1943: 'Geography Unshackled III'. *The New Yorker*, 9 October, 27–36.

Hennig, Richard 1928: *Geopolitik. Die Lehre vom Staat als Lebewesen*. Leipzig, Berlin: B. G. Teubner.

Hernández-Sandoica, Elena 1982: *Pensamiento burgués y problemas coloniales en la Restauración, 1875–1887*. PhD Dissertation, Universidad Complutense de Madrid. 2 vols.

Hertzberg, H. 1925: 'Die Deutschen; ein Kolonialvolk'. *Geographischer Anzeiger*, 26: 68–71.

Heske, H. 1987: 'Der Traum von Afrika. Zur politischen Wissenschaftsgeschichte der Kolonialgeographie'. In H. Heske (ed.), *Ernte-Dank? Landwirtschaft zwischen Agrobusiness, Gentechnik und traditionellem Landbau*, Giessen: Focus-Verlag, 204–22.

Hess, B. B. and Ferree, M. M. 1987: *Analyzing Gender*. Newbury Park, CA: Sage.

Hettner, Alfred 1929: 'Methodische Zeit-und Streitfragen, part V; Die Geopolitik und die politische Geographie'. *Geographische Zeitschrift*, 35: 332–6.

Heyward, DuBose and Peck, Daisy 1940: 'The American Virgins'. *National Geographic Magazine*, 78, 3: 273–308.

Hildebrand, J. R. 1919: 'The geography of games'. *National Geographic Magazine*, 36, 2: 84–144.

Hildebrand, Klaus 1969: *Vom Reich zum Weltreich, Hitler, NSDAP und koloniale Frage 1919–1945*. Munich: R. Oldenbourg.

Hobsbawm, E. 1987: *The Age of Empire 1875–1914*. New York: Pantheon.

Hofmeyr, I. 1990: 'Turning region into narrative'. In P. Bonner et al. (eds), *Holding their Ground*, Johannesburg: Ravan Press, 259–84.

Hollingsworth, L. 1953: *Zanzibar Under the Foreign Office, 1890–1913*. London: MacMillan.

Hollingsworth, L. 1965: *A Short History of the East Coast of Africa*. London: MacMillan, (original 1929).

Hollingsworth, L. and Seif, S. 1932: *Jiografia ya Unguja na Pemba* [A Geography of Zanzibar and Pemba Islands]. Zanzibar: UMCA Press.

hooks, b. 1990: *Yearning: Race, Gender and Cultural Politics*. New York: Between the Lines.

Horkheimer, Max and Adorno, Theodor W. 1972: *Dialectic of Enlightenment*. New York: Herder and Herder.

Horsey, Jerome 1598–1600: 'Coronation of the Emperor of Russia'. In Richard Hakluyt, *Principal Navigations, Voyages, Traffiques, and Discoveries of the English Nation*, 3 vols. London, vol. 1, 466–70.

Hudson, Brian 1977: 'The new geography and the new imperialism: 1870–1918'. *Antipode*, 9, 2: 12–19.

Hunt, James 1863: 'On ethno-climatology; or the acclimatization of man'. *Transactions of the Ethnological Society of London*, n.s. 2: 50–79.

Huntington, Ellsworth 1914: 'The adaptability of the white man to tropical America'. *Journal of Race Development*, 5: 185–211.

Huntington, Ellsworth 1917: 'Graphic representation of the effect of climate on man'. *Geographical Review*, 4: 401–3.

Huntington, Ellsworth 1924: 'Environment and racial character'. In M. R. Thorpe (ed.), *Organic Adaptation to Environment*. New Haven: Yale University Press, 281–99.

Huntington, Ellsworth 1924: *The Character of Races, as influenced by Physical Environment, Natural Selection and Historical Development*. New York: C. Scribner's Sons.

Hutcheon, J. 1915: 'Geography'. *The South African Journal of Science*, 327–32.

Hutcheon, J. 1915: 'Some aspects of climatic control'. *The Educational News*, May, 74.

Hyam, R. 1990: *Empire and Sexuality: The British Experience*. Manchester: Manchester University Press.

Iggers, G. G. 1958: *The Cult of Authority: The Political Philosophy of the Saint-Simonians – A Chapter in the Intellectual History of Totalitarianism*. The Hague: Martinus Nijhoff.

Iimoto, Nobuyuki 1925: 'Jinshutōsō no jijitsu to chiseigakuteki kōsatsu [The reality of racial conflicts and geopolitical considerations]'. *Chirigaku Hyōron*, 1: 155–75.

Iimoto, Nobuyuki 1928: 'Iwayuru chiseigaku no gainen [The concept of so-called geopolitics]'. *Chirigaku Hyōron*, 4: 76–99.

Iizuka, Koji 1942/1943: 'Geoporitiku no kihonteki seikaku (1), (2), (3)', *Keizai Ronsō*, 12: 816–44, 13: 486–96.

Iradier, Manuel 1887: *Africa. Viajes y trabajos de la Asociación Eúskara La Exploradora*. 1st edn; 2nd edn., Vitoria: Consejo de Cultura de la Diputación Foral de Alava, vol. 1.

Ishibashi, Gorō 1927: 'Seijichirigaku to chiseigaku [Political Geography and Geopolitics]'. *Chigaku Zasshi*, 500: 76–99.

Isida, Ryuzino 1984: *Nihon ni okeru kindai chirigaku no seiritsu* [Establishment of Modern Geography in Japan]. Tokyo: Taimeido.

Iwata, Koji 1942: *Chiseigaku* [Geopolitics]. Tokyo: Asahi Shimbun-sha.

Jacobsen, H.-A. 1979: *Karl Haushofer, Leben und Werk*, vols 1 and 2. Boppard am Rhein: Boldt.

Jacotin, Pierre 1822: 'Mémoire sur la carte de l'Égypte'. *Description de l'Égypte*, État moderne 2. Paris: Imprimerie royale, 2: 1.

James, C. L. R. 1983: *Beyond a boundary*. New York: Pantheon.

James, Preston E. and Martin, Geoffrey J. 1978: *The Association of American Geographers: The First Seventy-Five Years, 1904–1979*. Washington, DC: Association of American Geographers.

Janmohammed, K. 1975: 'African Laborers in Mombasa, c.1895–1940'. In Bethwell

A. Ogot (ed.), *Hadith 5: Economic and Social History of East Africa*. Nairobi: East African Literature Bureau, 154–76.

Jefferson, Thomas 1787: *Notes on the State of Virginia*. London. (Reprinted 1990.)

Jenkins, Hester Donaldson 1915: 'Bulgaria and its women'. *National Geographic Magazine*, 27, 4: 377–400.

Johnson, James 1821: *The influence of tropical climates on European constitutions; being a treatise on the principal diseases to Europeans in the East and West Indies, Mediterranean, and Coast of Africa*. London.

Johnson, Robert 1609: *Nova Britannia. Offering most excellent fruites by planting in Virginia*. London.

Johnston, (Sir) Harry 1896: Discussion, *Report of the Sixth International Geographical Congress* in London 1895: 603.

Johnston, (Sir) Harry 1909: 'Where Roosevelt Will Hunt'. *National Geographic Magazine*, 20, 3: 207–56.

Johnston, (Sir) Harry and Lyon, Ernest 1907: 'The Black Republic, Liberia'. *National Geographic Magazine*, 18, 5: 334–43.

Jomard, Edme F. 1809: 'Mémoire sur les Arabes de l'Égypte moyenne'. *Description de l'Égypte*, État moderne. Paris: Imprimerie impériale, 1: 545–76.

Jordana Morera, Ramón 1885. *Bosquejo Geográfico e Histórico-Natural del Archipiélago Filipino*. Madrid: Imprenta de Moreno y Rojas.

Jourdain, Charles 1857: *Le Budget de l'instruction publique et des établissements scientifiques et littéraires depuis la fondation de l'université impériale jusqu'à nos jours*. Paris: L. Hachette.

Julien, C.-A. 1979: *Histoire de l'Algérie Contemporaine*, 2nd edn, vol. 1: *La Conquête et les débuts de la colonisation, 1827–1871*, Paris: Presses universitaires de France, 64–163.

Kapferer, B. 1988: 'The anthropologist as hero: three exponents of post-modernist anthropology'. *Critique of Anthropology*, 8.

Kaplan, E. Ann 1983: 'Is the gaze male?' In Ann Snitow, Christine Stansell, and Sharon Thompson (eds), *Powers of Desire: The Politics of Sexuality*, New York: Monthly Review Press, 309–27.

Kappeler, Susanne 1986: *The Pornography of Representation*. Minneapolis: University of Minnesota Press.

Kass, Amalie M. 1983: 'Dr. Thomas Hodgkin, Dr. Martin Delany, and the "Return to Africa"'. *Medical History*, 27: 373–93.

Katz, Barry 1982: *Herbert Marcuse and the Art of Liberation: an intellectual biography*. London: Verso.

Katz, B. 1989: *Foreign Intelligence*. Cambridge, Mass.: Harvard University Press.

Katz, C. and Kirby, A. 1991: 'In the Nature of Things'. *Transactions of the Institute of British Geographers*, 16: 259–71.

Kawanishi, Masakane 1933: 'Fassho-chirigaku, geoporichiku hihan, sono hembō oyobi hōhōronnjo no gigi' [Fascist geography, criticism of geopolitics – its transformation and methodological problematics]. *Tskusyoku Daigaku Ronsō*, 3: 58–88.

Kayna-Forstner, Alexander Sydney 1969: *The Conquest of the Western Sudan. A Study of French Military Imperialism*. Cambridge: Cambridge University Press.

Kearns, G. 1984: 'Closed space and political practice: Frederick Jackson Turner and Halford Mackinder'. *Environment and Planning D: Society and Space*, 2: 23–34.

Kedourie, E. 1976: *In the Anglo-Arab Labyrinth: the MacMahon-Husayn correspondence and its interpretations, 1914–1939*. Cambridge: Cambridge University Press.

Kedourie, E. 1978: *England and the Middle East: the destruction of the Ottoman Empire 1914–1921*, 2nd edn, Brighton: Harvester Press.

Kemény, Anna 1973: *La Società d'Esplorazione Commerciale in Africa e la politica coloniale (1879–1914)*. Florence: La Nuova Italia.

Kennedy, Dane 1990: 'The Perils of the Midday Sun: Climatic Anxieties in the Colonial Tropics'. In John M. MacKenzie (ed.), *Imperialism and the Natural World*, Manchester: Manchester University Press, 118–40.

Kennedy, Emmet 1977: 'Destutt de Tracy and the Unity of the Sciences'. In *Studies on Voltaire and the Eighteenth Century*, Geneva: Institut et musée voltaire, 171: 223–39.

Kern, Stephen 1983: *The Culture of Time and Space*. Cambridge, Mass.: Harvard University Press.

Khan, Mirza Abou Taleb 1809: 'Preuves de la liberté des femmes en Orient, ou leur sort comparé à celui des Anglaises'. *Annales des voyages*, 9: 27–45.

Kimball, Warren F. 1984: For the Roosevelt–Churchill correspondence, *Churchill and Roosevelt*. Princeton: Princeton University Press.

King, A. 1976: *Colonial Urban Development*. London: Routledge and Kegan Paul.

Kinross, Lord 1968: *Between Two Seas: The Creation of the Suez Canal*. London: John Murray.

Kirby, A. (ed.) 1992: *The Pentagon and the Cities*. Newbury Park, CA: Sage.

Kirby, A. 1993: *Power/resistance: local politics and the chaotic state*. Bloomington: Indiana University Press.

Kirchhoff, A. 1882: *Schulgeographie*. Halle: Buchhandlung des Waisenhauses.

Kirk, John 1896: 'The extent to which tropical Africa is suited for development by the white races, or under their superintendence'. *Report of the Sixth International Geographical Congress*, held in London 1895, 526.

Kjellén, Rudolf 1899: 'Studier öfver Sveriges politiska gränser'. *Ymer*, 9: 283–332.

Kjellén, Rudolf 1917: *Der Staat als Lebensform*, tr. Margarethe Langfeldt. Leipzig: S. Hirzel.

Knodel, John E. 1974: *The Decline of Fertility in Germany, 1871–1939*. Princeton: Princeton University Press.

Knox, J. 1958: *The Historical Development of Geography as a Subject in the Schools of the Cape Province*. Unpublished MEd Thesis, Rhodes University.

Koch, H. W. 1984: 'Social Darwinism as a factor in the "New Imperialism"'. In H. W. Koch (ed.), *The Origins of the First World War: Great Power Rivalry and German War Aims*, 2nd edn, London: Macmillan.

Kohl, Louis von 1932: *Ursprung und Wandlung Deutschlands, Grundlagen zu einer deutschen Geopolitik*. Berlin: Deutsche Buch-Gemeinschaft.

Kohl, Louis von 1933: 'Biopolitik und Geopolitik als Grundlagen einer Naturwissenschaft vom Staate'. *Zeitschrift für Geopolitik*, 10: 304–10.

Kollm, G. 1897: 'Geographische Gesellschaften, Zeitschriften, Kongresse und Austellungen'. *Geographisches Jahrbuch*, 19: 403–13.

Kolodny, Annette 1975: *The Lay of the Land: Metaphor as Experience and History in American Life and Letters*. Chapel Hill: University of North Carolina Press.

Koloniale Reichsarbeitsgemeinschaft (ed.) 1928: *Wesen und Ziele der deutschen Kolonialbewegung, Verkündigung eines Allgemeinen Deutschen Kolonialprogramms der Kolonialen Reichsarbeitsgemeinschaft am 22. Juni 1928 in Köln a. Rh.* Berlin: Koloniale Reichsarbeitsgemeinschaft.

Komaki, Saneshige 1940: 'Nihon chiseigaku no shuchō' [Advocacy of Japanese geopolitics]. *Chirironsō*, 11: 3–6.

Komaki, Saneshige 1940: *Nihon chiseigaku sengen* [Manifesto of Japanese geopolitics]. Tokyo: Kobundo.

Konrad, Victor A. 1982: 'Introduction'. *The American Review of Canadian Studies*, 12, 2: 1–3.

Konvitz, Josef 1987: *Cartography in France, 1660–1848: Science, Engineering and Statecraft*. Chicago and London: University of Chicago Press.

Koonz, Claudia 1987: *Mothers in the Fatherland*. New York: St Martin's Press.

Korff, Alletta 1910: 'Where women vote'. *National Geographic Magazine*, 21, 6: 487–93.

Korinmann, M. 1991: *Continents perdus. Les Précurseurs de la géopolitique allemande*. Paris: Economica.

Kost, Klaus 1988: *Die Einflüsse der Geopolitik auf Forschung und Theorie der Politischen Geographie von ihren Anfängen bis 1945. Ein Beitrag zur Wissenschaftsgeschichte der Politischen Geographie und ihrer Terminologie unter Berücksichtigung von Militär-und Kolonialgeographie*. Bonn: Ferd. Dümmler.

Krahmann, Max 1927: 'Kapital, technik und geopolitik'. *Zeitschrift für Geopolitik*, 4: 859–61.

Kraus, Th. 1941: *Unsere Kolonien. Die Aufgaben der deutschen Wissenschaft in den Kolonien. Sonderheft von Deutschlands Erneuerung*. München: J. F. Lehmann Verlag.

Kristof, L. 1960: 'The origins and evolution of geopolitics'. *Journal of Conflict Resolution*, 4, 1: 15–51.

Kritzman, L. D. (ed.) 1988: *Politics, Philosophy, Culture*. New York: Routledge.

Kuhn, Helmut. 1980: 'Das geistige Gesicht der Weimarer Zeit'. In M. Stürmer (ed.), *Die Weimarer Republik: Belagerte Civitas*, 2nd edn. Königstein: Verlagsgruppe Athenäum, Hain, Scriptor, Hanstein, 214–23.

Kuntze, Paul 1938: *Das Volksbuch unserer Kolonien*. Leipzig: Georg Dollheimer Verlag.

Kupfer, Paul. 1930: 'Alles fängt mit dem Lande an'. *Übersee-und Koloniale Zeitung*, 42: 325–6.

la Hausse, P. 1990: 'Oral history and South African Historians'. *Radical History Review*, 46/7: 349–50.

Lacoste, Y. 1976: *La géographie, ça sert, d'abord, à faire la guerre*. Paris: Maspero.

Lacroix n. d. 'Walckenaer, Charles Anathase'. In *Biographie Michaud*, 44: 221–37.

Laffey, J. F. 1969: 'Roots of french imperialism in the nineteenth-century: the case of Lyon'. *French Historical Studies*, 6: 78–92.

Laffey, J. F. 1974: 'Municipal imperialism in nineteenth-century France'. *Historical Reflections/Réflexions Historiques*, 1: 81–114.

Laffey, J. F. 1975: 'Municipal imperialism in decline: the Lyon Chamber of Commerce, 1925–1938'. *French Historical Studies*, 9: 329–53.

Laffey, J. F. 1975: 'The Lyon Chamber of Commerce and Indochina during the Third Republic'. *Canadian Journal of History* 10: 325–48.

Lanchester, H. V. 1923: *Zanzibar: a Study in Tropical Town Planning*. Cheltenham: Burrow.

Lancret, M. A. 1809: 'Mémoire sur le système d'imposition territoriale et sur l'administration des provinces de l'Égypte dans les dernières années du gouvernement des Mamlouks'. *Description de l'Égypte*, État moderne. Paris: Imprimerie impériale, 1: 233–60.

Langhans, Paul 1931: 'Die 24. Tagung des Deutschen Geographentages zu Danzig'. *Petermanns Mitteilungen*, 77: 195–9.

Laqueur, Walter 1974: *Weimar: A Cultural History, 1918–1933*. New York: Weidenfeld and Nicolson.

Lattimore, O. 1959: *Studies in Frontier History*. Paris: Mouton.

Laurens, H., Gillespie, Charles C., Golvin, Jean-Claude, and Traunecker, Claude 1989: *L'Expédition d'Égypte, 1798–1801*. Paris: Armand Colin.

Lears, J. 1985: 'The concept of cultural hegemony: problems and possibilities'. *American Historical Review*, 90, 3: 567–93.

Lebovics, H. 1992: *True France: the wars over cultural identity, 1900–1945*. Ithaca: Cornell University Press.

Leclerc, G. 1972: *Anthropologie et colonialisme: essai sur l'histoire de l'Africanisme*. Paris: Éditions de Seuil.

Lefranc, Abel 1893: *Histoire du Collège de France*. Paris: Hachette.

Leiss, William 1972: *The Domination of Nature*. New York: George Braziller.

Leith, C. K. 1940: *Minerals in the Peace Settlement*. Geological Society of America.

Lejeune, D. 1982: 'La Société de Géographie de Paris: un aspect de l'histoire sociale française'. *Revue d'histoire moderne et contemporaine*, 29: 141–63.

Lemesle, R. 1986: 'De l'économie politique aux facultés de droit'. *Économies et sociétés*, 6: 223–36.

Lenin, V. I. 1966: *Imperialism, the Highest Stage of Capitalism*. Moscow: Progress Publications.

Leroy-Beaulieu, Pierre 1901: *Les nouvelles sociétés anglo-saxonnes; Australie, Nouvelle-Zélande, Afrique du Sud*. Paris: Armand Colin.

Leroy-Beaulieu, Pierre 1902: *De la colonisation chez les peuples modernes*. Paris: Armand Colin.

Leroy-Beaulieu, Pierre 1904: *Les États-Unis d'aujourd'hui*. Paris: Armand Colin.

Levy, B. 1984: *Geography Teaching in South African Schools for Whites, c.1800–1980.* Unpublished. MA thesis, University of the Witwatersrand.

Levy, F. J. 1964: 'The making of Camden's *Britannia*'. *Bibl. d'Humanisme et Renaissance,* 26: 76–92.

Lewis, D. 1989: 'Intellectuals, the working class and politics'. *Transformation,* 10: 64–9.

Lewis, J. 1990: 'South African labor history: a historiographical assessment'. *Radical History Review,* 46/7: 213–36.

Lewis, M. D. 1961–2: 'One hundred million Frenchmen: the assimilation theory in French colonial policy'. *Comparative Studies in Society and History,* 4: 129–53.

Liard, Louis 1894: *L'Enseignement supérieur en France 1789–1893.* Paris: Armand Colin. vol. 2.

Lincoln, D. 1979: 'Ideology and South African development geography'. *South African Geographical Journal,* 61: 99–110.

Linschoten, Jan Huygen van 1595–6: *Itinerario. Voyage ofte Schipvaert, van J. H. v. L. naer Oost ofte Portugaels Indien.* Amsterdam.

Lips, Julius 1932: 'Ethnopolitik und Kolonialpolitik'. *Koloniale Rundschau,* 530–8.

Lithgow, William 1614: *A most delectable and true discourse, of an admired and painful peregrination from Scotland to the most famous kingdomes in Europe, Asia and Affricke.* London.

Livingstone, David N. 1984: 'Natural theology and Neo-Lamarckism: the changing context of nineteenth century geography in the United States and Great Britain'. *Annals of the Association of American Geographers,* 74: 9–28.

Livingstone, David N. 1987: 'Human acclimatization: perspectives on a contested field of inquiry in science, medicine and geography'. *History of Science,* 25: 358–94.

Livingstone, David N. 1988: 'Science, magic and religion: a contextual reassessment of geography in the sixteenth and seventeenth centuries'. *History of Science,* 26: 269–94.

Livingstone, David N. 1990: 'Geography, tradition and the scientific revolution: an interpretive essay'. *Transactions of the Institute of British Geographers,* n.s., 15: 359–73.

Livingstone, David N. 1991: 'Of design and dining clubs: geography in America and Britain'. *History of Science,* 29: 153–83.

Livingstone, David N. 1991: 'The moral discourse of climate: historical considerations on race, place and virtue'. *Journal of Historical Geography,* 17, 4: 413–34.

Livingstone, David N. 1992: *The Geographical Tradition. Episodes in the History of a Contested Enterprise.* Oxford, and Cambridge, Mass.: Blackwell.

Livingstone, David N. 1992: *The Preadamite Theory and the Marriage of Science and Religion.* Philadelphia: American Philosophical Society.

Livingstone, David N. In press: 'In defence of situated messiness: geographical knowledge and the history of science'. *Geojournal.*

Lofchie, M. 1965: *Zanzibar: Background to Revolution.* Princeton: Princeton University Press.

Lorimer, D. 1988: 'Theoretical racism in late Victorian anthropology, 1870–1900'. *Victorian Studies,* 31: 405–30.

Louis, Roger Wm. 1978: *Imperialism at Bay: The United States and the Decolonization of the British Empire 1941–1945.* New York: Oxford University Press.

Luce, Henry, 'The American Century'. *Life,* February, 1941.

Lucena, Manuel 1990: 'Ciencia y crisis política: la doble creación de la Escuela de Náutica de Cartagena de Indias (1810–1822)'. *Revista de historia naval,* 30: 31–8.

Lutz, Catherine A. and Collins, Jane L. 1993: *Reading National Geographic.* Chicago: University of Chicago Press.

Lyautey, H. 1935: *Le rôle social de l'officier.* Paris: Librarie Plon. (First published 1891).

Lynam, Edward (ed.) 1946: *Richard Hakluyt and His Successors. A Volume issued to Commemorate the Centenary of the Hakluyt Society.* 2nd Series, 93. London: Hakluyt Society.

Lynn, John Albert 1984: *The Bayonets of the Republic: Motivation and Tactics in the Army of Revolutionary France, 1791–1794.* Urbana: University of Illinois Press.

Mabin, A. 1986: 'At the cutting edge: the new African history and its implications for historical geography'. *Journal of Historical Geography*, 12, 74–80.

McCarry, Charles 1988: 'Three men who made the magazine'. *National Geographic Magazine*, 174, 3: 287–316.

McCarthy, J. 1981: 'Research on neighbourhood activism: review, critique and alternatives'. *South African Geographical Journal*, 63: 107–31.

McCarthy, J. 1982: 'Radical geography, mainstream geography and southern Africa'. *Social Dynamics*, 8: 53–70.

McCarthy, J. 1983: 'The political economy of urban land use: towards a revised theoretical framework'. *South African Geographical Journal*, 65: 25–48.

McCarthy, J. 1986: 'Contours of capital's negotiating agenda'. *Transformation*, 1: 130–7.

McCarthy, J. and Smit, D. 1984: *South African City: Theory and Analysis in Planning*. Cape Town: Juta.

McCarthy, J. and Swilling, M. 1985: 'South Africa's emerging politics of bus transportation'. *Political Geography Quarterly*, 4: 235–50.

McCarthy, J. and Wellings, P. 1989: 'The regional restructuring of politics in contemporary South Africa'. *Social Dynamics*, 15: 75–93.

MacKay, D. V. 1943: 'Colonialism and the French geographical movement, 1871–1881'. *Geographical Review*, 33: 214–32.

MacKenzie, J. M. (ed.) 1990: *Imperialism and the Natural World*. Manchester: Manchester University Press.

MacKenzie, J. M. 1984: *Propaganda and Empire: the Manipulation of British Public Opinion, 1880–1960*. Manchester: Manchester University Press.

McLaren, A. 1983: *Sexuality and the Social Order: the Debate over the Fertility of Women and Workers in France, 1770–1920*. New York: Holmes and Meier.

MacLeod, R. and Lewis, M. (eds) 1988: *Disease, Empire and Medicine: Perspectives on Western Medicine and the Experience of European Expansion*. London: Routledge.

McNeil, William 1982: *The Pursuit of Power. Technology, Armed Force and Society Since Ad 1000*. Chicago: University of Chicago Press.

Magi, L. M. 1991: *Geography in Society: The Site of Struggle*. An Inaugural Address. The University of Zululand: University of Zululand Press.

Magri, Pier Gia 1968: 'Scopi geografici e retroscena politici della seconda spedizione Bottego'. *Bolletino della Società Geografica Italiana*, 605–24.

Malte-Brun, Conrad 1807: *Tableau de la Pologne ancienne et moderne*. Paris: Henri Tardieu, (1830 re-ed. by L. Chodzko).

Malte-Brun, Conrad 1810–1829: *Précis de géographie universelle, ou Description de toutes les parties du monde, sur un plan nouveau, d'après les grandes divisions naturelles du globe; précédée de l'histoire de la géographie chez les peuples anciens et modernes, et d'une théorie générale de la géographie mathématique, physique et politique; et accompagnée de cartes, de tableaux analytiques, synoptiques et élémentaires, et d'une table alphabetique de noms de lieux.* Paris: Chez Fr. Buisson.

Malte-Brun, Conrad (ed.) 1807: *Annales des voyages et de l'histoire: ou collection des voyages nouveau les plus estimés, ...; et des mémoires historiques sur l'origine, la langue, les moeurs et les arts des peuples, ainsi que sur le climat, les productions et le commerce des pays jusqu'ici peu ou mal connus accompagnée d'un bulletin où l'on annonce toutes les découvertes, recherches et entreprises qui tendent à accélérer les progrès des sciences historiques, spécialement de la géographie ...* Paris: Chez Fr. Buisson.

Malte-Brun, Conrad 1808: '[A review of] "Coup d'Oeil sur la statistique de la Pologne Varsovie 1807 brochure de 20 pages"'. *Annales des voyages*, 1: 399–405.

Malte-Brun, Conrad 1808: 'Aperçu des agrandissements et des pertes de la monarchie prussienne'. *Annales des voyages*, 1: 204–52.

Malte-Brun, Conrad 1809: 'Nouvelle description de la Kwarizmie ...', *Annales des voyages*, 4: 373.

Malte-Brun, Conrad 1809: '[A review of] *Voyage de découvertes aux Terres Australes*', 4: 282–8.

Malte-Brun, Conrad 1810: '[A review of] "Campagnes des armées françaises en Espagne et en Portugal pendant les années 1808 et 1809, sous le commandement de S. M. l'Empereur ... " ' *Annales des voyages*, 7: 277–80.

Malte-Brun, Conrad 1810: '[A review of Lapie's] "Carte reduite de la mer Mediterranée et de la mer Noire" '. *Annales des Voyages*, 5: 268–72.

Malte-Brun, Conrad 1810: 'Analyse de quelques Mémoires Hollandais sur l'Île de Formosa, [with a map by Lapie], Carte des Îles Formose Madjicosemah et Lieu-Kieu avec une partie de la Chine, des Philippines et du Japon'. *Annales des voyages*, 8: 344–75.

Malte-Brun, Conrad 1810: 'Aperçu de la monarchie autricienne'. *Annales des voyages*, 7: 281–355.

Malte-Brun, Conrad 1810: 'Description de l'Île de Bornholm et des islots d'Ertholm situés dans la mer Baltique'. *Annales des voyages*, 8: 95–125.

Malte-Brun, Conrad 1810: 'Moeurs et usages des anciens habitans de l'Espagne, avant la réunion de ce pays à l'Europe Romain'. *Annales des voyages*, 5: 278ff.

Malte-Brun, Conrad 1810: 'Periple de la Paphlagonie. Ou memoire sur les lieux indiques par les anciens et les modernes, sur la côte de la mer Noire ...' *Annales des Voyages*, 5: 210–31.

Malte-Brun, Conrad 1810: 'Sur un voyage inédit fait aux États Unis et aux Antilles, par M. Legris-Belle-Isle'. *Annales des voyages*, 6: 119–22.

Malte-Brun, Victor A. 1875: 'Aperçu de l'état de nos connaissances géographiques'. *Bulletin de la société de géographie de Paris*, 561–5.

Mani, L. and Frankenburg, R. 1985: 'The challenge of orientalism'. *Economy and Society*, 14: 174–92.

Mann, M. 1988: *States, War, and Capitalism: Studies in Political Sociology*. Oxford: Blackwell.

Manuel, F. E. 1963: *The New World of Henri Saint-Simon*. Notre Dame: Notre Dame Press.

Manuel, F. E. 1965: *The Prophets of Paris*. New York: Columbia University Press.

Maranelli, Carlo 1907: 'Sui rapporti economici con l'altra sponda dell'Adriatico'. *Atti del sesto congresso geografico italiano*. Venice, 1: 144–209.

Maranelli, Carlo 1915: 'Il problema dell'Adriatico'. *Unità*, 12 March.

Maranelli, Carlo and Salvemini, Gaetano 1918: *La questione dell'Adriatico*. Rome: Libr. della Voce.

Maranelli, Olinto 1926: 'Il problema coloniale'. *Bolletino della Società Geografica Italiana*, 353–72.

Marcus, G. and Fischer, M. (eds) 1986: *Anthropology as Cultural Critique: An Experimental Moment in the Human Sciences*. Chicago: University of Chicago Press.

Maree, J. 1989: 'Harnessing intellectuals: tensions between democracy and leadership in the independent trade unions in the 1970s'. *South African Sociological Review*, 1: 58–73.

Marglin, F. and S. 1990: *Dominating Knowledge: Development, Culture, and Resistance*. Oxford: Clarendon Press.

Marks, S. 1985: 'Southern and Central Africa, 1886–1910'. In R. Oliver and G. Sanderson (eds), *The Cambridge History of Africa*, vol. 6, Cambridge: Cambridge University Press, 422–92.

Marks, S. 1986: 'The historiography of South Africa'. In B. Jewsiewicki and D. Newbury (eds), *African Histories. What History for Which Africa?*, Beverly Hills, CA: Sage.

Marks, S. and Atmore, A. (eds) 1980: *Economy and Society in Pre-Industrial South Africa*. London: Longman.

Marks, S. and Rathbone, R. (eds) 1982: *Industrialization and Social Change in South Africa: African Class Formation, Culture and Consciousness 1870–1930*. London: Longman.

Marks, S. and Trapido, S. (eds) 1987: *The Politics of Race, Class and Nationalism in Twentieth Century South Africa*. London: Longman.

Marlowe, J. 1964: *The Making of the Suez Canal*. London: Cresset Press.

Marmocchi, Francesco Costantino 1840: *Raccolta di viaggi dalla scoperta del nuovo continente fino ai dì nostri*, 2 vols. Prato: Giachetti.

Marqués de Reinosa 1892: 'Algunas observaciones prácticas sobre colonización'. *Boletín de la Sociedad Geográfica de Madrid*, 186–96.

Marseille, J. 1984: *Empire Colonial et Capitalisme Française: histoire d'un divorce*. Paris: Albin Michel.

Martin, James Ranald 1856: *The influence of tropical climates on European constitutions, including practical observations on the nature and treatment of the diseases of Europeans on their return from tropical climates*. London: J. Churchill.

Martonne, E. de 1936: 'Les cartes d'Afrique du Service Géographique de l'Armée'. *Afrique française, renseignements coloniaux*, 46, 8: 1–8.

Marx, K. and Engels, F. 1970: *The German Ideology*, part 1. New York: International Publishers.

Mathur, G. 1989: 'The current impasse in development thinking: the metaphysic of power'. *Alternatives*, 14: 463–80.

Maull, Otto 1925: *Politische Geographie*. Berlin: Gebrüder Borntraeger.

Maull, Otto 1928: 'Friedrich Ratzel zum Gedächtnis'. *Zeitschrift für Geopolitik*, 5: 616–7.

Maull, Otto 1929: 'Review of R. Hennig's *Geopolitik*', *Zeitschrift der Gesellschaft für Erdkunde zu Berlin*, 61–2.

Mazzini, Giuseppe 1871: 'Politica internazionale'. *La Roma del popolo*, 6 (5 April): 2.

Mazzini, Giuseppe 1939: *Opere* (ed. L. Salvatorelli) 2 vols, Milan: Rizzoli.

Melcón, Julia 1989: 'Geografía en el sistema de instrucción de España, Puerto Rico y Filipinas (1838–1898)'. In J. L. Peset, *Ciencia, vida y espacio en Iberoamérica*, vol. 3, 267–92.

Melman, S. 1988: 'Economic consequences of the arms race: the second rate economy'. *Papers and Proceedings of the American Economics Association*, 78, 2: 55–9.

Mendyk, Stanley J. G. 1989: *Speculum Britanniae: Regional Study, Antiquarianism, and Science in Britain to 1700*. Toronto: University of Toronto Press.

Menon, R. 1978: *Zanzibar in the Nineteenth Century: Aspects of Urban Development in an East African Coastal Town*. MA Thesis, University of California, Los Angeles.

Mensua, Salvador 1956: *Bibliografía geográfica de Marruecos Español y zona International de Tanger*. Zaragoza: CSIC.

Mentelle, Edme and Malte-Brun, Conrad 1803: *Géographie mathématique, physique et politique de toutes les parties du monde*. Paris: Tardieu, an 12, 13.

Merchant, Carolyn 1980: *The Death of Nature: Women, Ecology and the Scientific Revolution*. New York: Harper and Row.

Merle, M. 1969: *L'Anticolonialisme Européen de Las Casas à Karl Marx*. Paris: Armand Colin.

Meyer, Hans 1926: 'Geopolitische Betrachtungen über Deutsch-Ostafrika [Tanganyika Territory] Einst und Jetzt'. *Zeitschrift für Geopolitik*, 3: 161–74.

Meynier, A. 1969: *Histoire de la pensée géographique en France*. Paris: Presses universitaires de France.

Meyrowitz, J. 1985: *No Sense of Place*. New York: Oxford University Press, 1985.

Miège, J. L. 1968: *L'impérialisme colonial italien de 1870 à nos jours*. Paris: Sedes.

Miles, M. and Crush, J. Forthcoming: 'Personal narratives as interactive texts: Collecting and interpreting migrant life-histories'. *Professional Geographer*.

Mill, Hugh Robert 1929: 'Geography'. *Encyclopaedia Britannica*, 14th edn. London, vol. 10.

Miller, A. Austin (1931) 1947: *Climatology*, 5th edn. London: Methuen.

Miller, C. 1985: *Blank Darkness: Africanist Discourse in French*. Chicago: University of Chicago Press.

Minamoto, S. 1984: 'Shiga Shigetaka, 1863–1927'. *Geographers: Biobibliographical Studies*, 8: 95–105.

Ministère de la guerre, État major de l'armée, Section historique 1901: *Liste chronologique des tableaux formant la collection du Ministère de la guerre (peinture, aquarelles, dessins) représentant les batailles, combats et sièges livrés par l'armée française 1628–1887*. Paris: Imprimerie nationale.

Mitchell, T. 1988: *Colonizing Egypt*. Cambridge: Cambridge University Press.

Mitchell, William 1924: 'Tiger-hunting in India'. *National Geographic Magazine*, 46, 5: 545–98.

Möller, Per Stig 1971: *La critique dramatique et littéraire de Malte-Brun*. Copenhagen: Munksgaard.

Monk, William 1858: *Dr. Livingstone's Cambridge Lectures together with a prefatory letter by the Rev. Professor Sedgwick*. Edited with introduction, life of Dr. Livingstone, notes and appendix. London.

Moore, W. Robert 1930: 'Among the hill tribes of Sumatra'. *National Geographic Magazine*, 57, 2: 187–227.

Moore, W. Robert 1931: 'Along the old Mandarin Road of Indo-China'. *National Geographic Magazine*, 60, 2: 157–99.

Moravia, Sergio 1967: 'Philosophie et géographie à la fin du XVIIIe siècle'. In Theodore Besterman *Studies on Voltaire and the Eighteenth Century*. Geneva: Institut et musée Voltaire, 57: 937–1011.

Morrill, Richard 1984: 'Recollections of the "Quantitative Revolution's" early years'. In M. Billinge et al. (eds), *Recollections of a Revolution*, London: Macmillan, 57–72.

Morissoneau, Christian 1978: *De la terre promise, le mythe du Nord québécois*. Montreal: Hurtubise HMH.

Morsy, M. (ed.) 1989: *Les Saint-Simoniens et l'Orient: vers la modernité*. Paris: Édisud.

Mrina, B. and Mattoke, W. 1980: *Mapambano ya Ukombozi Zanzibar* [Zanzibar's Liberation Struggle]. Dar es Salaam: Tanzania Publishing House.

Muchembled, Robert 1985: *Popular Culture and Elite Culture in France 1400–1750*. Baton Rouge and London: Louisiana State University.

Mudimbe, V. 1988: *The Invention of Africa*. Bloomington: Indiana University Press.

Mukerji, S. 1985: 'Voir le pouvoir: la cartographie au début de l'Europe moderne'. *Culture technique*, 14: 209–23.

Müller-Ross, Friedrich 1932: 'Verschlossene Welt'. *Übersee-und Koloniale Zeitung*, 44: 134.

Murchison, Roderick I. 1844: 'Address to the Royal Geographical Society'. *Journal of the Royal Geographical Society*, 14: xlv–cxxviii.

Murchison, Roderick I. 1853: 'Address to the Royal Geographical Society'. *Journal of the Royal Geographical Society*, 23: lxii–cxxxviii.

Muro, Ignacio 1992: *El pensamiento militar sobre el territorio en la España contemporánea*, 2 vols. PhD thesis, Madrid: Ministerio de Defensa.

Muroga, Nobuo 1942: 'Chirigaku no dōkō [Trends in Geography]'. *Rekishi Chiri*, 80: 466–72.

Muroga, Nobuo 1943: 'Daitōa chiseigaku shinron [A new geopolitics of Greater East Asia]'. *Chirironso*, 13: 1–15.

Murphy, A. 1948: *The Ideology of French Imperialism, 1871–1881*. Washington DC: the Catholic University of America Press.

Murphy, D. forthcoming 1995: *The Heroic Earth: Geopolitical Thought in the Weimar Republic*. Kent OH: Kent State University Press.

Murray, M. 1988: 'The triumph of Marxist approaches in South African social and labour history'. *Journal of African and Asian Studies*, 23: 79–101.

Naciri, M. 1984: 'La géographie coloniale: une "science appliquée" à la colonisation. Perceptions et interprétations du fait colonial chez J. Célérier et G. Hardy'. In J.-C. Vatin (ed.), *Connaissances du Maghreb: sciences sociales et colonisation*, Paris: Centre National de la Recherche Scientifique, 309–43.

Nadal, Francesc 1989: 'La formación de la Carta Geógrafo-Topográfica de Valcourt y los trabajos geográficos de las Comisiones de Estadística y División del Territorio de Cuba (1821–1868)'. In J. L. Peset (ed.), *Ciencia, vida y espacio en Iberoamérica*, vol. 3, 329–56.

Nadal, Francesc and Urteaga, L. 1990: 'Cartography and state: national topographic maps and territorial statistics in the nineteenth century'. *Geo crítica. Cuadernos críticos de geografía humana* (English Parallel series), 2.

Naitza, Giovanni 1975: *Il colonialismo nella storia italiana (1882–1949)*. Florence: La Nuova Italia.

Nazzi, Luisa 1969: *La Società Geografica Italiana nel primo ventennio del nostro secolo*. Milan: State University of Milan (thesis).

Nel, A. n.d.: *Die Natuurstreke van die Wêreld*. Cape Town: Nasionale Boekhandel Bpk.

Nelson, H. I. 1963: *Land and Power: British and Allied policy on Germany's Frontiers, 1916–19*. London: Routledge and Kegan Paul.

Neumann, F. 1942: *Behemoth: the structure and practice of National Socialism*. New York: Octagon Books.

Nicola-O., Nozawa, George and Hideki Nozawa 1992: *Shigetaka Shiga, Eratostene-Meridien*, 3, Lausanne: Eratostene.

Nordman, D. and Raison, J.-P. (eds) 1980: *Sciences de l'homme et conquête coloniale: constitution et usages des humanités en Afrique (XIXe et XXe siècle)*. Paris: Presses de l'École Normale Supérieure.

Norwine, J. and Gonzales, A. (eds) 1988: *The Third World: States of Mind, States of Being*. London: Unwin Hyman.

Nott, J. C. 1857: 'Acclimation; or, the comparative influence of climate, endemic and epidemic diseases, on the races of man'. In J. C. Nott and George R. Gliddon (eds), *Indigenous races of the earth; or, new chapters of ethnological inquiry*, Philadelphia: J. B. Lippincott, 353–401.

Nourse, Mary A. 1938: 'Women's work in Japan'. *National Geographic Magazine*, 73, 1: 99–132.

Nye, R. A. 1984: *Crime, Madness and Politics in Modern France: the medical concept of national decline*. Princeton: Princeton University Press.

Nye, R. A. 1989: 'Honor, impotence, and male sexuality in nineteenth-century French medicine'. *French Historical Studies*, 16: 48–71.

Obregón, Diana 1992: 'La sociedad de Naturalistos Neogranadinos o la invención de una tradicion'. *Interciencia Caracas*, 17, 3: 135–140.

Obst, Erich (ed.) 1941–3: *Afrika. Handbuch der praktischen Kolonialwissenschaften*, 13 vols. Berlin: W. de Gruyter.

Obst, Erich 1926: 'Warum brauchen wir Kolonien'? *Werknachrichten der Continental Caoutchouc- und Gutta-Percha-Compagnie*, 3–6.

Obst, Erich 1926: 'Wir fordern unsere Kolonien zurück!' *Zeitschrift für Geopolitik*, 3: 151–60.

Offen, K. 1984: 'Depopulation, nationalism, and feminism in *fin-de-siècle* France'. *American Historical Review*, 89: 648–75.

Ogawa, Takuji 1933: 'Jinmonchirigaku no ikka to toshite no seijichirigaku [Political Geography as a branch of human Geography]'. *Chikyu*, 9: 239–47.

Ogden, P. E. and Huss, M.-M. 1982: 'Demography and pronatalism in France in the nineteenth and twentieth centuries'. *Journal of Historical Geography*, 8: 283–98.

O'Hanlon, R. 1988: 'Recovering the subject: Subaltern Studies and histories of resistance in colonial South Asia'. *Modern Asian Studies*, 22.

Ohara, Keishi 1936: *Shakaichirigaku no kisomondai* [Fundamental Problems of Social Geography]. Tokyo: Kokon Shoin.

O'Keefe, P. 1983: 'South Africa in the global division of labor'. *Antipode*, 15, 2: 5–7.

O'Loughlin, J. and van der Wusten, H. 1986: 'Geography, war and peace'. *Progress in Human Geography*, 10: 484–510.

Omar, M. 1981: 'Historia ya Hadithi (Riwaya) na Maendeleo Yake' [The History and Development of Fiction and Novels]. In Haji, et al. (eds), *Misingi ya Nadharia ya Fasihi* [Foundations of Literary Theory], Zanzibar: Institute of Kiswahili and Foreign Languages, 56–60.

O'Neill, Henry E. 1885: 'East Africa, between the Zambesi and the Rovuma rivers: its people, riches and development'. *Scottish Geographical Magazine*, 1: 337–52.

Onselen, C. van 1976: *Studies in the Social and Economic History of the Witwatersrand, 1886–1914*, 2 vols. London: Longman.

Orozco y Berra, Manuel 1881: *Apuntes para la historia de la Geografía en México*. Mexico: Díaz de León, facsimile edition, Mexico, 1973.

Osborne, Michael 1987: *The Société Zoologique d'Acclimatation and the New French Empire: The Science and Political Economy of Economic Zoology during the Second Empire*. PhD thesis: University of Wisconsin-Madison.

O'Tuathail, G. O. 1986: 'The language and nature of the new geopolitics'. *Political Geography Quarterly*, 5, 1: 73–86.

Ozouf, M. and J. 1986: 'Le tour de France par deux enfants'. In P. Nora (ed.), *Les lieux de mémoire*, vol. 2, *La République*, Paris: Gallimard, 291–321.

Packard, R. 1989: 'The "healthy reserve" and the "dressed native": discourses on black health and the language of legitimation in South Africa'. *American Ethnologist*, 16.

Padgen, Anthony 1982: *The Fall of Natural Man*. Cambridge and New York: Cambridge University Press.

Palacios, Joaquín 1850: *Tratado elemental de Geografá astronómica, física y política, antigua y moderna*, 2nd edn. Sevilla: Imprenta y Librería Española y Extrangera de D. J. María Geofrín.

Parker, John 1965: *Books to Build an Empire. A Bibliographical History of English Overseas Interests to 1620*. Amsterdam: N. Israel.

Parker, Robert and Feagin, Joe 1992: 'Military spending in free enterprise cities: the military–industrial complex in Houston and Las Vegas'. In Andrew Kirby (ed.), *The Pentagon and the Cities*. Newbury Park, CA: Sage, 100–25.

Parkhurst, Anthony 1598–1600: 'Report of the true state and commodities of Newfoundland'. In Richard Hakluyt, *Principal Navigations, Voyages, Traffiques, and Discoveries of the English Nation*, 3 vols. London, 3: 31–45.

Parks, George Bruner 1930: *Richard Hakluyt and the English Voyages*. New York: American Geographical Society.

Parks, George Bruner 1974: 'Tudor Travel Literature: A Brief History'. In D. B. Quinn (ed.), *The Hakluyt Handbook*, London: Hakluyt Society, 97–132.

Parry, B. 1987: 'Problems in current theories of colonial discourse'. *Oxford Literary Review*, 9: 27–58.

Parry, William 1601: *A new and large discourse of the travels of Sir A. Sherley, Kt, by sea and overland to the Persian empire*. London.

Passarge, Siegfried 1939: 'Das Geographische Seminar des Kolonial-Instituts und der Hansischen Universität. Erinnerungen und Erfahrungen'. In *Mitteilungen der Geographischen Gesellschaft in Hamburg*. Hamburg: Friederichsen, de Gruyter and Co., vol. 46, 1–104.

Passarge, Siegfried 1951: *Aus achtzig Jahren. Eine Selbstbiographie*. Hamburg: unedited typescript, 522 pages.

Patrick, Mary Mills 1909: 'The emancipation of Mohammedan women'. *National Geographic Magazine*, 20, 1: 42–66.

Paul, H. W. 1972: *The Sorcerer's Apprentice: the French Scientist's Image of German Science 1840–1919*. Gainesville: University of Florida Press.

Pauly, Philip J. 1979: 'The world and all that is in it: The National Geographic Society, 1888–1918'. *American Quarterly*, 31, 4: 517–32.

Pearce, F. 1920: *Zanzibar: The Island Metropolis of Eastern Africa*. London: Fisher, Unwin.

Peet, R. 1985: 'The social origins of environmental determinism'. *Annals of the Association of American Geographers*, 75, 3: 309–33.

Pelzer, Karl 1951: 'Geography and the Tropics'. In T. Griffith Taylor (ed.), *Geography in the Twentieth Century. A Study of Growth, Fields, Techniques, Aims and Trends*, London: Methuen, 311–44.

Perret 1916: 'M. Dubois, Un grand géographe'. *Le Correspondant*, November, 88(265): 476–501.

Persell, S. M. 1983: *The French Colonial Lobby 1889–1938*. Stanford: Hoover Institute Press.

Peset, José Luis (ed.) 1989: *Ciencia, vida y espacio en Iberoamérica*, 3 vols, Madrid: CSIC.

Peset, José Luis 1989: *Ciencia y libertad. El papel del científico ante la independencia.* Madrid: CSIC.

Petzina, Dietmar, et al. (eds) 1978: *Sozialgeschichtliches Arbeitsbuch,* vol. 3, *Materialien zur Statistik des Deutschen Reiches 1914–1945.* Munich: C. H. Beck.

Peukert, Detlev 1987: *Die Weimarer Republik: Krisenjahre des Klassischen Moderne.* Frankfurt am Main: Suhrkamp.

Pick, D. 1989: *Faces of Degeneration: a European disorder, c.1848–c.1918.* Cambridge: Cambridge University Press, esp. 37–106.

Pickles, J. 1986: 'Geographic Theory and Educating for Democracy'. *Antipode,* 18, 2: 136–54.

Pickles, J. and Weiner, D. (eds) 1991: *Rural and Regional Restructuring in South Africa.* Special issue of *Antipode,* 23.

Pinchemel, Ph., Robic M.-C., and Tissier, J.-L. 1984: *Deux siècles de géographie française.* Paris: Bibliothèque nationale (CTHS).

Pirie, G. 1984: 'Political philosophy and political geography'. In P. Taylor and J. House (eds), *Political geography: Recent Advances and Future Directions,* Beckenham: Croom Helm, 227–36.

Polier, N. and Roseberry, W. 1989: 'Tristes tropes: post-modern anthropologists encounter the other and discover themselves'. *Economy and Society,* 18: 245–64.

Pommrich, Rudolf 1927: 'Geopolitische Ziele in der Luftpolitik'. *Zeitschrift für Geopolitik,* 4: 557–60.

Porch, D. 1984: *The Conquest of the Sahara.* Oxford: Oxford University Press.

Porter, B. 1968: *Critics of Empire: British radical attitudes to colonialism in Africa, 1895–1914.* London: Macmillan.

Pouwels, R. 1981: 'Sheikh Al-Amin bin Al Mazrui and Islamic modernism in Africa, 1875–1947'. *International Journal of Middle Eastern Studies,* 13: 329–45.

Prakash, G. 1990: 'Writing post-orientalist histories of the Third World: perspectives from Indian historiography'. *Comparative Studies in Society and History,* 32: 383–408.

Prakash, G. 1990: *Bonded Histories: Genealogies of Labour Servitude in Colonial India.* Cambridge: Cambridge University Press.

Prakash, G. 1992: 'Postcolonial criticism and Indian historiography'. *Social Text,* 31/32: 8–19.

Pratt, M. L. 1986: 'Scratches on the face of the country: or, what Mr. Barrow saw in the land of the Bushmen'. In L. Gates (ed.), *'Race', Writing and Difference,* Chicago: University of Chicago Press.

Pratt, M. L. 1988: 'Conventions of representation: where discourse and ideology meet'. In W. van Peer (ed.), *The Taming of The Text,* London: Routledge, 15–34.

Pratt, M. L. 1992: *Imperial Eyes.* London: Routledge.

Prévost, M. and d'Amat, Roman 1936: 'Chabrol, Gilbert-Joseph-Gaspard de'. In *Dictionnaire de biographie française.* Paris: Letouzey et Ane. 8: 152–3.

Prévost-Paradol, L.-A. 1981: *La France Nouvelle et pages choisis.* Paris: Éditions Garnier frères.

Putnam, George R. 1903: 'Surveying the Philippine Islands'. *National Geographic Magazine,* 14, 12: 437–41.

Pyenson, L. 1984: 'Astronomy and imperialism: J. A. C. Oudenmans, the topography of the East Indies, and the rise of the Utrecht Observatory, 1850–1990'. *Historia Scientiarum,* 26: 39–81.

Quaini, Massimo 1978: *Dopo la geografia.* Milan: Espresso Strumenti.

Quatrefages de Breau, Armand de 1863: 'Histoire de l'émigration européenne asiatique et africaine au XIXe siècle de M. Jules Duval'. *Bulletin de la Société de Géographie de Paris,* 5: 189–207.

Quimby, R. 1957: *The Background to Napoleonic Warfare.* New York: Columbia University Press.

Quinn, David B. (ed.) 1974: *The Hakluyt Handbook.* 2 vols, 2nd series, 144. London: Hakluyt Society.

Quinn, David B. 1955: *The Roanoke Voyages, 1584–1589.* London: Hakluyt Society.

Quinn, David B. 1974: 'Thomas Harriot and the New World'. In J. W. Shirley (ed.), *Thomas Harriot. Renaissance Scientist*, Oxford: Clarendon Press, 36–53.

Quynn, Dorothy Mackay 1945: 'The Art Confiscations of the Napoleonic Wars'. *American Historical Review*, 50, 1: 437–60.

Rabinow, Paul. 1989: *French modern: norms and forms of the social environment*. Cambridge, Mass.: MIT Press.

Rajan, R. 1990: 'The discourse of exploitation and the exploitation of discourse'. *Alternatives*, 15: 29–52.

Ramusio, Giovanni Battista, 1563, *Delle Navigatio*.

Ratzel, Friedrich 1884: *Wider die Reichsnörgler. Ein Wort zur Kolonialfrage aus Wählerkreisen*. Munich: Oldenbourg.

Ratzel, Friedrich 1897: 'Über den Lebensraum, eine biogeographische Skizze'. *Die Umschau*, 1: 363–7.

Ratzel, Friedrich 1897: *Politische Geographie*. Munich, Leipzig: Oldenbourg.

Ratzel, Friedrich 1898: *Deutschland. Einführung in die Heimatkunde*. Berlin, Leipzig: W. de Gruyter.

Ratzel, Friedrich 1900: *Das Meer als Quelle der Völkergrösse*. Munich, Leipzig: Oldenbourg.

Ratzel, Friedrich 1901: 'Der Lebensraum, eine biogeographische Studie'. In K. Bücher et al. (eds), *Festgaben für Albert Schäffle zur 70. Wiederkehr seines Geburtstages am 24. Februar 1901*, Tübingen: Verlag der Laupp'schen Buchhandlung, 101–89.

Ravenstein, E. G. 1891: 'Lands of the globe still available for European settlement'. *Proceedings of the Royal Geographical Society*, n.s. 13: 27–35.

Ravenstein, E. G. 1896: Discussion, *Report of the Sixth International Geographical Congress in London 1895*: 547.

Reclus, Élisée. 1887: *Nouvelle Géographie Universelle: la Terre et les Hommes, vol. XII, l'Afrique Occidentale*. Paris: Librairie Hachette et Cie.

Reintges, C. 1989: 'Philosophy and methodology in geography: a critical discussion'. In R. Fox and J. Daniel (eds), *50 Years of Geography at Rhodes University*, Grahamstown: Department of Geography, Rhodes University, 375–86.

Reintges, C. 1990: 'Urban movements in South African black townships: a case study'. *International Journal of Urban and Regional Research* 14: 109–34.

Renbourne, E. T. 1957: 'The history of the flannel binder and cholera belt'. *Medical History*, 1: 211–25.

Renbourne, E. T. 1962: 'Life and death of the solar topi'. *Journal of Tropical Medicine and Hygiene*, 65: 203–18.

Restrepo, Olga 1984: 'La Comisión Corográfica: un acercamiento a la Nueva Granada'. *Quipu*, 1, 3: 349–68.

Revelli, Paólo 1916: 'Una questione di geografia: l'Adriatico e il dominio del Mediterraneo orientale'. *Rivista Geografica Italiana*, 91–112.

Rhein, C. 1982: 'La géographie, discipline scolaire et/ou science sociale?' *Revue française de sociologie*, 23: 223–51.

Rice, E. 1990: *Captain Sir Richard Francis Burton*. New York: Scribners.

Robbins, B. (ed.) 1990: *Intellectuals: aesthetics, politics, academics*. Minneapolis: University of Minnesota Press.

Robequain, Charles 1929: *Le Than-Hoa. Étude géographique d'une région annamite*. Paris: Publications de l'École Française d'Extrème-Orient.

Roger, J. (ed.) 1979: 'Les néo-Lamarckiens français'. *Revue de synthèse*, special number, 95–6.

Rogerson, C. 1980: 'Internal colonialism, transnationalization and spatial inequality'. *South African Geographical Journal*, 62: 103–20.

Rogerson, C. 1981: 'Industrialization in the shadows of apartheid: a world-systems analysis'. In F. Hamilton and G. Linge (eds), *Spatial Analysis, Industry and the Industrial Environment*, vol. 2, London: John Wiley, 395–421.

Rogerson, C. 1983: 'South Africa in the global division of labor'. *Antipode*, 15.

Rogerson, C. 1985: 'Censorship and apartheid geography'. *Environment and Planning A*, 17: 723–8.

Rogerson, C. 1990: 'A new South Africa – a new South African Geography?' *Geojournal*, 22: 228.

Rogerson, C. and Beavon, K. 1988: 'Towards a geography of the common people in South Africa'. In J. Eyles (ed.), *Research in Human Geography*, Oxford: Blackwell, 83–99.

Rogerson, C. and Browett, J. 1986: 'Social geography under apartheid'. In J. Eyles (ed.), *Social Geography in International Perspective*, London: Croom Helm, 221–50.

Rogerson, C. and McCarthy, J. (eds) 1992: *Geography in a Changing South Africa*. Cape Town: Oxford University Press.

Rogerson, C. and Osborne, B. 1978: 'Conceptualizing the frontier settlement process: development or dependency'? *Comparative Frontier Studies*, 11: 1–3.

Rogerson, C. M. and Parnell, S. M 1989: 'Fostered by the laager: apartheid human geography in the 1980s'. *Area*, 21, 1: 13–26.

Roletto, Giorgio 1933: *Lezioni di geografia politica ed economica*. Padova: Cedam.

Rosaldo, R. 1989: *Culture and Truth*. Boston: Beacon.

Ross, Emory 1919: 'The climate of Liberia and its effect on man'. *Geographical Review*, 7: 387–402.

Ross, R. and Telkamp, G. 1985: *Colonial Cities: Essays on Urbanism in a Colonial Context*. Dordrecht: Martinus Nijhoff.

Rössler, Mechtild 1990: 'La géographie aux congrès internationaux: échanges scientifiques et conflits politiques'. *Rélations internationales*, 62, 183–99.

Rössler, Mechtild 1990: *Wissenschaft und Lebensraum. Geographische Ostforschung im Nationalsozialismus. Ein Beitrag zur Disziplingeschichte der Geographie*. Hamburg, Berlin: Dietrich Reimer Verlag.

Roth, M. S. 1989: 'Remembering forgetting: *Maladies de la mémoire* in nineteenth-century France'. *Representations*, 26: 49–68.

Rothwell, V. H. 1971: *British War Aims and Peace Diplomacy 1914–1918*. Oxford: Clarendon Press.

Rüger, Adolf 1977: 'Der Kolonialrevisionismus der Weimarer Republik'. In Helmuth Stoecker (ed.), *Drang nach Afrika*, Berlin: Akademie-Verlag, 243–72.

Rushdie, Salman 1991: *Imaginary Homeland*. New York: Granta Books.

Russell, Ruth B. 1958: *A History of the United Nations Charter. The Role of the United States 1940–1945*. Washington, DC: Brookings Institution.

Ryan, Mary P. 1990: *Women in Public: Between Banners and Ballots, 1825–1880*. Baltimore: Johns Hopkins University Press.

Sagra, Ramón de la 1842: *Historia física, política y natural de la isla de Cuba*, 2 vols. Paris: Lib. de Arthus Bertrand.

Sagra, Ramón de la 1851: *Historia económico-política y natural de la isla de Cuba, o sea de sus progresos en la población, la agricultura, el comercio y las rentas*. La Habana: Imprenta de la Viuda de Arazoza y Soler.

Said, Edward W. 1978: *Orientalism*. London: Routledge and Kegan Paul (New York: Vintage Books, 1979).

Said, Edward W. 1983: *The World, the Text and the Critic*. Cambridge: Harvard University Press.

Said, Edward W. 1985: 'Orientalism Reconsidered'. In Barker et al. (ed.), *Europe and its Others*, Colchester: University of Essex.

Said, Edward W. 1985: 'Orientalism Reconsidered'. *Race and Class*, 2: 1–15.

Said, Edward W. 1989: 'Representing the colonized: anthropology's interlocutors'. *Critical Inquiry*, 15: 205–25.

Said, Edward W. 1992: *Culture and Imperialism*. London: Chatto and Windus.

Salim, A. 1974: 'Early Arab-Swahili Political Protest in Colonial Kenya'. In Ogot (ed.), *Hadith 4: Politics and Nationalism in Colonial Kenya*, Nairobi: East African Literature Bureau, 71–84.

Sambon, Luigi Westenra 1897: 'Remarks on the possibility of the acclimatisation of Europeans in tropical regions'. *British Medical Journal*, 1: 61–6.

Sambon, Luigi Westenra 1898: 'Acclimatization of Europeans in tropical lands'. *Geographical Journal*, 12: 589–606.

Sambon, Luigi Westenra 1907: 'Tropical clothing'. *Journal of Tropical Medicine and Hygiene*, (15 February), 67–9.

Sandner, Gerhard 1989: 'The Germania-triumphans-syndrome and Passarge's Erdkundliche Weltanschauung'. *Political Geography Quarterly*, 8, 341–51.

Sandys, George 1615: *A relation of a journey begun An. Dom. 1610*. London.

Sangren, S. 1988: 'Rhetoric and the authority of enthnography'. *Current Anthropology*, 29: 405–24.

Sarrazin, H. 1985: *Elisée Reclus ou la passion du monde*. Paris: La Découverte.

Sasaki, Hikoichiro 1927: 'Geoporichiku to ekonomikku geogurafi' [Geopolitics and Economic Geography]. *Chirigaku Hyōron*, 3: 361–3.

Sato, Hiroshi 1933: *Keizaichirigaku sōron* [Economic Geography], Tokyo: Kokonshoin.

Sato, Hiroshi 1939: *Seijichirigaku gairon* [Outline of Political Geography]. Tokyo: Kajitani-shoin.

Saunders, C. 1988: *The Making of the South African Past*. Totowa, NJ: Barnes and Noble.

Schaefer, F. 1953: 'Exceptionalism in geography'. *Annals of the Association of American Geographers*, 43: 226–49.

Schiebinger, Londa 1988: 'Feminine icons: the face of early modern science'. *Critical Inquiry*, 14: 661–91.

Schirmer, H. 1891: 'La France et les voies de pénétration au Soudan'. *Annales de géographie* 1: 9–32.

Schirmer, H. 1891: 'La géographie de l'Afrique'. *Annales de géographie*, 1: 57–67.

Schirmer, H. 1892: 'La géographie de l'Afrique'. *Annales de géographie*, 2: 185–96.

Schmokel, Wolfe W. 1964: *Dream of Empire: German Colonialism 1919–1945*. New Haven: Yale University Press.

Schnee, Heinrich 1924: 'Die Koloniale Schuldlüge'. *Süddeutsche Monatshefte*, 21: 93–125.

Schnee, Heinrich 1932: 'Kolonialpolitischer Jahresrückblick'. *Deutsche Arbeit*, 31: 194–7.

Schnee, Heinrich n. d.: 'Braucht Deutschland Kolonien'? In Deutsche Kolonialgesellschaft and Interfraktionelle Koloniale Vereinigung (ed.), *Deutschland in den Kolonien. Ein Buch deutscher Tat und deutschen Rechtes*, Berlin: Otto Stollberg, 155–7.

Schneider, W. 1982: 'Toward the improvement of the human race: the history of eugenics in France'. *Journal of Modern History*, 54: 268–91.

Schneider, W. 1990: 'Geographical reform and municipal imperialism in France, 1870–80'. In J. M. MacKenzie (ed.), *Imperialism and the Natural World*, 90–117.

Schulte-Althoff, F.-J. 1971: *Studien zur politischen Wissenschaftsgeschichte der deutschen Geographie im Zeitalter des Imperialismus*. Paderborn: F. Schöningh.

Schultz, Hans-Dietrich 1980: *Die deutschsprachige Geographie von 1800 bis 1970. Ein Beitrag zur Geschichte ihrer Methodologie*. Berlin: Geographisches Institut der Freien Universität.

Schultz, Hans-Dietrich 1989: *Die Geographie als Bildungsfach im Kaiserreich*. Osnabrück: Fachgebiet Geographie.

Schulze, Hagen 1982: *Weimar: Deutschland, 1917–1933*. Berlin: Severin and Siedler.

Scott, D. 1986: 'Time, structuration and the potential for South African historical geography'. *South African Geographical Journal*, 68: 45–66.

Secord, J. A. 1982: 'King of Siluria: Roderick Murchison and the imperial theme in nineteenth-century British geology'. *Victorian Studies*, 25: 413–42.

Seidel, Rita, et al. (eds) 1981: *Universität Hannover 1831–1981. Festschrift zum 150 jährigen Bestehen der Universität Hannover*. vol. I and vol. II. Stuttgart: W. Kohlhammer.

Sekula, Alan 1984: 'Traffic in photographs'. In Alan Sekula (ed.), *Photography Against the Grain*, Halifax, Nova Scotia: The Press of Nova Scotia College of Art and Design.

Sellés, M., Peset, J. L., and Lafuente, A. (eds) 1988: *Carlos III y lan ciencia de la Ilustración*. Madrid: Alianza Editorial.

Semple, Ellen Churchill 1911: *Influences of Geographic Environment*. New York: H. Holt and Co.

Sen, G. 1987: 'Subaltern studies: capital, class and community'. *Subaltern Studies*, 5.

Sestini, Aldo 1961: *La Società di Studi Geografici e la Rivista Geografica Italiana*. Florence: Società di Studi Geografici.

Sewell, William H. Jr 1985: 'Ideologies and Social Revolutions: Reflections on the French Case'. *The Journal of Modern History*, 57, 1: 57–85.

Shapin, Steven and Schaffer, Simon 1985: *Leviathan and the air-pump. Hobbes, Boyle, and the experimental life*. Princeton, NJ: Princeton University Press.

Shay, Felix 1925: 'Cairo to Cape Town, overland: an adventurous journey of 135 days, made by an American man and his wife, through the length of the African continent'. *National Geographic Magazine*, 47, 2: 123–260.

Sheriff, A. 1987: *Slaves, Spices and Ivory in Zanzibar: Integration of an East African Commercial Empire into the World Economy, 1770–1873*. London: Heinemann.

Sherley, Sir Anthony 1600: *A true report of Sir A. Shierlies journey overland to Venice*. London.

Sherley, Sir Anthony 1613: *Relation of his travels into Persia*. London.

Sherwood, Robert E. 1948: *Roosevelt and Hopkins: An Intimate History*. New York: Harper and Bros.

Shiach, M. 1989: *Discourse on Popular Culture*. Cambridge: Polity Press.

Shiga, Shigetaka 1894: *Nihon Fukeiron*. In *Shiga Shigetaka Zenshū* [Collected Works of Shiga Shigetaka] vol. 4, Shiga Shigetaka Zenshū Kankokai, 1927, Tokyo: Seikyosha, 1–194

Shiga, Shigetaka 1908: *Chirigaku* [Geography]. In *Shiga Shigetaka Zenshū* [Collected Works of Shigetaka Shiga], vol. 4, Shiga Shigetaka Zenshū Kankokai, 1927. Tokyo: Seikyosha, 269–413.

Shirley, J. W. 1983: *Thomas Harriot. A Biography*. Oxford: Clarendon Press.

Siegfried, André 1904: *La démocratie en Nouvelle-Zélande*. Paris: Armand Colin.

Siegfried, André 1924: *L'Angleterre aujourd'hui*. Paris: Crès.

Simmer, Hans 1928: *Grundzüge der Geopolitik in Anwendung auf Deutschland*. Munich and Berlin: R. Oldenbourg.

Skocpol, Theda 1985: 'Cultural Idioms and Political Ideologies in the Revolutionary Reconstruction of State Power: A Rejoinder to Sewell' *The Journal of Modern History*, 57, 1: 86–96.

Skowronek, S. 1982: *Building A New American State*. Cambridge and New York: Cambridge University Press.

Smith, B. F. 1983: *Shadow Warriors*. New York: Basic Books.

Smith, Captain John 1608: *A True Relation of such occurrences as hath happened in Virginia*. London.

Smith, Captain John 1616: *A description of New England*. London.

Smith, D. (ed.) 1991: *Apartheid City and Beyond*. London: Routledge.

Smith, D. 1982: *Living under Apartheid*. London: Unwin Hyman.

Smith, Harrison W. 1919: 'Sarawak: the land of the white rajahs'. *National Geographic Magazine*, 35, 2: 110–67.

Smith, K. 1988: *The Changing Past: Trends in South African Historical Writing*. Halfway House: Southern Books.

Smith, Neil (1984) 1991: *Uneven Development: Nature, Capital and the Production of Space*. Oxford: Basil Blackwell.

Smith, Neil 1994: 'Geography, Empire and Social Theory'. *Progress in Human Geography* 18.

Smith, Thomas 1978: 'Manuscript and Printed Sea Charts in Seventeenth-Century London: The Case of the Thames School'. In Norman Thrower (ed.), *The Compleat Plattmaker*. Berkeley: University of California Press, 45–100.

Smith, Woodruff D. 1978: *The German Colonial Empire*. Capel Hill: University of North Carolina Press.

Smith, Woodruff D. 1986: *The Ideological Origins of Nazi Imperialism*. New York: Oxford University Press.

Smith, Woodruff D. 1987: 'Anthropology and German Colonialism'. In Arthur J. Knoll and Lewis H. Gann (eds), *Germans in the Tropics. Essays in German Colonial History*, New York: Greenwood Press, 39–57.

Società Geografica Italiana 1935: *L'Africa orientale*. Bologna: Zanichelli.

Soellner, Alfons 1990: 'From political dissent to intellectual integration: the Frankfurt School in American government, 1942–9'. In Bruce Robbins (ed.), *Intellectuals: Aesthetics, Politics, Academics*, Minneapolis: University of Minnesota Press, 225–43.

Soja, E. 1989: *Postmodern Geographies*. London: Verso.

Solf, W. H. 1920: *Afrika für Europa: Der koloniale Gedanke des 20, Jahrhunderts*. Neumünster: Holstein.

Somerville, Mary 1858: *Physical Geography*, 4th edn. London: Murray.

Sontag, Susan 1977: *On Photography*. New York: Delta.

Sori, Ercole 1979: *L'emigrazione italiana dall'unità d'Italia alla seconda guerra mondiale*. Bologna: il Mulino.

Soubeyran, Olivier n.d.: *Les dix premières années des 'Annales de Géographie'*. Typescript.

Soubeyran, Olivier 1992: 'Dubois, Gallois, Vidal: filiations et ruptures'. In Paul Claval (ed.), *L'Histoire de la géographie française au XIXe et au début du XXe siècle*, Paris: CNRS.

Southern African Studies Series, vols 1–6. Johannesburg: Ravan Press.

Speke, J. 1863: *Journal of the Discovery of the Source of the Nile*. London and Edinburgh: William Blackwood and Brothers.

Spelman, Elizabeth V. 1988: *Inessential Woman: Problems of Exclusion in Feminist Thought*. Boston: Beacon Press.

Spencer, J. 1989: 'Anthropology as a kind of writing'. *Man*, 24: 145–64.

Spinden, H. J. 1922–23: 'Civilization and the wet tropics'. *World's Work*, 45: 438–48.

Spivak, G. C. 1987: *In Other Worlds: Essays in Cultural Politics*. New York: Methuen.

Spivak, G. C. 1988: 'Can the Subaltern Speak?' In C. Nelson and L. Grossberg (eds), *Marxism and the Interpretation of Culture*, Chicago: University of Illinois Press, 271–313.

Spivak, G. C. 1990: 'Poststructuralism, marginality, post-coloniality and value'. In Collier, P. and Geyer-Ryan, H. (eds), *Literary Theory Today*, Ithaca: Cornell University Press.

Spivak, G. C. 1990: *The Post-Colonial Critic: Interviews, Strategies, Dialogues*. New York: Routledge.

Splenger, J.-J. 1979: *France Faces Depopulation*. Westport, Conn: Greenwood Press.

Stafford, Robert A. 1988: 'Roderick Murchison and the structure of Africa: a geological prediction and its consequences for British imperialism'. *Annals of Science*, 45: 1–40.

Stafford Robert A. 1989: *Scientist of Empire: Sir Roderick Murchison, scientific exploration and Victorian imperialism*. Cambridge: Cambridge University Press.

Stanley, Henry M. 1885: 'Inaugural address'. *Scottish Geographical Magazine*, 1: 1–17.

Stanley, Henry M. 1885: *The Congo and the founding of the Free State: A story of work and exploration*, 2 vols. New York: Harper and Brothers.

Staum, Martin S. 1980: 'The Class of Moral and Political Sciences, 1795–1803'. *French Historical Studies*, 11, 3: 371–97.

Stepan, Nancy Leys 1986: 'Race and gender: the role of analogy in science'. *Isis*, 77: 261–77.

Stevenson, D. 1982: *French War Aims Against Germany 1914–1919*. Oxford: Clarendon Press.

Stevenson, D. 1988: *The First World War and International Politics*. Oxford: Oxford University Press.

Stigand, C. 1913: *The Land of the Zinj*. London: Constable.

Stocking, George W. Jr 1982: 'The persistence of polygenist thought in post-Darwinian anthropology'. In *Race, Culture, and Evolution: Essays in the History of Anthropology*, Chicago: University of Chicago Press, 43–68.

Stocking, George W. Jr 1987: *Victorian Anthropology*. New York: Free Press.

Stockley, G. 1928: *Report on the Geology of the Zanzibar Protectorate*. Zanzibar: Government Printer.

Stoddart, D. R. 1975: 'The RGS and the foundation of geography at Cambridge'. *Geographical Journal*, 141, 216–39.

Stoddart, D. R. 1986: *On Geography and its History*. Oxford: Basil Blackwell.

Stoddart, D. R. 1991: 'Do we need a feminist historiography of geography – and if we do, what should it be?' *Transactions of the Institute of the British Geographers*, 16, 484–7.

Stoddart, D. R. 1992: 'Geography and War: the "New Geography" and the "New Army" in England, 1899–1914'. *Political Geography*, 11, 1: 87–99.

Stoecker, Helmuth (ed.) 1986: *German Imperialism in Africa. From the Beginning until the Second World War*. London: C. Hurst and Company.

Stone, J. C. 1988: 'Imperialism, colonialism and cartography'. *Transactions of the British Institute of British Geographers*, 13: 57–64.

Stone, Melville E. 1910: 'Race prejudice in the Far East'. *National Geographic Magazine*, 21, 12: 973–85.

Strobel, M. 1976: 'From Lelemama to Lobbying: Women's Associations in Mombasa, Kenya'. In Ogot (ed.), *Hadith 6: History and Social Change in East Africa*. Nairobi: East African Literature Bureau, 207–35.

Strong, Roy C. 1977: *The Cult of Elizabeth: Elizabethan Portraiture and Pageantry*. London: Thames and Hudson.

Strong, Roy C. 1986: *Henry, Prince of Wales and England's Lost renaissance*. New York: Thames and Hudson.

Sullivan, A. T. 1983: *Thomas-Robert Bugeaud, France and Algeria, 1784–1849: Politics, Power and the Good Society*. Connecticut: Archon Books, Hamden.

Sundiata, I. 1987: 'Twentieth Century Reflections on Death in Zanzibar'. *International Journal of African Historical Studies*, 20, 1: 45–60.

Surdich, Francesco 1979–80: *Esplorazioni geografiche e sviluppo del colonialisme nell'età della rivoluzione industriale*, 2 vols. Florence: La Nuova Italia.

Surdich, Francesco 1982: *L'esplorazione italiana dell'Africa*. Milan: il Saggiatore.

Sutcliffe, M. 1986: 'The crisis in South Africa: material conditions and the reformist response'. *Geoforum*, 17: 141–60.

Sutcliffe, M. and Wellings, P. 1985: 'Black worker "attitudes" and disinvestment: a critique of the Schlemmer report'. *TransAfrica Forum*, 3: 3–24.

Sutcliffe, M. and Wellings, P. 1985: 'Disinvestment and black workers' attitudes in South Africa: a critical comment'. *Review of African Political Economy*, 34: 68–82.

Sutcliffe, M. and Wellings, P. 1986: 'Attitudes and living conditions in Inanda: the context for unrest?' *Zululand Geographer*, 5: 5–22.

Sutcliffe, M. and Wellings, P. 1986: 'The widening rift: Buthelezi, Inkatha, and anti-apartheid policies in South Africa'. *TransAfrica Forum*, 3: 51–82.

Sutton, K. 1979: 'Augustin Bernard, 1865–1947'. In T. W. Freeman (ed.), *Geographers: biobibliographical studies*, 3: 19–27.

Swanson, M. 1977: 'The Sanitation Syndrome: Bubonic Plague and Urban Native Policy in the Cape Colony, 1900–1909'. *Journal of African History*, 18: 387–410.

Swayne, E. 1917: 'British Honduras'. *Geographical Journal*, 50: 161–79

Sykes, Ella C. 1910: 'A talk about Persia and its women'. *National Geographic Magazine*, 21, 10: 847–66.

Symonds, William, (ed.) 1612: *The proceedings of the English colonie in Virginia*. Oxford.

Taboulet, G. 1968: 'Aux origines du Canal de Suez: le conflit entre F. de Lesseps et les saint-simoniens'. *Revue historique*, 240, 287–8: 89–114, 361–92.

Taboulet, G. 1971: 'Le rôle des saint-simoniens dans le percement de l'isthme de Suez'. *Economies et sociétés*, 5: 1295–320.

Taboulet, G. 1973: 'Ferdinand de Lesseps et l'Égypte avant le canal (1803–1854)'. *Revue français d'histoire d'outre-mer*, 60, 219: 143–71, 364–407.

Takeuchi, Keiichi 1974: 'The origins of human geography in Japan'. *Hitotsubashi Journal of Arts and Science*, 15: 1–13.

Takeuchi, Keiichi 1980: 'Geopolitics and Geography in Japan: Re-examined'. *Hitotsubashi Journal of Social Studies*, 12: 14–24.

Takeuchi, Keiichi 1980: 'Some remarks on the history of regional description and the tradition of regionalism in modern Japan'. *Progress in Human Geography*, 4: 238–48.

Takeuchi, Keiichi 1984–5: 'Strategies of Heterodox Researchers in the National Schools of Geography and their Roles in Shifting Paradigms in Geography'. *Organon*, 21/22: 277–86.

Takeuchi, Keiichi 1984: 'Two outsiders: An aspect of Modern academic geography in Japan'. In Takeuchi, Keiichi (ed.), *Languages, Paradigms and Schools in Geography: Japanese Contributions to the History of Geographical Thought (2)*, Tokyo: Laboratory of Social Geography, Hitotsubashi University, 89–100.

Takeuchi, Keiichi 1987: 'How Japan learned about the outside world: the views other countries incorporated in Japanese School textbooks, 1968–1986'. *Hitotsubashi Journal of Social Studies*, 19: 1–13.

Takeuchi, Keiichi 1988: 'Nationalism and Geography in Modern Japan: With Special Attention to the Period between the 1880s-1920s'. In Hooson, David (ed.) *Geography and National Identity*, Oxford: Blackwell, 1994.

Takeuchi, Keiichi 1989: 'Paysage, langage et nationalisme au Japan du Meiji; Les langages de représentations géographiques'. *Actes du Colloque International*. Venice, 15–16 Octobre; *présentés par Gabriolo Zanotto*. Venice, 2: 171–84.

Takeuchi, Keiichi and Masai, Yasuo (eds) 1986: *Chirigaku wo manabu* [Experiences of Sixteen Senior Geographers]. Tokyo: Kokonshoin.

Tannenberg, O. R. 1911: *Gross-Deutschland, die Arbeit des 20. Jahrhunderts*. Leipzig-Gohlis: Bruno Volger.

Taton, René 1986: *Enseignement et diffusion des sciences en France pendant le dix-huitième siècle*. Paris: Hermann.

Taylor, Charles 1989: *Sources of the Self. The Making of Modern Identity*. Cambridge, Mass.: Harvard University Press.

Taylor, E. G. R. 1930: *Tudor Geography, 1485–1583*. London: Methuen.

Taylor, E. G. R. 1934: *Late Tudor and Early Stuart Geography, 1583–1650*. London: Methuen.

Taylor, E. G. R. 1935: *The Original Writings and Correspondence of the two Richard Hakluyts*, 2 vols. London: Hakluyt Society.

Taylor, E. G. R. 1947: 'Richard Hakluyt'. *Geographical Journal*, 109, 165–74.

Taylor, E. G. R. 1954: *Mathematical Practitioners of Tudor and Stuart England*. Cambridge: Cambridge University Press.

Taylor, T. Griffith 1914: 'The control of settlement by humidity and temperature'. *Bulletin of the Commonwealth Bureau of Meteorology*, Melbourne, no. 14.

Taylor, T. Griffith 1919: 'Climatic cycles and evolution'. *Geographical Review*, 8: 289–328.

Taylor, T. Griffith 1921: 'The evolution and distribution of race, culture, and language'. *Geographical Review*, 11: 54–119.

Taylor, T. Griffith 1930: 'Racial migration-zones and their significance'. *Human Biology*, 2: 34–62.

Taylor, T. Griffith 1936: 'The zones and strata theory: a biological classification of races'. *Human Biology*, 8: 348–67.

Taylor, T. Griffith 1957: 'Racial Geography'. In Griffith Taylor (ed.), *Geography in the Twentieth Century*, New York: Philosophical Library, 3rd edn, 433–62.

Thiong'o, Ngugi wa 1986: *Decolonising the Mind*. London: James Currey.

Thompson, E. P. 1978: 'Folklore, anthropology and social history'. *Indian Historical Review*, 3: 203–31.

Thomson, Joseph 1886: 'East Central Africa, and its commercial outlook'. *Scottish Geographical Magazine*, 2: 65–78.

Thomson, Joseph 1886: 'Niger and Central Sudan sketches'. *Scottish Geographical Magazine*, 2: 577–601.

Thorbecke, Franz 1934: 'Warum Kolonien?' *Kölnischen Zeitung*, 24 April, insert.

Tiffany, Sharon W. and Adams, Kathleen J. 1985: *The Wild Women: An Inquiry into the Anthropology of an Idea*. Cambridge, Mass.: Schenkman.

Tilly, C. 1990: *States, Coercion and Capital*. Oxford: Blackwell.

Tisdel, Edine Frances 1910: 'Guatemala, the country of the future'. *National Geographic Magazine*, 21, 5: 596–624.

Tocqueville, Alexis de 1935–40: *La démocratie en Amérique*, 2 vols. Paris: Gosselin.

Tocqueville, Alexis de 1988: *De la colonie en Algérie*. Brussells: Éditions Complexe.

Toniolo, Antonio Renato 1915: 'A proposito di un mio schizzo antropogeografico sulla Dalmazia'. *Rivista Geografica Italiana*, 151–5.

Torday, E. 1919: 'Curious and characteristic customs of central African tribes'. *National Geographic Magazine*, 36, 4: 342–68.

Toschi, Umberto 1937: *Appunti di geografia politica*. Bari: Macri.

Trade and Tourist Traffic Bureau of Zanzibar. 1949: *A Guide to Zanzibar*. Zanzibar: Trade and Tourist Traffic Bureau, (original 1932).

Trainer, F. 1989: 'Reconstructing radical development theory'. *Alternatives*, 14: 481–516.

Trewartha, Glenn T. 1926: 'Recent thought on the problem of white acclimatization in the wet tropics'. *Geographical Review*, 16: 467–78.

Troll, Carl 1939: *Deutsche Wissenschaft. Arbeit und Aufgabe*. Leipzig: Verlag S. Hirzel.

Troll, Carl 1974: 'Die Geographische Wissenschaft in Deutschland in den Jahren 1933 bis 1945. Eine Kritik und eine Rechtfertigung'. *Erdkunde*, 1: 3–47.

Trotter, D. 1990: 'Colonial subjects'. *Critical Quarterly*, 32: 3–37.

Truth, Sojourner 1976: 'Ain't I a woman'. In Bert James Loewenberg and Ruth Bogin (eds), *Black Women in Nineteenth Century America*, Philadelphia: Pennsylvania University Press, 235.

Uchimura, Kanzo 1894: *Chirigaku-ko* [Consideration of Geography]. In *Uchimura Kanzo Shiko Chosaku-shu* [Collected Works of Kanzo Uchimura], vol. 4. Tokyo: Kyobunkan, 1963, 5–105.

United Nations Center for Human Settlements. 1983: *The Stone Town of Zanzibar: A Strategy for Integrated Development*. Zanzibar: Ministry of Lands, Construction and Housing.

Vallette, J. 1976: *Socialisme Utopique et Idée Coloniale: Jules Duval (1813–1870)*. Lyon: Unpublished PhD Thesis, Université de Lyon II.

Van Onselen, C. 1976: *Studies in the Social and Economic History of the Witwatersrand, 1886–1914*, 2 vols. London: Longman.

Van Orman, Richard A. 1984: *The Explorers: Nineteenth Century Expeditions in Africa and the American West*. Albuquerque: University of New Mexico Press.

Vatin, J. C. (ed.) 1984: *Connaissances du Maghreb: sciences sociales et colonisation*. Paris: Centre National de la Recherche Scientifique.

Vidal de la Blache, Paul 1889: *Autour de la France. Pays et nations d'Europe*. Paris: De la Grave.

Vidal de la Blache, Paul 1899: 'Leçon de l'ouverture du cours de géographie'. *Annales de géographie*, 38: 97–109.

Vidal de la Blache, Paul 1903: 'La géographie humaine, ses rapports avec la géographie de la vie'. *Revue de synthèse historique*, 7: 219–240.

Vidal de la Blache, Paul 1903: *Tableau de la géographie de la France*. Paris: Hachette.

Vidal de la Blache, Paul 1917: *La France de l'Est (Lorraine-Alsace)*. Paris: Armand Colin.

Vidal de la Blache, Paul 1917: 'Nécrologie de Pierre Foncin'. *Annales de géographie*, 139: 67–9.

Vidal de la Blache, Paul 1922: *Principes de la géographie humaine*. Paris: A. Colin.

Vidal, S. 1874: *Memorra sobre el Ramo de Montes en las Islas Filipinas*. Madrid: Impr., estereotipia y galvanoplastia de Aribau.

Vinassa de Regny, Paolo. 1926: 'Mentalitá e coscienza coloniale'. *Bollettino della Società Geografica Italiana*, 373–90.

Vinci, Anna 1990: 'Storia e geografia al confine: l'esperienza di "Geopolitica" alle soglie della seconda guerra mondiale'. *Società e storia*, 47 (January–March): 87–127.

Volney, C. F. C., Comte de 1787: *Voyage en Syrie et en Égypte pendant les années 1783, 1784 et 1785*. Paris.

Volz, Wilhelm 1925: 'Lebensraum und Lebensrecht des deutschen Volkes'. *Deutsche Arbeit*, 24: 169–74.

Von Pfeil, Graf 1896: 'On tropical Africa in relation to white races'. *Report of the Sixth International Geographical Congress*, Delivered London 1895. London, 537–44.

Waibel, Leo 1926: 'Südwestafrika'. *Zeitschrift für Geopolitik*, 3: 187–200.

Walker, C. (ed.) 1990: *Women and Gender in Southern Africa to 1945*. Cape Town: David Philip.

Wallace, Michele 1979: *Black Macho and the Myth of the Superwoman*. New York: Dial Press.

Ward, Robert DeCourcy 1919: 'A new classification of climates'. *Geographical Review*, 8: 188–91.

Ward, Robert DeCourcy 1930: 'Fallacies of the melting pot idea and America's traditional immigration policy'. In Madison Grant and Chas Steward Davison (eds), *The alien in our midst or 'Selling our birthright for a mess of industrial potage'*, New York: The Galton Publishing Company, 230–6.

Ward, Robert DeCourcy 1931: 'Can the white race become acclimatized in the tropics'? *Gerlands Beiträge zur Geopolitik*, 32: 149–57.

Warner, Marina 1985: *Monuments and Maidens: The Allegory of the Female Form*. New York: Atheneum.

Watanabe, Akina 1942: 'Chiseigaku no naiyō ni tsuite' [On the Contents of Geopolitics]. *Chirigaku Kenkyu*, 1: 269.

Watsuji, Tetsuro 1934: *Fudo, ningengakuteki kōsatsu* [Climate, its Humanistic Considerations]. Tokyo: Iwanami-shoten.

Watts, M. J. 1991: 'Mapping meaning, denoting difference, imagining identity'. *Geografiska Annaler*, B, 73 (1): 7–16.

Waugh, Evelyn 1946: *When the Going Was Good*. London: Duckworth.

Webbe, Edward 1590: *The rare and most wonderful thinges which Edward Webbe an Englishman borne, hath seene and passed in his troublesome travailes*. London.

Weber, Eugen 1976: *Peasants into Frenchmen: the Modernization of Rural France 1870–1914*. Stanford, California: Stanford University Press.

Wegener, 1920: *Die geographischen Ursachen des Weltkrieges*,

Wehler, Hans-Ulrich 1969: *Bismarck und der Imperialismus*. Cologne, Berlin: Kiepenheuer and Witsch.

Wehler, Hans-Ulrich 1977: *Das deutsche Kaissereich 1871–1918*. Göttingen: Vandenhoek and Ruprecht.

Weiner, Douglas R. 1985: 'The roots of "Michurinism": Transformist biology and acclimatization as currents in the Russian life sciences'. *Annals of Science*, 42: 244–60.

Weisz, G. 1983: *The Emergence of the Modern Universities of France, 1863–1924*. Princeton: Princeton University Press.

Wellings, P. 1986: 'Geography and development studies in Southern Africa: a progressive prospectus'. *Geoforum*, 17: 119–31.

Wellings, P. and McCarthy, J. 1983: 'Whither Southern African human geography?'. *Area*, 15: 337–45.

Wellings, P. and Sutcliffe, M. 1984: ' "Developing" the informal sector'. *Development and Change*, 15: 517–70.

Wellings, P. and Sutcliffe, M. 1985: 'Worker militancy in South Africa: a sociospatial analysis of trade union activism in the manufacturing sector'. *Society and Space*, 3: 357–79.

Welliver, T. 1990: *The Clove Factor in Colonial Zanzibar*. PhD Dissertation, Northwestern University, Evanston.

Wesso, H. M. 1989: *People's education: towards a people's geography in South Africa*. Paper presented at Society for Geography Conference, Pretoria.

Wesso, H. M. 1991: *The colonisation of geography in South Africa: prospects for its decolonisation*. Paper presented at the South African Geographical Society Conference, Potchefstroom.

Western, J. 1984: 'Autonomous and Directed Cultural Change: South African Urbanization'. In Agnew, Mercer and Sopher (eds), *The City in Cultural Context*, Boston: Allen and Unwin, 205–36.

Western, J. 1984: 'Social Engineering through Spatial Manipulation: Apartheid in South Africa's Cities'. In Clarke, Ley and Peach (eds), *Geography and Ethnic Pluralism*, London: Allen and Unwin, 113–40.

Western, J. 1986: 'Places, Authorship, Authority: Retrospection on Fieldwork'. In L. Guelke (ed.) *Geography and Humanistic Knowledge*, Department of Geography, University of Waterloo, 23–38.

Westphal, Wilfried 1987: *Geschichte der deutschen Kolonien*. Frankfurt: Ullstein.

Whitaker, Alexander 1613: *Good newes from Virginia*. London.

White, Silva 1891: 'On the comparative value of African lands'. *Scottish Geographical Magazine*, 7: 191–5.

Whittelsey, D. 1941: 'War peace and geography – an editorial foreword'. *Annals of the Association of American Geographers*, 31, 2: 77–82.

Whittlesey, D., Hartshorne, R. and Colby, C. 1942: *German Strategy of World Conquest*. New York: Farrar and Rinehart.

Willes, Richard 1598–1600: 'Certain other reasons, or arguments to prove a passage by the Northwest, learnedly written by Mr. Richard Willes Gentleman'. In Richard Hakluyt *Principal Navigations, Voyages, Traffiques, and Discoveries of the English Nation*, 3 vols. London, vol. 3, 24–9.

Williams, G. 1960: 'The Concept of "egemonia" in the thought of Antonio Gramsci: some notes on interpretation'. *Journal of the History of Ideas*, 21, 4: 586–99.

Williams, Penry and Harriss, G. L. 1963: 'A Revolution in Tudor History'. Three articles in *Past and Present*, 25: 3–58.

Williams, R. 1977: *Marxism and Literature*. London: Verso.

Williams, R. 1980: *Problems in Materialism and Culture*. London: Verso.

Wilson, James C. 1934: 'Three-wheeling through Africa: Two adventurers cross the so-called dark continent north of Lake Chad on motorcycles with side cars'. *National Geographic Magazine*, 65, 1: 37–92.

Winchell, Alexander 1880: *Preadamites; or a demonstration of the existence of men before Adam; together with a study of their condition, antiquity, racial affinities, and progressive dispersion over the earth*. Chicago, 2nd edn.

Withers, C. 1988: *Gaelic Scotland: the Transformation of a Culture Region*. London: Routledge.

Wittfogel, Karl A. 1929: 'Geopolitik, geographischen Materiarismus und Marxismus'. *Unter dem Banner des Marxismus* 3: 26–64.

Witz, L. 1989: 'History of the people, for the people and by the people'. *South Africa International*, 19: 90–5.

Witz, L. 1990: 'The write your own history project'. *Radical History Review*, 46/7: 377–87.

Woodruff, Charles E. 1905: *The Effects of Tropical Light on White Men*. New York: Rebman

Young, R. 1990: *White Mythologies: Writing History and the West*. London: Routledge.

Zaghi, Carlo 1973: *L'Africa nella coscienza europea e l'imperialismo italiano*. Naples: Guida.

Zanzibar Protectorate. 1935: *Annual Medical and Sanitary Report of the Health Department*. Zanzibar: Government Printers.

Zanzibar Protectorate. 1937: *Annual Medical and Sanitary Report of the Health Department*. Zanzibar: Government Printers.

Zein, A. 1974: *The Sacred Meadows: a Structural Analysis of Religious Symbolism in an East African Town*. Evanston: Northwestern University Press.

Zimmermann, Peter 1976: 'Kampf um den Lebensraum. Ein Mythos der Kolonial-und der Blut-und-Boden Literatur'. In Horst Denkler and Karl Prümm (eds), *Die deutsche Literatur im Dritten Reich*, Stuttgart: Reclam, 165–82.

Index

Related Titles: List of IBG
Special Publications